美英报刊阅读教程(高级精选本)

(第二版)

Reading Course in American & British News Publications
(Advanced Level)

主　编　　端木义万
副主编　　杨晓冬　　郑志恒　　赵　虹　　张　琳　　沈　虹
编著者　　端木义万　陈　曦　　黄雅娟　　董明利　　庄　雪
　　　　　戴雨聪　　张庆轩　　范若瑜　　高一丹　　李宇华
　　　　　胡中健　　殷东豪　　陈若雨　　王雪阳　　韩晓星
　　　　　程子航　　季　锋　　黄　原　　黄　莹　　陈　倩
　　　　　陈兴圆　　张茂林　　李　栋　　王　坚

本书编委（姓氏笔画为序）

马　兴	王少琳	王亚民	王传经	王　波	王健玲	王　萍	王慧玉
尹富林	白济民	冯艳荣	石运章	孙金华	何　树	谷　蕾	李文军
李明英	李昌标	李贵苍	李德俊	李　静	李霄翔	刘金玲	刘　苋
牟　珊	孙金华	陈光祥	肖　辉	严轶伦	张一峰	张　权	张　莉
邹卫宁	林　劲	杜　辉	孟伟根	苏　勇	邰庆燕	汪学磊	吴建清
肖　凡	郭影平	郝雁南	胡美馨	贾陆依	贾　磊	唐宪义	葛　红
楼　毅	鲁　莉	路玮丽	臧玉福	薛洲堂	魏福平	端木义万	

图书在版编目(CIP)数据

美英报刊阅读教程：高级精选本/端木义万主编. —2版. —北京：北京大学出版社，2015.2
（大学美英报刊教材系列）
ISBN 978-7-301-25561-2

Ⅰ.①美… Ⅱ.①端… Ⅲ.①英语–报刊–阅读教学–高等学校–教材 Ⅳ.① H319.4

中国版本图书馆CIP数据核字(2015)第031067号

书　　名	美英报刊阅读教程(高级精选本)(第二版)
著作责任者	端木义万　主编
责任编辑	刘　爽　叶　丹
标准书号	ISBN 978-7-301-25561-2
出版发行	北京大学出版社
地　　址	北京市海淀区成府路205号　100871
网　　址	http://www.pup.cn　新浪微博：@北京大学出版社
电子信箱	nkliushuang@hotmail.com
电　　话	邮购部 62752015　发行部 62750672　编辑部 62759634
印　刷　者	北京圣夫亚美印刷有限公司
经　销　者	新华书店
	787毫米×1092毫米　16开本　26.5印张　600千字
	2009年9月第1版
	2015年2月第2版　2025年1月第8次印刷
定　　价	59.00元

未经许可，不得以任何方式复制或抄袭本书之部分或全部内容。
版权所有，侵权必究
举报电话：010-62752024　电子信箱：fd@pup.pku.edu.cn
图书如有印装质量问题，请与出版部联系，电话：010-62756370

主编主要著作介绍

本书主编端木义万系南京国际关系学院英语资深教授,博士生导师,全国优秀教师,享受政府特殊津贴专家,从事外报外刊教学与研究近五十年,其主要著作如下:

一、教材系列

*《美英报刊阅读教程》(南京大学出版社,1994,迄今已20次印刷)
《美英报刊阅读教程(第二版)》(南京大学出版社,2007,已6次印刷)
▲《美英报刊阅读教程(第三版)》(南京大学出版社,2012,已5次印刷)
*《美英报刊阅读教程(高级本)》(北京大学出版社,2001,已14次印刷)
《美英报刊阅读教程(高级本)教师参考书》(北京大学出版社,2001,已3次印刷)
《美英报刊阅读教程(高级本)(精选版)》(北京大学出版社,2009,已6次印刷)
《新编美英报刊阅读教程(中级本)》(中国社会科学出版社,1999,已8次印刷)
*《美英报刊阅读教程(中级本)(精选版)》(北京大学出版社,2005,已8次印刷)
*《美英报刊阅读教程(中级本)(精选版)教师参考书》(北京大学出版社,2005,已2次印刷)
**《美英报刊阅读教程(中级本)(精选第二版)》(北京大学出版社,2010,已7次印刷)
**《美英报刊阅读教程(中级本)(精选第二版)教师参考书》(北京大学出版社,2010)
《大学英语外报外刊阅读教程》(北京大学出版社,2003,已18次印刷)
《大学英语外报外刊阅读教程教师参考书》(北京大学出版社,2003)
《大学英语外报外刊阅读教程(第二版)》(北京大学出版社,2011,已5次印刷)
▲《大学英语外报外刊阅读教程》(北京大学出版社,2011,已3次印刷)
《新编美英报刊阅读教程(普及本)》(世界图书出版公司,2005,已9次印刷)
***《美英报刊阅读教程(普及精选本)》(南京大学出版社,2008,已9次印刷)
《美英报刊阅读教程(普及本修订本)》(南京大学出版社,2013,已3次印刷)
《21世纪报大学英语报刊阅读教程》(世界图书出版公司,2005,已3次印刷)

(以上标有*的书曾列为国家级教学成果二等奖主干教材;标有**的书为国家级规划教材;标有***的书获中国大学出版社优秀教材一等奖;标有▲的书为全国教育科学"十一五"规划2010年教育部重点课题)

二、专著系列

《传媒英语研究》(中国社会科学出版社,2000)
《美国传媒文化》(北京大学出版社,2003,已2次印刷)
《美国社会文化透视》(南京大学出版社,1999)
《高校英语报刊教学论丛》(北京大学出版社,2000)
《高校英语报刊教学论丛(第二版)》(北京大学出版社,2006)
《高校英语报刊教学论丛(第三版)》(北京大学出版社,2010)

三、学术论文58篇

第二版前言

承蒙广大读者厚爱，我所编著的《美英报刊阅读教程（高级本）》自 2001 年出版和《美英报刊阅读教程（高级精选本）》自 2009 年出版以来，总共印刷了 20 次。近几年来，世界政治格局、经济形势、社会文化、文教科技等方面又出现了一些新的重要情况，不少高校同行建议我根据新的形势对原教材部分课文作相应替换更新，这便使我萌发了编写"高级精选本"第二版的想法。

笔者从事高校英语报刊教学已近五十年，对报刊英语的研究也有三十余年。

多年的教学实践证明，英语报刊是十分理想的教学资料。报刊具有贴近时代、贴近大众、贴近现实、贴近生活的特点。作为教学资料，英语报刊具有以下四点显著优势：内容新颖、语言现代、资料丰富、词语实用。

伴随着国际交流的迅猛增加，英语报刊课程的重要性日趋突出，越来越多的高校为英语专业和非英语专业学生开设了这门课程。

教育部对英语报刊教学给予高度重视。教学大纲的四、六、八级阅读项目都明确将阅读英美报刊水平作为评定阅读能力的标准。

为了适应形势的需求，自 20 世纪 90 年代初以来我们先后编著出版了针对大学不同层次学生水平的英语报刊系列教材（详见"主编主要著作介绍"）。这套教材融入了我多年外报外刊的教学和研究成果，它们的共同之处在于突出学生能力的培养。

选材所坚持的标准是：题材覆盖面广、文章内容典型、语言质量上乘、知识含量丰富、使用时效较长。

为了突出能力培养，本书每篇课文之后共设七个部分：

1. 课文生词（New Words）
2. 知识介绍（Background Information）
3. 难点注释（Notes to the Text）
4. 语言简说（Language Features）
5. 内容分析（Analysis of the Content）
6. 问题思考（Questions on the Article）
7. 话题讨论（Topics for Discussion）

"知识介绍"部分根据课文内容，简明系统地提供文章相关专题的内容，旨在拓宽读者社会文化和科技等方面的知识。"语言简说"部分结合课文，简单扼要地介绍报刊英语和现代英语的常见语言现象，意在帮助读者熟悉外报外刊语言的规律和特点。这两个部分有助于学生构建和丰富外报外刊语言和文化的认知结构，引导他们步入轻松自如阅读英语报刊的理想境界。"内容分析"部分提供课文内容和语言的多项选择练习，目的在于帮助学生培养深入理解、分析推断和综合归纳能力。"话题讨论"部分提供与课文内容相关且有一定深度的宏观讨论题，意图在于培养学生的思辨能力和表述能力，增加口头交际实践的机会。

这是一本体现媒介素养教育理念的教材。为了帮助学生提高媒介素养水平，教材在"语言简说"栏目提供了西方常见报刊的最新简况，系统介绍了西方报刊版面与图片的功能和意识形态的表现形式。"内容分析"和"话题讨论"栏目力图引导学生培养深层次的分析能力和对作者观点的剖析和批评能力。

为了减轻授课老师的备课负担,本书配有教学参考资料,提供"内容分析"与"问题思考"两项练习的答案和课文篇章层次的分析。使用本书的教师可以登录网址:http://www.pup.cn,下载这些参考资料。

本书凝结着许多人的深情厚谊和汗水心血。高校英语报刊教学界的许多同仁和我的博士生、硕士生们为此书献计献策,我的夫人郭荣娣同志为我创造理想的工作环境,全力保障我的教学和科研。

尤为值得一提的是,本书修订过程中得到学院各级领导的热情鼓励和鼎力支持。在此,谨向为此书做出贡献的所有人士致以诚挚、深切的谢意。

由于对本书锤炼仍显不足,书中定有不少疏漏和错误,竭诚欢迎并殷切期望高校英语教师和广大读者提出宝贵意见。

还有一点需要说明:教材中有的文章个别地方用词值得商榷,主编不揣鄙陋提出修改拙见。为表示对原文作者的尊重,主编保留原文用词,而在认为有问题的用词之后的括号内标出修改意见,以供老师和读者们鉴别选择。

端木义万
2014年9月28日

目 录

第一单元 社会群体

Lesson 1	A Nation in Full	1
	知识介绍：美国人口的增长	7
	语言简说：新闻英语特色	10
Lesson 2	The New Greatest Generation	13
	知识介绍：内战后的几代人	20
	语言简说：《时代》周刊介绍	25
Lesson 3	Asians in the Promised Land	27
	知识介绍：亚裔美国人	32
	语言简说：《新闻周刊》介绍	36

第二单元 政治体制

Lesson 4	Closing the Gap	39
	知识介绍：传媒与选举	44
	语言简说：词语文化内涵	49
Lesson 5	Occupy Wall Street	52
	知识介绍：占领华尔街运动	58
	语言简说：《经济学家》简介	62
Lesson 6	D. C. Influentials	64
	知识介绍：美国的游说政治	71
	语言简说：《基督教科学箴言报》简介	76
Lesson 7	Republic or Empire	79
	知识介绍：军事凯恩斯主义	85
	语言简说：复合词	88

第三单元 信仰观念

Lesson 8	Accepting "The New Normal"	91
	知识介绍：9·11事件及其影响	94
	语言简说：《美国新闻与世界报道》介绍	98
Lesson 9	The Real Truth about Money	101
	知识介绍：金钱与幸福	104
	语言简说：报刊翻译常见错误	107

Lesson 10	The State of Our Unions	110
	知识介绍:婚姻观念	113
	语言简说:《今日美国》报简介	116
Lesson 11	The Elusive Big Idea	119
	知识介绍:网络与思维	124
	语言简说:《纽约时报》简介	128

第四单元　衣食住行

Lesson 12	How the World Eats	131
	知识介绍:快餐与慢食	135
	语言简说:借词	138
Lesson 13	Road Warriors	140
	知识介绍:美国交通	145
	语言简说:"说"意动词	148
Lesson 14	The Boom Towns and Ghost Towns of the New Economy	151
	知识介绍:美国带状区	158
	语言简说:《大西洋月刊》简介	162

第五单元　行为风尚

Lesson 15	Battle of the Binge	165
	知识介绍:学生酗酒	168
	语言简说:常用俚语	171
Lesson 16	The Share Economy	173
	知识介绍:分享经济	180
	语言简说:外刊与文化	184
Lesson 17	The Casino Next Door	187
	知识介绍:美国赌博业	196
	语言简说:《商业周刊》简介	199

第六单元　社会问题

Lesson 18	The Next Gun Fight	201
	知识介绍:美国枪支问题	207
	语言简说:版面与图片	211
Lesson 19	Homeless Sprawl	214
	知识介绍:美国住房问题	218
	语言简说:派生构词	221
Lesson 20	Sex on the Job	224
	知识介绍:性骚扰	226
	语言简说:委婉语	229

Lesson 21	Crooks Find Net Fertile Ground for Cyber Crime	232
	知识介绍：网络犯罪	236
	语言简说：网络新词常用词缀	239

第七单元　文教娱乐

Lesson 22	Secrets of Success	241
	知识介绍：美国高等教育	246
	语言简说：新闻英语常用典故	250
Lesson 23	Tuning Out TV	252
	知识介绍：美国广告	255
	语言简说：缩略词	259
Lesson 24	Our Titanic Love Affair	261
	知识介绍：美国电影史	266
	语言简说：报刊用喻特色	270

第八单元　企业经济

Lesson 25	What Price Reputation?	272
	知识介绍：企业形象	278
	语言简说：标题句式	283
Lesson 26	Tech's Kickback Culture	286
	知识介绍：商业贿赂	291
	语言简说：词义变化	294
Lesson 27	The Last Kodak Moment?	297
	知识介绍："柯达"的破产与"富士"的幸存	302
	语言简说：词性转化	304
Lesson 28	How One Red Hot Retailer Wins Customer Loyalty	307
	知识介绍：经营观念	312
	语言简说：嵌入结构	316

第九单元　科技军事

Lesson 29	The Internet Has Created a New Industrial Revolution	319
	知识介绍：创客运动	324
	语言简说：《卫报》简介	327
Lesson 30	Think Again: American Nuclear Disarmament	329
	知识介绍：美国核裁军	336
	语言简说：外报外刊中意识形态的表现	339
Lesson 31	On the Horizon: Are the next generation of UAVs ready to take off?	342
	知识介绍：无人机的发展趋势	348
	语言简说：前置定语	354

Lesson 32	Big Power Goes Local	356
	知识介绍：能源与环境	361
	语言简说：习语活用	364

第十单元　世界报道

Lesson 33	A Hopeful Continent	367
	知识介绍：非洲的崛起	373
	语言简说：拼缀词	377
Lesson 34	Return of the Samurai	379
	知识介绍：日本军国主义的复活	386
	语言简说：借代	390
Lesson 35	The Lost Youth of Europe	392
	知识介绍：困扰欧洲的两大问题	395
	语言简说：名词定语	397
Lesson 36	At Daggers Drawn	400
	知识介绍：世贸组织	406
	语言简说：经贸常用术语	409

Lesson 1

A Nation in Full

Within days, America will pass the 300-million mark in population. Behind the numbers, the changes are dramatic. A look at the biggest:

By Silla Brush

    It took the United States 139 years to get to 100 million people, and just 52 years to add another 100 million, back in 1967. Now, one day in October — after an interval of just 39 years — America will claim more than 300 million souls. The moment will be hailed as another symbol of America's boundless energy and unique vitality. It is that, of course. But it is also true America has grown every time the Census Bureau has taken a measurement, starting in 1790, when the Founders counted fewer than 4 million of their countrymen — about half the population of New York City today.

    The recent growth surge has been extraordinary. Since 2000 alone, the nation has added some 20 million people. Compared with western Europe, with birth rates plunging, or Japan, its population shrinking, America knows only growth, growth, and more growth. It now has the third-largest population in the world, after China and India. "Growth is a concern that we have to manage," says Kenneth Prewitt, former head of the Census Bureau, "but it's much easier to manage than losing your population."

    Examine the numbers closely, and three broad trends emerge. The first is migration. As the industrial base of the Northeast and Midwest has declined, millions of Americans have moved to the South and the West, now home to more than half the population — and growing strong. Immigration is next. Over the past four decades, immigrants, primarily from Mexico and Latin America, have reshaped the country's ethnic makeup; of the newest 100 million Americans, according to Jeffrey Passel of the Pew Hispanic Center[1], 53 percent are either immigrants or their descendants. Last are the much-ballyhooed boomers, many now on the cusp of retirement. America, says the nonprofit Population Reference Bureau, "is getting bigger, older, and more diverse."

    The implications are both vast and varied, affecting America's culture, politics, and economy. One obvious example is the stormy debate on immigration now roiling Congress. Another: As population shifts continue, congressional redistricting will follow, tipping the geographical balance of power.[2] A markedly older America will also have a profound effect on government spending — all three issues giving a new Congress and, before too much longer, a new president, plenty to ponder.

THE NEW MIGRATION

    BOISE, IDAHO — Sitting between the Rocky Mountain foothills[3] to the northeast and the Great Basin[4] desert to the south, between big sky and dusty desert, Boise has always been a pioneer town. In the early 1800s, legend has it, French-Canadian fur trappers came upon a clump of trees and exclaimed "Les Bois!" — the woods. And so Boise grew up a mining, logging, and farming hub, the capital city of one of the most rural states in America.

Those laid-back days are long gone. The 1970 census reported that Idaho had become more urban than rural; only a few years later, Micron, one of the world's largest superconductor producers and now the state's largest private employer, was founded here, and Hewlett-Packard's printer plant[5] was on the way. The main industry now is growth and how to manage it.[6] The Boise metro area's population has grown 79 percent just since 1990. Onion and beet farms abut subdivisions not even half finished[7]; on Chinden Boulevard, a main artery, a sign proclaiming "Hay for Sale" stands across from a flashy placard advertising the new Paramount housing development[8].

The challenge for city planners is as difficult as it is stark[9]: find enough room, housing, and jobs for more than double — or perhaps even triple — Boise's metropolitan area population, 530,000, as it charges toward 2030, when the population could reach 1.5 million people. "What we have today, we have to find room for again... That's daunting," says James Grunke, economic development manager at the Chamber of Commerce[10], looking out his eighth-floor conference room windows toward the foothills.

Daunting perhaps, but such growth is the envy of most mayors, though truth be told not all that uncommon among Grunke's regional peers.[11] For four decades, at the expense of the Northeast and Midwest, the South and West have taken off as America's fastest-growing areas, buoyed by immigration, lower costs, and recreational opportunities. Between 1990 and 2000, all five of the fastest-growing states were out West: Nevada (66 percent), Arizona (40 percent), Colorado (31 percent), Utah (30 percent), and Idaho (29 percent). Between 2004 and 2005, Florida, Georgia, North Carolina, and Texas were also among the fastest-growing states. Massachusetts, by contrast, declined in population between 2000 and 2005.

"It's so cheap," says Patrick Sweeney, bike messenger and bartender, who left San Francisco two years ago and bought a house in Boise for $121,000. "And the traffic isn't anything like California. That's why I got out." Adds Sue Williams, 49, who used to work at AT&T but left Redmond, Wash., for Boise less than two months ago and is renting an apartment with her 10-year-old son as she looks for a house: "We wanted to buy a house, and you can't buy in Redmond for less than $500,000." Over 80 percent of Boise residents say recreational opportunities are one of the city's top draws[12]; 125,000 people floated through the center of town on the Boise River last year.

Seattle, Portland, and California's biggest cities provide the majority of new Boise residents each year. Unemployment in Idaho's Treasure Valley region, including Boise, Meridian, Nampa, Caldwell, and surrounding towns, rests at 3 percent. And though still a relative bargain, housing prices skyrocketed 29 percent in the past year, the second-fastest rate in the country behind Bend, Ore.

At first glance, it's hard to imagine the nation's most isolated metropolitan area running out of room. Drive less than 5 miles southeast from the city on Warm Springs Avenue: Cow pastures lie to the north, a small mini storage park to the south. Yes, there is still a lot of land left. But it's being purchased at a feverish pace by developers. In Ada

County, one of the two largest counties in the region, 19 planned communities are either proposed or under construction. That has led to lengthy discussion about land use and economic development.

Two years and $1 million later, the valley region has yet to finalize a comprehensive plan to manage growth. Each municipality has its own vision. It might as well be the Old West in Boise's sprawling suburbs[13], such as Meridian — which since 1990 has grown six times in size to 66,000 people. The suburbs, says Ada County Commissioner Fred Tilman, are in an "annexation war" to acquire more land. Economic planners are also concerned about how to ensure that Boise is attracting solid jobs[14]. "I do have some worries that we're an economy of people building houses for people building houses," says Jeffrey Jones, Boise's head of economic development. The region is spending $5 million over the next five years to attract 5,000 highly skilled jobs and stay ahead of perennial regional threats: Albuquerque, N.M.; Reno, Nev.; Colorado Springs and Fort Collins, Colo.; and Salt Lake City. Then there is the traffic problem. Only one highway serves the region and almost no one uses public transportation; that could change with a light rail system, but only if planners are able to raise enough money to get one built.

Horace Greeley's[15] 1850s paraphrased proverb of manifest destiny[16], with a bit of a southern flavor added, still rings true today: "Go West and South, young man, and grow up with the country."

A WAVE OF IMMIGRANTS

FORT WAYNE, IND. — Matthew Schiebel was born just three blocks from Northwood Middle School here in northeastern Fort Wayne, a gritty rust belt[17] city of 220,000 formerly known as a canal and rail gateway to the West. When Schiebel, 41, attended grade school 20 years ago, "we used to think of diversity as black-white," he says. Now Northwood, where Schiebel is principal, is 13 percent Hispanic. Each year the number of students taking classes in English as a second language increases; this year, it's 90 students out of a total of 802. Thirty-two flags hang from the lobby ceiling, each representing a student's ethnicity. Among those added recently: Rwanda, Portugal, and Honduras. The United Hispanic Americans, a community organization, sends four to five tutors to the school twice a week.

The Hoosier State's[18] second-largest city is still overwhelmingly black (16 percent) and white (74 percent). But immigration growth is rapidly transforming Fort Wayne. Since 1990, its Hispanic population has grown about four times to 16,500. With fertility rates tumbling in the 1980s and 1990s (and projected to stay low through 2050), immigration has become the main driver of population growth[19]. Since 2000 alone, there has been a 16 percent rise in the number of immigrants living in American households.

In 1967, at the time of the 200 million mark, the biggest immigration story was about "brain drain[20]" from western Europe to the United States. After President Johnson signed the Immigration and Naturalization Act in 1965 to stop racial and ethnic quotas for new immigrants, and once the Mexican economy tanked in the 1970s, immigration, both legal and illegal, skyrocketed. In Fort Wayne, nearly 80 percent of Hispanics are Mexican. An estimated 12 million undocumented immigrants now live in America, up from 5 million just a decade ago. Prior to the early 1990s, a third of new immigrants came to California, and a full three quarters wound up either there or in just five other states: Illinois, New Jersey,

Florida, New York, and Texas. But in the past 15 years, immigrants have spread out. States like Georgia have seen massive increases. Demographers have also noticed a third wave of dispersion to the meatpacking plants in Iowa and Nebraska and to farming, manufacturing, construction, and service-sector jobs in places like Fort Wayne.

When Zulma Prieto moved 16 years ago from Colombia to Goshen, Ind., a farming and RV-manufacturing town[21] an hour west of Fort Wayne, there were only three Hispanic stores in the area. "It was almost a surprise to see someone speak Spanish," she says. There were some migrant farmworkers, but in the early 1990s, the Chamber of Commerce started advertising for workers. "All of a sudden a lot of people started to come," says Prieto, editor of the newspaper *El Puente*[22].

Goshen's population is now about 30 percent Hispanic. Los Galanes, a Spanish market with piñatas hanging from the ceiling, sits about 2 miles from one of the first Wal-Marts in the country to provide stables for Amish horse and buggies. Each year, the Mexican consulate in Chicago sends a "mobile consulate" to issue IDs. In Fort Wayne, Sam Hyde, who runs Hyde Brothers Booksellers, can remember the first Mexican restaurant opening 40 years ago at a truck stop. In the past six years, a Mexican restaurant and a bakery opened across from his store on Wells Street, the city's hip arts neighborhood[23]. "The biggest business on this street is wiring money[24]," Hyde says. Mega 102.3, the first Spanish radio station in the area, opened last month with an estimated audience of 50,000.

But the influx has brought accompanying tensions. St. Patrick's Church in Fort Wayne, the area's only church with a full Spanish service, has seen its congregation grow from a couple of hundred to standing room only on Sundays, with more than 900 people attending. When the church moved to a heavily Hispanic neighborhood, many white members left. "It was a big change, and a lot of people were really hurt," says Blanca Navarro, who works at the church. According to a survey done for Republican Rep. Mark Souder, who represents Fort Wayne and Goshen, 76 percent of his district's residents think there should be a fence along the Mexican border. "We have Ku Klux Klan here," says Goshen Mayor Allan Kauffman. "So of course everyone isn't accepting... It's getting more integrated, but it hasn't been the smoothest transition."

THE GRAYING OF AMERICA

WILMINGTON, N.C. — It's a cliché, elderly parents telling their kids how they "don't want to be a burden" to them. Right out of *Guilt Trip 101*.[25] Well, if the number crunchers[26] are right, all those aging baby boomers — the first ones turned 60 this year — probably shouldn't waste their breath. Economist Laurence Kotlikoff of Boston University is typical. He describes the onslaught of 77 million aging boomers as a "generational storm" that will pose "a crushing burden for the country."

The United States is growing dramatically older. Back in 1900, the median age in the United States was 22.9 years. But with people having fewer babies, that number started to climb. Lower fertility rates mean older populations. The baby boom caused a brief pause in this movement during the 1950s and 1960s, but the aging trend has since resumed. The median age is up to 36.5 and is expected to rise to 39 by 2030 before leveling off. Or, to put it another way, America in 2030 will look like Florida does today. Some 12.4 percent of Americans are 65 or older today — up from 9.9 percent in 1970 — but that number will rise to 19.6 percent of Americans in 2030.

But at the local level, the perspective's a little different. Seniors a burden? That sure isn't how his gray-haired residents look to Mayor Bill Saffo of Wilmington. "They're a real asset to us," he says. "The seniors retiring here are active in our community. They're involved in nonprofits, but they are also working part time or creating businesses."

Wilmington, on the Cape Fear coast, has become a magnet for retirees, thanks to its great beaches, low cost of living, and abundant golf courses. During the 1990s, a decade when the city grew 35 percent, Wilmington saw its over-65 population grow 46 percent, the eighth-fastest rate for any metro area with a population under 1 million residents, according to research by demographer William Frey. Wilmington also saw its pre-elderly population — ages 55 to 64 — jump 52 percent, the seventh-fastest rate for any city in America. And there are few signs the river of older residents has abated.

Wilmington also has plenty of what some urban experts call "street corner strange," a quirky, artsy atmosphere fed by the presence of the University of North Carolina — Wilmington and its role as a frequent Hollywood film location. On a recent rainy morning, not far from Saffo's office, Wilmington's main drag was narrowed by the bulky presence of large vans used in filming TV's *One Tree Hill*.[27]

Among the folks now making their home here are Bill and Mary Lou Bryden, who moved to Wilmington from Britain six years ago when Bill retired from Lockheed, where he worked on air-traffic-control automation systems.[28] In addition to the great boating opportunities, "we really loved the fact this was a college town," says Bill, 71. The Brydens hardly fit the "round of golf, dinner at 4 o'clock" stereotypes of retirees. Bill serves on the local transportation board, a railroad museum board, a charity board, and a bank board. Mary Lou, 70, still designs and sells stained-glass windows[29]. "You move here with different talents and abilities, and the city wants you to keep using them," she says.

There's no doubt that seniors have been a boost to economic activity. Prof. William Hall, senior economist at the Center for Business and Economics Services at UNCW[30], estimates that retirees — often well-to-do — generate $2 in economic activity for every $1 they spend. And there are indirect benefits, too. Connie Majure-Rhett, president of the Greater Wilmington Chamber of Commerce, says it's no coincidence the area's health services are getting an upgrade. The New Hanover Regional Medical Center, based in Wilmington, is undergoing a $200 million expansion. As a matter of fact, Saffo says he's hard-pressed to think of any downside to the flood of seniors here.[31]

A CHALLENGING FUTURE

Demographers say America's growth will only accelerate further. By around 2043, or in less than another 40 years, the nation's population is expected to reach 400 million. And many of the trends now altering the American landscape will become even more pronounced.

The South and West will be home to roughly two thirds of the country's population: The Phoenix and Tucson metropolitan areas, for instance, are projected to merge, and the population of those regions is projected to double to 10 million.

Demographers expect that the impact of births by new immigrants in coming years will be an even larger force than the impact of immigrants actually crossing the border. For the 2000–2005 period, Latino births surpassed the number of new Latino immigrants nationally for the first time since the 1960s. "I expect that over the next 50 years, we'll see more Latino births than immigrants," says Passel. "In the next 100 million [in population], the role of future immigration will be a bit less." And according to one calculation, those children will help push the country to the brink of becoming a "majority minority" nation[32], just as California, the District of Columbia, Hawaii, New Mexico, and Texas are now. Whites could make up just about half of the population, down from two thirds now. The black population could grow 50 percent, and the Hispanic and Asian populations could each more than double. "For the past half of the 20th century, we were more or less a suburban middle-class society," says demographer Frey, a visiting fellow at the Brookings Institution[33]. But now, he says, we're headed back to more of a melting pot.

Over the course of the next 25 years, the over-65 population is expected to double to 71.5 million. As a result, the Social Security and Medicare systems are headed for trouble. Each year, the overseers of Social Security and Medicare, the two largest entitlement programs, warn that they're on the cusp of bankruptcy.[34] Why the pessimism? Starting somewhere around 2017 or 2019, the Social Security program will pay out more money in benefits than it takes in from taxes. Then by around 2041 to 2046, the Social Security trust fund will run dry. There are plans to change how Social Security works — the retirement age, for example, could be extended or future initial benefit increases could be linked to inflation rather than wages — but the fight is sure to be bruising.

Medicare starts drawing down its reserves a whole lot sooner — in 2010. If the national debt sounds staggering, at $8.5 trillion, try Medicare's projected shortfall of $32.4 trillion over 75 years. Not only does Medicare have to deal with the same demographic challenges as Social Security; it's also plagued by the complex and politically vexing problem of rising healthcare costs. "I could give you a plan to fix Social Security," says Rand Corp.[35] economist Michael Hurd. "But nobody has a very good plan for fixing healthcare." Turns out the new America has more than its share of both opportunities and challenges. Meeting the latter may determine how quickly America reaches its next milestone.

With James M. Pethokoukis

From *US News & World Report*, October 2, 2006

Ⅰ. New Words

abate	[ə'beit]	v.	to become less strong; to decrease
annexation	[ˌænek'seiʃən]	n.	合并,并吞
artsy	['ɑːtsi]	adj.	装作爱好艺术的
ballyhoo	['bælihuː]	v.	过分宣扬
buggy	['bʌgi]	n.	AmE 四轮单马轻便车
buoy	[bɔi]	v.	to keep sth at a high level
clump	[klʌmp]	n.	丛,簇
cusp	[kʌsp]	n.	交接时段;转折点
hub	[hʌb]	n.	the central part
influx	['inflʌks]	n.	arriving in large numbers
laid-back	['leidbæk]	adj.	*informal* calm and relaxed
metro	['metrəu]	n.	a large or capital city

nonprofit	[ˌnɒn'prɒfit]	*adj.*	非赢利的
onslaught	['ɒnslɔːt]	*n.*	a strong or violent attack
perennial	[pə'renjəl]	*adj.*	continuing for a long time
piñata	[piːn'jɑːtə]	*n.*	〈西〉(墨西哥人用于装糖果或玩具等陶质或纸质的)彩罐
pronounced	[prə'naunst]	*adj.*	obvious
quirky	['kwɜːki]	*adj.*	strange and unusual
roil	[rɔil]	*v.*	to make disturbed and confused
stable	['steibl]	*n.*	马厩
superconductor	[ˌsjuːpəkən'dʌktə]	*n.*	[物]超导(电)体
tank	[tæŋk]	*v.*	*AmE informal* to suffer a sudden decline or failure
tip	[tip]	*v.*	使倾斜
tumble	['tʌmbl]	*v.*	to fall downwards
wind	[waind]	*v.*	~ **up** to find oneself in a particular place or situation

Ⅱ. Background Information

美国人口的增长

1790年,美国人口仅为390万,主要集中于大西洋沿岸。1880年美国人口上升到5,000万,1915年突破1亿,1967年超过2亿,2006年10月17日达到3亿。截至2014年1月1日美国人口总数为3.17亿。

美国人口增长共分四个阶段(four chapters)。

第一阶段(1790—1840年):这一阶段移民数量有限,有时一年仅有6,000,最多一年也未超过79,000,但是人口增长率却很高,每十年增长率在28%和30%之间。人口增长的主要因素是高生育率。这一阶段,美国妇女平均每人生育7个孩子。

第二阶段(1841—1865年):这个阶段大批西欧移民来到美国。爱尔兰土豆灾荒(potato famine)导致100多万难民移居美国。此外,许多欧洲人为了逃避政治迫害而来到美国。1830—1848年德国革命失败之后,大批知识分子逃到美国。据统计,这一阶段共有330万移民来到美国,约占原先人口的16%。

第三阶段(1866—1944年):南北战争造成大批人员伤亡,人口一度下降。但是战争结束后移民浪潮再次形成。19世纪70年代移民数量多达270万,80年代为520万,90年代为370万,1900—1914年有1,340万。原先移民基本来自西欧,1890年后的移民主要来自南欧、中欧和东欧。在人口流动方面,虽然北部工资大大高于南部,但是很少有南方人迁往北部。20世纪20年代,移民限制政策使得移民数量大幅下降。30年代又出现了经济大萧条(the Great Depression),美国人口增长率降至7%。第二次世界大战后,美国经济步入繁荣时期,人口出生也呈现了高峰(baby boom),这一时期持续将近20年。与此同时,人口流动比较活跃,除了由东往西方向的流动,在种族隔离结束之后还出现了由北向南方向的流动。据统计,20世纪40年代,加利福尼亚州、得克萨斯州和佛罗里达州人口分别为1,060万、640万、190万,而第四阶段(1970—　):20世纪60年代末开始,美国白人生育率急剧下降,但是美国人口却大幅攀升。其原因是大量移民的到来。1965年,美国颁布了"移民归化法"(the Immigration and Naturalization Law)。移民政策的放宽带来了一次大规模的移民潮(immigration wave)。70年代新移民数量超过660万,使美国人口增长了3%,80年代又有大约800万移民的到来,使人口增加了3.3%。这一阶段的移民主要来自拉丁美洲和亚洲。人口流动依然保持向西、向南趋势。2000年,加利福尼亚州、得克萨斯州和佛罗里达州人口分别增加到3,400万、2,090万和1,600万。

近几十年来,由于新的移民源源不断流入,加之少数种族生育率高于白人,美国人口的结构大大改变。2006年,美国西班牙裔人数量为4,420万,占总人口比例为14.8%,非洲裔人数量为3,830万,占12.8%,亚裔人数量为1,310万,占4.4%,印第安人数量290万,约占1%。少数种族人口总数为1亿70万,占总人口比例为33.5%。截至2012年7月,少数族裔人口上升至1.16亿,占全国总人口(3.14亿)比例为37%。据专家预计,本世纪中期之前,美国非西班牙裔白人(non-Hispanic white)人口比例将低于50%,成为少数种族。

纵观美国人口发展史,可以说美国是一个"移民之国"(a nation of immigrants)。

Ⅲ. Notes to the Text

1. the Pew Hispanic Center — 皮尤西班牙裔美国人研究中心(一家非赢利性研究西班牙裔美国人相关情况的机构)
2. As population shifts continue, congressional redistricting will follow, tipping the geographical balance of power. — 随着人口继续变化,国会选举区域就会重新划分,这将改变区域权力的平衡。(redistrict — to change the election districts according to population shifts)
3. Rocky Mountain foothills — 落基山脉丘陵
4. the Great Basin — 大盆地(指美国西部落基山脉和内华达山脉之间的盆地区)
5. Hewlett-Packard printer plant — 惠普打印机制造厂
6. The main industry now is growth and how to manage it. — 现在主要企业是迅速发展的企业和企业发展管理型行业。(growth industry — an industry which grows faster than other industries under the same conditions)
7. Onion and beet farms abut subdivisions not even half finished — 种植洋葱和甜菜的农场毗连尚未建好一半的住宅小区(subdivision — *AmE* an area of land that has been divided for building houses on)
8. the new Paramount housing development — 新建的派拉蒙住宅区(housing development — housing estate)
9. The challenge for city planners is as difficult as it is stark — 城市规划者面临的是既困难又苛刻的挑战。(stark — harsh)
10. Chamber of Commerce — 商会
11. Daunting perhaps, but such growth is the envy of most mayors, though truth be told not all that uncommon among Grunke's regional peers. — 这或许使人感到可怕,但是这种快速发展是大部分市长所羡慕的。然而说实话,在类似格兰克的地区,这种情况并非鲜见。

12. one of the city's top draws — one of the city's greatest attractions
13. It might as well be the Old West in Boise's sprawling suburbs —博伊西市郊区的无序扩张就像早期西部的发展。(Old West — referring to the West of the U.S. during its early stage of fast development)
14. solid jobs — 有价值的工作(solid — of practical value)
15. Horace Greeley — 霍勒斯·格里利(1811—1872,纽约《论坛报》创办人)
16. manifest destiny — 天定命运论(the belief that US people had the right and the duty to take land in North America from other people, because this was God's plan. This phrase was used by journalists and politicians in the 19th century when US citizens moved west across North America.)
17. rust belt — 衰落地带(a region that used to have a lot of industry, but has now decreased in importance and wealth)
18. the Hoosier State — 山地人之乡(美国印第安纳州的别称,因旧时来该州定居者为肯塔基州山地人而得名)
19. immigration has become the main driver of population growth — 移民已成为人口增长的主要因素(driver — one of the factors that causes sth to make progress)
20. brain drain — 人才外流(the movement of highly-skilled and qualified people to another country where they can work in better conditions and earn more money)
21. RV-manufacturing town — 休闲车制造业城市(RV — recreational vehicle, a large vehicle designed for people to live and sleep in when they are travelling)
22. *El Puente* —《假日报》
23. hip arts neighborhood — 时尚工艺品街(hip — fashionable)
24. The biggest business on this street is wiring money — 这条街最重要的商业就是电汇业务。(wire money — to send money from one bank to another using an electronic system)
25. Right out of *Guilt Trip 101*. — 刚刚出自《罪恶感101》栏目(① guilt trip — feeling of guilt or shame; ② 101 — All college courses have a three-digit number assigned to them, preceded by the course name. Freshman courses are in the 100s, so the number "101" means: the most basic or elemental form.)
26. number cruncher — 数字计算者(crunch numbers — to do a lot of calculations using a calculator or a computer)
27. Wilmington's main drag was narrowed by the bulky presence of large vans used in filming TV's *One Tree Hill*. —威尔明顿市主街当电视剧《独树山》拍摄所用的那种大型货车通过时显得狭窄。(main drag — *AmE informal* the most important or busiest street in a town)
28. Bill retired from Lockheed, where he worked on air-traffic-control automatic systems. — 比尔已从洛克希德公司退休,他在这家公司干的是空中交通管理自动控制系统生产线工作(Lockheed — 美国一家主要航空航天公司,创建于1912年)
29. stained-glass windows 彩色玻璃窗(stained-glass — glass of different colors)
30. the Center for Business and Economics Services at UNCW — 北卡罗来纳州立大学威尔明顿分校商业与经济服务中心
31. ... he's hard-pressed to think of any downside to the flood of seniors here. — ……他很

难想出大批老人移居这里有任何坏处。(downside — the disadvantage or less positive aspects of sth)

32. And according to one calculation, those children will help push the country to the brink of becoming a "majority minority" nation — 据预测,这些(新出生的)孩子将促使美国即将成为少数种族人口占多数的国家。

33. a visiting fellow at the Brookings Institution — 布鲁金斯学会访问研究员(①fellow — research fellow;②Brookings Institution — 美国一个带有自由主义色彩的非赢利的政治学与经济学研究所)

34. the overseers of Social Security and Medicare, the two largest entitlement programs, warn that they're on the cusp of bankruptcy. — (美国)政府经办的"社会保障"和"医疗照顾"两大福利项目的管理者们警告说,这两个项目即将破产。〔①Social Security — 社会保障制度(1935年美国政府通过"社会保障"条例,对老年或残疾人员及贫苦儿童、失业人员等给予最低额救济金);②Medicare — 老年医疗保险,指政府为65岁以上老人设置的医疗费减免制度〕

35. Rand Corp. — 兰德公司〔美国一家思想库,专门为政府(特别是空军)做战略情报分析研究服务〕

Ⅳ. Language Features

新闻英语特色

英语新闻刊物多种多样:有新闻报纸(newspaper),也有新闻杂志(news magazine),还有电子报纸(electronic newspaper,简称 e-paper)和电子杂志(electronic magazine,简称 e-zine)。报纸可细分为日报(day newspaper),晨报(morning newspaper),晚报(evening newspaper),半周报(semiweekly),周报(weekly)和双周报(biweekly);城市报(metropolitan newspaper),郊区报(suburban newspaper)和乡村报(rural newspaper);严肃(高级)报(quality newspaper)和通俗小报(tabloid)。

翻开报纸我们便会发现,就是同一种报纸所载文章体裁也是纷繁复杂的:有纯新闻报道(straight news report)、解释性报道(interpretative report)、调查性报道(investigative report)、精确性报道(precision report),还有特写(feature)、社论(editorial)、读者来信(letters to the editor)和广告(advertisement)等。

不同新闻刊物有不同办刊风格,不同类型文章也有不同语言特色。因此,不容易对新闻刊物的语言特色作出全面概述。这里所谈的新闻语体是指新闻刊物最为常见的和最有代表性的体裁——新闻报道,而且主要是指纯新闻报道。

新闻英语主要受五个因素制约:大众性、节俭性、趣味性、时新性和客观性。

报刊是大众传媒,写作必须适合广大读者水平,语言必须通俗易懂。

报业十分珍惜版面,要求新闻写作人员在有限的篇幅内提供尽可能多的信息,读者看报珍惜时间,希望在很短的时间得到所要的信息,这就迫使新闻写作人员养成文字简洁的风格。

西方新闻界一向注重趣味性,报刊又面临电视、广播、网络传媒的巨大挑战,要稳住报业市场就得加强趣味性,因而新闻报道必须写得生动有趣。

时新性是新闻价值之一。新闻报道在提供最新消息的同时也传播了相关的新词。此外，不少新闻写作人员为了增加文章的吸引力，在语言上刻意求新，因而新闻英语具有新颖活泼的特色。

客观性是纯新闻报道所遵循的准则，没有客观性，报道就要丢掉可信性，也就会失去读者。客观性要求新闻报道文字准确具体，避用情感词语和夸张手法。

初读美英报刊的人往往会遇到很多困难。之所以如此，主要是因为他们对报刊英语特点了解不够。譬如，新闻标题短小精悍，在句式和用词上都有相应的省略手段。又如，新闻报道为了节约篇幅，采用一系列手段浓缩、精练句式。较常见的有前置定语、名词定语、身份同位语前置、词性转化、借代、缩略词等。再如，为使语言生动、活泼，报刊常常使用比喻和成语活用手段。新闻刊物不仅是报导新闻的媒介，而且是"使用新词的庞大机器和杜撰新词的巨大工厂"。这些特点会给读者带来理解上的困难。为了帮助读者克服这些困难，本书把新闻英语特色分成若干细目，结合每篇课文，逐一进行介绍。

应该指出的是，英语报刊种类繁多，针对不同读者群体的报刊会有相应的不同语言特色。此外，同一份报刊中的不同类型文章在语言方面也存在相应的差异。

《高级本》文章基本选自针对教育水平较高读者群体的报刊，一般都是特稿和评论。这些文章除篇幅较长之外，还具有一定思想深度和语言难度。请广大读者阅读时充分注意这一点。

V. Analysis of the Content

1. The term "solid jobs" in the 12th paragraph refers to _____.
   A. service-sector jobs　　　　　　　B. house-building jobs
   C. well-paid jobs　　　　　　　　　D. highly-skilled jobs
2. According to the article, America's population reached 100 million in _____.
   A. 1907　　　　　　　　　　　　　B. 1915
   C. 1790　　　　　　　　　　　　　D. 1928
3. Of the newest 100 million Americans, the largest group is _____.
   A. immigrants or their descendants　　B. white people
   C. African-Americans　　　　　　　D. Hispanics
4. Demographers believe that the major factor which will lead America to the brink of becoming a "majority minority" nation is _____.
   A. the influx of new immigrants　　　B. births by new immigrants
   C. decrease of white American's fertility rate　　D. longer life expectancy
5. Which of the following statements is False?
   A. About two thirds of America's population will live in the South and the West.
   B. Births by new immigrants will have a greater impact than new immigrants.
   C. The over-65 population will show a big increase.
   D. The new America will have more challenges than opportunities.

VI. Questions on the Article

1. What are the three big milestones for America's population?

2. How fast has America's population been growing in recent years?
3. What are the three population trends in America?
4. What have buoyed the fast growth of the South and the West?
5. What is the major factor in the population growth?
6. What is the most striking difference between the immigration before 1967 and the immigration after that?
7. What problem has the influx of new immigrants caused according to the article?
8. How has the median age been changing in America?
9. Why do people like Mayor Bill Saffo consider the senior citizens as a real asset?
10. What are the main attractions of Wilmington?
11. What impacts does the enlarged senior population have on Social Security and Medicare?

VII. Topics for Discussion

1. Is the American society a melting pot?
2. Is the increase of immigrants a boon or a curse to America's economy?

Lesson 2

The New Greatest Generation
Why Millennials Will Save US All

By Joel Stein

(Abridged)

I am about to do what old people have done throughout history: call those younger than me lazy, entitled, selfish and shallow. But I have studies! I have statistics! I have quotes from respected academics! Unlike my parents, my grandparents and my great-grandparents, I have proof.

Here's the cold, hard data: The incidence of narcissistic personality disorder[1] is nearly three times as high for people in their 20s as for the generation that's now 65 or older, according to the National Institutes of Health[2]; 58% more college students scored higher on a narcissism scale in 2009 than in 1982. Millennials got so many participation trophies growing up that a recent study showed that 40% believe they should be promoted every two years, regardless of performance. They are fame-obsessed: three times as many middle school girls want to grow up to be a personal assistant to a famous person as want to be a Senator, according to a 2007 survey; four times as many would pick the assistant job over CEO of a major corporation. They're so convinced of their own greatness that the National Study of Youth and Religion found the guiding morality of 60% of millennials in any situation is that they'll just be able to feel what's right. Their development is stunted: more people ages 18 to 29 live with their parents than with a spouse, according to the 2012 Clark University Poll of Emerging Adults[3]. And they are lazy. In 1992, the non-profit Families and Work Institute[4] reported that 80% of people under 23 wanted to one day have a job with greater responsibility; 10 years later, only 60% did.

Millennials consist, depending on whom you ask, of people born from 1980 to 2000. To put it more simply for them, since they grew up not having to do a lot of math in their heads, thanks to computers, the group is made up mostly of teens and 20-somethings. At 80 million strong, they are the biggest age grouping in American history.[5]

They are the most threatening and exciting generation since the baby boomers brought about social revolution, not because they're trying to take over the Establishment but because they're growing up without one.[6] The Industrial Revolution made individuals far more powerful—they could move to a city, start a business, read and form organizations. The information revolution has further empowered individuals by handing them the technology to compete against huge organizations: hackers vs. corporations, bloggers vs. newspapers, terrorists vs. nation-states, YouTube directors vs. studios, app-makers vs. entire industries[7]. Millennials don't need us. That's why we're scared of them.

In the U.S., millennials are the children of baby boomers, who are also known as the Me Generation, who then produced the Me Me Me Generation, whose selfishness technology has only exacerbated.[8] Whereas in the 1950s families displayed a wedding photo, a school photo and maybe a military photo in their homes, the average middle-class American family today walks amid 85 pictures of themselves and their pets. Millennials have come of age in the era of the quantified self, recording their daily steps on Fit Bit, their whereabouts every hour of every day on PlaceMe and their genetic data on 23 and Me.[9] They have less civic engagement and lower political participation than any previous group. This is a generation that would have made Walt Whitman[10] wonder if maybe they should try singing a song of someone else.

They got this way partly because, in the 1970s, people wanted to improve kids' chances of success by instilling self-esteem. It turns out that self-esteem is great for getting a job or hooking up at a bar but not so great for keeping a job or a relationship.[11] "It was an honest mistake," says Roy Baumeister, a psychology professor at Florida State University and the editor of *Self-Esteem: The Puzzle of Low Self-Regard*[12]. "The early findings showed that, indeed, kids with high self-esteem did better in school and were less likely to be in various kinds of trouble. It's just that we've learned later that self-esteem is a result, not a cause." The problem is that when people try to boost self-esteem, they accidentally boost narcissism instead. "Just tell your kids you love them. It's a better message," says Jean Twenge, a psychology professor at San Diego State University, who wrote *Generation Me and The Narcissism Epidemic*. "When they're little it seems cute to tell them they're special or a princess or a rock star or whatever their T-shirt says. When they're 14 it's no longer cute." All that self-esteem leads them to be disappointed when the world refuses to affirm how great they know they are. "This generation has the highest likelihood of having unmet expectations with respect to their careers and the lowest levels of satisfaction with their careers at the stage that they're at," says Sean Lyons, co-editor of *Managing the New Workforce: International Perspectives on the Millennial Generation*[13]. "It is sort of a crisis of unmet expectations."

What millennials are most famous for besides narcissism is its effect: entitlement. If you want to sell seminars to middle managers, make them about how to deal with young employees who e-mail the CEO directly and beg off projects they find boring.[14] English teacher David McCullough Jr.'s address last year to Wellesley High School's graduating class, a 12-minute reality check[15] titled "You Are Not Special," has nearly 2 million hits on YouTube. "Climb the mountain so you can see the world, not so the world can see you," McCullough told the graduates. He says nearly all the response to the video has been positive, especially from millennials themselves; the video has 57 likes for every dislike.

Though they're cocky about their place in the world, millennials are also stunted, having prolonged a life stage between teenager and adult that this magazine once called twixters and will now use once again in an attempt to get that term to catch on. The idea of the teenager started in the 1920s; in 1910, only a tiny percentage of kids went to high school, so most people's social interactions were with adults in their family or in the workplace. Now that cell phones allow kids to socialize at every hour—they send and receive an average of 88 texts a day, according to Pew—they're living under the constant influence of their friends. "Peer pressure is anti-intellectual. It is anti-historical. It is anti-eloquence," [16] says Mark Bauerlein, an English professor at Emory, who wrote *The Dumbest Generation: How the Digital Age Stupefies Young Americans and Jeopardizes Our Future (Or, Don't Trust Anyone Under* 30). "Never before in history have people been able to grow up and reach age 23 so dominated by peers. To develop intellectually you've got to relate to older people, older things: 17-year-olds never grow up if they're just hanging around other 17-year-olds." Of all the objections to Obamacare[17], not a lot of people argued against parents' need to cover their kids' health insurance until they're 26.

Millennials are interacting all day but almost entirely through a screen. You've seen them at bars, sitting next to one another and texting. They might look calm, but they're deeply anxious about missing out on something better. Seventy percent of them check their phones every hour, and many experience phantom pocket-vibration syndrome. "They're doing a behavior to reduce their anxiety," says Larry Rosen, a psychology professor at California State University at Dominguez Hills and the author of *iDisorder*[18]. That constant search for a hit of dopamine ("Someone liked my status update!") reduces creativity.[19] From 1966, when the Torrance Tests of Creative Thinking[20] were first administered, through the mid-1980s, creativity scores in children increased. Then they dropped, falling sharply in 1998. Scores on tests of empathy similarly fell sharply, starting in 2000, likely because of both a lack of face-to-face time and higher degrees of narcissism. Not only do millennials lack the kind of empathy that allows them to feel concerned for others, but they also have trouble even intellectually understanding others' points of view.

What they do understand is how to turn themselves into brands, with "friend" and "follower" tallies that serve as sales figures. As with most sales, positivity and confidence work best. "People are inflating themselves like balloons on Facebook," says W. Keith Campbell, a psychology professor at the University of Georgia, who has written three books about generational increases in narcissism (including *When You Love a Man Who Loves Himself*). When everyone is telling you about their vacations, parties and promotions, you start to embellish your own life to keep up. If you do this well enough on Instagram, YouTube and Twitter, you can become a microcelebrity.[21]

Millennials grew up watching reality-TV shows, most of which are basically documentaries about narcissists. Now they have trained themselves to be reality-TV-ready. "Most people never define who they are as a personality type until their 30s. So for people to be defining who they are at the age of 14 is almost a huge evolutionary jump," says casting director Doron Ofir, who auditioned participants for "Jersey Shore, Millionaire Matchmaker," "A Shot at Love" and "RuPaul's Drag Race,"[22] among other shows. "Do you follow me on Twitter?" he asks at the end of the interview. "Oh, you should. I'm fun. I hope that one day they provide an Emmy for casting of reality shows—because, you know, I'd assume I'm a shoo-in. I would like that gold statue. And then I will take a photo of it, and then I will Instagram it." Ofir is 41, but he has clearly spent a lot of time around millennials.

While the entire first half of this article is absolutely true (I had data!), millennials' self-involvement is more a continuation of a trend than a revolutionary break from previous generations. They're not a new species; they've just mutated to adapt to their environment.

For example, millennials' perceived entitlement isn't a result of overprotection but an adaptation to a world of abundance. Twixters put off life choices because they can choose from a huge array of career options, some of which, like jobs in social media, didn't exist 10 years ago. What idiot would try to work her way up at a company when she's going to have an average of seven jobs before age 26? Because of online dating, Facebook circles and the ability to connect with people internationally, they no longer have to marry someone from their high school class or even their home country. Because life expectancy is increasing so rapidly and technology allows women to get pregnant in their 40s, they're more free to postpone big decisions. The median age for an American woman's first marriage went from 20.6 in 1967 to 26.9 in 2011.

In fact, a lot of what counts as typical millennial behavior is how rich kids have always behaved. The Internet has democratized opportunity for many young people, giving them access and information that once belonged mostly to the wealthy. When I was growing up in the 1980s, I thought I would be a lawyer, since that was the best option I knew about for people who sucked at math in my middle-class suburb, but I saw a lot more options once I got to Stanford. "Previously if you wanted to be a writer but didn't know anyone who is in publishing, it was just, Well, I won't write. But now it's, Wait, I know someone who knows someone," says Jane Buckingham, who studies workplace changes as founder of Trendera, a consumer-insights firm[23]. "I hear story after story of people high up in an organization saying, 'Well, this person just e-mailed me and asked me for an hour of my time, and for whatever reason I gave it to them.' So the great thing is that they do feel entitled to all of this, so they'll be more innovative and more willing to try new things and they'll do all this cool stuff."

Kim Kardashian[24], who represents to nonmillennials all that is wrong with her generation, readily admits that she has no particular talent. But she also knows why she appeals to her peers. "They like that I share a lot of myself and that I've always been honest about the way I live my life," she says. "They want relationships with businesses and celebrities. Gen X was kept at arm's length from businesses and celebrity." When you're no longer cowed by power, you are going to like what a friend tells you about far more than what an ad campaign does, even if that friend is a celebrity trying to make money and that friendship is just a reply to one tweet.

While every millennial might seem like an oversharing Kardashian, posting vacation photos on Facebook is actually less obnoxious than 1960s couples' trapping friends in their houses to watch their terrible vacation slide shows. "Can you imagine if the boomers had YouTube, how narcissistic they would've seemed?" asks Scott Hess, senior vice president of human intelligence for Spark SMG[25], whose Ted X speech[26], "Millennials: Who They Are and Why We Hate Them," advised companies on marketing to youth. "Can you imagine how many frickin' Instagrams of people playing in the mud during Woodstock we would've seen?[27] I think in many ways you're blaming millennials for the technology that happens to exist right now." Yes, they check their phones during class, but think about how long you can stand in line without looking at your phone. Now imagine being used to that technology your whole life and having to sit through algebra.

Companies are starting to adjust not just to millennials' habits but also to their atmospheric expectations. Nearly a quarter of DreamWorks'[28] 2,200 employees are under 30, and the studio has a 96% retention rate. Dan Satterthwaite, who runs the studio's human-relations department and has been in the field for about 23 years, says Maslow's hierarchy of needs[29] makes it clear that a company can't just provide money anymore but also has to deliver self-actualization. During work hours at DreamWorks, you can take classes in photography, sculpting, painting, cinematography and karate. When one employee explained that jujitsu is totally different from karate, Satterthwaite was shocked at his boldness, then added a jujitsu class.

Millennials are able to use their leverage to negotiate much better contracts with the traditional institutions they do still join. Although the armed forces had to lower the physical standards for recruits and make boot camp less intensive, Gary Stiteler, who has been an Army recruiter for about 15 years, is otherwise more impressed with millennials than any other group he's worked with. "The generation that we enlisted when I first started recruiting was sort of do, do, do. This generation is think, think about it before you do it," he says. "This generation is three to four steps ahead. They're coming in saying, 'I want to do this, then when I'm done with this, I want to do this.'"

Here's something even all the psychologists who fret over their narcissism studies agree about: millennials are nice. They have none of that David Letterman irony and Gen X ennui.[30] "The positivism has surprised me. The Internet was always 50—50 positive and negative. And now it's 90—10," says Shane Smith, the 43-year-old CEO of Vice[31], which adjusted from being a Gen X company in print to a millennial company once it started posting videos online, which are viewed by a much younger audience. Millennials are more accepting of differences, not just among gays, women and minorities but in everyone. "There are many, many subcultures, and you can dip into them and search around. I prefer that to you're either supermainstream or a riot grrrl[32]," says Tavi Gevinson, a 17-year-old who runs *Rookie*, an online fashion magazine, from her bedroom when she's not at school. It's hard, in other words, to join the counterculture when there's no culture. "There's not this us-vs.-them thing now. Maybe that's why millennials don't rebel," she says.

There may even be the beginning of a reaction against all the constant self-promotion. Evan Spiegel, 22, co-founder of Snapchat, an app that allows people to send photos, video and text that are permanently erased after 10 seconds or less, argues that it's become too exhausting for millennials to front a perfect life on social media. "We're trying to create a place where you can be in sweatpants, sitting eating cereal on a Friday night, and that's O.K.," he says.

But if you need the ultimate proof that millennials could be a great force for positive change, know this: Tom Brokaw, champion of the Greatest Generation[33], loves millennials. He calls them the Wary Generation, and he thinks their cautiousness in life decisions is a smart response to their world. "Their great mantra has been: Challenge convention. Find new and better ways of doing things. And so that ethos transcends the wonky people who are inventing new apps and embraces the whole economy," he says. The generation that experienced Monica Lewinsky's dress, 9/11, the longest wars in U.S. history, the Great Recession and an Arab Spring that looks at best like a late winter is nevertheless optimistic about its own personal chances of success.[34] Sure, that might be delusional, but it's got to lead to better results than wearing flannel, complaining and making indie movies about it.[35]

So here's a more rounded picture of millennials than the one I started with. All of which I also have data for. They're earnest and optimistic. They embrace the system. They are pragmatic idealists, tinkerers more than dreamers, life hackers.[36] Their world is so flat that they have no leaders[37], which is why revolutions from Occupy Wall Street to Tahrir Square have even less chance than previous rebellions. They want constant approval—they post photos from the dressing room as they try on clothes. They have massive fear of missing out and have an acronym for everything (including FOMO[38]). They're celebrity obsessed but don't respectfully idolize celebrities from a distance. (Thus US magazine's "They're just like us!" which consists of paparazzi shots of famous people doing everyday things.) They're not into going to church[39], even though they believe in God, because they don't identify with big institutions; one-third of adults under 30, the highest percentage ever, are religiously unaffiliated. They want new experiences, which are more important to them than material goods. They are cool and reserved and not all that passionate. They are informed but inactive: they hate Joseph Kony but aren't going to do anything about Joseph Kony.[40] They are probusiness. They're financially responsible; although student loans have hit record highs, they have less household and credit-card debt than any previous generation on record—which, admittedly, isn't that hard when you're living at home and using your parents' credit card. They love their phones but hate talking on them.

They are not only the biggest generation we've ever known but maybe the last large birth grouping that will be easy to generalize about. There are already microgenerations within the millennial group, launching as often as new iPhones, depending on whether you learned to type before Facebook, Twitter, iPads or Snapchat. Those rising microgenerations are all horrifying the ones right above them, who are their siblings. And the group after millennials is likely to be even more empowered. They're already so comfortable in front of the camera that the average American 1-year-old has more images of himself than a 17th century French king.

So, yes, we have all that data about narcissism and laziness and entitlement. But a generation's greatness isn't determined by data; it's determined by how they react to the challenges that befall them. And, just as important, by how we react to them. Whether you think millennials are the new greatest generation of optimistic entrepreneurs or a group of 80 million people about to implode in a dwarf star of tears when their expectations are unmet depends largely on how you view change.[41] Me, I choose to believe in the children. God knows they do. —WITH REPORTING BY JOSH SANBURN

From *TIME*, May 20th, 2013

I. New Words

atmospheric	[ˌætməˈsferik]	adj.	有(或产生)独特气氛的
array	[əˈrei]	n.	a group or collection of things
banality	[bəˈnæləti]	n.	平庸,(因千篇一律)乏味
befall	[biˈfɔːl]	v.	(of sth unpleasant) to happen to sb
blogger	[ˈblɒgə]	n.	博客写手
boost	[buːst]	v.	to make sth increase
catch	[kætʃ]	v.	~ **on** to become popular
catchy	[ˈkætʃi]	adj.	pleasant and easily remembered
champion	[ˈtʃæmpjən]	n.	~ **of sth** a person who speaks in support of sth

cocky	['kɔki]	adj.	too confident about yourself in a way that annoys other people
coddle	['kɔdəl]	v.	to pamper or overprotect
counterculture	['kauntə'kʌltʃə]	n.	反正统文化(指20世纪60年代和70年代美国青年中形成的一种文化群落)
cute	[kjuːt]	adj.	*informal* clever
dip	[dip]	v.	~ **into sth** to read or watch only part of sth
dumb	[dʌm]	adj.	*informal* stupid
delusion	[di'luːʒən]	n.	a false belief or opinion
empower	[im'pauə]	v.	to give sb more control over a situation
Emmy	['emi]	<美>	艾美奖(美国电视界最高奖项)
exacerbate	[ig'zæzəbeit]	v.	*formal* to make sth worse
ethos	['iː,θəs]	n.	*formal* the distinctive feature of a particular group
fret	[fret]	v.	~ **about sth** to be worried about sth
herd	[həːd]	n.	<贬> a large group of people
jeopardize	['dʒepədaiz]	v.	to put in danger
mantra	['mæntrə]	n.	祷文,符咒
mutate	[mjuːˈteit]	v.	to change into a new form
Karate	[kəˈraːti]	n.	<日> 空手道
jujitsu	[dʒuːˈdʒitsuː]	n.	<日> 柔术,柔道
leverage	['liːvəridʒ]	n.	the ability to influence what people do
paparazzi	[papaˈraːtsi]	n.	<意> 专门追逐名人偷拍照片的摄影者
rant	[rænt]	n.	大话,夸夸其谈
rookie	['ruki]	n.	新手
shoo-in	['ʃuːˌin]	n.	*AmE informal* a person or team that will win easily
suck	[sʌk]	v.	*slang* to be contemptible or very bad
stupefy	['stjuːpifai]	v.	to make unable to think
sullen	['sʌlən]	adj.	unwilling to talk or be sociable
stunt	[stʌnt]	v.	to prevent sb/sth from growing or developing
sweatpants	['swetpænts]	n.	宽松长运动裤
subculture	[ˌsʌbˈkʌltʃə]	v.	亚文化群
tally	['tæli]	n.	a record or count of a number of things
transcend	[trænˈsend]	v.	*formal* to be or go beyond the usual limits of sth

twixter	['twikstə]	n.	a new generation of Americans trapped between adolescence and adulthood
unmet	[ʌn'met]	adj.	not satisfied
unaffiliated	[ʌnə'filieitid]	adj.	~ **with sth** not belonging to or concerned with a large organization
wonky	['wɔŋki]	adj.	not steady, unreliable

Ⅱ. Background Information

内战后的几代人

美国内战后分别有传教士一代(Missionary Generation)、迷惘的一代(Lost Generation)、大兵的一代(G. I. Generation)、沉默的一代(Silent Generation)、婴儿潮代(Baby Boom Generation)、第十三代(Thirteenth Generation)和千禧代(Millennial Generation)。他们身上分别深深地打上了各个时期的烙印。了解他们有助于认清内战后美国社会演变轨迹和现代美国社会纷繁交错的景象。

1. 传教士一代(1860—1882年出生)

美国内战摧毁了阻碍社会经济发展的南方奴隶制度,促进了北方大资产阶级和大工业的发展。生活水平的提高使这一代人受到良好教育。这一代人具有强烈的使命感。他们在国内开展禁酒和女权运动,在国外积极传播基督教。

2. 迷惘的一代(1883—1900年出生)

这一代人出生、成长于世纪之交,正逢美国各种道德观念交织的时代,在其成长过程中出现了一系列无法解释的灾难(如旧金山大地震、"泰坦尼克号"客轮沉没、美国大流感)。他们成年不久,第一次世界大战爆发。战争冷酷无情,彻底打破了他们心中的理想,使他们对现实深感失望。"迷惘的一代"源自Gertrude Stein对海明威说的话:"You are all a lost generation."

3. 大兵的一代(1901—1924年出生)

美国历史学家伦纳德·凯恩认为,1900年是个代际分水岭,这之后出生的孩子受到明显多的关心和照顾。第二次世界大战锻炼了他们的意志,战争的胜利又使他们深感自豪。这一代人对自己信心十足。有较强的责任感。他们中产生了7位美国总统,从肯尼迪到布什,控制白宫达50年。GI这两个大写字母是"Government Issue"(政府配发)的缩写。在这一代人身上可以明显看出政府的作用。

4. 沉默的一代(1925—1945年出生)

这一代人生活在历史夹缝中。"要想成为二战英雄,出生得太晚;要想成为越战时期的学生激进分子,又出生得太早。"这一代人从小就被培养得循规蹈矩、唯命是从。他们大多不愿意从政,对时事不太关心。

5. 婴儿潮代(1945—1964年出生)

二战后,美国出现生育高峰,这一代人有7,600万。他们被称为婴儿潮代(Baby-boom Generation),他们还常被称为"以我为中心的一代"(Me Generation)、"动辄抗议的一代"(Protest Generation)或"摇滚的一代"(Rock Generation)。

这一代人普遍蔑视父辈的社会、宗教、道德和政治价值观。60年代许多人参加反越战运动,还有很多人愤世嫉俗、听摇滚乐、吸大麻,被称为"嬉皮士"(hippies)。80年代,这一代人中有一批又成为"雅皮士"(yuppies),他们注重自我,追求享受。

这一代人已经进入美国领导层。1992年,二战后出生的克林顿击败了大兵一代的布什,入主白宫。他们已成为美国社会的中坚。

6. 第十三代(1965—1981年出生)

1964—1974年是美国生育低谷期,出生总人数只有4,600万。因此,第十三代又常被称作"低谷代"(Babybust Generation)。此外,还有人称这一代人为"后代人"(Posters 意指"婴儿潮"后出生的一代),"逃避责任的人"(Slackers),"二十多一点毛头小伙"(Twenty Somethings)。这些称呼多少带点儿贬义,因而也引起这一代人的不满。

美国内战后至此,共经历了13代,尽管西方人普遍忌讳13。但这一代人对此并不介意,似乎更乐于接受"第13代"(Thirteenth Generation)或"第13代人"(thirteeneers 或 13-ers)的说法。有社会学家把第13代的时间划得更宽,定为1961—1981年出生者。小说家道格拉斯·库普兰(Douglas Coupland)称这一代人为"无名代"(Generation X)。这个称呼多少带点贬义,因而也引起这代人的不悦。若按这一时间域计算,第13代人多达7,900万。这一代人是在毒品泛滥、离婚频频、经济吃紧的环境中长大的,他们更善理财,珍惜金钱。

7. 千禧代(1982—2000年出生)

由于这一代人一般都是"X代人"的子女,按字母顺序他们被称作"Y代人"(Generation Y)。这一代人还由于他们擅长使用网络,又被称作"网络代"(Net Generation)。此外,由于这一代人数量为7,600万,与"婴儿潮代"相同,并且20世纪80年代美国也出现生育高潮,他们还被称为"回声潮代人"(Echo Boomers)。

Ⅲ. Notes to the Text

1. narcissistic personality disorder—自恋性人格障碍(也称利己型人格障碍,其特征是把自己看得过于重要,应该享有特权;渴望被别人注意和赞美;喜欢自我显示和炫耀,不顾他人感受和权利;对别人一贯嫉妒)

2. the National Institution of Health—(美国)国家卫生研究院(NIH is America's medical research agency, and one of the world's foremost medical research centers.)

3. the 2012 Clark University Poll of Emerging Adults—克拉克大学2012年对新成年人的民意测验

4. the non-profit Families and Work Institute—非营利性家庭与工作关系研究所

5. At 80 million strong, they are the biggest age grouping in American history.—人数有8,000万,是美国有史以来数量最大的年龄群体。

6. They are the most threatening and exciting generation since the baby boomers brought about social revolution, not because they're trying to take over the Establishment but because they're growing up without one.—他们是自婴儿潮代发起社会革命以来最具威胁、最引人关注的一代,其原因不是他们试图推翻统治集团,而是他们是在没有权势集团的环境下成长的。(the Establishment—the people who has influence and power over a society)

7. YouTube directors vs. studios, app-makers vs. entire industries—YouTube视频网站导演对付电影公司,应用软件制作者对付整个企业(① YouTube——一家设在美国全球著名让使用者上传、观看及分享影片和短片的网站;② app—a piece of software)

8. In the U.S. millennials are the children of baby boomers, who are also known as the Me Generation, who then produced the Me Me Me Generation, whose selfishness technology has only exacerbated.—美国的千禧代人是婴儿潮代人的孩子,婴儿潮代人也

被称作"唯我代",他们的孩子是"更加唯我的一代",技术使得这一代人自私程度更重。(Me Generation—a group of young adults who are selfishly concerned only with their own affairs and interests, and pay no attention to the lives and problems of other people)

9. Millennials have come of age in the era of the quantified self, recording their daily steps on Fit Bit, their whereabouts every hour of every day on PlaceMe and their genetic data on 23 and Me. —千禧代人是在量化个人生活时代成年的,用 Fit Bit 健身追踪器记载每天运动步数,PlaceMe 软件记录每天每时每刻所在地点,23 and Me 个人基因服务网站记录他们的基因数据。(① Fit Bit—a wireless-enabled wearable device that measure data such as the number of steps walked; ② PlaceMe—a free app that always remembers the places you visit; ③ quantified self—a movement to incorporate technology into data acquisition on aspects of a person's life in terms of input; ④23 and Me—a privately-held personal genomics and biotechnology company based in Mountain View California that provides rapid genetic testing)

10. Walt Whiteman—沃尔特·惠特曼(1819—1892, a U.S. writer known for his poetry about the beauty of nature and the value of freedom. He is regarded as one of the greatest and most influential U.S. poets, and his best-known work is *Leaves of Grass*.)

11. It turns out that self-esteem is great for getting a job or hooking up at a bar but not so great for keeping a job or a relationship. —结果表明自尊对找工作和酒吧里勾搭很起作用,但对保住工作或维持关系却不起什么作用。(hook up—referring to casual sexual contact)

12. *Self-Esteem: The Puzzle of Low Self-regard*—《自尊——低自尊难题解析》(该书综合归纳了过去 20 年有关低自尊专题的科研成果,着重讨论导致自尊心弱者疏离社会的因素)

13. *Managing the New Workforce: International Perspectives on the Millennial Generation*—《新一代劳力的管理:从国际视角看千禧代》

14. If you want to sell seminars to middle managers, make them about how to deal with young employees who e-mail the CEO directly and beg off projects they find boring. —如果你想要中层管理人员参加专题讨论会,讨论专题就得是如何应对给执行总裁直接发电子邮件恳求免去自己讨厌项目的年轻雇员。(① sell seminars to sb—to persuade sb to attend seminars; ② beg off projects—to ask to be allowed to be relieved of projects)

15. reality check—an occasion when you consider the facts of a situation, as opposed to what you would like or what you have imagined

16. Peer pressure is anti-intellectual. It is anti-historical. It is anti-eloquence. —同龄人的压力是反心智、反历史、反理性的。(eloquence—the ability to persuade)

17. Obamacare—奥巴马医改方案(即 Patient Protection and Affordable Care Act,简称 PPACA。该法案要求美国所有公民都必须购买医疗保险,否则将需缴纳一笔罚款,除非因宗教信仰或经济困难原因而被豁免。法案还对医保行业和公共医保项目进行了改革,将 3000 万没有医保的公民纳入了医保覆盖范围。)

18. *iDisorder*—书的全名为 *iDisorder—Understanding Our Obsession with Technology and Overcoming Its Hold on Us*

19. That constant search for a hit of dopamine ("Someone liked my status update!") reduces creativity. —不断寻求快乐情绪的刺激("有人喜爱我的更新状态!")使创造力下降。(① dopamine—一种脑内分泌物,属于神经递质,可影响一个人的情绪,由于它传递快乐、兴奋情绪的功能,又被称作快乐物质;② status update—a change of one's posting on a social

networking website that indicates a user's current situation, state of mind or opinion about sth)

20. the Torrance Tests of Creative Thinking—托兰斯创造性思维测试(该测试是美国明尼苏达大学心理学教授托兰斯编制,是目前应用最广的创造力测试)

21. If you do this well enough on Instagram, YouTube and Twitter, you can become a microcelebrity.—如果你在Instagram,YouTube和推特网站上做得十分好,你可以成为小名人。(① Instagram—an online photo-sharing, video-sharing and social networking service; ② microcelebrity—a celebrity whose fame is relatively narrow in scope and is likely to be transient)

22. casting director Doron Ofir, who auditioned participants for "Jersey Shore," "Millionaire Matchmaker," "A Shot at Love" and "RuPaul's Drag Race"—为(真人秀节目)《泽西海岸,为百万富翁做媒》《爱情赏试》和《鲁·保罗变装皇后》挑选参与者的星探多伦·奥菲尔(① casting—the process of choosing actors for a play or film; ② audition—to cause sb to give a performance as a test of suitability for a particular job)

23. a consumer-insights firm——家消费者研究公司(该公司专门从事消费文化分析和消费趋势预测)

24. Kim Kardashian—金·卡尔达希安(1980— an American television personality, fashion designer, model and actress)

25. senior vice president of human intelligence for Spark SMG—Spark SMG公司人力智能部高级副总裁

26. Ted X speech—Ted X演讲(Ted指technology, entertainment, design 技术、娱乐、设计,是美国一家私有非营利机构,该机构以它所组织的TED演讲大会著称。它在美国召集众多科学、设计、文学、音乐等领域的杰出人物演讲,让人们分享他们的成果和思想。从2006年起,Ted演讲的视频上传到网上。Ted X是Ted于2009年推出的一个项目,旨在鼓励世界各地Ted粉丝自发组织Ted风格的活动。)

27. Can you imagine how many frickin' Instagrams of people playing in the mud during Woodstock we would've seen?—你能想象出伍德·斯托克音乐节期间我们会在Instagram网站看到有多少显示人们在泥潭中嬉闹的照片？(① Woodstock—a music festival held over three days in 1969 near the town of Woodstock in New York state, where about 500,000 young people went to see Rock, Pop, and Folk singers and bands. It's remembered especially for the Hippies who attended it, and is seen as a very typical example of the hippie culture; ② frickin's—the polite way of saying the "F" word, used to give force to an expression)

28. DreamWorks—梦工厂(a US film and television company in Los Angeles and started in 1994 and started by Steven Spielberg and others)

29. Maslow's hierarchy of needs—马斯洛需求层次(理论)(马斯洛提出心理层次共分五种. physiology needs 生理需求; safety needs needs 安全需求; love and belonging needs 社交需求; esteem needs 尊重需求; self-actualization needs 自我实现需求。他还在晚年又提出了self-transcendence needs 自我超越需求。)

30. They have none of that David Letterman irony and Gen X ennui.—他们没有大卫·莱特曼那种冷嘲热讽和无名代人表现出的百无聊赖。(① David Letterman—an American late-night talk show host, noted for his absurd irony; ② ennui—tiredness and dissatisfaction caused by lack of interest and having nothing to do)

31. Vice—founded in 1994 as a "punk zine" and has since expanded into a leading global

youth media company with bureaus in over 30 countries

32. I prefer that to you're either superrmainstream or a riot grrrl. —我喜欢这种情况而不是要么超级主流要么强悍好斗。(grrrl—*slang* a young woman perceived as independent and strong or aggressive, especially in her attitude to men or in her sexuality)

33. Tom Brokaw, champion of the Greatest Generation—"最伟大一代"的倡导者汤姆·布罗考(① Tom Brokaw—美国全国广播公司晚间新闻节目主持人,深得美国观众信赖;② champion—a person who fights or speaks for a person or a cause)

34. The generation that experienced Monica Lewinsky's dress, 9/11, the longest wars in U.S. history, the Great Recession and an Arab Spring that looks at best like a late winter is nevertheless optimistic about its own personal chances of success. —这一代人经历过克林顿总统与莱温斯基的性丑闻、9.11 事件、美国历史上最长的战争、大衰退和看上去最好也只能算是晚冬的"阿拉伯之春"。然而他们却对自己成功的可能持乐观态度。(① Monica Lewinsky's dress—referring to the Monica Lewinsky's blue dress with Clinton's semen serving as indisputable evidence of Clinton's sexual affair; ② the Great Recession— referring to the global economic recession that began in December 2007; ③ Arab Spring—指 2010 年底在北非和西亚的阿拉伯国家和其他地区的一些国家所发生的一系列以"民主"和"经济"等为主题的反政府运动,这场运动波及突尼斯、埃及、利比亚、也门、叙利亚等国)

35. Sure, that might be delusional, but it's got to lead to better results than wearing flannel, complaining and making indie movies about it. —当然这或许是种错觉,但现实要求必须改善状况而不是自我欺骗、怨天尤人,独立制作反映这种状况的影片。(① delusional—characterized by false beliefs or opinions about the situation; ② wearing flannel—saying nice things to evade an issue; ③ indie—produced by a small independent company at low cost)

36. They are pragmatic idealists, tinkerers more than dreamers, life hackers. —他们是讲究实效的理想主义者,喜爱小发明的实干家而不是空想家,生活黑客。(① tinkerer—a person who makes small changes, especially when trying to repair or improve sth; ② life hacker—a person who uses technology to improve personal organization and increase personal efficiency)

37. Their world is so flat that they have no leaders... —他们的世界十分平等,因而没有领导者……

38. FOMO—*slang* fear of missing out

39. They're not into going to church... —They're not interested in going to church...

40. They are informed but inactive: they hate Joseph Kony but aren't going to do anything about Joseph Kony. —他们富有见识,但不愿采取行动。他们仇恨约瑟夫·科尼,但却不打算采取任何行动。(Joseph Kony—乌干达游击队首领,圣主抵抗军的领导者,欲建立一个基于十诫和阿乔利传统的政教合一政府,自 1986 年叛乱以来,绑架和强迫约 66,000 名儿童加入战争,迫使国内约 200 万人流离失所,2005 年国际刑事法庭以战争罪和反人类罪起诉,但潜逃至今。)

41. Whether you think millennials are the new greatest generation of optimistic entrepreneurs or a group of 80 million people about to implode in a dwarf star of tears when their expectations are unmet depends largely on how you view change. —你是认为千禧代是乐观企业家辈出的新的最伟大一代,还是当自己期望未能实现时只会号啕大哭而要崩溃的 8000 万人的群体,这在很大程度上取决于你是如何看待变化。(①

implode—to explode inwards; ②dwarf star—used metaphorically to emphasize huge amounts of tears)

Ⅳ. Language Features

《时代》周刊介绍

现今《时代》周刊共有四种版本,除美国版之外,还有欧洲版(*Time Europe*,伦敦印刷)、亚洲版(Time Asia,香港印刷)和南太平洋版(The South Pacific Edition,悉尼印刷)。该刊读者主要是受过良好教育的专业人士和高级管理人员、中产阶级。

《时代》周刊创刊于1923年。1989年时代股份有限公司与华纳通讯公司合并,该刊成为时代华纳(Time Warner)公司一部分。

《时代》周刊编辑方针是不仅为读者提供一周重要消息,而且要提供相关景背解释和评论,使读者不仅能充分理解,而且从中得以启发。《时代》周刊的写作风格也不同于报纸。它是把新闻事件作为故事来描述,而不是按照倒金字塔模式。文字力求生动活泼,情节富有趣味。

《时代》周刊在西方新闻界享有很高声誉,其发行量很长时间保持在400万份左右,据称美国国内读者有2,000万,全球读者有2,500万,是美国最大的一家新闻杂志。经过多年发展,它已形成独特的写作风格。语言学家称之为《时代》周刊风格(Timestyle)。这种风格的特色是:报道夹叙夹议,句式常用倒装,大量使用前置定语,用词力求新颖活泼。尤为值得一提的是其句式倒装。《时代》周刊常将句子谓语中的分词提到句首,这种倒装形式在其他刊物中十分少见。沃尔科特·吉布斯(Wolcott Gibbs)曾在《纽约人》杂志刊登一篇文章嘲讽模仿了《时代》周刊常用的倒装句式:"Backward ran sentences until reeled the mind... Where it all will end, knows God!"

受新媒体的冲击,该刊发行量从1997年开始出现下滑,由原先的420万份跌至340万(2009)。最近几年《时代》周刊版面出现了较大变化。改版的目的是"为读者提供更清晰、更为睿智、更为前瞻的观点(provide readers with a clearer, smarter and more forward-looking take on the world),主要做法是使《时代》周刊传统特色适合21世纪"(take the DNA of *Time* and adapt it to the 21st century)。

新版《时代》周刊主要有三大版面:新闻简介版(Briefing);特稿版(Features);文化版(The Culture)

改版后的《时代》周刊保留和加强了创刊以来的传统特色,提供一周重大事件有深度和力度的特稿,其中有解释性报道、调查性报道、精确性报道、新闻特写。与此同时,新版《时代》周刊还具有以下四个新的特色:

(1)内容方面加强了"商务和旅游服务"报道;
(2)生活栏增设了"饮食"等专题,生活气息更浓;
(3)语言风格更加简洁明快,新闻简介篇幅一般都较短小;
(4)版面更加活泼。新版内页插图照片增多,图片色泽鲜艳,夺人眼球,增加了文章的吸引力。

《时代》周刊1927年推出年代风云人物版,自此之后一直延续至今成为该刊特色品牌,原先称为 The Man of the Year,20世纪60年代后改为 The Person of the Year。这项评选颇受全球关注。1999年12月31日该刊评选出科学家爱因斯坦为"世纪风云人物"(The Person of the Century)。

该刊长期坚持反华反共立场。近些年来,伴随我国改革开放规模的扩大,该刊态度有所转变,不但增加了有关我国的新闻篇幅,而且报道比较深入充分,但也常常出现反映西方新闻价值观,显示其意识形态的偏见。

《时代》周刊的网址是 www.time.com。

V. Analysis of the Content

1. The meaning of the word "hard" in the sentence "Here's the cold, hard data."(Para. 2) is _____.
   A. very severe
   B. definitely true
   C. difficult to understand
   D. without sympathy
2. The effect of technology on Millenials' selfishness is _____.
   A. restraining it
   B. making it worse
   C. making it known to all
   D. making it difficult to prove
3. Which of the following is NOT listed as the effect on Millenials produced by interaction through a screen? _____
   A. Enlarging the social network.
   B. Reducing empathy.
   C. Reducing creativity.
   D. Leading to a higher degree of narcissism.
4. The author's overall attitude towards the Millenial Generation is _____.
   A. negative
   B. positive
   C. objective
   D. unknown
5. The article is _____.
   A. a straight news report
   B. a news comment
   C. an expository essay
   D. an interpretative news report

VI. Questions on the Article

1. What kind of people does the Millenial Generation refer to? How large is it?
2. What data can prove the narcissism of America's Millenial Generation?
3. What proves the stunted development of the Millenial Generation?
4. Why does the author say the Millenial Generation are the most threatening and exciting generation since the baby boomers brought about social revolution?
5. Why did people instill self-esteem into kids in the 1970s? What adverse effects does self-esteem boost produce?
6. What kind of relationship exists between narcissism and entitlement?
7. What effects does peer pressure have on Millenials according to Mark Bauerlien?
8. What does the term "twixters" mean? Why do twixters put off life choices?
9. What does Tom Brokaw think of Millenials?
10. What is a more rounded picture of Millenials?
11. What does the author think, is the way to determine a generation's greatness?

Lesson 3

Asians in the Promised Land[1]

America should be their Golden Mountain[2], but along with success as the "model minority" have come immense struggles

By Tony Emerson

    Of all the images broadcast from the Los Angeles riots, one in particular burned into the minds of Asian-Americans[3]: on the third day of the disturbances, a Korean merchant crouched on a rooftop, aiming an automatic weapon into the chaos below. From the Chinatowns in San Francisco and New York to the flourishing Little Saigons in San Diego and outside Washington, D. C. , the defenders' defiance and isolation sank home.[4] "Those who attack see only Asian," said Chinese-American author Betty Lee Sung in New York. If Korean-American shop owners cannot depend on the U. S. police or military, "we should send troops to L. A. to protect our brethren," Seoul resident Yang Jae Ryong, 37, told *The Korean Herald*. "Who will protect them in a land far away from home?"

    That is the dilemma: for a growing number of Asian-Americans, America is home. Nearly 2.5 million Asians arrived in the United States during the 1980s, helping to double the Asian-American population to 7.3 million. Asians are now the fastest-growing ethnic group, led by the Koreans and the Vietnamese. Some of the immigrants will try to make their fortune and return home. Most will stay. About half are settling on the Pacific Coast, while hundreds of thousands move on to New York and dozens of cities in between. But nobody could escape the message of L. A.[5], where Korean stores faced some of the worst of the burning and looting. For many Asian-Americans, the riots represented an assault on their faith in America.

    All the vices: They used to say America was a land of freedom, the "Golden Mountain" in the Chinese phrase. Many still do, though the Chinese were first brought in large numbers to the United States in the 1860s to work on continental railroads[6]. Vilified then as "a population befouled with all the social vices," as one newspaper put it in 1865, Asians have come a long way.[7] In 1965 the ban on free Asian immigration was loosened for the first time.[8] Now Asians are seen as the "model minority" — superior to other Americans in habits of study and work. No less a patriot than Ronald Reagan once told a group of Asian-Americans that they embodied the American Dream of hard work, thrift and success.[9] One widely repeated statistic shows, in fact, that Asian families earn an average of $35,900 per year — more than the average for American white families.

    Asians, however, rebel against the model-minority label as another insidious stereotype.[10] It's seen as a subtle racist excuse not to help underprivileged Asians and to hold back even average Asians — on the ground that they already have "natural" advantages.

Ronald Takaki, professor of ethnic studies at the University of California, Berkeley, points out that Asian families are large, so their per capita income is actually less than that of white families, and most of them live in high-wage areas on the coasts, which further skews the statistics. Still, on average, Asians in the United States are undeniably well off. What many Asians can't square with experience is the implication that they are fully welcome in America.[11] Takaki tells of a Virginia taxi-driver who once asked him how long he had been in the States. "My family has been here for over 100 years," replied Takaki, who speaks no Japanese. "Your English is excellent," responded the cabdriver. "It's a myth," Takaki concludes, "that we've gained social acceptance in this society."

The Asians' success in the United States has singled them out for resentment.[12] In white communities, workers smash Japanese cars. In black communities, anti-Asian violence has been on the rise for years. The ill feelings go beyond the issue of economic power. In "Confessions of a Chinatown Cowboy," Chinese-American author Frank Chin writes that as far as blacks are concerned, Asians are "the Uncle Toms[13] of nonwhite people... We're hated by blacks because the whites love us for being everything the blacks are not. Blacks are a problem: badass[14]. Chinese-Americans are not: kissass."

In Atlanta, Georgia, two weeks ago, television broadcast a scene much like the one in Los Angeles: a Korean couple scrambling to the roof of their liquor store as looters banged at the doors and police stood by. Once again, Asians felt besieged by blacks, abandoned by whites. "What if the people trapped had been white? What then? It makes me crying inside," said Edward Lee, a Korean-American convenience-store owner.[15] "It's getting scary. They are picking on Koreans and Asians wholesale." In fact, many Asians had come to Atlanta as the home of the civil-rights movement — a symbol of peaceful protest and American freedom,[16] said pastor Henry H. Jee. "What do we tell our children now?" he asked.

In New York and Los Angeles, blacks have boycotted successful Asian businesses, accusing them of mistreating blacks and taking money out of the community. Koreans, in particular, are on the front line in blighted urban neighborhoods where they have set up shops. In Atlanta, about 20 Korean store owners have been shot since 1980. In Detroit, "It's worse than it was 10 years ago," says Charles Yang, a business leader in a city where Koreans own more than half the remaining downtown stores. His message to fellow Koreans: "They are better off there in Korea."

But in many Asian countries, homeownership is very difficult to secure, and access to universities and careers is strictly limited. So they keep looking for the American Dream. If current trends continue, the Asian-American population will increase fivefold to 36 million by 2050, according to the Population Reference Bureau[17] in Washington, D. C. The Vietnamese are bringing jasmine rice to Virginia, the Hmong are bringing Laotian culture to Minneapolis-St. Paul. Increasingly diverse, the Asian-American community is also increasingly dominated by new arrivals[18]: more than two thirds are now foreign born. And the newcomers are often impoverished refugees from Indochina, a trend that is widening an already significant income gap among Asian-Americans. In 1980, the median Chinese family income was $22,000, four times more than that of the Laotians.

Hard work: As the first generation gives way to the second, many Asian-American parents worry that their children are abandoning Asian values of honor, hard work and thrift for American materialism.[19] Euihang Shin, a sociology professor at the University of South Carolina, says Asian-Americans are becoming "legalistic" — pushing the limit of what the law allows, rather than following a rigid code of personal honor.[20]

For Asian-Americans, the pull of two cultures can create an identity crisis.[21] Lydia C. Fontan, a college teacher from San Jose, California, calls herself a "Filipoamerican"[22] — no hyphen. Proud of her Filipino heritage, Fontan is also proud of being American, and a hyphen would suggest she's "half and half — that's negative," she says. For others, the question can't be resolved. Reverend Jee in Atlanta is 52 and has lived in the United States for 20 years. "I cannot be an American, even though I was educated here. I am still Korean, Korean-American. When I visit Korea, it's frustrating. I cannot identify with the culture. Both times I board the plane, I feel I am coming home."

Some young people are on a desperate search for authentic Asianness. Like many Asian-American children, Davis Yee, now 21, took Saturday Chinese classes when he was a boy, but isn't proficient enough to be accepted as an Asian "from the motherland." "People would call me banana, yellow on the outside, white on the inside,[23]" he recalls. But he didn't feel accepted by the white American culture either. Now Yee is also known as Nunchuck C, one of a growing number of young Asian rap musicians attacking the model-minority image and Asians who forget where they came from. The conformists are branded "Charlie Chans."[24] "They don't know their culture," says Yee. "They're whitewashed." In a song called "Yellow Peril," the Seattle-based Seoul Brothers pick up the refrain, "Not a coolie slave on a sugar plantation... I'm a bona fide Asian."[25]

But while the rappers celebrate their independence, there are still plenty of Asians who are overwhelmingly poor, working in sweatshops and living in warrenlike apartments recalling the 19th century. It seems safe to say that the least assimilated of Asian-Americans include the residents of New York's sprawling Chinatown, many of whom never learn English and rarely move out of the community. "Chinatown is a voluntary and involuntary ghetto," says Shirley Hung, associate provost at Hunter College in New York. That is, Chinese willingly join the ethnic community but then, in most cases, can't escape.

Racial slurs: Many would like to. But it's not easy to be accepted in the white mainstream. Often newcomers don't speak English well. There are also hurdles of skin color. Siu Hung Cheng, owner of the Viet Royale Restaurant in Falls Church, Virginia, has a BMW and a fine house and says success has inured him to racial slurs. But he worries for his kids. "I think my children will be the same as American boys," says Hung. "but from the outside, my children will always be Asian. No matter how long you've been here, they look at your face."

Ha Nguyen, too, is trying to fit in. He emigrated from Vietnam to Chicago in 1984 and goes out to Wrigley Field to watch baseball games. Yet he feels lonely in a wildly cheering crowd. "We know the rules and everything, but we don't have the excitement or feeling that we're part of the game," says Nguyen.

In some respects, though, the newcomers are very American; in particular, they thrive in the entrepreneurial atmosphere of their new homeland. Korean-Americans have virtually taken over the greengrocer business in New York and Los Angeles. They comprise half the lottery agents in Washington, D.C. and they own one in four U.S. dry cleaners, estimates Bill Seitz, executive director of the Neighborhood Cleaners Association. Pyong Gap Min, an associate sociology professor at Queens College in New York, estimates that 40 to 50 percent of adult Koreans in the United States are self-employed. That compares with about 9 percent of white Americans.

Yet in many cases, Koreans strike out on their own because they have hit, or afraid they will hit, a "glass ceiling" in American corporations.[26] Min's estimates suggest that 60 percent of the greengrocers have college degrees. Many would be working in the professions if they thought they had a fair shot at promotion. As one Asian graduate student put it, Americans tend to see Asians as "high-tech coolies," fit for technical jobs but unable for upper management.

Unemployed Asian youths, particularly the Indochinese, are fueling a different growth industry: street gangs. In Boston, there are perhaps 100 Southeast Asian youths in gangs with names like the Oriental Street Boys and the Tiny Rascals, says Ratha Yem, a special assistant to the Massachusetts attorney general. Some have no home, and a majority have witnessed the death of a family member in violence back in Indochina. In New York, similar but even larger groups are challenging the Mafia as a leading mob threat. The desperation of these youths points to other holes in the model-minority image: by one estimate, the influx of refugees in the 1980s raised the number of Asian-Americans living close to or below the poverty line to 20 percent.

Martyrs: It's perhaps not surprising then that some Asian-Americans see themselves as brothers in suffering with African-Americans. In some areas, there are real parallels. Both groups have their martyrs. The Asians' Rodney King was Vincent Chin, a 27-year-old Chinese-American beaten to death in Detroit by a white autoworker and his stepson who reportedly called Chin a "Jap." His attackers got off in 1983 with three years on probation and a small fine on manslaughter charges — a slap on the wrist that still upsets the Asian-American community.

Another link is Christianity. Atlanta has 60 Korean churches, and scores of primarily black churches. "Blacks have souls, we have hearts,[27]" says Reverend Jee. "We have the same spiritualities." Asian rappers would like to think so, too — so they are deeply distressed at anti-Asian outbursts from blacks, particularly the L. A. riot. Responding to a threat form black rapper Ice Cube against Asian merchants, Seattle rapper Michael Park fumes, "He's rich. Why doesn't he open a store in South-Central L. A. ? Only Koreans would have the guts to come into a crazy urban jungle[28] like that."

As a whole, Asian-Americans have had a far easier time shrugging off the legacy of discrimination than African-Americans have had. True, a series of vicious anti-Chinese attacks took place in the late 19th century. The worst was the Snake River Massacre of 1887, in which 31 Chinese miners were robbed and murdered in Oregon. (By comparison, two Asians died in the Los Angeles riots.) In perhaps the most notorious injustice, 120,000 Japanese-Americans were interned in California during World War II.[29] But most African-Americans are descended from slaves. Most Asian-Americans are newcomers who applied for an entry visa.

If there's one piece of the model-minority picture that arouses little controversy, it is this: the typical first-generation Asian immigrant is incredibly hardworking and thrifty. Man Kwai, 51, came to the New York area from Hong Kong in 1978 as the cook and nanny for an American family. Since then, she has taken two days off, but still recalls the trip as "a dream." Unable to read or speak English well, she got around New York by memorizing mass-transit routes. She put in 16 hours as a maid each Sunday, her day off, and saved a small bundle, while quietly learning the banking ropes[30] from Chinese friends. One day she stunned her employers by opening up a cigar box with $3,000 inside and asking, "Please put it in an interest-bearing CD[31]." Eventually she was juggling four different CDs. In 1987 she bought a $259,000 house with $100,000 down. Two months ago she managed to get a green card for her 20-year-old nephew, who now has a room in her house. To this day she barely speaks English.

Credit clubs: That's how many Asian communities have survived in the United States: by wits and strong family connections. A key link in the system is the rotation credit association, known in Korean as the kye, but common to the Chinese, Japanese and Vietnamese as well. These are informal credit clubs in which members contribute a set sum — say $100 each month — and take turns borrowing from the group fund. By one estimate, 80 percent of Korean-Americans belong to at least one kye, and they have financed thousands of businesses in inner cities.

What the Asian mosaic lacks is a larger sense of unity.[32] Many Asian groups bring ancient rivalries from their native countries — Chinese vs. Japanese, and so on — and these rivalries are only partly submerged in the United States. Most Asian support groups are based on nationality, or even smaller units. In New York, the Chinese break down into groups from the mainland, Hong Kong and Taiwan, and even family association, such as the Wong Family Benevolent Association and the Lee Family Benevolent Association. Mainly they are social clubs, but they help in a pinch. "If you're sick and need money, members will help. If you need a loan, you ask for it," explains association member Thomas Wong. "The concept is based on trust."

The system is also inherently limiting. Asian-Americans are underrepresented at all levels of American government. Unless Asians' numbers grow even faster and they start voting for one another, that's unlikely to change. As of now, the Filipinos tend to vote Democratic, and so on, without regard to Asian-American issues. "The thing that unites Asian-Americans of different ethnicities is not being Asian — it's being American," says Marshall Wong, a second-generation Chinese-American and chairman of the Afro-Asian Relations Council in Washington, D. C. "It's the sensation of being different in America that is the common ground."

In politics that's not a bad thing necessarily. America is a celebration of differences.[33] But after the Los Angeles riots, there was a moment when Asians seemed to see themselves in terms of their bonds, not their differences. Certainly many people recognized the attacks on Korean-Americans as a threat to Asian-Americans. That recognition has not quickly translated into a wider political movement. But as time and generations pass, groups tend to meld more easily into one another — and into America, says Kathleen Hom, an Asian adviser to the mayor of Washington. Sooner or later, she says, Asian-Americans have to ask themselves: "Are we a nation unto ourselves? Are we misplaced Asians?" The answer is No. Asian immigrants have chosen to become Americans — though many are still searching for a way to fit in.

With Daniel Glick in Washington, Patricia King in San Francisco, Michael Mason in

Atlanta, Jay Mathews and Jason Shaplen in New York, Nichole Christian in Detroit, Robin Bulman in Seoul and bureau reports

From *Newsweek*, May 18, 1992

Ⅰ. New Words

badass	['bædæs]	n.	*slang* bum, rascal 无赖
befoul	[bi'faul]	v.	to make dirty; cover with filth
benevolent	[bi'nevələnt]	adj.	kind and generous
brethren	['breðrən]	n.	*plural old-fashioned* brothers
crouch	['krautʃ]	v.	蹲伏
defiance	[di'faiəns]	n.	open refusal to obey
entrepreneurial	[ˌentrəprə'nəːriəl]	adj.	企业家的
ethnicity	[eθ'nisəti]	n.	ethnic status, quality or character
Hmong	[hmɔŋ]	n.	(居住在泰国北部省份的)苗族
influx	['inflʌks]	n.	the arrival of large numbers of people
insidious	[in'sidiəs]	adj.	sly; tricky; crafty
inure	[i'njuə]	v.	to make someone become used to something unpleasant
kissass	['kisæs]	n.	*AmE* 马屁精, 谄媚者
meld	[meld]	v.	to unite; to merge
Minneapolis	[ˌmini'æpəlis]	n.	明尼阿波利斯[美]
mosaic	[mou'zeiik]	n.	a pattern
provost	['prɔvəst]	n.	教务长
rap	[ræp]	n.	说唱乐
rapper	['ræpə]	n.	someone who speaks the words of a rap
Reverend	['revərənd]	n.	教士; 教士大人
scramble	['skræmbl]	v.	to climb
skew	[skjuː]	v.	to distort; to twist
slur	[sləː]	n.	unfair criticism
spirituality	[ˌspiritju'æləti]	n.	the quality of being interested in religion or religious matters
stereotype	['steriətaip]	n.	a fixed idea or image
sweatshop	['swet-ʃɔp]	n.	血汗工厂

Ⅱ. Background Information

亚裔美国人

最早移居美国的亚洲人是中国人。早在美国独立前,1571—1784 年间就有华工为当时西班牙殖民者(Spanish colonists)雇佣,在加利福尼亚从事造船业。此后,由于清政府腐败,加之天灾战乱,以及对新大陆充满美好幻想,又有不少华人移居美国。1848年在旧金山附近发现金子的消息在5个月后传入中国。从1850年开始,华人大批涌入加州。19世纪60年代美国西部铁路建设劳力严重短缺,中国合同工(Chinese contract workers)源源不断而来。到1880年进入美国境内的中国移民已逾10万。19世纪60年代日本开始向美国移民。其他亚洲国家也有移民陆续到美国寻求发展机会。

1882年5月美国通过了排华法案,在很长一段时期内华人很难进入美国。

1965年在民权运动(Civil Rights Movement)影响下,美国国会通过了一项移民与归化法(Immigration and Naturalization Law)。新法使亚洲人像其他人一样享受移居美国的平等权利,于是产生了亚洲移民的高潮。

根据2006年美国人口统计,亚裔美国人已增至1,310多万,占全国人口总数的4.4%。

亚裔美国人所包含的成分很多,这些成分各自所占亚裔美国人的比例如下表所示:

种族	华人	菲律宾人	日本人	印度人	韩国人	越南人	其他
比例	24%	21%	10%	17%	10.6%	10.6%	8%

近几年,亚裔人口又有较大幅度增长。到2012年7月亚裔人口为1570万,占美国人口的比例是5%。

亚裔人的成就在美国是有目共睹,有口皆碑。

亚裔学生几乎所有学科的成绩都超过其他少数民族和大部分白种人。在1990年的全国4年级、8年级和12年级三个层次所组织的数学考试中,亚裔学生的成绩超过其他所有各族学生。1990年的全国高考中,亚裔学生的平均数学成绩比全国平均成绩高61分。亚裔美国人虽然只占全国人口的3.6%,但在一流大学新生中的比例却高达20%。

亚裔美国人在事业上竞争力也很强,许多人在各项领域作出了非凡的贡献。据美国马丁·韦尔伯博士统计,至少有1,333名华人被列入《美国科学名人录》。其中有世界著名的建筑天才贝聿铭,获得诺贝尔奖金的物理学家李政道、杨振宁、丁肇中,还有举世闻名的物理学家吴健雄和她的夫婿袁家骝。最近一些年,有的华人进入政界高层,如能源部长朱棣文,商务部长骆家辉等。

在美国历史上仇视亚洲移民或亚裔人的情况屡有发生。1882年美国国会通过一项《排斥华工案》,规定10年不接受华工移民,并对非美国出生的所有华人后裔的国籍不予承认。

每当美国失业率上升、经济不景气时,亚裔人较多遭到社会攻击甚至暴行。民权运动以来,亚裔人境况有所改善。但在就业和晋升方面,亚裔人较多遇到障碍,相对而言,较难进入商界和政界决策层。

亚裔美国人有相当多生活在贫困之中。2003统计资料显示:亚裔人中生活在贫困线以下(below the poverty line)者比例为11.8%,而白人中同类人比例是8.2%。亚裔美国人由于成分较为复杂,整体凝聚力较弱,政治参与率也较低。

III. Notes to the Text

1. Asians in the Promised Land — 乐土中的亚裔人 (the Promised Land — a place of expected happiness)

2. Golden Mountain — a place for making fortunes and achieving successes（金山原指加州。有的学者认为早期华工移居美国是加州金矿发现所激发的黄金梦所致。）

3. Of all the images broadcast from the Los Angeles riots, one in particular burned into the minds of Asian-American... — Among all the TV pictures transmitted from the Los Angeles, one has left a particularly deep impression on Asian-Americans. （① burn into — to make an indelible impression；② the Los Angeles riots — 洛杉矶骚乱。这次骚乱的直接原因是种族歧视，以及警察施暴、司法不公等严重弊端。1992年4月29日洛杉矶地方法院全由4名白人组成的陪审团，无视确凿无疑的现场录像证据，判定一年前4名狂暴殴打驾车超速的黑人青年罗德尼·金的白人警察无罪，从而导致黑人群众强烈愤懑，促使一场大规模的种族冲突的爆发。据报道，持续数日的骚乱使五十多人丧生，2,000多人受伤，10,000多人被捕，5,200多座房屋烧毁或遭严重破坏，经济损失不下7亿美元。在骚乱中，不少黑人趁机劫掠亚裔人经营的商店。）

4. From the Chinatowns in San Francisco and New York to the flourishing Little Saigons in San Diego and outside Washington, D. C., the defenders' defiance and isolation sank home. — Asian-Americans across the United States became conscious of the defenders' unyielding attitude and isolated position. （① Chinatown — an area in a city where there are Chinese restaurants, shops and clubs and where many Chinese people live；② Little Saigon — a place in a city where Vietnamese shops are located and a lot of Vietnamese people live）

5. But nobody could escape the message of L. A. — But no one could fail to understand what the Los Angeles riots meant to them.

6. continental railroads — 横贯北美大陆的铁路（19世纪60年代，美国为促进经济发展，建造横贯北美大陆的铁路。由于工程时间紧张，条件艰苦危险，铁路公司难以从本土找到足够数量劳工，因而大批引进华工。）

7. Vilified then as "a population befouled with all the social vices," as one newspaper put it in 1865, Asians have come a long way. — 当时亚裔人被污蔑为"染有社会上所有恶习的民族"，1865年一家报纸就是这么写的。与那时相比，现在亚裔人的境况取得了很大的改进。（Asians have come a long way. — Asians have made a lot of progress in status.）

8. In 1965, the ban on free Asian immigration was loosened for the first time. — 1965年在民权运动的影响下，美国国会通过了一项"移民与归化法"（Immigration and Naturalization Law）。新法使亚洲人像其他地区人一样具有移居美国的平等权利，于是产生了亚洲人移民的高潮。

9. No less a patriot than Ronald Reagan once told a group of Asian-Americans that they embodied the American Dream of hard work, thrift and success. — Even the former president Ronald Reagan whose patriotism was unquestionable once told a group of Asian-Americans that they served as a good example of achieving success through hard work and thrift. （embody — to be an example of）

10. Asians, however, rebel against the model-minority label as another insidious stereotype. — 然而亚裔人反对模范少数民族这一称号，认为它是一种非常有害的成见。（rebel against — to oppose）

11. What many Asians can't square with experience is the implication that they are fully welcome in America. — Many Asians' personal experience contradicts the indirect suggestion that they are fully welcome in America. (square with — to be or cause to be consistent)

12. The Asians' success in the United States has singled them out for resentment. — 亚裔人在美国取得的成功使得他们突出显眼,遭人忌恨。(single sb out — to choose sb from among a group of similar people or things, esp. in order to praise or criticize them)

13. Uncle Tom — the central character of the antislavery novel *Uncle Tom's Cabin*, a humble, pious and long-suffering Negro slave. The term is now often used in the sense of a black person who holds a humble, timid and servile attitude.

14. badass — *AmE slang* a bum, an idle or good-for-nothing person

15. convenience-store — *AmE* a shop where one can buy food, alcohol, magazines etc. and that is often open 24 hours each day

16. In fact, many Asians had come to Atlanta as the home of the civil rights movement — a symbol of peaceful protest and American freedom. — 事实上,许多美国人来到亚特兰大是由于它是民权运动的发源地,是和平式抗议和美国自由的象征。[亚特兰大在南方城市中比较特殊,黑人民权运动较为活跃,政治势力一直比较强大。1973 年产生第一位黑人市长,1986 年市委员会 18 名成员中黑人占了 11 位。由于这些原因,亚特兰大被称为黑人的"麦加"(Mecca)。]

17. the Population Reference Bureau — 人口资料局

18. Increasingly diverse, the Asian-American community is also increasingly dominated by new arrivals. — 亚裔美国人种类越来越多,亚裔社区也越来越被新来者影响所控制。

19. ... many Asian-American parents worry that their children are abandoning Asian values of honor, hard work and thrift for American materialism. — 许多亚裔家长担心孩子正在放弃亚洲人的荣誉、勤奋和节俭等价值观而接受美国人的物质主义价值观。(materialism — the tendency to leave out or forget the spiritual side of things, the belief that money and material possessions are more important than art, religion, moral goodness etc.)

20. Asian-Americans are becoming "legalistic" — pushing the limit of what the law allows, rather than following a rigid code of personal honor. — 亚裔美国人变得"按法律条文办事"——将自己行为控制在法律容许的极限范围内,而不是严格依照个人荣誉的准则行事。

21. For Asian-Americans, the pull of two cultures can create an identity crisis. — 对于亚裔美国人两种文化的影响会造成文化认同危机。(pull — influence)

22. Filipoamerican — Americans of Filipino heritage 菲律宾裔美国人

23. ... banana, yellow on the outside, white on the inside... — 黄皮白心的香蕉 (It is a racist remark meaning: Though Asians' skin color is yellow, different from that of white people, they have accepted the white American culture.)

24. The conformists are branded "Charlie Chans." — 循规蹈矩者被蔑称为"张查理"。(① conformist — a person who acts according to laws or rules; ② Charlie Chan — referring to a fictional detective in a series of popular films in the late 1930s and 1940s.

He spoke English with a Chinese accent and wore western-style suits.)

25. ... the Seattle-based Seoul Brothers pick up the refrain, "Not a coolie slave on a sugar plantation...I'm a bona fide Asian." — 总部设在西雅图的"汉城兄弟会"采用叠句:"我不是甘蔗园的苦力……我是真正的亚洲人。"(refrain — part of a song that is repeated, especially at the end of each verse)

26. Yet in many cases, Koreans strike out on their own because they have hit, or afraid they will hit, a "glass ceiling" in American corporations. — Many Koreans start their own businesses because they already face or fear to meet with an invisible barrier for promotion in American big companies.

27. Blacks have souls, we have hearts. — Blacks and Asians have similar religious beliefs. (The black community have adopted the term "soul" to refer to the unique ethnic elements of their culture and religion. The Asians use the term "heart" also to refer to their emotional religious practice. In fact, there is not much difference.)

28. urban jungle — an urban area where it is difficult to succeed or trust anyone

29. In perhaps the most notorious injustice, 120,000 Japanese-Americans were interned in California during World War Ⅱ. — 二战期间有12万美籍日本人在加州被拘留,这可能是最臭名昭著的不公正行为。(二战日本偷袭珍珠港事件爆发后不久,许多日裔人被怀疑进行间谍活动,为了"清除隐患",一场大规模扣押日裔人行动便开始了。这一行动不仅给许许多多无辜日裔人造成很深的精神创伤,也使他们经济上蒙受巨大损失。)

30. learning the banking ropes — learning the knowledge about how to benefit from depositing money

31. CD — certificate deposit 定期存款,证券存款

32. What the Asian mosaic lacks is a larger sense of unity. — 亚裔群体缺乏大团体观念。(mosaic — Here, it means: a group of various kinds of ethnic groups that are seen or considered as a whole.)

33. America is a celebration of differences. — It is an emphatic way of saying that the U.S. does more than accept differences. It suggests that America welcomes and eulogizes different cultures and political viewpoints.

Ⅳ. Language Features

《新闻周刊》介绍

《新闻周刊》(Newsweek)原名为 News-Week,是新闻企业家托马斯·马丁(Thomas John Martyn)于1933年创办。它模仿《时代》杂志,将一周国内外大事分门别类加以综合叙述。1937年,该刊与《今日》(Today)杂志合并,取消原名连字符,更名为 Newsweek。

1961年《新闻周刊》转手给《华盛顿邮报》公司(The Washington Post Company)。主权易手之后,资金投入增多。编辑队伍充实,竞争力量加强。目前每期发行量为300万份左右,在美国三大新闻周刊中名列第二。

近些年来,在电子媒体的强大冲击下,《新闻周刊》与其他报刊一样,广告收入急剧减少。

为了扭亏为盈,该刊裁减了 1/4 员工。除此之外,该刊还采取了几项新的措施。为了应对网络新闻时新性强的优势,该刊更加突出观点和评论,更多依赖知名度高的记者和专栏作家撰写文章,该刊对其读者群重新定位,缩小了读者订阅规模。2008 年初,从以前的 310 万减少到 260 万,2009 年 7 月又进一步缩减到 190 万。杂志提高了订阅价格,受众定位在中上层。改版后的《新闻周刊》党派倾向性更为明显。为此,杂志又丢失了不少读者。

这些措施均未改变杂志经济亏损局面。2009 年财务数据显示 2009 年杂志亏损为 1,600 万美元,2009 年亏损额升至 2,930 万美元。2010 年 8 月 2 日《华盛顿邮报》公司决定将该刊出售给音响制造商悉尼·哈曼(Sidney Harman)。后又经过 3 个月的协商,《新闻周刊》于 11 月份与新闻网站 The Daily Beast 合并。原网站总编 Tina Brocon 兼任该刊主编。

2011 年 3 月《新闻周刊》版面做了新的调整。新版共设 5 大版块:1. 专栏版(Columns)。该版刊登专栏作家、编辑和特邀作者的文章,一般篇幅较短。2. NewsBeast 版。改版体现网站 The Daily Beast 特色,刊登可供读者快速阅读文字的简洁明快的新闻报道、新闻人物访谈和具有网站风格的鲜明图表。3. 特写版。改版所占篇幅较多,刊登体现原《新闻周刊》特色的详细报道、解释性报道和新闻特写。4. 文化版(Omnivore)。改版刊登艺术、音乐、书籍、影视、戏剧、饮食、旅游等专题的报道和评论。5. 号外版(Plus)。该版刊登读者来信、历史回忆和城市介绍。

从 2013 年开始该刊停止发行纸质版,只发行电子版,其网址是 www.newsweek.com。

风光 80 年享有国际盛名的纸质版《新闻周刊》的消失凸显了新闻杂志业的发展趋势。路透社在 2012 年 10 月 18 日报道《新闻周刊》即将停止出版纸质版的消息时这样评论道:在新闻日益商品化和新闻滚动 24 小时无停歇的情况下,更多的消费者喜欢用平板电脑和手机浏览媒体的电子版而不是纸媒。不少美国传播学专家认为,新闻周刊正面临两种选择。一种选择是把新闻解释和分析市场做强做好。另一种是融合网络优势,将重点放在电子版上。前一种选择的理由是新闻周刊的核心优势是新闻解释和分析,周刊这一优势与美国人生活节奏基本相符,多数美国人没有时间和兴趣阅读所有信息,他们对海量信息感到困惑,渴望得到指导,这就给新闻解释和分析市场提供更好的商机,因而新闻类周刊依然存在发展空间。

Ⅴ. Analysis of the Content

1. Among Asian-Americans, the fastest growing groups are _____.
   A. Chinese and Filipinos   B. Vietnamese and Koreans
   C. Chinese and Koreans   D. Cambodians and Vietnamese
2. According to the author, the Asians are singled out for resentment because of their _____.
   A. success   B. different culture
   C. higher social status   D. unwillingness to be assimilated
3. The author of the article thinks that the pull of the two different cultures on Asian-Americans results in _____.
   A. frustration against the system B. cultural diversification
   C. an identity crisis   D. faster assimilation
4. The word "white-wash" in the article means to _____.
   A. clean thoroughly   B. assimilate into white people's culture

C. cover with white coat   D. bleach
5. Many Koreans start up their own businesses mainly because _____.
    A. they want to be their own bosses   B. they want to make more money
    C. they want to be entrepreneurs   D. they have hit or are afraid to hit a glass ceiling

VI. Questions on the Article

1. What was the message Asian-Americans got from the attacks on Korean-Americans in the Los Angeles riots?
2. Tell something about the population of Asian-Americans.
3. How were the earliest Chinese immigrants treated?
4. How do Asian-Americans compare with white people in family income and per capita income?
5. Why are Asian-Americans called the "model minority"? According to the article, how do they feel about it?
6. Why do some blacks call Asian-Americans Uncle Toms?
7. How are some young Asians searching for authentic Asianness?
8. What are the hurdles to Asians' full acceptance by the society?
9. Among the Asians, which group is most noted for street gangs? What is the main cause of street gang expansion?
10. Tell something about the ties among Asian-Americans.
11. What, do you suggest, Asian-Americans should do to enhance their political status?

VII. Topics for Discussion

1. Does the label of model minority help Asian-Americans to improve their situation?
2. Is America a country celebrating differences?

Lesson 4

Closing the Gap

Media, Politics, and Citizen Participation
By Muir, Janette Kenner

It's primary election[1] night in Manchester, New Hampshire. Bright lights of media tents beckon political thrill seekers, most of whom are trying to catch a glimpse of their favorite candidate or media celebrity. The lights cast an eerie glow on the dark night, as cameras, posed in various places, wait with anticipation. Important things are happening here in this snowy town, located in an ardently independent and politically active state. As election results are reported, political candidates begin to sort themselves out — the best rising to the top, the remainder wondering how much longer they can spend precious resources chasing a dream that only a few will ever achieve.

New Hampshire managed to retain its "First in the Nation" primary status in 2008, amidst attempts by other states to close in on this treasured position.[2] Despite protestations from across the country, there is good reason for starting here. From the interplay of candidates and the press to the frenetic energy of campaign volunteers, no other state provides as many opportunities to see politics in action. As the political campaign process unfolds, there are numerous ways to directly connect with candidates, which is something that becomes increasingly difficult as the primary season progresses and the frontrunners are anointed. This primary also provides an early view of the political energy associated with this campaign year, making it feel different from previous elections. One only needs to look around to see the myriad of political signs dotting the highway, dozens of people standing on street corners cheering for their favorite candidate, and the campaign buses and press trucks creating traffic jams to know that something profound is happening here. There seems to be a movement afoot, a passionate desire for change, and a hope for a new perspective. For some it is the search for a new conservative heart. For others it is the promise of a completely new direction for the country.

In January, I had the privilege of traveling to New Hampshire with 18 others for a course called, "On the Campaign Trail."[3] Our goal was to see and learn about as many political candidates as possible and observe their relationships with media and potential voters. Spending a week trudging through snow, attending candidate events, and talking with the press and citizens alike, one cannot help but take away from that experience the firm realization that politics and media are inextricably linked. As with previous elections, the political reality that candidates attempt to create is directly wedded to the way that reality is mediated by journalists.[4]

Politics and media are clearly intertwined in shaping the national political agenda.

Adding to this complexity, however, is a greater public voice utilizing various means to engage citizen participants in the unfolding story. This year, citizen engagement is another strong source of influence, manifested through Internet social networks and blogging sites. As this voice grows, it becomes more challenging for media outlets to garner the kind of influence they held in past presidential campaign seasons. These challenges have significant implications for elections throughout the world.

Every campaign season generates discussion about the ways that media influence the political process and shape public debate. From the earliest US broadsides and editorial cartoons, media have played important roles in framing campaign issues and personalities.[5] In US politics specifically, the press has gone through various stages of influence and now it faces perhaps it (**its**) greatest identity crisis as it redefines its role in media-saturated society.[6] To understand the ways the media impacts US politics, the potential for citizen engagement in the process, and the evolution of international politics, it is helpful to understand the nature of media influence.

Early Aristotelian writing about the art of persuasion and the common places a speaker may draw from to appeal ethically, logically, and emotionally to an audience, underscores the idea that effective political oratory is carefully crafted and delivered for the greatest persuasive impact.[7] Since the time of the printing press, rhetors have depended on media forms to transmit and reinforce this political persuasion, thereby enabling media influence to grow substantially over time. In order to understand this influence, three areas of media are worth noting: plurality, ownership, and technological development.

Media Plurality

An assumption many people make when trying to understand media influence is to think of the media as a conglomeration of messages.[8] Critics often blame media for the ills of society and believe "it" to be the bane of political existence, destroying the art that Aristotle so brilliantly delineated.[9] Yet "media" is a plural noun; this word describes the multitude of channels that bombard us on a daily basis. As the media inundate the public with messages from all directions, the impact of any single message is often diffused as audiences selectively tune in and pay attention to only certain messages. This selective exposure affects the ways different media outlets attempt to attain the public's attention and how candidates stage events for the greatest political benefit.

In the days when there were only three major news networks and trusted media personalities graced our living rooms every evening on the nightly news, media theory suggested that the masses were greatly influenced by what they saw on the news.[10] Early deterministic theories depicted an all-powerful media capable of shaping human behavior in significant ways. Now with more than 400 channels to view, the ability to Tivo favorite shows, and nonstop 24/7 news networks, it is more difficult to gauge the influence of any particular media form on shaping attitudes, especially regarding elections.[11] Contemporary media theorists, responding to this complexity, have begun to highlight media ecology and the systemic interplay of attention, influence, and power in a world of "datasmog" as a way to make sense of these new realities.

Media Ownership

In 1983, approximately 50 corporations owned media outlets. Now due to continually shifting business exchanges, media ownership is primarily controlled by only a handful of major corporations such as Time Warner, Disney, Rupert Murdoch's News Corporation, Bertelsmann of Germany, Viacom, and General Electric.[12] This ownership provokes much criticism over who owns the airwaves and what biases occur as a result of these business deals. For example, a local radio station in a small US Midwest town could be owned by a corporate conglomerate[13]. As a result, there may be strict guidelines in place about what can be aired and what products will be endorsed.

The impact of this ownership is two-fold. First, it underscores the fact that most media outlets are profit-generating enterprises. They are in the business to gain advertisers and maintain stock holders; therefore, creating news coverage that can enhance ratings and increase viewership is always the first goal.[14] Furthermore, these profit-making goals often directly contrast with the requirements of responsible, objective journalism. A second impact of limited ownership is the lack of diversity. As corporation ownership narrows, power lies in the hands of a few, making it difficult for diverse voices to be heard. These monopolies tend to create a mainstream mentality that makes it especially difficult for marginalized voices to gain publicity.[15]

Technological Development

The sophistication of the Internet is leading to a major transformation in political elections, particularly in the availability of information and the potential for active engagement in the process. Interactive technology is ushering in a whole new way of thinking about civic engagement in politics. One area of significant relevance is blogging. Often called "the Sixth Estate[16]," bloggers — who can provide an added level of transparency to the process of reporting — are transforming how we access and absorb political news. Through careful fact-checking, scathing critiques, and dialogue, these web journals written by journalists, professors, and average citizens provide another layer of influence as they attempt to ensure that political claims are substantiated and well-developed.[17]

Another technological development transforming the election process is the personalization of electronic messages between the candidate and potential voters. Through email and websites, candidates can often bypass traditional media and directly interact with the public in an electronic form of direct mail that is relatively inexpensive and far more expedient. Candidates and their surrogates send daily e-mail messages to supporters and potential voters, keeping them apprised of critical moments, popularity surges, and the need to send more money to maintain momentum. Websites such as Facebook and MySpace generate armies of political supporters willing to give money and work locally for their candidates.[18] Electronic bulletin boards keep voters informed about candidate sightings and other political events.[19] Given these technological developments and the ability of some political candidates to embrace these new technologies, it is easy to understand the growing interest among young people in this year's US presidential election and the increasing use of the Internet for gathering political information.

Global Media, Politics, and Citizenship

Evidence for shifting influences in media and increased citizen involvement can be found in the international arena as well. Throughout the world, political candidates are learning ways to stage political events for the largest possible influence, as gauged through media coverage and public attention. Looking at the elections in Russia, Pakistan, and Kenya further highlights this phenomenon.

Consider the visual snapshots of Vladimir Putin and his successor, Dmitry Medvedev, standing together for a mediated moment following the Russian presidential election.[20] The victory pose of these two leaders, aired throughout Russia and around the globe, illustrates the role visual power has in establishing authority and credibility for the incoming president. The message this image projects contrasts greatly with Russian bloggers' interpretations of this election and the subsequent government that will result. The uncritical media coverage of Putin's anointed predecessor (successor) angered many bloggers as they attempted to identify the characteristics of the First Deputy Prime Minister and his relationship with Putin, while also pointing out the merits of other political candidates. Greater government control of the Russian news media through state-owned corporations and wealthy loyal investors has greatly influenced what ends up on Russian television. On the other hand, bloggers are significantly contributing to reporting the reality of the situation, often through the use of sarcasm and unfiltered remarks[21]. Though Medvedev has won the election, there is evidence to suggest that the Kremlin may be concerned about the uncontrolled nature of the Internet and is considering legislation to regulate this kind of "extremist material."

Bloggers also responded to the election in Pakistan. Many websites captured the anger citizens felt toward US involvement in the election process,[22] responding to editorials in Pakistani newspapers that accused the United States of meddling in the country's affairs. Websites such as Voice of America News and Human Rights Watch provided stories underscoring the role of the people in changing the course of Pakistan's election. Though the election was a highly contentious one, the outcome represented a transformation in Pakistani politics that points to a more engaged citizenry.[23]

Similarly, Kenya's blogging community has been praised as one of the most vibrant in sub-Saharan Africa. Over 60 blog sites devoted specifically to the Kenyan election process discuss the violence and unrest that has (**have**) resulted from perceived fraudulent activities, involving vote tabulations that put incumbent president Mwai Kabaki (**Kibaki**) back in power.[24] When the government instituted a media blackout, blogs were critical in spreading the latest news. Even after the blackout was lifted, bloggers were faster and more detailed in their reporting about the latest clashes than were other news sources. Blogs, along with mobile phones, are attempting to tell the story in ways that reflect the pain and struggle of the Kenyan people.

While critics will argue that access to the Internet is still minimal in many countries — with limited numbers of personal computers, slow connections, and a complete lack of access in poorer areas — the Internet's influence and potential to reach people has only just begun to be explored in many societies. The amazing growth of public voices telling the stories that most of the world does not get to see, speaks to the tremendous potential the Internet has in shaping future campaigns and elections. One can only imagine the possibilities for future elections as more and more people acquire better access to technology. As this access grows, so does the potential for elections to run in a more fair and open manner. Information is ubiquitous and expansive. While various countries may struggle with reaching the electorate, there are many media outlets, converging on the Internet, that play important roles in disseminating news about the political process.[25]

What of the Future?

As influence continues to shift, politics and media converge on new technologies. Given these realities, campaigns must continue to seek out the simplest and most effective ways to transmit and receive messages. In turn, media outlets must consider multiple ways to feed consumers and new ways to maintain viability. In 2008, candidates have found growing support in online social networks such as Facebook and MySpace. There are even Facebook groups formed to support Kenyan peace efforts and efforts to create a Russian version of Facebook. The Pakistani Facebook claims over 145,000 friends in its network; includes all sorts of commentary and YouTube[26] videos. These networks are bound to continue their growth and influence in future elections.

As consumers of politics, we can increase our political literacy by becoming more aware of these integrated systems. We can learn how to analyze the ways candidates shape messages to acquire media attention and how media outlets support much of this shaping. Political literacy requires that we understand the economics of the process as well as the ways persuasive messages are created and sustained. It also means that we need to dig deeper to address the short attention spans of the public and encourage people to grapple with the actual ideas of the candidate.

A positive feature that results this year from observing US politics and the rise of public voices in presidential campaigns is the creation of a more civil discourse that attempts to bypass more mediated environments to directly respond to individual concerns. As the pool of presidential candidates evolves, it will become increasingly necessary to determine the best ways to address race, gender, class, and religious differences in a manner that advances constructive political dialogue. The transparency of blogging may help to keep discourse on a civil level[27]—or at the very least, bloggers will challenge unfair claims on all sides of the political spectrum and tell the stories that need to be heard. There is hope that with the right access, political transparency will continue to spread worldwide.

Does the art of political persuasion still exist? One need only look to the sweeping oratory of Barack Obama, the careful event staging of John McCain, or the one-on-one interpersonal style of Hillary Clinton to know that there is clearly an art to doing it right.[28] The rhetoric may not always be aesthetically pleasing, but it is intentional, creative, and passionate. Journalistic reports of politics must take into account these same needs to persuade and inspire, and the Internet is becoming the place where citizens can lend their voice to the public debate. Democracy is not a perfect system; it can be a messy construct. But politics and media are permanent businesses in American society that will continue to evolve with time, technological advances, and true believers.

From *Harvard International Review*, April 1, 2008

Ⅰ. New Words

afoot	[ə'fut]	*adj.*	being planned, happening
airwave	['ɛəweiv]	*n.*	（无线电或电视的）广播
anoint	[ə'nɔint]	*v.*	*formal* to choose sb to do a particular job
apprise	[ə'praiz]	*v.*	*formal* to inform about sth
bane	[bein]	*n.*	sth that causes trouble

beckon	['bekən]	v.	*formal* to appear very attractive to sb
blackout	['blækaut]	n.	(新闻等的)封锁,不准发表,不准广播
blog	[blɔg]	n.	网络日志,博客
conglomeration	[kɔn,glɔmə'reiʃən]	n.	*AmE* 聚集物,混合体
datasmog	['deitəsmɔg]	n.	信息烟雾(尤指通过因特网检索得到的过多信息)
delineat	[di'linieit]	v.	*formal* to describe sth carefully so that people can understand it
deterministic	[di,tə:mi'nistik]	adj.	〔哲〕决定论的
diffuse	[di'fju:z]	v.	*formal* to spread sth widely in all directions
eerie	['iəri]	adj.	strange, mysterious
expedient	[ik'spi:diənt]	adj.	useful or necessary for a particular purpose
fraudulent	['frɔ:djulənt]	adj.	欺骗性的
frenetic	[fri'netik]	adj.	involving a lot of energy and activity
garner	['gɑ:nə]	v.	*formal* to obtain or collect sth
grace	[greis]	v.	to make sth more attractive
grapple	['græpl]	v.	~ **with** to try to find a solution to a problem
incumbent	[in'kʌmbənt]	adj.	现任的,在职的
inextricably	[in'ekstrikəbli]	adv.	(绳结)解不开地,分不开地
interplay	['intəplei]	n.	相互影响,相互作用
inundate	['inʌndeit]	v.	to give or send sb so many things that he/she cannot deal with them all
Kenya	['kenjə]	n.	肯尼亚
myriad	['miriəd]	n.	*literary* an extreme large number
protestation	[,prəutes'teiʃən]	n.	抗议,异议,反对
rhetor	['ri:tə]	n.	演说家
scathing	['skeiðiŋ]	adj.	bitterly severe
sub-Saharan	[,sʌbsə'hɑ:rən]	adj.	(非洲)撒哈拉沙漠以南的
surrogate	['sʌrəgət]	n.	*formal* a person acting in place of sb
ubiquitous	[ju'bikwitəs]	adj.	seeming to be everywhere at the same time
tabulation	[,tæbju'leiʃən]	n.	排成表格式,列表
viability	[,vaiə'biləti]	n.	独立生存性,独立发展性
vibrant	['vaibrənt]	adj.	exciting and full of activity

Ⅱ. Background Information

传媒与选举

当今美国,传媒发挥监督政府、引导舆论、影响受众等重要作用,常被称作"第四权力"。

在美国新闻史中起重要影响的理论是自由主义理论、客观主义理论和社会责任理论。自由主义理论认为媒介不受政府干涉,拥有对政府的监督权,强调社会大众的信息知晓权和新闻媒介的传播权。客观主义理论要求新闻反映客观事实,必须与意见分开,新闻不得夹杂观点、表现个性。社会责任论要求传媒真实客观地报道新闻，承担社会成员之间交流思想的责任，反映社会各阶层的风貌。

媒体与选举关系密不可分。竞选者选举是否成功取决于三个"M"，即 message（信息）、media（媒体）和 money（金钱）。"信息"主要指竞选纲领、竞选者资格和业绩。信息必须借助媒体传播，从而广为人知，使竞选人得到民众的了解和支持。然而，美国绝大多数媒体是私营的，借助媒体传播信息是需要花许多资金购买印刷媒体版面篇幅（buy space）、电子媒体时段（buy time）。所以，在某种程度上来说，竞选是一场"金钱大战"。

政治广告类似商品广告，有硬销售（hard sell）和软销售（soft sell）。硬销售是明确呼吁选民投自己的票，软销售主要是塑造竞选人良好形象，从而赢得选民的好感和支持。

媒体是竞选广告的载体。广告是媒体主要经济来源。据统计，广告收入占报纸总收入的72%，占杂志总收入的60%，占几乎电视的全部收入。竞选是民众所关心的内容，也为媒体带来大量的广告收入。

美国早期的竞选广告重点放在讨论候选人的资格和品德。20世纪60年代后，美国竞选广告转入"形象时代"，重点转到塑造候选人形象方面。一般来说，竞选广告内容有以下四种：陈述政见、攻击对手、反驳对手、塑造形象。最近一些年，美国竞选出现了一个值得关注但又是很有争议的现象：负面竞选（negative campaigning），即刊登或播放针对竞选对手的负面广告（negative advertising），目的在于诋毁对手形象，抬高自身形象。

为了更好地运用媒体，取得最佳宣传效果，竞选人都有专家作为顾问。总统竞选人会有选举策划人、传播主任、民意测验专家、媒体顾问、演讲写作人、广告制作人、游说辩士、助选名嘴组成的顾问团。

竞选广告媒体常见形式为报纸杂志、广播、电视和网络。报纸杂志具有一览性、便携性、易存性特点，但由于是印刷媒体（print media），效果较为单一。广播广告声情并茂，制作方便，广告价格较为低廉。电视广告声、色、形兼备，感官效果强烈。电视是大众最喜爱的媒体，也是获取新闻的主要途径；但电视广告费用比较昂贵。网络媒体的最大特点是信息的透明和双向交流。伴随个人电脑的普及、网络技术的变革，网络的优势日趋显著。竞选人充分利用网络加强与选民的联系和沟通，民众也充分运用博客（blogging）、播客（podcasting）和社会网络（SNS）表达观点。可以预见，网络在竞选中的作用还会持续增加。

Ⅲ. Notes to the Text

1. primary election — (in the US) an election in which people in a particular area vote to choose a candidate for a future important election 初选
2. New Hampshire managed to retain its "First in the Nation" primary status in 2008, amidst attempts by other states to close in on this treasured position. — 2008年，新罕布什尔州成功卫冕"初选全国第一州"地位，其他州都试图要夺取这个宝座。（①primary — primary election；②close in on — to come near from all sides to snatch the position）
3. course called, "On the Campaign Trail" — 被称为"竞选路径"的课程（trail — a route that is followed for a particular purpose）
4. As with previous elections, the political reality that candidates attempt to create is directly wedded to the way that reality is mediated by journalists. — 与先前的选举一样，

候选人试图创造的政治现实与新闻记者传播现实的方式是直接关联的。（①wedded to sth — *literary* combined with sth；②mediate — to be the medium for effecting a result）

5. From the earliest US broadsides and editorial cartoons, media have played important roles in framing campaign issues and personalities. — 从美国最早期的激烈抨击和政治讽刺画以来,传媒在构想竞选议题和创造名人方面发挥了重要作用。[①the earliest US broadsides and editorial cartoons — 这里作者指美国新闻早期的政党报时期（the Party Press Period）,当时报纸绝大多数依附于党派,为党派利益服务,故而称作"政党报"（partisan newspaper）,其特色是宣传党派观点、纲领,展开激烈争论,常常伴有谩骂污蔑、人身攻击的情况,这些报不是以报道事实为主,而是以宣传观点为主,因此也被称作"观点报"（viewspapers）；②broadside — a strong or abusive written attack]

6. ..., the press has gone through various stages of influence and now it faces perhaps it (**its**) greatest identity crisis as it redefines its role in media-saturated society. — 新闻业的影响经过了各种不同阶段,现在是媒体充斥的社会,新闻业正在重新确定自己的功能,因而面临着或许最大的性质认同危机。（①identity crisis — a psychological term used here to refer to the uncertainty of the press about its role in society；②media-saturated society — a society with a huge number of media forms）

7. Early Aristotelian writing about the art of persuasion and the common places a speaker may draw from to appeal ethically, logically, and emotionally to an audience, underscores the idea that effective political oratory is carefully crafted and delivered for the greatest persuasive impact. — 早期亚里士多德有关劝说技巧和演说者为了在道德上、逻辑上和情感上打动听众而常用手法的写作中强调的观念是成功的政治演说是讲稿要精心准备,演讲能够产生最大的劝说效果。[Aristotle — 亚里士多德（384—322,BC）是西方古典修辞学中最著名的一位修辞学家。他提出：演说要想打动听众,要靠三个因素：内容、文辞、演说技巧。他认为,演说要具有三种感染力（persuasive appeals）,伦理道德的（ethical）、情感的（emotional）和逻辑的（logical）。他把演说分为五个步骤：觅材取材、布局谋篇、确定风格、牢记在心、进行演讲。]

8. An assumption many people make when trying to understand media influence is to think of the media as a conglomeration of messages. — 许多人在试图搞清媒体影响的时候头脑中是把传媒看作传播信息的聚合体。（conglomeration — *formal* a group of many different things gathered together）

9. Critics often blame media for the ills of society and believe "it" to be the bane of political existence, destroying the art that Aristotle so brilliantly delineated. — 批评者责怪传媒造成社会弊病,认为传媒是导致政治权术的祸根,它毁掉了亚里士多德所精辟阐述的演说艺术。(Here, the word "political" is used in the derogatory sense of being skilled at using different situations to try to get power or advantage for oneself without much consideration of principles.)

10. In the days when there were only three major news networks and trusted media personalities graced our living rooms every evening on the nightly news, media theory suggested that the masses were greatly influenced by what they saw on the news. — 在只有三大电视网,人们在客厅里观看所信赖的著名播音员的晚间新闻的时代,传媒理论

认为:大众的观点在很大程度上受电视新闻节目内容的影响。[three major news networks — referring to the three TV networks: National Broadcasting Company (NBC); CBS (Columbia Broadcasting System) and ABC (American Broadcasting Company)]

11. Now with more than 400 channels to view, the ability to Tivo favorite shows, and nonstop 24/7 news networks, it is more difficult to gauge the influence of any particular media form on shaping attitudes, especially regarding elections. — 现在观众可以观看的频道有400多个,可以用 Tivo 挑选自己所喜爱的节目,新闻网络每周7天,每天24小时不间断地播放,因而要对任何特定媒体形式对观众,尤其关于选举问题态度的影响进行判定更加困难(Tivo ——一种可以帮助人们筛选电视上播放节目的数字录像设备)。

12. ..., media ownership is primarily controlled by only a handful of major corporations such as Time Warner, Disney, Rupert Murdoch's News Corporation, Bertelsmann of Germany, Viacom, and General Electric. — 媒体所有权主要控制在少数几家大公司手中,比如时代—华纳公司、迪斯尼公司、默多克的新闻公司、德国的贝塔斯曼集团、维亚康姆公司和通用电气公司。[①Time Warner—时代—华纳公司,是世界上最大的媒体与娱乐公司,2000年与美国在线(AOL)公司合并成为美国在线时代—华纳公司,其业务范围包括美国在线、电视与广播、有线电视、出版、影视娱乐和音乐;②Disney — 全称为 the Walt Disney Cosney Company,是全球最大的娱乐媒体公司之一,营业额仅次于时代—华纳公司,拥有影视娱乐业、主题公园与度假区、媒体网络、ABC广播公司、消费品品牌、儿童书籍出版业;③News Corporation — 新闻集团公司,是世界上规模最大、国际化程度最高的综合性传媒公司之一;④Bertelsmann — 德国贝塔斯曼集团,是世界四大传媒巨头之一,拥有欧洲最大的广播集团——RTL集团、全球最大的图书出版集团——兰登书屋、欧洲最大的杂志出版集团、单曲唱片发行公司;⑤Viacom — 维亚康姆公司,是国际传媒巨头,涉及电影、电视、出版和娱乐相关的零售业务,旗下有哥伦比亚广播公司(CBS)、派拉蒙电影公司等;⑥General Electric — 美国通用电气公司,是世界上最大的多元化服务性公司]

13. corporate conglomerate — 合股联合大企业(conglomerate — a large company formed by joining together different firms 近几十年来西方传媒垄断步伐加快,联合大企业兼并新闻业情况日趋增多。一些传播学者指出:联合大企业经办新闻业的结果是忽视新闻质量和限制新闻自由。为了谋求更大利润,联合大企业会减少严肃新闻,加大软新闻、煽情新闻含量。此外,新闻业掌握在联合大企业手中必然维护企业本身利益、排斥不同观点,造成呼声单一、观点单一的情况。)

14. They are in the business to gain advertisers ... always the first goal. — 他们的意图就是争取广告客户,保持持股人数不降,因此,制作能够提高收视率、增加观众数量的新闻报道永远是其首要目的。(the ratings — a set of figures that show how many people watch or listen to a particular television or radio program)

15. These monopolies tend to create a mainstream mentality that makes it especially difficult for marginalized voices to gain publicity. — 这些垄断企业往往会产生主流心态,使得受排斥的声音特别难得到公众关注。(mentality — the particular attitude or way of thinking of a group)

16. the Sixth Estate — 第六等级/权力 [美国原有 the Fourth Estate(第四等级/第四权力)之说,指的是报刊、广播、电视新闻界拥有监督政府三大权力(executive, legislative and judicial)部门的权力。博客的影响扩大促使一些专家的关注,他们称博客为第五等级/权力。最近资深传媒专家 Stephen D. Cooper 撰写了一本专论博客影响的书,题为 *Watching the Watchdog: the Fifth Estate*。此外,美国社会也有人使用 the Fifth Estate 表示"科学界"。]

17. ... they attempt to ensure that political claims are substantiated and well-developed. — 他们试图确保所提出的政治主张有根有据,成熟完善。(substantiated — *formal* to provide information or evidence to prove that sth is true)

18. Websites such as Facebook and MySpace generate armies of political supporters willing to give money and work locally for their candidates. — 像脸谱网和聚友网之类网站产生出大批愿意为他们所拥护的候选人提供选金和当地服务的竞选支持者。[Facebook and MySpace — Facebook(脸谱网)与 MySpace(聚友网)是并列为全球最大的社交网站。2008年脸谱网用户增加到1.15亿,其中6,200万是美国用户;聚友网美国用户为7,300万。前者特色是现实生活信息交流,后者特色是突出自我表现。]

19. Electronic bulletin boards keep voters informed about candidate sightings and other political events. — 电子公告板使选民了解候选人所出现的场合和其他政治活动。(sighting — an occasion when sb sees sb)

20. Consider the visual snapshots of Vladimir Putin and his successor, Dmitry Medvedev, standing together for a mediated moment following the Russian presidential election. — 仔细品味弗拉基米尔·普京和他的接班人德米特里·梅德韦杰夫在俄罗斯总统选举后特意站在一起让媒体所拍下的快照。(a mediated moment — a moment which has been arranged)

21. unfiltered remarks — original remarks

22. Many websites captured the anger citizens felt toward US involvement in the election process, ... — 许多网站反映了公民对美国介入其选举过程的愤怒情绪。(capture — to reflect)

23. Though the election was a highly contentious one, the outcome represented a transformation in Pakistani politics that points to a more engaged citizenry. — 虽然巴基斯坦选举是一个很有争议的问题,但其结果却显示巴基斯坦政治向着公民更高参与率方向转变。(①engaged — more active in participation;②the election — 此处指2008年2月18日所举行的巴基斯坦国会选举,原定于2008年1月8日举行,后因贝娜齐尔·布托遇刺事件而后延。这次选举穆沙拉夫所领导的巴基斯坦穆斯林联盟所得席位少于巴基斯坦人民党,选举之后巴基斯坦这两大党组成联合政府,推选 Yosaf Raza Gillaini 为总理。)

24. Over 60 blog sites devoted specifically to the Kenyan election process discuss the violence and unrest that has(**have**) resulted from perceived fraudulent activities, involving vote tabulations that put incumbent president Mwai Kibaki back in power. — 具体报道肯尼亚选举过程的60多个博客站讨论公众所了解的选举舞弊行为所导致的暴力和动乱,舞弊行为包括使原任总统姆瓦伊·齐贝吉得以重新当选的选票统计。(the Kenyan election — 指肯尼亚2007年大选。据媒体报道,齐贝吉总统操纵选票汇总统计程序。

第一批选票揭晓的结果是反对派赢得席位数量大大高于齐贝吉,然而选票汇总后报出的统计总数却完全不同。在反对派试图质疑不一致现象时,肯尼亚选举委员会却匆匆宣布齐贝吉大选获胜。此后,反对者走上街头游行抗议,后遭政府镇压,抗议行动中有数百人丧生。)

25. ... there are many media outlets, converging on the Internet, that play important roles in disseminating news about the political process. — 因特网上还汇聚许多媒体的网站,他们在传播竞选进程相关新闻方面发挥了重要作用。(①converge on — to move towards a place from different directions and meet;②many media outlets, converging on the Internet — referring to the websites of newspapers, television stations, etc.)

26. YouTube — (设立在美国的)世界最大视频分享网站,可供网民下载观看和分享视频短片。

27. The transparency of blogging may help to keep discourse on a civil level — 博客的透明性会有助于使劝说保持在文明的水平上。

28. One need only look to the sweeping oratory of Barack Obama, ... to know that there is clearly an art to doing it right. — 你只要留意巴拉克·奥巴马的铿锵有力的演讲,约翰·麦凯恩的竞选活动的精心安排,或是希拉里·克林顿的一对一人际交流方式,你就会知道有效的政治劝说显然是要有技巧的。(①event staging — referring to the arrangement of election campaign activities;②sweeping — forceful)

Ⅳ. Language Features

词语文化内涵

本文中的"political campaign"并非表示"政治运动"之意,而是指"竞选活动"。

语言与文化存在血肉相连的关系。语言是文化的载体,语言中渗透着文化。因此,我们在学习一门外语时,必须熟悉这种语言的相关文化。

美英报刊题材面广,内容丰富,涉及政治、经济、军事、宗教习俗、社会风尚、价值观念、家庭观念、人际关系和生活方式等方面,各个方面的文化差异必然影响外刊阅读的理解。

由于文化差异,英汉语中有不少词语虽然概念意义相同,但却具有不同的关联意义,赋有不同感情色彩,不了解这些关联意义和感情色彩,就会产生误解。

譬如:英语中,"peasant""politics""propaganda"这三个词常常带有贬义,而汉语中的对应词却毫无贬义。

此外,英语中有些词含有丰富的关联意义,"cowboy"所包含的意思决非是词典中注释的"放牛娃"或"牛仔"所能准确表达的,它还具有以下关联意义:吃苦耐劳、酷爱自由、敢于冒险。再如"sin taxes"并非指对犯罪者征税,而是特指(烟、酒、赌博所征收的)罪孽税。

外刊中这类情况甚多,大量词语看上去与某些汉语词相似,但实际上是"貌合神离"。不了解这些词语真正内涵,根据结构望而生义就会造成误解。

例:couch potatoes ≠ 沙发上的土豆,而是电视迷
　　senior citizens ≠ 地位高的公民,而是老年公民
　　street-walker ≠ 街道散步的人,而是街头拉客的妓女

do-gooder ≠ 做好事的人，而是不现实的慈善家
baby-kisser ≠ 亲吻孩子的人，而是善于笼络人心的政客
easy meat ≠ 可嚼的肉，而是容易上当受骗的人
open housing ≠ 开放式的住房，而是住房方面取消种族隔离
call-girl ≠ 传呼姑娘，而是电话应召女郎、妓女
whistle-blower ≠ 吹哨者，而是告密者
busybody ≠ 大忙人，而是爱管闲事的人
hard money ≠ 硬币，而是合法政治献金
gay marriage ≠ 幸福的婚姻，而是同性婚姻
Individualism ≠ 个人主义，强调自主、自信、独立、个人权利

Ⅴ. Analysis of Content

1. The term "primary election" in the article refers to _____.
   A. the final election for the president
   B. the state's election for the governor
   C. the election to choose a presidential candidate
   D. the most important election

2. The phrase "something profound" in the sentence "One only needs to look around to see… to know that something profound is happening here."（Para. 2）refers to _____.
   A. the sharp rise of citizen participation in politics
   B. big changes in mass media
   C. major corporations' control of mass media
   D. great improvement of news coverage

3. The author suggests that, to be more effective, present-day election campaigns should _____.
   A. seek out the simplest and most effective ways to transmit and receive messages
   B. spend more money on political advertising
   C. spend more time on the campaign
   D. encourage the public to be more actively involved in politics

4. It can be inferred from the article that major corporations' control of mass media has the effect of _____.
   A. improving the quality of news coverage
   B. boosting the status of mass media
   C. increasing mass media's political influence
   D. reducing objectivity of news coverage

5. The article is intended to _____.
   A. criticize the monopolization of mass media

B. eulogize the positive effects of media's technology development
C. elaborate the changes in the relationship between media, politics and citizen participation
D. clarify major theories on mass media's functions

VI. Questions on the Article

1. Why does the author think New Hampshire should retain its "First in the Nation" primary status?
2. What was the aim of the course "On the Campaign Trail"?
3. What kind of relationship exists between politics and media? What makes the relationship even more complex?
4. How does media plurality affect media's influence?
5. According to early deterministic theories, what functions did media play?
6. What are the impacts of major corporations' control of the media?
7. Why are bloggers often called "the Sixth Estate"?
8. In what way does personalization of electronic messages affect election process?
9. According to the author, what does the victory pose of Putin and Medvedev illustrate? What was the bloggers' response to the media coverage of Medvedev?
10. What role has Kenya's blogging community been playing in the country's politics?
11. Considering the new realities, what must media outlets do?
12. How can the public increase their political literacy?

VII. Topics for Discussion

1. Does corporation ownership of mass media help to improve the quality of news reporting?
2. Is there complete press freedom in the western countries?

Lesson 5

Occupy Wall Street

A protest against a broken economic compact
By Amy Dean

During the early months when Occupy Wall Street maintained tent cities in lower Manhattan[1] and other metropolitan areas around the country, the occupations attracted an array of young counter-culturalists and itinerant radicals. To many people seeing the images of the encampments on the news, it looked like a motley assembly, not something out of the American mainstream.

But while some of the images of Zuccotti Park[2] that defined Occupy Wall Street in its infancy may have appeared to depict a fringe, the movement as a whole is far bigger than any of its encampments. In truth, the Occupy movement is a protest against a broken economic compact that reaches into the very middle of America and that is resonating in other parts of the world as well.

With the movement's permanent occupations now largely disbanded, the protesters are looking for ways to escalate and keep the spotlight on their issues. But regardless of what strategies they adopt(**for**) moving forward, they have already left behind a transformed framework for public debate in America. Occupy Wall Street has struck a chord with a wide swath of the country by highlighting issues that had been all but hidden in mainstream news coverage prior to the street protests.[3] According to a poll conducted by *The Hill*[4] in October 2011, 74 percent of likely voters say that inequality is a problem in the country, with the great bulk of that group indicating that it is a big one. Moreover, a Gallup poll from February 2011 reveals that in large majorities, Americans believe that corporations should have less influence on our politics.

The same thing that gives Occupy Wall Street strong appeal in the United States also gives the movement international resonance. In an integrated international economy, profound inequality is a global phenomenon. Virtually anywhere protests have emerged—whether in Europe, Asia, or the Americas—participants can point to examples of how the most affluent members of their societies have benefitted at the expense of the majority. They can tell stories that bring to life the reality of how economic downturn has affected their families and their communities.

Back in the United States, even leaders in the financial community credit Occupy Wall Street protesters with pinpointing concerns that are central to our democracy. In mid-November of last year, former Treasury Secretary Robert Rubin[5] said that the occupations "identified issues that are really central to what's going to happen to our economy and our society." President Obama, after being confronted by protesters during a speech, stated, "There is a profound sense of frustration about the fact that the essence of the American

Dream—which is if you work hard, if you stick to it, that you can make it—feels like that's slipping away. And it's not the way things are supposed to be."

How Things Should Be: Linking Productivity and Wages

Both Rubin and Obama's reaction to the Occupy movement point (points) to something important and often overlooked. The central slogan of the Occupy movement, the call of "We Are the 99 Percent," has led many people to focus on inequality as the central issue. Indeed, this is an important concern, as economists such as Nobel Laureate Joseph Stiglitz[6] have persuasively argued. In a May 2011 article in *Vanity Fair*[7], Stiglitz wrote, "The upper 1 percent of Americans are now taking in nearly a quarter of the nation's income every year. In terms of wealth rather than income, the top 1 percent control 40 percent ... Twenty-five years ago, the corresponding figures were 12 percent and 33 percent." The division between the top one percent and the rest of the population is particularly apparent among political officeholders. As Stiglitz further explained, many senators and representatives in the House "are members of the top 1 percent when they arrive, are kept in office by money from the top 1 percent, and know that if they serve the top 1 percent well they will be rewarded by the top 1 percent when they leave office."

Yet inequality is only part of the picture, and perhaps not the most important part. Republicans have seized upon denunciations of inequality to claim that protesters are calling for class warfare and unfair redistribution. But what Americans are truly speaking out against is not that some affluent people have done well in our economy. It is that they have left the rest of the country, behind. While inequality is a symptom, the root imbalance leading to the protests that have swept the country is the severing of increasing economic productivity and the wellbeing of most Americans[8].

Historically—and particularly during the post-World War II economic boom that created a vibrant middle class in our country—productivity increases have translated into tangible benefits for ordinary working people. As Steven Greenhouse and David Leonhardt of the *New York Times* wrote in a 2006 article, "For most of the last century, wages and productivity—the key measure of the economy's efficiency—have risen together." But in the last three decades that linkage between workers' wages and their productivity, a core component of America's economic compact, has been severed. A March 2011 study by the Economy Policy Institute[9] stated that "the typical worker [in both public and private sectors] has had stagnating wages for a long time, despite enjoying some wage growth during the economic recovery of the late 1990s." The same study indicated that "while productivity grew 80 percent between 1979 and 2009, the hourly wage of the median worker grew by only 10.1 percent, with all of this wage growth occurring from 1996 to 2002, reflecting the strong economic recovery of the late 1990s."

Young people who have entered the labor market in the last ten years, burdened with historically onerous student debts, have experienced the broken compact in a particularly striking way. As the same report notes, "The fading momentum of the 1990s recovery failed to propel real wage gains for college graduates, from 2002 to 2010, despite productivity growth of 20.2 percent over the same period." It is little surprise that students and recent graduates have identified in large numbers with Occupy Wall Street.

Although the encampment in Zuccotti Park provided a focal point for the movement, one of the great strengths of the Occupy efforts is that they have allowed even people who live far from Wall Street to identify targets in their local communities that embody our economy's imbalances. Unlike in the 1990s, when activists followed trade meetings to Seattle or Genoa[10], the Occupy movement has allowed protesters to stay at home and to demonstrate ways in which a wide range of communities have been directly affected by an economic system that no longer translates rising productivity into widely shared gain. It has provided a framework for translating national and international data into local action.[11]

No Sharing of Risk

As a result, in hundreds of cities and towns people have been motivated to decry how changes in the economy have taken a measurable toll. The consequence of productivity being de-linked from rising wages indicates a marked increase in economic insecurity. A Rockefeller Foundation[12] team led by Yale University Professor Jacob Hacker confirms this concern about economic security as one that "has only grown amid the deepest downturn in decades." Hacker's team defines economic insecurity as "1) Experiencing a major loss in income, 2) Incurring large out-of-pocket medical expenses, or 3) Lacking adequate financial wealth to buffer the first two risks." Economic insecurity is an issue that has not only worsened over the last couple of decades; it is a phenomenon that has dramatically intensified over the last few years. Hacker's study reveals that in 1985, 12.2 percent of Americans could be classified as insecure. In the early 2000s, this number had increased to 17 percent in conjunction with the recession. In 2007, before the downturn we currently face, the group of insecure Americans had improved to 13.7 percent, but measured insecurity still remained higher than in the 1980s. After the economic crash of 2008, all indications are that it has shot up again.

In times of relative security and stability in America, private businesses, the public sector, and individual workers all bore some part of the insecurity, inherent in our economic system. Yet in recent decades, we have had a dismantling of the institutions that allowed a sharing of the risk associated with the undulations of the capitalist business cycle. Since the 1980s, our social safety net has been unraveled. Moreover, union density has sharply declined, leaving workers without the ability to collectively negotiate the terms of their employment with management. Hence, individuals have been left to carry the vast bulk of the risk burden. This widespread insecurity in our citizenry is what has fueled the Occupy movement.

The political protests have provided an important reminder that the economic situation we find ourselves in was not inevitable. Past periods of relative economic security resulted from a different set of policy choices than those our elected officials have pursued since the 1980s. It was not pre-ordained in prior eras that we would have a social safety net that would catch people when volatility took place. The safety net that allowed workers who were disconnected from a job not to hit rock bottom and be able to reenter the workforce was something that was won in large part thanks to social movements of the past, specifically the activism that led up to the New Deal.[13] Nor was it pre-ordained that jobs in auto, steel, textile, and apparel sectors would create middle-class jobs in America. The institution of collective bargaining allowed for these.[14]

To remedy today's economic imbalances, some liberals have advocated increasing revenue to government through a measure of more progressive taxation[15], such as the Buffett Tax[16]—a tax on the wealthy named after billionaire financier and tax advocate Warren

Buffett. Sadly, serious discussion of such a measure is difficult to find in Washington. But even if this proposal were on the table, it is not adequate to address the core economic issues in question.[17] In order to return to a situation in which the risks of the business cycle are shared by all major actors in our economy, we must rebuild the institutions that gave working people a voice. In particular, we must revive collective bargaining. In a new economy, resurrected institutions of collective bargaining may not look like the unions of old. Especially in situations where work is part-time, contingent, or performed by independent contractors, we will need new ways to restore balanced risk. But until we endeavor to find these new forms, we cannot be surprised to see public protests spread.

Radicalism and Reform

The lack of voice that most Americans experience in the economic sphere—exacerbated by the decline of institutions such as trade unions—is also present in our political life. Unions provided one of the major institutional vehicles for working and middle class people to express their interests in the public sphere. While unions have been under continual attack, few new forces have emerged that can challenge the unchecked political influence of corporate America. The resulting sense of political disenfranchisement is another factor that has fueled Occupy Wall Street.

The protests have highlighted the fact that formal channels of democratic influence appear accessible only to those who can afford lush campaign donations and well-paid Washington lobbyists. Changes in the American economy have taken place at a far greater pace than often-gridlocked decision-making in the nation's capital has been able to respond.[18] This has created a gap between perennial hopes that elected officials might pursue the type of reform agenda that might rebuild the institutions of risk sharing in the economy and a reality of persistent disappointment.

The Occupy movement has emerged at a moment when that gap has been particularly severe. In a historic election, voters elected President Obama and endorsed a strong mandate of change. Yet, in Washington, the ideology of economic neoliberalism is so dominant that no substantive proposals for reining in corporate influence over politics or correcting the imbalance that has placed individuals as sole risk-bearers in the economy are part of serious discussion.[19] The fact that Obama's jobs proposals this past fall had no chance of passing through Congress shows how far off we are. Far beyond creating jobs, we need to be talking about how to transform poor jobs into good jobs—a conversation nowhere on the current political map.[20]

The rise of inequality and the de-linking of productivity and wages are trends that have been emerging(**thing**) for decades. So why have protests emerged now?

For one, amid a global economy in turmoil, people are feeling the effects of these economic trends in a direct and local way. Protest movements in Spain, Greece, and other countries that emerged in response to the economic crisis set the stage for protests at the heart of the global financial system. And now, demonstrations in the United States have reverberated back abroad, inspiring further anti-corporate protests from London to Rome to Melbourne.

Yet, in the United States, the raised expectations of the 2008 elections have been at least as significant as the latest economic downturn. Seeing business continue as usual under an administration elected on a platform of change has convinced many Americans that their discontent must be expressed outside of the normal channels of electoral politics. Throughout our history, radicalism has appeared when reformism has failed. In a November 2011 *New York Times* article, economist Jeffrey Sachs called for a "New Progressive Movement."[21] He argues that Ronald Reagan's overlooking of "the rise of global competition in the information age" thirty years ago led to "a nation singularly unprepared to face the global economic, energy, and environmental challenges of our time." The cause and continuation of the problem can be blamed on "both parties ... who above all else insist on keeping low tax rates on capital gains, top incomes, estates and corporate profits." Our present political situation has created fertile ground for dissent.

The situation that we face today does not stand unprecedented in history. Sachs remarks that twice before, in the Gilded Age of the late 1800s and again in the Roaring 1920s, "powerful corporate interests dominated Washington and brought America to a state of unacceptable inequality, instability, and corruption."[22] Both times, society was able to successfully recover through "a social and political movement [that] arose to restore democracy and shared prosperity."

Indeed, throughout the 20th century, radical movements in America have presaged most serious reform efforts. During President Franklin Delano Roosevelt's first years in office, the president faced growing Communist and Socialist parties, insurgent populist voices from left and right, and even armed resistance to foreclosure in the countryside. The sweeping programs of the New Deal[23] were instituted in the face of such resistance. In the 1960s, radical movements revolutionized national conceptions of race, gender, and sexual preference, bringing marginalized groups an influence and power long denied them. The globalization protests of the 1990s set the stage for today's Occupy movement by recognizing sweeping economic transformations in our economy and fostering relationships between progressive groups (such as the famous "Teamsters and Turtles" alliance[24] on display at the 1999 Seattle protests against the World Trade Organization) that have helped to bolster the most recent round of demonstrations.

In each case, the pace of political reform had failed to catch up to wider economic and cultural transformation, and social unrest reflected the disjuncture.[25]

Recreating the American Compact

Establishing a renewed period of social stability, democratic enfranchisement, and shared economic risk in America will require a new approach to economic policy-making in Washington, or at least a return to a mentality that prevailed prior to the 1980s. In the postwar decades that witnessed the greatest growth of our country's middle class, elected officials crafted economic policy with an eye to fostering both competitiveness and public wellbeing. Since then the latter goal has been abandoned, and competitiveness has been adopted as the sole objective worthy of concern. Institutions such as collective bargaining that might have given working people a greater voice in insisting that social wellbeing remain a part of economic policy-making were dismantled.

The result is our broken economic compact. The protests that have swept the country are a reflection of it. Their significance is bigger than any of the camps that appeared this past fall. So long as Washington remains unwilling to consider a program of reform that rebuilds the institutions that allowed for stability and shared prosperity in America, growing unrest will be the only avenue open for placing these issues back on the agenda.

AMY DEAN is a best-selling, award-winning author and a champion of the labor movement. Dean served as president and CEO of the South Bay AFL-CIO Labor Council[26] for a decade. She is president of ABO Ventures, a consulting firm that creates innovative strategies for social change organizations.

From *Harvard International Review*[27], Spring 2012

Ⅰ. New Words

apparel	[ə'pærəl]	n.	clothing
array	[ə'rei]	n.	a group or collection of things or people
bolster	['bəulstə]	v.	to support or strengthen
buffer	['bʌfə]	n.	a thing that protects sb/sth or lessens a shock
business cycle			商业周期
counter-culturalist	['kauntəkʌltʃəlist]	n.	反正统文化者,反传统文化者
craft	[krɑːft]	v.	to make sth using special skills
decry	[di'krai]	v.	to express open disapproval
delink	[di'liŋk]	v.	to disconnect
denunciation	[di,nʌnsi'eiʃən]	n.	open condemnation
depict	[di'pikt]	v.	to represent or show in a picture or as if in a picture
disband	[dis'bænd]	v.	to break up
disenfranchise	[disin'fræntʃaiz]	n.	to take away sb's rights, especially their right to vote
disjuncture	[dis'dʒʌŋktʃə]	n.	分离,分裂
downturn	['dauntəːn]	n.	a fall in the amount of business that is done
encampment	[in'kæmpmənt]	n.	营地
enfranchisement	[in'fræntʃaizmənt]	n.	the act of giving sb the right to vote
foreclosure	[fɔː'kləuʒə(r)]	n.	丧失抵押品赎回权
foster	['fɔstə]	v.	to help sth to grow or develop
incur	[in'kə]	v.	招致,引起
inherent	[in'hiərənt]	adj.	existing as an inseparable part
insurgent	[in'səːdʒənt]	adj.	反叛的,反抗的
integrated	['intigreitid]	adj.	整体的,互相协调的
itinerant	[ai'tinərənt]	adj.	traveling from place to place, especially to find work
lush	[lʌʃ]	adj.	rich
mandate	['mændeit]	n.	the right or power given to the government or any body of people
marginalize	['mɑːdʒinəlaiz]	v.	to cause a group of people to become unimportant or powerless in a society

motley	[ˈmɒltli]	adj.	made up of people of different kinds
onerous	[ˈəʊnərəs]	adj.	*formal* causing trouble or worry
perennial	[pəˈreniəl]	adj.	continuing for a long time
pinpoint	[ˈpɪnpɔɪnt]	v.	to find and show the exact position of sth
populist	[ˈpɒpjulɪst]	n.	平民主义者
preordained	[ˌpriːɔːˈdeɪnd]	adj.	already decided or planned by God or by fate
presage	[ˈpresɪdʒ]	v.	*literary* to be a sign or a warning that something will happen
resonance	[ˈrezənəns]	n.	回响，回荡
resurrect	[ˌrezəˈrekt]	v.	to bring back to life from death
reverberate	[rɪˈvɜːbəreɪt]	v.	发出回声，回响
stagnate	[ˈstægˌneɪt]	v.	to stop developing or making progress
turmoil	[ˈtɜːmɔɪl]	n.	a state of great confusion
unchecked	[ʌnˈtʃekt]	adj.	未受约束的
undulation	[ˌʌndjuˈleɪʃn]	n.	movement like a series of waves
unravel	[ʌnˈrævəl]	v.	拆散
volatility	[ˌvɒləˈtɪləti]	n.	liability to sudden change

Ⅱ. Background Information

占领华尔街运动

占领华尔街运动系指自 2011 年 9 月 17 日起，一些美国示威者在华尔街及其附近举行示威、静坐和宿营抗议的行动。这次行动最初规模较小，但随着 10 月 1 日纽约警方大举出动，一度逮捕 700 多名示威者和 10 月 8 日示威者发动的、号称"万人大游行"的活动，这次示威呈现升级趋势，三周后扩展到了美国近千个城镇和世界 110 多个国家，逐渐演变成席卷全美乃至全世界的群众性社会运动。11 月 15 日凌晨，纽约警方对运动大本营祖科蒂公园实施了强制清场，此后美国其他城市和其他国家相继采取类似行动，运动告以结束。

自 2008 年华尔街金融行业因自身不负责任的行为酿成国际金融危机以来，美国社会对华尔街的非议和谴责就从未平息。如今，华尔街金融界已恢复元气，却未能和普通民众共度时艰，反而热衷于内部分红，这使得积蓄已久的民怨最终爆发。而占领华尔街的直接导火索正是华尔街大银行要向消费者收取更高的账户费用，从而转嫁前一年通过的金融监管改革法给银行带来的成本负担。该活动旨在通过占领象征美国金融中心的华尔街，以反抗贫富不均、政治腐败等一系列不公平的社会现象。组织者宣称"我们代表社会的 99%，我们不再忍受那 1% 的贪婪与腐败"，并试图通过占领该地以形成一场对体制反思的运动，并在占领过程中以直接民主的方式去讨论问题。

位于加拿大的广告克星媒体基金会首先提议举行和平的集会活动，反抗美国政府的不作为。随后，该活动通过互联网得以发展壮大，包括纽约市大型集会（NYC General Assembly）

和美国愤怒日(U.S. Day of Rage)在内的其他组织也都给予积极响应。

　　对于这场抗议运动,美国民主、共和两党的态度有明显差别。民主党许多官员都明确表示理解或同情。总统奥巴马称,"抗议运动表达了美国人民对金融系统的不满",并借机将矛头指向共和党人,指责国会中的共和党人在过去一年中一直阻挠金融监管改革法案的实施。而共和党的态度截然相反,不少议员公开指责占领示威者是"破坏公共秩序的暴徒"。

　　占领华尔街运动既没有统一的组织和领导,也没有共同的行动目标和纲领,因而很难取得具体的成果。但是,它使越来越多的美国民众认识到美国社会的不公,民主制度的扭曲,以及维护"1％"利益集团的联邦政府的真实面目。从表面上看,这次运动是向金融界发起的抗争活动,但实际上它却反映了美国社会酝酿已久的思潮。它向社会发出强大的警示:金融界监管必须加强;贫富巨大差距必须遏制。这场运动在美国的历史上留下了不可磨灭的一页。

Ⅲ. Notes to the Text

1. tent cities in lower Manhattan——下曼哈顿帐篷城(① tent city——a temporary housing facility which is often set up by homeless people or protesters;② lower Manhattan——the southernmost part of the island of Manhattan, the main island and center of business and government of the city of New York)

2. Zuccotti Park——祖科蒂公园(原名自由广场公园,位于华尔街金融区,2011年9月开始成为占领华尔街示威者的宿营地)

3. Occupy Wall Street has struck a chord with a wide swath of the country by highlighting issues that had been all but hidden in mainstream news coverage prior to the street protests.——占领华尔街运动突显了那些主流新闻媒体在街头抗议行动之前一直几乎掩盖的问题,在美国引起了广泛共鸣。(① strike a chord with sb——to say or do sth that makes people feel sympathy or enthusiasm;② swath——a large area;③ all but——almost)

4. *The Hill*——《国会山》(a congressional newspaper published since 1994. It is written for and about the US Congress with a special focus on business and lobbying, political campaigns and other events on Capital Hill.)

5. Treasury Secretary Robert Rubin——美国财长罗伯特·鲁宾

6. Joseph Stiglitz——约瑟夫·斯蒂格利茨(美国经济学家,哥伦比亚大学教授,2001年诺贝尔经济学奖获得者)

7. *Vanity Fair*——《名利场》杂志(美国著名生活杂志,主要宣扬当代文化)

8. the severing of increasing economic productivity and the wellbeing of most Americans——经济生产力的提高与大多数美国人生活的改善两者关系被割断(sever——to break off a tie or relationship)

9. the Economy Policy Institute——美国政治经济研究所(a non-profit, non-partisan think tank, founded in 1986, to broaden discussions about economic policy to include the needs of low-and-middle-income workers)

10. activists followed trade meetings to Seattle or Genoa——激进分子跟随贸易会议到(美国)西雅图和(意大利)热内亚市(referring to the anti-globalization movement: Anti-globalization activists forced the 1999 Seattle WTO Ministerial Conference to end early

and their demonstration during 3 days of the 2001 27th G8 summit in Genoa, Italy became one of the bloodiest protests in Western Europe's recent history.)

11. It has provided a framework for translating national and international data into local action. —它提供了一个把国内和国际形势的信息转化为当地行动的基准体系。(framework—a set of ideas or rules that is used for making judgments, decisions)

12. Rockefeller Foundation—洛克菲勒基金会(美国最早的私人基金会,该机构通过资助美国政治、经济、军事、外交等专题研究,对美国政府决策施加影响)

13. The safety net that allowed workers who were disconnected from a job not to hit rock bottom and be able to reenter the workforce was something that was won in large part thanks to social movements of the past, specifically the activism that led up to the New Deal. —安全网使失业者不至于跌入谷底,而是能再次找到工作,它在很大程度上是过去的社会运动,特别是导致罗斯福新政出台的运动所赢得的成果。(① safety net—an arrangement that helps to prevent disaster; ② New Deal—a program of economic and social changes that was introduced by President Franklin D. Roosevelt in 1933, in order to help people who had lost jobs and property as a result of the Great Depression)

14. The institution of collective bargaining allowed for these. —这些都是劳资双方谈判机制所处理的事。(① collective bargaining—discussions between employers and employees in order to reach agreements on wages, working conditions etc.; ② allow for sth—to consider /include sth in calculation)

15. progressive taxation—累进税制(① 税率随课税对象收入数额的增进而提高税率的税制,累进税制有利于公平税负,调整社会贫富差距;② taxation—the system of collecting money by taxes)

16. the Buffett Tax—巴菲特税(The plan suggested by Buffett would apply a minimum tax rate of 30% on individuals making more than a million dollars a year. The new tax rate would directly affect 0.3% of taxplayers.)

17. But even if this proposal were on the table, it is not adequate to address the core economic issues in question. —但是,即使这一提议已被提交讨论,它也不足以解决当前经济的核心问题。(on the table—having been suggested for discussion)

18. Changes in the American economy have taken place at a far greater pace than often-gridlocked decision-making in the nation's capital has been able to respond. —美国经济变化速度很快,而美国政府决策常常陷入僵局,根本不能应对这些变化。(gridlocked—stalemated)

19. Yet, in Washington, the ideology of economic neoliberalism is so dominant that no substantive proposals for reining in corporate influence over politics or correcting the imbalance that has placed individuals as sole risk-bearers in the economy are part of serious discussion. —但在华盛顿,经济新自由主义理论占据统治地位,任何要控制公司的政治影响或要纠正使个人成为经济风险唯一承担者的不平衡的重要提议都无法成为认真讨论的内容。(① rein sth in—to start to control sth more strictly; ② substantive—dealing with real, important, or serious matters; ③ economic neo-liberalism—a set of economic policies that have become widespread during the past 25 years or so. The main

points of neo-liberalism are the rule of the market, reduction of government regulation and privatization.)

20. Far beyond creating jobs, we need to be talking about how to transform poor jobs into good jobs—a conversation nowhere on the current political map.—我们需要讨论的内容远不只是提供就业机会,而是如何把报酬差的工作转变为报酬好的工作,它已大大超出提供就业的范畴,这个议题在当前的政府工作计划中根本就没有。(beyond—more than)

21. economist Jeffrey Sachs called for a "New Progressive Movement"—经济学家杰弗里·萨克斯呼吁进行一场"新进步运动"(① Jeffrey Sachs—an American economist, a world-renowned professor of economics at Columbia University ② the Progressive Movement—1900—1918, an effort to cure many of the ills of American society that had developed during the great spurt of industrial growth in the last quarter of the 19th century)

22. Sachs remarks that twice before, in the Gilded Age of the late 1800s and again in the Roaring 1920s, "powerful corporate interests dominated Washington and brought America to a state of unacceptable inequality, instability, and corruption."—萨克斯说,"强大的公司利益集团曾经两次控制了美国政府,使美国落入不可接受的不平等、不稳定和腐败的局面:一次是在19世纪晚期"镀金时代",另一次是在20世纪的"兴旺的20年代"。(① Gilded Age—the 35 years following the Civil War, marked by a shift to a rapid economic growth and high concentration of wealth; ② Roaring 1920s—the years from 1920 to 1929, considered as a time when people were confident and cheerful)

23. New Deal—(美国)新政(the policies and measures advocated by President Franklin D. Roosevelt as a means of helping people who had lost their jobs or their property as a result of the Great Depression)

24. "Teamsters and Turtles" alliance—工会会员与环境保护者联盟 [Here: Teamsters (the largest union in the US) and Turtles (symbol of the Sierra Club, the largest environment protection group in the US, whose members are dressed as sea turtles) are used to stand for trade unions and environment protection organizations in the US. During the Seattle WTO protests, hundreds of thousands of Sierra Club activists and union members marched to demand that human and environmental concerns be included in discussions of global free trade regimes. Trade unionists and environmentalists formed an alliance to advance their common causes.]

25. In each case, the pace of political reform had failed to catch up to wider economic and cultural transformation, and social unrest reflected the disjuncture.—每次情况都是政治改革的步伐跟不上更为广泛的经济和文化转变的步伐,社会动乱便反映了这种脱节。(disjuncture—state of being disconnected)

26. *the South Bay AFL-CIO Labor Council*—南湾劳联-产联劳工联合会(AFL-CIO—American Federation of Labor and Congress of Industrial Organizations)

27. *Harvard International Review*—《哈佛国际评论》(a quarterly journal of international relations published by the Harvard International Council at Harvard University)

Ⅳ. Language Features

《经济学家》简介

《经济学家》(*The Economist*)周刊创刊于1843年9月,迄今已有160多年历史。该刊创刊人是詹姆斯·威尔逊(James Wilson),现在该刊属经济学家集团(The Economist Group)所有。该集团是一家私人企业,一半股份由私人股东控制,另一半由《金融时报》拥有。其经济收入一半来自读者订阅,另一半来自广告。

该刊在西方享有较高声誉。2012年发行量为150万,其中50%在北美,20%在欧洲大陆,15%在英国,10%在亚洲。

《经济学家》自称是报纸,但其版面却更像是新闻周刊。其创刊的目的是"参与一场推动前进和阻碍我们进步的卑劣、胆怯的无知之间激烈博弈"(take part in a severe contest between intelligence, which presses forward, and an unworthy, timid ignorance obstructing our progress),这句话仍印在每期目录页的左下角处。

该刊一直奉行所刊登文章不署名(editorial anonymity)的做法。据称,这样做的目的是突出"协作成果"(collaborative effort)和"集体观点"(collective voice)。该刊读者定位是受过高等教育,富有独立见解的精英,声称其读者群中许多是经理和决策者。

自创刊以来,《经济学家》始终保持自己的独特风格:注重数字、图表,强调新闻事实,看重理性分析。它很少刊登广告,这与广告充斥的其他新闻刊物形成了鲜明对照。

《经济学家》每期第5—6页是这期杂志文章的目录,主要有两大部分,一部分是世界政治和时事(World Politics and Current Affairs),下分:亚洲、美国、美洲、国际、欧洲、英国。另一大部分涉及企业、金融和科技。目录页还标出该期杂志的封面故事(cover story)、重要文章(leaders)、一周新闻概要(briefing)、亚洲(Asia)、美国(United States)、南北美洲(The Americas)、中东和非洲(Middle East and Africa)、欧洲(Europe)、英国(Britain)、商业(Business)、金融与经济(Finance and Economics)、科学技术(Science and Technology)、图书艺术(Books and Arts)。此外,还有读者来信(Letters)等。

《经济学家》清晰、简洁的写作风格独树一帜,西方杂志中很少有与其媲美者。它的文字精练,简明易懂,对于复杂的社会问题、世界重大事件,它能以浅显的语言、较短的篇幅、清楚的图表把来龙去脉、前因后果交代出来,条理自然,表达清晰,令人叹服。

美国新闻写作学家卡彭在《美联社写作指南》一书中高度赞赏《经济学家》的文笔:"英国《经济学家》深受称赞,虽然它所报道的是严肃题材,但它所用的文字却简洁明快,许多导语所含句子的平均长度只有16个词,文章大部分句子较短,平均在16—19个词之间。"(Rene J. Cappon,1991:51)

《经济学家》的另一大特色是其英国式的幽默与辛辣讽刺。它对美国社会文化的报道、对其政治形势的评论常常夹杂一些讥讽,使得美国知识分子感到不是滋味。

该刊声称坚守超党派立场。在英国大选中,该刊既支持过工党(2005),也支持过保守党(2010);对于美国大选,既支持共和党的一些候选人,也支持民主党的一些候选人。从其长期的报道和评论中可以看出该刊支持自由市场、经济全球化、同性婚姻、免费教育;主张管控枪支,征收碳排放税;但也支持毒品和卖淫合法化。

该刊对我国报道往往注重负面,常常显示偏见。

V. Analysis of the Content

1. The meaning of the word "density" in the sentence "Moreover, union density has sharply declined, leaving workers without the ability ... management." (Para. 12) is _____.
   A. authority
   B. activity
   C. thickness
   D. strength
2. Which of the following points is NOT included in the definition of economic insecurity given by Hacker's team?
   A. Experiencing a major loss in income.
   B. Incurring large out-of-pocket medical expenses.
   C. Lacking education or job skills.
   D. Lacking adequate financial wealth to buffer financial risks.
3. To the author's mind, the root cause of the protests is _____.
   A. economic inequality
   B. unfair social system
   C. severing of increasing economic productivity and the wellbeing of most Americans
   D. the US government's corruption
4. Which group of people has been particularly affected by the broken economic compact?
   A. Young people.
   B. The aged.
   C. Women.
   D. The middle class
5. Which of the following is the author's view on the Occupy Wall Street Movement?
   A. A movement against the capitalist system.
   B. A protest against a broken economic compact.
   C. A motley assembly.
   D. A counter-culturalists' movement.

VI. Questions on the Article

1. What impact has the Occupy Wall Street Movement produced on America?
2. Why did the movement fast spread to many other countries?
3. How did even leaders in the financial community respond to the movement?
4. What is a core component of America's economic compact?
5. What did the 2011 study by the Economic Policy Institute find?
6. What accounts for lack of risk sharing in the American society?
7. Why did protests emerge in 2011?
8. What was the problem with radical movements in America throughout the 20th century according to the author?
9. What solution does the author suggest?

VII. Topics for Discussion

1. Is the Occupy Wall Street Movement a success or a failure?
2. Is globalization to blame for the problem of inequality?

Lesson 6

D. C. Influentials

Who are "speclal interests"[1]? You and me, Say the lobbyists who help shape every law that congress passes. 'And they're key players in the biggest policy battle in a generation—healthcare reform.

By David T. Cook and Gail Russell Chaddock

If labor lobbyist Robert "Bobby" Juliano didn't move away from his stakeout just off the Senator floor from time to time, he might be mistaken for a statue.

Other lobbyists have moved on to BlackBerrys and instant messaging.[2] (He calls them "the thumb generation[3].") But for Mr. Juliano, who has been in the thick of every big labor issue in the past 36 years, there's no substitute for face-to-face contact with members of Congress.

"I'm not going to be sitting in an office when my workbench is the seat of power for the whole world," he says, standing in the ornate Senate reception room where lobbyists mingle with members before and after floor votes[4].

The lobbying world has shifted dramatically since Juliano came to Washington in 1973 to lobby for the Hotel Employees and Restaurant Employees and Bartenders International Union, shaking hands and trading stories with such labor allies as Hubert Humphrey, Jacob Javits, and Edward Kennedy[5], and pushing issues ranging from the minimum wage[6] to healthcare and comprehensive immigration reform.

But, now representing an expanded labor group, UNITED (**UNITE**) HERE[7], he says the fundamentals are the same: Get there early. Stuff your pockets with business cards. And if it's a tax issue, don't come in unless you've got legislative language, committee support on both sides of the aisle, and a start laying the groundwork on the Senate side.[8]

Lobbyists like Juliano and their efforts to shape policy are back in the spotlight this year, as Congress works a legislative agenda of historic size and scope. The battle over reform of the nation's healthcare system is the biggest effort to influence national policy in nearly a quarter century.

Some 3,300 lobbyists have registered on the healthcare issue alone, all striving to shape the outcome in their clients' interest. With the equivalent of six healthcare lobbyists for each member of Congress, experts say the battle today is larger than that over President Clinton's 1993 healthcare reform[9] push.

The fight over healthcare is "the largest lobbying effort" since the 1986 battle royal[10] over tax reform during the Reagan administration, says Sheila Krumholz, executive director of the Center for Responsive Politics (CRP)[11], which tracks the impact of money and lobbying on government policy.

The struggle over healthcare has a far-reaching and profound impact "on the corporations involved, on the interest groups involved, and on each and every American," she says.

Also looming is a major battle over climate and energy legislation that narrowly passed in the House of Representatives last June and is expected to come up for Senate action this fall. It faces stiff resistance from business groups who say the House version of the legislation would raise energy prices and result in lost jobs.

Since the earlist days of the nation, lobbyists have been popular political villains. Their current image is that of highly paid, well-fed white men in expensive suits and tasseled loafers working to game the system on behalf of the rich and well-connected—the dreaded special interests. [12]

For example, Washington tailor Georges de Paris sells suits that range in price from $3,500 to $25,000 and says 80 percent of his business is with lobbyists.

But lobbyists are also people like Fred Wertheimer, dressed for an interview like a college professor in a button-down shirt and slacks. He ran Common Cause for many years and now leads—and lobbies for—Democracy 21[13], which has as its stated goal to lessen the impact of money on politics.

"Money is the core issue in this city when it comes to lobbying," he says.

Most members of Congress are loath to talk about their relationships with lobbyists, who are a vital source of campaign funds for legislators who aspire to a leadership position. The most effective lobbyists are constituents "who are personally involved in something important to them," argues three-term Sen. Jack Reed (D) of Rhode Island. "They are a lot more central and crucial to a lot that you're doing than someone paid in Washington."

Still, in addition to concerned and vocal citizens CRP says there are 12,552 professional lobbyists working the halls of Congress on behalf of what might be called special interests.

But the meaning of special interest is in the eye of the beholder. [14] The groups that hire lobbyists range widely in motives and funding levels. Some seek special advantage and a chance for their clients to feast at the federal-spending trough[15]. Others seek to protect the old, the infirm, the wilderness, and religious freedom. It is hard to find a segment of American society that does not lobby—from bakers to bankers, chicken breeders to independent colleges, and even the church that publishes the Monitor.

"The media has done a pretty good job demonizing us," says David Wenhold, president of the American League of Lobbyists[16]. "I love the term 'special interest groups are behind this.' Is Greenpeace[17] a special interest group? Clean Coal[18]? The Girl Scouts of America[19]? Because they *are*. That term gets thrown around, but they are all lobbyists."

In fact, many who work to influence events in Washington do not fall under the formal rules for registering as a lobbyist. For example, law firms hire former senior government officials to function as "senior advisers" rather than have them register as lobbyists. One notable example is former Senate majority leader Tom Daschle[20].

Registered lobbyists account for only a small portion of the cost of influence and advocacy in Washington, says James A. Thurber, director of American University's Center for Congressional and Presidential Studies[21].

Last year, lobbying—defined narrowly by those who must register with Congress—was a $3.4 billion industry, according to CRP statistics. But when the cost of grass-roots efforts and of strategic advisers are all counted, total spending on influencing policy in Washington approaches $9.6 billion a year, he estimates.

Combing Senate records, Bloomberg News[22] determined that 3,300 lobbyists signed up to work on healthcare and that more than 1,500 organizations have healthcare lobbyists. Spending on healthcare lobbying was $263.4 million in the first six months of 2009, up from $241.4 million in the same period of 2008, according to CRP figures.

What do lobbyists do in return for that kind of money? The American League of Lobbyists says its members research and analyze legislation or regulatory proposals, monitor and report on developments, attend congressional or regulatory hearings, work with coalitions interested in the same issues, and then educate not only government officials but also employees and corporate officers as to the implications of legislative changes.

"The next few months are going to be huge with lobbying [on] healthcare," says Mr. Wenhold. "Every lobbyist is going to have some part of it in one way or another."

And if some version of healthcare reform passes, demand for lobbyists will probably increase.

"This is the tip of the iceberg." Wenhold says. If health reform passes, doctors and companies involved in healthcare "are going to need a huge lobbying presence to make sure their voices are heard in Washington" as new healthcare regulations are first written and then enforced, he says.

While the healthcare lobbying battle is perhaps the most visible effort to shape national policy at the moment, the influence industry touches virtually all aspects of public policy.

The so-called "iron triangle" of defense industries, Congressional defense-related committees, and Pentagon officials is one of the best known areas.

Lobbyists also attempt to shape US foreign policy, with the American Israel Public Affairs Committee (AIPAC)[23] being perhaps the most powerful single force in that field, spending $2.5 million on lobbying in 2008, according to CRP statistics.

In 2008, lobbyists for foreign interests reported more than 22,000 contacts with various branches of the federal government, seeking favorable policies on a wide variety of issues. That estimate comes from an analysis of filings under the Foreign Agents Registration Act by the Sunlight Foundation and ProPublica, an independent journalism organization.[24]

Lobbying is rooted in the U.S. constitution which prohibits Congress from making laws that restrict the people's right to "petition the Government for a redress of grievances."

And lobbying has been around since the nation's earliest days. During the First Congress, Pennsylvania Sen. William Maclay wrote in his diary that New York merchants employed "treats, dinners, attentions" to delay passage of a tariff bill, according to a detailed 1980 speech on the history of lobbying given by Sen. Robert Byrd (D) of West Virginia as part of a series of addresses on Senate history and operations.

Even influence-industry watchdog groups see great merit in lobbyists' ability to provide detailed expertise to Congress.[25] The typical member often lacks the highly detailed knowledge needed in drafting legislation.

"Lobbyists play very valuable and helpful and important roles here in terms of expertise and information and strategic advice—the ability to help the various players on the Hill know what everyone is doing,"[26] says Mr. Wertheimer.

Given the ongoing national debate about healthcare, it's not surprising that healthcare companies were the sector of the economy that spent the most on lobbying from 2006 through 2009.

The financial sector is another major force in lobbying activity—ranking second in 2006 and 2007, third in 2008, and second again so far this year. Last year, financial-sector firms—including those in the fields of finance, insurance, and real estate—spent $459 million on lobbying.

The US Chamber of Commerce[27], representing 3 million businesses, is Washington's lobbying powerhouse. Among individual organizations, the Chamber "is the No. 1 spender on lobbying over time and again this year so far," says Ms. Krumholz. "If there ever is a corporate battle, they are at the head of it. This is what they do best."

In 2008, the Chamber spent $91.7 million on lobbying, according to CRP. Part of the Chamber's power comes from the presence of local chambers in congressional districts around the country. In Washington the Chamber has a deep bench of policy experts and an in-house law firm, the National Chamber Litigation Center, which works to shape legal policy.[28]

The other top individual spenders on lobbying in recent years: Exxon Mobil, the Pharmaceutical Research and Manufacturers Association, AARP, the American Medical Association, and the American Hospital Association[29].

It is clear that the Chamber does not cower before the Obama administration.

"I have a good relationship with the White House. We are dealing with them on all kinds of things," says Chamber President Thomas Donohue. "We are trying to be fair and helpful, but that doesn't mean we roll over and play dead just because they are excited about something when in fact we know it ain't going to work,[30]" he said at a recent lunch sponsored by the Monitor[31].

R. Bruce Josten, executive vice president for government affairs at the Chamber, tracks some 300 legislative issues of interest to his employer. "Solid, sound research and information counts for something in this town... where facts matter and people are important," he says.

And Mr. Josten notes the formidable grass-roots efforts the Chamber can mount using its capacity to mobilize local businesses.

"We generated 208,000 letters against the House healthcare plan in six weeks," he says, which is an impressive volume even on such a controversial issue.

Some critics question the effectiveness of big lobbying budgets focused on Washington.

"Every dollar that the Chamber of Commerce spends on a lobbyist is a waste of money," argues Grover Norquist, president of Americans for Tax Reform[32] and himself a registered lobbyist.

He stressed the importance of building support for legislative initiatives through grass-roots efforts rather than working the halls of Congress.

"The Christian Coalition[33] in the 1990s had three people in D.C.—everyone else was in the field," says Mr. Norquist. "They were a power and they won elections. K Street[34] is here, they're grouped in big buildings, but they have no grass-roots capacity."

Those who compete with the Chamber and other well-funded entities stress the key role of grass-roots efforts to build support for action in Washington. "We know we can't match the money that is being spent by the opposition," John Sweeney, AFL-CIO[35] president, said at a recent Monitor breakfast.

"Our strongest asset is our rank-and-file activist. To have 250,000 people in the field, as we did during the [2008 presidential] campaign and [that] we have now on healthcare, that is the strongest weapon that we have, and the more we strengthen that, the stronger we will be."

A number of industries have trimmed lobbying expenditures because of the weak economy. Data from the CRP show revenues at several major Washington lobbying firms dropped 10 percent or more in the first half of 2009. The home building, defense, and transportation industries have all trimmed their lobbying efforts, and the number of registered lobbyists in Washington now stands at 12,552, down 2,248 from a year ago.

Another factor making the life of a lobbyist less pleasant is stiffer rules on lobbying imposed by the Obama administration.

"They applied unprecedented rules to their own administration," Democracy 21's Wertheimer says. Among other things, the administration imposed rules barring administration appointees from leaving office and seeking lobbying jobs while Barack Obama is president. They also forbid new officials from making policy on matters involving their former employers or clients for two years or working for an agency they lobbied within two years.

The administration also barred executive branch officials from speaking to lobbyists seeking economic stimulus funds under the American Recovery and Reinvestment Act[36].

After a protest from the lobbying community, the Obama administration later revised the rules, narrowing the time frame when the ban applied and expanding it to cover everyone seeking to exert influence on contract awards, not just lobbyists.

Reviews are mixed on the effectiveness of the new rules. Reporting requirements on those seeking stimulus funds are off to a slow start.[37] In August, the government reported only eight lobbying contacts on the $787 billion stimulus bill, according to the Associated Press. The Pentagon, which controls $7.4 billion in stimulus spending, reported only one contact from a lobbyist so far this year.

The White House argues that the low number of reported interactions shows the rules are working. "This is a good thing, not a bad thing," White House counsel Norm Eisen told the Associated Press. But one lobbyist said that rather than visit the Energy Department herself to seek stimulus funds, she sent her client, who wasn't a registered lobbyist. So the low number of reported interactions may indicate some lobbyists have found a way around the rules.

Administration rules trying to slow the revolving door between government and lobbying firms received high praise from influence-industry watchdog groups.

"They demonstrated that President Obama was serious and cared about these issues," says Wertheimer. "No one has come close to doing what they have done in terms of the revolving-door provisions for people who leave the administration."

But the revolving-door rules also make it difficult for lobbyists for nonprofit causes to work on issues to which they have devoted their lives.

"I'm disappointed that the president has adopted such a restrictive policy," says Ralph

Neas, chief executive officer of the National Coalition on Health Care[38] and a longtime civil rights activist. "It is a tragedy... too many good people have been kept out."

In some cases, the Obama administration ran into what CRP executive director Krumholz calls "the cold, harsh reality of the onerous task of filling political appointments" and did end up hiring lobbyists for key positions.

A *National Journal* tabulation shows 30 of Mr. Obama's top appointees—11 percent— had been lobbyists within the past five years. Among the exceptions the administration made in its revolving-door rules: Former Raytheon[39] lobbyist William Lynn, who was named deputy Defense secretary.

The revolving-door rules matter because experts say the most effective tool for affecting legislation is hiring a former member of Congress or a key congressional staffer.

"The healthcare battle is instructive in the sense that we know that the vast majority of players who care about this battle have hired at least one insider," says Krumholz. "So they have got the revolving door working for them... former members are golden if you can get them."

In her view, the next most effective lobbying tool is the ability to bundle campaign cash for a candidate or a member of Congress. The current limit for individual giving is $2,400.

"If you can multiply that by 100 people, [it means] that you can deliver a big message to a candidate or a member of Congress," Krumholz says. "In that way, you can funnel money to the targets that are most valuable to you as chairman or ranking members of key committees that can move your legislative agenda forward fastest."

"Lobbyists catch us when they catch us, and that's usually at a fundraiser[40]," says former 11-term Rep. Chris Shays (R) of Connecticut. "The dollars don't buy votes, they buy a better shot at access.[41] There's a distortion but a much different one than most people think."

The practice of plying legislators with food and drink and taking them to sporting events has fallen off in the wake of tough new rules adopted because of the lobbying scandal surrounding Jack Abramoff[42], who was convicted of fraud, tax evasion, and conspiracy to bribe public officials by trading gifts, meals, and sports trips for political favors. The 2007 Honest Leadership and Open Government Act[43] has a provision some in Washington sarcastically refer to as "The Jack Abramoff Reform" that prohibits members of Congress from receiving gifts, including gifts of meals, entertainment, and travel, from lobbyists.

Measuring the success of lobbying efforts is difficult, experts say.

"Members of Congress almost never make up their minds, first, on any one thing, or based on what a single lobbyist is saying to them," Wertheimer says. "There is a hell of a lot of smoke blown in Washington by lobbyists to their clients about what they have single-handedly accomplished."

And, of course, sometimes the battle in Washington is to keep things from happening, which can be harder to track than an action in favor of some industry.

For example, Krumholz cites the success of oil company executives in warding off legislative action when oil prices were high. "Although they were the target of such public ire and although they were marched up to Capitol Hill to explain themselves and their high profits at a time of high gas prices, they were able to diffuse the issue, and I think lobbying and campaign contributions had a lot to do with that."

Another example of lobbying success, Wertheimer says, is the battle to impose tougher regulation on cigarettes. It was, he says, "a David and Goliath battle against enormous resources."[44]

From *The Christian Science Monitor*, September 27, 2009

I. New Words

bundle	['bʌndl]	v.	to supply
button-down	['bʌtəndaun]	adj.	（衬衫等）领尖钉有纽扣的
comb	[kəum]	v.	to search sth carefully in order to find sth
cower	['kauə(r)]	v.	to bend low and move back because of fear
demonize	['diːmənaiz]	v.	to describe sb as evil or dangerous
diffuse	[di'fjuːz]	v.	to spread
enforce	[in'fɔːs]	v.	to make sure that people obey a law or rule
formidable	['fɔːmidəb(ə)l]	adj.	very great and frightening; difficult to deal with
fraud	[frɔːd]	n.	欺骗行为
fundraiser	['fʌnd,reizə]	n.	资金筹集会
funnel	['fʌnl]	v.	to make sth move through
grass-roots	['graːs 'ruːts]	n.	the ordinary people
grievance	['griːvəns]	n.	苦情，冤情；怨愤
ire	['aiə(r)]	n.	anger
loath	[ləuθ]	adj.	~ **to do sth** not willing to do sth bad
loom	[luːm]	v.	to appear threatening and likely to happen soon
mount	[maunt]	v.	to increase in intensity or in quantity
onerous	['əunərəs]	adj.	difficult
ornate	[ɔː'neit]	adj.	having a great deal of decoration
petition	[pə'tiʃən]	v.	请愿
ply	[plai]	v.	~ **sb with** to keep supplying sb with
powerhouse	['pauəhaus]	n.	an organization that has a lot of power
redress	[ri'dres]	v.	to correct sth that is unfair or wrong
revolving door			旋转门
slack	[slæk]	n.	便裤，宽松长裤
stakeout	['steikaut]	n.	监视；监视区
tabulation	[,tæbjə'leiʃən]	n.	列表
tariff	['tærif]	n.	关税

time frame			时间范围，期限
trim	[trim]	v.	to reduce by cutting what is unnecessary
trough	[trɔf]	n.	a container (usually in a barn or stable) from which cattle or horses feed
ward	[wɔːd]		~ **sth off** to prevent sth bad
watchdog	['wɔtʃ,dɔg]	n.	监督人；监督机构
wilderness	['wildənəs]	n.	in the wilderness 在野，不掌权
workbench	['wəːk,bentʃ]	n.	a long heavy table used for doing practical jobs

Ⅱ. Background Information

美国的游说政治

"游说"(lobbying)一词最初起源于17世纪中叶的英国，lobby原指英国议会大厅的门廊。一些想要推动某项议程的人聚集于此，期待和议员们会面交谈，渐渐地这些游说政客的人就被称为 lobbyists。

美国民主体制中的院外游说活动由来已久。针对国会议员的游说活动原先集中在首都华盛顿威拉德饭店的大厅。众多说客乘议员从国会山返回饭店的间隙，在大厅里对他们进行各种方式的游说，由此 lobby 一词指代"游说"的用法在美国流传开来。

游说业在许多国家都存在，但在美国最为发达。在K街（华盛顿说客之街）登记的专业游说公司有3,700多家，说客有8,200人，客户有9,800家。

通常而言，在华盛顿从事院外游说活动的角色主要有公关公司、律师事务所以及大公司、利益集团的代表处。游说的对象包括国会议员、政府部门高级公务员，甚至是联邦总统。

院外游说与美国的利益集团(interest groups)政治密不可分。美国政治其实就是各个利益集团与政客之间相互利用、相互妥协的一种博弈游戏。通过游说，实现各自的政治诉求，获得政策倾斜，最终获取高额的经济利益，这是所有利益集团展开游说活动的共同目的。

美国游说业的存在有以下四个原因。

第一，美国法律的明确规定。宪法第一修正案规定，人民有"向政府请愿"(petition)的权利。游说因此就具有它的合法性。

第二，美国是个社团国家。任何有利益共同点的人都可以组成大大小小的社团组织。为了声张自己的利益，让决策者制定有利于本团体利益的政策，这些团体需要在华盛顿游说能够影响国家政策的人士。

第三，利益集团的积极推动。利益集团通过游说国会可以以小付出换来大收益。

第四，国会自身的立法需求。由于国会议员对于很多立法领域都很陌生，议员们需要说客提供的各种信息，以帮助他们了解有关领域的利益需求，据此制定出的法律就可能更客观。

院外游说活动方式主要有以下几种：

直接游说(inside lobbying, or direct lobbying)是最为传统和古老的政治游说手段，但至今仍是最为有效和常用的政治策略。公民、利益集团代表本人或委托专业游说人员通过面对面的方式与决策者发生接触,传递信息、表达观点、施加影响。在直接游说活动中采用的主要方式有:登门拜访政府官员或国会议员、在政策听证会上发言、向决策部门递送材料等等。

间接游说(outside lobbying, or indirect lobbying)是一种迂回的政治战略,通过广告、宣传、公众舆论、群众示威等手段向决策者发送信息。间接游说在更大程度上是一个公开的信息传递过程,这些信息不仅针对决策者,而且也面向公众,并试图通过吸引群众的注意来强化对决策者的影响。由于秘密的直接游说经常涉及道德和法律方面的风险,尤其是大公司与政府之间的"钱权交易"历来受美国民众的憎恶,为了树立良好的公众形象,争取公众的支持,广泛和公开的间接游说成为利益集团常用的政治手段。

草根游说(grass-roots lobbying)指的是普通公民通过信函、电话、传真、电子邮件等手段比较广泛和集中地向决策者表达政治意愿的行为。然而在现实中,自发的、自然的草根游说根本不可能发生,这种大规模的群众运动必然有某些利益集团在背后进行运作、组织和发动。有组织的草根游说被称为"草尖游说"(grass-tops lobbying),为了使游说行动更有说服力,这些"草尖"总是尽量假装成草根。

其他方式包括政治行动委员会以委员会的形式向候选人捐款,进行政治捐赠;通过智库和研究机构进行政策分析引导等等。

Ⅲ. Notes to the Text

1. special interests—special interest groups 特别利益集团 (groups of people seeking to protect their interests, especially by means of a lobby)
2. Other lobbyists have moved on to BlackBerrys and instant messaging.—其他说客已经改用黑莓手机和即时通讯。(instant messaging—是一个终端服务,允许两人或多人使用网络即时传递文字信息、档案、语音与视频的交流)
3. the thumb generation—拇指代 (referring to the generation born after 1985, who as teens and adolescents communicated by use of mobile devices such as cell phones)
4. floor votes—全体议员投票 (votes taken among the entire membership of the House or Senate)
5. Hubert Humphrey, Jacob Javits, and Edward Kennedy—休伯特·汉弗莱、雅各布·贾维茨和爱德华·肯尼迪(① Hubert Humphrey—1911—1978, an American politician who served as the 38th Vice President under President Lyndon Johnson; ② Jacob Javits—1904—1986, U. S. Senator from 1957 to 1981; ③ Edward Kennedy—1932—2009, U. S. senator for 47 years.)
6. minimum wage—最低工资 (In the U. S., workers generally must be paid no less than the statutory minimum. As of July 2009, the federal government mandates a nationwide minimum wage level of $7.25 per hour.)
7. UNITED (UNITE) HERE—(a labor union in the U. S. and Canada with more than 265,000 active members, who work mainly in the hotel, food service, laundry, warehouse and casino gaming industries. The union was formed in 2004 by the merger of two former unions Unite and Here.)
8. And if it's a tax issue, don't come in unless you've got legislative language, committee

support on both sides of the aisle, and a start laying the groundwork on the Senate side. ——如果事关税务法案,那么除非你通晓税法内容,得到了委员会双方的支持,并且在参议院那边已经开始打基础,否则你就不要进这个门。

9. President Clinton's 1993 healthcare reform——克林顿总统1993年的医疗改革[1993年,刚刚当选总统的克林顿着手对美国的医疗保险制度进行改革,试图建立一个普惠的全民医疗保险制度(Universal Health Care)。但是,由于方案过于复杂,著名的"哈里与露易丝"广告激发了中产阶级的忧虑,以及其他一些原因,最终彻底失败。]

10. battle royal——*formal or literary* a fierce battle or struggle

11. executive director of the Center for Responsive Politics (CRP)——(美国)回应政治研究中心执行主任(the Center for Responsive Politics——a non-partisan, non-profit research group based in Washington, D.C. which tracks money in U.S. politics and its effect on election and public policy)

12. Their current image is that of highly paid, well-fed white men in expensive suits and tasseled loafers working to game the system on behalf of the rich and well-connected——the dreaded special interests. ——他们目前的形象就是身材富态,穿着昂贵西服,脚踏流苏乐福鞋的高收入白人,他们代表富有的权贵,那些令人惧怕的特别利益集团,为他们进行政治博弈。(① well-fed——fat; ② well-connected——having important or rich friends or relatives)

13. He ran Common Cause for many years and now leads——and lobbies for——Democracy 21... ——他主管同道会多年,现在又担任Democracy 21机构领导和说客……(① Common Cause——an American non-partisan, non-profit liberal advocacy organization, founded in 1970, based in Washington, D.C.. The group aims at establishing greater transparency and accountability in U.S. political institutions; ② Democracy 21——a non-profit organization in the U.S. that works to remove the influence of private money from politics)

14. But the meaning of special interest is in the eye of the beholder. ——然而"特别利益集团"的定义,则是仁者见仁,智者见智,各方说法不一。(Note the author's creative use of the idiom, "Beauty is in the *eye of the beholder*.")

15. feast at the federal-spending trough——从联邦政府开支中分一杯羹。(trough——a long open container, especially one for animals' food or water)

16. the American League of Lobbyists——美国说客联盟(a preeminent national organization that represents lobbying, public policy and advocacy professionals)

17. Greenpeace——绿色和平组织(an international organization whose members work actively to protect the environment from damage by industrial processes or military activities)

18. Clean Coal——清洁用煤协会(a group that advocates use of technology for reducing emission of CO_2 and other greenhouse gases)

19. The Girl Scouts of America——女童子军(a youth organization for girls in the U.S. and American girls living abroad)

20. Senate majority leader Tom Daschle——参议院多数党领袖汤姆·达施勒(1947—   , a policy advisor, lobbyist, former U.S. Senator from South Dakota, a member of the Democratic Party. He was elected to the U.S. House of Representatives and served four

73

terms. In 1986, he was elected to the Senate and served as minority leader from 2003. In 2004, the Democratic Party gained the majority and he became the Senate majority leader. Defeated for reelection, he took a position as a policy advisor with a lobbying firm, and also became a senior fellow at the Center for American Progress.)

21. director of American University's Center for Congressional and Presidential Studies——美国大学国会和总统研究中心主任

22. Bloomberg News——彭博新闻社（an international news agency headquartered in New York and a division of Bloomberg L. P.）

23. the American Israel Public Affairs Committee (AIPAC)——美国以色列公共事务委员会（a lobbying group that advocates pro-Israel policies to Congress and Executive Branch of the U. S.）

24. That estimate comes from an analysis of filings under the Foreign Agents Registration Act by the Sunlight Foundation and ProPublica, an independent journalism organization.——估计数出自阳光基金会和独立新闻机构 ProPublica 根据外交代理人登记法所做的文档分析。（① Sunlight Foundation——a non-profit organization with the goal of increasing transparency and accountability of the U. S. Congress and the executive branch in state and local governments; ② ProPublica——an independent non-profit newsroom that produces investigative journalism in the public interest）

25. Even influence-industry watchdog groups see great merit in lobbyists' ability to provide detailed expertise to Congress.——甚至游说业监督组织也认为说客能给国会提供详细的专业知识非常有益。（① influence industry——referring to the lobbying industry exerting great influence on the government; ② watchdog——an organization that tries to guard against evil acts; ③ expertise——expert knowledge）

26. Lobbyists play very valuable and helpful and important roles here in terms of expertise and information and strategic advice—the ability to help the various players on the Hill know what everyone is doing.——就专门知识、提供信息和策略咨询而言，说客不仅很有价值，很有益处，并且十分重要。他们能够帮助国会里的各种政客了解各行各业的具体情况。

27. The US Chamber of Commerce——美国商会，简称 USCC（a business federation representing companies business associations, state and local chambers in the U. S.）

28. In Washington the Chamber has a deep bench of policy experts and an in-house law firm, the National Chamber Litigation Center, which works to shape legal policy.——美国商会在华盛顿市有一大批政策专家和一个机构内部的法律公司——美国商会诉讼中心,该组织力图影响法律政策的制定。（① in-house——existing within an organization; ② a deep bench of——a large number of; ③ litigation——the process of making or defending claims in a court; ④ shape——to have an important influence on the way that sth develops）

29. Exxon Mobil, the Pharmaceutical Research and Manufacturers Association, AARP, the American Medical Association, and the American Hospital Association——埃克逊·美孚公司、药物研究与制造协会、美国退休人协会、美国医学会和美国医院协会（① Exxon Mobil——the world's largest publicly traded international oil and gas company;

②AARP—the American Association of Retired Persons)

30. ... but that doesn't mean we roll over and play dead just because they are excited about something when in fact we know it ain't going to work. —然而这并不意味着我们会因为(白宫里的)那帮人对某事件一时兴起,在明知此事行不通时会装傻充愣,听命于他们。(①roll over—to stop resisting and do what the other person wants them to do; ②play dead—to pretend to be ignorant or dead)

31. the Monitor—referring to the Christian Science Monitor

32. Americans for Tax Reform—美国税制改革协会(a tax payer group whose stated goal is "a system in which taxes are simpler, flatter, more visible and lower than they are today")

33. the Christian Coalition—基督教联盟[a U.S. Christian advocacy group which includes Christian fundamentalists(原教旨主义者), neo-evangelicals(新福音教派), and conservative charismatics(灵恩运动者)]

34. K Street—K街(a street located in Washington D.C., known as a center for numerous think tanks, lobbyists and advocacy groups)

35. AFL-CIO—美国劳工总会与产业劳工组织(American Federation of Labor and Congress of Industrial Organizations)

36. American Recovery and Reinvestment Act—《美国复苏与再投资法案》(an economic stimulus package aiming at saving and creating jobs)

37. Reporting requirements on those seeking stimulus funds are off to a slow start. —对于公司寻求经济刺激资金情况必须报告的规定已经慢慢开始执行。

38. the National Coalition on Health Care—全国医疗联盟(a coalition of groups lobbying to achieve comprehensive health system reform, founded in 1990, a non-profit alliance of more than 80 organizations)

39. Former Raytheon—雷神公司(美国大型国防合约商,该公司在世界各地雇员数量为73,000,营业总额为200亿美元)

40. Lobbyists catch us when they catch us, and that is usually at a fundraiser. —那些说客一旦联系上你,就给你施加影响,这通常是在(竞选)资金筹集会上。(Note the author's use of the word "catch" in the senses of "influence" and "manage to contact" respectively.)

41. The dollars don't buy votes, they buy a better shot at access. —金钱并非是买投票而是买更好的门路。[①这句话源自美国政治行动委员会专家拉里·萨巴托(Larry Sabato),他指出,政治捐款与其说是为了"买投票",不如说是为了"买门路";②shot—a chance or attempt to do sth]

42. lobbying scandal surrounding Jack Abramoff—杰克·阿布拉莫夫游说腐败案(阿布拉莫夫,美国共和党人,长期从事美国院外游说活动的知名人士,有美国游说业"教父"之称。为换取议员在国会对他的客户作出有利的言行,阿布拉莫夫向一些议员提供竞选政府职位的资金支持、国内外豪华旅行、高尔夫娱乐项目、体育比赛门票、高档餐厅免费用餐机会以及向其亲属提供就业机会等等,总值高达数千万美元。2006年1月3日,阿布拉莫夫承认共谋、欺诈和逃税三项重罪,为换取减轻刑责,成为检方证人,配合调查收受贿赂的国会人员。)

43. Honest Leadership and Open Government Act—《正直领导与开放政府法案》(The act

strengthens public disclosure requirements concerning lobbying activity and funding, places more restriction on gifts for members of Congress and their stuff, and provides for mandatory disclosure of earmarks in expenditure bills.)

44. It was, he says, "a David and Goliath battle against enormous resources."—他说:"这是对付具有巨额资源一方的以弱胜强之战。"(a David and Goliath battle—an allusion. In the Old Testament of the Bible, Goliath, a Giant was killed by a boy called David, who later became King David.)

Ⅳ. Language Features

《基督教科学箴言报》简介

《基督教科学箴言报》由基督教科学会(the Church of Christ, Scientist)创始人玛丽·贝克·埃迪(Mary Baker Eddy)于1908年在波士顿创办,该报由基督教科学出版社出版。她之所以要办这一报纸是为了抵制当时美国社会所盛行的低级趣味煽情新闻(Yellow Journalism)风潮。

该报虽有"基督教"字样,但它并非是纯宗教性报刊,而是面向"世俗"的一般性报纸,其报道内容很广,辟有政治、文学、艺术、文化、科学、教育、生活等方面的特稿专栏。它极少直接宣讲宗教教义,而是通过报纸文章感化和启迪读者,其宣称的办报方针是"不伤害任何人,帮助所有人"。(To injure no man, but to bless all mankind.)该报读者以美国中上层知识分子和国际问题研究人员为主,其报道和分析颇受国会和政府部门的重视。

《基督教科学箴言报》原先是大报(broadsheet),后改为小报形式(tabloid format)。自2009年4月开始,该报转型,停止纸质日报,改为周报,但该报通过网站和电子邮件继续每日提供新闻。

《基督教科学箴言报》具有以下四点特色:
1. 内容较为严肃。该报内容上明显没有美国其他报纸那种一味追逐读者、迎合社会的倾向,一般不登有暴力、色情内容的文章。该报一般不接受烟酒、咖啡等广告,广告篇幅仅占所有版面的25%。
2. 报道注重正面。该报不同于其他美国媒体关注冲突和矛盾,而是比较关注人类永恒的福祉。有关科学和人文方面的文章比其他报纸要多。在报道灾难、犯罪事件时,该报一般回避细节描写,注重事件分析。
3. 注重解释分析。该报比较重视解释性报道、新闻评论,其分析具有一定力度,颇受政界和知识界的重视。美国业内人士称其特点是提供"冷静的分析,而不是片段的新闻"。
4. 语言简洁朴实。该报文章短小精悍,句式简单,可读性较强。

《基督教科学箴言报》曾7次获得普利策新闻奖,其总编三次当选美国报业最高荣誉"全美编辑人协会"主席职务。

自20世纪60年代开始,该报一直设法增加发行量,1970年鼎盛时期上升到22.3万,此后一直下滑,2011年降至7.5万,目前纸质报发行量保持在5万份左右,但其网站的点击率却有所上升,每月浏览量为500万人次。

该报头版一般是5篇文章左右,3—4张图片,每篇文章都有转版标示。有的文章仅有一句话便转到内页另一版。

《基督教科学箴言报》网址是 http://www.csmonitor.com。

Ⅴ. Analysis of the Content

1. The meaning of the word "floor" in the sentence "... reception room where lobbyists mingle with members before and after floor votes." is _____.
   A. the surface of a room where people walk on
   B. the right to speak during a discussion or a debate
   C. the entire membership of the House or Senate
   D. the hall of Congress

2. Which of the following is a non-profit interest group?
   A. The National Coalition on Health Care.
   B. The U.S. Chamber of Commerce.
   C. The American Medical Association.
   D. The Pharmaceutical Research and Manufacturers Association.

3. To the mind of R. Bruce Josten, the most effective way of lobbying is _____.
   A. building support for legislative initiatives through grass-roots efforts
   B. making contribution to candidates during election campaigns
   C. doing research and providing legislators with detailed knowledge
   D. providing legislators with food and drink, and taking them to sports events

4. Which of the following statements is NOT true?
   A. the lobbying world has changed greatly.
   B. lobbying does no good.
   C. lobbying has been around since America's earliest days.
   D. money plays a very important role in lobbying.

5. which of the following is NOT on the list of new rules imposed by the Obama Administration on lobbying?
   A. Barring administration's appointees from leaving office and seeking lobbying jobs during Obama's presidency.
   B. Forbidding new officials from making policy on matters involving their former employers.
   C. Reporting requirements on those seeking stimulus funds.
   D. Establishing a system to measure the success of lobbying efforts.

Ⅵ. Questions on the Article

1. What devices of communication have many lobbyists shifted to in making contacts with members of Congress?
2. What are the same fundamentals according to Robert Juliano?
3. What is the biggest effort to influence America's national policy in nearly a quarter century? How large is the force of lobbyists working on this issue?
4. Why is the issue on climate and energy legislation gaining so much attention from

lobbyists?
5. What is the current image of lobbyists?
6. How large is the spending on lobbying in America?
7. What is America's lobbying rooted in?
8. What are the factors that make the life of a lobbyist less pleasant?
9. Why do revolving-door rules matter?
10. Why is measuring the success of lobbying efforts difficult?

VII. Topics for Discussion

1. Does lobbying lead to government corruption?
2. Should lobbying be banned?

Lesson 7

Republic or Empire

A National Intelligence Estimate¹ on the United States
By Chalmers Johnson²

KEY JUDGMENTS

The United States remains, for the moment, the most powerful nation in history, but it faces a violent contradiction between its long republican tradition and its more recent imperial ambitions.

The fate of previous democratic empires suggests that such a conflict is unsustainable and will be resolved in one of two ways. Rome attempted to keep its empire and lost its democracy. Britain chose to remain democratic and in the process let go its empire. Intentionally or not, the people of the United States already are well embarked upon the course of non-democratic empire.³

Several factors, however, indicate that this course will be a brief one, which most likely will end in economic and political collapse.

Military Keynesianism

The ongoing U.S. militarization of its foreign affairs has spiked precipitously in recent years, with increasingly expensive commitments in Afghanistan and Iraq.⁴ These commitments grew from many specific political factors, including the ideological predilections of the current regime, the growing need for material access to the oil-rich regions of the Middle East, and a long-term bipartisan emphasis on hegemony as a basis for national security⁵. The domestic economic basis for these commitments, however, is consistently overlooked. Indeed, America's hegemonic policy is in many ways most accurately understood as the inevitable result of its decades-long policy of military Keynesianism.

During the Depression that preceded World War II, the English economist John Maynard Keynes, a liberal capitalist, proposed a form of governance that would mitigate the boom-and-bust cycles⁶ inherent in capitalist economies. To prevent the economy from contracting, a development typically accompanied by social unrest, Keynes thought the government should take on debt in order to put people back to work. Some of these deficit-financed government jobs might be socially useful, but Keynes was not averse to creating make-work tasks if necessary. During periods of prosperity, the government would cut spending and rebuild the treasury. Such countercyclical planning was called "pump-priming."

Upon taking office in 1933, U.S. President Franklin Roosevelt, with the assistance of Congress, put several Keynesian measures into effect, including socialized retirement plans,

79

minimum wages for all workers, and government-financed jobs on massive projects, including the Triborough Bridge[7] in New York City, the Grand Coulee Dam[8] in Washington, and the Tennessee Valley Authority[9], a flood-control and electric-power-generation complex covering seven states. Conservative capitalists feared that this degree of government intervention would delegitimate capitalism — which they understood as an economic system of quasi-natural laws — and shift the balance of power from the capitalist class to the working class and its unions. For these reasons, establishment figures tried to hold back countercyclical spending.[10]

The onset of World War II, however, made possible a significantly modified form of state socialism[11]. The exiled Polish economist Michal Kalecki attributed Germany's success in overcoming the global Depression to a phenomenon that has come to be known as "military Keynesianism." Government spending on arms increased manufacturing and also had a multiplier effect[12] on general consumer spending by raising worker incomes. Both of these points are in accordance with general Keynesian doctrine. In addition, the enlargement of standing armies absorbed many workers, often young males with few skills and less education. The military thus becomes an employer of last resort, like Roosevelt's Civilian Conservation Corps[13], but on a much larger scale.

Rather than make bridges and dams, however, workers would make bullets, tanks, and fighter planes. This made all the difference. Although Adolf Hitler did not undertake rearmament for purely economic reasons, the fact that he advocated governmental support for arms production made him acceptable not only to the German industrialists, who might otherwise have opposed his destabilizing expansionist policies, but also to many around the world who celebrated his achievement of a "German economic miracle."

In the United States, Keynesian policies continued to benefit workers, but, as in Germany, they also increasingly benefited wealthy manufacturers and other capitalists. By the end of the war, the United States had seen a massive shift. Dwight Eisenhower, who helped win that war and later became president, described this shift in his 1961 presidential farewell address...

Eisenhower went on to suggest that such an arrangement, which he called the "military-industrial complex[14]," could be perilous to American ideals. The short-term economic benefits were clear, but the very nature of those benefits — which were all too carefully distributed among workers and owners in "every city, every statehouse, every office of the federal government" — tended to short-circuit Keynes's insistence that government spending be cut back in good times[15]. The prosperity of the United States came increasingly to depend upon the construction and continual maintenance of a vast war machine, and so military supremacy and economic security became increasingly intertwined in the minds of voters. No one wanted to turn off the pump.

Between 1940 and 1996, for instance, the United States spent nearly $4.5 trillion on the development, testing, and construction of nuclear weapons alone. By 1967, the peak year of its nuclear stockpile, the United States possessed some 32,000 deliverable bombs. None of them was ever used, which illustrates perfectly Keynes's observation that, in order to create jobs, the government might as well decide to bury money in old mines and "leave them to private enterprise on the well-tried principles of laissez faire to dig them up again." Nuclear bombs were not just America's secret weapon; they were also a secret economic weapon.

Such spending helped create economic growth that lasted until the 1973 oil crisis. In the 1980s, President Ronald Reagan once again brought the tools of military Keynesianism to bear, with a policy of significant tax cuts and massive deficit spending on military projects, allegedly to combat a new threat from Communism. Reagan's military expenditures accounted for 5.9 percent of the gross domestic product in 1984, which in turn fueled a 7 percent growth rate for the economy as a whole and helped reelect Reagan by a landslide.

During the Clinton years military spending fell to about 3 percent of GDP, but the economy rallied strongly in Clinton's second term due to the boom in information technologies, weakness in the previously competitive Japanese economy, and — paradoxically — serious efforts to reduce the national debt. With the coming to power of George W. Bush, however, military Keynesianism returned once again. Indeed, after he began his war with Iraq, the once-erratic relationship between defense spending and economic growth became nearly parallel.[16] A spike in defense spending in one quarter would see a spike in GDP, and a drop in defense spending would likewise see a drop in GDP.

To understand the real weight of military Keynesianism in the American economy today, however, one must approach official defense statistics with great care. The "defense" budget of the United States — that is, the reported budget of the Department of Defense — does not include: the Department of Energy's spending on nuclear weapons ($16.4 billion slated for fiscal 2006), the Department of Homeland Security's[17] outlays for the actual "defense" of the United States ($41 billion), or the Department of Veterans Affairs' responsibilities for the lifetime care of the seriously wounded ($68 billion). Nor does it include the billions of dollars the Department of State spends each year to finance foreign arms sales and militarily related development or the Treasury Department's payments of pensions to military retirees and widows and their families (an amount not fully disclosed by official statistics). Still to be added are interest payments by the Treasury to cover past debt-financed defense outlays. The economist Robert Higgs estimates that in 2002 such interest payments amounted to $138.7 billion.

Even when all these things are included, Enron-style accounting[18] makes it hard to obtain an accurate understanding of U.S. dependency on military spending. In 2005, the Government Accountability Office[19] reported to Congress that "neither DOD nor Congress can reliably know how much the war is costing" or "details on how the appropriated funds are being spent." Indeed, the GAO found that, lacking a reliable method for tracking military costs, the Army had taken to simply inserting into its accounts figures that matched the available budget. Such actions seem absurd in terms of military logic. But they are perfectly logical responses to the requirements of military Keynesianism, which places its emphasis not on the demand for defense but rather on the available supply of money.

The Unitary Presidency

Military Keynesianism may be economic development by other means, but it does very often lead to real war, or, if not real war, then a significantly warlike political environment. This creates a feedback loop[20]: American presidents know that military Keynesianism tends to concentrate power in the executive branch, and so presidents who seek greater power have a natural inducement to encourage further growth of the military-industrial complex. As the phenomena feed on each other, the usual outcome is a real war, based not on the needs of national defense but rather on the domestic political logic of military Keynesianism.[21] As U.S. Senator Robert La Follette Sr. observed, "In times of peace, the war party insists on making preparation for war. As soon as prepared for war, it insists on making war."

George W. Bush has taken this natural political phenomenon to an extreme never before experienced by the American electorate. Every president has sought greater authority, but Bush — whose father lost his position as forty-first president in a fair and open election — appears to believe that increasing presidential authority is both a birthright and a central component of his historical legacy. He is supported in this belief by his vice president and chief adviser, Dick Cheney.

In pursuit of more power, Bush and Cheney have unilaterally authorized preventive war against nations they designate as needing "regime change[22]," directed American soldiers to torture persons they have seized and imprisoned in various countries, ordered the National Security Agency to carry out illegal "data mining" surveillance of the American people,[23] and done everything they could to prevent Congress from outlawing "cruel, inhumane, or degrading" treatment of people detained by the United States. Each of these actions has been undertaken for specific ideological, tactical, or practical reasons, but also as part of a general campaign of power concentration.

Cheney complained in 2002 that, since he had served as Gerald Ford's chief of staff, he had seen a significant erosion in executive power as post-Watergate presidents were forced to "cough up and compromise on important principles[24]." He was referring to such reforms as the War Powers Act of 1973[25], which requires that the president obtain congressional approval within ninety days of ordering troops into combat; the Budget and Impoundment Control Act of 1974[26], which was designed to stop Nixon from impounding funds for programs he did not like; the Freedom of Information Act[27] of 1966, which Congress strengthened in 1974; President Ford's Executive Order 11905 of 1976, which outlawed political assassination; and the Intelligence Oversight Act of 1980[28], which gave more power to the House and Senate select committees on intelligence. Cheney said that these reforms were "unwise" because they "weaken the presidency and the vice presidency," and added that he and the president felt an obligation "to pass on our offices in better shape than we found them."

No president, however, has ever acknowledged the legitimacy of the War Powers Act, and most of these so-called limitations on presidential power had been gutted, ignored, or violated long before Cheney became vice president. Republican Senator John Sununu of New Hampshire said, "The vice president may be the only person I know of that believes the executive has somehow lost power over the last thirty years."

Bush and Cheney have made it a primary goal of their terms in office, nonetheless, to carve executive power into the law[29], and the war has been the primary vehicle for such actions. John Yoo, Bush's deputy assistant attorney general[30] from 2001 to 2003, writes in his book *War By Other Means*[31], "We are used to a peacetime system in which Congress enacts laws, the President enforces them, and the courts interpret them. In wartime, the gravity shifts to the executive branch." Bush has claimed that he is "the commander" and "the decider" and that therefore he does not "owe anybody an explanation" for anything.

Failed Checks on Executive Ambition

The current administration's perspective on political power is far from unique. Few, if any, presidents have refused the increased executive authority that is the natural byproduct of military Keynesianism. Moreover, the division of power between the president, the Congress, and the judiciary — often described as the bedrock of American democracy — has eroded significantly in recent years. The people, the press, and the military, too, seem anxious to cede power to a "wartime" president, leaving Bush, or those who follow him, almost entirely unobstructed in pursuing the imperial project.

Congress: Corrupt and indifferent, Congress, which the Founders[32] believed would be the leading branch of government, has already entirely forfeited the power to declare war. More recently, it gave the president the legal right to detain anyone, even American citizens, without warrant, and to detain non-citizens without recourse to habeas corpus, as well as to use a variety of interrogation methods that he could define, at his sole discretion, to be or not be torture.[33]

The Courts: The judicial branch is hardly more effective in restraining presidential ambition. The Supreme Court was active in the installation of the current president, and the lower courts increasingly are packed with judges who believe they should defer to his wishes. In 2006, for instance, U.S. District Judge David Trager dismissed a suit by a thirty-five-year-old Canadian citizen, Maher Arar, who in 2002 was seized by U.S. government agents at John F. Kennedy Airport and delivered to Syria, where he was tortured for ten months before being released. No charges were filed against Arar, and his torturers eventually admitted he had no links to any crime. In explaining his dismissal, Trager noted with approval an earlier Supreme Court finding that such judgment would "threaten 'our customary policy of deference to the President in matters of foreign affairs'."[34]

The People: Could the people themselves restore constitutional government — A grassroots movement to break the hold of the military-industrial complex and establish public financing of elections is conceivable. But, given the conglomerate control of the mass media and the difficulties of mobilizing the United States' large and diffuse population, it is unlikely.[35] Moreover, the people themselves have enjoyed the Keynesian benefits of the U.S. imperial project and — in all but a few cases — have not yet suffered any of its consequences.

Bankruptcy and Collapse

The more likely check on presidential power, and on U.S. military ambition, will be the economic failure that is the inevitable consequence of military Keynesianism. Traditional Keynesianism is a stable two-part system composed of deficit spending in bad times and debt payment in good times. Military Keynesianism is an unstable one-part system. With no political check, debt accrues until it reaches a crisis point.[36]

In the fiscal 2006 budget, the Congressional Research Service estimates that Pentagon spending on Operation Enduring Freedom and Operation Iraqi Freedom[37] will be about $10 billion per month, or an extra $120.3 billion for the year. As of mid-2006, the overall cost of the wars in Iraq and Afghanistan since their inception stood at more than $400 billion. Joseph Stiglitz, the Nobel Prize-winning economist, and his colleague, Linda Bilmes, have tried to put together an estimate of the real costs of the Iraq war. They calculate that it will cost about $2 trillion by 2015. The conservative American Enterprise Institute[38] suggests a figure at the opposite end of the spectrum — $1 trillion. Both figures are an order of magnitude larger than what the Bush Administration publicly acknowledges.[39]

At the same time, the U.S. trade deficit, the largest component of the current account deficit, soared to an all-time high in 2005 of $782.7 billion, the fourth consecutive year that America's trade debts set records. To try to cope with these imbalances, on March 16, 2006, Congress raised the national debt limit from $8.2 trillion to $9 trillion. This was the fourth time since George W. Bush took office that the limit had to be raised. Had Congress not raised it, the U.S. government would not have been able to borrow more money and would have had to default on its massive debts.[40]

It is difficult to predict the course of a democracy, and perhaps even more so when that democracy is as corrupt as that of the United States.

It appears for the moment, however, that the people of the United States prefer the Roman approach and so will abet their government in maintaining a facade of constitutional democracy until the nation drifts into bankruptcy.

Of course, bankruptcy will not mean the literal end of the United States any more than it did for Germany in 1923, or Argentina in 2001. It might, in fact, open the way for an unexpected restoration of the American system, or for military rule, revolution, or simply some new development we cannot yet imagine. Certainly, such a bankruptcy would mean a drastic lowering of the current American standard of living, a loss of control over international affairs, a process of adjusting to the rise of other powers. The American people will be forced to learn what it means to be a far poorer nation and the attitudes and manners that go with it.

From *Harper's Magazine*, January 2007

I. New Words

abet	[ə'bet]	v.	to help sb do sth wrong
accrue	[ə'kru:]	v.	自然增加
averse	[ə'və:s]	adj.	strongly disliking; opposed to
bipartisan	[bai,pɑ:ti'zæn]	adj.	两党（或派）的
birthright	['bə:θrait]	n.	生来就有的权利
cede	[si:d]	v.	to give sb power, a right, unwillingly
conceivable	[kən'si:vəbl]	adj.	able to be believed or imagined
countercyclical	[,kauntə'saiklikəl]	adj.	[经]反周期的
defer	[di'fə:]	v.	~ **to sb** 遵从，听从
delegitimate	[,di:li'dʒitimət]	v.	使丧失合法性（或权威）
diffuse	[di'fju:z]	adj.	松散的
façade	[fə'sɑ:d]	n.	（尤指给人以假象的）表面，外观
forfeit	['fɔ:fit]	v.	没收；丧失
governance	['gʌvənəns]	n.	the activity of governing a country
gut	[gʌt]	v.	to destroy the inside or contents of sth
habeas corpus	['heibjəs'kɔ:pəs]	n.	人身保护权
impound	[im'paund]	v.	to take sth away from sb
improvisation	[,imprəvai'zeiʃən]	n.	即席创作

inception	[in'sepʃən]	n.	开始
inducement	[in'dju:smənt]	n.	引诱;引诱力
inherent	[in'hiərənt]	adj.	being a basic or permanent part of sth
Keynesianism	['keinziənizəm]	n.	凯恩斯主义
laissez faire	[ˌleisei'fɛə]	n.	the policy of allowing private businesses to develop freely
mitigate	['mitigeit]	v.	to make sth less harmful, serious
onset	['ɔnset]	n.	the beginning of sth, especially sth unpleasant
perilous	['periləs]	adj.	very dangerous
plowshare	['plauʃɛə]	n.	[农](犁)铧,铧头
precipitously	[pri'sipitəsli]	adv.	sharply, very rapidly
predilection	[ˌpri:di'lekʃən]	n.	*formal* a liking
pump-priming	['pʌmp'praimiŋ]	n.	刺激国民经济的政府投资
short-circuit	[ˌʃɔ:t'sə:kit]	v.	使短路
spectrum	['spektrəm]	n.	a wide range
stockpile	['stɔkpail]	n.	积蓄,库存
unitary	['ju:nitəri]	adj.	中央集权制的

II. Background Information

军事凯恩斯主义

1929—1933年的大萧条之后不久,凯恩斯主义成了西方经济学的主流学派,从此,凯恩斯主义登上了历史舞台。针对"有效需求不足"的问题,凯恩斯提出扩大政府开支、赤字预算为内容的财政政策来增加总需求。然而,面对"滞涨",这些措施难以奏效。于是,一种新型的凯恩斯主义即军事凯恩斯主义渐渐地滋生起来。

美国军事凯恩斯主义的主要根源在于美国经济体制与经济结构的变化。二战以来,美国的经济体制不断发生变化,尤其是冷战以后,军民一体化成为美国的经济体制的突出特征,军民一体化的经济体制是美国军事凯恩斯主义的经济基础。从第二次世界大战开始,特别是冷战时期,美国一直对关系国家安全与军事优势的军工产品生产和尖端军事技术的研制给予高度重视,大量的国家资源被用于支撑军用技术的突破性进展,而军用技术的突破性进展也为民用技术的开发及新兴产业部门的建立与发展(如飞机制造业、核能发电业、计算机与集成电路产业等)提供了强大的技术支持。一方面,民用技术和产业向军用技术和产业渗透;另一方面,军工产业大举进入商业市场,从而形成了美国军民一体化的经济体制。

美国军事凯恩斯主义主要表现在以下两个方面:(1)巨额的军事预算和军事支出。(2)扩大军品贸易。扩大军事产品贸易可以保证军事科研和军工生产的稳定发展,解决部分就业问题,还可以通过军工产品与民用产品的关联性,拉动整个产业出口增长,推动产业结构升级,促进经济发展。因而,近些年来,美国政府一方面为扩大军品贸易制造环境(如制造地区不稳定因素),另一方面寻找各种借口,发动对外武装干涉或对外战争,从而增进国际市场对军事产品的需求,促进美国军工产品出口贸易的增长。

冷战结束后,对于美国来说,传统意义上的军事威胁已经消除,过去的敌对国或敌对集团已经不再对美国形成任何军事威胁,主要威胁是来自恐怖主义者。美国军事开支的绝大部分已经超出了保护美国公民的需要,其实质在于内在的经济动因。为了达到促进经济发展目的,美国需要军事行动,其中包括全球范围内的干涉行动。

III. Notes to the Text

1. National Intelligence Estimate — 国家情报评估(written judgment concerning a national security issue prepared by the Director of Central Intelligence)
2. Chalmers Johnson — The author served as an outside consultant to the CIA's Office of National Estimates from 1967 to 1973.
3. Britain chose to remain democratic ... embarked upon the course of non-democratic empire. — 英国宁愿保留民主制,与此同时放弃了帝国制。美国则有意无意地彻底走上了非民主制帝国的道路。(① embark — to put on board a ship or other vehicle;② well — thoroughly and completely)
4. The ongoing U. S. militarization of its foreign affairs has spiked precipitously ... in Afghanistan and Iraq. — 正在继续的美国外交事务军事化近些年随着美国在阿富汗和伊拉克投入代价不断提高显得非常突出,十分危险。(spike — to rise sharply)
5. a long-term bipartisan emphasis on hegemony as a basis for national security — 两党长期以来强调霸权是国家安全的基础。
6. the boom-and-bust cycles — 经济繁荣与萧条的周期
7. the Triborough Bridge — 三区桥(The Triborough Bridge is a complex of three bridges connecting the New York City boroughs of the Bronx, Manhattan, and Queens.)
8. the Grand Coulee Dam — 大古力水坝(It is the largest electric power producing facility in the United States, and the largest concrete structure in the U. S.)
9. the Tennessee Valley Authority — 田纳西河谷管理局(a federally owned corporation created in 1933 to provide navigation, flood control, electricity generation, fertilizer manufacturing, and economic development in the Tennessee River Valley)
10. For these reasons, establishment figures tried to hold back countercyclical spending. — 出于这些原因,权势集团人物设法制止反周期的开支。(establishment — an organization which has power and influence in a society)
11. state socialism — 国家社会主义(a form of socialism involving government control, management or ownership of all or certain enterprises with the purpose of improving social conditions)
12. multiplier effect — [经]倍数效应(指国民总收入变量可达国家总投资变量若干倍的效应)
13. Civilian Conservation Corps — (美国)民间资源保护队(a work relief program designed to help combat the poverty and unemployment of the Great Depression)
14. military-industrial complex — 军工联合体(由政府中的军事部门和军需品供应部门联合组建并控制美国的经济和外交政策的集团)
15. short-circuit Keynes's insistence that government spending be cut back in good times — 回避凯恩斯所坚持的一点,即政府要在经济好的时期削减财政投入(short-circuit — to

bypass, avoid)

16. Indeed, after he began his war with Iraq, the once-erratic relationship between defense spending and economic growth became nearly parallel. — 实际上,自伊拉克战争开始以后,国防开支与经济增长曾经不确定的关系变得几乎并存。(① erratic — not happening at regular times; ② parallel — taking place at the same time)

17. the Department of Homeland Security — 国土安全部(It is a cabinet department established in 2002 with the responsibility of protecting the territory of the United States from terrorist attacks.)

18. Enron-style accounting 安然公司式的假账(Enron — 美国安然公司,曾为世界最大能源公司之一,2001 年被揭露虚报利润,掩盖巨额债务的财务丑闻,12 月被迫申请破产保护。此后 Enron 变成了"欺骗"的代名词。)

19. Government Accountability Office — (美国)政府问责署(an investigative arm of Congress, charged with auditing and evaluation of government programs and activities)

20. a feedback loop — 反应循环

21. As the phenomena feed on each other ... military Keynesianism. — 这些现象相互激化,通常导致发动真正战争,这种战争并非基于国防的需要,而是基于军事凯恩斯主义国内政治理由。(feed on sth — to become stronger because of sth)

22. regime change — a euphemism for the overthrow of a government (or regime) considered illegitimate by an external force (usually military), and its replacement with a new government according to the ideas and/or interests promoted by that force. It was popularized by George W. Bush, in reference to Saddam Hussein's regime.

23. ordered the National Security Agency to carry out illegal "data mining" surveillance of the American people — 命令国家安全局对美国公民通过非法的"数据挖掘"手段进行监视(data mining — originally a term in computing, here used in the sense of collecting information and sharing it on files about suspects)

24. cough up and compromise on important principles — 在原则性问题上让步和妥协(cough up — to yield)

25. the War Powers Act of 1973 — 《战争权限法》(1973 年国会为避免总统滥用统帅权进行不宣而战的战争,通过了这一法案,规定如无国会的宣战,总统自行决定打的战争不得超过 60 天)

26. the Budget and Impoundment Control Act of 1974 — 《预算与扣压拨款控制法》

27. the Freedom of Information Act — 《信息自由法》(1996 年通过,规定政府除国家机密、商业机密和个人隐私等 9 种信息之外其他信息在公众请求时都必须公开)

28. the Intelligence Oversight Act of 1980 — a United States federal law that amended the Hughes-Ryan Act and requires United States government agencies to report covert actions to the House Permanent Select Committee on Intelligence (HPSCI) and the Senate Select Committee on Intelligence (SSCI).

29. carve executive power into the law — 将总统的权力深深地印在法律上(总统运用自己的权力左右法律)

30. deputy assistant attorney general — 司法部长副助理

31. *War By Other Means* — 此书全名为 *War by Other Means — Building Complete and Balanced Capabilities for Counterinsurgency*

32. Founders — Founding Fathers (members of the group who wrote the Constitution of the U.S. in 1787)

33. More recently, it gave the president the legal right … at his sole discretion, to be or not be torture. — 最近,国会赋予总统以下权力:可以在没有逮捕证情况下拘留任何人,甚至美国公民,可以无需考虑人身保护权扣押非美国公民。还可以采用各种手段进行审讯,至于使用的手段是否是酷刑全由总统自己判定。(① habeas corpus — the right of sb in prison to come to a court of law so that the court can decide whether he should stay in prison; ② at sb's discretion — according to sb's decision)

34. In explaining his dismissal, Trager noted … in matters of foreign affairs'." — 在解释拒绝受理此案原因时,特拉格赞许地提到先前最高法院的裁决:此类案件的审理会"威胁到'我们在外交事务上惯常遵从总统的政策'"。

35. But, given the conglomerate control of the mass media and the difficulties of mobilizing the United States' large and diffuse population, it is unlikely. — 但是,鉴于大众传媒控制在联合大企业手中,美国人口数量众多,居住分散,动员工作存在困难,这一点(组织基层民众运动)是不可能的。

36. With no political check, debt accrues until it reaches a crisis point. — 如果没有政治势力的制约,债台就会增高,直到产生危机。

37. Operation Enduring Freedom and Operation Iraqi Freedom — the official names used by the U.S. government for its war on terrorists in Afghanistan and its 2003 War on Iraq

38. the American Enterprise Institute — 全称为 the American Enterprise Institute for Public Research,美国企业公共政策研究所(是美国最大和最重要的思想库之一,也是保守派的重要政策研究机构)

39. Both figures are an order of magnitude larger than what the Bush Administration publicly acknowledges. — 两个数字都远远高出布什政府所公开承认的数额。(an order of magnitude — a great degree)

40. Had Congress not raised it, the U.S. government would … default on its massive debts. — 如果国会不提高债务限额,政府就没有可能借更多的钱,就得拖欠巨额债款。(default on a debt — to fail to pay debt as required by law)

IV. Language Features

复合词 (Compounds)

本文使用了较多复合词,如:short-circuit,pump-priming,make-work,feedback。

复合法是英语古老的构词法之一,它是把两个或两个以上的词结合在一起构成新词的方法。在整个英语发展的过程中,复合法在构词方面起着积极的作用。它所构成新词的数量仅次于派生法(affixation)。在现代英语中,这一构词法依然十分活跃。美国语言学家门肯曾在书中写道:"美国人所表现的一种最突出的倾向是他们惯于使用合成这个简易方法构词。"

复合法可以起到使语句精炼生动的作用。正是由于这种功能使得它备受新闻写作人员的喜爱。从下列几个例子中可以看出这种作用。

dynamic pay— pay intended to improve worker morale and achievement（奖金）

team-teach—to teach in cooperation with others（协作教学）

depth interview—an interview which is designed to probe attitudes, feelings or motives（深度访谈）

house-boat—a boat which is fitted up for living in（可供居住的船）

复合词按词性分类有复合名词、复合形容词、复合动词、复合介词、复合副词、复合代词、复合数词，但数量较多的是前三种。

1. 复合名词：identity crisis（性格认同危机）；website（网址）；checkbook participation（支票参战；出钱不出兵的参战）；retirement baby（老妇所产婴儿，停经后妇女通过卵子移植方式受孕所产的婴儿）；suicide bomber（人肉炸弹）；Lewinsky effect（莱温斯基效应，担心婚外性关系败露）；people person（人缘好的人）；hush money（封口费）；glass ceiling（妇女等面临的）隐形升迁障碍；one-off（一次性的）；high-end（高端的）

2. 复合形容词：war-weary（厌倦战争的）；top-heavy（头重脚轻的）；sizzling hot（极热的）；bitter-sweet（又苦又甜的，又苦又乐的）；wring wet（湿淋淋的）；freezing cold（冰冷的）

3. 复合动词：wallet X-ray（钱袋透视，指收治病人前对其支付能力的审查）；handcarry（手提）；vacuum clean（真空吸尘）；mass produce（成批生产）；green wash（绿刷洗，指塑造关心环境保护的形象）；fast-talk（花言巧语企图说服）；tape-record（用磁带为……录音）；date-rape（约会强奸）；marry up（结婚高攀）

Ⅴ. Analysis of the Content

1. The warning sounded by Dwight Eisenhower in his presidential farewell address was about _____.
   A. the perilous effects of the military-industrial complex
   B. the possible decline of America's military power
   C. America's economic bankruptcy in the future
   D. the increasing profits gained by the arms manufacturers and other capitalists

2. By saying that nuclear bombs were also a secret economic weapon, the author means that _____.
   A. they could be used to overthrow the government of a hostile country
   B. they could be used to frighten other countries into making concessions in trade
   C. they could be sold for huge profits
   D. spending on nuclear arms industry helped create economic growth

3. Those reforms such as the War Powers Act of 1973 were intended to _____.
   A. give the president more power in times of war
   B. help further develop America's armaments industry
   C. force the president to cough up and compromise on important principles
   D. restrain the executive branch from abusing its power in times of conflicts

4. The author believes that the leading branch, according to the Founders of the

Constitution, is _____.

A. the Congress B. the President C. the courts D. the people

5. To the author's mind, the more likely check on U.S. presidential power and on U.S. military ambition will be _____.

A. the Congress B. the Courts C. the mass media D. economic failure

VI. Questions on the Article

1. What contradiction does the U.S. face? How will the contradiction be resolved? Which way has the U.S. chosen?
2. What idea did John Keynes propose?
3. How did Franklin Roosevelt apply Keynes's theory?
4. How much did the U.S. spend on nuclear weapons? What's the author's view on the nuclear stockpile?
5. What factor should be taken into consideration when evaluating the real weight of military Keynesianism in the American economy today?
6. What does the author mean by the term "feedback loop"?
7. What have Bush and Cheney done in pursuit of more power?
8. What does the War Powers Act require the president to do? Has it been strictly observed?
9. How does the gravity of power shift in war time according to John Yoo?
10. Is the judicial branch effective in restraining presidential ambition?
11. What effects will economic bankruptcy have on America according to the author?

VII. Topics for Discussion

1. Is Britain's political system more democratic than America's political system?
2. Does military Keynesianism work in the interest of the U.S.?

Lesson 8

Accepting "The New Normal"[1]

We mourned, united, and adapted. But five years after 9/11, we are divided once again.

The snuffing out of nearly 3,000 lives on that perversely beautiful September morning five years ago brought one consolation.[2] For a time, at least, the American people put aside their differences and embraced their common citizenry. And we were not alone. "We are all Americans," a headline in France's *Le Monde*[3] declared. People disagree about how much, or even whether, America has changed since 9/11. But one thing is almost beyond dispute: That early sense of solidarity is largely gone.

Some would say it is an inevitable story. A nation of pragmatists, we are also a disputatious tribe, prone to impatience and quick to point the finger[4] when things go wrong — even when things don't go right fast enough. Yet at first, everything seemed to go so well so fast. George W. Bush, after some initial discombobulation, rallied the nation with a declaration of war on the terrorists and those who harbored them. No more minimalist responses; no more law-enforcement-style half measures.[5] Yet it was a curious war footing.[6] There would be no draft, no large material sacrifices expected of the citizenry. Americans were under orders to act normally, as though doing otherwise would be conceding victory to the terrorists.

Big Brother. For the most part, Americans began to adapt to the "new normal" even before the administration launched military operations in Afghanistan, an invasion supported by well over 80 percent of the public. Adjusting to long lines in airports, color-coded risk advisories, and Big Brotherish highway signs urging drivers to report suspicious behavior, a usually inward-looking people consumed record numbers of books on Muslims and the Middle East, learning to distinguish between true Islam and its corrupted form.[7] Irony and humor, said to be fatal casualties of 9/11, made their comeback, helped along by the good news from Afghanistan. A dashing little war in which horse-mounted Special Forces combined with smart bombs[8] to produce marvelously swift results, it was marred only by the unfinished business at Tora Bora, where Osama bin Laden[9] eluded death or capture. Yet the noose, we were assured, was tightening.[10]

Back at home, Americans were eager to do their part, even if that meant sacrificing some of their liberties. Shortly after the Patriot Act[11] was signed into law in October 2001, 53 percent of respondents in one poll expressed concern that the government would be too protective of civil rights in its pursuit of terrorists. Americans were equally supportive of using extraordinary measures against the enemy. While critics around the world carped at the treatment of prisoners in Guantanamo, 55 percent of Americans in one early 2002 survey deemed it appropriate.

If World War II gave rise to the national security state, September 11 created the homeland security state.[12] Morphing from an office into a full-fledged cabinet-level department, the Department of Homeland Security was the institutional expression of a new national obsession.[13] While many warned of bureaucratic bloat, wasteful spending, and even more dangerous consequences — later confirmed by FEMA's[14] performance in the handling of Hurricane Katrina[15] — a course was irrevocably set.

The urge to prevent future attacks found further expression in the demand for an independent 9/11 investigation to study what went wrong. But even as the 9/11 commission moved toward its first meeting in January 2003, the nation was growing queasy about a military venture far more ambitious than the one in Afghanistan. In one poll, 59 percent responded that invading Iraq would increase the risk of terrorism against the United States, while only 12 percent thought it would decrease it. Americans had to digest a lot in the year preceding the invasion of Iraq: Saddam Hussein and WMDs and U.N. resolutions; rumors of ties between Iraq and al Qaeda; the Bush Doctrine[16] and pre-emptive war; the growing rift with "old" Europe[17]. There were so many questions, so many risks.

Regime change. But many went along, including leaders of the Democratic Party. The idea of bringing democracy to the failed autocratic states of the Middle East wasn't bad in principle, even if, in the case of Iraq, it had to be sold in conjunction with a dubiously established threat of WMDs.[18] Still, many asked, was this the best way to win Muslim hearts and minds? And why did U.S. attempts at public diplomacy seem so feeble? Some wondered why more wasn't being done to stop the Saudi-funded Wahhabi religious establishment[19] from indoctrinating more Muslims into the most intolerant strain of Islam. Others pointed to the growing instability in Pakistan, a nation with nuclear weapons. And even if many of the al Qaeda top brass[20] had been rounded up or killed, bin Laden and his sidekick Ayman al-Zawahiri remained at large while organizational clones of al Qaeda kept popping up around the globe.[21]

Some charged that America was succumbing to a dangerous idealism and forgetting its tradition of foreign policy realism[22]. Even the president's father thought his son should listen to a wider circle of advisers. Americans, however, saw ever widening rifts within the administration, the more cautious heads in the State Department and the CIA losing out to the full-speed-ahead gang in the vice president's office and the Pentagon.[23] If there was no clear, universally agreed-upon plan for postwar Iraq, well, that would take care of itself later.

And then came the swift deposing of Saddam Hussein, briefly silencing the naysayers and doubters at home and abroad. But the looting of the Baghdad museums was an ominous flicker of a greater lawlessness to come. The failure of the liberating forces to move swiftly in re-establishing order and normalcy in the Iraqi economy and society gave renewed credence to all those pre-war warnings about the need for greater troop strength, a more thoroughly worked out plan, and the full cooperation of all our traditional allies.

As Iraq began to unravel into the civil war that we see today, American confidence further suffered from the disclosures of the 9/11 commission.[24] Why so many clear warnings ignored? Why such poor communication between (and even within) organizations like the CIA and the FBI? And why, apart from Richard Clarke[25], a former White House counterterrorism official, did nobody seem to take full responsibility for the many institutional failures? The looming question, set forth in the commission's many recommendations, was how well the administration and the nation would address such troubling deficiencies. (Grades on 41 areas of performance issued by the 9/11 commission in its December 2005 "report card" were not particularly encouraging: Twenty-four were C or below, and there was only one A minus.)

"Big bang." It didn't take the 2004 presidential election to prove that America was once again a riven nation, but it showed that red and blue Americans were now also deeply and evenly divided over the incumbent's handling of the war on terrorism.[26] Bush's supporters could — and still can — point to one indisputable fact: not one successful act of terrorism on American soil since September 11. Yet the charges of incompetent leadership would grow ever sharper, many coming from traditional conservatives. "Five years into the global war on terror," says Loren Thompson, a military analyst at the Lexington Institute, "and trillions spent on the military has done remarkably little for its long-term health."

Strategically, Bush's plan for a "Big Bang" transformation of the Middle East[27] is also receiving low marks from some of its earlier backers. Thomas Barnett, author of The Pentagon's New Map and Blueprint for Action, faults the administration for accumulating more and more "postwar situations" — in Afghanistan, Iraq, and now, through encouragement of Israel, Lebanon? without solving any of them. "That is the path I've been warning against," Barnett says, "because if it seems cumulative, the American public gets tired." And that is to say nothing about how these postwar situations are serving as recruitment ads and training grounds for the swelling ranks of jihadists.[28]

To keep track of the growing threat, U.S. intelligence agencies, particularly the CIA, have been on a hiring binge[29], adding hundreds and hundreds of new analysts and case officers[30]. But the CIA is suffering from a dearth of experienced hands, many of whom were driven out or retired during the troubled tenure of former Director Porter Goss. Domestically, it still seems very much in doubt that the FBI can effectively add counterterrorism to its law enforcement responsibilities.

Meanwhile, the American public is resigned to the inevitability of further attacks[31], says Karlyn Bowman, a resident fellow at the American Enterprise Institute[32] who has tracked polling data on attitudes toward terrorism-related subjects since 9/11. "But no one should have expected public opinion to be simple," she adds. "They believe it's a more dangerous world, but also feel they are safer. They give some credit for things like airport security, though they are still worried about other areas like port security." Bowman finds Americans are willing to put up with inconvenience, discomfort, and even some encroachment upon their civil liberties. Perhaps that is because most believe we are in for a long struggle, one that, in their view, neither side is currently winning. "We are resilient," Bowman says, "but there seems to be a deep hangover — a deep level of pessimism."

Or call it the realism of the aging new normal. "I think the terrorists have discovered that they have great power over our daily lives, our material lives, even over our imagination of the present and future. This is significant power," says Walter Reich, a professor of international affairs at George Washington University. But the way Americans have hardened themselves to the terrorist threat is also a source of power. Many believe that our tactics and strategy are badly in need of overhaul — and high percentages disapprove of the president's leadership — but very few think this is a struggle that we can or will lose.

From *U.S. News & World Report*, September 11, 2006

Ⅰ. New Words

autocratic	[ˌɔːtəˈkrætik]	adj.	独裁的,专制的
bloat	[bləut]	n.	膨胀,臃肿
carp	[kɑːp]	v.	~ **at** to keep complaining about
credence	[ˈkriːdəns]	n.	belief in the truth of a statement
cumulative	[ˈkjuːmjulətiv]	adj.	累积的,渐增的
dashing	[ˈdæʃiŋ]	adj.	full of energy and spirit
dearth	[dəːθ]	n.	*formal* a lack of sth
depose	[diˈpəuz]	v.	to remove from office or power
discombobulation	[ˌdiskʌmbɔbjuːˈleiʃən]	n.	困惑
disputatious	[ˌdispju(ː)ˈteiʃəs]	adj.	tending to argue
elude	[iˈluːd]	v.	to avoid or escape from sb or sth
flicker	[ˈflikə]	n.	忽隐忽现,闪现
hangover	[ˈhæŋˌəuvə]	n.	a feeling that remains from the past
irrevocable	[iˈrevəkəbl]	adj.	不能取消的
mar	[mɑː]	v.	to damage or spoil sth good
morph	[mɔf]	v.	to change
naysayer	[neiˈseiə]	n.	反对者,否认者
normalcy	[ˈnɔːməlsi]	n.	常态
overhaul	[ˌəuvəˈhɔːl]	n.	a thorough examination for making changes
queasy	[ˈkwiːzi]	adj.	slightly nervous or worried
resilient	[riˈziliənt]	adj.	有弹性的;恢复活力的
rift	[rift]	n.	a serious disagreement that stops relationship from continuing
riven	[ˈrivən]	adj.	split violently apart
strain	[strein]	n.	a particular type
trillion	[ˈtriljən]	n.	万亿

Ⅱ. Background Information

9·11 事件及其影响

  2001年9月11日上午,两架被恐怖分子劫持的民用飞机先后撞击纽约世贸中心大楼,造成南北双楼倒塌。这个举世震惊的事件造成了2,792人丧生,1,000多亿美元的经济损失。

  9·11事件使美国看到国防体制的不安全因素,促使政府加强对此类袭击和对生化武器与核武器的防范措施。为此,美国新设了国土安全部(Department of Homeland Security)。政府还设定了十项重点保护机构和设施,启动颜色标示和恐怖袭击警报系统(color-coded terrorist-alert system)。

这次袭击是继日本袭击珍珠港事件之后美国本土所遭受的最沉重的一次打击,给美国民众心理上造成了巨大创伤,使他们看到美国安全体系的脆弱之处。他们感到超级航母、精确导弹、先进电子、高级枪炮无法提供可靠的安全保护。许多人变得情绪紧张、焦虑、恐惧。9·11事件之后,美国又遭遇了一系列炭疽袭击事件,政府不断发出恐怖袭击警报。一段时期,美国许多人处于惊恐状态之中,纷纷储存食品和日用品,安装住房安全设施,尽量减少外出旅行。

　　9·11事件促使美国人的爱国情绪迅速高涨。青年们对国际事务表现出浓厚的兴趣。有关中东、伊斯兰教派书籍十分畅销。这些专题讨论会吸引了很多大学生。许多建筑物上挂起了大国旗,汽车上插着小国旗。年青一代增强了社会责任感,立志要为国家效力,准备投身于科技、医疗事业的人数明显增加。

　　伴随反恐战争的展开,美国政府极力扩张权力。在国际事务处理上奉行单边主义。2002年国情咨文(the State of the Union Message)中,布什总统将伊朗、伊拉克和朝鲜列为"邪恶轴心"(Axis of Evil)。2003年3月20日美国未经安理会授权,不顾世界多数国家的反对,发动了伊拉克战争。战争不仅造成军队人员伤亡,还造成大批民众丧生。2004年美军在阿布格莱布监狱多张令人触目惊心的虐囚照片的曝光使美国在国际的形象大损,使美国更加孤立。

　　在国内,美国民众对政府的一系列反恐政策和措施的怀疑情绪日益增强,对政府部门所表现的无能越来越感到失望。他们清醒地意识到美国存在许多不安全因素,也意识到无法改变这种处境,他们所能做的便是期待上帝的保佑。

Ⅲ. Notes to the Text

1. The New Normal — 新常态(①It refers to the big switch of Americans' lifestyle after 9/11; ②normal — *n.* the usual state)

2. The snuffing out of nearly 3,000 lives on that perversely beautiful September morning five years ago brought one consolation. — 五年前9月份那个偏偏天气美好的上午,近3,000人的生命一下就消失了,这个悲剧也给我们带来一种慰藉。(① perverse — *disapproving* strange and not what most people would expect or enjoy; ②snuff out — to suddenly end one's life)

3. *Le Monde* — 法国《世界报》

4. A nation of pragmatists, we are also a disputatious tribe, prone to impatience and quick to point the finger — 我们美国人是实用主义者,也是喜好争论者,往往缺乏耐心,动辄指责。(pragmatism是美国人崇尚奉行的价值观,其要义是把获得实际效果作为追求的最高目标。)

5. No more minimalist responses; no more law-enforcement-style half measures. — 不再尽量减少军事行动,采取行动不再心慈手软。(①minimalist — here used in the sense of taking as little action as possible; ②half measures — a policy or action that is weak and does not do enough)

6. Yet it was a curious war footing. — 但这却是种奇怪的战备状态。(war footing — readiness to go to a war)

7. Adjusting to long lines in airports, color-coded ... learning to distinguish between true

Islam and its corrupted form. —— 美国人正在适应机场排长队,由颜色标示的(恐怖)危险等级告示以及高速路出现类似专制国家所用的敦促司机举报可疑行为的标语。过去他们一向只关心国内的事情,现在却开始空前大量地购买关于穆斯林和中东的书,试图把真正的伊斯兰教和它的异化邪恶教派区分开。[①color code —— America uses the following five color codes, each representing a different level of threat: red(severe), orange(high), yellow(elevated), blue(guarded) and green(low); ②Big Brother —— 老大哥(英国作家乔治·奥威尔讽刺小说《1984》中的独裁者,现常用作"独裁政权""专制国家"之意)]

8. smart bomb —— 〈美〉灵巧炸弹(激光制导炸弹)

9. Osama bin Laden —— 本·拉登(基地组织头目)

10. Yet the noose, we were assured, was tightening. —— 然而我们所得到的保证是,对本·拉登的包围圈正在不断缩小。

11. the Patriot Act —— 爱国者法案(a U.S. law which was introduced in October 2001 as a reaction to the terrorist attacks in the U.S. on September 11, 2001. It gives the authorities more power to find out information about people who they think may be terrorists. It also allows them to put someone who is not a U.S. citizen in prison for as long as they wish and without trial if he is believed to be a threat to national security.)

12. If World War II gave rise to the national security state, September 11 created the homeland security state. —— 如果说第二次世界大战导致了美国奉行国家安全政策,那么9·11事件则促使美国推行国土安全政策。(美国二战后和冷战期间奉行国家安全政策,重点在加强军备,保卫国防。9·11事件后转为国土安全政策,重点在对付恐怖主义,密切观察可疑分子行为,采取一切行动阻止恐怖行动在本土发生。)

13. Morphing from an office into a full-fledged cabinet-level department, the Department of Homeland Security was the institutional expression of a new national obsession. —— 美国国土安全部由一个办公室转变为完完全全内阁级的部门,这从机构方面体现出美国新的关注。

14. FEMA —— Federal Emergency Management Agency[(美国)紧急事务处管理局]

15. Hurricane Katrina —— "卡特里娜"飓风(该飓风发生于2005年8月29日,引发洪水成灾,共计造成883人死亡,100余万人无家可归,700亿至1300亿美元的经济损失)

16. the Bush Doctrine —— "布什主义"(以先发制人,政权变更,单边主义和追求霸权为主要特色,其思想基础是新保守主义)

17. "old" Europe —— "旧欧洲"(美国入侵伊拉克,德法坚决鲜明的反对立场被美国国防部长Rumsfeld讥讽为"旧欧洲",意指"不识时务"。反之,支持美国开战的英国、波兰、西班牙则被视作与时俱进,称为"新欧洲"。)

18. it had to be sold in conjunction with a dubiously established threat of WMDs. —— 这种观念必须与尚无根据就确立的大规模杀伤武器威胁论同时兜售。(①dubiously —— uncertainty; ②WMD —— *abbr.* weapons of mass destruction)

19. Wahhabi religious establishment —— 瓦哈比教派(a very conservative Islamic group that rejects innovation that occurred after the third century of Islam)

20. the al Qaeda top brass —— 基地组织领袖人物

21. bin Laden and his sidekick Ayman al-Zawahiri remained at large while organizational

clones of al Qaeda kept popping up around the globe. — 本·拉登和他的助手阿亚曼·扎瓦赫里依旧逍遥法外,而基地组织的各种复制版在全球范围内不断出现。[①pop up — to appear suddenly and unexpectedly; ②sidekick — sb who helps another person more important]

22. Some charged that America was succumbing to a dangerous idealism and forgetting its tradition of foreign policy realism. — 一些人指责美国正在屈从于一种危险的理想主义,而忘记美国外交政策现实主义的传统。(理想主义是美国威尔逊总统所提出的理论,主张加强民主、自由、贸易,通过贸易促进和平,在国际和平方面主张裁军、建立国际组织,这里具体指布什政府包括变更政权的大中东民主改造计划。现实主义强调国家之间的权力争夺是永不停止的,主张通过均势、联盟和军备来维持安全。)

23. Americans, however, saw ever widening rifts ... the full-speed-ahead gang in the vice president's office and the Pentagon. — 但是,美国人看到的却是政府内分歧的不断扩大,国务院和中央情报局的谨慎派在失去权势,而副总统办公室和国防部中的激进派权势却在飞速增长。(full-speed-ahead — with all your energy and enthusiasm)

24. As Iraq began to unravel ... the 9/11 commission. — 当伊拉克局势开始失控,向现在所出现的内战方向发展的时候,9·11事件调查委员会所公布的事实使美国人对政府的信任感进一步受到损害。[unravel into — to break up and develop into]

25. Richard Clarke — 美国白宫网络安全特别顾问

26. red and blue Americans were now also deeply and evenly divided over the incumbent's handling of the war on terrorism. — 支持共和党的美国人与支持民主党的美国人对现任总统在领导反恐战争问题上的分歧很大,人数各占一半。(red and blue Americans refer to Americans supporting the Republican party and Democratic party respectively)

27. "Big Bang" transformation of the Middle East — 对中东"大爆炸"式的改变(big bang — the great explosion that many scientists believe created the universe)

28. these postwar situations are serving as recruitment ads and training grounds for the swelling ranks of jihadists. — 这些战后的糟糕状况为伊斯兰教好战分子队伍壮大发挥了招募广告和培训基地的作用。

29. on a hiring binge — 大量招人(binge — an occasion when an activity is done in an extreme way)

30. case officer — 办案人员(亦可为案件官员,其职责是在国外招募间谍,还常用作"签证官"之意)

31. the American public is resigned to the inevitability of further attacks — 美国民众对美国未来定会再遭攻击抱着听天由命的态度(to resign oneself to sth — to make oneself accept sth that is unpleasant but cannot be changed)

32. resident fellow at the American Enterprise Institute — 美国企业研究所的专聘研究员(the American Enterprise Institute 全称为 the American Enterprise Institute for Public Policy,是美国最重要思想库之一,也是美国保守派重要研究机构)

Ⅳ. Language Features

《美国新闻与世界报道》介绍

辛迪加专栏作家大卫·劳伦斯(David Lawrence)于1933年创办了《美国新闻》(*US News*)刊物,1946年又创办了《世界报道》(*World Report*)刊物。1948年,劳伦斯将这两个刊物与《美国周刊》(*US Weekly*)三合为一,更名为《美国新闻与世界报道》(*US News & World Report*)。

在美国三大新闻周刊中,《美国新闻与世界报道》一直屈居第三,无法与其他两家杂志相抗衡。

1995年,为了顺应时代发展,该刊开设了电子版。电子版《美国新闻与世界报道》内容比纸质版丰富得多,网页超过10万。此外,电子版的信息不断更新。这些优势使得电子版的读者数量不断增加。据统计,该刊电子版每月读者数量为500万,是纸质版的3倍。

该刊报纸版从2008年7月改成双周刊,2009年2月又改为周刊。与此同时,该刊在版面、风格方面也有重大变化。《美国新闻与世界报道》的月刊报道具有专题单一、重点突出、深度加大的特色。例如:2009年9月期刊所有文章围绕大学教育专题。"编者按"(Editor's Note)谈的是消费者选择大学必须谨慎。"正反观点栏"(Two Tasks)的辩论题是:高考是否必要? 本期报道内容下分四个子题:(1)如何改进大学教育(How To Fix Higher Education);(2)大学面貌变化(Changing Face of College);(3)大学教育费用的支付(Paying For College);(4)大学排行榜(The Rankings)。每一子题包含一组文章,报道该子题各方面的情况。读者通过这一期文章的阅读可以获得美国高等教育专题较为完整、全面、清晰的画面。电子版的《美国新闻与世界报道》版面较为固定,每期都设有:国内外新闻版(Nation & World);观点版(Opinion);金融商务版(Money & Business);健康卫生版(Health)和教育版(Education)。有时根据形势发展,电子版还会增设其他版面。总的说来,改版后的纸质版《美国新闻与世界报道》的语言更为简明,阅读更加轻松,内容更强调服务性、实用性。

从2011年1月开始,《美国新闻与世界报道》停止发行纸质版,只发行电子版。其电子版仍然保留原先实用性、服务性的特色。

该刊在政治观点上支持共和党右翼;经济方面反对增税,反对增加联邦政府权力;军事方面主张加强美国军事实力。

《美国新闻与世界报道》特色品牌有:① 美国最佳大学(America's Best Colleges,自1985年每年一次延续至今,是美国引用最多的大学排行榜);② 美国最佳医院(America's Best Hospitals,1911年开始延续至今);③ 美国最佳中学(America's Best High Schools,2007年开始延续至今)。

《美国新闻与世界报道》的网址是www.usnews.com。

V. Analysis of the Content

1. The term "case officers" in the 13th paragraph refers to people handling _____.
   A. visas   B. social problems
   C. technical problems   D. security problems
2. The reason why record numbers of books on Muslims were sold in the U.S. is that many Americans _____.
   A. wanted to distinguish between true Islam and its corrupted form
   B. wanted to convert Muslims to Christianity
   C. wanted to convert themselves to Islam
   D. were eager to improve their relations with Muslims
3. The American majority's early response to the government's anti-terrorist measures was _____.
   A. support   B. opposition
   C. doubt   D. resignation
4. Which of the following is NOT on the list of the disclosures of the 9/11 commission?
   A. Ignoring many clear warnings.
   B. Poor communication between organizations.
   C. Unwillingness to take responsibility for institutional failures.
   D. Lack of knowledge about terrorist groups.
5. It can be inferred from the article that the American public's overall attitude toward future terrorist strikes is _____.
   A. disbelieving   B. optimistic
   C. escapist   D. fatalistic

VI. Questions on the Article

1. What was the consolation brought by 9/11?
2. How did George W. Bush respond to the terrorist strikes according to the author?
3. What was the American public's early response to the measures taken by the U.S. government against terrorists?
4. What did Americans think of the Patriot Act according to the opinion poll?
5. What did many Americans warn of when the Department of Homeland Security was established?
6. What did the poll show about the American public's opinion on the invasion of Iraq before the Iraq war?
7. What kind of situation has Iraq been led into? What impact have the disclosures of the 9/11 commission produced on Americans?
8. What did the 2004 presidential election show?
9. What does the term "big bang" in the article refer to? What is Americans' response to Bush's strategic plan for the Middle East?
10. What does the term "the new normal" mean? What does the author think of the impact

of "the new normal"?

Ⅶ. Topics for Discussion

1. Was the U. S. war on Iraq an anti-terrorist war?
2. Is the idea of changing regimes in the Middle East a good idea?

Lesson 9

The Real Truth about Money

Why we remain keen for cash[1] even though it often gives us more social anxiety than satisfaction
By Gregg Easterbrook

   If you made a graph of American life since the end of World War II, every line concerning money and the things that money can buy would soar upward, a statistical monument to materialism[2]. From 1960 to the late 1980s, for example, the country's GDP quintupled, the fastest growth in history up to that point. Filling one's belly and getting a paying job were difficult enough dreams after a war that left the nation in ashes[3]; nowadays, Japanese own more than one car per household, and spend almost $1,000 a year each on recreational travel. Hybrid cars[4], personal electronics[5] and other items that didn't even exist a half-century ago are today affordable. No matter how you chart the trends in earning and spending, everything is up, up, up. But if you made a chart of happiness in the same period, the lines would be as flat as the roof of a Lexus LS 430[6]. Even before the bubble burst[7] in the early 1990s, polls in Japan showed remarkably little change in well-being since the country began its economic resurgence[8].

   Japan isn't alone. South Korea went through its own economic miracle in the past few decades, yet surveys have shown that happiness has stagnated even as GDP soared. In polls taken by the U.S.'s National Opinion Research Centre[9] in the 1950s, about the one-third of Americans described themselves as "very happy." The centre has conducted essentially the same poll periodically since then, and the percentage remains almost identical today, even after per-capita GDP has more than doubled. The same trend holds true in Europe, too. In the U.K., GDP has surged from $34 billion to more than $2 trillion over the past 50 years, but the measure of domestic progress — a broad measure of life satisfaction — is still where it was in the mid-1970s. In Germany, the Allensbach polling agency[10] found that 57% of those surveyed were "content with their life as it is," while in 2001, that figure had crept up only to 59%. Money jangles in our wallets and purses as never before[11], but we are basically no happier for it. How can that be?

   Of course, we've all been told that our money can't buy happiness. Yet we don't act as though we listened.[12] Millions of us spend more time and energy pursuing the things money can buy than engaging in activities that create real fulfillment, like cultivating friendships, helping others and developing a spiritual sense.[13] We behave as though happiness is one wave of a credit card away.[14]

   There is ample evidence that being poor causes unhappiness. Studies by Ruut Veenhoven, a professor of happiness studies at Erasmus University in Rotterdam[15], show that those living in poor countries — where the average income is less than about $10,000 a year — are unhappy. In countries where the average annual income exceeds $10,000 or so, Veenhoven found that money and happiness decouple and cease to have much to do with each other. This may be somewhat less true in places where wealth is relatively recent but on the whole, it seems the platitudes about the best things in life being free are probably true, even in supposedly materialistic Asia.

Over the past two decades, in fact, an increasing body of social-science and psychological research has shown that there is no significant relationship between how much money a person earns and whether he or she feels good about life. A *TIME* poll carried out in the U.S. in December found that happiness tended to increase as income rose to $50,000 a year. After that, more income did not have a dramatic effect.[16] Edward Diener, a psychologist at the University of Illinois, interviewed members of the *Forbes* 400,[17] the richest Americans. He found the Forbes 400 group was only a tiny bit happier than the public as a whole. "We pursued economic development and we got it," says Dylan Evans in Bristol and author of the book *Emotion: The Science of Sentiment*. "But there is much more to happiness than financial security."

Money doesn't guarantee happiness, in part because of a phenomenon that sociologists call reference anxiety. According to that thinking, most people judge their possessions in comparison with others'. Our soaring reference anxiety is a product of the widening gap in income distribution.[18] In other words, the rich are getting richer faster, and the rest are none too happy about it. America is a textbook case.[19] The majority of its citizens used to live in small towns or urban areas, where conditions for most people were approximately the same — hence low reference anxiety. Especially since those who were living higher on the hog did so behind high fences, closed doors and damask curtains.[20]

But in the past few decades, new economic forces have changed all that. Rapid growth in income for the top 5% of households has created a substantial moneyed elite[21] that lived notably better than the middle class, amplifying the latter's reference anxiety. That wealthier minority is occupying ever larger homes and spending more on each change of clothes than others spend on a month's rent. It all feeds middle-class anxiety, even when the middle is doing O.K. In nations with higher levels of income equality, like the Scandinavian countries, well-being tends to be higher than in areas with unequal wealth distribution, such as the U.S. or Hong Kong. Meanwhile, television, lifestyle magazines and the Web make it easier to know how the very well-off live. (Never mind whether they're happy.) Want to glimpse the glamorous lives of Hollywood divas or Canto-pop superstars[22]? Just open a glossy gossip rag.[23]

Paradoxically, it is the very increase in money — which creates the wealth so visible in today's society — that triggers dissatisfaction. As material expectations keep rising, more money may engender only more desires. "What people want in terms of material things and life experiences has increased almost exactly in lockstep with the postwar earnings curve,[24]" Diener notes. As men and women move up the economic ladder, most of them almost immediately stop feeling grateful for their elevated circumstances and focus on what they still don't have. Suppose you lived in a two-bedroom house for years and dreamed of three bedrooms. You finally get that three-bedroom house. Will it bring you happiness? Not necessarily. Three bedrooms will become your new norm, and you'll begin to long for a four-bedroom abode.

Polls show that Americans, whatever their income level, feel that they need more to live well. Even those making large sums said still larger sums were required. But Robert MacCulloch, a professor of economics at the London Business School, has found that poor people in the U.S. are less unhappy about their lot than their European counterparts, despite the fact that Europeans enjoy far greater welfare provisions than Americans and therefore are more insulated against reference anxiety. The difference is that "poor Americans think that one day they are going to get rich," he says. "They think that if they work hard, they will be the next Bill Gates." MacCulloch contends that, in contrast, poor Europeans find the barriers to wealth much harder to surmount: "They feel that they will never get rich, that they're stuck at the bottom.[25]" Asians in freewheeling economic environments may have attitudes that are similar to Americans', says MacCulloch. So poor Hong Kongers see wealthy tycoons less as objects of envy than models to admire. They think they can become the next Li Ka-shing[26].

The power of positive thinking is important because if we believe our lot is improving, happiness tends to follow. Carol Graham, an economist at the Brookings Institution in Washington, D. C.[27], found that people's expectations about the future may have more influence on their sense of well-being than their current state does. People living modestly but anticipating better days to come, Graham thinks, are likely to be happier than people living well but not looking forward to improvements in their living standards. Consider two people: one earns $50,000 a year and foresees a 10% raise, and the other makes $150,000 but does not expect any salary increase. The second person is much better off in financial terms, but the first is more likely to feel good about life.

And guess what? Income growth has almost come to a halt for the middle class in many wealthy countries. In real terms, although median household income in the U.S. is higher than ever, it has increased only about 15% since 1984. Since the bubble burst in Japan, middle-class incomes have stagnated. Most people in such countries have never had it better but do not expect any improvement in the near future, and so they're likely to accentuate the negative.

Living standards, education levels and other basic measures of U.S. social well-being have improved so much so quickly in the postwar era that further big leaps seem improbable in developed countries. But because we are all conditioned to think there's something wrong if we don't make some money each year, high standards of living may, paradoxically, have become an impediment to happiness.[28] Fixated on always getting more, citizens of rich countries fail to appreciate how much they have. Of course, in the grand scheme it's better that there are large numbers of us who are materially comfortable, if a bit whiny about it, than large numbers who are destitute.

Poverty remains a stark reality amid affluence, yet even among the very poor, reference anxiety can play a decisive role. A study of homeless people in Calcutta and Fresno, California, found that the Indian street people were happier than their counterparts in America. Hetan Shah, program director at British think tank the New Economics Foundation[29], says that's because Americans have a higher degree of reference anxiety as they compare themselves with people who are more affluent. In India, the gap between rich and poor is narrower. "Sometimes we think we will be putting developing countries at a disadvantage if we compare them with us," Shah says. "But, in fact, it's the other way around[30]: we learn the shortcomings of our own culture."

One of these shortcomings may be that we chase money at the expense of meaning[31]. Too many in the developed world have made materialism and the cycle of work and spend their principal goals.[32] Then they wonder why they don't feel happy.

With reporting by Helen Gibson and Kate Noble/London, Hanna Kite and Bryan Walsh/Hong Kong and Ursula Sautter/Bonn

From *Time*, February 28, 2005

Ⅰ. New Words

abode	[ə'bəud]	n.	*formal* the place where sb lives
accentuate	[æk'sentjueit]	v.	to emphasize sth
decouple	[di'kʌpl]	v.	*formal* to end the connection between two things
destitute	['destitju:t]	adj.	having no money, no food, and nowhere to live
engender	[in'dʒendə]	v.	*formal* to make a feeling or situation exist
fixated	['fikseitid]	v.	~ **on** always thinking about
freewheeling	['fri:'hwi:liŋ]	adj.	*informal* 自由放纵的
impediment	[im'pedimənt]	n.	妨碍,障碍
insulate	['insjuleit]	v.	(from) 使绝缘,隔离(以免受影响)
jangle	['dʒæŋgl]	v.	(使)发出刺耳声
lockstep	['lɔkstep]	n.	紧密步伐
norm	[nɔ:m]	n.	标准
provision	[prə'viʒən]	n.	(尤指政府提供的)钱或物资
quintuple	['kwintju(:)pl]	v.	to become five times bigger
stagnate	['stægneit]	v.	to stop developing or making progress
stark	[stɑ:k]	adj.	unpleasantly clear; harsh
surmount	[sə:'maunt]	v.	to overcome
whiny	['waini]	adj.	好发牢骚的

Ⅱ. Background Information

金钱与幸福

在物质主义为主导的(materialism-dominated)西方社会,金钱往往与成功和权力紧密联系在一起。金钱常被视作成功的主要标准。字典给"成功"通常所下的定义是:获得财富达到目标。金钱与幸福感之间究竟存在什么关系一直是社会学者所关注的课题。

美国学者 Lewis Yoblonsky 在《钱的情感意义》(*The Emotional Meaning of Money*)书中提出的观点是：对于自己经济状况满足与否，不在于实际所得金钱多少，而在于自己对钱的感觉。他把美国社会的金钱观分为以下五种。

1. 知足常乐型：对自己现在所拥有的金钱、权力和成就感到满意者，人数占25%。
2. 量力而为型：对自己所定的金钱、权力和成功的目标合理可行，人数占24%。
3. 冷静打拼型：尽力争取可能得到的财富、权力和成就，但不会受金钱折磨，人数占20%。
4. 激昂奋斗型：所定目标是出人头地、有钱有势，不达目的情绪便备受煎熬，人数占14%。
5. 永不满足型：所追求的和所得到的存在鸿沟，感到精神痛苦。

Yoblonsky 把前三种类型通称为"满足型"，后两种为"不满足型"。他的调查发现满足与不满足的人比例在各个收入阶层相差不大。这说明，金钱观在很大程度上影响了人的满足感。调查还发现，同类人(peer group)之间的攀比是导致不满足的主要因素。这是因为人的期望层次通常受限于所属群体，这个群体是衡量成败的主要标准。

20世纪90年代中期，《美国新闻与世界报道》杂志曾刊登了一篇幸福感的研究报告，提供了一个幸福指数表(The Happiness Index)。表中列入的相关因素和其质商(Quality Quotient)如下：精神生活(spiritual life：8.25)；家庭生活(family life：8.18)；居住房子(their homes：8.12)；情感生活(romantic life：7.71)；身体状况(their health：7.68)；工作职业(their jobs：6.82)；闲暇时间(leisure time：6.14)；经济状况(financial situation：5.98)。

2003年英国《新科学家》刊登了一篇幸福感调查报告。作者共列入10个幸福感相关的报告。这些因素重要性排列如下：基因区别(genetic variation)；婚姻(marriage)；交友(making and valuing friends)；降低期望(low aspirations)；乐于助人(do someone a good turn)；宗教信仰(religious belief)；容貌(looks)；金钱(money)；年龄(age)和智力(intelligence)。作者认为有的人生性乐观，有的生性悲观。这是决定幸福感的首要因素。其次便是结婚，结婚者比不结婚者幸福感强。乐于交友和降低期望是影响幸福感较为重要因素，最后四个因素较为次要。从这份研究报告可以看出金钱对幸福的影响比较有限。

III. Notes to the Text

1. keen for cash — very eager to have cash
2. a statistical monument to materialism —（monument to sth — a thing that remains as a good witness）统计图线对物质主义的见证
3. Filling one's belly and getting a paying job were difficult enough dreams after a war that left the nation in ashes. — 在一个被战争夷为废墟的国家，填饱肚皮、找份挣钱的工作是非常难以实现的梦想。
4. Hybrid cars — 混合动力车
5. personal electronics — 个人电子器件
6. Lexus LS 430 — 雷克萨斯车系第三代豪华汽车，其车顶形态扁平
7. the bubble burst — 好景破灭（the bubble bursts — the good situation suddenly ends）
8. economic resurgence — 经济复苏
9. the U.S.'s National Opinion Research Centre — 美国国民舆论研究中心
10. the Allensbach polling agency — 德国阿兰斯巴赫民意调查所

11. Money jangles in our wallets and purses as never before — 我们腰包里的钱比任何时候都多。
12. Yet we don't act as though we listened. — 然而我们所作所为却不像我们听信了这些话。
13. Millions of us spend more time ... helping others and developing a spiritual sense. — 我们中的许许多多人将更多时间和精力用于追求金钱所能购买的东西,而不是从事那些能够获得真正满足感的事情,例如培养友情,帮助他人以及陶冶情操。
14. We behave as though happiness is one wave of a credit card away. — 我们表现得好像只要用信用卡一阵狂热购物便可获得幸福。(wave — a sudden increase of a particular activity)
15. Erasmus University in Rotterdam — (荷兰)鹿特丹伊拉斯姆斯大学(该校是荷兰最著名的综合性大学,以 15 世纪荷兰著名人文主义学者的名字命名)
16. A *TIME* poll carried out in the U.S. ... more income did not have a dramatic effect. — 《时代》周刊 12 月份在美国所做的民意测验发现年收入在 5 万美元之内,幸福感往往随工资上升而增加。但在这个数额以上,收入增多没有很大的影响。(dramatic — impressive)
17. *Forbes* 400 — 《福布斯》400 富豪榜(《福布斯》杂志所发布的全美 400 富豪榜)
18. Our soaring reference anxiety is a product of the widening gap in income distribution. — 我们剧增的攀比心理是收入差距增大而造成的结果。
19. America is a textbook case. — 美国是个典型范例(textbook case — typical example)
20. Especially since those who were living higher on the hog did so behind high fences, closed doors and damask curtains. — 特别是因为那些阔佬住在高墙院内,大门紧闭,房间整天拉上花缎窗帘,其豪华生活外人不知。(high on the hog — *informal* in a lavish manner, luxuriously)
21. moneyed elite — 富裕的上层人士(monied — rich)
22. Hollywood divas or Canto-pop superstars — 好莱坞的大牌女歌星或是粤语流行音乐超级明星(①diva — a famous woman singer; ②canto-pop — *SEAsian E* a type of popular music that combines Cantonese words and western pop music)
23. Just open a glossy gossip rag. — 只要翻开一本光纸印刷的名人隐私的报刊看看就知道了。(rag — *informal* a newspaper of low quality)
24. What people want in terms of material things and life experiences has increased almost exactly in lockstep with the postwar earnings curve. — 人们在物质享受和生活经历方面欲望的增长几乎完全与显示战后收入的曲线相一致。(in lockstep with — in exactly the same way as)
25. ... they're stuck at the bottom. — 他们被困在社会的底层(stuck — in an unpleasant situation that you cannot escape from)
26. Li Ka-shing — 李嘉诚(亚洲最富有的企业家)
27. the Brookings Institution in Washington, D.C. — 华盛顿的布鲁金斯学会(该学会是非赢利的政治学与经济学研究机构,带有自由主义色彩)
28. ... high standards of living may, paradoxically, have become an impediment to

happiness. — 似乎矛盾的是,更高的生活水平反而有可能成为获得幸福感的障碍。
29. the New Economics Foundation — 新经济基金会
30. it's the other way around — It's the opposite situation.
31. we chase money at the expense of meaning — 我们追求金钱但忽视了生活的意义。(at the expense of sth — with loss or damage to sth)
32. Too many in the developed world have made materialism and the cycle of work and spend their principal goals. — 发达国家太多的人把物质享受、工作挣钱、花钱购物当作生活的主要目标。

Ⅳ. Language Features

报刊翻译常见错误

阅读报刊译文时常常发现误译情况,造成误译的因素主要有以下四点:

一、语法概念不清

例:At the same time that commercial loans are becoming harder to get, the developing nations' own funding has been devastated by the slump in commodity prices.

原译:与此同时,商业信贷越来越难以得到了,发展中国家本身的资金由于商品价格下跌而受重创。

改译:商业信贷越来越难以得到,与此同时……

二、词义理解偏差

例:After a 10-year bender of gaudy dreams and Godless consumerism, Americans are starting to trade down.

原译:经过10年绚丽的梦和不信神的消费的大转弯,美国人开始减少消费。

改译:经过10年绚丽的梦和罪恶的高消费的一场狂热,美国人开始减少消费。

本句中bender是俚语,表示"狂热"。外刊中俚语常常出现,应引起翻译者的注意。

例:All told, the US military is spending roughly $6 billion each year on its virtual side, embracing the view, as author Tom Chatfield put it, that "Games are the 21 century's most serious business."

原译:美国军方每年大约在虚拟项目上花费60亿美元。按照作家汤姆·菲尔德的说法啊,军方认为"游戏是21世纪最危险的勾当"。

文章报道电子游戏软件的诸多军用价值。为此,美国国防部高度重视,不仅投入大量资金研发,而且鼓励官兵大量运用这类软件。译者未能把握全局造成"误译"。

改译:电子游戏是21世纪最正经的事。

三、有关知识缺乏

例:The radio broadcast patriotic messages and coded orders for military personnel.

原译:电台广播了爱国发言和给军事人员的命令。

改译:电台播送激发爱国情绪的讲话和给军事人员的加密的命令。

四、语言知识缺乏

例1:The Libyan strongman flashed hot and cold, warning that the waters off Tripoli would become "a red gulf of blood" if the Nimitz stayed too close—yet protesting that he had no intention of attacking his neighbor...

原译：利比亚铁腕人物<u>大为恼怒</u>。他警告：假如"尼米兹号"舰驶得太近，那么，的黎波里的近海流域将成为"血腥的海湾"——然而，他又抗议说，他没有袭击邻国的意图……

改译：这个利比亚铁腕人物<u>反复无常</u>……然而，他又表白……

这里，作者活用习语 blow hot and cold。习语活用在美英报刊中较为常见。

例 2：The Chinese government is expected to support the opening of roughly 35,000 more screens over the next five years, up from the current 5,000 in the country.

原译：在今后 5 年中，中国政府预计将支持另外大约 3.5 万块屏幕投入使用。中国政府目前拥有 5,000 块屏幕。

改译：预计中国政府在今后 5 年中将支持另外大约 3.5 万个影院的营运。目前中国只有 5,000 个影院。

本句作者使用提喻修辞手法（synecdoche），screen 指的是"movie theater"。

第一、二类错误是英语基本功问题，第三、四类错误是知识结构问题。上述例子说明：要想提高外刊理解和翻译水平，就得做到语法概念清晰，词义理解准确，文化知识广博，语言知识丰富。

Ⅴ. Analysis of the Content

1. The phrase "in real terms" in Paragraph 11 means _____.
   A. in terms of material things   B. as a matter of fact
   C. in terms of real pay   D. after taking account of price rises
2. More and more researches in the past two decades show that the relationship between money and happiness _____.
   A. does not exist   B. is very close
   C. is not great   D. is very significant
3. It can be inferred from Paragraphs 6 and 7 that high reference anxiety results from _____.
   A. fast growth of income   B. the widening gap in income
   C. sharp price increase   D. high level of income equality
4. Which of the following countries has higher levels of income equality?
   A. The U.S.   B. Sweden.
   C. South Korea.   D. Japan.
5. Which of the following statements is False about Americans?
   A. Poor Americans are less happy than poor Europeans.
   B. Americans of all income levels feel that they need more to live well.
   C. The moneyed elite lives notably better, which feeds the middle class anxiety.
   D. About one third of Americans feel very happy.

Ⅵ. Questions on the Article

1. How fast did America's GDP increase from 1960 to the late 1980s?
2. How did the living conditions of Japanese improve from the end of WWII to now? Has the improvement of living conditions increased their sense of well-being?
3. What did the polls periodically taken by the US's National Opinion Research Center show?
4. What do Professor Veenhoven's studies find about happiness?
5. What did Edward Diener find about the *Forbes* 400 group?
6. Tell what you know about the term "reference anxiety".
7. Why is the middle class Americans' reference anxiety greatly increased in the US even when they are doing OK?
8. What triggers dissatisfaction in today's society?
9. Who feel less unhappy, poor Americans or poor Europeans? Why?
10. Why are high standards of living an impediment to happiness for citizens of rich countries?

Ⅶ. Topics for Discussion

1. Can money buy happiness?
2. Is reference anxiety the most important factor in unhappiness?

Lesson 10

The State of Our Unions[1]

Divorce, cohabitation and adultery have hurt institution of marriage
By Rick Hampson

President Bush wants a constitutional amendment to preserve marriage. But what, exactly, would it preserve? Unlike Mom, the flag and apple pie[2], there's something about marriage that Americans want to attack and to protect, to restrict and to expand, to exalt and to ridicule.

What the president called civilization's "most fundamental institution" is, in America, a rather peculiar one.

It's an institution that 59% of us currently inhabit and that more than 9 in 10 of us eventually embrace, at least once and for a little while. It correlates with health, wealth and happiness. It's the acknowledged gold standard for raising children. It has been extolled in cultural touchstones from *Father Knows Best to Sex and the City*.[3]

But it's also an institution that over the past four decades has been increasingly severed by divorce and mocked by adultery. It has been ignored by couples who live together and have children out of wedlock. And it has been postponed by those who marry later in life.

The nation that introduced the concepts of the seven-year itch, the starter marriage and *Who Wants to Marry a Millionaire*, is also one that believes love and marriage go together like a horse and carriage.[4] Feelings about marriage are complex, and only an amendment to the national psyche would change that.

Marriage is such a great idea that Americans seem to love it too much — the idea, that is. The reality of marriage — crumbs in the bed, toilet seat up (or down), meatloaf again — suffers in comparison. And, since the introduction of no-fault divorce[5] in California in 1969, it has gotten easier and easier across the nation to leave a real marriage behind and move on in search of the ideal one.

Everyone is an expert on marriage. Here's Homer, 29 centuries ago: "There is nothing more admirable than two people who see eye-to-eye keeping house as man and wife, confounding their enemies and delighting their friends.[6]"

And here's twice-divorced Donald Trump[7], two years ago: "Marriage is a great institution if you get it right."

A lot happened between the ages of these sages. Marriage turned into a contract. Television, in its first 30 years, was fixated on the perfect marriage as the basis for the perfect family. But anyone who compared their marriage to the Seavers found it wanting.[8]

A "sacred obligation"

What the Supreme Court in the 19th century referred to as a "sacred obligation" had by 1965 become merely "an association of two individuals."[9] Then came the sexual revolution[10] and women's liberation.

At the moment, the institution is beset by these maladies:

Divorce. As many as 50% of new marriages end in divorce. The divorce rate leveled off in 1990s. There's no question divorce has become more common: A Census study showed that 90% of women who married between 1945 and 1949 reached their 10th anniversary, compared to 73% of those who married between 1980 and 1984.

Peggy Vaughan, the author of the *The Monogamy Myth*[11] says marriage's meaning "is getting diluted and polluted. We have serial monogamy as multiple marriages become the norm." She says that the expectation of a long-term marriage is fading and that "somebody has to be willing to say the emperor is not wearing any clothes.[12]" But maybe not at a $25,000 wedding for a couple of twentysomethings, which may turn out to be a "starter marriage" that ends before the couple has children and before they even turn 30.

Cohabitation. At least half of all newlyweds have lived together first, researchers say. And David Popenoe, a Rutgers University sociologist, estimates that two-thirds of people who marry have lived with somebody else first.

Live-in unions are more fragile than marital unions[13], and many live-ins have children. About 41% of opposite-sex couples[14] living together have children younger than 18 at home. But sociologists Pamela Smock and Wendy Manning have found that children born to couples who live together have about twice the risk of seeing their parents split than those with married biological parents.

Children out of wedlock. About a third of children are born out of wedlock, and roughly the same percentage live with only one parent.

Later marriages. President Bush married at age 31 — past the median age of 27. John Wall, a professor of ethics and religion at Rutgers University-Camden, says the children of baby boomers, themselves often scarred by divorce, now are reluctant to try marriage themselves.

Adultery. Although there are no good statistics on the subject, Vaughan estimates that 60% of both husbands and wives have had an affair during either their current marriage or a previous one. Others (**Other**) trend-trackers say the percentages are much smaller.

"A lot of people in the '60s and '70s thought they could escape the gravitational pull of marriage," says Robert Thompson, who studies and teaches pop culture at Syracuse University[15]. "But it proved to be a lot stronger than they thought. The society had too much invested in it."

Too many old wedding photos, too many bridal gowns in the attic, too many stories about the time "when your father and I ..." Americans may be dissatisfied with marriage, but we don't know anything else. Marriage fills a certain need, and there's nothing to take its place.

"The alternatives — single parenting and cohabitation — are available to people, but they are making a bargain that requires less of them and gives them less in return," says Linda Waite, a University of Chicago sociologist and co-author of *The Case for Marriage*[16].

David Blankenhorn, founder of the Institute for American Values[17], a think tank on the family, calls marriage "our society's most pro-child institution... If you want kids to do well, then you want marriage to do well."

Marriage is, by many measures, doing just fine.

According to the most recent figures, 65% of men and 71% of women marry by age 30. By age 60, those figures rise to 97% for men and 95% for women.

"The institution of marriage itself strikes men as being in no trouble at all," says Robert Lang, a demographer at Virginia Tech[18]. "How many things do 95% of people do?... They should have a defense of voting act." (The "Defense of Marriage Act,"[19] which defines marriage as a union between a man and a woman, has been passed by Congress and 38 states.)

Lang says he suspects "a large share of the people not married in a lifetime are gay, or they're Ralph Nader[20]."

Similarly, sales and production of homes for single people are down. The housing market is preoccupied with the desire of married couples and families for large houses, not putting up apartments for recent divorces.

Speaking of which: Lang says the divorce rate is artificially inflated by people with multiple divorces.[21] The actress and serial bride Zsa Zsa Gabor, he says, could have gone into a town and "lifted the divorce rate to 50% on her own."

Strengthening the institution

Many of those who divorce more than once also try again, and thus spend much of their life, for better or worse, married.

In recent years there have been many attempts to strengthen marriage. Florida requires marriage education courses in high school. Louisiana, Arkansas and Arizona have approved "covenant marriages[22]" in which couples voluntarily limit their ability to divorce. Arizona provides state funds to help couples attend privately run marriage-skills workshops. Oklahoma has used welfare money to reduce the divorce rate.

There is a National Marriage Project at Rutgers[23] that studies and promotes marriage, a national, non-partisan Marriage Movement and all sorts of courses in marriage, from Marriage 101 at Northwestern University[24] to "Couple Communication" in suburban Maryland[25].

What stumps some people is why, if marriage is such a bedrock of traditional values, the franchise should not be expanded to gay men and lesbians.[26]

"Because it's morally wrong," says Terry Calhoun, 47, a Roman Catholic who lives in Stockton, III. with his second wife. "Marriage has slipped a lot," he says, "and reserving it for straight people[27] would strengthen it."

This makes no sense to John Plessis, 69, of Scottsdale, Ariz. He's a retired steamship company executive who says he has lived with several women over the years but never married. "Gays are people, too," he says. "I don't see what difference it makes if they're allowed to get married."

Cheryl Jacques, president of the Human Right Campaign, a gay civil rights organization, says same-sex marriages taking place in San Francisco and ordered by the court in Massachusetts starting in May will reassure marriage's protectors. When gays and lesbians marry, she says, "for the vast majority of Americans, absolutely nothing bad happens. ... gay or lesbian family is made stronger, safer and more secure."

Lang, the Virginia Tech demographer, notes that "there was a time when you couldn't marry between races. It was always to protect marriage. Isn't that what this is going to be 10—20 years from now? Culture absorbs redefinition of marriage.[28]"

Contributing: Karen S. Peterson, Haya El Nasser and Paul Overberg

From *USA Today*, February 26, 2004

I. New Words

adultery	[ə'dʌltəri]	n.	通奸
bedrock	[ˌbed'rɔk]	n.	坚岩；坚实的基础
covenant	['kʌvənənt]	n.	a formal agreement
crumb	[krʌm]	n.	碎屑
demographer	[diː'mɔɡrəfə]	n.	人口学家
exalt	[iɡ'zɔːlt]	v.	to praise sb/sth very much
extol	[iks'təul]	v.	to praise sth highly
fixated	[fik'seitid]	adj.	~ **on sth** always thinking and talking about one particular thing
gravitation	[ˌɡrævi'teiʃən]	n.	引力
malady	['mælədi]	n.	疾病，不健康状态
meatloaf	['miːt'ləuf]	n.	（用肉糜做成的）肉糕
monogamy	['mɔnəɡəmi]	n.	一夫一妻制
newlywed	['njuliwed]	n.	新近结婚的人
psyche	['saiki]	n.	心灵，精神
pull	[pul]	n.	吸引力
sever	['sevə]	v.	to completely end a relationship with sb
twentysomething	['twenti'sʌmθiŋ]	n.	二十好几的人
trend-track	['trend'træk]	v.	跟踪趋势
wedlock	['wedlɔk]	n.	婚姻 **born out of wedlock** 私生的

II. Background Information

婚姻观念

上世纪40年代，美国社会学教科书上写明："离婚是公认的个人生活失败。"60年代初之前，美国家庭结构比较固定，离婚率低于10%。

然而，60年代中期开始，美国离婚率明显上升，到1979年已增长到23%，自此以后一直居高不下。目前，100对婚姻中会有一半以离婚告终。

造成离婚率增长的因素除妇女就业率上升，经济依赖丈夫情况大大减少之外，主要是美国人的婚姻观念的改变。原先，大多数美国人认为离婚是件不光彩的事，即使夫妻感情不和，为了孩子的利益，也不应该离婚。然而到了60年代，美国出现了反正统文化运动（counter-culture movement）和性解放运动（sexual liberation movement），传统的婚姻观念和性观念受到了巨大冲击。追求理想的婚姻和个人欢乐成为主流,越来越多的人认为"父母本人快乐,才能使孩子真正快乐。"许多人对于个人、夫妇、孩子三方利益的处理原则是:个人利益首位,夫妇利益次位,孩子利益末位(self-interest first, spousal interest second and kids' interest last)。有的社会学者认为婚姻的关键是使男女双方获得各自最大的满足,提出了所谓"开放式婚姻"(open marriage)的理念。大众媒介对于婚姻观念的变化起了推波助澜的作用,把离婚颂扬为个人的新生和解放。价值观的改变也引起了相关法律的更改。加州率先通过"无过失婚姻法",规定夫妻分开半年以上,声明彼此感情不和、关系破裂,便可离婚。因此,离婚变成了一件比较容易的事。

然而,离婚率的上升并非意味着美国人否定了婚姻的价值。据统计,离婚的美国人中有80%会再次结婚,其中又会有一半多再次离婚。二婚者中还会有一半第三次结婚。社会学者称这类周而复始婚姻为"阶段婚姻"(serial marriage),或"连续性婚姻"(sequential marriage)。

离婚再婚率的上升导致了继亲家庭(step family)、双核家庭(binuclear family)和混合家庭(blended family)数量的增加。

上世纪60年代以来,美国家庭结构呈现了多元化现象。已婚有孩家庭(married couples with own children)数量,2000年占总数比例为24.1%;已婚无孩家庭(married couples without children)数量,2000年所占比例为28.7%。此外还有大量单亲家庭(single-parent family),1993年,美国有1,090万个这类家庭,其中单身母亲家庭(female-headed family)占86%,单身父亲家庭(male-headed family)仅占14%。还有一些同性婚姻(same sex marriage)所建立的同性恋者家庭(gay family)。许多美国人未婚同居(cohabitation),据统计,大约2/3人结婚之前有此经历,不少人称此经历为"试婚"(trial marriage)。

这些年来,美国晚婚现象比较明显,据统计,1970年女性第一次结婚者平均年龄为20.8岁,男性为23.2岁。2003年这两个数字分别上升到25.3岁和27.1岁。

Ⅲ. Notes to the Text

1. The State of our Unions — 我们的婚姻状况
2. Unlike Mom, the flag and apple pie — These refer to the issues least likely to cause controversy. (①the flag — symbol of love for the motherland; ②apple pie — considered by Americans to be sth that is typically American)
3. It has been extolled in cultural touchstones from *Father Knows Best* to *Sex and the City*. — 它在《父亲是权威》和《欲望都市》这些典型(婚姻)文化影视剧中被高度颂扬。(①*Sex and the City*——《欲望都市》,电视连续爱情喜剧,曾获艾美最佳电视喜剧奖。该剧内容是:4个成功的女人,时髦漂亮,虽不再年轻但自信,魅力四射。她们面临的共同问题是在充满欲望和诱惑的都市里寻找真正的爱情和归属。②*Father Knows Best* — a popular family comedy portraying an idealized version of the middle-class American family)
4. The nation that introduced the concepts ... like a horse and carriage. — 美国人首创"七年之痒""初婚"和"谁想嫁给百万富翁"的婚姻观念,同时他们也深信婚姻离不了爱情就像马车少不了马一般。[①seven-year itch — *informal* a feeling of dissatisfaction with one's marriage after about seven years; ②starter marriage — a first marriage that lasts

a short time and that ends in a clean (i. e. no kids, no property, no acrimony) divorce; ③*Who Wants to Marry a Millionaire?* — 2002 年初推出的电视娱乐节目,42 岁的富豪里克•洛克威尔征婚之后收到 1,000 多名女性的录像带,从中挑出 5 名预选对象,最后选中了 1 名急诊室护士,但这桩婚姻只持续两个星期。该节目收视率很高,观众高达 2,200 万。]

5. no-fault divorce — (基于婚姻关系已经破裂事实的)无过失离婚

6. Here's Homer 29 centuries ago: "There is nothing more admirable... delighting their friends." — 荷马 29 世纪之前就说过:"最值得赞美的是心心相印、朝夕相处、仇敌见之羞愧、朋友为之高兴的夫妻二人。"(①Homer   a Greek poet who lived around 800 to 700 years B. C. had great poet with great influence on European literature;②confound — to make uneasy and ashamed)

7. Donald Trump — 唐纳德•特朗普(纽约地产大亨)

8. But anyone who compared their marriage to the Seavers found it wanting. — 但是任何人如果把自己的婚姻与希瓦夫妇相比就会觉得还很不理想。[Seavers — 电视连续剧《成长的烦恼》(*Growing in Pains*)中的一对夫妻。]

9. What the Supreme Court in the 19th Century referred to as a "sacred obligation" had by 1965 become merely "an association of two individuals." — 19 世纪最高法院所称之为的"神圣结合"到 1965 年已仅仅是"两个个体的组合"。

10. sexual revolution — (反对传统的性约束和性禁忌,尤指反对一夫一妻制的)性革命

11. *The Monogamy Myth* —《一夫一妻制的神话》(作者 Peggy Vaughan 在书中指出美国有 55%—65% 的丈夫,45%—55% 的妻子在 40 岁之前有婚外情。)

12. somebody has to be willing to say the emperor is not wearing any clothes. — 总得要有人愿意说出皇帝没穿衣服的事实。(Note the author's use of allusion to a fairy tale. "The emperor has no clothes on!" is often used to describe a situation in which people are afraid to criticize sth because everyone else seems to think it is good or important.)

13. Live-in unions are more fragile than marital unions. — 同居关系比婚姻关系更为脆弱。

14. opposite-sex couples — 异性伴侣(opposite-sex couple 相对于 same-sex couple)

15. Syracuse University — 锡拉丘兹大学(一所著名私立大学,由于该大学坐落的地方每年平均降雪量为 2.89 米,故又得名"雪城大学")

16. *The Case for Marriage* —《婚姻存在的理由》(case for — a set of facts or arguments that support a view)

17. the Institute for American Values — 美国价值观研究所

18 Virginia Tech — 弗吉尼亚理工学院

19. The Defense of Marriage Act — 婚姻保护法(该法于 1996 年由联邦政府颁布,它不仅拒绝同性恋婚姻获取与婚姻相关的联邦福利,而且授权各州拒绝承认同性恋婚姻)

20. Ralph Nader — 拉尔夫•纳德(1934 —   , an American political activist of Lebanese origin, as well as an author, lecturer and attorney; an Independent candidate for President of the US in 2008, 2004, 2000, 1996)

21. Speaking of which: Lang says the divorce rate is artificially inflated by people with multiple divorces. — 谈到这点,Lang 说美国离婚率被多次离婚者不真实地抬高了。(指

一些多次离婚者由于多次出现在离婚统计表中,使所统计的美国人离婚率提高。后一句中女演员 Zsa Zsa Gabor 是典型一例,到 1986 年她已经结婚 8 次。)

22. covenant marriage — 契约婚姻(美国路易斯安那州首先提出,要求男女双方婚前进行法律商议,签订契约,对离婚作以苛刻的限制)

23. Rutgers — 罗格斯大学(创建于 1766,坐落在新泽西州)

24. Marriage 101 at Northwestern University — 西北大学婚姻基础课程(Marriage 101 — a course on marriage for freshmen. College courses in America are numbered starting with the most basic ones numbered 101. Sophomore courses begin with 2, juniors with 3 and seniors with 4.)

25. "Couple Communication" in Suburban Maryland — 南马里兰州"夫妻交流"课

26. What stumps some people is why ... gay men and lesbians. — 使一些人难以理解的是,既然婚姻是传统价值观的坚实基础,那为什么婚姻范畴不能扩大,容许男女同性恋者结婚。(① franchise — permission by a government; ② gay men — homosexual men; ③ lesbian — a female homosexual)

27. straight people — 异性恋者

28. Culture absorbs redefinition of marriage. — 社会会采纳婚姻的新的定义。

Ⅳ. Language Features

《今日美国》报简介

《今日美国》报创刊于 1982 年 9 月 15 日,它是美国唯一的全国综合性日报。

当甘尼特报业集团(The Gannett Group)总裁纽哈思(Al Neuharth)宣布创办这份报纸的决定时,许多办报人都认为这是一个十分错误的决定。他们的担忧是很有道理的。从历史情况来看,美国只适宜经办地方性报纸,全国性报纸经济上一般都是亏本。

然而,《今日美国》报创办之后获得成功,销售长期名列全国之首。但近些年销量下滑,2012 年跌至 180 万,落后于《华尔街日报》,屈居第二。

《今日美国》报(国际版)每期共有 16—24 页(周一为 16 页,周二—周五均为 24 页),下分两大版块:A 版和 B 版,篇幅各占一半。A 版是新闻版,主要栏目有全国新闻(Nation);国际新闻(World);各州新闻(State by State);经济新闻(Money)和评论(Opinion)。B 版主要栏目有生活报道(Life);体育报道(Sports),全球气象报道(Weather)和智力游戏(Puzzles)。

《今日美国》报具有下列鲜明特色:

1. 版面固定清晰

该报头版除刊登 3 篇新闻报道外还提供新闻目录(Newsline),清晰标示主要新闻报道所在页面。此外经济版、生活版和体育版还分别提供自己的内容目录:Moneyline, Lifeline 和 Sportsline。报纸所有文章位置展示清楚,便于读者查找。

2. 语言简明凝练

当今美国报纸为了与电子媒介争雄,转向深度报道,因而一般篇幅较长。而该报新闻报道突出新闻,少写背景,篇幅较短,语言十分精练,简洁明了。最长文章篇幅不超过 35 句,1000 个词。文字按美联社可读性专家弗莱斯制定的可读性公式(Readability Formula)测定,属于

"较为易读"(Fairly Easy)类别。语言简明凝练,可节约篇幅,刊登更多新闻,更好满足忙碌的人们对信息的渴望。

3. 图片彩色鲜艳

该报图片色彩鲜艳,使报纸版面生动、形象、活泼。新闻摘要栏中每一条新闻前都标有实心点符号,显得十分醒目。该报开创了大量富含信息的照片和图表来表现新闻的先河,富有"报纸中的电视"的称号。

4. 图表数据丰富

该报图表形象鲜明。每日"快照"既是生动的图表,又是新鲜及时的新闻,迎合读者通过形象方法快速获取信息的习惯。报中的数据十分详尽。该报有一大整页气象图表,股市行情和50个州体育比赛成绩。

5. 内容注重正面

美国传统新闻界一向以"社会监督者"(watch dog)自居,倾向报道阴暗面。而该报奉行的是"希望新闻"(Hoping Journalism),注重"新闻平衡""好坏搭配",让读者看到希望和光明。

虽然该报获得很大成功,褒扬者众多,但也不乏贬斥者。有的新闻学者指出该报的新闻报道内容浅薄,具有粉饰太平倾向。还有的嘲笑它是"大型小报"。

Ⅴ. Analysis of the Content

1. What is false about the American society according to the article?
    A. Adultery is rather common.
    B. Percentage of newlyweds with prior cohabitation experience is rather high.
    C. Americans hate the idea of marriage.
    D. Most Americans now marry rather late.
2. It can be seen from the article that children living with only one parent in America amount to about _____.
    A. 41%
    B. about one third
    C. 90%
    D. 73%
3. No-fault divorce law was introduced first in _____.
    A. Arizona
    B. Virginia
    C. Florida
    D. California
4. Same-sex marriage is legal in _____.
    A. Massachusetts only
    B. Massachusetts and San Francisco
    C. Louisiana and Arkansas
    D. New York and Arizona
5. To the author's mind, America's marriage institution _____.
    A. is in a rather peculiar state
    B. is free from any problem
    C. remains firm and healthy
    D. still keeps the original form

Ⅵ. Questions on the Article

1. What kind of amendment does President Bush want?
2. Does divorce mean that Americans are fed up with marriage itself?

3. Tell something about America's divorce problem.
4. How common is cohabitation in America?
5. How strong is the live-in union?
6. Why are baby-boomers' children more reluctant to marry?
7. How prevalent is adultery in America according to Vaughan?
8. What impact does marriage have on children?
9. What is Robert Lang's view on America's marriage institution?
10. What are the measures taken by state governments and the society to strengthen the marriage institution?
11. What is Lang's prediction about the same-sex marriage?

Ⅶ. Topics for Discussion

1. Is divorce the best solution to marital problems?
2. Should same-sex marriage be allowed in the society?

Lesson 11

The Elusive Big Idea

By Neal Gabler

Neal Gabler is a senior fellow at the Annenberg Norman Lear Center at the University of Southern California[1] and the author of *Walt Disney: The Triumph of the American Imagination*.

The July/August issue of *The Atlantic* trumpets the "14 Biggest Ideas of the Year." Take a deep breath. The ideas include "The Players Own the Game" (No. 12), "Wall Street: Same as It Ever Was" (No. 6), "Nothing Stays Secret" (No. 2) and the very biggest idea of the year, "The Rise of the Middle Class — Just Not Ours," which refers to growing economies in Brazil, Russia, India and China.[2]

Now exhale. It may strike you that none of these ideas seem particularly breathtaking. In fact, none of them are ideas. They are more on the order of observations.[3] But one can't really fault *The Atlantic* for mistaking commonplaces for intellectual vision. Ideas just aren't what they used to be. Once upon a time, they could ignite fires of debate, stimulate other thoughts, incite revolutions and fundamentally change the ways we look at and think about the world.

They could penetrate the general culture and make celebrities out of thinkers — notably Albert Einstein, but also Reinhold Niebuhr, Daniel Bell, Betty Friedan, Carl Sagan and Stephen Jay Gould, to name a few.[4] The ideas themselves could even be made famous: for instance, for "the end of ideology," "the medium is the message," "the feminine mystique," "the Big Bang theory," "the end of history."[5] A big idea could capture the cover of *Time* — "Is God Dead?" — and intellectuals like Norman Mailer, William F. Buckley Jr. and Gore Vidal would even occasionally be invited to the couches of late-night talk shows.[6] How long ago that was.

If our ideas seem smaller nowadays, it's not because we are dumber than our forebears but because we just don't care as much about ideas as they did. In effect, we are living in an increasingly post-idea world — a world in which big, thought-provoking ideas that can't instantly be monetized are of so little intrinsic value that fewer people are generating them and fewer outlets are disseminating them, the Internet notwithstanding.[7] Bold ideas are almost passé.

It is no secret, especially here in America, that we live in a post-Enlightenment age[8] in which rationality, science, evidence, logical argument and debate have lost the battle in many sectors, and perhaps even in society generally, to superstition, faith, opinion and orthodoxy. While we continue to make giant technological advances, we may be the first generation to have turned back the epochal clock — to have gone backward intellectually

119

from advanced modes of thinking into old modes of belief. But post-Enlightenment and post-idea, while related, are not exactly the same.

Post-Enlightenment refers to a style of thinking that no longer deploys the techniques of rational thought. Post-idea refers to thinking that is no longer done, regardless of the style.

The post-idea world has been a long time coming, and many factors have contributed to it. There is the retreat in universities from the real world, and an encouragement of and reward for the narrowest specialization rather than for daring — for tending potted plants rather than planting forests.

There is the eclipse of the public intellectual in the general media by the pundit who substitutes outrageousness for thoughtfulness, and the concomitant decline of the essay in general-interest magazines.[9] And there is the rise of an increasingly visual culture, especially among the young — a form in which ideas are more difficult to express.

But these factors, which began decades ago, were more likely harbingers of an approaching post-idea world than the chief causes of it. The real cause may be information itself. It may seem counterintuitive that at a time when we know more than we have ever known, we think about it less.

We live in the much vaunted Age of Information. Courtesy of the Internet, we seem to have immediate access to anything that anyone could ever want to know.[10] We are certainly the most informed generation in history, at least quantitatively. There are trillions upon trillions of bytes out there in the ether — so much to gather and to think about.

And that's just the point. In the past, we collected information not simply to know things. That was only the beginning. We also collected information to convert it into something larger than facts and ultimately more useful — into ideas that made sense of the information. We sought not just to apprehend the world but to truly comprehend it, which is the primary function of ideas.[11] Great ideas explain the world and one another to us.

Marx pointed out the relationship between the means of production and our social and political systems. Freud[12] taught us to explore our minds as a way of understanding our emotions and behaviors. Einstein rewrote physics. More recently, McLuhan[13] theorized about the nature of modern communication and its effect on modern life. These ideas enabled us to get our minds around our existence and attempt to answer the big, daunting questions of our lives.

But if information was once grist for ideas, over the last decade it has become competition for them.[14] We are like the farmer who has too much wheat to make flour. We are inundated with so much information that we wouldn't have time to process it even if we wanted to, and most of us don't want to.

The collection itself is exhausting: what each of our friends is doing at that particular moment and then the next moment and the next one; who Jennifer Aniston is dating right now; which video is going viral on YouTube this hour; what Princess Letizia or Kate Middleton is wearing that day[15]. In effect, we are living within the nimbus of an informational Gresham's law[16] in which trivial information pushes out significant information, but it is also an ideational Gresham's law in which information, trivial or not, pushes out ideas.

We prefer knowing to thinking because knowing has more immediate value. It keeps us in the loop, keeps us connected to our friends and our cohort.[17] Ideas are too airy, too impractical, too much work for too little reward. Few talk ideas. Everyone talks information, usually personal information. Where are you going? What are you doing? Whom are you seeing? These are today's big questions.

It is certainly no accident that the post-idea world has sprung up alongside the social networking world. Even though there are sites and blogs dedicated to ideas, Twitter, Facebook, Myspace, Flickr, etc.[18], the most popular sites on the Web, are basically information exchanges, designed to feed the insatiable information hunger, though this is hardly the kind of information that generates ideas. It is largely useless except insofar as it makes the possessor of the information feel, well, informed.[19] Of course, one could argue that these sites are no different than conversation was for previous generations, and that conversation seldom generated big ideas either, and one would be right.

BUT the analogy isn't perfect. For one thing, social networking sites are the primary form of communication among young people, and they are supplanting print, which is where ideas have typically gestated. For another, social networking sites engender habits of mind that are inimical to the kind of deliberate discourse that gives rise to ideas. Instead of theories, hypotheses and grand arguments, we get instant 140-character tweets about eating a sandwich or watching a TV show.[20] While social networking may enlarge one's circle and even introduce one to strangers, this is not the same thing as enlarging one's intellectual universe. Indeed, the gab of social networking tends to shrink one's universe to oneself and one's friends, while thoughts organized in words, whether online or on the page, enlarge one's focus.

To paraphrase the famous dictum, often attributed to Yogi Berra, that you can't think and hit at the same time, you can't think and tweet at the same time either[21], not because it is impossible to multitask but because tweeting, which is largely a burst of either brief, unsupported opinions or brief descriptions of your own prosaic activities, is a form of distraction or anti-thinking.

The implications of a society that no longer thinks big are enormous. Ideas aren't just intellectual playthings. They have practical effects.

An artist friend of mine recently lamented that he felt the art world was adrift because there were no longer great critics like Harold Rosenberg and Clement Greenberg to provide theories of art that could fructify the art and energize it.[22] Another friend made a similar argument about politics. While the parties debate how much to cut the budget, he wondered where were the John Rawlses and Robert Nozicks[23] who could elevate our politics.

One could certainly make the same argument about economics, where John Maynard Keynes remains the center of debate nearly 80 years after propounding his theory of government pump priming[24]. This isn't to say that the successors of Rosenberg, Rawls and Keynes don't exist, only that if they do, they are not likely to get traction in a culture that has so little use for ideas, especially big, exciting, dangerous ones, and that's true whether the ideas come from academics or others who are not part of elite organizations and who challenge the conventional wisdom. All thinkers are victims of information glut, and the ideas of today's thinkers are also victims of that glut.

But it is especially true of big thinkers in the social sciences like the cognitive psychologist Steven Pinker[25], who has theorized on everything from the source of language to the role of genetics in human nature, or the biologist Richard Dawkins[26], who has had big and controversial ideas on everything from selfishness to God, or the psychologist Jonathan

Haidt[27], who has been analyzing different moral systems and drawing fascinating conclusions about the relationship of morality to political beliefs. But because they are scientists and empiricists rather than generalists in the humanities, the place from which ideas were customarily popularized, they suffer a double whammy: not only the whammy against ideas generally but the whammy against science, which is typically regarded in the media as mystifying at best, incomprehensible at worst.[28] A generation ago, these men would have made their way into popular magazines and onto television screens. Now they are crowded out by informational effluvium.

No doubt there will be those who say that the big ideas have migrated to the marketplace, but there is a vast difference between profit-making inventions and intellectually challenging thoughts. Entrepreneurs have plenty of ideas, and some, like Steven P. Jobs of Apple[29], have come up with some brilliant ideas in the "inventional" sense of the word.

Still, while these ideas may change the way we live, they rarely transform the way we think. They are material, not ideational. It is thinkers who are in short supply, and the situation probably isn't going to change anytime soon.

We have become information narcissists, so uninterested in anything outside ourselves and our friendship circles or in any tidbit we cannot share with those friends that if a Marx or a Nietzsche[30] were suddenly to appear, blasting his ideas, no one would pay the slightest attention, certainly not the general media, which have learned to service our narcissism.

What the future portends is more and more information — Everests of it.[31] There won't be anything we won't know. But there will be no one thinking about it.

Think about that.

From *The New York Times*, August 13, 2011

I. New Words

airy	['eəri]	adj.	seeming not to be related to real conditions
analogy	[ə'næclədʒi]	n.	a comparison of one thing with another
blast	[blɑːst]	v.	to criticize
byte	[bait]	n.	[计] 字节
cognitive	['kɔgnitiv]	adj.	认知的
cohort	['kəuhɔːt]	n.	a group of people sharing a common feature
commonplace	['kɔmənpleis]	n.	a remark that is not new or interesting
counterintuitive	[ˌkauntərin'tjuːitiv]	adj.	反直觉的,反直观的
daunting	['dɔːntiŋ]	adj.	making sb feel nervous and less confident about doing sth
deliberate	[di'libərət]	adj.	done slowly and carefully
deploy	[di'plɔi]	v.	to use sth effectively
discourse	['diskɔːs]	n.	(口头的或书面的)交流

dumb	[dʌm]	adj.	*informal* stupid
effluvium	[eˈfluːviəm]	n.	恶臭；废料，垃圾
elusive	[iˈluːsiv]	adj.	difficult to find or achieve
empiricist	[imˈpirisist]	n.	经验主义者，经验论者
Enlightenment	[inˈlaitnmənt]	n.	启蒙
epical	[ˈepikəl]	adj.	史诗的
epochal	[ˈepəkəl]	adj.	（重要）时期的，划时代的
ether	[ˈiːθə]	n.	以太网
forebear	[ˈfɔːˌbeə]	n.	祖宗，祖先
gab	[gæb]	n.	idle talk, chatter
genetics	[dʒiˈnetiks]	n.	遗传学
glut	[glʌt]	n.	a larger supply than is needed
gestate	[dʒesˈteit]	v.	孕育（计划，思想等）
harbinger	[ˈhaːbindʒə]	n.	*formal* a sign that shows that sth is going to happen soon
ideational	[aidiˈeiʃənəl]	adj.	概念的，观念的
ignite	[igˈnait]	v.	to make sth start to burn
incite	[inˈsait]	v.	to encourage sb to do sth violent
inimical	[iˈnimikl]	adj.	*formal* harmful to sth
insatiable	[inˈseiʃəbl]	adj.	always wanting more of sth
inundate	[ˈinʌndeit]	v.	~ **sb**（**with sth**）to give sb so many things that they cannot deal with them all
loop	[luːp]	n.	**in the** ~ part of a group of people dealing with sth important
mode	[məud]	n.	a particular way of thinking, or doing sth
multitask	[ˌmʌltiˈtaːsk]	v.	to do several things at the same time
nimbus	[ˈnimbəs]	n.	光轮，光环
orthodoxy	[ˈɔːθədəksi]	n.	正统观念，正统信仰
passé	[paːˈsei]	adj.	no longer fashionable
pundit	[ˈpʌndit]	n.	专家，权威，学者
propound	[prəˈpaund]	v.	*formal* to suggest an idea for people to consider
prosaic	[prəˈzeiik]	adj.	ordinary or not showing any imagination
tidbit	[ˈtidbit]	n.	a small but interesting piece of news
traction	[ˈtrækʃn]	n.	吸引
tweet	[twiːt]	v.	to send messages by using Twitter
trillion	[ˈtriljən]	n.	万亿，兆
vaunted	[ˈvɔːntid]	adj.	*formal* proudly talked about or praised

Ⅱ. Background Information

网络与思维

当今时代,互联网已全面渗入我们的社会,成为我们生活中必不可少的一部分。网络如同一个规模浩大、随时开放、使用便捷、提供新知的图书馆,极大地满足了人们日益增长的信息需求。无限的搜索引擎让人们有限的大脑实现任意衔接,轻松自如获取无限的信息。

网络为人们获取信息提供了方便。但与此同时人们也可能形成搜索成瘾,网络依赖。不少学者指出,网络的普遍使用带来了人们认知能力削弱的负面效应。美国 Temple 大学神经决策系统研究中心主任安吉利卡·达莫卡(Angelika Dimoka)的研究发现,无止境的搜索往往形成信息过剩(surfeit of information),导致认知和信息过载(cognitive and information overload),使人们决断能力负荷过重(overtaxing people's decision-making abilities)造成在有"更多的信息情况下做出更差的决定"。

斯坦福大学心理学教授克利福德·纳斯(Clifford Nass)认为,大量信息的不断输入使得人们的大脑不停地做出即刻反应,导致大脑决断时牺牲缜密和深思(sacrificing accuracy and thoughtfulness)。

网络阅读还改变了人们原先的思维方式和交际模式。美国 Tufts 大学发展心理学家(developmental psychologist)马丽安娜·沃尔夫(Maryanne Wolf)认为:"我们是什么样的人不仅由我们的阅读内容而且由我们的阅读方式所决定。"(We are not only what we read. We are how we read.)深层次的阅读促成深层次的思考。网络短小精悍、碎片化的信息,跳跃式的阅读习惯不仅分散了读者的专注力(diffuse concentration),也使读者丧失了阅读长篇文章的耐心和能力。此外,网络使得信息获取便捷,简单的输入便可使相关信息一览无遗。这便容易导致人们不愿记忆资料,不去思考问题,形成思维惰性。《哈佛商业评论》原执行主编尼古拉斯·卡尔认为:"(网络时代)在丢失《战争与和平》,丢失羊皮圣经,丢失报纸杂志,丢失托尔斯泰心灵的同时,人类正在丢失的是大脑。"

不少学者哀叹道:"网络时代流行的文化是快餐文化,这样的环境很难构建出独特的思想体系,很难再出思想大师。"

然而,也有的学者认为互联网时代人类社会框架没有变,只不过网络这种开放、多元、虚拟的交流方式使我们的思维随着技术的发展进入新的阶段。只要人们注意克服网络的负面影响,科学调节对信息的欲望,网络最终会成为人们思想的延伸与交流利器。

Ⅲ. Notes to the Text

1. a senior fellow at the Annenberg Norman Lear Center at the University of Southern California—南加州大学安嫩伯格·诺曼·尼尔研究中心高级研究员
2. The ideas include "The Players Own the Game" (No. 12), "Wall Street: Same as It Ever Was" (No. 6), "Nothing Stays Secret" (No. 2) and the very biggest idea of the year, "The Rise of the Middle Class — Just Not Ours," which refers to growing economies in Brazil, Russia, India and China.—这些思想包括"游戏者控制游戏"(排名

12),"华尔街一切如常"(排名 6),"无事能保密"(排名 2)和本年最大思想"中产阶级的崛起——只不过不是美国的",指的是巴西、俄罗斯、印度和中国不断增长的经济。(2011 年《大西洋月刊》7-8月期刊中列出以下 14 个大思想:1. The Rise of the Middle Class — Just Not Ours; 2. Nothing Stays Secret; 3. The Rich Are Different from You and Me; 4. Elections Work; 5. The Arab Spring Is a Job Crisis; 6. Wall Street:Same As It Ever Was; 7. Public Employee, Public Enemy; 8. Grandma's in the Basement; 9. The Next War Will Be Digitized; 10. Bonds Are Dead; 11. Gay Is the New Normal; 12. The Players Own the Game; 13. The Maniac Will Be Televised; 14. The Green Revolution Is Neither)

3. They are more on the order of observations. —它们更加类似评述。(① on the order of—similar to; ② observation—a spoken or written remark about sth noticed)

4. They could penetrate the general culture and make celebrities out of thinkers — notably Albert Einstein, but also Reinhold Niebuhr, Daniel Bell, Betty Friedan, Carl Sagan and Stephen Jay Gould, to name a few. —它们可以渗进大众文化,使思想家名扬社会,特别是阿尔伯特·爱因斯坦,还有莱茵霍尔德·尼布尔、丹尼尔·贝尔、贝蒂·弗里丹、卡尔·萨根和斯蒂芬·杰伊·古尔德等。(①Albert Einstein—1879—1955,美籍德国物理学家,创立狭义相对论和广义相对论,提出光子概念;②Reinhold Niebuhr—1892—1971,美国神学家,鼓吹"基督教现实主义",著有《道德的个人,不道德的社会》;③Daniel Bell—1919—2011,美国最重要思想家之一,提出了西方社会深具影响的三大观念:"意识形态的终结""后工业社会"和"资本主义文化矛盾";④Betty Friedan—1921—2006,美国女权主义者、作家,著有《女性的奥秘》;⑤Carl Sagan—1934—1996,美国天文学家、科普学家,著有《宇宙间的智能生物》;⑥Stephen Jay Gould—1941—2002,美国古生物学家、科学史学家、进化论研究者,提出"间断平衡"进化理论)

5. The ideas themselves could even be made famous:for instance, for "the end of ideology," "the medium is the message," "the feminine mystique," "the Big Bang theory," "the end of history." —这些思想本身就会闻名,例如"意识形态的终结""媒介即信息""女性的奥秘""大爆炸理论""历史的终结"等。(①the end of ideology—In the book *The End of Ideology:On The Exhaustion of Political Ideas* published in 1960, Daniel Bell suggests that the older, grand-humanistic ideologies derived from the 19th and early 20th centuries had been exhausted, and the new, more parochial ideologies would soon arise;②the medium is the message—a phrase coined by Marshall McLuhan meaning that the form of a medium embeds itself in the message, creating a symbiotic relationship by which the medium influences how the message is perceived;③ the feminine mystique—the title of a book by Betty Friedan, which is widely credited with starting the Women's Movement in the 1960s;④the Big Bang theory—a theory which maintains that the universe originated in a cosmic explosion of hydrogen, which became condensed into the galaxies;⑤the end of history—an essay written by Francis Fakuyama and published in the 1989 *International Affairs* journal, which argues that the advent of western liberal democracy may signal the endpoint of humanity's sociocultural evolution and the final form of human government.)

6. A big idea could capture the cover of *Time* — "Is God Dead?" — and intellectuals like Norman Mailer, William F. Buckley Jr. and Gore Vidal would even occasionally be invited to the couches of late-night talk shows. —大思想能成为《时代》周刊封面故事——《上帝死了?》,像诺曼·梅勒,小威廉·法兰克·巴克利和戈尔·维达尔一类有真知灼见的人甚至偶尔会被电视台邀请为深夜访谈节目嘉宾。(①"Is God Dead?"—cover story for the April 8,1966 issue of *Time*, which looked in great depth at the problems facing modern theologians; ②Norman Mailer—1923— , a U. S. writer and journalist, known for dealing with social and political subjects and criticizing U. S. society; ③William F. Buckley Jr.—1925—2008, a well-known U. S. political writer who started *the National Review*; ④Gore Vidal—a well-known U. S. novelist, dramatist and essayist)

7. In effect, we are living in an increasingly post-idea world — a world in which big, thought-provoking ideas that can't instantly be monetized are of so little intrinsic value that fewer people are generating them and fewer outlets are disseminating them, the Internet notwithstanding. —实际上,我们生活在后思想世界:在这个世界中,令人深思但不能立即转化为金钱的大思想自身价值很低,因而产生这些大思想的人越来越少,尽管现在有互联网,传播这些思想的媒体也在减少。(①monetize—to turn into money; ②outlets—referring to media that disseminate news and ideas; ③disseminate—to spread information, ideas)

8. a post-Enlightenment age—后启蒙时代(Enlightenment—启蒙运动,尤指18世纪欧洲以推崇"理性"、怀疑教会权威和封建制度为特点的文化思想运动)

9. There is the eclipse of the public intellectual in the general media by the pundit who substitutes outrageousness for thoughtfulness, and the concomitant decline of the essay in general-interest magazines. —大众媒体中公共知识分子已黯然失色,得宠的是那种追奇逐怪而不是深入思考的学者。与此同时,综合性杂志的文章质量也在下降。(①eclipse—a loss of importance or power etc. especially because sb else has become more important or powerful; ②outrageous—extremely unusual or unconventional; ③public intellectual—a common term for an intellectual addressing and responding to the problems of the society and thus expected to rise above the partial preoccupation with one's own profession and engage in the global issues of the truth, judgment and taste of the time; ④concomitant—happening at the same time)

10. Courtesy of the Internet, we seem to have immediate access to anything that anyone could ever want to know. —由于互联网的使用,我们似乎可以获取想要知道的一切信息。(courtesy of sth—as a result of sth)

11. We sought not just to apprehend the world but to truly comprehend it, which is the primary function of ideas. —我们力图不仅了解世界,而且真正理解世界,这是思想的主要功能。(comprehend—to recognize)

12. Freud—弗洛伊德(1856—1939,奥地利精神病学家,精神分析学派、心理学创始人)

13. McLuhan—麦克卢汉(1911—1980,加拿大传播理论家,著作有《人的延伸》《媒介即信息》等)

14. But if information was once grist for ideas, over the last decade it has become

competition for them. —然而，虽然信息本是提取思想的原料，但过去十年里却成了思想的竞争对手。(grist—sth that can be used for a particular purpose)

15. who Jennifer Aniston is dating right now; which video is going viral on YouTube this hour; what Princess Letizia or Kate Middleton is wearing that day—珍妮弗·阿尼斯顿现在与谁约会，YouTube视频网站此刻哪个视频最为流行，西班牙王储妃莱蒂齐亚或者英国王妃凯特·米德尔顿那天穿的什么服装(①Jennifer Aniston—1969—   ，美国著名演员、制片人、导演、监制、企业家；②viral—A viral video is any clip of animation or film that is spread rapidly through online sharing；③YouTube—世界最大的视频分享网站)

16. Gresham's law—[经]格雷欣法则(亦称劣币驱逐良币法则，指两种实际价值不同的金属货币同时流通时，实际价值较高的良币必被实际价值较低的劣币所排斥)

17. It keeps us in the loop, keeps us connected to our friends and our cohort. —它使我们在消息圈内，把我们与朋友和同事联系在一起。(①in the loop—Am. E. part of a group knowing about sth that is happening；②cohort—group, company)

18. ...sites and blogs dedicated to ideas, Twitter, Facebook, Myspace, Flickr, etc. —用于交流思想的网站和博客，如推特网、脸谱网、聚友网、Flickr网等(①Twitter——家社交网络和微博客服务网站，2006年创办，总部位于美国旧金山；②Facebook—创办于2004年，总部位于美国加州帕罗奥图市，是世界排名第一的照片分享站点；③Myspace—全球第二大社交网站，2003年创办，总部位于美国加州贝弗利山；④Flickr—雅虎旗下图片分享网站)

19. It is largely useless except insofar as it makes the possessor of the information feel, well, informed. —这种信息只是让信息占有者觉得信息灵通而已，基本上没有价值。(insofar—to such an extent or degree)

20. Instead of theories, hypotheses and grand arguments, we get instant 140-character tweets about eating a sandwich or watching a TV show. —我们得到的不是理论、假设和大论点，而是通过推特用140个符号即刻发出内容有关吃三明治、看电视节目的短信。(①tweets—messages sent by using twitter；②140-character—referring to the maximum of characters which is allowed in using Twitter)

21. To paraphrase the famous dictum, often attributed to Yogi Berra, that you can't think and hit at the same time, you can't think and tweet at the same time either... —有句常被认为出自约吉·贝拉的名言：一个人不能同时思考和击球。这句话我们可以变换为：一个人也不能同时思考和发短信。(①Yogi Berra—an American former Major League Baseball catcher, outfielder and manager；②tweet—to send messages by using twitter)

22. An artist friend of mine recently lamented that he felt the art world was adrift because there were no longer great critics like Harold Rosenberg and Clement Greenberg to provide theories of art that could fructify the art and energize it. —我的一个艺术家朋友最近哀叹道，他觉得艺术界十分茫然，因为再也没有哈罗德·罗森堡和克莱门特·格林伯格一类的批评家提供可以供给艺术养料和能量的艺术理论。(①adrift—without direction or an aim in life；②fructify—to fertilize or make it bear fruit；③lament—to say with great sadness or disappointment；④Harold Rosenberg—an American writer, educator, philosopher and art critic, remembered as one of the most incisive and supportive critics of Abstract Expressionism；⑤Clement Greenberg—a renowned American art critic of the

twentieth century)

23. John Rawlses and Robert Nozicks—约翰·罗尔斯们和罗伯特·诺齐克们(①John Rawls—one of America's most important political philosophers;②Robert Nozick—an American political philosopher, who was very prominent in the 1970s and 1980s)

24. John Maynard Keynes remains the center of debate nearly 80 years after propounding his theory of government pump priming—Please refer to the Background Information of Lesson 7.

25. cognitive psychologist Steven Pinker—认知心理学家史蒂文·平克(Steven Pinker—a Canadian experimental psychologist, cognitive scientist, linguist and popular science author)

26. the biologist Richard Dawkins—生物学家理查德·达金斯(an English ethologist, evolutionary biologist and author)

27. the psychologist Jonathan Haidt—心理学家乔纳森·海德特(an American social psychologist at New York University's Stern School of Business)

28. But because they are scientists and empiricists rather than generalists in the humanities, the place from which ideas were customarily popularized, they suffer a double whammy: not only the whammy against ideas generally but the whammy against science, which is typically regarded in the media as mystifying at best, incomprehensible at worst.—但是,因为他们是科学家和经验主义者,而不是人文学科的通才,而思想通常是从人文学科推广的,他们遭受不仅是普遍对思想而且是对科学的双重打击,在媒体中这一般最好也只被认为令人惊奇,最差则是不可理解。(whammy—the act of striking)

29. Steven P. Jobs of Apple—苹果公司的史蒂夫·P.乔布斯(美国苹果公司联合创办人、前行政总裁、著名发明家、企业家)

30. Nietzsche—Friedrich Wilhelm Nietzsche(1844—1990,德国哲学家、诗人、唯意志论的主要代表)

31. What the future portends is more and more information — Everests of it.—未来预示着越来越多的信息——浩若大山的信息。(①portend—to be a sign of sth that is going to happen in the future; ②Everest—something resembling a great mountain in size or amount)

Ⅳ. Language Features

《纽约时报》简介

《纽约时报》(*The New York Times*),由亨利·雷蒙德于1851年创办。1896年该报由A. S. 奥克斯所收买。1935年奥克斯去世后,由其婿索尔茨伯格家族所有,1969年起从家族企业变为纽约时报公司(The New York Times Company),成为拥有多家美国报纸、杂志、电视台、广播电台和国外联合企业的大报团。它与《华盛顿邮报》(*The Washington Post*)、《洛杉矶时报》(*The Los Angeles Times*)并列为美国最有影响的三家大报。也有不少人称它为美国"第一大报"。该报所获美国新闻普利策奖(Pulitzer Prize)的数量雄踞榜首,到2012年共获112

项奖。

  《纽约时报》读者多属于美国上层社会,包括政府官员、国会议员、工商业家和高级知识分子等。它的平日发行量为 107 万份,星期日发行量为 163 万份,它的印张最多,平日版有 60—100 页,星期日版达 300 页以上。

  该报资料雄厚,文章内容充实。20 世纪 70 年代,《纽约时报》进行了一次版面改革,在与社论版相对的一页上设"社论相对版"(Op-ed-Page),刊登报外人士评论。报纸平日版(周一至周五)内容由原来的两部分改为四部分:

  A 组——国内、国际、纽约新闻、社论

  B 组——经济新闻

  C 组——文化艺术新闻

  D 组——专题报道,每天刊登一个专题,星期一为体育,星期二为科技,星期三为生活,星期四为家庭,星期五为周末版

  有时,周三会增加 F 组(金融新闻),周四会增加 E 组(时尚相关新闻)。周日版除了新闻报道之外,还包括许多专栏,如饮食、旅游、艺术和其他文化专题。

  星期日版包括两大副刊:《纽约时报杂志》(*The New York Times Magazine*)和《纽约时报书评》(*The New York Times Review*)。此外,该报还发行几种郊区版,内容比较庞杂。

  阅读《纽约时报》时,首先应看一下 A 组第一页左下方"内页栏"(Inside),从这一栏可以看出这一天版面情况。在第二部分,即 B 组第一页有新闻摘要及索引。一日重大新闻分类归纳在内,并标有页数和栏数。读者可从中找出自己所感兴趣的新闻。

  该报一贯标榜客观公正,其口号是"刊登一切适合刊登的新闻"。(All the news that's fit to print.)其网站将这一口号改为"All the news that's fit to click"。该报风格比较严肃,享有新闻来源较为可靠的声誉。其观点比较自由开放,有时发表一些批评政府政策的报道和评论。1971 年,该报曾连续刊登五角大楼秘密文件,揭露政府蓄意扩大越战规模。2004 年,该报报道伊拉克战争"情报门事件",挑战攻击伊拉克的正当性。但该报也出现过不少失误,2003 年该报承认其记者杰森·布莱尔多年新闻报道作假。2004 年 5 月 26 日,该报承认在伊拉克战争爆发前的报道错误促使公众更进一步相信伊拉克拥有"大规模杀伤性武器"的谎言。该报与东部大财团关系密切,其报道和评论基本代表垄断集团的利益。

Ⅴ. Analysis of the Content

1. Which of the following is NOT on the author's list of functions of ideas in the past?

   A. Stimulating other thoughts.

   B. Igniting fires of debate.

   C. Increasing work efficiency.

   D. Giving rise to revolutions.

2. Which of the following is NOT listed as a big thinker?

   A. Steven P. Jobs.

   B. McLuhan.

   C. Carl Sagan.

   D. Freud.

3. The author believes that the real cause of an approaching post-idea world is _____.

A. universities' retreat from the real world

   B. an encouragement of and reward for the narrowest specialization

   C. decreasing value of ideas

   D. information

4. The meaning of the word "dumb" in the sentence "If our ideas seem smaller nowadays, it's not because we are dumber than..." (Para. 5) is _____.

   A. unable to speak

   B. stupid

   C. silenced by surprise

   D. unwilling to speak

5. Which of the following statements is False about social networking sites?

   A. Social networking sites can help develop ideas.

   B. Social networking sites may enlarge the social circle.

   C. Social networking sites are the primary form of communication among young people.

   D. Social networking sites can help exchange information.

VI. Questions on the Article

1. What does the author think of the "14 Biggest Ideas of the Year" listed in the July/August issue of *The Atlantic*?
2. Why do ideas seem smaller nowadays?
3. What is the difference between post-idea and post-Enlightenment?
4. What accounts for the fact that at a time when we know more than we have ever known, we think about it less?
5. Why do people prefer knowing to thinking?
6. Why did the author's art friend lament that he felt the art world was adrift?
7. Does it mean that the successors of Rosenberg, Rawls and Keynes don't exist?
8. How is the situation for big thinkers in the social sciences?
9. Are profit-making inventions and intellectually challenging thoughts the same?
10. What does the future portend about information and ideas?

VII. Topics for Discussion

1. Is information the real cause of the post-idea world?
2. Does the use of special networking sites weaken the ability to think?

Lesson 12

How the World Eats

In the face of urbanization and Westernization, families across the globe are abandoning ancient diets and dining habits

By Bryan Walsh

Noriko Yanagihara is putting the finishing touches on a work of simplicity, beauty and good nutrition. The single porcelain bowl she's working on holds a fistful of baby potatoes and a slim cut of Kobe beef drizzled with an egg yolk sauce.[1] A Japanese cooking teacher whose husband and son are both celebrity chefs, Yanagihara works to preserve and promote her nation's cuisine, and she can rhapsodize endlessly about the meaning of a Japanese dinner table. "Cuisine is the essence of a country," she says at her family's home in Tokyo. "So if you study the characteristics of Japanese cuisine, you are studying the essence of Japanese culture." That means a celebration of simplicity — fresh and seasonal ingredients, in small and well-balanced proportions, artfully presented.[2] Though the food being photographed in Yanagihara's dining room is at the highest of high ends, even a basic home meal is meant to strive for the same spirit.[3]

At least, that's the idea. But thanks to the spread of fast-paced lifestyles, such meals are disappearing from Japanese dinner tables, crowded out by convenient, Westernized food.[4] Though Japanese cuisine is still celebrated in glossy magazines and expensive restaurants, traditional eating habits — the essence of the culture — are slowly being lost.[5] "The technique has not been passed on from grandmother to mother, mother to daughter," says Yanagihara. "But more importantly, pride in food, the confidence that our food is beautiful, we have forgotten to pass this on as well."

Japan is not alone. Food and diet are the cornerstones of any culture, one of the most reliable symbols of national identity. Think of the long Spanish lunch followed by the afternoon siesta, a rhythm of food and rest perfectly suited to the blistering heat of the Iberian peninsula in summer.[6] Think of the Chinese meal of rice, vegetables and (only recently) meat, usually served in big collective dishes, the better for extended clans to dine together. National diets come to incorporate all aspects of who we are: our religious taboos, class structure, geography, economy, even government. When we eat together, "we are ordering the world around us and defining the community most important to us," says Martin Jones, a bioarchaeologist at Cambridge University and author of the new book *Feast: Why Humans Share Food*.

Even the traditions we learn from others we adopt and adapt in ways that make them our own. Japan received chopsticks from China and tempura from Portugal. Tomatoes, that staple of pasta and pizza, arrived in Southern Europe only as part of the Columbian Exchange (so-called because of Christopher Columbus' journeys to the New World, where tomatoes originated). "A lot of what we think of as deeply rooted cultural traditions are really traceable back to global exchange," says Miriam Chaiken, a nutritional anthropologist at Indiana University of Pennsylvania[7].

In an era of instant communication and accelerated trade, those cultural exchanges have exploded, leading to something closer to cultural homogenization.[8] That's bad for not only the preservation of national identities but the preservation of health too. Saturated fats[9] and meats are displacing grains and fresh vegetables. Mealtimes are (**Mealtime is**) shrinking. McDonald's is everywhere. From Chile to China, the risk of obesity, diabetes and heart disease is on the rise as the idiosyncratic fare that used to make mealtime in New Delhi, Buenos Aires and Sydney such distinctive experiences is vanishing.[10] This, in turn, is leading to a minimovement in some countries to hold fast to traditional food culture, even as their menu grows ever more international. Says Jones: "With every change there's nostalgia for what's gone before."

Such longing for what was may be only natural, but before we get too misty over the way we used to eat, it's important to remember that the first purpose of food is to keep us alive — something that used to be a lot harder than it is today. For thousands of years, humans were chiefly agrarian, which meant that you ate only what you could grow or slaughter yourself or trade for locally. Geography was culinary destiny.[11]

Africa, which strains under so much political and economic hardship, is the place where this ancient reality is in greatest evidence today.[12] Throughout much of the continent, people remain tied to the land and therefore dependent on it. Most meals are keyed around a single calorie-rich starch — in East Africa, it's often cornmeal or flour made into a stiff porridge — with extra food added if available.[13] Meat remains a rare indulgence, something reserved for holidays and feasts. Even relatively well-fed populations like the Iraqw of Tanzania, who typically eat three full meals a day, must brace for periods when that is impossible. "In times of food insecurity — right before a harvest — or in a bad year, they will reduce this to two or one meals," says Crystal Patil, an anthropologist at the University of Illinois in Chicago[14]. "If there are several bad years in a row, it can be devastating." Often, the only sure foods are largely useless ones, those sloshing over from the well-fed world outside. "I've never seen a village where you couldn't find a Coke," says Chaiken.

All human cultures may have started out with this kind of day-to-day, harvest-to-harvest existence, but the better environmental hand that people of other regions drew — richer soil, fewer droughts, milder temperatures — allowed them to tame their land, meaning that the food they ate and the lives they lived could evolve together.[15] In agrarian, preindustrial Europe, for example, "you'd want to wake up early, start working with the sunrise, have a break to have the largest meal, and then you'd go back to work," says Ken Albala, a professor of history at the University of the Pacific. "Later, at 5 or 6, you'd have a smaller supper."

This comfortable cycle, in which the rhythms of the day helped shape the rhythms of the meals, gave rise to the custom of the large midday meal, eaten with the extended family, that is still observed in pockets of Southern and Western Europe.[16] "Meals are the foundation of the family," says Carole Counihan, an anthropologist at Millersville University in Pennsylvania and author of *Around the Tuscan Table*, "so there was a very important interconnection between eating together" and cementing family ties.

Since industrialization, maintaining such a slow cultural metabolism has been much harder, with the long midday meal shriveling to whatever could be stuffed into a lunch bucket or bought at a food stand. [17] Certainly, there were benefits. Modern techniques for producing and shipping food led to greater variety and quantity, including a tremendous increase in the amount of animal protein and dairy products available, making us more robust than our ancestors. In contemporary China, where tens of millions were starving less than 50 years ago, meat has become far more common, and Chinese youth are on average 6 cm taller than they were just three decades ago. "China has gone from a sparse diet to a point where it's got almost too much," says James Watson, professor of Chinese society and anthropology at Harvard University. "As a nutritionist, you have to be outraged. As a historian, you have to consider it one of the biggest success stories on the planet."

Yet plenty has been lost too, even in cultures that still live to eat. Take Italy. It's no secret that the Mediterranean diet — with its emphasis on olive oil, seafood and fresh produce — is healthy, but it was also a joy to prepare and eat. Italians, says Counihan, traditionally began the day with a small meal called *colazione*, consisting of light baked goods and coffee. The big meal came at around 1 p. m. and included a first course of pasta, rice or soup; a second of meat and vegetables; a third, fruit course and, of course, wine. In between the midday meal and a late, smaller dinner came a small snack, the *merenda*. Today, when time zones (**meal times**) have less and less meaning, there is little tolerance for offices' closing for lunch, and worsening traffic in cities means workers can't make it home and back fast enough anyway. [18] So the formerly small supper after sundown becomes the big meal of the day, the only one at which the family has a chance to get together. "The evening meal carries the full burden that used to be spread over two meals," says Counihan.

South Americans are struggling with similar changes. John Brett, a nutritional anthropologist at the University of Colorado at Denver and Health Sciences Center[19], says that many Latin Americans too prefer a large family meal at midday, heavy on starchy grains like quinoa or plants like yucca. But migration from the country to the cities has made that impossible. "They don't have the luxury of two hours of lunch," says Brett. "The economy moves on." NOT only do these changes add stress for families, but nutritional quality declines as well. "They tend to eat whatever is cheap and quick," says Chaiken.

Paradoxically, the thing that has contributed the most to the deterioration of food culture may be one of the very things that has helped turbocharge countries in so many other ways[20]: the presence of women in the workforce. "If women are working, they can't shop and cook and prepare a meal," says Counihan. "In the old days, you might have had the grandmother doing it, but family size is shrinking." And the less exposure younger generations have to the food their grandparents ate, the less they develop the sensitive palates that allow them to appreciate it. [21] In Latin America, says Jeffery Sobal, a professor of nutritional science at Cornell University, "parents complain that they make [traditional] dishes, but the kids won't eat them. They want the things they see on television."

It shouldn't be surprising that the societies that have been most successful at retaining food cultures are the ones that have also resisted the pull of Westernization[22] — for better and worse. In many Middle Eastern countries, extended families still live together, and women stay in the home preparing the kinds of traditional meals that women elsewhere no longer can. Diets in the Middle East also show the influence of religion; besides widely observed taboos on pork and alcohol, the fasting month of Ramadan alters Middle Eastern eating habits. While Muslims fast from sunup to sundown, Ramadan nights are marked by calorie-heavy indulgence.[23] "The level of food consumption during Ramadan is much higher than during ordinary months," says Sami Zubaida, co-author of the book *Culinary Cultures of the Middle East*. Ramadan is "the fasting month that is really a feasting month," Zubaida says, hence the tendency for Ramadan weight gain.[24]

Outside the most conservative nations in the Muslim world, it has proved difficult to hold on to the pleasures of traditional eating. But that's not to say that people don't long for the old ways all the same, inspiring movements in some nations to rediscover how Mom used to prepare a meal. In Europe, Asia and the U. S., the Slow Food movement[25] — a kind of alimentary Greenpeace — campaigns against fast food while championing traditionally prepared meals. Bolivians regularly hold food fairs[26] that celebrate South American staples even as they develop ways to speed up the time-intensive preparation of native meals so that Bolivians can enjoy the dishes of the past at the pace of today. Yet while we might — indeed must — clean up the worst of the fast-food excesses, trying to preserve the diets that keep us both culturally and physically healthier, no one pretends we're ever going to turn back the clock entirely. "Nobody has time anymore," laments Harvard's Watson. "Not even the French."[27]

Nor do the harried Japanese, although there are exceptions. At a trim home in northwest Tokyo, where commuter trains rumble just outside the window, homemaker Estsuko Shinobu, 60, prepares a proper Japanese lunch, using fresh ingredients she bought that morning at the nearby supermarket. The mother of two grown children pads around the kitchen in slippers and a violet kimono, chopping Japanese radishes and carrots, carefully packing a sushi cake with tuna and vinegared rice. She serves dishes arranged on an individual tray just so, down to the direction of each set of chopsticks. She looks happy, even serene as she works, but when asked whether she has passed these skills on to her daughter, she sighs. "Of course not," Shinobu says. "She's far too busy for this."

With reporting by Elisabeth Salemme/New York, Toko Sekiguchi/Tokyo, Ishaan Tharoor/Hong Kong and Christopher Thompson/London

From *Time*, June 25—July 2, 2007

Ⅰ. New Words

alimentary	[ˌæliˈmentəri]	*adj.*	饮食的
blistering	[ˈblistəriŋ]	*adj.*	extremely hot
diabetes	[ˌdaiəˈbiːtiːz]	*n.*	[医]糖尿病
harried	[ˈhærid]	*adj.*	被困扰的
idiosyncratic	[ˌidiəsinˈkrætik]	*adj.*	特殊的，独特的
kimono	[kiˈməunəu]	*n.*	[日]和服
Kobe	[ˈkəubi]	*n.*	神户（日本本州岛西南岸港口城市）

metabolism	[me'tæbəlizəm]	n.		新陈代谢
misty	['misti]	adj.		full of tender emotion; sentimental
obesity	[əu'bisiti]	n.		过度肥胖；[医]肥胖症
pad	[pæd]	v.		to walk softly and quietly
pasta	['pɑːstə]	n.		意大利面食
quinoa	['kiːnəuə]	n.		[植]昆诺阿苋（南美一种谷物）
radish	['rædiʃ]	n.		[植]萝卜
rhapsodize	['ræpsədaiz]	v.		to talk with great enthusiasm
siesta	[si'estə]	n.		a rest or nap after the midday meal
slosh	[slɔʃ]	v.		(of liquid) to move in a noisy way
sushi	['suːʃiː]	n.		[日]寿司
tempura	['tempuˌrɑː]	n.		[烹]面拖油炸鱼虾（一种日本菜肴）
tuna	['tjuːnə]	n.		金枪鱼
yucca	['jʌkə]	n.		[植]丝兰

Ⅱ. Background Information

快餐与慢食

快节奏的生活与工作，使美国人在饮食上追求快捷方便，养成偏爱快餐的特点。为了适应大众对快速(fastness)和便捷(convenience)的需求，美国快餐业飞速发展起来。

美国快餐业十分发达，约有13万个快餐连锁店星罗棋布全国各地。平均每天有1/5的美国人在这里用餐。美国饮食业营业额为2,000多亿，快餐业营业额就高达500多亿，占有1/4的比例。

快餐馆预先准备好饭菜，环境简朴洁净，服务熟练迅捷。在这类餐馆就餐，顾客无需付小费，吃完饭后把残羹剩饭倒入杂物桶便可。

快餐馆中，"麦当劳"(MacDonald's)连锁店独占鳌头，占据快餐市场42％份额，成为快餐业的象征。其他著名的快餐店有"汉堡包大王"(Burger King)、"温迪"(Wendy's)、"肯德基"(KFC)、"比萨饼屋"（又译为"必胜客"）(Pizza Hut)和"阿比快餐馆"(Arby's)等。

这些年来，美国的快餐文化风靡世界，"麦当劳"之类的快餐馆遍布全球。然而，也有许多的人认识到快餐不利健康，导致肥胖，称快餐食品为垃圾食品(junk food)。随着健康意识的提高，人们对快餐的抵制力也就增强。"慢食运动"(slow food movement)便是一种大规模的抵制行动。

慢食运动始于1986年，意大利美食专栏作家和社会活动家Carlo Petrini向世人提出"为什么我们的生活要这么快？""即使在最繁忙的时候，也不要忘记享受家乡美食。"三年后，"国际慢食运动"在法国巴黎正式启动。20多个国家代表签署了《慢食宣言》，坚持不懈地鼓励人们放慢节奏，享受生活，不接手机，不看手提电脑的信息，在放松的环境下享用精心烹制的食品。慢吞吞并非"慢食"的目标，"慢"的真义是指人们能够掌握自己的生活节奏，培养一种懂得珍惜和欣赏的生活态度。

国际慢食协会的标志是一只缓慢爬行中的蜗牛。慢食运动既是一种美食态度，也是一种生活态度。从精神层面上讲，人们可以静静地体味以六个 M 为内涵的慢食文化：Meal(美味的佳肴)，Menu(精致的菜单)，Music(醉人的音乐)，Manner(周到的礼仪)，Mood(高雅的氛围)，Meeting(愉悦的面谈)。从生理层面而言，细嚼慢咽能产生大量唾液，而唾液中富有的 15 种特殊酶，能有效降解食物中的致癌物质。同时，经慢慢咀嚼后的食物对胃的刺激比较缓和，有利于降低餐后高血糖。专家建议，每口食物咀嚼 20 次以上，每顿饭的进餐时间在 45 分钟以上，是对健康的基本保证。

近年来，在许多国家，这种"细嚼慢咽"的慢食运动正在逐渐蔚然成风。

Ⅲ. Notes to the Text

1. The single porcelain bowl ... drizzled with an egg yolk sauce. —— 她正在做的料理盛在一只瓷碗里：一把小土豆和薄薄的一片浇上蛋黄沙司的神户牛肉。

2. a celebration of simplicity —— fresh and seasonal ingredients, in small and well-balanced proportions, artfully presented. —— 崇尚的是简朴风格——新鲜的时令菜肴，分量不多，搭配均衡，色形美观。

3. Though the food being photographed ... strive for the same spirit. —— 虽然在 Yanagihara 的餐厅里拍摄的食物是日本烹饪的最高水平，即使家里简单的膳食也是努力体现同样的精神。

4. But thanks to the spread of fast-paced lifestyles, such meals are disappearing from Japanese dinner tables, crowded out by convenient, Westernized food. —— 由于快节奏生活方式的普及，这样的（传统）食物受到方便、西化食品的排斥，正从日本人的餐桌上消失。

5. Though Japanese cuisine is still celebrated ... are slowly being lost. —— 虽然日本美食在时尚杂志和豪华餐厅里依然受到赞美，但是作为文化精髓的传统饮食习惯却在逐渐消失。（glossy magazines —— 用优质有光纸印刷并有许多图片的杂志；时尚杂志）

6. a rhythm of food and rest perfectly suited to the blistering heat of the Iberian peninsula in summer. —— 完全顺应伊比利亚半岛夏季的酷热天气的进餐和休息的节奏。

7. Indiana University of Pennsylvania —— 宾州印第安纳大学

8. In an era of instant communication ... cultural homogenization. —— 在通讯快捷和贸易加速的时代，文化交流猛增，导致一种近似文化同质化的现象。（①explode —— to increase quickly；②homogenize —— to change sth so as to make it seem the same）

9. saturated fats —— 饱和脂肪

10. From Chile to China, ... such distinctive experiences is vanishing. —— 从智利到中国，随着新德里、布宜诺斯艾利斯和悉尼等地那些使进餐成为非常独特享受的特色食品的消失，人们患肥胖症、糖尿病和心脏病的危险性在上升。

11. Geography was culinary destiny. —— The place where people lived decided what kind of food they had.

12. Africa, ... in greatest evidence today. —— 非洲饱受沉重政治经济磨难，这种长期存在的状况现在依然十分明显。

13. Most meals are keyed around a single calorie ... with extra food added if available. —— 大多数膳食以单一的高热量的淀粉为主（在东非，通常是玉米粉或面粉煮成的稠粥），如

果有的话,再配上点儿别的食物。

14. the University of Illinois in Chicago —— 伊利诺伊州立大学芝加哥分校

15. All human cultures ... could evolve together. —— 所有的人类文化恐怕都是从这种日复一日、春种秋收的生存方式开始的,但其他地区的人得益于更好环境(土地更加肥沃、旱灾较少发生、气候更加温和),从而能够开垦土地,这意味着他们的饮食和他们的生活可以同时改善。

16. the custom of the large midday meal, eaten with the extended family, that is still observed in pockets of Southern and Western Europe. —— 这种大家庭共同享用丰盛午餐的习俗在南欧和西欧的局部地区依然奉行。(pocket —— small area that is different from its surroundings)

17. Since industrialization, ... bought at a food stand. —— 自工业化以来,维持这样缓慢的文化节奏变得越来越困难了,曾经长时间的午餐已经缩短成为快速进步,吃的是自带午饭盒装的或食品摊上买的东西。(shrivel —— to become smaller)

18. Today, when time zones (**meal times**) have less and less meaning, ... back fast enough anyway. —— 今天时区(吃饭时间)的概念日益淡化,人们几乎无法容忍办公室因午餐而停止办公,而且城市交通越来越差,员工也无法赶回家吃饭再及时赶回来上班。

19. the University of Colorado at Denver and Health Sciences Center —— 科罗拉多州立大学丹佛分校健康研究中心

20. Paradoxically, the thing that has contributed the most to the deterioration of food culture may be one of the very things that has helped turbocharge countries in so many other ways. —— 奇怪的是,导致饮食文化衰退的最重要因素或许正是其他很多方面促使国家高速发展的其中一个因素。(turbocharge —— to add power so as to increase the speed)

21. And the less exposure younger generations ... allow them to appreciate it. —— 年青一代对他们祖父母辈吃的食物尝的越少,他们欣赏这些食物的胃口也就越差。(palate —— the sense of taste)

22. resisted the pull of Westernization —— 抵制西方化的影响(pull —— *informal* influence)

23. While Muslims fast from sunup to sundown, Ramadan nights are marked by calorie-heavy indulgence. —— 斋月期间,虽然穆斯林白天斋戒,但是夜间却是放开肚子大吃高热量食物。

24. Ramadan is "the fasting month that is really a feasting month," hence the tendency for Ramadan weight gain. —— 斋月是禁食的一个月,但其实却是吃饕餮大餐的一个月,因此人们过斋月体重往往增加。

25. the Slow Food movement —— 慢食运动(Please refer to Background Information)

26. food fairs —— 食品展销会

27. "Nobody has time anymore," laments Harvard's Watson. "Not even the French." —— 哈佛大学的沃森惋惜地说,"没有人再有时间了,连法国人也不例外。"(法国被视为美食王国,法国人将"吃"视为人生一大乐事。他们花在餐桌上的时间较多。)

Ⅳ. Language Features

借词

本文在谈到日本和意大利饮食文化时几处使用日语借词（Japanese loanwords），如 sushi, kimono, *colazione*, *merenda*。这些借词的使用有助营造日本和意大利的文化特色。

语言学家的研究表明，英语词汇数量已逾百万，在西方语言中雄居榜首。而这些词汇中大部分是来自其他语言。据统计，英语中外来词的比例高达 80%。纵观英语发展史，我们不难发现英语"具有吸收外来语的特异能力"。长时期的兼收并蓄使英语形成了词汇国际性的特色。

借词分早期借词和近期借词。早期借词的拼写和发音都已英语化（Anglicized）。人们使用这些词时根本感觉不到它们是异国之物。譬如：A large part of the vocabulary of contemporary English consist of borrowed rather than native elements.（当代英语词汇大部分是由借用语成分而不是本族语成分所组成。）这一句话中只有 7 个词是英语本族词（其中"of"出现了 3 次，"the"出现了 2 次），6 个词是法语借词。

现代英语仍然源源不断地从其他语言中吸收新词，这些近期借词依然保留自己的拼写和发音，因而易于识别。

外刊上时而可见外来词，这些借词的使用主要有以下两个目的。

1. 无对等词时表达新概念

例如：American bars-and living rooms — may never be the same, now that a Japanese sing-along fad known as <u>Karaoke</u> has begun to infiltrate American popular culture.

Karaoke（卡拉 OK）发源于日本，英文中无对等词表达这一概念。

2. 营造特定文化气氛

例如：Mr. Peter Broke was yesterday morning recovering from a press of work and steeling himself for the task of instilling a little <u>perestroika</u> into Conservative Central Office in his new role as party chairman.

本段文字摘自报道苏联经济改革的文章，俄语词 perestroika（改革）的使用增添了异国情调。

应该指出的是，借词的使用虽然有助于活跃语言，增强表达效果，但也带来一定的阅读困难。一般来讲，新闻报道由于强调文字通俗易懂，因此尽量少用或不用新的借词，这些词较多出现在新闻周刊所刊载的解释性报道或评论之中。

Ⅴ. Analysis of the Content

1. According to the article, the essence of the Japanese food culture is _____.
   A. use of fresh and seasonal ingredients B. traditional eating habits
   C. artful presentation D. small and well-balanced proportions
2. By saying "As a nutritionist, you have to be outraged," James Watson means that the food the Chinese youth have today _____.
   A. is too much to be good for their health B. is too little to be good for their health

C. has little variety   D. has insufficient nutrition
3. The reason for the disappearance of Japanese cuisine from dinner tables in Japan is _____.
   A. women's presence in the workforce   B. popularity of foods advertised on TV
   C. migration from the country to the cities   D. the spread of fast-paced lifestyle
4. The main reason for the disappearance of the large family midday meal in Latin America was _____.
   A. the popularity of fast food   B. migration from the country to the cities
   C. women's presence in the workforce   D. adoption of foreign food cultures
5. Which of the following can NOT serve as a reason for the gradual disappearance of traditional food culture?
   A. Westernization.   B. Women's presence in the workforce.
   C. Industrialization.   D. The change of climate.

VI. Questions on the Article

1. What are the main features of Japanese food according to the article?
2. What does Yanagihara think of cuisine?
3. What does the author think of food and diet?
4. What does the author mean by saying "Geography was culinary destiny."?
5. What does the author think of the explosion of food culture exchange?
6. What gave rise to the custom of the large midday meal during the agrarian age?
7. What is the major change in the diet habit of Italians? What is the reason for the change?
8. What change has taken place in the diet of many Latin Americans?
9. What effects does women's presence in the workforce have on food culture according to the article?
10. Is it easy to preserve the traditional food culture according to the author? Why or why not?

VII. Topics for Discussion

1. Is modern food culture worse than the traditional food culture?
2. Is women's presence in the workforce the most important factor in the deterioration of food culture?

Lesson 13

Road Warriors

Tie-ups. Backups. Gridlock.[1] **The American commute has never been so painful. Is there any solution?**

By Will Sullivan

For Kathy Kniss, staying calm while getting to and from work is about sticking to her rules. The 29-year-old publicist must be out the door of her Long Beach, Calif.[2], home by 7:45 a.m. at the latest. Some car-choked neighborhoods are just off limits. When leaving her office in Culver City, she must shut down her computer by 5:54 p.m., so she can be in her car by 6:00 to avoid the traffic buildup on side streets[3] and make it to La Cienega Boulevard[4] before 6:15.

Five years ago, Kniss says, commuting caused so much stress that she had panic attacks on the road and had to see a hypnotherapist. But moving closer to her office is out of the question. "I live on the beach, and I pay the same amount for a two-bedroom that I would be paying in the middle of Los Angeles for a complete dump," she says.[5]

It's only about 25 miles from Kniss's office to her home, but driving to her little bit of heaven in the evenings is a grueling 75 minutes, meaning that, on average, her speedometer is hovering just above zero. That's on a good day, when weather, accidents, or bad luck don't interfere. "It's Murphy's Law[6]," Kniss laments about her drive. "If something can go wrong, it will."

The status of the City of Angels[7] as a commuting hell is nothing new. But by 2030, according to some estimates, driving in Atlanta, Minneapolis, and nine other urban areas will be worse than present-day Los Angeles. Nationwide, more and more people will see their roads clogged for longer periods of time. With Mayor Michael Bloomberg's rollout last week of a plan to charge hefty tolls for driving in most of Manhattan, New York became the most recent city to try to fight back.[8] Others are investing in mass transit or high-tech traffic management. Across the country, new technology, new thinking, and cold cash are being leveraged in aggressive efforts to combat congestion.[9]

But serious doubts linger about whether any of these plans will amount to more than a finger in the dike.[10]

People have been complaining about congestion since the time of Julius Caesar[11], who banned some traffic from downtown Rome. But in America, the 50-year-old Interstate Highway System[12] is showing its age, more people are on the roads, and traffic has grown dramatically worse. Americans spent 3.7 billion hours in traffic in 2003, the last year for which such figures are available — more than a fivefold increase from just 21 years earlier. The amount of free-flowing travel is less than half what it was in the '80s, and the average commuter now loses 47 hours to congested traffic every year.

Disconnect. The issue mainly boils down to population growth outpacing road building.[13] America has about 70 million more people than it did a quarter century ago, but highway miles have increased by a little more than 5 percent in that time. The Department of Transportation estimates that the demand for ground transportation — either by road or rail — will be 2½ times as great by 2050, while highway capacity is projected to increase by only 10 percent during that time.[14]

Changes in consumer behavior also aggravate traffic congestion. A strong economy has driven car ownership to new heights; the average household now has slightly more cars, 1.9, than drivers, 1.8. High property values and restrictive zoning[15] in many areas have made finding quality housing near one's workplace virtually impossible for many, and the quest for affordable housing has sent people to ever more-distant locales. Commuters to New York City increasingly call the Pocono Mountains[16] of Pennsylvania, two hours away, home, while workers in Washington have streamed into Gettysburg, Pa., a full 85 miles away.

Folks in places like these are considered "extreme commuters," those traveling 90 minutes or more to work every day. According to the U.S. Census Bureau, more than 3 million people — about 2.8 percent of workers — now have such commutes, a 95 percent increase from 1990.

Dave Givens, 47, hits the road[17] at 4:30 a.m. each day for a three-hour drive from his home in Mariposa, Calif., on the edge of Yosemite National Park[18], to his job at Cisco Systems[19] in San Jose, Calif. It's an hour before he even stops for his first coffee and picks up his carpool partner. He adds 372 miles to the odometer daily. "It's kind of a daily mind game of what's on the radio traffic reports," says Givens, who won first place in an "America's Longest Commute" contest run by Midas Inc[20]. Givens says the drive is a small price to pay to live in the town his family has inhabited since the Gold Rush[21]. And he says he enjoys the rural lifestyle.

But all that driving takes a toll on a commuter's time, money, and peace of mind.[22] David Lewis, a British scientist who studies the brain's response to stress, found that the tension commuters experience when stuck in traffic is comparable to that felt by first-time parachutists. Part-time New York cabdriver Sol Soloncha knows that all too well. "I'm a Buddhist," he says. "I do yoga, I practice meditation, and weekday traffic gets so bad that even I can't keep my composure during it."

Traffic can be more than an annoyance. Medical symptoms ranging from sleep deprivation to digestive problems are linked to long commutes, and a 2004 article in the *New England Journal of Medicine* found that being stuck in a traffic jam more than doubles one's chance of experiencing a heart attack in the subsequent hour.

Consequences. Traffic inflicts social costs as well. Harvard public policy Prof. Robert Putnam found that community involvement falls 10 percent for every 10 minutes spent driving to work. And leisure pursuits are casualties, too. "It sort of turns me off to have to go far to see any sort of entertainment or any arts, or even to go to the beach," says Donald Pierce of Granada Hills, Calif. "Any good day at the beach, there's going to be a lot of traffic."[23]

Major improvement in traffic congestion not only requires massive government intervention but also involves getting all political forces on the same page.[24] And that can be an insurmountable hurdle. In Virginia, years of fierce legislative battling over who should foot the bill[25] for traffic relief in heavily congested Northern Virginia finally resulted in a compromise between Gov. Tim Kaine and antitax Republican legislators in April. The bill authorizes $3 billion in borrowing for statewide improvements, such as widening highways and improving rail service, and lets car-choked regions raise taxes and fees for local projects. But even backers urged Virginians not to set their hopes too high, with a Republican state Senate leader calling the bill "one of the ugliest bastard stepchildren" to pass the Senate.

Some cities, including Houston, have embarked on aggressive programs of road building, trying to stay ahead of their swelling populations. But significantly increasing capacity is just not feasible for metropolitan areas with high population densities. Building more roads in places like Chicago or Philadelphia would involve either leveling buildings or tunneling — an option that is now virtually unthinkable after Boston's troubled, and fabulously expensive, Big Dig project[26]. Even when new roads are built, they are often quickly filled to the point of congestion by drivers who previously traveled at other times, took other roads, or used public transportation, says Brookings Institution traffic expert Anthony Downs.

With that in mind, more cities are looking to enhance public transportation options. In January, Denver opened new lines that more than doubled the miles covered by its light rail system, to 33. By 2017, the city hopes to have laid down 119 miles of track and 18 miles of bus rapid transit, at a cost of $4.7 billion. Charlotte, N.C., will unveil the first of what is expected to be a five-line rail system in November, joining cities like Salt Lake City and Dallas, whose low population densities don't make them obvious candidates for rail.

Perhaps most surprisingly, Los Angeles, where driving is almost a religion[27], is undergoing a veritable transit boom, furiously digging new subway tunnels and expanding a rapid bus system that will let buses zoom down their own designated lanes. Mayor Antonio Villaraigosa is pushing hard for his dream of a "subway to the sea," a Metro line running under the notoriously jammed Wilshire Boulevard[28]. "This city will one day have a world-class transportation system, period," he proclaims.[29]

There is cause for optimism. Less than 18 months after the October 2005 opening of the city's Orange Line — a high-speed bus line using an old railroad right of way to avoid traffic — ridership had reached the city's 2020 projections. And unlike nearly every other city, Los Angeles drivers spend less time in traffic now than they did a decade ago, thanks to both mass transit and aggressive traffic management.

But experts are skeptical that public transportation offers a real solution to congestion problems. In the 2000 census, just 4.7 percent of people said they used public transit to get to work, and transit represents only 2 percent of daily trips in Southern California. In most cities, even if the percentage of trips using transit tripled, which is not likely, the resulting drop in congestion would be overwhelmed by the projected growth in population. And it would no doubt be extraordinarily expensive. Villaraigosa estimates that a public transit system that would seriously reduce congestion, rather than just slowing its growth, would require funding "that has heretofore been unprecedented. I'm talking about ... tens of billions of dollars and beyond." That's in Los Angeles alone.

The prohibitive cost of alleviating gridlock is one factor behind the Department of Transportation's new congestion initiative, announced last year. The department hopes to partner with cities to show the usefulness of charging tolls based on the level of congestion, raising the price during rush hour to deter some commuters from traveling during peak times. DOT believes this would keep highways near capacity without descending into gridlock, and increase the number of cars able to travel on a road daily by 40 percent. "What we are trying to do is push states to be as aggressive as they can be," says Transportation Secretary Mary Peters.

Cordons. That includes encouraging the implementation of "cordon tolls,"[30] which would charge drivers for entering crowded urban areas. Such systems are already in place in London and Singapore, but Bloomberg's proposed $8 charge for daytime driving in Manhattan, assessed using E-ZPass[31] technology and cameras, would be a first for America. In announcing his push for tolling, Bloomberg conceded that he had once been a skeptic himself but said he had come to see it as necessary.

The proposal faces an uphill battle in the state Legislature. Trucking unions are already griping because trucks would be charged a whopping $21 for entering Manhattan, and politicians in the city's outer boroughs are unmoved by the mayor's pledge to increase public transit to compensate for the charge.

DOT Secretary Peters concedes that cordon tolling is not politically palatable in most cities and that perhaps the most realistic option is so-called HOT lanes[32], converted carpool lanes where drivers willing to pay a variable fee can ride with carpools and buses. Though often derided as "Lexus lanes"[33] for the wealthy, they have proved effective in several states as a means of letting those willing to pay avoid gridlock. In Minnesota, which opened its first HOT lanes in 2005, drivers in the lanes travel at an average speed of 50 miles per hour 95 percent of the time. But HOT lanes lack the major benefit of other tolling options for reducing congestion; since people can still use the untolled lanes free, the lanes don't discourage drivers from hitting the road during peak hours, limiting congestion relief. And even congressional Republicans who preach limited government are skeptical that market forces are enough to bust the nation's bottlenecks.

The DOT's plan also encourages states to follow a growing trend of seeking private financing for building or managing roads. An Australian-Spanish consortium paid $1.8 billion for a 99-year lease of the Chicago Skyway[34] in 2004, and a number of states have inked long-term leases of toll roads[35] or are considering it. Both the New Jersey and Pennsylvania turnpikes could go on the auction block soon.[36]

However, both the American Automobile Association and the American Trucking Associations are wary of leasing highways, and previous leases have sometimes borne out their concerns. The deals often forbid government to build roads that would compete with the private toll road. After selling a private company the right to operate HOT lanes on the Riverside Freeway[37] for $120 million in the late '80s, officials in Orange County, Calif., had to buy them in 2003 for more than $200 million to make improvements on the road's untolled lanes. In Indiana, the Republican loss of its House majority in November was blamed in part on Gov. Mitch Daniels's unpopular 75-year lease of the Indiana Toll Road, which led to a toll hike.

"There is certainly a strongly held belief in this country that roads are for the public benefit ... and that they are free," says Bill Graves, the president of the ATA and former governor of Kansas.

With few appealing options, many traffic experts suggest that the growth of congestion is inevitable. That might not be the end of the world, says traffic expert Downs. To remain efficient and prosperous, people largely have to be traveling to the same places at the same times of day. Traffic is simply the equivalent of waiting in line. Downs contends that only a serious economic downturn — such as the one that sent congestion plummeting in Silicon Valley after the tech bubble burst — can reverse the cycle of rising congestion.

That doesn't mean government is helpless. Many cities are looking to Los Angeles for lessons in how to slow traffic's growth. To avoid blockages, the city has stopped road construction during rush hour, stiffened penalties for parking illegally, and deploys a roaming fleet of tow trucks to quickly clear stalled or damaged cars off the freeways.

Tech fix[38]. New technology also gives the city an edge.[39] Its Automated Traffic Surveillance and Control system[40] uses sensors buried in the road to measure traffic flow and can automatically adjust 3,400 of the city's 4,400 traffic lights to ease congestion. The system can, for example, extend a green light for a bus that is behind schedule or an emergency vehicle rushing to an accident. At its high-tech command center, buried four stories under City Hall East in downtown Los Angeles, ATSAC operators can view bottlenecks from hundreds of cameras throughout the city and make their own adjustments.

The system has given Los Angeles unprecedented power to respond to unusual traffic patterns, from the Academy Awards[41] to the 1994 earthquake that collapsed key sections of the city's freeway system. And the city is hoping to use some of its share of California's recently approved $19.9 billion transportation bond — the largest bond in state history — to link the remaining lights to ATSAC.

The city has most likely shaved minutes off its frustrated citizens' commutes, but such measures can go only so far. Each morning and evening, despite all their efforts, ATSAC operators still watch freeways clog and Wilshire Boulevard turn as suffocating as the La Brea Tar Pits[42] it runs beside. "We're maxing out what our roads are able to do[43]," says John Fisher, assistant general manager of the Los Angeles Department of Transportation.

How bad can traffic in American cities get? Los Angeles's long-range transportation plan is a grim look at the future. By 2025, Los Angeles County is projected to have 3 million more people, which could prompt a 30 percent increase in car trips. At that rate, the report suggests, "congestion will last nearly all day long." None of the city's innovative solutions — from new subway lines to traffic management systems — are likely to change that. And at the rate traffic in other cities is snarling, they won't be far behind.

From *U.S. News & World Report*, May 7, 2007

I. New Words

borough	['bʌrə]	n.	自治的村、镇、区
bust	[bʌst]	v.	*informal* to break
carpool	['kɑːpuːl]	v. & n.	合伙使用汽车,拼车
consortium	[kən'sɔːtjəm]	n.	财团,联营企业
cordon	['kɔːdən]	n.	警戒线,屏障

deprivation	[ˌdepriˈveiʃən]	n.	a lack of sth one needs
freeway	[ˈfriːwei]	n.	〈美〉高速公路
grueling	[ˈgruəliŋ]	adj.	very difficult and tiring
hover	[ˈhɔvə]	v.	to stay very close to sth
hypnotherapist	[ˌhipnəˈθerəpist]	n.	催眠术治疗家
locale	[ləuˈkɑːl]	n.	a place or area
odometer	[ɔˈdɔmitə]	n.	（汽车等的）里程表
palatable	[ˈpælətəbl]	adj.	pleasant, acceptable
plummet	[ˈplʌmit]	v.	to fall suddenly from a high level
publicist	[ˈpʌblisist]	n.	广告人员，公关人员
quest	[kwest]	n.	*literary* a long search for sth
ridership	[ˈraidəʃip]	n.	公共交通工具乘客（人数）
shave	[ʃeiv]	v.	to cut a small amount off
snarl	[snɑːl]	v.	(of traffic) to make cars unable to move
speedometer	[spiˈdɔmitə]	n.	速度计，里程计
stall	[stɔːl]	v.	to make a car stop suddenly
uphill	[ˈʌpˈhil]	adj.	艰难的
veritable	[ˈveritəbl]	adj.	名副其实的，十足的
whopping	[ˈwɔpiŋ]	adj.	*informal* very big

Ⅱ. Background Information

美国交通

美国号称"车轮上的国家"（a country on wheels），汽车最为普遍，人们以车代步，上下班、购物、参加活动都靠汽车。驾车出行已是美国人生活的重要一部分。美国政府一直致力于交通发展。从18世纪90年代开始，全美范围内兴起了改善公路运输的运动，特别注重收费公路的修建。在铁路建成以前，收费公路在一定的程度上改善了交通运输，一度成为通往美国西部的主要干道。从19世纪20年代开始，美国政府大力修建铁路，1914年，美国铁路的总长度已超过欧洲铁路总和，成为世界上铁路线最长的国家。直到20世纪50年代，铁路运输在美国的交通运输系统中占据了主导地位。从20世纪60年代开始，美国政府开始修建和完善高速公路网络。经过几十年的发展，美国公路系统已经完备，高速公路和主次干道纵横交错，辅助设施配置齐全，停车场遍布城乡各处。

可是，美国的道路发展难以跟上人口和汽车的迅猛增长。1976年美国人口为2亿，2006年又突破3亿。随着美国城市的扩张，人们对汽车的依赖性不断增加。如今每个美国家庭平均就拥有两辆汽车。如此多的车辆让美国很多大城市饱受交通拥挤的困扰。一项调查结果显示：从1982年到2000年，美国各城市交通堵塞造成的时间和汽油浪费不仅带来了每年高达680亿美元的经济损失，而且还消耗了大量的能源，造成了空气污染，导致了非常严重的环境问题。在美国主要城市中，第二大城市洛杉矶在高峰期间的塞车状况最为严重。在该市市区驾车上班的人平均每年在路上遇到堵车的时间为136小时。其他名列堵车最严重的十大城市或地区分别为旧金山、奥克兰、芝加哥、华盛顿、西雅图、迈阿密、波士顿、硅谷、丹佛和纽约。

面对日益严重的堵车状况,美国政府和社会一直积极采取应对措施,除建设新的公路和地铁之外,还注意改善城市交通管理和控制。美国已于2007年底开始在迈阿密、明尼阿波利斯、纽约、旧金山和西雅图五个大城市进行试点,寻求解决城市交通拥挤问题的措施,包括拥挤(城区)收费(congestion pricing)、公共交通和专线道路收费(tolling)。此外,改善和发展公共交通、运用新技术疏导交通、弹性工作制(flexible work schedules)、电脑联勤(telecommuting)等也是大城市减轻高峰时段交通拥挤的主要措施。

Ⅲ. Notes to the Text

1. Tie-ups. Backups. Gridlock. — 暂时受阻,车排长队,全面堵塞(① tie-up — a temporary problem that delays traffic;② backup — an accumulation of cars caused by clogging or by a stoppage;③ gridlock — a traffic jam in which no vehicular movement is possible)

2. Long Beach,Calif — 加州长滩市(加州西南部的一座港市)

3. side streets — 小街

4. La Cienega Boulevard — 该街道位于加州好莱坞,这里聚集许多高级餐厅,故又称作"餐厅街"

5. "I live on the beach,..." she says. — 她说:"我住在海边,租了一套两居室的公寓,而在洛杉矶市中心地区同样的钱只能租到一个十分蹩脚的地方。"(dump — *slang*, a dirty, shabby and unpleasant place)

6. Murphy's Law — 墨菲法则(a statement of the fact that if anything can possibly go wrong, it will go wrong)

7. the City of Angels — referring to the city of Los Angeles

8. With Mayor Michael Bloomberg's rollout last week ... try to fight back. — 上周纽约市长迈克尔·布隆伯格展示了最新的计划:对驶入曼哈顿大部分地区车辆征收很高的过路费,纽约成了美国最新整治交通的城市。(① rollout — *informal* the first public showing of sth new;② hefty—large in amount)

9. Across the country, new technology ... combat congestion. — 整个美国都在采用新的技术、新的理念和投入现金,积极努力解决交通堵塞问题。[① cold cash — 现金(hard cash);② leverage — to use]

10. But serious doubts linger about whether any of these plans will amount to more than a finger in the dike. — 但是人们依然十分怀疑这些计划所起的作用不过只是"指堵堤穴"传说而已。(① to amount to — to be same as;② a finger in the dike—referring to the tale about a boy who saved Holland from a disastrous flood by putting a finger in the dike)

11. Julius Caesar — 尤利乌斯·恺撒(100 B.C.—44 B.C.)(a Roman politician, military leader and writer who took control of the government of Rome and changed it from a Republic to an Empire, making himself the first Roman emperor)

12. Interstate Highway System — referring to the Dwight D. Eisenhower National System of Interstate and Defense Highways. (It has almost 70,000 kilometers of roads. It

crosses more than 55,000 bridges and can be found in 49 states. Eisenhower signed the bill creating the highway system in 1956.)

13. The issue mainly boils down to population growth outpacing road building. —问题产生的主要原因是人口增长速度超过道路建设速度。(to boil down to sth — sth is the main reason)

14. The Department of Transportation estimates ... increase by only 10 percent during that time. —交通部预计，到2050年美国地面交通（公路和铁路）的需求将会增长1.5倍，而公路的通行能力预计只能提高10%。

15. restrictive zoning —限制性分区制(zoning — the act of deciding what particular use an area should have)

16. Pocono Mountains — a range of the Appalachian system in northeast Pennsylvania and also a popular year-round resort area

17. hit the road — *informal* to start a journey

18. Yosemite national park —优胜美地国家公园(a national park in California which is famous for its waterfalls and rock formations)

19. Cisco Systems —思科系统公司（该公司是全球领先的电信网络设备供应商）

20. Midas Inc. —美国麦达斯控股集团（全称Midas Holdings, Inc, 该集团主要从事直接投资）

21. the Gold Rush — a period of feverish migration of workers into the area of a dramatic discovery of commercial quantities of gold

22. But all that driving takes a toll on a commuter's time, money, and peace of mind. —但是长时间的驾驶浪费了通勤者的时间和金钱，也搅乱了他们平和的心情。(take a toll on sth — to have a bad effect on sth)

23. "It sort of turns me off ... there's going to be a lot of traffic." —"无论是观看娱乐节目还是艺术展览，甚至是去海滩，都得要走很远的路，这使我有些不感兴趣，"家住加利福尼亚州格拉纳达山的唐纳德·皮尔斯说，"只要海边天气好，路上车流量就会大。"(turn sb off — to cause sb to be bored or disgusted by sth)

24. Major improvement in traffic congestion not only requires massive government intervention but also involves getting all political forces on the same page. —交通阻塞状况要有较大改善不仅需要政府大规模干预而且需要所有政治势力齐心协力。(be on the same page — to agree about what they are trying to achieve)

25. foot the bill — to pay for something, especially something expensive

26. the Big Dig project — referring to a 15-billion-dollar project, the most expensive highway project in the U.S. history. It involved building new tunnels to support an 8-to-10-lane underground expressway as well as new bridges.

27. driving is almost a religion —开车几乎必不可少(religion — an activity which sb is extremely enthusiastic about and does regularly)

28. a Metro line running under the notoriously jammed Wilshire Boulevard —一条运行在以交通堵塞出名的威尔希尔大道下的地下铁路(① Metro — an underground train system; ② Wilshire Boulevard — one of the principal east-west arterial roads in Los Angeles)

29. "This city will one day have a world-class transportation system, period," he

proclaims. — 他声称,"一句话,这座城市总有一天会有世界水平的交通系统。"(period — used at the end of a sentence for emphasis)

30. the implementation of "cordon tolls" — 实施"区域性收费"

31. E-ZPass — 电子射频收费系统(the electronic toll collection system used on most toll bridges and toll roads in the northeastern United States)

32. HOT lanes — 高乘载收费车道[referring to high occupancy toll lanes, designed for single-occupant vehicles which want to use lanes or entire roads that are designated for the use of high-occupancy vehicles (HOVs, also known as carpools)]

33. Lexus lanes — referring to HOT lanes, because in the United States many critics view HOT lanes as a perk for the rich(Lexus — a type of large comfortable car made by Toyota, which is often driven by wealthy business people)

34. the Chicago Skyway — referring to Chicago Skyway Toll Bridge System (a 12.5 k.m. long toll way bridging Interstate 90 at the Dan Ryan Expressway on the west, and the Indiana Toll Road on the east with a feature of 800 m. long steel truss bridge, known as the "High Bridge")

35. inked long-term leases of toll roads — 签署收费道路长期租约(ink — to sign)

36. Both the New Jersey and Pennsylvania turnpikes could go on the auction block soon. — 新泽西和宾夕法尼亚州的收费公路不久要进行拍卖。(① turnpike — a main road for the use of fast traveling traffic, especially one which drivers must pay to use; ② go on the block — to be offered for sale, especially at an auction)

37. the Riverside Freeway — the assigned name of a segment of California east-west freeway, located entirely within Southern California

38. Tech fix — 技术措施(referring to the use of new technology to solve the problem)

39. New technology also gives the city an edge. — 新技术同样也给城市带来了优势。(an edge — an advantage)

40. Automated Traffic Surveillance and Control system — 自动交通监控系统

41. Academy Awards — 奥斯卡金像奖颁奖典礼

42. La Brea Tar Pits — 拉布瑞亚焦油坑(a famous cluster of tar pits located in Hancock Park in the urban heart of Los Angeles, California, USA)

43. We're maxing out what our roads are able to do — 我们在最大限度地使用公路(max out — *AmE informal* to reach the limit at which nothing more is possible)

Ⅳ. Language Features

"说"意动词

本文"说"意动词较为丰富,除了"say"之外,还用了"lament""suggest""contend" "concede"和"proclaim"。

新闻报道经常转述、援引新闻相关人物的谈话,因而频频出现"说"意动词。这些动词虽然在表示"说"这个总的概念方面是相同的,但是同中有异,在语义、情感、文体上存在不同程度区

别,这些词如果使用妥帖,就会产生以下效果:

1. 有助语言准确

例 1 "We're not making any progress," concludes Dallas officer Nabors. (conclude 推断说)

例 2 "I need my creative space behind closed doors," she explains. (explain 解释说)

2. 有助语言简洁

例 1 "And mine, too!" hastened Little Lucas. (hasten — say in a hurry 急急忙忙地说)

例 2 Addressing foreign journalists here, he emphasized the ANC would not revert to violence… (emphasize 强调说)

3. 有助态度鲜明

例 1 "We're tennis fanatics: we love it," cheers Christie Ann's aunt… (cheer 喝彩说)

例 2 "One of the finest speeches I've ever heard," praised Ford speaking of the brief, touching text drafted by Reagan. (praise 赞扬说)

4. 有助语言生动

例 1 "The next guy who hollers 'Headache!', I'm gonna kick his ass," sputters a winded James. (sputter 因激动、愤怒唾沫飞溅地说)

例 2 Shrugged a Defense Department official: "The Soviets are the ones who walked out of the arms limitation talks." (shrug 耸了耸肩不满地说)

常见的"说"意动词有:

acknowledge	承认	admit	承认	add	又说
affirm	肯定	allege	断言	agree	同意
announce	宣布	argue	争辩	ask	询问
assert	宣称	boast	夸口说	claim	声称
complain	抱怨	challenge	提出异议	conclude	最后说
contend	争论	declare	宣称	elaborate	详述
emphasize	强调	enquire	询问	explain	解释
imply	暗示说	insist	坚持说	joke	开玩笑说
maintain	断言	object	反对说	observe	评述
pledge	保证	promise	许愿	refute	反驳
reply	回答	retort	反诘	reveal	透露
state	说,声称	stress	强调	suggest	建议说

相比之下,纯新闻由于强调客观公正,含有情感意思的"说"意动词一般少用或不用,而解释性报道(interpretative reporting)、特写(features)和新新闻(new journalism)类写作中含有情感意思的"说"意动词使用较多。

Ⅴ. Analysis of the Content

1. The word "religion" in the sentence "… driving is almost a religion" (in Para. 17) means _____.

   A. belief in the existence of God

    B. an activity which is extremely important in life
    C. worship of a god   D. an interesting hobby
 2. The subhead "Disconnect" refers to the fact that _____.
    A. the government is out of touch with reality
    B. commuters have no contact with the community
    C. commuters' homes are distant from work places
    D. the government is not concerned about traffic congestion
 3. According to the article, the main reason for traffic congestion in many American cities is _____.
    A. Americans' propensity for better housing in the suburbs
    B. the fast increase of cars
    C. poor traffic surveillance and control
    D. population's growth outpacing road building
 4. Which of the following is NOT on the author's list of costs caused by traffic congestion?
    A. air pollution   B. loss of time
    C. loss of money   D. stress
 5. The author's view of traffic congestion in the future is _____.
    A. optimistic   B. unknown
    C. objective   D. pessimistic

Ⅵ. Questions on the Article

 1. Why does Kathy Kniss live in Long Beach and spend much time commuting under great stress?
 2. What is New York's recent measure to tackle the congestion problem?
 3. Is Los Angeles an isolated case in traffic congestion? How is the traffic situation in many other American cities?
 4. What are the costs of traffic congestion?
 5. According to the author, what does major improvement in traffic congestion require? Is it easy?
 6. Why is it infeasible to significantly increase traffic capacity of metropolitan areas with high population densities?
 7. How is Los Angeles trying to improve its traffic?
 8. Why are experts skeptical that public transportation offers a real solution to congestion problems?
 9. What is the new congestion initiative announced by the Department of Transportation?
 10. What do HOT lanes refer to? What is the effect of those lanes?
 11. What is the future of Los Angeles County's traffic?

Ⅶ. Topics for Discussion

 1. Is traffic congestion an unsolvable problem in the U. S. ?
 2. Is it a sensible idea to charge tolls based on congestion level?

Lesson 14

The Boom Towns and Ghost Towns of the New Economy

New York, Houston, Washington, D. C.—plus college towns and the energy belt—are all up, while much of the Sun Belt is (still) down. Mapping the winners and losers since the crash.

By Richard Florida

America's economic map is ever changing. Great migrations—settlers westward; African Americans northward; urbanites outward to greener suburbs, then back again—have shaped the country's history. Cities have heaved skyward; boom towns have come and gone.

Back in the spring of 2009, I wrote in these pages that the financial crisis would "permanently and profoundly alter the country's economic landscape." Some cities and regions "will eventually spring back stronger than before," I predicted. "Others may never come back at all."

It might have sounded apocalyptic, but tectonic shifts of this kind are not unprecedented. They are the geographic counterpart to what the economist Joseph Schumpeter dubbed "creative destruction"—the great gales of change that level some companies and industries, and give rise to others.[1] As powerful as they might seem in the moment, it is only when we look back through the lens of history that the full extent of economic and geographic changes becomes clear.

Five years after the crash, with the national economy just beginning to return to something resembling normalcy, we can begin to trace the outlines of America's emerging economic map—and take inventory of the places that are thriving, those that are declining, and those that are trying, in novel ways, to come back.

The American economy is enormous, and enormously complicated. It comprises scores of industries harboring hundreds of occupations, spread across more than 350 metro economies, large and small. A variety of measures can be used to divine the health and prospects of these different places—population growth, job growth, housing prices, and the unemployment rate are among the more common. Each of these measures has its uses, but some of them can conceal as much as they reveal. Population growth, for instance, tells you nothing about the skills and education of the people arriving; job growth says nothing about whether the new jobs are good or bad.

Throughout this article, I will draw on some of these measures. But I'll lean most heavily on three measures less commonly seen in the popular press, but perhaps more telling: the composition of job growth (high-wage, mid-wage, or low-wage); productivity growth (which is the basis for improvements in the standard of living); and venture-capital funding (a proxy for the sort of entrepreneurial innovation that can power future growth).

Taken together, the patterns revealed by these measures provide a fine-grained picture of America's post-crisis geography. The economic landscape is being reshaped around two kinds of hubs—centers of knowledge and ideas, and clusters of energy production. Overwhelmingly, these are the places driving the economic recovery. Outside them, the economy remains troubled and weak.

New York City was widely expected to be devastated by the financial crisis. Wall Street's collapse, the conventional wisdom went, would bring the whole city down with it. In 2009, I predicted that New York would in fact prove to be one of the country's most resilient places. Even so, the speed and strength of its rebound has surprised me—its explosive growth as a start-up center especially so.

New York's financial sector did shrink somewhat—before the 2008 crash, finance and insurance accounted for 44 percent of Manhattan's payroll; in 2009, 37 percent—but the city has retained its perch as a preeminent global finance center, and the reduction of the finance industry's footprint has provided the spur and the space for other industries to grow.[2]

New York has incredibly high concentrations of management, media, design, and creative occupations. Since the crash, it has gained ground in its competition with Los Angeles as a center for media and entertainment (the imminent return of *The Tonight Show*, which decamped for Burbank, California, in 1972, is one result). Brooklyn—the setting for the HBO megahit *Girls*—has emerged as a major trendsetter for everything from film and television to indie rock and artisanal food.[3]

The crash was supposed to send real-estate values plummeting throughout the city, and prices did dip. But today Manhattan and nearby sections of Brooklyn not only are booming, they have surpassed pre-crisis peaks. And as anyone who has noticed how many windows are dark in Manhattan's luxury high-rises might have guessed, New York is not just a playground for the global elite, but a locus for their investments—including high-end properties where they reside for a small part of the year.[4]

Then there is tech. Wall Street has always provided capital to high-tech businesses, but until recently, its investment dollars were typically exported to other regions. Yet over the past 10 years, greater New York's share of the nation's start-ups funded by venture capital has more than doubled, from 5.3 percent to 11.4 percent, far outpacing Silicon Valley's rate of growth, with much of the growth occurring after the crash. In 2011, the city attracted more venture-capital investment than any other save San Francisco, nearly double Palo Alto's, almost four times Boston's, and more than six times Seattle's.

Tech clusters have sprouted in Manhattan, mostly in lower neighborhoods like the Flatiron District, and Chelsea and the Meatpacking District down to SoHo and Tribeca on the West Side.[5] All of these neighborhoods are diverse places, filled with old buildings like the former Port Authority building that now serves as Google's nearly $2 billion New York headquarters. Their repurposing as tech hubs only makes the city stronger and more diverse.

New York's rise as a tech center signals a major shift in the locus of venture-capital-fueled innovation. For a long time, high-tech start-ups have clustered in suburban office parks along freeways, places that are sometimes called "nerdistans."[6] But since the crisis, start-ups have taken an urban turn. San Francisco, which has fared extremely well since the crash, is a striking case in point. Over the past several years, Twitter has established its headquarters downtown, Pinterest has moved from Silicon Valley to San Francisco[7], and even Yahoo has created a new facility in the old *San Francisco Chronicle*[8] building in the South of Market neighborhood. The legendary Silicon Valley investor Paul Graham saw this coming. "For all its power, Silicon Valley has a great weakness," he wrote in 2006, "its soul-crushing suburban sprawl."[9] Today, San Francisco proper tops Silicon Valley as a center for venture-capital investment, by a wide margin. The same shift has happened in greater Boston, where venture-capital investment and start-up activity are now more concentrated in Cambridge and downtown Boston than in the suburbs along Route 128.

What's surprising is that tech stayed in the suburbs for so long. The urbanist Jane Jacobs long ago noted how cities, with their deep wells of intellectual and entrepreneurial capital, and their density and diversity, provide ideal ecosystems for entrepreneurial innovation. Nineteenth-century Pittsburgh and Henry Ford's Detroit were the Silicon Valleys of their time.

Suburban tech parks, of course, aren't all about to be shuttered. Big, established companies like Google, Apple, and Facebook need the large amounts of space that their suburban campuses provide. Company shuttles will continue to run between San Francisco, where more and more workers prefer to live, and Cupertino[10] or Mountain View[11]. But new entrepreneurial activity is increasingly bubbling up from within the urban core.

America's "knowledge metros," large and small, make up perhaps the biggest group of winners, overall, since the crash. Data provided by Economic Modeling Specialists International[12] show that a handful of knowledge metros have an overwhelming lead in generating the high-wage jobs (those paying more than $21 an hour) that America needs. Nearly two-thirds of San Jose's[13] new jobs have been high-wage, as have nearly half of the new jobs in nearby San Francisco. San Jose also leads the nation in productivity growth, with a nearly 10 percent increase between 2009 and 2011, based on comprehensive data from the Bureau of Economic Analysis[14]. Portland, Oregon, posted the second-highest level of productivity growth among large metros, nearly 7 percent, belying its *Portlandia* caricature as a place for slackers[15]. Austin's tech-fueled economy combined the fastest job growth of all large metros (10.5 percent between 2009 and 2013) with well-above-average growth in productivity and in high-wage jobs.

College towns such as Boulder, Colorado; Ann Arbor, Michigan; Charlottesville, Virginia; Champaign-Urbana, Illinois; and Lawrence, Kansas, number among the nation's leading centers for start-up activity on a per capita basis. And in general, college towns have combined low unemployment rates with stable economies. The strength of these smaller centers suggests that the future does not belong to large superstar cities alone.

Knowledge, it turns out, is what allows metros to generate good high-wage jobs. Across America's metro regions, I have found that high-wage jobs are closely related to several key markers of regional knowledge economies: the share of adults who are college grads; the share of the workforce in professional, technical, and creative jobs; the levels of innovation and venture-capital investment.

That brings us to Washington, D. C. As the urbanist Aaron Renn wrote recently, Washington is well on its way to becoming America's "second city," on track to displace Chicago and Los Angeles "in terms of economic power and national importance." Greater Washington has had among the nation's lowest rates of unemployment, the most-stable housing prices, and high overall job growth since the crash. A whopping 59 percent of all new jobs created there since 2009 have been high-wage jobs, second only to San Jose. The Washington metro area includes six of the 10 most affluent counties in the nation.

Washington's economy has clearly prospered from federal spending; lobbying and government contracts are significant sources of its wealth. But its economy is not entirely or even predominantly parasitic. The decline in the federal workforce over the past several years (a result of austerity) has not substantially altered the region's economic trajectory. The ultimate source of the region's wealth is Washington's unparalleled human capital. The population is the best educated of any large metro's in the United States; about half the region's adults hold bachelor's degrees, and nearly a quarter have graduate degrees.

Greater Washington is much more economically diverse than its reputation suggests. It is a major center for media and real-estate finance, and is home to a small but growing cluster of high-tech activity, in the city as well as in outlying Maryland and Northern Virginia. The greater Washington metro area consistently ranks among the nation's leading centers of venture-capital-backed start-ups, alongside noted tech hubs like Austin, San Diego, and Seattle. For well-educated professionals, especially those with families, D. C. offers tremendous quality of life and a raft of opportunities at a fraction of Manhattan prices. And indeed, it is the southern terminus of the vibrant economic corridor stretching all the way up to Boston, which produced more than $2.5 trillion in economic output in 2011, more than all of the United Kingdom or Brazil.

One thing I didn't foresee in 2009 was the stunning rise of America's energy belt—a region stretching from Houston to Oklahoma City to New Orleans and their surrounding areas that in 2011, by my estimation, produced some $750 billion in total economic output, more than Switzerland or Sweden. The Sun Belt features two kinds of regional economies: declining real-estate economies and booming energy economies. Energy stands alongside knowledge as the second pillar of America's recovery.

Cities like Sioux Falls, South Dakota, and Bismarck and Fargo in North Dakota have experienced strong growth since the crisis, and fracking has brought flush times to out-of-the-way places in North Dakota, Wyoming, and other parts of the country[16]. Several commentators have argued that places with energy-based economies or natural-resource-based economies, not knowledge metros, have been the real stars of the recovery. That goes too far. To put things in perspective, the economist Paul Krugman[17] noted in March 2012 that while "employment in oil and gas extraction has risen more than 50 percent since the middle of the last decade... that amounts to only 70,000 jobs, around one-twentieth of one percent of total U.S. employment."

Still, the energy economy involves more than just extraction. Houston has clocked the third-fastest rate of job growth of all large metros since the recession, 9 percent. Between 2009 and 2013, it gained more than 250,000 new jobs, 5.6 percent of all new jobs added nationwide. And its job growth has been balanced, with 24 percent coming from high-wage jobs (again, those paying more than $21 an hour), 48 percent from mid-wage jobs ($14 to $21 an hour), and 27 percent from low-wage jobs (less than $14 an hour).

Houston's high-wage-job growth stems from two main sources—the fossil-fuel industry and information technology. The city is home to more than a third of the country's petroleum engineers and by far the highest concentration of geoscientists. From 2009 to 2012, Houston added 30,000 jobs in a mix of industries related to oil and gas extraction and scientific and technical consulting services. These pay an average salary of $124,000. Houston has also seen rapid growth in software-development jobs (16 percent) and information-technology jobs (12 percent), along with consistent growth in its medicine-and-health-care sector.

Opinions vary on just how long the shale boom will last—especially in specific localities. And while energy metros have generated jobs, my analysis of all U. S. metros finds that in general, energy economies are not notable for high-wage-job growth. Nonetheless, the fracking boom illustrates how energy and technology are combining. Unlike some oil booms of the past, which turned on the discovery of new oil fields, we've known about these shale deposits for a long time. It was new technology that made exploiting them possible. Much has been made of the so-called resource curse—the syndrome whereby countries that are endowed with an abundance of natural resources get lazy, rest on their inherited riches, and fail to invest in the kinds of research, education, and innovation that are key to long-run development. That's not what has happened in the United States. America's leading energy hubs prosper not just because of the stuff they pump out of the ground, but because of their ability to combine resources with technology and knowledge.

Cheap energy, especially from natural gas, has been a boon to the broader economy in the past several years, and still is today. Knowledge centers like Houston make it quite plausible that as the fracking boom eventually goes bust, other technologies will arise to provide new sources of inexpensive energy—and the growth that comes along with them.

Back in 2009, I predicted that the crisis would exact its steepest toll in "the interior of the country—in older, manufacturing regions whose heydays are long past," and "in newer, shallow-rooted Sun Belt communities whose recent booms have been fueled in part by real-estate speculation, overdevelopment, and fictitious housing wealth."

Sadly, the data bear me out. Just before the crisis, greater Las Vegas was one of the nation's leaders in population growth; today it has the highest concentration of fast-food jobs in the nation. Palm Coast, Florida, the metro with the fastest population growth since 2001, has seen the nation's worst rate of growth in economic output per person since that same year (negative 3.2 percent through 2011).

Population growth alone has never proved a sufficient foundation for future prosperity—not when many of the new arrivals are retirees or modestly educated people looking to get in on a real-estate boom. But since the crash, even that imperfect engine has failed many Sun Belt cities. Buffeted by the effects of the housing-and-real-estate collapse, both Phoenix and Las Vegas saw their population growth stall in the wake of the crisis. And Sun Belt metros that were once rapidly growing, like Las Vegas, Reno, Miami, and Orlando, all saw their productivity decline between 2009 and 2011. The Harvard economist Edward Glaeser argued in April 2011 that "human capital follows the thermometer," but the crisis appears to have broken this connection.[18] My analysis, focused on the past four years, finds no association whatsoever between warmer temperatures and high-wage-job growth.

The metros where low-wage jobs make up the largest share of job growth since 2009 are in the Rust Belt and the Sun Belt: St. Louis (where 90 percent of new jobs are low-wage); California's so-called Inland Empire of Riverside[19]—San Bernardino (where nearly three-quarters of new jobs are low-wage); New Orleans; Tampa; Orlando; Columbus, Ohio; and Rochester, New York (where more than half of new jobs are low-wage). Temp jobs account for an extraordinarily large share of recent job growth in Memphis, Birmingham, Cincinnati, Milwaukee, and Cleveland.

It is striking, nonetheless, how some of the hardest-hit places have begun to sow the seeds of recovery in ways few people, including myself, would have predicted.

Detroit has been a case study in industrial decline and white flight for decades.[20] Long before the economic crisis, its population had cratered and its city services had collapsed. In many ways, things have gone from terrible to even worse in the wake of the crisis. As of July, the city is officially bankrupt, with the fates of thousands of municipal pensioners hanging in the balance.

Yet amid all of that truly dreadful news are signs of a comeback. Despite the continuing exodus of its residents, Detroit has posted the third-highest rate of productivity growth of any large metro since the crash. And while the greater Detroit region is home to affluent suburbs and has world-class research and knowledge communities like Ann Arbor just outside its borders, reinvestment in the city's once-burned-out core is spurring a partial recovery in Detroit itself.[21] The past several years have seen a flow of new residents into the downtown area, including architects, designers, techies, and innovative musicians.

Much of the immediate impetus for the boom has been provided by Quicken Loans, whose billionaire founder, Dan Gilbert, has been taking advantage of Detroit's real-estate collapse to amass millions of square feet of real estate. A major new initiative is under way to animate the business districts with dozens of pop-up food markets, cafés, restaurants, and shops[22]. Though these developments don't begin to erase the city's misery, the fact that some green shoots[23] are pushing upward is astonishing.

America's emergent growth model, which is taking shape around its knowledge and energy hubs, may be more powerful than its old one. That pre-crash model depended on the continual building of debt-financed houses with bigger and bigger footprints, sprawling ever outward.[24] It was dirty, resource-inefficient, crisis-prone, and ultimately unsustainable.

Clear away the rubble, and one can better see the country's formidable strengths. The recovery has been more robust in the United States than many expected, much more so than in Europe. That's partly a result of America's willingness to print money and run substantial deficits. But what other nation has even one start-up ecosystem that can rival Silicon Valley's, San Francisco's, New York's, or Boston's—to say nothing of Seattle's or Austin's? What other nation boasts the number of world-class universities and college towns that America has? What other advanced nation can combine such knowledge resources with such abundant energy resources?

The main threats to America's growth model don't come from other countries, but from domestic contradictions. The more talented people cluster, the greater the economic returns they produce. But as these clusters of highly educated people form and grow, they tend to push out the middle class, resulting in a ruthless sorting of people and places. As great as its potential may be, this new economic landscape is also notable for its widening fissures.

The cultural, political, and economic gulfs that separate advantaged and disadvantaged people and places go well beyond the wage gap. [25] Knowledge workers benefit from living in neighborhoods with better schools, better amenities, and lower crime rates, while less advantaged groups are sometimes stuck in place, with limited prospects for climbing even one rung up the economic ladder, and insufficient resources to move out of stagnant areas. Americans have seen a dramatic decline in economic mobility, overall. But a poor person from a knowledge center like San Jose or San Francisco has twice the chance of becoming wealthy as a poor person from some Rust Belt or Sun Belt centers like Cleveland or Atlanta.

Reckoning with these deepening class and geographic divides, finding and implementing a set of policies that can build a sustainable prosperity for everyone, is the toughest and, at the same time, most urgent challenge we face.

From *The Atlantic*, October, 2013

Ⅰ. New Words

apocalyptic	[əˌpɔkə'liptik]	adj.	预示大动乱（或大灾变）的
austerity	[ɔː'steriti]	n.	（国家财政开支的）紧缩
belie	[bi'lai]	v.	to give a false impression of sb/sth
boon	[buːn]	n.	sth that is very helpful
bust	[bʌst]	adj.	bankrupt
caricature	['kærikətʃuə]	n.	漫画，讽刺画，讽刺文章
cluster	['klʌstə]	n.	a group of things of the same type
crater	['kreitə]	v.	to form a large hole
decamp	[di'kæmp]	v.	to leave a place suddenly, often secretly
divine	[di'vain]	v.	*formal* to find out sth by guessing
dub	[dʌb]	v.	to give sb/sth a particular name
endow	[in'dau]	v.	**be ~ed with sth** to naturally have a particular feature, quality
exodus	['eksədəs]	n.	(many people) leaving a place at the same time
fine-grained	['fain'greind]	adj.	细致的
fissure	['fiʃə]	n	a long deep crack in sth, especially in rock
fraction	['frækʃən]	n.	a small part or amount of sth
gale	[geil]	n.	an extremely strong wind
geoscientist	[dʒi(ː)əu'saiəntist]	n.	地球科学家
heave	[hiːv]	v.	to rise heavily
hub	[hʌb]	n.	the central, most important part of a place or activity
locality	[ləu'kæliti]	n.	a particular area

metro	['metrəu]	n.	大都市
migration	[mai'greiʃ(ə)n]	n.	the movement of large numbers of people from one place to another
normalcy	['nɔːməlsi]	n.	正常状态,常态
novel	['nɔv(ə)l]	adj	new
outpace	[aut'peis]	v.	to go, rise faster than
parasitic	[,pærə'sitik]	adj.	寄生的
plummet	['plʌmit]	v.	to fall suddenly and quickly from a high level or position
proxy	['prɔksi]	n.	~ **for sth** sth used to represent sth else
raft	[rɑːft]	n.	**a ~ of sth** a large number or amount of sth
rebound	['riːbaund]	n.	弹回,反弹;回复,回升
repurpose	[,riː'pəːpəs]	v.	to change sth slightly in order to make it suitable for a new purpose
resilient	[ri'ziliənt]	adj	富有弹性的;富有活力的
shale	[ʃeil]	n.	页岩
slacker	['slækə]	n.	a person who is very lazy and avoids work
tectonic	[tek'tɔnik]	adj.	connected with the structure of the earth's surface
trajectory	[trə'dʒektəri]	n.	(射体)轨道
terminus	['təːminəs]	n.	the last station of the end of a railway
trendsetter	['trend,setə]	n.	a person who starts a new fashion or make it popular
urbanist	['əːbənist]	n.	城市规划专家
urbanite	['əːbənait]	n.	城市居民
vibrant	['vaibrənt]	adj	full of life and energy
whopping	['hwɔpiŋ]	adj.	very big

Ⅱ. Background Information

美国带状区

美国有三个主要城市带:美国东北部地区城市最为集中,形成一个城市连绵带,像"城市的海洋"。这个庞大的都市群北起波士顿,南到华盛顿,绵延700公里,宽约100公里,被称为"波士华氏",即取两城市首字而成。还有五大湖南部的工业地带,都市化程度也很高。从密尔沃基开始,经过芝加哥、底特律、克利夫兰到匹兹堡,形成又一个城市连绵带。在那里许多大城市地区已经连成一片,往往这个城市的延伸部分也是另一个城市的发展部分,形成了卫星城镇和工业区相互交错的局面。第三个城市连绵带在加利福尼亚州。它北起旧金山湾区,经洛杉矶、圣地亚哥直到墨西哥边境,形状像个哑铃。

这三大城市连绵带的规模都在世界前列。其中"波士华氏"是美国也是世界最早、最大的城市连绵带,是美国政治经济文化的中心。加州是美国经济实力最强的州,人口3,800万,相当于美国人口的1/8,国内生产总值等均居全美第一,它的城市化水平达到90%,高居美国各州之首,完全具备了富可敌国的实力,在美国经济中的地位可谓举足轻重。

美国幅员辽阔,因此还产生了很多极具特色的带状地区。有因地区特产得名的如香蕉带(Banana Belt),玉米带(Corn Belt),棉花带(Cotton Belt),松树带(Pine Belt),水果带(Fruit Belt),也有因信仰情况得名的如圣经地带(Bible Belt),无教堂地带(Unchurched Belt)等等。其中比较著名的有:

铁锈地带(Rust Belt),指美国包括伊利诺伊州、俄亥俄州、密歇根州、印第安纳州和威斯康星州部分地区的北部地带。该地带许多大型老式工厂,特别是钢铁和汽车制造业的衰老、倒闭,导致了人员外流。

阳光带(Sun Belt)是指美国南部北纬37度以南的地区,西起加利福尼亚州东至北卡罗来纳州和南卡罗来纳州一带,这些地区的日照时间较长。

圣经地带(Bible Belt)是美国南部基督教基要派流行的别称,该派主张恪守《圣经》全部文句;亦指任何基要派流行的地区。

能源带(Energy Belt)覆盖从休斯敦到俄克拉荷马、新奥尔良及其周边区域。据本文作者估计,2011年该地区的经济总产值为7,500亿美元。

Ⅲ. Notes to the Text

1. They are the geographic counterpart to what the economist Joseph Schumpeter dubbed "creative destruction" —the great gales of change that level some companies and industries, and give rise to others. —它们是经济学家约瑟夫·熊彼得命名的"创造性破坏"的地理对应词语——巨大的变革之风毁灭一些公司和企业,同时催生其他的公司和企业。[Joseph Schumpeter — 约瑟芬·熊彼得(1883—1950),奥地利裔美籍经济学家,哈佛大学教授(1932—1950),提出用以解释资本主义特征的"创新理论"。著有《经济发展理论》《资本主义、社会主义与民生》]

2. ... but the city has retained its perch as a preeminent global finance center, and the reduction of the finance industry's footprint has provided the spur and the space for other industries to grow. —但这座城市保住了全球突出的金融中心地位,金融业腐败的减少给其他行业的发展提供了动力和空间:(① perch—position; ② spur—incentive, driving force; ③footprint—gas emission; corruption)

3. Since the crash, it has gained ground in its competition with Los Angeles as a center for media and entertainment (the imminent return of *The Tonight Show*, which decamped for Burbank, California, in 1972, is one result). Brooklyn—the setting for the HBO megahit *Girls*—has emerged as a major trendsetter for everything from film and television to indie rock and artisanal food. —金融危机发生之后,它在与洛杉矶之间的传媒业和娱乐业中心地位的竞争中已站稳脚跟(1972年迁到加州伯班克市的《今夜秀》节目拍摄场即将回归就是其中一例。)布鲁克林区作为HBO电视网杰作《衰姐们》的故事背景,已经成为从电影和电视到硬地摇滚和手工制作的食品的主要潮流风向标。(① *The*

Tonight Show—an American late night talk show that has aired on NBC since 1954; ② HBO—Home Box Office 一家总部位于纽约的有线电视网络媒体公司; ③ megahit—sth extremely successful; ④*Girls*—HBO 于 2011 年推出的一档女性励志剧; ⑤ indie rock—independent rock—也称硬地摇滚,指有别于主流唱片公司独立创作的摇滚乐; ⑥ artisanal food—food produced by non-industrialized methods, often handed down through generations)

4. And as anyone who has noticed how many windows are dark in Manhattan's luxury high-rises might have guessed, New York is not just a playground for the global elite, but a locus for their investments—including high-end properties where they reside for a small part of the year. —任何注意到曼哈顿的豪华高层建筑有多少房间未开灯的人都可能猜想到,纽约不仅是全球精英的度假胜地,而且是他们投资的地方,包括购买那些他们每年只住一小段时间的高端房产。(① Manhattan—an island and borough of New York City in New York Bay; ② high-rise—a very tall building with many floors; ③ locus—a place where sth happens)

5. Tech clusters have sprouted in Manhattan, mostly in lower neighborhoods like the Flatiron District, and Chelsea and the Meatpacking District down to SoHo and Tribeca on the West Side. —技术集群已在曼哈顿生根,主要集中在南部社区,如熨斗区、切尔西和肉库区,并一直延伸到西边的苏荷区和翠贝卡。[① Flatiron District—熨斗区(纽约市曼哈顿区的一个街区,得名于熨斗大厦); ② Chelsea—a neighborhood on the west side of Manhattan; ③SoHo—苏荷区(美国纽约曼哈顿休斯敦街南面,以先锋派艺术、音乐、电影和时装款式等著称); ④ Tribeca—shortening of Triangle Below Canal Street]

6. For a long time, high-tech start-ups have clustered in suburban office parks along freeways, places that are sometimes called "nerdistans." —很长时期以来,高技术新创公司都聚集在沿高速公路而建的办公楼区,这些地方有时被称作"讷第斯坦"。(① start-up—a company that is just beginning to operate; ② office park—an area in which a number of office buildings are constructed together, often on landscaped grounds; ③cluster—to gather; ④ nerdistan—a locus of high-tech industry, particularly a town or suburb areas where many high-tech workers live 计算机精英领地)

7. Pinterest has moved from Silicon Valley to San Francisco—Pinterest 公司已经从硅谷迁到旧金山(① Silicon Valley—a place known as a center of the computer industry; ② Pinterest——家图片社交平台)

8. *San Francisco Chronicle*—《旧金山纪事报》(1865 年创立,是北加利福尼亚地区发行量最大的报纸)

9. "For all its power, Silicon Valley has a great weakness," he wrote in 2006, "its soul-crushing suburban sprawl." —他在 2006 年写道:"尽管硅谷实力很强。但它存在很大弱点:令人沮丧的郊区无序扩张。"(① suburban sprawl—ill-planned, disorderly expansion of suburbs; ② soul-crushing—depressing)

10. Cupertino—库比蒂诺市[加利福尼亚州旧金山湾区南部,圣塔克拉拉县西部的城市,硅谷核心城市之一,也是苹果(Apple Inc.)、赛门铁克(Symantec)等大公司总部所在地]

11. Mountain View—山景城(美国加州旧金山湾区西南部硅谷主要组成部分)

12. Economic Modeling Specialists International—经济建模专家国际公司（该公司专门提供全球劳动市场数据分析）
13. San Jose—（美国加州）圣何塞市（The third largest city in California. Its location within the booming local technology industry earned the city the nickname "Capital of Silicon Valley"）
14. Bureau of Economic Analysis—经济分析局
15. belying its *Portlandia* caricature as a place for slackers—证实《波特兰迪亚》喜剧将其讽刺为"懒汉之地"是不真实的（① belie—to show sth to be untrue；② caricature—a description which exaggerates for comic effect；③ *Portlandia*—该剧讲述男女平等主义者的书店老板、自行车信使、庞克摇滚夫妻等各种奇特角色之间发生的喜剧故事）
16. fracking has brought flush times to out-of-the-way places in North Dakota, Wyoming, and other parts of the country—开采页岩气给北达科他州、怀俄明州和美国其他地区的偏僻地方带来了繁荣时代（① fracking—extracting natural gas from shale rock layers through fracking rock by pressurized liquids；② flush—having a lot of money；③ out-of-the-way—far from a city）
17. Paul Krugman—保罗·克鲁格曼（美国经济学家，普林斯顿大学经济系教授，2008 年获诺贝尔经济学奖）
18. The Harvard economist Edward Glaeser argued in April 2011 that "human capital follows the thermometer," but the crisis appears to have broken this connection.—哈佛经济学家爱德华·格莱泽在 2011 年 4 月说道："人力资本随气候而变"，但金融危机看上去已经打破了这种关联。（①Edward Glaeser—爱德华·格莱泽，哈佛大学经济学教授；② human capital follows the thermometer—referring to warm-weather areas' attraction for human capital）
19. Inland Empire of Riverside—"内陆帝国"河滨县（河滨县与毗邻的圣伯纳迪县共同组成所谓的"内陆帝国"，是一个位于南加州，约有 400 万人口的内陆都会区）
20. Detroit has been a case study in industrial decline and white flight for decades.—几十年来，底特律一直是工业衰落和白人迁移的个案研究对象。（① case study—a detailed study of a person or a group, especially in order to learn about the development and relationship；② white flight—large numbers of middle class white people leaving an area, usually because of fears that black families are coming to live there）
21. And while the greater Detroit region is home to affluent suburbs and has world-class research and knowledge communities like Ann Arbor just outside its borders, reinvestment in the city's once-burned-out core is spurring a partial recovery in Detroit itself.—虽然大底特律区是富裕郊区的所在地，并与世界级研究和知识社区比邻相依，但对该市一度衰竭的核心的再投资只是刺激了底特律本身经济的部分恢复。（① affluent—wealthy；② spur—to make sth happen faster；③Ann Arbor—安阿伯，美国密歇根州东南部城市，密歇根大学所在地。）
22. pop-up food markets, cafés, restaurants and shops—（短期经营）的时尚食品市场、咖啡馆、餐厅和商店
23. green shoots—复苏绿芽（referring to the fresh start of economic recovery）

24. That pre-crash model depended on the continual building of debt-financed houses with bigger and bigger footprints, sprawling ever outward.—金融危机之前的发展模式依靠的是不断建造借贷购房,造成越来越多的碳排放,城市不断无序向外扩张。(footprints—referring to carbon footprints, greenhouse gas emissions)
25. The cultural, political, and economic gulfs that separate advantaged and disadvantaged people and places go well beyond the wage gap.—文化、政治和经济领域里将优势和弱势人群和地区隔开的鸿沟已经远远超过了工资上的差距。

Ⅳ. Language Features

《大西洋月刊》简介

《大西洋月刊》由 M. D. 菲利普斯于1857年11月在波士顿创办。创刊资助者中有一些是著名作家,如爱默生、霍尔姆斯、朗费罗斯托、惠蒂尔。洛威尔担任该刊第一任主编。

《大西洋月刊》创刊宣言中称自己为"一本有关文学、政治与艺术的杂志",该刊登载高质量小说文学和文化评论文章,在文学刊物中居于前列,为年轻作者成就创作事业提供了理想的平台。它所登的作品许多成为美国文学的瑰宝、政论的名篇。该刊在19世纪刊登过梭罗、霍桑、爱默生等人的作品,发表过马克·吐温、亨利·詹姆斯的小说;20世纪发表了伍德罗·威尔逊和西奥多·罗斯福等人的论文,马丁·路德·金的《伯明翰监狱来信》的手稿。

该刊创刊时就宣称"坚持无党派、无偏见的原则",如今每一期第三页上端都印有"不属任何政党和派系"(Of No Party Or Clique)。但是该刊强烈关注政治,南北战争时期十分坚定地支持废奴主义(Abolitionism)。在关注文学和政治的同时,该刊对于新兴的技术显示了浓厚的兴趣。它是最早评价计算机带来的人工智能的杂志。

《大西洋月刊》1980年由波士顿房地产业巨头莫蒂默·朱克曼收购,1999年所有权又被转移给全国期刊集团。近些年来的财团困难和一系列所有权的变更使该刊转变为综合性评论杂志。涉及的内容为外交、政治、经济、技术、文化、艺术和生活。虽然内容面域更广,但是该刊的主要特色仍旧未变。现任执行主编加仑·默非把《大西洋月刊》特色总结为四点,其内容概要如下:1. 为公众提供关于这个国家各个层面的深思熟虑的看法和观点;2. 充当众多小说作者和诗人从无名小卒到大名鼎鼎之间的中转站;3. 成为政治、商业与文化精英们的(精神)餐桌;4. 发挥类似通才教育的功能。

通观近些年《大西洋月刊》的版面设计和文章内容,该刊具有以下三点特色:

1. 版面清晰、生动活泼。该刊主要版面有特稿(Features)、新闻报道(Dispatches)、专栏(Departments)、文化生活(The Culture Life)、散文(Essays)、诗歌(Poetry)和本月网站主要内容(This Month From The Atlantic Digital)。目录中文章除采用彩色标示页码之外还附有高度精练的内容简介和相关图片,文章中也插入彩色图片。版面内容一目了然,视觉效果强烈,不仅便于读者翻阅,同时也增强阅读兴趣。

2. "特稿"文章颇具特色,该刊特稿版的文章中许多颇有力度,不仅提供某新闻事件或某一文化问题的清晰解释,而且还有较为深入的分析。例如,该刊的2013年1—2月期刊题为《美国银行的内幕》(What's Inside America's Banks)的文章中,作者基于对美国银行详细深入的调查和其运营机制的全面科学的分析指出,虽然金融危机阶段已经结束,但金融业巨大风险依然存在。文章解释清楚,分析有力。

3. 评论文章富有文采。该刊的文学和文化评论文章中不少是精品,这些文章思维角度独特,内容充满智慧,语言生动有力,富有幽默感和艺术感。

经过近160年的努力,《大西洋月刊》已经成为"美国最受尊敬的杂志",它所赢得的"全国杂志奖"(National Magazine Awards)在美国杂志中高居榜首。当今的发行量为48万,每期读者人数在160万左右。该刊总的来说政治立场倾向保守。

Ⅴ. Analysis of the Content

1. Which city had the highest percentage of productivity between 2009 and 2011?
   A. New York.   B. San Jose.
   C. Washington, D. C.   D. San Francisco.
2. Which city will soon become America's second city in terms of economic power and national importance?
   A. Chicago.   B. Los Angeles.
   C. Washington, D. C.   D. San Francisco.
3. Which of the following is NOT listed among more telling measures?
   A. The composition of job growth.   B. Productivity growth.
   C. Venture-capital funding.   D. Population growth.
4. The list of key markers of regional knowledge economies which high-wage jobs are closely related to does NOT include _____.
   A. share of adults with doctoral degrees
   B. share of adults who are college grads
   C. share of the work force in professional, technical and creative jobs
   D. the levels of innovation and venture-capital investment
5. What the author didn't foresee in 2009 was _____.
   A. the stunning rise of America's energy belt
   B. that the financial crisis would permanently and profoundly alter the country's economic landscape
   C. that New York would prove to be one of America's most resilient places
   D. that the crisis would exact its steepest toll in the interior of the country

Ⅵ. Questions on the Article

1. What is the author's prediction for America's cities in the spring of 2009?
2. What is the author's finding about America's post-crisis economic landscape?
3. What impact did many people expect the financial crisis would produce on New York? Has the prediction proved to be true?
4. How fast has New York been growing as a start-up center?
5. What does New York's rise signal?
6. Which places make up the biggest group of winners since the crash?
7. How diverse is America's economy?
8. According to Paul Krugman, how important are energy-based economies in job growth?

9. How important has job growth alone been to a place's prosperity?
10. What was the author's prediction about the financial crisis' impact on the interior of the U. S. older manufacturing regions and Sun Belt communities? What do the data show?
11. Where do the main threats come from?

Ⅶ. Topics for Discussion

1. Do clusters of highly-educated people inevitably lead to widening social fissures?
2. Will the new economic landscape stay for long?

Lesson 15

Battle of the Binge[1]

A fatal night of boozing[2] at a Louisiana university stirs up the debate over the drinking culture in America's colleges. Are they doing enough to change it?

By Adam Cohen

Benjamin Wynne, 20, underwent two of the most time-honored rites of passage[3] at Louisiana State University last week. He received a pledge pin from the fraternity that voted him into the brotherhood, and he got rip-roaring drunk to celebrate.[4] Wynne and his fellow Sigma Alpha Epsilon brothers began their bacchanalia[5] with an off-campus keg party featuring "funneling"[6], in which beer is shot through a rubber hose into the drinker's mouth. Next came a communal bender[7] at Murphy's bar, a frat hangout[8] a few hundred meters from L. S. U. There, the libation of choice was "Three Wise Men," a high octane mix of 151-proof rum, Crown Royal whiskey and Jagermeister liqueur.[9] Wynne "was staggering, but no more than a lot of other people," says a college woman who was there. The festivities ended with upperclassmen wheeling the pledges out of the bar in shopping carts[10], because they were too far gone to walk. "They were like firemen carrying people out of a burning building," says Christopher Sule, an L. S. U. student who works at a sandwich shop next door. When police were called to the frat house hours later, they found almost two dozen men passed out on the living-room floor. By early morning, Wynne was dead of alcohol poisoning, and three of his fraternity brothers had been hospitalized. An autopsy found that Wynne, who downed the equivalent of about 24 drinks, had a blood alcohol level six times the amount at which the state considers a person intoxicated.[11]

Wynne's death last week sent a tremor down L. S. U.'s fraternity row[12] and set off a round of back-to-school soul searching about binge drinking on campuses all over the U. S. Just days before the incident, The Princeton Review had ranked L. S. U. as No. 10 in the nation on a list of "top party schools." L. S. U. officials protest that their school is no worse than many others, which underscores the larger issue[13]. A Harvard survey of 18,000 undergraduates found that 44% said they had engaged in binge drinking — four to five drinks in a row[14] — in the previous two weeks. "Most schools realize they are just one tragedy away from being in the spotlight[15] themselves," says Debra Erenberg, an alcohol-policy associate[16] at the Center for Science in the Public Interest. To combat excessive drinking, colleges in recent years have taken such steps as establishing alcohol-free dorms and writing letters to parents of hard-drinking students. But critics contend the L. S. U. tragedy shows the schools are still not doing enough. The incident also illustrates that although the drinking age is now 21 everywhere in America, making most college students underage, alcohol remains widely available — and highly promoted — to students of all ages.

Colleges today are among the nation's most alcohol-drenched institutions. America's 12 million undergraduates drink 4 billion cans of beer a year, averaging 55 six-packs apiece[17], and spend $446 on alcoholic beverages — more than they spend on soft drinks and textbooks combined. Excessive drinking among college students has been blamed for at least six deaths in the past year. Studies show that excessive drinking affects not only the bingers but also fellow students, who are more likely to report lost sleep, interrupted studies and sexual assaults on campuses with high binge-drinking rates. Several schools, including the University of Colorado, the University of Iowa and Ohio State, have recently been the site of "beer riots," some set off by toughened alcohol policies. At Colorado, scores of police and students were injured when a mob of 1,500 threw bricks and Molotov cocktails[18] over a three-day period last May to protest a crackdown on drinking.

From the moment freshmen set foot on campus, they are steeped in a culture that encourages them to drink, and drink heavily. At many schools, social life is still synonymous with alcohol-lubricated gatherings at fraternities and sororities, as well as the tailgate-party and hip-flask scene that accompanies athletic events.[19] But increasingly the pressure to drink is coming from bars catering to students, which aggressively promote themselves on school grounds. College newspapers, which get 35% of their advertising revenues from alcohol-related ads, are filled with come-ons for nickel pitchers of beer and "ladies drink free" specials[20]. Bars distribute handbills to students as they walk between classes and put flyers under doors in freshman dorms. On many campuses, bars send shuttle buses to round up students. "There really are establishments that prey on youth," says Frances Lucas-Tauchar, vice president for campus life at Atlanta's Emory University. "We ask them to stop, and sometimes we're effective; sometimes we're not."

The fact that many college students, like Wynne, are under the legal drinking age is rarely an obstacle. Many drink at private parties off campus, with an older student buying the alcohol. Bars' enforcement of the drinking age can be lax, false IDs are common, and legal-age friends are often willing to buy the drinks and bring them back to the table. In fact, raising the legal drinking age from 18 to 21, a movement that swept all 50 states over the past two decades, may actually have made the binging problem worse. Instead of drinking in well-monitored settings, the young often experiment in private homes and bars, where there are few checks in place to deter dangerous practices. And research suggests that making alcohol illegal may give it an illicit thrill[21] for younger drinkers. "By setting a high drinking age, what we have inadvertently[22] done is say that drinking is an adult activity, and that makes it especially appealing to younger people," says David Hanson, a sociologist who specializes in alcohol abuse and education. Fraternity parties are famous for drinking games that make a sport of quick and excessive consumption. Bars in college neighborhoods pull in students with all-you-can-drink policies[23] — $6.50 for as much beer as a customer can hold — that make binge drinking a cost-effective strategy. With "beat the clock" and "ladder pricing," the prices start low and increase as the night wears on, encouraging students to drink fast while the booze is cheap. And bar owners are constantly thinking up new binge-friendly promotions[24], like "bladder busts"[25], in which drinks are inexpensive until someone in the bar has to go to the bathroom, which raises the price for everyone.

Many colleges have been getting tougher on the issue. Schools are still handing out literature and holding workshops[26], but they know that education is not enough to solve the problem. "Vague know-when-to-say-when messages just don't mean a lot to students," says Erenberg. Administrators have become quicker to penalize campus groups that sponsor reckless parties. And more than 50 colleges now permit students to avoid temptation and rowdy behavior[27] by living in alcohol-free dorms. "It's an effort to break into the campus alcohol culture and say it is possible to have a fulfilling college experience without drinking," says Alan Levy, a spokesman for the University of Michigan, where 30% of undergrads[28] choose the alcohol-free option.

Some colleges have decided that the way to combat alcohol abuse is to ban consumption on campus entirely. In 1995, after finishing at the top of The Princeton Review's party-school rankings two years in a row, the University of Rhode Island banned alcohol at all campus social events. Combined with tougher penalties for violations and greater efforts to educate students about responsible drinking, U. R. I. administrators say the new policy has changed the culture of the school. "For a long time, this community was going through a period of denial[29]," says vice president for student affairs John McCray. Now, he adds, alcohol-related problems are down, "the SATs (entrance exams) of the entering class are up, and our students are more serious."

But banning alcohol on campus does nothing about the dangers that lurk just outside[30]. "You can have a perfect program on campus, but if you don't do anything about the liquor store across the street that sells to minors or the bar that serves intoxicated students, you haven't solved the problem," says William DeJong, a professor at the Harvard School of Public Health. The most important area for schools to focus on now, he says, is working with the larger community to ensure that students cannot abuse alcohol at private homes and bars.

In fact, some experts say that rather than driving students into the outside world by banning alcohol, colleges should encourage at least those who are of legal drinking age to drink responsibly on campus. L. S. U. had a schoolwide no-alcohol policy in effect the night Wynne died. But neither that policy nor the fact he was underage stopped him from finding a private party and an off-campus bar to serve him enough alcohol to end his life. As recently as five years ago, L. S. U. permitted fraternities to hold open-air beer blasts[31] under the watchful eyes of campus police. "We had some injuries, mostly from horseplay and wrestling in the mud[32]," says L. S. U. police captain Ricky Adams. "We never had anyone die."

With reporting by Greg Fulton/Atlanta, Lisa McLaughlin/New York, Bill Walsh/Baton Rouge and Richard Woodbury/Denver

From *Time*, September 8, 1997

I. New Words

autopsy	['ɔːtəpsi]	n.	an examination of a dead body to find the cause
binge	[bindʒ]	n.	*informal* a bout of excessive drinking
cost-effective	['kɔstɪ'fektɪv]	adj.	providing adequate financial return in relation to outlay

crack-down	['krækdaun]	n.	severe action taken to deal with a problem
dorm	[dɔːm]	n.	*informal* a dormitory
enforcement	[in'fɔːsmənt]	n.	the act or process of forcing people to obey or putting into force
flyer	['flaiə]	n.	a sheet of paper advertising something
fraternity	[frə'təːnəti]	n.	(at some American universities) a club of male students
hip-flask	[hip-'flæsk]	n.	可放在身后裤袋里的酒瓶
intoxicated	[in'tɔksikeitid]	adj.	drunk
keg	[keg]	n.	a round wooden container for storing beer
monitor	['mɔnitə]	v.	to carefully watch and check a situation in order to see how it changes
rowdy	['raudi]	adj.	behaving in a noisy, rough way
shuttle	['ʃʌtl]	n.	a plane, bus, or train that makes regular journeys between two places
sorority	[sə'rɔrəti]	n.	女生联谊会
steep	[stiːp]	v.	to soak or be soaked in a liquid
synonymous	[si'nɔniməs]	adj.	having the same or nearly the same meaning; closely associated with

Ⅱ. Background Information

学生酗酒

在西方国家中,法国、意大利、西班牙是酒的盛产国。在法国,几乎人人饮酒,因而有人讽刺法国人说他们生下的孩子不会吃奶,就会喝酒。

然而,论中毒比例,美国却大大高于法国,每到周末聚会、节日宴会,许多"老美"开怀畅饮,有时是整瓶往下灌,直到灌倒在地,不省人事。酒精中毒死亡情况屡见不鲜。

美国大学的酒文化气氛很重,步入大学便置身于浓郁的酒文化之中,许多大学的社交活动也就是酒会。不仅校外而且校内有众多酒吧。业主们促销手段很多,大登广告提供优惠券,实行女生免费,诱惑更多学生饮酒。大学是美国酒的最大消费市场之一,1,200万大学生一年要喝掉40亿听啤酒,平均每人每年要喝6听装55盒。他们人均年消费额为446美元,大大高于全国平均数。

美国《普林斯顿评论》刊物每年要对数千名大学生作以详细调查,并评出全美十大酒会高校(Top 10 Party School),1995年的十大酒会高校是:

1. West Virginia University 西弗吉尼亚大学
2. University of Wisconsin, Madison 威斯康星大学麦迪逊分校
3. State University of New York, Albany 纽约州立大学奥尔巴尼分校
4. University of Colorado, Boulder 科罗拉多州立大学博尔德分校
5. Trinity College, Conn. 康涅狄格州特里尼蒂学院
6. Florida State University 佛罗里达州立大学
7. Emory University 埃默里大学

8. University of Kansas   堪萨斯大学
9. University of Vermont   佛蒙特大学
10. Louisiana State University   路易斯安那州立大学

　　据调查,2005年美国大约有1,080万12—20岁的青少年喝酒,占这一年龄群体的28.2%,其中有720万是狂饮者(binge drinkers)。大学本科生中有44%喝酒达到狂饮水平(at the binge level),接近¼的学生每个月喝酒有10次以上,29%的学生每月至少醉3次。

　　大学生酗酒带来许多问题。首先,酗酒扰乱正常教学秩序,促使旷课率、退学率上升,学生成绩下降。酗酒导致暴力行为发生,大学校园的性攻击(sexual assault)事件往往与酗酒相关。1996年5月美国科罗拉多州警察在强行取缔一场历时3天的狂欢酒会时,与学生发生暴力冲突,导致多人受伤。酗酒常造成酒精中毒,有的导致死亡。据2005年的调查资料,美国40%以上大学生承认前一个月有酗酒经历,这一年有1,700名大学生死于酒后驾车所引起的车祸,近30,000名大学生饮酒过量接受治疗。

　　美国政府为刹住无节制饮酒之风,采取了措施,在过去20年中美国50个州的饮酒合法年龄从18岁提高到21岁。许多大学还设立"无酒寝室"(alcohol-free dormitories)。

　　但是,这些措施未能根本解决大学生的酗酒成风的问题。

Ⅲ. Notes to the Text

1. binge — 狂饮

2. a fatal night of boozing — 酗酒一夜致死（booze — *informal* to drink a lot of alcohol）

3. ... underwent two of the most time-honored rites of passage ... — (他)经历了两个最为传统的、标志人生进入新阶段的仪式 ……（① undergo — to experience；② rite of passage — a special ceremony that is a sign of a new stage in somebody's life especially when a boy starts to become a man）

4. He received a pledge pin from the fraternity that voted him into the brotherhood, and he got rip-roaring drunk to celebrate. — 他被大学男生联谊会接纳,领到一枚徽章,为了表示庆祝他喝得烂醉。（① brotherhood — an organization formed for a special aim；② rip-roaring drunk — *informal* very drunk）

5. bacchanalia — 狂饮的闹宴（*literary* a party or celebration involving alcohol）

6. an off-campus keg party featuring "funneling" — 校外啤酒桶晚会的特点就是"猛灌"（funnel — to pass a large amount of something through a narrow opening）

7. a communal bender — 集体狂饮（① communal — shared by a group；② bender — *informal* drinking a lot of alcohol at one time）

8. a frat hangout — 联谊会喜欢光顾的地方（① frat — *informal* fraternity；② hangout — *informal* a place people like to go to often）

9. There, the libation of choice was "Three Wise Men," a high-octane mix of 151-proof rum, Crown Royal whiskey and Jagermeister liqueur. — 在那儿,他们选择的奠酒叫"东方三博士",这是一种含有大量辛烷的混合饮料,成分有151度的朗姆酒、皇冠威士忌和贾格迈斯特利口酒。（① libation — a gift of wine to god, here it is a satirical expression for the wine the students drank；② proof — 标准酒精度,90度的威士忌含有45%的酒

精,依此推算,151 度的朗姆酒的酒精含量约为 75.5%,为烈性酒）③ liqueur — a sweet and very strong alcoholic drink, drunk in small quantities after a meal）

10. The festivities ended with upperclassmen wheeling the pledges out of the bar in shopping carts ... — 高年级学生用购物车把立誓入会者推出了酒吧,庆祝活动随之结束 …… （① festivities — things like drinking, dancing, eating etc. done to celebrate a special occasion; ② upperclassmen — *American* students in the last two years at a school）

11. ... who downed the equivalent of about 24 drinks, had a blood-alcohol level six times the amount at which the state considers a person intoxicated. — 他喝下了大约有 24 杯酒,血液中的酒精含量是该州所定酒醉标准的六倍。（① down — to drink something quickly; ② equivalent — having the same amount; ③ intoxicated — drunk）

12. ... sent a tremor down L. S. U. 's fraternity row ... — ……引起了路易斯安那州立大学男学生联谊会成员们的震动……（① tremor — a small earthquake; ② row — a line of people next to each other, referring to "a lot of people" in the context）

13. underscore the larger issue — 强调更重要的问题（underscore — to emphasize）

14. in a row — at one time, one after another

15. in the spotlight — receiving a lot of attention in the media

16. alcohol-policy associate — 酒精管理政策办公室副主任（associate — associate director）

17. 55 six-packs apiece — 每人喝 55 盒 6 罐装的啤酒

18. Molotov cocktails — 莫洛托夫燃烧弹（用一瓶汽油和引燃布条等制成）

19. ... social life is still synonymous with alcohol-lubricated gatherings ... accompanies athletic events. — 社交依然是除了观看球赛前聚会、赛时边看边以酒助兴就是男、女生联谊会相聚时灌酒。（① lubricated — *slang* drunk; ② tailgate-party — a party before an American football game where people eat and drink in the parking lot of the place where the football game is played）

20. come-ons for nickel pitchers of beer and "ladies drink free" specials — 五美分一罐啤酒廉价促销,"女士免费喝酒"的特别促销（① come-on — *informal* something a business offers cheaply or free in order to persuade you to buy something; ② pitcher — 有柄有口的罐; ③ special — *informal* a lower price than usual for a particular product for a short period of time）

21. an illicit thrill — 因叛逆而产生的兴奋（illicit — strongly disapproved of by society）

22. inadvertently — without knowing what you are doing

23. all-you-can-drink policies — "开怀畅饮"策略

24. binge-friendly promotions — 导致酗酒的促销手段

25. "bladder busts" — "膀胱爆炸"（bust — *v.* to break）

26. handing out literature and holding workshops — 分发手册,举办专题讨论会

27. rowdy behavior — 粗鲁的行为（rowdy — rough and noisy）

28. undergrad — *informal* undergraduate

29. a period of denial — a period during which alcohol was not allowed

30. the dangers that lurk just outside — the dangers which exist off-campus without being heeded

31. hold open-air beer blasts —— 举行露天啤酒狂欢活动（blast —— *AmE informal* an enjoyable and exciting experience）
32. horseplay and wrestling in the mud —— 在泥地里摔跤、互相打闹（horseplay —— rough noisy behavior in which older children play by pushing or hitting each other for fun）

Ⅳ. Language Features

常用俚语

本文多处使用俚语,例如:rip-roaring drunk(酩酊大醉);a communal bender(集体狂欢);binge drinking(狂饮作乐);come-ons(诱人上当的东西);frat house(大学生联谊会);dorm(宿舍);boozing(纵酒);funneling(用橡皮管通入口腔灌酒)。

俚语是现代英语词汇中不可缺少的一部分。《美国俚语词典》编者弗莱克斯纳(S. B. Flexner)在该词典的前言中写道:"普通美国人的词汇量一般估计为 10,000—20,000……据我的保守估计,其中有 2,000 个词是俚语,它们是最经常使用的词汇中的一部分。"换句话说,俚语占常用词语的 1/10。可见,俚语在英语中是起重要作用的。

20 世纪被称作为"普通人的世纪",过于高雅的语言往往使读者望而生厌。为了迎合读者口味,缩短与大众之间情感距离,报刊许多文章采用通俗口语体语言,可以使语言亲昵、自然、幽默、活泼,"产生共同情感联系"(create the common touch)。美英报刊上,较为常见的俚语有:

buck(美元);bust(降职,降级);grand(一千美元);kneejerk(不假思索的);pro(专业人员);poor mouth(哭穷);jawbone(施加压力);cool(酷、时髦、帅);lowdown(内幕真相);ego trip(追名逐利);yuck(令人厌恶的事物);green(钱);mugger(抢劫犯);pink slip(解雇通知单);buddy(哥们儿);nerd(讨厌的人);jack up(抬高物价);hype(促销);highbrow(文化修养高的人);turn-on(使人兴奋的事);quick fix(权宜之计);upscale(高档消费层次的);sobstuff(伤感文章);fence straddler(保持中立);nab(抓住、捉拿);nuts(疯狂的;古怪的);goody-goody(正人君子);binge(狂欢);goof(傻瓜);prof(教授);uptight(紧张的);nuke(核武器);posh(豪华的);savvy(精明的);muckraking(揭丑新闻);yuppies(雅皮士);go-go(兴隆的;精力充沛的);odds-on(大有希望赢的);whopping(巨大的)

必须指出的是,对待俚语必须持慎重态度。使用得当可以产生新颖时髦、生动诙谐、形象有力的效果,但使用不当则有损效果,给人以轻佻之感,或使人觉得怪诞可笑,不伦不类。

Ⅴ. Analysis of the Content

1. Wynne drank a lot of wine because _____.
   A. he liked off-campus keg party featuring "funneling"
   B. he enjoyed his birthday party
   C. he had been accepted by the fraternity
   D. he had won a grand prize
2. According to the article, Wynne's death _____.

171

A. did not produce any impact

B. helped LSU to become one of the 10 top party schools

C. led to the arrest of the party's sponsors

D. set off a debate over the drinking problems of America's colleges

3. In a year, the undergraduates of the U.S. _____.

A. spend more money on textbooks than on soft drinks

B. spend more money on textbooks and soft drinks combined than on alcoholic drinks

C. spend more money on alcoholic beverages than on soft drinks and textbooks combined

D. spend less money on alcoholic beverages than on beer

4. Raising the legal drinking age _____.

A. has made the problem of binge drinking less serious

B. has made students drink in well-monitored settings

C. has helped to prevent dangerous practices

D. may actually have made the problem of binge drinking worse

5. From the article, we know that banning alcohol on campus _____.

A. has totally solved the problem of binge drinking

B. has ensured that students cannot abuse alcohol

C. has greatly improved college education

D. has not really solved the problem of binge drinking

Ⅵ. Questions on the Article

1. What did the doctors find in the autopsy?
2. According to the article, what are the influences of excessive drinking?
3. What is the most important factor in American college students' binge problem?
4. Can the act of raising the legal drinking age from 18 to 21 solve the problem of binge drinking?
5. How do colleges solve the problem of binge drinking?
6. Has alcohol ban on campus produced satisfactory effects?
7. What do you think is the best solution to excessive drinking on American campuses?

Ⅶ. Topics for Discussion

1. Should alcohol consumption be banned on campus?
2. Is raising the legal drinking age an effective way to solve the problem of binge drinking?

Lesson 16

The Share Economy
Consumers are building multibillion-dollar market places for sharing cars, homes, bicycles, driveways and tools. In looking for a better deal and extra income, they're reshaping business.

By Tomio Geron

On paper, Frederic Larson is just one data point in five years of U. S. government statistics showing underemployment in dozens of industries and stagnant income growth across the board. The 63-year-old photographer with two children in college was downsized by the *San Francisco Chronicle*[1] in 2009. He now spends his time teaching at Academy of Art University[2] with occasional lecturing gigs in Hawaii. A far cry from the salary, benefits and company car he used to have.[3]

But Larson is also a data point in an economic revolution that is quietly turning millions of people into part-time entrepreneurs, and disrupting old notions about consumption and ownership. While Airbnb is the best-known example of this phenomenon (to most casual observers, it's the only example). Twelve days per month Larson rents his Marin County home on website Airbnb for $100 a night, of which he nets $97. Four nights a week he transforms his Prius into a de facto taxi via the ride-sharing service Lyft, pocketing another $100 a night in the process.

It isn't glamorous—on nights that he rents out his house, he removes himself to one room that he's cordoned off, and he showers at the gym—but in leveraging his hard assets into seamless income streams, he's generating $3,000 a month. "I've got a product, which is what I share: my Prius and my house," says Larson. "Those are my two sources of income." He's now looking at websites that can let him rent out some of his camera equipment.

The "gig economy," the plethora of microjobs fueled by online marketplaces offering and filling an array of paid errands and office chores, has been well-documented, and sites like TaskRabbit, Exec and Amazon's Mechanical Turk continue to grow apace.[4] What Larson finds himself in, however, is something lesser-noticed and potentially far more disruptive—a share economy, where asset owners use digital clearing houses to capitalize the unused capacity of things they already have, and consumers rent from their peers rather than rent or buy from a company.

Over the past four years at least 100 companies have sprouted up to offer owners a tiny income stream out of dozens of types of physical assets[5], without needing to buy anything themselves. "The sharing economy is a real trend. I don't think this is some small blip," says Joe Kraus, a general partner at Google Ventures[6] who has backed two car-sharing sites, RelayRides and Sidecar. "People really are looking at this for economic, environmental and lifestyle reasons. By making this access as convenient as ownership, companies are seeing a major shift."

The sharing concept has created markets out of things that wouldn't have been considered monetizable assets before. A few dozen square feet in a driveway can now produce income via Parking Panda. A pooch-friendly room in your house is suddenly a pet penthouse via DogVacay. On Rentoid, an outdoorsy type with a newborn who suddenly notices her camping tent never gets used can rent it out at $10 a day to a city slicker who'd otherwise have to buy one. On SnapGoods, a drill lying fallow in a garage can become a $10-a-day income source from a homeowner who just needs to put up some quick drywall. On Liquid, an unused bicycle becomes a way for a traveler to cheaply get around while visiting town for $20 a day.

Getting into the share economy was the reason Avis Budget Group last month chose to pay a whopping $500 million for Zipcar, despite the fact that the pioneering rent-by-the-hour startup generated a paltry profit of $4.7 million over the past year. But Zipcar in some ways misses the larger point of what's going on: Its fleet, as with Avis', has been centrally owned. A more profitable model may lie in peer-to-peer car-sharing services such as RelayRides and Getaround, which mimic Hertz or Avis except that the service itself owns nothing. Their fleets, about 50,000 combined at last count, draw from the tens of millions of autos idling in America's driveways. SideCar and Lyft slice that market finer, monetizing an empty seat by letting owners tote along fee-paying passengers on routes they may already be taking.

Just as YouTube did with TV and the blogosphere did to mainstream media, the share economy blows up the industrial model of companies owning and people consuming, and allows everyone to be both consumer and producer, along with the potential for cash that the latter provides. Shervin Pishevar, a venture capitalist at Menlo Ventures[7] and an investor in Getaround, TaskRabbit, Uber and other startups in this space, believes these services will have a major impact on the economics of cities. "This is much bigger than any specific app," he says. "This is a movement as important as when the web browser came out."

FORBES estimates the revenue flowing through the share economy directly into people's wallets will surpass $3.5 billion this year, with growth exceeding 25%. At that rate peer-to-peer sharing is moving from an income boost in a stagnant wage market into a disruptive economic force. Technology has vastly improved on the newspaper classifieds that brokered the sweating of assets for a century. Ebay's much-duplicated rating system bestows commercial credibility on individuals.[8] With Facebook you can go further, checking people's profiles before renting to them. Smartphone apps let sharers transact anywhere, see what's being shared nearby and pay on the spot. "We're moving from a world where we're organized around ownership to one organized around access to assets," says Lisa Gansky, who started the Ofoto photo-sharing site, before selling it in 2001 to Eastman Kodak.

Dozens of startups chasing the trend will fail, as market places like these always prove winner-take-all.[9] The leaders are, as expected, absorbing blows from anxious regulators and incumbents. Airbnb is fighting to prove its legality in New York and San Francisco. New York City officials are going after short-term rentals—but only when they get complaints.[10] In 2012 the city did 828 inspections and issued 2,239 violations for short term rentals. This year, fines for repeat offenders go up to a maximum of $25,000. Lyft and SideCar, meanwhile, were cited by California utility commissioners[11] recently for operating without a license. Big issues also have yet to be worked out over how these services are taxed and whether they protect customers sufficiently from liability and fraud. And who's to say whether what works among the hipsters in Brooklyn and San Francisco translates in between.

But for all the doubters, Airbnb cofounder Brian Chesky can point to the figurative heartland, Peoria, where his company has three hosts willing to rent their place for as low as $40 a night. "People providing these services in many ways are entrepreneurs or micro-entrepreneurs," he says. "They're more independent, more liberated, a little more economically empowered."

Even in Peoria.

The genesis of the modern-day share economy is best traced to San Francisco in 2008, where Chesky and Joe Gebbia, recent Rhode Island School of Design[12] graduates who had fled west, thought they could make some pocket cash by housing attendees at an industrial design conference on air beds in their apartment. They put up a site, Airbedandbreakfast.com, to advertise their floor space. After three people bunked with them that week, they decided to max out their credit cards and build a bigger site with more listings. [13] "We never considered the notion we were participating in a new economy," Chesky says. "We were just trying to solve our own problem. After we solved our own problem, we realized many other people want this."

To beef up their tech chops[14] the two designers brought in Nathan Blecharczyk, Gebbia's former roommate. Early on, the trio focused their site—rechristened Airbnb—on large events where hotels were sold out, such as the 2008 Democratic and Republican conventions. In 2009 they got into the hot Silicon Valley accelerator Y Combinator, yet cofounder Paul Graham was dubious. [15] The Airbnb partners impressed him with wacky gambits like "Obama O's" and "Cap'n McCain's" breakfast cereals, which they first gave away to bloggers to get publicity, then ended up selling for $40 a box to support the company. [16] "We were skeptical about the idea but loved the founders," says Graham. Chesky and crew then won over Sequoia Capital, which came up with $600,000 in seed funding.

Airbnb started slowly, facing the critical mass problem that all marketplaces do—buyers want more sellers and vice versa. [17] There was also a social stigma around sharing. A lot of people told Chesky that renting to strangers was a "weird thing, a crazy idea." To attract more hosts the Airbnb founders went to New York in 2009, where many of its users lived, to meet them personally—the opposite of what an Internet company typically does—and learn how to improve.

That year the site ended with 100,000 guest nights booked, but growth started to tick up faster after adding features like escrow payments and professional photography services, and allowing different kinds of spaces such as whole houses, driveways and even castles and tree houses[18]. By 2010 the site had gone international and guest nights booked rose to 750,000. By 2011 it passed 2 million total nights booked. Critical mass had been achieved.

Airbnb has a broker's model. In exchange for providing the market and services like customer support, payment handling and $1 million in insurance for hosts, Airbnb takes a 3% cut from the renter and a 6% to 12% cut from the traveler, depending on the property price.

Last year guest nights booked fell in the range of 12 million to 15 million, estimates Wedbush Securities analyst[19] Michael Pachter. On New Year's Eve alone, 141,000 people worldwide stayed at an Airbnb. In single-occupancy terms that's almost 50% more than can fit in all the rooms in all the hotels on the Las Vegas Strip.[20] To be sure, those figures still pale next to the entire U.S. hotel industry[21], which according to research firm STR sold 1 billion nights alone between January and November 2012.

But if you add Airbnb's 300,000 listings to the equivalent type of places available on vacation-oriented sites like HomeAway, suddenly house-sharing is larger in terms of room count than all the Hilton-branded hotels in the world.[22] Pachter believes that Airbnb will eventually get to 100 million nights per year, a figure that would likely produce revenue of more than $1 billion, up from an estimated $150 million in 2012.

Focused on expansion, the site likely lost money last year, but that's an easy thing to do when Silicon Valley is throwing cash at you. Chesky and crew have raised $120 million to date from Sequoia, Greylock Partners, Andreessen Horowitz and Y Combinator.[23] A $112 million funding round in 2011 gave the startup a $1.3 billion valuation. Chesky and his partners are currently trying to raise another $150 million at a valuation of $2.5 billion, a figure that could make their stakes worth about $400 million each, with a shot at becoming the first billionaires of the share economy. "The potential is huge," says Sequoia's Greg McAdoo. "In 20 years we won't be able to imagine a world where we didn't have access to things through collaborative consumption."

Airbnb had great timing and fast-moving founders but benefited equally from a sea change over the past five years in consumer attitudes about ownership, a shift that could prove to be the longest-lasting legacy of the Great Recession.[24]

The lesson learned was basic and deeply ingrained: borrowing to buy assets above your means is a sketchy proposition[25], as the recent owners of 16.5 million foreclosed houses will attest. Ownership, the root of the American Dream, took a hit. "It's changed, especially with the younger generation," says Shannon King, chair for strategic planning at the National Association of Realtors[26]. "Also they like the idea of not being tied into a property. They can move to different areas of town and live a more flexible lifestyle."

And that new paradigm trickled down far past real estate. With cars, for example, the old ideal of buying a ride after high school to squire friends and dates is eroding. The share of new cars bought by Americans 18 to 34 dropped from 16% in 2007 to 12% last year, according to Lacey Plache, chief economist of Edmunds.com[27].

Millennials, the ascendant economic force in America, have been culturally programmed to borrow, rent and share.[28] They don't buy newspapers; they grab and disseminate stories a la carte via Facebook and Twitter. They don't buy DVD sets; they stream shows. They don't buy CDs; they subscribe to music on services such as Spotify or Pandora (or just steal it). Sabrina Hernandez, 23, used to work at Starbucks, but she isn't going back after averaging $1,200 a month this fall hosting strangers' dogs in her apartment through website DogVacay. "It's so much more rewarding than working in a customer-service setting."

Once you get beyond homes and cars, though, creating peer marketplaces for smaller-ticket items proves more challenging, since the transaction has to be easy enough to justify the owner's effort. Some startups have had success in high-value niches like high-end sporting goods, food-related products and music equipment and instruments. "The value proposition here is not to rent anything from anyone," says Ron J. Williams, cofounder and CEO of SnapGoods, a neighbor-to-neighbor lending service launched in 2010. "You have to serve a particular kind of person like a photographer who's traveling and needs equipment."

To ramp up usage Williams is currently going a step further: partnering with manufacturers and retailers[29] those crimped by the share economy, to turn his site's efforts into a try-before-you-buy sales tool, with consumers getting a credit toward a purchase.

Williams will surely find a receptive market. While hotels so far are letting regulators do the dirty work of targeting Airbnb, other industries are pivoting, most notably the auto industry.[30] Besides the Avis acquisition of Zipcar, Mercedes-owner Daimler is rapidly expanding its car2go service that rents its Smart Fortwo cars by the minute.[31]

The service debuted in 2009 in Hamburg, Germany and Austin, Tex., and is now in 18 cities including 9 in North America. Car2go charges 38 cents per minute including fuel, insurance and parking and is designed for shorter rides than at Zipcar. Car2go customers don't have to return the auto to where they got it and don't have to reserve in advance. Says Nicholas Cole, CEO of car2go North America: "Interest from other cities has been remarkable. We're in discussions with a number of cities in North America and other parts of the world."

Meanwhile, Home Depot also has a unit that rents out products, in about half of its 2,000 stores, from trucks to drills and saws. The company emphasizes keeping its rental stock in top condition, which is one advantage over peer-to-peer, says Michael Jones, Home Depot's director of tool rental.

But again, that's corporate America mimicking the share economy. General Motors[32] has fully embraced the peer-to-peer market. In late 2011 General Motors invested in a $3 million round in RelayRides, which is in thousands of cities. The reason? Marketing. GM hopes people sharing a Chevy will eventually buy one. Additionally, GM can incentivize sales by promoting the idea that a new car can now come with a rental income stream attached. You can even open your GM car with RelayRides' iPhone app using GM's OnStar system[33]. "The partnership allows GM to sell consumers what they're looking for: mobility," says RelayRides founder Shelby Clark.

Economists remain perplexed as to how to measure all this activity. "We're going to have to invent new economics to capture the impact of the sharing economy," says Arun Sundararajan, a professor at the Stern School of Business at NYU[34] who studies this phenomenon. The largest question for academics is whether this all creates new value or just replaces existing businesses.

The answer is surely both. It's classic creative destruction. There may be a short-term negative for the economy because a person isn't buying a car. (A UC Berkeley[35] study shows that for every vehicle used by companies like Zipcar, 9 to 13 cars are being ditched by car owners.) But long-term economic efficiencies result, and that's ultimately good for everyone. Airbnb commissioned a study of its economic impact on San Francisco last year and found a "spillover effect."[36] Because an Airbnb rental tends to be cheaper than a hotel, people stay longer and spent $1,100 in the city, compared with $840 for hotel guests; 14% of their customers said they would not have visited the city at all without Airbnb.

"It's never been the case in our economy that utilizing assets more efficiently leads to fewer jobs," says Robert Atkinson, president of the Information Technology & Innovation Foundation[37]. "If I were in hotels I wouldn't lose a lot of sleep over it."

And perhaps it's artificial to even divide the world into the individual versus the corporation. Many critics deride Airbnb and the like as short-term fads for slow economic times. (Airbnb's report found that 42% of hosts use the income to pay everyday living expenses.) Safety, value, customer service and quality of goods remain areas where these sites could stumble.

There are also regulatory issues: New York and San Francisco, fueled by pressure from annoyed neighbors, have enacted laws that try to crimp short-term house rentals. California has been citing ride-sharing services for operating without a taxi license. And there are all sorts of tax questions, such as whether an Airbnb stay should be hit with a local hotel tax. SideCar CEO Sunil Paul, who has sold two startups including FreeLoader, which he cofounded with Mark Pincus in 1995 and sold for $38 million, believes it's a matter of time before regulators catch up to innovation. "Regulators need to recognize that the rules the PUC[38] is using were literally invented in the era of highways and telephones. We are now moving into a new era," he says.

But human beings have been swapping before money even existed. New technologies only grease the wheels of these ancient transactional instincts.[39] Even if growth levels off, it doesn't change the fact that peer exchanges are simply another way for entrepreneurs to reach customers.

Dylan Rogers, a 27-year-old sales executive in Chicago, began renting out his BMW 6 series on RelayRides because he wasn't using it as much as he intended. Now that he's making $1,000 per month from it—well above what it costs to finance and maintain—he recently bought a Jeep and plans to add a Charger specifically to rent out, with the goal of netting $40,000 a year for his three-car fleet.[40] "I want vehicles that are useful for the marketplace," he says. Is he an entrepreneurial individual, or a small car rental company? Either way, there's nothing to stop him from using the tools of the share economy to create the next Hertz.

From *Forbes*, February 11, 2013

I. New Words

a la carte		*French*	according to the menu
apace	[ə'peis]	*adv.*	happening quickly
Airbnb			空中食宿(成立于2008年8月,是一个短期旅行房屋租赁社区)
Avis Budget Group Car			艾维士巴吉集团租车公司(一家经营汽车租赁的大型跨国集团)
blip	[blip]	*n.*	a temporary change
BMW		*n.*	宝马品牌轿车
Chevy	['tʃevi]		雪佛兰品牌轿车

clearing house		n.	(情报等的)交流中心
cordon	[ˈkɔːdən]	v.	~ **sth off** to surround an area with soldiers or vehicles
commission	[kəˈmiʃən]	v.	委托
crimp	[krimp]	v.	to restrict the growth or development of sth
deride	[diˈraid]	v.	*formal* to treat sth as ridiculous
debut	[ˈdeibjuː]	n.	首次进入社交界;(商店等的)开张
drywall	[ˈdraiwɔːl]	n.	干墙
downsize	[ˈdaunsaiz]	v.	to reduce the number of employees for cutting costs
DogVacay	[ˈdɔgvəkei]		一家宠物短期寄养服务公司
ditch	[ditʃ]	v.	to get rid of
fad	[fæd]	n.	sth that people are interested in for only a short period
fallow	[ˈfæləu]	adj.	not used
foreclose	[fɔːˈkləuz]	v.	取消抵押品赎回权
genesis	[ˈdʒenisis]	n	beginning or origin of sth
Getaround	[ˈgetəraund]	n.	a peer-to-peer car sharing and local car rental business
Hertz	[həːtz]	n.	赫兹公司(美国汽车租赁巨头,在世界145个国家有 8,000 个左右租车店)
Home Depot			一家美国著名在线度假酒店租赁服务网
hipster	[ˈhipstə]	n.	追求时髦的人
incumbent	[inˈkʌmbənt]	n.	在职者,现任者
ingrained	[inˈgreind]	adj.	根深蒂固的,难以改变的
Lyft	[lift]	n.	美国一家互助租赁公司
Liquid	[ˈlikwid]	n.	一家自行车租赁网站
monetizable	[ˈmʌnitizəbəl]	adj.	可以货币化的
net	[net]	v.	to earn an amount of money
outdoorsy	[ˈautdɔːzi]	adj.	爱好户外活动的
paltry	[ˈpɔːltri]	adj.	(of an amount)too small to be considered important
Pandora	[pænˈdɔːrə]	n.	潘多拉网站(是一个仅在美国、澳大利亚和新西兰提供的自动音乐推荐系统服务的公司)
paradigm	[ˈpærədaim]	n.	范式
Parking Panda			一家停车位租赁服务公司
Peoria	[ˈpiəriə]	n.	皮奥尼亚(美国伊利诺伊州中部城市)
Prius	[priəs]	n.	普锐斯品牌车(丰田汽车公司的一款混合动力车)
plethora	[ˈpleθərə]	n.	过多,过剩
pooch-friendly	[puːtʃˈfrendli]	adj.	讨狗喜欢的
RelayRides	[riːˈleiraidz]	n.	一家网上共享或租车公司

Rentoid	[ˈrentɔid]	n.	澳大利亚最大的网上租赁市场
Sidecar	[ˈsaidkɑː]	n.	一家拼车服务公司
SnapGoods	[ˈsnæpgudz]	n.	一家物品租赁网络
Spotify	[ˈspɔtifai]	n.	网站(一个起源于瑞典的音乐平台,提供约3,200万支歌曲的流媒体服务)
squire	[ˈskwaiə]	n.	殷勤伴护女子的人;情人
stagnant	[ˈstægnənt]	adj.	not developing or growing
Starbucks	[ˈstɑːbʌks]	n.	星巴克(全球最大的咖啡连锁店,总部设在美国华盛顿西雅图)
stigma	[ˈstigmə]	n.	耻辱
swap	[swɔp]	v.	to give sth to someone and get sth in return
tote	[təut]	v.	to carry sth especially heavy
Uber	[ˈjuːbə]	n.	"优步"交通网络公司
valuation	[vælju'eiʃən]	n.	股价,估定的价值
whopping	[ˈhwɔpiŋ]	adj.	*informal* very large
Zipcar	[ˈzipkɑː]	n.	一家网上共享式租车公司

II. Background Information

分享经济

分享经济(sharing economy 或 share economy)指能够让商品、服务、数据以及才能等有共享渠道的经济社会体系。这些体系形式各异,但都是运用信息技术让人们可以分配、共享及再利用过剩的商品和服务。

分享经济的商业模式来自于我们人类最古老的本能——合作、共享、慷慨、个人选择以及灵活多变,具体模式包括租赁、易物、借贷、赠送、交换以及合作组织等所有权共享形式。很多受欢迎的模式都是基于所谓的"双面市场",该市场是由第三方研发、建立并维护的一个信息技术平台,其功能为共享各类经济活动信息。其创业项目一般需要具有四项前提条件:1、存在闲置资源;2、供给和需求在中长期的场景中,能形成许许多多小市场的聚合;3、交易的成本不能太高;4、信任机制建立的门槛不应过高。

近年来一股新兴的"分享经济"浪潮,已催生了200余家新企业,并得到了20亿美元风险资本的注资。借助简便易用的软件,新一代的科技初创企业已使分享模式变得比以往任何时候都更具吸引力。这些投资项目出现在经济下行周期,消费者们被迫找寻省钱的新途径。

此外,年轻群体的文化也发生了变化,年轻人对与自己的朋友和邻居做生意更感兴趣,而不太喜欢从毫无个性的企业那里购买产品和服务。Airbnb初步成功后,分享经济逐步渗透很多领域,人们试图向客户出租的已不仅仅是房间,还包括办公场所以及驾车出行的座位,甚至将电钻、割草机等闲置资产变成了收入来源。有些人还会出售自己的时间,承接遛狗、取回干洗衣物或组装宜家(Ikea)家具等杂活。

不过,这种新兴商业模式将在多大程度上颠覆酒店、汽车以及出租车服务等传统行业,目前尚不明了。它们的发展过程遭遇到不少阻力。传统行业对这类新兴竞争对手发起了反击,声称这种个人对个人的房屋租赁以及自驾拼车违反了有关住房和交通的国家及地方法规。税务机关也盯紧了初创企业财务收入中的应纳税部分。分享经济面临这样一个问题:在新兴企业的业务与旨在确保服务质量和安全的交易法规之间,界限究竟划在哪里。

分享经济还面临诸多问题,需要通过创新来解决。总结起来有:最早期的一批供给怎么获取以及最早期的用户从哪里来?服务规范如何制定?服务一致性的标准在哪个高度上制定?信任机制是永远的难题,这还不仅仅是网站内部的信用体系建设,还涉及整个社会是否有健全的信用机制。安全上的隐患和政府监管政策也是必须面对的问题。

Ⅲ. Notes to the Text

1. *San Francisco Chronicle*—《旧金山纪事报》(又称《旧金山新闻》,北加利福尼亚地区发行量最大的报纸)
2. Academy of Art University—(美国)旧金山艺术大学
3. A far cry from the salary, benefits and company car he used to have. —与他曾经享有的薪金、福利以及公司配车的待遇相比简直是天壤之别。(a far cry from sth—completely different from sth)
4. The "gig economy," the plethora of microjobs fueled by online marketplaces offering and filling... continue to grow apace. —短工经济,即网络市场提供和承接许多付酬的差事和杂活所增加的大量零碎工作,种类十分丰富,类似"跑腿",Exec和"亚马逊土耳其机器人"这类网站持续迅速增加。(①gig—a temporary job;②fuel—to increase;③Task Rabbit——家利用任务发布和认领形式打造的劳务平台;④Exec——家政服务网站;⑤Amazon's Mechanical Turk——一个网络服务应用程序接口)
5. physical assets—实体资产
6. Google Ventures—谷歌风险投资部门(a venture capital investment arm of Google Inc. that provides seed, venture and growth stage funding to technology companies)
7. Menlo Ventures—门罗风险投资公司(a company that provides long-term capital and management support to early-stage and emerging growth companies)
8. Ebay's much-duplicated rating system bestows commercial credibility on individuals. —广泛复制的电子湾评级系统给个人授予商业信誉。(① Ebay—全球最大的拍卖网站,也是全球最大的电子商务公司之一;② bestow— to give sth to sb, especially to show how much they are respected)
9. Dozens of startups chasing the trend will fail, as market places like these always prove winner-take-all. —赶浪潮的新兴企业中许多会失败,因为这类市场结果总是"赢家通吃"。
10. New York City officials are going after short-term rentals—but only when they get complaints. —纽约市官员只是在接到投诉之后才调查短期租赁公司。(① go after— to chase or follow sb; ② rental — a company engaged in renting business)
11. California utility commissioners—加州公共事业委员会委员
12. Rhode Island School of Design—罗得岛设计学院

13. After three people bunked with them that week, they decided to max out their credit cards and build a bigger site with more listings. ——那周他们就有三位宿客,此后他们决定刷爆信用卡,建立有更多项目的更大网站。(① bunk ——to sleep;②max out ——to reach the limit at which nothing more is possible;③listing—— a list of things printed)

14. beef up their tech chops ——to improve their technical skills

15. In 2009 they got into the hot Silicon Valley accelerator Y Combinator, yet cofounder Paul Graham was dubious. ——2009 年他们对广受欢迎的硅谷催创公司 Y Combinator 很感兴趣,但该公司共同创始人保罗·格雷厄姆对其持有怀疑态度。(①Y Combinator ——美国一家著名投资种子阶段初创公司业务的创投公司;② get into—to develop a strong interest in;③hot—very popular)

16. The Airbnb partners impressed him with wacky gambits like "Obama O's" and "Cap'n McCain's" breakfast cereals, which they first gave away to bloggers to get publicity, then ended up selling for $40 a box to support the company. ——Airbnb 公司创业合伙人采用精心策划的怪招来打动他,如提供"奥巴马奥氏"和"船长麦凯恩式"品牌早晨谷餐,这些谷物原本是创名气而赠送给博客的,最后为了给公司提供资金又以 40 美元一盒出售。(①wacky ——funny or amusing in a slightly crazy way;②gambit—a move designed to gain an advantage later)

17. Airbnb started slowly, facing the critical mass problem that all marketplaces do—buyers want more sellers and vice versa. ——Airbnb 公司一开始生意进展缓慢,面临所有市场都遇到的规模做大的关键问题,即买家想要更多的卖家,反之亦然。

18. but growth started to tick up faster after adding features like escrow payments and professional photography services, and allowing different kinds of spaces such as whole houses, driveways and even castles and tree houses—在增加第三方托管,专业摄影服务和容许客户选择诸如整个房子、车行道甚至宅邸和树上小屋不同类型场所这类特色后,投宿人数开始增加。[① escrow payment ——(为增加交易可靠安全性)买方将贷款付给买卖双方之外的第三方;②tick up— to increase]

19. Wedbush Securities analyst—韦德布什证券公司分析员(Wedbush Securities——one of the largest securities firms and investment banks in the US)

20. In single-occupancy terms that's almost 50% more than can fit in all the rooms in all the hotels on the Las Vegas Strip. ——就单人房而言,这几乎是拉斯维加斯大道所有宾馆全部客房数的一倍半。(①single-occupancy— single resident occupancy. It is a rate charge for one person occupying the room;② Las Vegas Strip —an approximately 4.2 mile stretch of Las Vegas Boulevard. Many of the largest hotels in the world are located here with a total of over 62,000 rooms.)

21. To be sure, those figures still pale next to the entire U.S. hotel industry... ——诚然,这些数字与美国的整个酒店行业相比依然显得逊色……(pale next to sth—to seem less important when compared with sth else)

22. But if you add Airbnb's 300,000 listings to the equivalent type of places available on vacation-oriented sites like HomeAway, suddenly house-sharing is larger in terms of room count than all the Hilton-branded hotels in the world. ——但是如果将 Airbnb 清单

上的 300,000 间房加入像 HomeAway 一类在线度假酒店提供的同类房间,那么房屋分享业的房间数量就多得出奇,超过全世界所有希尔顿酒店。(① Homeaway —美国著名在线度假酒店租赁服务商家;②equivalent—same)

23. Chesky and crew have raised $120 million to date from Sequoia, Greylock Partners, Andreessen Horowitz and Y Combinator. —切斯基和其他工作人员从 Sequoia 风险投资公司、Greylock 合股风险投资公司、Andreessen Horowitz 风险投资公司和 Y Combinator 创投公司迄今已经筹措了 1 亿 2 千万美元。(① Sequoia— Sequoia Capital,a venture capital firm;② Greylock Partners —one of the largest early-stage venture-capital firms;③Andreessen Horowitz— a venture-capital firm cofounded by Mare Andreessen and Ben Horowitz)

24. Airbnb had great timing and fast-moving founders but benefited equally from a sea change over the past five years in consumer attitudes about ownership, a shift that could prove to be the longest-lasting legacy of the Great Recession. —Airbnb 把握了极好的时机并且拥有当机立断的决策者,但同样程度受益于过去五年间消费者对于所有权看法的巨大改变,这种转变可能会是大衰退最持久的影响。(the Great Recession—从 2007 年开始的经济大衰退,是一场在 2007 年 8 月浮现的金融危机所引发的经济衰退)

25. The lesson learned was basic and deeply ingrained: borrowing to buy assets above your means is a sketchy proposition... — 所吸取的教训是重要深刻的,超出经济能力借钱购买资产是十分草率的做法……(①ingrained —deep-rooted;②sketchy—done very roughly)

26. National Association of Realtors—全国房地产经纪人协会(该协会代表 100 多万住宅和商业房地产行业成员)

27. chief economist of Edmunds.com—Edmunds.com 汽车资讯网站首席经济学家

28. Millennials, the ascendant economic force in America, have been culturally programmed to borrow, rent and share. —千禧代是美国日趋重要的一支经济力量,其成长环境决定了他们会借、租和分享。(program —to make a person behave in a particular way so that it happens automatically)

29. To ramp up usage Williams is currently going a step further: partnering with manufacturers and retailers... —为提高利用率,威廉斯目前正采取进一步措施:与制造商和零售商合伙……(①ramp up— to make sth increase in amount;②partner with— to own a business and share profits together with other people)

30. While hotels so far are letting regulators do the dirty work of targeting Airbnb, other industries are pivoting, most notably the auto industry. —尽管酒店业目前在让管理机构出面艰苦对付 Airbnb,但是其他行业,尤其是汽车行业正在采取措施应对。(①dirty work —unpleasant work that no one wants to do;② pivot —to make proper arrangements so as to deal with sth difficult)

31. Besides the Avis acquisition of Zipcar, Mercedes-owner Daimler is rapidly expanding its car2go service that rents its Smart Fortwo cars by the minute. —除了安飞士公司收购 Zipcar 租车公司之外,梅赛德斯-奔驰公司业主戴姆勒集团正在迅速扩张其 Car2go 按分钟计价的 Smart Fortwo 时尚微型车的租赁服务。(①Smart Fortwo —是由戴姆勒集团微型车公司设计生产的时尚的两座汽车;②Car2go— a subsidiary of Daimler A. G. that

provides car-sharing service)
32. General Motors—(通用汽车公司世界最大汽车公司之一,2009年申请破产保护)
33. OnStar system—"安吉星"安全信息通讯系统
34. Stern School of Business at NYU—纽约大学史登商学院
35. UC Berkley—加州大学的伯克利分校(是加州大学9所分校中历史最久、最著名的一所)
36. "spillover effect"—溢出效应(the external outcome of an economic activity which can affect those not directly involved)
37. Information Technology & Innovation Foundation—信息技术与创新基金会(a non-partisan think tank whose mission is to formulate and promote public policies to advance technological innovation and productivity)
38. PUC— Public Utilities Commission 公共事业委员会
39. New technologies only grease the wheels of these ancient transactional instincts.—新技术只是更加促进了我们从古就有的交易本能。(① grease —to cause sth to run smoothly by greasing; ②transactional —of business activity)
40. ...he recently bought a Jeep and plans to add a Charger specifically to rent out, with the goal of netting $40,000 a year for his three-car fleet.—他最近买了辆吉普牌车,还打算买特别为了出租的Charger牌车,他为这三辆车组合的车队设定的目标是一年收入4万美元。(①net —to earn an amount of money ;②specifically— exactly)

Ⅳ. Language Features

外刊与文化

社会语言学家认为,语言渗透着民族的生活经验,储存了民族的价值观念,蕴含着民族的思维方式。对于第一语言使用者而言,他们在习得这门语言的过程中,由于自身生活在相关文化之中,其思维和行为一直受到该文化的熏陶,因而他们在彼此的交际中基本上不存在文化障碍。然而,对于第二语言习得者而言,情况就大不相同。他们往往用自己的生活经验,自己所认同的价值观和思维方式去"比附"外国文化,套用到外语交际中去。套用的结果便形成文化干扰和交际障碍。外报外刊涉及英语国家文化诸多方面,不了解这些情况便会造成理解困难。

例1:Violence in language has become almost as casual the possession of handguns. 语言粗鲁几乎就像持枪一样十分随意。不了解美国的枪支文化就很难理解作者为什么把语言粗鲁看得更为严重。

例2:Busibodies:New Puritans

这是《时代》周刊1991年8月21日一篇文章的标题。不了解清教徒的价值观和美国人对清教主义的看法就无法理解这个标题。

清教主义主张节俭、勤奋(thrift and hard work)。清教牧师强调只有勤劳、节俭,人才能得到上帝的拯救。这种勤奋、节俭价值观在美国发展时期起过积极作用,对今日的美国人也有一定影响。但美国社会中有很多人认为清教主义倡导禁欲苦行。美国名作家H.L.门肯就曾嘲笑过清教徒,称他们是"不让自己也不让别人过高兴日子的好管闲事的人"。

例3:Early retirement trend to quit working at 65 or sooner:Sterling Phillips, 65, spends 30 hours a month at an on-and-off job … Spurgeon Wilson, 61, was considering a six-week job … George Garrett, 60… prefers playing in local golf tournaments and traveling.

这段文字所举三例,按我国标准,应该属于退休行列,若说是推迟退休之例(cases of late retirement)那很好理解,说成提早退休(early retirement)就较难接受了。可在美国法定退休年龄为 65 岁,为了激励更多老人 65 岁之后继续工作,最近政府还有新的奖励措施:65 岁之后每多工作一年,退休金增加 8%。

When I screw up, she just raises her pretty chin and snorts. It's very British.

(每当我把事搞糟时,她只是撇一下可爱的下巴轻蔑地哼一声,表现地十分像英国人。)这一句说的是一位美国父亲对其女儿受过英国高等教育归国后行为改变的印象。不了解美国人对英国受过良好教育上层人士的定型观念是矜持寡言、一般不表露自己想法,是很难理解这句话的。

上述实例说明,外刊阅读过程中确实存在文化干扰。因而,要想增强外刊理解能力,不但要提高语言水平,还要扩充文化背景知识。

V. Analysis of the Content

1. The meaning of the word "fuel" in the sentence "The 'gig economy,' the plethora of microjobs fueled by online marketplaces offering and filling an array of paid errands and office chores… to grow apace."(Para. 4) is _____.
   A. to supply with fuel
   B. to provide with power
   C. to increase
   D. to produce
2. Which of the following is a peer-to-peer car-sharing website?
   A. Airbnb.
   B. Avis.
   C. Zipcar.
   D. RelayRides.
3. The best known example of share economy, according to the article, is _____.
   A. Airbnb
   B. Retoid
   C. Lyft
   D. Getaround
4. Which of the following statements is NOT true about the share economy?
   A. Economists find it difficult to measure the impact of the share economy.
   B. The share economy may lead to a short-term negative for the economy but will result in long-term economic efficiencies.
   C. The share economy is a real trend.
   D. The share economy will end when the world economy recovers.
5. The author's purpose in citing the example of Dylan Rogers is to _____.
   A. show that share economy will continue
   B. prove the importance of share economy
   C. show that it is easy to start up a website rental
   D. illustrate Americans' interest in starting up businesses of their own

VI. Questions on the Article

1. What does Frederic Larson do with his house and his Prius?
2. Why did Avis Budget Group Car choose to pay a whopping $500 million for Zipcar? What was the larger point which Zipcar in some ways missed?
3. What effect does the share economy produce on the industrial model of companies owning and people consuming?
4. What was the share economy's impact on people's income according to Forbes?
5. By what means did Airbnb founders attract more hosts in 2009, and increase its business?
6. What were the factors in Airbnb's success?
7. What was the lesson learnt by Millenials about consumption?
8. How are America's big corporations responding to the share economy?
9. What are the prospects of share economy?

VII. Topics for Discussion

1. Is share economy ultimately good for manufacturing businesses?
2. Does share economy have great staying power?

Lesson 17

The Casino Next Door

How slot machines snuck into the mall, along with money laundering, bribery, shootouts, and billions of profits.

(Abridged)

By *Felix Gillette*

Inside a one-story building on the edge of a strip mall[1] in central Florida, Joy Baker calculates the sum total of her morning bets. It's almost noon, and she's down $5. Not bad. Her husband, Tony, sits a few feet away. "This is the most fun we've had in 20 years," says Joy, who is 78 and retired. "At our age, we can't hike. You can't pay him to go to the movies. This gives us a reason to get up in the morning."

Tony concurs. "We enjoy this," he says. "We will be very bitter if the politicians take this away from us. I will take it personally."

It's a Wednesday morning in mid-March, and the Bakers are sitting inside Jacks, a new type of neighborhood business that is flourishing in shopping malls throughout Florida — and across America. Jacks bills itself as a "Business Center and Internet Cafe," but it looks more like a pop-up casino.[2]

Jacks is about the size of a neighborhood deli. There is a bar next door and a convenience store around the corner. Inside, jumbo playing cards decorate the walls. The room is filled with about 30 desktop computers. Here and there, men and women sit in office chairs and tap at the computers. They are playing "sweepstakes" games that mimic the look and feel of traditional slot machines.[3] Rows of symbols — cherries, lucky sevens, four-leaf clovers — tumble with every click of the mouse.[4]

John Pate, a 50-year-old wearing a Harley-Davidson T-shirt[5], says he is wagering the equivalent of 60 cents a spin. "This place is pretty laid-back," says Pate. "You can come here and get your mind off everything. You're not going to win the mortgage. You're not going to lose the mortgage. It's pretty harmless."

Local law enforcement disagrees. Jacks is located in the town of Casselberry, in the heart of Seminole County, a former celery-growing region that is now a suburb of nearby Orlando. For the past couple of years, the vice squad of the local sheriff's department[6] has been investigating Jacks and seven other similar businesses around the county for potentially violating state prohibitions on gambling. The cafe owners contend that what they are offering is not technically gambling but rather a form of "sweepstakes" promotions, which are currently legal under Florida state law. In January, after consulting with the sheriff's department, the five members of the local Board of County Commissioners[7] passed an ordinance designed to shut down the mini-casinos.

The legal fight did not end there. As the commissioners soon learned, along with local officials throughout the U. S., getting rid of Internet sweepstakes cafes[8] is not easy. Shortly after passing the ordinance, the commissioners were hit with multiple civil lawsuits filed in federal court. An attorney representing a chain of sweepstakes cafes headquartered in St. Augustine, Fla., filed a 49-page complaint alleging, among other things, that the ordinance unfairly restricted the cafes' First Amendment rights to free speech[9]. A lawyer working for a sweepstakes software company in New Jersey filed a 20-page complaint alleging that the commissioners had violated the commerce clause of the U. S. Constitution[10].

More than two months later, Seminole County awaits a court ruling. In the meantime, the sweepstakes cafes remain open.

The fight over the legality of the pop-up casinos in Seminole County is part of a broader battle that has been fought for six years in counties across the nation from North Carolina to Texas to Massachusetts. Along the way, cops have raided numerous sweepstakes cafes, confiscated computers and seized safes full of cash. In September, cops in Virginia Beach, Va., raided a dozen game rooms and confiscated more than 400 computers. In March, police in West Valley City, Utah, shut down two sweepstakes cafes, detained 67 people, and seized 80 computers. Lawmakers in North Carolina passed legislation last year outlawing the business model. In February, Virginia did the same. In April, the Massachusetts attorney general[11] submitted emergency regulations to shut down the businesses.

And yet the sweepstakes cafes keep spreading.

James Mecham, the managing director of SweepsCoach, a Sacramento, Calif., company that provides startup services to new sweepstakes cafes, says he has helped open some 200 around the country in recent years. Mecham says the number continues to grow and estimates that there are now somewhere between 3,000 and 5,000 operating in the U. S. On Google Maps, a search for "sweepstakes cafe" turns up 2,823 results in North America. Those are just the ones listing their services.

"Phones are ringing off the hook," Mecham says. "Everybody wants to open one."

It's a high-margin, cash-rich business.[12] According to Mecham, each terminal at a thriving cafe typically grosses $1,000 to $5,000 per month. A medium-size business with, say, 100 machines would therefore gross around $250,000 a month, or in the ballpark of $3 million a year. All of which would suggest that in less than a decade, Internet sweepstakes cafes in the U. S. have grown into a collective $10 billion to $15 billion industry.

Once populated by shadowy figures operating at the margins of society, the industry now attracts entrepreneurs operating openly.[13] The co-owner of Jacks is a friendly fellow named Darryl Agostino who formerly owned a construction business. Like many of his peers, he advocates for regulation rather than prohibition. "If they regulate it and there's money to be made from this for the government, I'm fine with that," he says. Regulating the businesses, however, would also mean further legitimizing them — not to mention possibly expanding legalized gambling's reach into every shopping mall, every neighborhood, every county in the state and perhaps the entire country.

Scott Plakon, a member of the Florida House of Representatives, thinks that's a bad idea. He believes the sweepstakes cafes are a predatory form of "convenience gambling" that hurt those who can often least afford it: the poor and the elderly.

In March, Plakon introduced a bill aiming to clarify state law in order to shut down sweepstakes cafes throughout Florida. He knows chasing the industry out of the Sunshine State [14] won't be easy. "They're hiring regulators; they're hiring lobbyists; they're hiring lawyers," says Plakon. "In the meantime, our communities are paying the price for this."

Cafes started popping up in South around 2005

The first Internet sweepstakes cafes started popping up in small towns throughout the South sometime around 2005. At the time, James Mecham and his partners were running a business out of Sacramento that designed and operated traditional Internet cafes. The small retail stores, born in the wake of the first Internet boom of the late 90s, catered to adults wanting to check their e-mail over coffee and teenagers wanting to play video games. There were no games mimicking slot machines. There was no betting.

About five years ago, according to Mecham, he started getting phone calls from people around the country interested in opening Internet sweepstakes cafes. At first, he and his partners were baffled. The calls kept coming. "The frequency increased to the point where we thought, 'OK, maybe we're missing the boat here,'" says Mecham.

They did some research and found that a handful of software companies based in states such as Texas and Oklahoma were making "sweepstakes" games that looked and felt like digital slot machines and were designed to take advantage of state laws that prohibited slot machines but allowed sweepstakes promotions. Demand for the games was spiking.

The software companies, according to Mecham, weren't thrilled about the logistical headaches of helping clients set up new mini-casinos in states where politicians, cops, and lawmakers didn't want them. Mecham and his partners saw a potential niche: They would market, sell and install sweepstakes terminals for new cafes in exchange for payments from the software companies.

"When we first got into the sweepstakes, for the first six months we were taking a hide-in-the-bushes strategy," says Mecham. [15] "We didn't want to go to jail. I have a mortgage and a wife and five kids. I'm not going to jail over this. Now that I've been in it long enough, I realize it's pretty darn safe."

SweepsCoach has since set up numerous businesses in states around the country. Right now, says Mecham, Ohio is particularly hot. As part of the installation process, SweepsCoach provides new cafes with "compliance training" for its employees, which is geared toward keeping them out of jail. [16]

Wherever Mecham sets up sweepstakes businesses, he says, somebody soon tries to shut them down. "I tell people, 'If you're looking for a reason not to do this, read the news,'" says Mecham. "But if you're looking for a reason to do it, look at someone's bank account who is in it. These guys make tons of money."

Mecham says SweepsCoach recently set up a top-of-the-line cafe with 50 computers that made $20,000 profit in its first weekend. Once a cafe is set up, operational costs (rent, potato chips, soda) are minimal. Staffing is cheap. Cafe employees typically work for around $10 an hour. The major cost is the software.

According to Mecham, sweepstakes cafes typically pay around 25 percent to 35 percent of their net take[17] back to the software companies as part of long-term revenue-sharing agreements, with some of that money going back to installers like Mecham. He says that when they started in the business, there were only three companies making sweepstakes software. Now there are roughly 50. "There are at least 40 that are just two guys in their garage," says Mecham.

Some of the new companies, according to Mecham, are peddling lousy products. One of the key challenges for Internet sweepstakes cafe designers is to calibrate the prize percentage just right. Software that pays out too much can drag down a cafe's profits. Software that pays out too little will drive customers elsewhere. As with traditional slot machines, the "return to player" varies from company to company. But successful sweepstakes companies, says Mecham, typically pay out in the low 90 percent range, i. e., for every $1 million patrons collectively wager, roughly $900,000 is returned in prizes. A customer's chance of winning at a reputable sweepstakes cafe should be more or less on par with his chance of winning at a slot machine in Vegas[18].

Customers are easy to find. Mecham says sweepstakes cafes cater primarily to two demographics: the old and the poor. "Lower-income customers are coming in because they're bad at math," he says. "It's like the lottery. The lottery is a tax on people who are bad at math. They're coming in to try and catch a big break."[19]

Every so often, one state or another tries to ban the businesses, but even if a state assembly cracks down, says Mecham, it's possible to keep the cash flowing. This past July, after various legal skirmishes, the North Carolina assembly passed legislation aiming to get rid of the Internet sweepstakes cafes once and for all. The ban went into effect in December. "Everybody was very sad in the industry," says Mecham. "Our very conservative attorney told us to get out of the state. We promptly did."

A couple of months passed, says Mecham, and SweepsCoach noticed that none of its competitors had left North Carolina. Mecham met with his lawyer again and told him they wanted to go back in. The lawyer said it was dangerous. "Well, define dangerous," says Mecham. "Nobody is getting in trouble. So we're going back into North Carolina and starting to open them up again."

"It's very, very rare that you hear of any serious criminal issues or major fines," says Mecham. "It's very difficult to pin this down, since it's a technology-based thing. There's going to be nine ways around whatever they come up with usually."[20]

Occasionally, convictions do happen. In July 2010, federal attorneys successfully prosecuted three men who had been operating a ring of Internet sweepstakes cafes throughout East Texas. The trial came on the heels of a joint investigation into the cafes conducted by local officials and the FBI. After the 10-day trial, a jury found the defendants guilty of conspiracy to operate an illegal gambling enterprise and money laundering. In March, one of the men, Daniel Patrick Davis, was sentenced to 12 months and one day in federal prison. He is appealing the verdict. According to a public information officer with the U. S. Justice Dept., the other two defendants were sentenced to multiple years of probation.

In central Florida, cafes started popping up sometime around 2007. Shortly thereafter, according to April Kirsheman, the general counsel for the Seminole County Sheriff's Office, complaints started rolling in. "Citizens were calling and saying, 'I don't understand. There's a gambling house next to the dry cleaners. Why is it there?'" says Kirsheman. The sheriff's vice squad launched an investigation.

Over the past six years, the debate over the legality of Internet sweepstakes cafes has occasionally made its way into courtrooms, revealing the inevitable marriages of money and politics that were also on display in the wake of the FBI's recent crackdown on three major online poker sites. [21] In one of the early legal challenges to the cafes, in 2006, a trial judge in Alabama ruled in favor of a sweepstakes business, called MegaSweeps, which had been shut down by a local sheriff. It was run by a racetrack owner named Milton McGregor.

Shortly thereafter, however, the Alabama Supreme Court reversed the decision. The state's high court found that the sweepstakes cafe business model was a roundabout way of trying to take what was in essence a slot machine operation and reconfigure it to take advantage of weaknesses in the law. "It is axiomatic that one may not lawfully do indirectly what is unlawful to be done directly," read the court's unanimous decision. The ruling provided a blueprint for sweepstakes cafe opponents looking for a solid legal argument to counter the industry's standard defense. Opponents of the game rooms also correctly predicted that the blow to the industry in Alabama would be only temporary. The legal justification would mutate.

Sure enough, it did. Before long, Milton McGregor, the former owner of MegaSweeps, opened a parlor — once again filled with games that mimicked the look and feel of traditional slot machines — at his greyhound racetrack outside Montgomery. McGregor no longer billed the video slot machines as legal sweepstakes. Now he insisted they were "electronic bingo" machines, and legal.

In the months to come, while the money poured in (the racetrack operated more than 6,000 terminals), McGregor escalated the push toward legality, forming with industry colleagues an advocacy group, the Sweet Home Alabama Coalition, which lobbied state lawmakers on behalf of electronic bingo business interests. In January 2010, members of the Alabama state legislature introduced a bill aiming to amend the constitution of Alabama to recognize the legality of electronic bingo.

The push to amend the constitution, according to the Associated Press[22], passed in the Senate but eventually floundered in the House after news leaked out that the FBI was investigating. In October 2010, federal authorities arrested McGregor and 10 other people, including four current and former state legislators and a handful of lobbyists. They were charged with buying and selling votes related to pro-gambling legislation. The indictment, based in part on covert wiretaps, detailed an extensive conspiracy to try and legalize video slot machine-like games in Alabama.

Among other charges, prosecutors allege that the defendants would "provide campaign contributions, campaign appearances by country music celebrities, political polls, media buys, fundraising assistance ... and other things of value" to state lawmakers in return for their votes on specific bills. [23] Prosecutors allege that in February 2010 one of the lobbyists charged in the conspiracy told a state legislator that if he voted for a pro-gambling bill, they would provide him with side work[24] at a public-relations firm that would pay him $1 million a year. McGregor has pled not guilty and is awaiting trial.

Elsewhere around the country, law enforcement officers are still struggling to pin down the Internet sweepstakes cafe business model long enough to ban it. After listening to Bass and Mathis in January, the Seminole County commissioners passed an ordinance banning the use of what the county dubbed "simulated gambling devices."

"Based on what we saw and what we were learning from the experts, the problem is the highly addictive method of these video displays that are gambling or simulated gambling," says Kirshe-man, the general counsel for the sheriff's department in Seminole County, who helped draft the ordinance. "We took the approach that whatever it is—whether it's going to be declared gambling by some court or not—we don't want these in Seminole County because of the quality of life issues that they're presenting."

Kirsheman points out that whatever you think of the cafes, gambling remains illegal in the state. Narrowly defined exceptions have been made, she says, in cases where the benefit was thought to outweigh the costs. "What the industry has done is take certain parts of those statutes and just mixed (**mix**) them up by taking a safe harbor from one statute and sort of applying it to the law in the other," she says. "There is no court that has found that this is lawful."

On Feb. 1, a U.S. District Court in Florida granted a temporary restraining order and preliminary injunction allowing Allied Veterans and the other sweepstakes game rooms to remain open until a judge could rule on the legality of the county ordinance.

Back in Apopka, a copy of the court injunction hangs on the front door of the Allied Veterans #67. At the front desk there is a stack of business cards[25], decorated with a palm tree and the words "Save Our Internet Cafes" and directing patrons to an online petition. Two of the room's computers have been set aside specifically for petition signers. As I leave the business on Tuesday night, I ask the security guard by the door about the cafe's hours. "We never close," he says.

Industry lobbies against regulations

About two years ago, Scott Plakon, a father of six and Republican member of the Florida House of Representatives, was getting his hair cut at a shopping center in Deltona, Fla. He noticed that something called an Internet sweepstakes cafe was about to open in the mall. He'd never heard of such a thing. His hair cutter told him she (sometimes) frequented the Allied Veterans cafe in the neighboring county. She gave him the lowdown.

Shortly thereafter, Plakon heard about sweepstakes cafes from another source: his local sheriff. The more Plakon learned, the more he became convinced the pop-up casinos were a bad idea. The cafes often catered to low-income residents. Plakon says he was disturbed to learn that the ATMs in some of the game rooms accepted Quest cards — the debt cards with which the state of Florida distributes public assistance[26]. Plakon kept talking about it to his hair cutter. "She asked me to shut these down because some of her friends were starting to have gambling issues," says Plakon.

In March, after months of consulting with sheriffs, district attorneys, and the state's attorney general's office, Plakon introduced a bill into the Florida House of Representatives designed to shut down the sweepstakes cafes. After an initial hearing, the business and consumer affairs subcommittee voted 10-5 in favor of the bill, which must now pass through several more committees before it can reach a chamber-wide vote. For the ban to become law, a sister bill must also pass in the Florida Senate. Plakon expects the counter-lobbying to be fierce.

Industry money is already pouring into the state capital. The disclosure forms for state lobbyists brim with substantial donations from Internet sweepstakes cafes. According to state records, since January 2009, Allied Veterans alone has given somewhere between $120,000 and $280,000 to the Tallahassee lobbying firm Capital City Consulting, and $230,000 to $290,000 over the same period to a lobbying firm called Cruz & Co. In

February, two new political fundraising groups popped up in Tallahassee, raising money from sweepstakes cafes and then redirecting the donations to state politicians. Since Feb. 10, a group called Save Our Internet Access has raised $70,000, while Floridians for Internet Access has raised $17,700.

A month after Plakon introduced his bill into the statehouse, the legislation has already gotten bogged down in the state Senate. There the bill was assigned to the Committee on Commerce and Tourism[27]. Republican Senator Nancy Detert, chair of the committee, has not yet introduced the bill into committee — essentially putting the whole legislative effort on ice[28].

State records show that in January, Detert formed a new fundraising group. So far it has received three contributions worth $15,000 total. Two of the three donations appear to have come directly from the Internet sweepstakes industry. Most recently, on Mar. 2, Save Our Internet Access gave Detert's group $5,000. Detert did not respond to several requests for an interview.

Pat Fowler, the head of the Florida Council on Compulsive Gambling[29], a nonprofit organization that operates a 24-hour help line providing support for problem gamblers, says the calls involving the pop-up casinos began coming in about two years ago. Unlike resort casinos[30], says Fowler, the cafes can be hard for compulsive gamblers to avoid in everyday life. She cites a 1999 report commissioned by the U.S. Congress in which The National Gambling Impact Study Commission found that "the presence of a gambling facility within 50 miles roughly doubles the prevalence of problem and pathological gamblers."

"This is positioned within the community," says Fowler. "They are in the neighborhoods, by the laundromat, next door to the hair salon where people go to conduct their day-to-day lives. For those who develop problems, it's impossible for them to avoid."

The council recently published the results of a survey based on more than 60 individuals who had called the help line experiencing problems due to the sweepstakes cafes. The survey found that 89 percent of the callers were suffering from depression, 24 percent were either unemployed or disabled, and 37 percent said they had committed illegal acts to finance their sweepstakes fix.[31] The average household income was $26,000. The average amount they reported losing on gambling was just over $34,000.

Sweepstakes cafe proponents criticize the survey's small sample size and say that those who develop a problem are a minority of the customers. Supporters also accuse opponents in the legislature of hypocrisy. After all, while gambling per se remains illegal in Florida, the state has made various exceptions. Betting is allowed at more than 30 establishments across the state, including at horse and dog racing tracks, jai alai arenas, and casinos run by the Seminole Indians "It's ridiculous," says Seminole County resident Gwenn Flannery. "The state just wants to get a cut from this. Pretty soon they'll be taxing the air."

Like many of the regulars in Seminole County, Flannery also takes the bus two or three times a year to the Seminole Hard Rock casino in Tampa, but she enjoys the ease and convenience of the Empire Internet Café. To her, it's the same thing, only closer. "It's gambling," she says. "I don't care what they call it."

Larry Godden, a 67-year-old retired resident from Nebraska, agrees that the Internet sweepstakes cafe nomenclature is absurd. "That's a joke," says Godden. "It's gambling."

Godden says he doesn't see anyone losing serious money at the cafes. Once a week, he and his wife head over to the Cyber City Café in Winter Park and spend a couple of hours playing games like Wheel O' Treasure, Prize Is Right and Cobra Cash. On an average night, says Godden, they may lose between $40 and $60. Along the way he has become friends with some of the managers and customers. "It's a family place," says Godden. "There's no vulgarity. I go in planning to lose, and I'm never disappointed."

The cops in Seminole County have come to believe that the parlors create quality of life issues. Not long ago they released an internal study, which found that the arrival of sweepstakes cafes resulted in a 22 percent rise in calls to the police and a 55 percent rise in crimes at the shopping malls where they operated.

Part of the problem, general counsel Kirsheman says, is that the cash-rich businesses have proven to be tempting targets to would-be robbers. In December 2010, a man walked into the Empire Internet Café in Lake Mary brandishing a spray bottle filled with gasoline and a lighter, attempting to rob the place. The clerk at the sweepstakes cafe pulled out a gun and opened fire. The assailant fled.

Around 1 a.m. on the morning of Apr. 19, two men entered the Allied Veterans #67 and got into an altercation with the security guard. As captured on security cameras, one of the men started shooting.[33] The security guard returned fire, hitting one of the assailants, Gary Bryant, in the back. The men retreated to the parking lot and fired several more shots at the business before driving off. Police later found Bryant's body at a nearby hotel. Shortly thereafter, he was pronounced dead.

"These businesses are a bad idea for their communities," says Kirsheman.

Those who try and stop the spread often feel overpowered. "We're completely outgunned moneywise,"[34] says Kirsheman. "Part of the industry strategy is clearly to utilize the court system to bully local governments."

In the meantime, the sweepstakes industry will continue to recruit new entrepreneurs to the ranks. On his website, sweepstakesmachines.com, James Mecham advises newcomers that in the end the rewards of getting into the business outweigh the potential risks. "There will ALWAYS be people sitting on the sidelines afraid to get into the Internet sweepstakes business," he writes. "Our answer is this ... there have been people trying to shut this business down for years. And it's still going. And people that got into it years ago are now sitting under a palm tree on a tropical island somewhere enjoying a piña colada[35]."

From *Bloomberg Businessweek*, April 25th—May 1st, 2011

Ⅰ. New Words

advocacy	[ˈædvəkəsi]	n.	the act of supporting an idea, a person or a way of life
altercation	[ˌɔːltəˈkeiʃən]	n.	a noisy argument or disagreement
ATM			automated teller machine (自动取款机)
axiomatic	[ˌæksiəˈmætik]	adj.	true in an obvious way
baffle	[ˈbæfl]	v.	to confuse sb completely
ballpark	[ˈbɔːlpaːk]	n.	a number that is approximately correct

brim	[brim]	v.	~ **with sth** to be full of
calibrate	['kæli‚breit]	v.	to mark units of measurements on an instrument
cater	['keitə]	v.	~ **to sb** to provide the things a particular type of person wants
celery	['seləri:]	n.	芹菜
crack	[kræk]	v.	~ **down on sb/sth** to take strong and severe action to deal with sb/sth bad
commission	[kə'miʃən]	v.	to officially ask sb to do sth for you
concur	[kən'kə:]	v.	*formal* to agree
conviction	[kən'vikʃən]	n.	the act of finding sb guilty of a crime in court
deli	['deli]	n.	delicatessen（熟食店）
darn	[da:n]	adv.	damn; extremely
demographics	[‚demə'grə'fiks]	n.	人口统计数据
dub	[dʌb]	v.	to give sb/sth a particular name, often in a humorous or critical way
flounder	['flaundə]	v.	to be in danger of failing completely
fundraising	['fʌnd‚reiziŋ]	n.	资金筹集（工作）
gross	[grəus]	v.	to earn as a total amount
hike	[haik]	v.	to go for a long walk in the country
indictment	[in'daitmənt]	n.	控告
injunction	[in'dʒʌŋkʃən]	n.	an official order given by a court
jumbo	['dʒʌmbəu]	adj.	*informal* larger than others of the same kind
laid-back	[lieidbæk]	adj.	calm and relaxed
launder	['lɔ:ndə]	v.	洗钱
laundromat	['lɔ:ndrə‚mæt]	n.	a place where you can wash and dry clothes in machines
legitimize	[li'dʒitimaiz]	v.	to make sth legal
low-down	['ləu‚daun]	n.	*informal* true facts about sb/sth, especially those considered most important to know
minimal	['miniməl]	adj.	very small in size or amount
mutate	[mju:'teit]	v.	to change into a new form
niche	[nitʃ]	n.	（有利可图的）的专业市场
nomenclature	[nəu'menklətʃə]	n.	*formal* a system of naming things, especially in a branch of science
ordinance	['ɔ:dinəns]	n.	an order or rule made by a government
par	[pa:]	n.	equal level
predatory	['predə‚təri:]	adj.	using weaker people for financial advantage
per se			by itself
probation	[prə'beiʃən]	n.	（律）缓刑（期）

patron	['peitrən]	n.	（商店等）主顾
prohibition	[ˌprəuhi'biʃən]	n.	a law or rule that stops sth being done or used
promotion	[prə'məuʃən]	n.	activities done in order to increase the sales of a product or service
racetrack	['reis,træk]	n.	跑道；赛马场
reconfigure	[ˌriːkən'figə]	v.	to make changes to the way that sth is arranged to work
reverse	[ri'vəːs]	v.	to change sth completely so that it is opposite of what it was before
skirmish	['skəːmiʃ]	n.	a short argument, especially between political opponents
spike	[spaik]	v.	to rise quickly
terminal	['təːminəl]	n.	（计）终端，终端机
technically	['teknikəli]	adv.	strictly by the law
top-of-the-line	['tɔpəvðə,lain]	adj.	the best of its kind
wager	['weidʒə]	v.	to bet money
vulgarity	[vʌl'gæriti]	n.	庸俗，粗俗

Ⅱ. Background Information

美国赌博业

美国的赌博文化氛围十分浓厚。据 2009 年的统计，美国人一年在赌馆和彩票合法性赌博活动中所花的钱总额高达 1,600 亿美元，其中购买彩票钱的总数为 600 多亿美元，平均每户为 600 美元，花在合法经营赌馆里的钱总额是 1,000 亿美元，平均每户为 950 美元。美国赌博业规模庞大。据 2012 年统计，合法经营赌馆所聘用的工作人员总数高达 33 万，一年所开出的工资总额为 132 亿美元。

美国的赌博方式形形色色，有"吃角子老虎机"(slot machine)，轮盘赌(roulette)，21 点牌(black jack)，电视抽彩机(video lottery machine)，宾果(bingo)，基诺(keno)，回力球(jai-alai)，幸运转盘(wheel-of-fortune)。

美国不仅有赛马赌博(betting on horse races)，还有赛狗赌博(betting on greyhound races)和赛鼠赌博(betting on rat races)。不仅有陆上赌馆(land-based casino)，还有水上赌馆(river-based casino, casino boat)。

在这个科技高度发达的国家，高科技手段也用于赌博。互联网赌博(online gambling)十分活跃。据 2011 年统计，美国互联网共有 3,000—5,000 个博彩网吧(sweepstakes cafes)，这些网吧利润十分肥厚。据报道，每台电脑一个月可获 1,000—5,000 美元利润。2011 年博彩网吧总利润额为 100 亿美元。这些网吧为美国国内的赌客提供了极大方便，网吧设置一排排电脑，少至几台，多至近百台。有的网吧为了激励赌客延长玩的时间，为他们提供免费餐饮。

赌博狂潮兴起的原因有：美国民族喜欢冒险、政府积极支持赌业、宗教领袖默许认可、业主美化自身形象。

赌博带来的危害主要有：

1. 赌博使穷者更穷。从实际情况来看，穷人用于抽奖的金额比富人大得多。因此，赌博业所掠夺的对象正是那些最需要社会帮助的落魄者。

2. 赌博将青少年引入歧途。美国几项研究表明全国赌博成性的青少年占其参与赌博者比率为 9.4%，远高于成人的 3.8% 的比率。对纽约高中生的调查发现有 86% 的学生参加赌博。青少年一旦对赌博产生兴趣，就会荒废学业，还会出现不良行为。

3. 影响社会安定。实践证明，凡有赌博活动的地方犯罪率也必然很高。一篇题为《美国赌博热》的文章指出：美国平均每 10,000 人犯罪数为 593 起，而有赌博活动的地方则为每 10,000 人 1,092 起犯罪。

赌博还导致个人前途丧失、家庭破裂。亨利·莱西尔教授的调查发现：赌徒中有 20% 由于赌博离婚或家庭破裂，34% 丢掉工作，44% 偷钱还债，21% 破产，18% 由于赌博导致犯罪被捕，66% 产生自杀念头，16% 企图自杀。

Ⅲ. Notes to the Text

1. a strip mall—a row of shops built together, with a large area for parking cars in front of it（前面带有停车场的路边）一排商店
2. Jacks bills itself as a "Business Center and Internet Cafe," but it looks more like a pop-up casino.—Jacks 自称是"商务中心网吧"，但看上去更像时尚赌馆。（①bill—to advertise or describe in a particular way；②pop-up casino—a casino that, unlike the traditional casinos, pays out in prizes such as T-shirts, gift vouchers）
3. They are playing "sweepstakes" games that mimic the look and feel of traditional machines.—他们在玩样子和感觉像传统的吃角子老虎机的"博彩"赌博。（mimic—to look and behave like sth else）
4. Rows of symbols—cherries, lucky sevens, four-leaf cloves—tumble with every click of the mouse.—鼠标一点，（屏幕上）一排排的符号便开始滚动：红樱桃、幸运 7 和四叶草。（tumble—to roll）
5. Harley-Davidson T-shirt—（哈雷—戴维森公司生产的有张嘴鹰标志的）哈雷 T 恤
6. the vice squad of the local sheriff's department—当地警局缉捕队
7. Board of County Commissioners—县管理委员会（It serves as a legislative and policy-setting body for county government, enacts county-wide laws and authorizes programs and all expenditures of county funds.）
8. Internet sweepstakes cafes—博彩网吧
9. First Amendment rights to free speech—（美国宪法）第一修正案所赋予的言论自由权利
10. the commerce clause of the U.S. Constitution—美国宪法中的商务条款
11. attorney general—检察总长
12. It's a high-margin, cash-rich business.—这是一种高利润、赚钱多的行业。（①high-margin—high-profit；②cash-rich—getting a lot of money）
13. Once populated by shadowy figures operating at the margins of society, the industry now attracts entrepreneurs operating openly.—过去这一行是由隐秘的人偷偷摸摸地干，现在引入企业家公开经营。（at the margins of the society—outside socially accepted norms）
14. the Sunshine State—referring to Florida

15. "When we first got into the sweepstakes, for the first six months we were taking hide-in-the-bushes strategy," says Mecham. —米查姆说:"我们刚进入博彩业的头六个月采用的办法是偷偷地干。"(taking a hide-in-the-bushes strategy—operating in a covert way)

16. As part of the installation process, SweepsCoach provides new cafes with "compliance training" for its employees, which is geared toward keeping them out of jail. —作为安装程序的一个部分,Sweeps Coach 公司为新开张的博彩网吧雇员提供"遵守法规培训",其目的是使他们不被监禁。(①compliance — the practice of obeying laws and rules; ②gear sb toward—to prepare sb for a particular purpose)

17. net take—净收入

18. Vegas—an informal name for Las Vegas, a city known for its casinos

19. They are coming in to try and catch a big break. —他们参与(博彩活动)试图大赚一把。(break —opportunity)

20. There's going to be nine ways around whatever they come up with usually. —他们会在通常提出的理由基础上再编出许多理由。(come up with—to think of a reply)

21. ... revealing the inevitable marriages of money and politics that were also on display in the wake of the FBI's crackdown on three major online poker sites. —揭示了金钱与政治必然的密切关系,这些关系在联邦调查局对三大扑克赌博网站打击之后也显现出来。(marriage—close connection)

22. the Associated Press—简称 AP,美国联合通讯社,简称美联社(该社是美国最大的通讯社,每天用6种文字向全世界播报新闻和经济信息)

23. Among other charges, prosecutors allege that the defendants would "provide campaign contributions, campaign appearances by country music celebrities, political polls, media buys, fundraising assistance ... and other things of value" to state lawmakers in return for their votes on specific bills. —检察官声称,其他指控包括:原告作为回报,将给具体议案投票的州议员提供选金、安排乡村音乐歌星助阵、选民民意测验、购买媒体广告、协助筹措资金和其他有价值的服务。(political poll—a sampling of opinions organized during elections)

24. side work—an activity in addition to one's job for extra money

25. business card—商业名片(印有企业名称、地址等)

26. the debit cards with which the state of Florida distributes public assistance—佛罗里达州政府用以发放政府补助的借记卡(①debit card—a plastic card that can be used to take money from your bank account when you pay for sth.; ② public assistance—US government payments under Social Security to needy persons such as the aged, the blind and the disabled)

27. the Committee on Commerce and Tourism—商业旅游业事务委员会

28. essentially putting the whole legislative effort on ice—in reality leaving the whole legislative effort out of consideration

29. the Florida Council on Compulsive Gambling—佛罗里达州成瘾性赌博研究会 (compulsive gambling — gambling which is out of one's control)

30. resort casinos—度假胜地赌馆

31. ... they had committed illegal acts to fiance their sweepstakes fix. —为了搞钱去博彩网吧过赌瘾,他们干过不法活动。(Here, the author likens gambling to drug injection)

32. ... horse and dog racing tracks, jai alai arenas, and casinos run by the Siminole Indians—赛马和赛狗场，回力球竞技场和西米诺尔族印第安人经营的赌馆

33. As captured on security cameras, one of the men started shooting.—电子探头摄影显示，其中一个人开始射击。（capture—to film）

34. We're completely outgunned moneywise.—我们在资金方面根本比不过他们。（①outgun—to overpower；②moneywise—in the aspect of money）

35. Piña colade—椰香鸡尾酒

Ⅳ. Language Features

《商业周刊》简介

美国《商业周刊》(*Business Week*)是当今世界很有影响的商业类杂志。据统计，该刊物发行量为120万，读者人数超过560万。自1975年以来，该刊每年刊登的广告页超过美国其他杂志。

《商业周刊》创刊于1929年，由美国麦格劳-希尔出版公司（McGraw-Hill Inc.）出版。2009年该刊由彭博新闻收购，从此更名为《彭博新闻周刊》(*Bloomsberg Business Week*)。它在亚洲和欧洲出版国际版，发行范围超过140个国家。1986年《商业周刊》与我国外贸部合作，创办了中文版《商业周刊》，由彭博资讯、中国商务出版社和美国麦格劳-希尔公司合作出版社运营。这一刊物已成为我国工商界很有影响的商业杂志。

《商业周刊》具有商业性、新闻性和服务性特色。它致力于报道美国和世界商业、工业、财经、科技、贸易等领域重大事件，提供深入独到的见解和细微详尽的商业信息，帮助专业人士在商业、财经和投资方面做出更为明智的抉择。读者可以从其报道分析掌握商务大事、了解金融趋势、知晓科技动态，因而它是许多商界人士必读之物，其读者群包括政府官员、制造业、通讯业、经贸业、金融业的精英。

每期《商业周刊》都有一页目录（Contents），从中可以了解这一期内容布局、文章安排。该刊物一般设有以下六个栏目：全球经济（Global Economics）；公司与企业（Companies and Industries）；政治与政策（Politics and Policy）；技术（Technology）；市场与金融（Market & Finance）；特稿（Features）和其他类型（Etc）。前四栏篇幅一般在6页左右，每一栏中都有一篇深度报道，其他为简要报道。特稿篇幅较多，约占20页，所刊文章均有解释和分析。封面故事（Cover Story）也在其中，是每一期的重中之重，篇幅最长，报道广度、思想深度、分析力度均比较突出。

值得一提的是《商业周刊》所刊登的广告明显多于其他周刊，所占篇幅接近总篇幅的1/3。

《商业周刊》"最佳商学院"排名在美国很有影响。原先，只是评选商学院研究生项目。后来扩大到本科生项目。《商业周刊》的其他排名项目有"全球企业1200强""全球IT百大""新兴市场200强"等排行榜。这类信息也颇能引起世界各国的关注。

Ⅴ. Analysis of the Content

1. The Internet sweepstakes cafes mainly cater to _____.
   A. college students   B. teenagers
   C. the elderly and the poor D. rich businessmen

2. It can be seen from the article that regulating sweepstakes cafes would in fact produce the effect of _____.
   A. stopping the spread of sweepstakes cafes
   B. keeping sweepstakes cafes under government control
   C. gradually legalizing sweepstakes cafes
   D. chasing sweepstakes cafes out of the community
3. The sentence "phones are ringing off the hooks."(Para. 12) suggests that _____.
   A. many customers want to reserve places at sweepstakes cafes.
   B. many people want to get into the Internet sweepstakes business
   C. the phones have gone out of order
   D. law enforcement officers frequently make investigations
4. It is hard for compulsive gamblers to avoid sweepstakes cafes because _____.
   A. the games there are really interesting
   B. they are positioned within the community
   C. the payout rate of sweepstakes cafes is very high
   D. they get full respect there
5. The author believes that the most important factor in Florida's failure to shut down sweepstakes cafes is _____.
   A. Americans' strong interest in gambling
   B. the First Amendment of the Constitution
   C. the effective promotions of sweepstakes cafés
   D. the powerful lobbying by the Internet sweepstake industry

Ⅵ. Questions on the Article

1. What kind of business is Jacks in?
2. How do the Internet sweepstakes cafe owners in Florida try to justify their business?
3. What efforts have law-makers and law-enforcement officers across the U. S. done for the past six years about the Internet sweepstakes cafes?
4. Have those efforts stopped the spread of the sweepstakes cafes?
5. What kind of business did James Mecham and his partners operate before 2005? What kind of company has his business become?
6. Why did federal authorities arrest McGregor and 10 other people?
7. Why has Plakon's bill for shutting down sweepstakes cafes got bogged down in the state senate?
8. What is the impact of sweepstakes cafes' arrival on social order?
9. What is James Mecham's view on the prospects of the Internet sweepstakes café business?

Ⅶ. Topics for Discussion

1. Is gambling a form of harmless entertainment?
2. Should the Internet sweepstakes cafes be banned?

Lesson 18

The Next Gun Fight
Will a new campaign for gun laws quell the mass shootings that are routine in America?[1]
By Michael Scherer

 The next great American gun fight began this month with handshakes and smiles in a reunion of old foes at the Vice President's ceremonial office. Joe Biden knew the drill.[2] Two decades ago, he led the last major gun-control effort in the Senate, enacting a 10-year ban on sales of certain semiautomatics and imposing background checks for gun purchasers using licensed dealers. It was a defining experience.[3] "Guns! Guns! Guns!" he called out from the Senate floor in August 1994. "The single most contentious issue in the 22 years I have been here that relates to the criminal-justice system."

 Now it was starting again, in another gilded room and with many of the same players still sitting on opposite sides of the table, including James Jay Baker, a top advocate for the National Rifle Association.[4] The Vice President's views on guns hadn't changed much over the years: "The NRA gained power, and he gained disdain for them," explains one former aide. But Biden arrived, as always, looking to win the room.[5]

 So he began with charm, praising Baker for his fairness regarding some issue they both worked on in Delaware. He made a crack to the other gun-owner advocates—"gunners," he used to call them—about the difficulty of getting Hollywood and the video-game industry to talk about their addiction to violence. Then he laid out the contours of the fight to come, deflecting the harshest policy disagreements to his boss's judgment. "I am the Vice President, not the President," he said.

 Biden wanted to send a message, one he had been honing since December in meetings with cops, gun-control groups, clergy, mayors, educators and medical professionals. Ever since President Obama decided to pursue new gun controls after the massacre of 20 first-graders and six staff members at Sandy Hook Elementary[6], Biden and his staff knew they faced an uphill battle in Congress[7]. Democrats from rural districts remain wary of gun restrictions, and the Republican House[8] is so dysfunctional that it can't even pass its own bills, let alone one written by the White House. Even Obama treated guns as swing-state kryptonite during his re-election campaign, hardly mentioning the issue on the trail.[9]

 So the public fact-finding mission that Biden undertook in late December was given a second, more vital purpose: to lay the groundwork for a new grassroots movement, a lasting national campaign that would bring together various interest groups to win new limits on firearms—new penalties for gun trafficking, new prosecutions of gun crimes, limits on the types of guns available for sale, requirements for background checks for private and gun-show[10] purchases, regulations for ammunition and limits on the size of gun magazines.

 Biden and Obama laid their proposal before the public Jan. 16, with more than a hint of other battles to come. The President immediately signed 23 Executive Orders[11] to prevent future gun violence and proposed new legislation that would, if enacted, amount to the biggest change in gun laws since 1968. "This is our first task as a society—keeping our children safe," Obama said. "This is how we will be judged."

The White House does not expect to win many judgments soon. Instead it wants to change the entire conversation about gun politics in America. Republicans in both chambers, resistant to betraying a key constituency, will have to feel the sting of sustained public outrage.[12] And Democrats will have to risk short-term ballot-box backlash and take votes they too have resisted for at least 20 years. No one expects either campaign to be easy. "It falls into the larger context of the Republicans' fighting rearguard battles on immigration and the role of government and on this," said one Administration official about the coming gun fight. "That's going to be hard to sustain over time."

But even some Republicans admit that the Newtown, Conn., massacre may have changed the fundamental chemistry of gun politics in the U.S.[13] Before the end of the year, polls were shifting slightly, showing majorities in the country in favor of new regulations on assault weapons, high-capacity magazines and universal background checks[14]. A Time/CNN poll found in mid-January that 55% of the country supported stricter gun control, while 44% opposed it. As Biden put it before his meeting with the gun-owner groups, "There is nothing that has gone to the heart of the matter more than the visual image people have of little 6-year-old kids riddle[15]—not shot by a stray bullet but riddled, riddled—with bullet holes in their classroom." In his meetings with the gun lobbyists, Biden asked his guests to consider the shifting terrain after Sandy Hook. Even evangelical leaders, he said, traditionally a source of Republican influence, were expressing concern about guns. "It's going the other way," he told the men across the table. It was a warning and, in its way, a threat.

Kiss My Constitution

For Baker and the rest of the NRA brass, the Biden effort had the feel of a dark prophecy finally fulfilled.[16] For a year, NRA executive vice president Wayne LaPierre had been warning Americans of "a massive Obama conspiracy to deceive voters and hide his true intentions to destroy the Second Amendment[17]." He said gun owners needed to ready themselves for an assault on their rights if Obama was re-elected. And the uptick in gun and ammunition purchases across the country after the election suggested that many gun owners agreed. At rallies LaPierre would warn that Americans had been lulled to sleep in the first term. "That lying, conniving Obama crowd can kiss our Constitution[18]!" he would call out to applause. Now it was happening.

"They see this as their best shot[19], and it is a shot that they are taking, and they are coming right at us," David Keene, the NRA's president, said a few days later in an interview with *Time*. The group, which says it has more than 4 million members and spent about $20 million in the 2012 election cycle, was getting ready—reviewing the polls, keeping in touch with its members and calibrating message strategy. "We're doing all the things you would do if you were expecting a really serious battle," he said.

Keene welcomed some of the ideas Biden was preparing, like increased federal funding for school security and more aggressive prosecution for felons who illegally attempt to buy weapons. Keene was even willing to entertain an expansion of the background-check system for gun shows, where roughly 40% of gun sales take place. "I'm interested to see how such a proposal would be workable," he said. But he expressed concern about the entire approach of the Administration and about anything that sought to limit the types of firearms and magazines available for law-abiding citizens. "We are saying the question that Americans are asking is 'How do we protect our kids?' The question is not 'How do we ban guns we don't like?'"

Most worrisome for the NRA was the clear sense that something else had changed since the 1990s, something Biden didn't harp on in the meeting but was counting on nonetheless: leverage.[20] "They, for the first time, have money and coordination that they did not have before," Keene said. Millionaires and billionaires were stepping forward. Gun-victim groups were organizing. Social-networking campaigns were being prepared. Celebrities had been recruited to carry the message. This new fight over guns would be fought over old fault lines but on new terrain, with new tools, many of which were just proved very effective in the heat of a nationwide campaign.[21] Biden, this time, had backup. "The public wants us to act," he said.

"This Is Different"

On the day of the Sandy Hook shooting, Mark Kelly, the husband of former Representative Gabby Giffords[22], was traveling in China. He awoke in a Beijing hotel at 3 a.m., saw the news on television and called his wife, who was in Arizona, continuing her recovery from the gunshot wound to her brain—the work of another madman with a high-capacity gun. She was shaken, changed. "She said, 'We need to do something. We've got to stop just talking about this,'" Kelly remembers.

Until then, the couple had decided to avoid the activist path, treating the 2011 Tucson shooting largely as a personal trauma that needed to be dealt with in private. "It's not what we wanted to do," he said. But now they went all-in, drawing up plans for two new organizations: a nonprofit to build grassroots support for changes to gun laws and a super PAC[23] to run ads supporting members of Congress on the issue. Kelly decided to start working full time on the effort and began calling those he thought could help.

One of his first calls was to SteveMostyn, a wealthy trial-lawyer friend from Houston who happens to be one of the biggest contributors to Democratic super PACs. Like Kelly and Giffords, Mostyn is a gun owner. He sleeps with a handgun by his bed, in a safe that opens by his fingerprint. He has a gun range[24] on his West Texas ranch and invites friends out to shoot. But when Kelly called, Mostyn had just dropped off his 5-year-old daughter at school. "I told him it was time," Mostyn says.

The subject of gun laws was on his mind even before Sandy Hook. A few months earlier, he bought a couple of pistols, both with high-capacity magazines, and 3,000 rounds of ammunition for his gun collection at a local gun store. "The kid who walks me out to the car says to me, 'It looks like you are going to start a war,'" Mostyn says, noting his shock at how easy it was to stock up on enormous amounts of lethal firepower.

"I'm not anti-gun. I'm just not pro-dumbass,[25]" he continues, citing the more than 30,000 Americans who die every year from guns, mostly from suicide. "We've got a gun problem. That's what differentiates us from other cultures." He told Kelly he would seed the new group, which they called Americans for Responsible Solutions[26], with $1 million and begin fundraising with a goal of more than $14 million to support members of Congress in the 2014 elections who cast tough gun votes. "If a representative wants to vote their conscience, we are not going to allow you to bully," he said of the NRA.[27] "We will counter."

At the same time, in New York City, Mayor Michael Bloomberg was working from the same playbook.[28] With a net worth estimated at $25 billion, his contribution was potentially far greater than Mostyn's. In 2012 he challenged Mitt Romney and Obama to lay out their plans for curbing gun violence. Neither took Bloomberg up on the offer, but he went ahead and seeded a super PAC of his own, Independence USA, to flex his muscle on the gun issue.[29] The group spent about $10 million on five races around the country and won four, including the primary defeat of a veteran pro-NRA Democratic Representative in California, Joe Baca. Another group funded by Bloomberg, Mayors Against Illegal Guns, began an advertising campaign called Demand a Plan, with spots running in communities that had been affected by gun violence.

"The NRA is only powerful if you and I let them be powerful," Bloomberg tells *Time*. He says he wants to force votes on Capitol Hill so he can take the issue to the 2014 congressional elections. "I want the Congress to have to stand up and say, 'I'm with the NRA and support killing our children' or 'No.' And if the answer is, 'I'm going to take on that fight,' I've got their back,'" he says. He will not say how much more money he will spend, other than that it will be a substantial sum. "He described the $10 million as putting his toe in the water," says Howard Wolfson, one of Bloomberg's political advisers. "I don't know what the full foot is worth."[30]

Other groups are also organizing. The Brady Campaign to Prevent Gun Violence[31] raised $5 million since late December and announced a new ad campaign built around the slogan "We are better than this." A coalition of liberal gun-violence groups targeted North Dakota Senator Heidi Heitkamp with ads last month after the Democrat criticized the President's proposals, and California Senator Dianne Feinstein, who authored the 1994 ban on certain semiautomatic guns, is planning her own media push for the end of January. "This is different," she says. "I did not get calls about 'How do we organize?' I get those now."

But the opposition to gun control has grown stronger as well. Compared with the early 1990s, the NRA has strengthened its hand in the halls of Congress, and since Sandy Hook it has added 250,000 new members. More Americans agree with the positions of the NRA than disagree, in the new TIME/CNN poll, and of the half of people with guns in their homes, a majority feel that the government is trying to take their firearms away, even though Obama has not proposed any such measure. "Stand and fight," runs the tagline of a new television ad the NRA released in advance of the Biden task-force announcement.[32] The spot calls Obama an "elite hypocrite" and attacks him for supporting armed guards for his daughters but not at other schools, a deceptive charge given the President's decision to increase federal funding for school security. (In response, the White House denounced the ad as "repugnant and cowardly" for mentioning the President's children.) Keene suggests more tough talk is on the way and says he is actively seeking wealthy donors to counter the new money on the left.

The landscape in Congress, meanwhile, tilts against new regulation. The assault-weapons ban passed the Senate in 1993 with 56 votes. The thought of filibustering that proposal was seen at the time as out of bounds.[33] That is probably no longer the case. In the Senate, Democratic majority leader Harry Reid, who has long supported gun owners, has discouraged the idea of trying to renew the assault-weapons ban. The key question for the coming months is whether all the outside efforts can change the underlying physics of gun politics. Grover Norquist, a Republican organizer and an NRA board member, says the left often mistakes voter preference for voter intensity on the gun issue. While polls might show that a majority of Americans support a given gun regulation, come election time, it is usually only the opponents who base their vote on that issue. "We've been through this before," he notes, saying the power of the NRA has never been anchored in the number of television ads it buys in campaigns[34]. "People who care about the Second Amendment know where people are on guns. It's not a vote-moving issue on the left." The TIME/CNN poll suggests that dynamic is still at work. Only 14% of Democrats said they would vote for candidates only if they shared their view on guns, compared with 22% of Republicans.

310 Million Guns

But the White House is not counting votes in Congress just yet. It is counting instead on fostering a change in attitudes that will force politicians to take notice. "There will be pundits and politicians and special-interest lobbyists publicly warning of a tyrannical all-out assault on liberty," Obama said when he announced his recommendations. "The only way we will be able to change is if their audience, their constituents, their memberships say this time must be different."

To do that, the White House will have to sell the idea that its solutions will address the problem of mass shootings. But on that most important question, the verdict is vague. For decades, the frequency of mass shootings and the number of gun-related suicides in the U. S. have been consistent, while gun homicides have declined with the general crime rate. On average, there are 20 shootings a year with more than four victims killed, according to James Alan Fox, a professor at Northeastern University in Boston. On the same day that Biden met with the gun industry, a 16-year-old walked into his high school in Southern California and fired two rounds from a shotgun, allegedly trying to kill two students he believed were bullying him. He hit one of his targets and missed the second, killing no one, so the crime will not be counted in the statistics.

Eliminating all firearms in the U. S. would eliminate the ability to kill with firearms, but that is not anything like a realistic option. The Supreme Court ruled in 2008 that the Second Amendment bestows on U. S. citizens a right to possess firearms for lawful purposes. That right, just like those guaranteed in the First Amendment, can be subject to restrictions, but guns will never be removed from civilian circulation. And the number of guns out there continues to grow. In 1968 there was one gun in civilian hands for every two Americans. As of 2009, there were more guns in the U. S. than people: 114 million handguns, 110 million rifles and 86 million shotguns. Nothing proposed would take away those guns.

And most mass shooters don't use assault weapons anyway. They prefer pistols, often with many bullets in the clip. The shooters, more often than not, lack criminal records, suggesting that background checks applied to all sales might not deter them. But Biden and Obama have set a low bar for the legislation they propose, speaking only about diminishing the probability of more attacks, not eliminating them altogether. "If there is even one life that can be saved," Obama says, "then we've got an obligation to try."

On that score, there is evidence to support the idea that more rules might prevent individual cases of mass violence or at least lessen the damage. The disturbed man who shot

Giffords was tackled while reloading his gun, having spent 33 rounds. Nine-year-old Christina-Taylor Green was shot sometime after bullet No. 12, says Kelly, who has reviewed the criminal records. "If Jared Loughner didn't have access to a high-capacity magazine, there would be less people dead," he says.

Improving the scope and quality of background checks, with better mental health and more recent criminal records, could help prevent criminal and disturbed individuals from acquiring weapons. Also, better coordination between schools, mental-health officials and the police could flag potential shooters. [35] Both Loughner and James Holmes, the movie-theater shooter in Aurora, Colo., raised alarm bells at their respective schools before they struck. Obama has promised to pursue several education efforts about mental illness and guns as part of his Executive actions.

But the big questions on gun control will soon move out of Washington and be placed before the American people. "I will put everything I've got into this, and so will Joe," said Obama. "But I've got to tell you that the only way we can change is if the American people demand it." It will be a long fight. But it is a fight that has begun again.

From *Time*, January 28, 2013

I. New Words

backlash	[ˈbæklæʃ]	n.	a strong negative reaction
backup	[ˈbækʌp]	n.	extra support or help
ballot-box	[ˈbælətbɔks]	n.	投票箱
calibrate	[ˈkælibreit]	v.	校订；调整
contentious	[kənˈtenʃəs]	adj.	likely to cause argument
contour	[ˈkɔntuə(r)]	n.	the outline of the shape or form
conniving	[kəˈnaiviŋ]	adj.	acting slyly and unpleasantly so as to harm others
crack	[kræk]	n.	俏皮话
curb	[kəːb]	v.	to control or limit sth
deflect	[diˈflekt]	v.	*figurative* to turn sb away from his intended course of action
disdain	[disˈdein]	n.	complete lack of respect
dysfunctional	[disˈfʌŋkʃənl]	adj.	not working properly or normally
evangelical	[ivænˈdʒelikəl]	adj.	（美国）福音主义教派的
fact-finding	[ˈfæktˌfaindiŋ]	adj.	实情调查的
felon	[ˈfelən]	n.	someone who is guilty of a serious crime
homicide	[ˈhɔmisaid]	n.	killing of one person by another
hone	[həun]	v.	to develop or improve sth, over a period of time
hypocrite	[ˈhipəkrit]	n.	伪善者，伪君子
lethal	[ˈliːθəl]	adj.	causing or able to cause death
lull	[lʌl]	v.	to make sb relaxed and calm

penalty	[ˈpenəlti]	n.	a punishment for breaking a law
prosecution	[ˌprɒsɪˈkjuːʃn]	n.	起诉,告发
pundit	[ˈpʌndɪt]	n.	a person who is an authority on a subject; an expert
rearguard	[ˈrɪəˌgɑːd]	adj.	后卫的;无望取胜的
repugnant	[rɪˈpʌgnənt]	adj.	causing strong dislike or disgust
riddle	[ˈrɪdl]	v.	to make many holes in sb/sth
seed	[siːd]	v.	to promote the growth of sth
traffick	[ˈtræfɪk]	v.	to carry on trade, especially of an illegal kind
trial-lawyer	[ˈtraɪəlɔːjə(r)]	n.	Am.E(初审)出庭律师
trauma	[ˈtrɔːmə]	n.	an injury
uptick	[ˈʌptɪk]	n.	a small increase
verdict	[ˈvɜːdɪkt]	n.	裁定

Ⅱ. Background Information

美国枪支问题

美国是世界上唯一法律允许私人拥有枪支的国家。目前,美国有近17万家枪械专卖店,每年的枪支交易量约在300—500万支之间。售枪广告随处可见,公民只需交35美元的登记费,就可以轻松取得为期三年的持枪执照。据2012年数据,有1.1亿户拥有至少2.8亿支枪。目前大约40%的美国家庭拥有枪支,而在美国南部,70%的家庭都有枪。

枪杀已成为美国第11大死亡因素,2011年死于枪口之下的人数为32,163人,美国枪杀事件频频发生。2007年4月16日,弗吉尼亚理工大学发生恶性校园枪击案,韩裔男子赵承熙在9分钟内用两把手枪170发子弹夺去了32人的生命,并将最后一颗子弹留给了自己。此外,2012年7月20日,美国丹佛市举行《蝙蝠侠前传3:黑暗骑士崛起》的首映现场发生枪击事件,至少造成14人死亡,50人受伤。2012年8月5日,美国威斯康星州奥克里克一座锡克教寺庙内,发生枪击事件,造成7人死亡,多人受伤,包括与警方交火中丧生的一名犯罪嫌疑人。2012年12月14日,康涅狄格州西部纽镇的桑迪·胡克小学枪击案造成28人丧生,其中包括20名儿童。2013年一年,美国发生了多次校园枪击案:2月,一名17岁的男孩在俄亥俄州沙登高中咖啡馆开枪,造成3名学生死亡;4月,一名曾在加州奥克兰市的奥伊科斯大学就读的学生冲入校园,向学生开枪扫射,造成7人死亡。本文是在桑迪·胡克小学枪击案发生以后不久,控枪问题再次成为美国全国上下关注的焦点问题的大背景下刊登的。

事实上,每次枪击案后,美国社会都会掀起加强枪支管控(gun control)甚至禁枪的呼声。桑迪·胡克小学血案发生后,纽约州州长科莫呼吁,美国全社会应该"团结起来管控枪支";纽约市长布隆伯格也呼吁"立即行动",并表示美国总统奥巴马不能只是向遇难者家属送去同情,更应向国会送去法律草案来解决非法拥有枪支问题。

然而,"控枪"在美国一直是无法实现的"奢望"。这其中一个原因就是美国宪法第二修正案(the Second Amendment to the Constitution)中有"人民持有和携带武器的权利不受侵犯(The right of the people to keep and bear Arms shall not be infringed.)"的条款。2008年和

2010 年最高法院的裁决更加强了这一宪法权利。极度崇尚个人自由的美国民众担心,如果"控枪",个人的权利就很可能受到侵蚀和威胁。美国政治中一直有这样一种趋势,就是基于个人权利的观点总是胜过提倡社会责任的呼吁。

美国难以"控枪"的另一个重要原因是利益集团(interest groups)。其中最为著名的就是财大气粗的全国步枪协会(National Rifle Association, NRA),该机构总部设在弗吉尼亚,是美国最大的枪械拥有者组织。NRA 认为,拥有枪支的权利是受美国宪法第二修正案保护的民权,这构成了它的政治活动的理论基础。它自称是"美国历史最悠久、规模最大的民权维护组织",根据 NRA 官网的数字,目前该组织拥有会员数近 400 万人。虽然 NRA 是非党派性、非营利性的组织,但是它积极参加美国政治活动,在美国政治中具有巨大的影响力。美国《财富》(Fortune)杂志曾声称,全国步枪协会是美国最具影响力的院外游说集团(lobby),它每年花在美国国会的游说经费都在百万美元以上。这是"控枪派"(gun-control advocates)所无法匹敌的势力。

III. Notes to the Text

1. Will a new campaign for gun laws quell the mass shootings that are routine in America? — 新一轮的控枪法案运动会平息美国已经习以为常的大规模枪击事件吗?(① gun law — a law that pertains to firearms and weapons. ② quell — to bring to an end, especially by force ③ mass shootings — shootings killing or injuring many people)

2. Joe Biden knew the drill. — 乔·拜登知道这套程序。(drill — the correct and usual way to do sth)

3. It was a defining experience. — 这是关键性时刻。(defining experience — an experience which clearly shows the beginning of a situation change)

4. Now it was starting again, in another gilded room and with many of the same players still sitting on opposite sides of the table, including James Jay Baker, a top advocate for the National Rifle Association. — 如今枪支问题斗争再度展开,地点换到了另一个富丽堂皇的房间,许多老对手依然坐在谈判桌的对面,其中包括詹姆斯·贝克,美国步枪协会的头号辩护者。(gilded — coated with or as if with gold)

5. But Biden arrived, as always, looking to win the room. — 但拜登的意图一如既往,期待赢得参会者的支持。(look to win the room — expect to get the support of those present)

6. the massacre of 20 first-graders and six staff members at Sandy Hook Elementary — 在桑迪·胡克小学发生的枪杀 20 名一年级学生和 6 名学校工作人员的事件

7. Biden and his staff knew they faced an uphill battle in Congress — 拜登和他的工作班子知道他们在国会面临一场艰苦的斗争(uphill battle — a struggle that is difficult to win and takes a lot of effort or a long period of time)

8. Republican House — 共和党控制下的众议院

9. Even Obama treated guns as swing-state kryptonite during his re-election campaign, hardly mentioning the issue on the trail. — 就连奥巴马再度竞选总统时,也把枪支问题视为摇摆州的致命弱点,所以在竞选系列活动中很少提及。(①swing state — a state in

which no candidate has overwhelming support; ② kryptonite — the ultimate natural weakness of Superman. In popular culture, it has become synonymous with Achilles' heel, the one weakness of an otherwise invulnerable hero.)

10. gun-show — a temporary exhibition or gathering in the U.S. where firearms are displayed, bought, sold and traded 枪支展销会

11. Executive Orders — orders issued by the president of the United States of America and having the force of laws

12. Republicans in both chambers, resistant to betraying a key constituency, will have to feel the sting of sustained public outrage. — 两院共和党人由于拒绝背叛自己的主要支持者,必然会被公众持续痛批。(① resistant — showing refusal; ② sting — a sharp pain; ③ constituency — a particular group likely to support a person; ④ outrage — a strong feeling of shock and anger)

13. But even some Republicans admit that the Newtown, Conn., massacre may have changed the fundamental chemistry of gun politics in the U.S. — 但是,甚至一些共和党人也承认康涅狄格州纽顿镇的枪杀案可能改变了美国枪支政治的基本形势。(chemistry — referring to situation)

14. new regulations on assault weapons, high-capacity magazines and universal background checks — 对购买攻击性武器和大容量弹夹以及普遍性背景调查新的规定(magazine — the part of a gun that holds bullets before they are fired)

15. There is nothing that has gone to the heart of the matter more than the visual image people have of little 6-year-old kids riddled... — 年仅6岁的孩子被枪打得满身弹眼,这种场景最能使人们看到问题的实质……(riddle — to make many holes in sb)

16. For Baker and the rest of the NRA brass, the Biden effort had the feel of a dark prophecy finally fulfilled. — 对于贝克和全国步枪协会其他头目而言,拜登所取得的成果使人感到令人沮丧的预言最终得以实现。(① dark — gloomy; ② prophecy — a statement telling sth that will happen in the future)

17. the Second Amendment — The amendment runs as follows: A well regulated militia being necessary to the security of a free state, the right of the people to keep and bear arms shall not be infringed. (对此法案有两种解读:一种认为该法案保障个人拥有枪支的权利,另一种认为该法案指的是民兵群体拥有枪支的权利。)

18. kiss our Constitution — This phrase appears to claim that the NRA and its followers own the Constitution and enjoy its protection.

19. they see this as their best shot — 他们把这次事件当做最好的机会(shot — a chance)

20. Most worrisome for the NRA was the clear sense that sth else had changed since the 1990s, something Biden didn't harp on in the meeting but was counting on nonetheless: leverage. — 全国步枪协会清楚地意识到自20世纪90年代以来,另外一种情况也发生了变化,拜登虽未在会上喋喋不休地讲,但却对此很有把握,那就是影响力,这种意识使他们最为担忧。(① harp on — to keep talking about sth in a boring or annoying way; ② count on — to be sure that sth will happen; ③ leverage — the ability to influence what people do)

21. This new fight over guns would be fought over old fault lines but on new terrain, with new tools, many of which were just proved very effective in the heat of a nationwide campaign. — 这场新的枪支问题之战会围绕老的分歧,但形势和手段却是新的,这些手段在许多全国性运动最激烈时刻使用证明是十分有效的。(①fault lines — a metaphor referring to potentially divisive issues; ②new terrain — a metaphor referring to new situation)

22. Gabby Giffords — (1970—   ), a retired American politician, elected to Congress 3 times. On January 8, 2011, she was critically injured by a gun shot at a supermarket near Tucson, Arizona. The criminal was Loughner, who killed 6 people and injured 13 in the shooting.

23. super PAC — 超级政治行动委员会(政治行动委员会在接受捐款和使用捐款时受到严格规定和限制。然而,超级政治行动委员会可以无限制接受捐款,也可以无限制花钱,所受到的唯一限制是不得直接资助个人竞选,而只能做政治广告之类的宣传活动)

24. gun range — 靶场

25. I'm just not pro-dumbass. — 我只是不支持蠢货。(dumbass — *U. S.*, *vulgar*, *slang*, a person marked by stupidity or foolishness)

26. Americans for Responsible Solutions — 支持负责可靠解决方案协会

27. "If a representative wants to vote their conscience, we are not going to allow you to bully," he said of the NRA. —他针对全国步枪协会说:"如果议员要按良心投票,我们不会允许你们威吓他们。"

28. At the same time, in New York City, Mayor Michael Bloomberg was working from the same playbook. — 与此同时,纽约市长麦克•布隆伯格也以同样的方式在活动。(from the same playbook — in the same way)

29. Neither took Bloomberg up on the offer, but he went ahead and seeded a super PAC of his own, Independence USA, to flex his muscle on the gun issue. —(罗姆尼和奥巴马)两人都没有接受布隆伯格的建议,但他继续努力,创建了自己的超级政治行动委员会"独立美国",以显示他在枪支问题方面的影响。(① take Bloomberg up on the offer — to accept Bloomberg's offer; ②flex his muscle — to show his strength or power)

30. "He described the $10 million as putting his toe in the water," says Howard Wolfson, one of Bloomberg's political advisers. "I don't know what the full foot is worth." — 布隆伯格的政治顾问霍华德•沃尔森说:"他把1,000万美元投入说成是牛刀小试,我不知道他的全部资金投入会是多少。"(Note the author's use of sustained metaphor.)

31. the Brady Campaign to Prevent Gun Violence — 布雷迪阻止枪支暴力运动(a non-profit organization, named after James "Jim" Brady, who was press secretary and permanently disabled as a result of the 1981 assassination attempt on President Ronald Reagan. His wife, Sarah Brady served as a leader of the organization from 1989 until 2012.)

32. "Stand and fight," runs the tagline of a new television ad the NRA released in advance of the Biden task-force announcement. —全国步枪协会新的电视广告主题句是"站起来战斗",这个广告在拜登特别工作组宣布之前就已经开始播放。(①tagline — A tagline is a variant of an advertising slogan typically used in movie marketing, commercials, and

websites；② task-force — a group of people who are brought together to deal with a particular problem)

33. The thought of filibustering that proposal was seen at the time as out of bounds. — 采用冗长演说的方式阻挠这个提案通过的想法在当时显得越轨。(filibuster — to try to prevent action in a law-making body by making very slow long speeches)

34. the power of the NRA has never been anchored in the number of television ads it buys in campaigns — 全国步枪协会的力量从来不是基于(宣传)运动中所购买的电视广告数量 (anchor sth in sth — to firmly base sth on sth else)

35. Also, better coordination between schools, mental-health officials and the police could flag potential shooters. — 此外，如果学校、心理健康官员和警察之间能更好地协作，就可以引起对可能持枪射击者的注意。(flag — to draw attention to sb)

Ⅳ. Language Features

版面与图片

报刊的意识形态除表现在文字之中，还体现在版面和图片上。

一篇新闻报道的篇幅数量、所在位置、标题所用字体形式、所占栏目多少都能显示报社对这篇新闻的看法。通常，报社认为最重要的新闻报道会安排在头版(front page)，使用通栏标题(banner headline)，标题采用粗体字(boldface type letters)。每期新闻杂志最重要文章的图片会醒目显示在封面上，成为该期封面故事(cover story)。

新闻图片"看上去是客观记录的现实"，给人的印象是"原原本本的视觉呈现"，因而增强新闻报道的客观性。然而，"图片的选择是一个高度意识形态化的程序"。报社编辑选用图片不仅是为了活泼版面、吸引读者，而且是为了突出文章主题。编辑们在撰写图片说明时"是把图片和新闻导语紧密联系在一起考虑"。许多编辑认为，图片说明"在某种程度上是他们每天所写的最重要的文章"。

本文是《时代》周刊2013年1月28日期刊所刊载的一篇特别报道(Special Report)。这篇报道配有一幅图片和八幅图表。一幅共占两整页的图片展现堆积如山的子弹壳。第一幅图表显示美国人所持有的持枪数量(3.1亿支)；第二幅图表显示2008年拥有枪支的选民总数(5,500万)；第三幅显示美国持有经营执照的枪支销售商数量(129,817)；第四幅显示世界人均持枪数比率最高的五个国家的排行(美国高居榜首)；第五幅显示美国1993年和2011年死于枪口之下的人数(分别为39,596和32,163)；第六幅显示美国每年制造和进口的枪支数量(分别为5,459,240和3,252,404)；第七幅显示一支AR-15型半自动步枪一分钟可射出的子弹数量(45发)；第八幅显示的是美国2013年1月拥有至少一支枪的家庭所占家庭总数的百分比(49%)。这些图表和图片所表达的主题是美国枪支泛滥，枪祸十分严重，但持枪派具有较大政治影响，控枪之路困难重重。

{ V. Analysis of the Content }

1. The meaning of the word "shot" in the sentence "They see this as their best shot, and it is a shot that they are taking..."(Para. 10)_____.
   A. the act of firing a gun
   B. a metal bullet
   C. a scene in a movie
   D. a chance
2. The more important purpose of the meeting organized by Biden was _____.
   A. to lay the ground work for a new grassroots movement to win new limits on firearms
   B. to know public opinion on gun control
   C. to change the views of the gun-rights group
   D. to announce the White House's proposal for new gun legislation
3. The list of new limits the White House intends to win on firearms does NOT include _____.
   A. limits on the types of guns available for sale
   B. requirements for background checks
   C. limits on the number of guns owned by each American
   D. limits on the size of gun magazines
4. Which of the following statements is NOT true?
   A. The gun issue was an issue avoided by Democratic candidates during an election campaign.
   B. The gun issue is a highly divisive issue.
   C. As a result of the Sandy Hook massacre, it will be easy to win new gun-control regulations.
   D. The gun fight in the U.S. will remain tough.
5. The author's view on gun-control rules' effect on reduction of mass violence is _____.
   A. positive
   B. negative
   C. unknown
   D. uncertain

{ VI. Questions on the Article }

1. What is Biden's stand on the gun issue?
2. Why does the author say Biden and his staff knew they faced an uphill battle in Congress?
3. What impact may the Sandy Hook School massacre have produced on the gun issue?
4. How large is the NRA? How was it preparing for the gun fight in 2012?
5. How did Keene respond to Biden's ideas?
6. What was most worrisome for the NRA?
7. Who was the victim of the 2011 Tucson shooting? How did she and her husband take the shooting? What was the couple's reaction to the Sandy Hook massacre?
8. How has the opposition to gun control become?
9. What is the White House counting on?
10. What does the author think the White House will have to do in order to foster a change in attitudes?

11. What are the prospects of the next gun fight?

VII. Topics for Discussion

1. Does gun possession enhance Americans' safety?
2. Is it possible for the U.S. government to solve the problem of gun violence?

Lesson 19

Homeless Sprawl

The City of Angels struggles to deal with a devil of a place

By Betsy Streisand

It was nothing unusual; just a high-voltage electrical box[1], 3 feet deep in trash, surrounded by a chain-link fence and wedged between two windowless warehouses on a downtown Los Angeles Street. It hardly merited a passing glance, or got one, from anyone other than Los Angeles Police Capt.[2] Andrew Smith. After years of patrolling Skid Row[3], the city's sprawling 50-square-block homeless encampment[4], Smith has a way of seeing things that others might miss, like the pair of muddy feet peeking out from a mountain of garbage. "C'mon outta there,"[5] Smith called out as he rapped the fence with his nightstick. "Don't you see that high-voltage sign? You're gonna get hurt.[6]"

"Don't worry. I'm not going to electrocute myself. I worked in construction for years," the man called back, relying on the résumé that once kept his life afloat to qualify him instead to set up house in a reeking pile of filth next to a box of live wires. Rail thin and jumpy, Jack, 51, said he had gone to college and worked in construction, but then bad things started happening in the late 1980s and he landed on Skid Row. He has been there ever since, one of 12,000 homeless people living in the shelters, tent cities[7], cardboard condos[8], and flophouses that give Skid Row the dubious distinction of having the nation's largest concentration of homeless.

Like more than 1,000 other longtime street dwellers, Jack is what's known in the trade as "services resistant," a controversial term applied mostly to drug addicts and the mentally ill, who for a variety of reasons refuse to go into a shelter or program. (Nearly 10,000 Skid Row residents sleep in shelters and cheap hotels at night and return to the streets during the day.) "I don't mind being outside," Jack said as he unchained a bicycle piled high with his belongings. "I don't want to go to a mission and have people telling me what to do. I'd rather live out here."

But living on the streets of Skid Row is becoming an increasingly iffy proposition as police crack down on crime and camping and lift (**put**) the lid on what has become a massive homeless gulag in downtown L.A.[9] Out of view in an industrial district, Skid Row has been operating under the radar for decades.[10] But it's on everyone's agenda now. Flashy Los Angeles Police Chief William Bratton is on a crusade to conquer crime in Skid Row. Developers are circling with blueprints for high-priced hotels and condos. Even L.A.'s politicians are working together — sort of — to find a solution for what new Mayor Antonio Villaraigosa has labeled a "national disgrace." Still, success is far from assured.

History. Skid Row, at the end of what was once the railroad line, has been around since the late 1800s when transient men who had come to the West looking for work would live in its cheap hotels. Then came the bars, the brothels, and the religious missions. Through the Depression and two world wars, Skid Row evolved as the place to bring together those who needed help — alcoholics, addicts, and the mentally ill — and the social-service providers who could give it to them. But after more than 100 years, it has become a containment zone for some of society's most desperate and a magnet for those who prey on them. [11] "While the best of intentions may have been used in centralizing services in Skid Row, they have produced the worst possible solution," says Tom Gilmore, a developer and a former commissioner of the Los Angeles Homeless Services Authority[12]. "Years of flawed policies have enabled Skid Row to become the most obscene environment for the homeless in America."

Skid Row is also a haven for prostitutes, drug addicts, and a rich assortment of criminals. One fifth of the city's narcotics arrests were made on Skid Row in 2005. And Los Angeles jails release 1,600 prisoners a month directly into downtown. There are thousands of parolees, including hundreds of registered sex offenders[13], living on "the Row," which is also a breeding ground for infectious diseases like AIDS and hepatitis[14]. And because of the availability of so many services, hospitals frequently dump indigent patients there. Similarly, cities all over Los Angeles County, now the homeless capital of the nation with 90,000 transients, point their street people in the direction of Skid Row.

But that's starting to change, albeit slowly. Los Angeles is in the midst of a sweeping downtown revitalization that is headed Skid Row's way. [15] Spurred by huge developments like the Staples Center arena[16], the Walt Disney Concert Hall[17], and the upcoming $1.8 billion Grand Avenue project, downtown has become a giant construction zone. From the lofts in the historic Rosslyn Hotel to the apartments of the converted Pacific Electric Building — both on the fringes of Skid Row — more than 7,000 new housing units have been added to downtown since 1999, with many more in the works. Martini bars and trendy bistros are moving in. The area is starting to feel, well, hot. "We have managed against all odds to make this happen[18]," says Carol Schatz of the Central City Association, which represents more than 400 local businesses and has been instrumental in fueling downtown's rebirth. "But we believe we could have even more downtown investment... if it weren't for the Skid Row problem."

Enter Bratton, who has a bit of experience with urban disorder. As New York police commissioner, he was instrumental in taking back Times Square from prostitutes and street swindlers and making way for its commercial rebirth[19]. He also cleared Gotham streets of the windshield-washing "squeegee men" who would materialize at traffic lights to ambush unwitting drivers. [20] Relying on the "broken windows" approach to policing — stop the small crimes first and it will be easier to prevent big ones — the NYPD[21] stepped up arrests in Times Square for crimes like littering and loitering. Residents started walking the streets again, and businesses began to flourish.

Stay the course[22]. Skid Row, OK, is not Times Square. The LAPD, by any measure, is vastly understaffed. [23] And while the city of L.A. has begun to set aside more money for the homeless, New York outspends L.A. in that area by more than 10-fold. But Bratton's approach is essentially the same: Reduce the crime on Skid Row and clean the place up, and then there's at least a foundation in place to tackle the underlying causes of homelessness —

theoretically, anyway. "This city has turned a blind eye to the scale of the Skid Row problem, because it was out of sight and out of mind," Bratton told U.S. News. "But it's in full view now."

In September, Bratton added 50 more cops to the 350-person Central Division, which includes most of Skid Row. Serious crimes dropped almost immediately and are now down 18 percent for the year. There have been more than 3,000 arrests since September, the vast majority for felony narcotics charges. "'The Show,' as they call it down here, is over," says Captain Smith. "The drugs, drinking, prostitution, and hanging out by the campfire with your buddies is finished." Since September, the LAPD has also been walking a legal tightrope[24] by enforcing a sidewalk sleeping ban during the day, which means that tents and other improvised shelters must be collapsed from 6 a.m. to 9 p.m. The number of people sleeping on the street dropped from 1,876 in mid-September to under 1,200 in December. It's a start. The streets are now cleaner, and the sidewalks, once so crowded with tents and cardboard cities that they were impassable, are clear. Many homeless people have complained of being hassled, and homeless advocates have accused the cops of harassment. But others are thankful. "It's better this way, safer, and you can walk on the sidewalk," said Frank (who didn't want his last name used), who says he's been on the street for 2½ years.

For Malcolm Quon, a manager for his family's firm, the Umeya Rice Cake Co., simply being able to enter his warehouse without stepping past heroin addicts shooting up[25] is a big improvement. Umeya, which makes fortune cookies[26] and other Asian snacks, has been on Skid Row since the end of WWII. "It's hard to attract new customers ... because people come down here and they are not comfortable," says Quon, who doesn't schedule meetings until late morning and alerts his neighborhood LAPD officer every time he has a client coming, so that there is no one camped out close to his entryway. "Things have gotten much better in the last six months," Quon says. "But that just means someone else's problem got worse. It's not like it has disappeared."

No one is more aware of that than Bratton. "This is a big and complex problem that needs a big fix.[27] Busting up the crime is an aspect, but it's not the solution," he says. "You can't arrest your way out of it."[28]

Even if he wanted to, he couldn't. In 2003, the American Civil Liberties Union[29] sued the police chief and the city to stop enforcement of an ordinance that prohibited people from camping on streets and sidewalks at any time of the day. In April, the U.S. Ninth Circuit Court of Appeals[30] sided with the ACLU in ruling that the law amounted to cruel and unusual punishment. With not enough shelter beds, the court argued, the city was in effect criminalizing homelessness.

The decision set in motion one of L.A.'s signature political polkas, featuring the city, the county, the mayor, the business community, and the police chief.[31] At first, the city was going to appeal, with Bratton's support. Then he joined forces with Villaraigosa, who wanted to settle with the ACLU. (Villaraigosa is a past president of the ACLU of Southern California.) A settlement that would have called for only a partial, daytime sleeping ban was proposed in September but shot down by the City Council[32]. Then came a similar plan to allow sleeping on the streets between 9 p.m. and 6 a.m. — but the mayor withdrew from that one amid widespread worry the agreement would create a permanent homeless sanctuary in Skid Row.

Even the ACLU admitted that formalizing Skid Row as a city within a city probably wasn't a great idea. "The [proposed] settlement was not a very good settlement," says Ramona Ripston of the ACLU of Southern California. "No one thinks that sleeping on the street is a solution. But we thought it was a step toward getting more shelter beds, more services, and more low-cost housing."

The parties are still talking, and for the moment, the LAPD feels it's on safe legal ground[33] in enforcing a sleeping ban during the day. But virtually everyone agrees that the only real solution is to offer more supportive housing[34], where those with mental illnesses and drug addictions can get help. Services also need to be spread throughout the county. That way, the financial burden can be shared, and the growing numbers of homeless women and children can be placed in a better environment. Homeless people with drug problems would also be farther away from Skid Row's temptations. "The city can take the easy route and say all the crap is already here on Skid Row, so let's just make better crap," says Gilmore. "Or, it can make the hard decision to fund supportive housing, with services, and to distribute it geographically rather than create a ghetto."

Rays of hope. That has proved to be a difficult task in a county where not-in-my-backyardism[35] is so strong that the city of Santa Clarita had actually planned to bus its entire homeless population to Los Angeles. (The plan was aborted last year after bad publicity.) "People need to be realistic. Every elected official needs to accept permanent supportive housing in their district," says L.A. City Councilwoman Jan Perry, whose district includes Skid Row. "Two thirds of Los Angeles County is not in compliance. If I were a lawyer for the ACLU, I'd be looking at that."

But there is some good news. Union Rescue Mission[36] on Skid Row recently bought Hope Gardens, a former retirement home in the San Fernando Valley, to provide housing and services for elderly women and for mothers and children. With day care and other services, women living at Hope Gardens would be able to go to school while their kids were cared for. The project was nearly done in by local opposition[37], even though it is separated by several miles from the nearest neighborhood. It is the kind of place Crystal Harper, 33, and the hundreds of other mothers with children on Skid Row would welcome. "My kids are terrified to go outside down here, and so am I," said Harper, as she waited outside the Union Rescue Mission for the school bus with her 6-year-old son. Harper is in a yearlong "second step" program, which includes job training and other life skills. She and her two children share a room with another single mother and her kids. Harper believes she could turn her life around if she could catch her breath away from Skid Row.

Hope Gardens will happen. And so will several other small projects here and there around the county. A recent vote by the county board of supervisors will direct $100 million toward new homeless programs in the next year. And Villaraigosa has proposed to the City Council that $4.6 million in new money be spent to fund 372 beds at emergency shelters. The mayor has also pushed for help from the state. But when it comes to the big fix — long-term supportive housing — the best hope went down the drain in the November election[38]. Measure H, a bond issue[39] that would have created $1 billion for supportive housing, fell just short of the required two-thirds majority. "There is plenty of goodwill," says Douglas Mirell, a commissioner on the Los Angeles Homeless Services Authority. "But... it will be at least two years before we see another bond measure like that."

In the meantime, Skid Row will continue to bedevil the City of Angels[40]— especially when the sun goes down, the tent cities go up, and the homeless try to find their way in the dark.

From U.S. News and World Reports, December 10, 2006

Ⅰ. New Words

afloat	[əˈfləut]	*adj.*	able to survive
albeit	[ɔːlˈbiːit]	*conj.*	even though
assortment	[əˈsɔːtmənt]	*n.*	*AmE* a collection of different kinds
bistro	[ˈbistrəu]	*n.*	小酒馆，小咖啡店
buddy	[ˈbʌdi]	*n.*	伙伴
bust	[bʌst]	*v.*	~ **up** to prevent sth from continuing
compliance	[kəmˈplaiəns]	*n.*	依从，顺从
crap	[kræp]	*n.*	things that are useless or unimportant
electrocute	[iˈlektrəkjuːt]	*v.*	触电致死
felony	[ˈfeləni]	*n.*	a serious crime
flashy	[ˈflæʃi]	*adj.*	（性子）火爆的
flophouse	[ˈflɔphaus]	*n.*	（贫民区供流浪者投宿的）廉价旅馆
formalize	[ˈfɔːməlaiz]	*v.*	to make sth official
hassle	[ˈhæsl]	*v.*	骚扰
indigent	[ˈindidʒənt]	*adj.*	*formal* very poor
loiter	[ˈlɔitə]	*v.*	闲逛，游荡
Martini	[mɑːˈtiːni]	*n.*	马提尼酒
mission	[ˈmiʃən]	*n.*	（宗教团体设在贫民区的）慈善会堂
nightstick	[ˈnaitstik]	*n.*	警棍（原先在夜间携带，故名）
ordinance	[ˈɔːdinəns]	*n.*	法令
parolee	[pə,rəuˈliː]	*n.*	获假释者，假释犯
rap	[ræp]	*v.*	to hit or knock sth quickly and lightly
reek	[riːk]	*v.*	to smell very strongly of sth unpleasant
sanctuary	[ˈsæŋktjuəri]	*n.*	避难所
swindler	[ˈswindlə]	*n.*	诈骗者，骗子
transient	[ˈtrænziənt]	*n.*	短暂居住者，流浪者
wedge	[wedʒ]	*v.*	to force sth firmly into a narrow place

Ⅱ. Background Information

美国住房问题

20世纪30年代罗斯福总统实行新政之前，美国政府对住房问题很少干预。30年代的经济危机把大量失业者抛到街头巷尾。为了缓和社会矛盾,在罗斯福的推动下国会批准了一系列为贫困家庭修建公共住房的项目。60年代后期,150个城市发生居民骚乱,住房问题再次引起国家重视,政府增加了对低收入家庭的住房补贴,增加了政府补助的建房项目。卡特总统执政期间,联邦政府鼓励老城市复苏。1977年住房和社会发展立法获得通过。

70多年来,美国人的居住条件有了较大改善。1950年,美国平均每个人拥有1.5个房间,1981年又增加到近两个房间。按照美国公认标准,如果住房每个房间超过1人就被定为"过分拥挤"(over-occupied)。

然而,美国住房依然存在不少问题,最为严重的是住房分配不均。一方面巨富们拥有大庄园和豪宅,另一方面却有不少人住在过分狭小拥挤的房间,甚至流落街头。

无家可归是美国社会长期以来存在的问题。据较新数据,美国共有350万人有过无家可归的经历。这个群体成分较为复杂,其成分和特点如下表所示:

构成	比例	种族	比例	特点	比例
单身男性	41%	白人	35%	精神病患者/残疾者	22%
单身女性	14%	黑人	49%	酗酒吸毒者	30%
带孩子家庭	40%	西班牙裔人	13%	退伍军人	23%
无家长陪伴孩子	5%	印第安人/亚裔人	2%	有工作者	25%

造成无家可归问题的主要因素有四个:1) 消费价格上涨过快。据统计,1999—2004年期间,美国消费品价格指数(CPI)上升13%,增幅大大高于工资涨幅。医疗费用上涨尤为突出,是同期通货膨胀率的3倍多,美国人的医疗支出占全国GDP的16%。消费价格上涨削弱了美国人的租房、买房能力。2) 住房市场租金过高。1999—2004年期间,美国房租增加19%。据调查,一个每年工作52周,每周工作40小时,每小时工资5.15美元(当时法定最低工资)的工人无法支付单卧室套房(one-bedroom apartment)的租金。3) 廉价住房十分匮乏。由于建造低档住房利润很低,房地产开发商不愿介入经济适用房(affordable housing)和低收入家庭住房(low income housing)项目,造成廉价房产严重匮乏。据统计,2003年低价房缺额高达170万套。4) 诸多相关社会问题。不少美国社会学者指出,无家可归问题(homelessness)不等同于无房可住问题(houselessness),它是与失业、贫困、家庭破裂、种族歧视、吸毒、酗酒、赌博、心理疾病等社会问题密切相关。这些社会问题不解决,无家可归问题就会永远存在下去。

III. Notes to the Text

1. high-voltage electrical box — 高压变电箱
2. Los Angeles Police Capt. — 洛杉矶警局副巡官
3. skid row — 贫民区 (a poor dirty part of a town where vagrants and drunks live)
4. the city's sprawling 50-square-block homeless encampment — 散乱分布在50号方形街段的无家可归者的宿营地 (sprawl — to spread in an untidy way)
5. C'mon outta there. — Come on out of there.
6. You're gonna get hurt. — You're going to get hurt.
7. tent cities — 帐篷城 (referring to places where a large number of tents serve as shelters)
8. cardboard condos — 纸板公寓 (referring to places where many homeless people use cardboard boxes as shelters)
9. But living on the streets of Skid Row is becoming an increasingly iffy proposition as

police crack down on crime and camping and lift (**put**) the lid on what has become a massive homeless gulag in downtown L.A. — 但是由于警方打击犯罪、露宿，取缔洛杉矶市中心地段所形成的大规模无家可归者集中营，能否在贫民区街边居住将是越来越难说的事。(①gulag — a concentration camp for political prisoners, here used in a metaphorical way; ②iffy — *informal* not certain; ③put the lid on sth — to end, or eliminate sth)

10. Out of view in an industrial district, Skid Row has been operating under the radar for decades. — 由于地处工业区域，并非引人注目，贫民区数十年来一直暗中运行。(under the radar — out of view)

11. it has become a containment zone for some of society's most desperate and a magnet for those who prey on them. — 这已成为社会上一些最困苦人的集中营，对于那些想从他们身上骗钱的人来说也是一个很有吸引力的地方。(prey on — to hurt or deceive a group of people, especially people who are weak)

12. commissioner of the Los Angeles Homeless Services Authority — 洛杉矶市无家可归者服务局局长

13. registered sex offenders — 记录在案的性犯罪者

14. a breeding ground for infectious diseases like AIDS and hepatitis — 像艾滋病和肝炎一类的传染病的滋生地

15. Los Angeles is in the midst of a sweeping downtown revitalization that is headed Skid Row's way. — 洛杉矶市商业区正在大规模复兴，工程建设正向贫民区延伸。

16. Staples Center arena — 斯台普斯球馆(NBA 球队洛杉矶湖人队和洛杉矶快船队的主场)

17. Walt Disney Concert Hall — 迪斯尼音乐厅

18. We have managed against all odds to make this happen — 尽管困难重重我们还是设法办成了。

19. ... he was instrumental ... for its commercial rebirth. — 他在治理时报广场方面发挥了重要作用，将妓女和骗子清除出去，为商业复兴腾出了地方。[①Times Square — 时报广场(位于《纽约时报》报社附近)；②instrumental — important in making sth happen]

20. He also cleared Gotham streets ... ambush unwitting drivers. — 他还清除了纽约市街道的抹车仔，这些人红灯一亮便突然出现，不待车主知晓就强行洗抹挡风玻璃。(①Gotham — an informal name for New York city; ② materialize — to appear in an unexpected way)

21. NYPD — New York Police Department

22. stay the course — *informal* to finish sth in spite of difficulties

23. The LAPD, by any measure, is vastly understaffed. — 洛杉矶警局无论怎么计算都是严重缺编。(LAPD — Los Angeles Police Department)

24. The LAPD has also been walking a legal tightrope. — 洛杉矶警局还采取了有可能触犯法律的举措。

25. stepping past heroin addicts shooting up — 从注射海洛因的瘾君子身边走过(shoot up — *slang* to take illegal drug by using a needle)

26. fortune cookies — 〈美〉签饼(中国餐馆内小的脆甜点，内有写着预测运气的纸条)

27. This is a big and complex problem that needs a big fix. — 这是一个大而复杂的问题，需要采取力度大的措施。(fix — *informal* solution to a problem)

28. You can't arrest your way out of it. — 不能光靠逮捕就会把问题解决。

29. the American Civil Liberties Union — 美国公民自由同盟(一个民权保障团体)

30. the U.S. Ninth Circuit Court of Appeals — 美国第九巡回上诉法庭

31. The decision set in motion … and the police chief. — 该决议引发了市、县、市长、企业界和警局局长参与,具有洛杉矶特色的快速政治行动。(①signature — a particular quality that makes sth different from other similar things; ②polka — a very quick, simple dance)
32. but shot down by the City Council — 但被市议会断然否决(shoot down — to refuse to accept without giving any consideration)
33. on safe legal ground — 有法律根据
34. supportive housing — 支援性住房(a program designed to support individuals, not just with housing but with services that help homeless people to become independent)
35. not-in-my-backyardism — "别在我的后院搞"观念(It refers to local officials' opposition to the supportive housing program for the homeless people in their district for fear that their stay will pose a threat to the safety of the community.)
36. Union Rescue Mission — 联合教会慈善救济会堂
37. The project was nearly done in by local opposition — 由于当地人的反对,该计划险些夭折(do in — to kill)
38. long-term supportive housing — the best hope went down the drain in the November election — 在十一月选举中,长期支援性住房这个最好的解决方案落了空。(go down the drain — to be left out)
39. bond issue — 债券发行
40. Skid Row will continue to bedevil the City of Angels — 贫民区问题将会继续困扰这座"天使之城"(①the City of Angles — *informal* referring to the city of Los Angeles; ②bedevil — to cause a lot of problems and difficulties)

Ⅳ. Language Features

派生构词(derivation)

本文中的"outspend""homelessness""understaff"三个词分别是"spend""homeless"和"staff"加前缀 out-,后缀-ness,前缀 under-所构成的派生词。

派生词是把词根(root)与前缀(prefix)或后缀(suffix)相结合所构成的新词。派生法是现代英语构词最多的形式。它所构成的词占新词总数的 30%—34%。

在词缀中构成能力较强的后缀有-able(例:xeroxable 可复印的;livable 适宜居住的;portable 可携带的)、-er(diner 用餐的人;encoder 编码员,编码器)、-less(例:smokeless 无烟雾的;thankless 吃力不讨好的;topless 袒胸的)。构词能力较强的动词后缀有-ise/-ize(例:computerize 使计算机化;mechanize 使机械化;authorize 核准,认可)。

在报刊上较为活跃的后缀还有:

-ism(表示"对歧视"):ageism 对老年人的歧视;sexism 对女性的歧视;heightism 对矮个子人的歧视;weightism 对胖人的歧视;intelligencism 对低智商人的歧视

-wise(表示"在……方面"):personalitywise 在个性方面;experiencewise 就经验而言;budgetwise 在预算方面

较为活跃的前缀有:

anti-(1)(表示"反对"):anti-human 反人类的;anti-inflation 反通货膨胀的;anti-establishment 反政府的;anti-abortion 反对堕胎的

(2) (表示"非正统的""反传统的"):antihero 非传统派主角;antiart 非正统派艺术;antimusic 非正统派音乐

de-(表示"离开""除去"):detrain 下火车;debug 拆除窃听器;de-air 消除(敌方)空战能力;deconflict 散开避免撞击

dis-(表示"否定""相反"):disincentive 起抑制作用的行动;disinformation(以假乱真的)假情报;disinflation 通货紧缩

eco-(表示"生态"):ecocide 生态灭绝;ecocrisis 生态危机;ecofreak 一味关注生态的怪人;ecothug 破坏生态的坏蛋

non- (1) (表示"无""非""不"):nonpolitical 非政治的;non-profit 非赢利的 nondegree 非学位的

(2) (表示"不重要的""无价值的"):nonevent 不重要的事;nonperson 没有社会地位的人;nonbook 无价值的书

out-(表示"超过"):outgun 在武器上超过;outscore 分数超过;outproduce 生产上超过;outtrade 贸易上超过

over-(表示"超量""过分"):overcapacity 生产能力过剩;overkill 过大的核武器杀伤力量;overpurchase 过量购买

pro-(表示"赞成……的"):pro-gun 赞成持枪支的;pro-life 要生命的,反对堕胎的;pro-reform 赞成改革的

info-(表示"信息"):infoglut 信息过剩;info-tech 信息技术的;infoweapon 信息武器

cyber-(表示"与电脑相关的"):cyberculture 电脑文化;cyberhead 电脑迷

e-(表示"与电子相关的"):e-paper 电子报;e-cash 电子货币

post-(表示"……之后的"):post-industrialist 后工业主义的;post-feminism 后女权主义;post-structuralism 后结构主义;post-90s 90 后的人

Ⅴ. Analysis of the Content

1. The word "hot" in the sentence "The area is starting to feel, well, hot" (Para. 7) means _____.
   A. high in temperature
   B. quick to get angry
   C. popular
   D. seething with activity
2. The "big fix" in the text refers to _____.
   A. total elimination of Skid Row
   B. arrests of all the criminals
   C. long-term supportive housing
   D. rehabilitation of all the shelters and cheap hotels in Skid Row
3. The number of homeless people sleeping in shelters and cheap hotels at night in Skid Row is _____.
   A. 10,000   B. 1000   C. 2000   D. 12,000
4. Which of the following is NOT true about Skid Row?
   A. a containment zone for some of the society's most desperate people
   B. a haven for prostitutes, drug addicts and criminals
   C. a breeding ground for infectious diseases like AIDs
   D. an area crowded with casinos and gambling houses

5. The author's attitude toward the future of the homeless people in Skid Row is _____.
   A. optimistic
   B. indifferent
   C. unknown
   D. pessimistic

Ⅵ. Questions on the Article

1. What does Skid Row refer to?
2. How many homeless people are there in Skid Row? Where do they live?
3. What kind of people is the term "services resistants" applied to?
4. Why is living on the streets of Skid Row becoming an increasingly iffy proposition?
5. How has Skid Row developed from the railroad line into the present concentration camp for the homeless?
6. What experience does Britain have in dealing with urban disorder?
7. What difficulties did Bratton encounter in cleaning up Skid Row?
8. What measures did Bratton take in dealing with the Skid Row problem?
9. What are the effects of the clean-up acts?
10. Why was the ACLU strongly opposed to the sidewalk sleeping ban?
11. What is the real solution to the Skid Row problem according to the author?

Ⅶ. Topics for Discussion

1. Is homelessness the same as houselessness?
2. Is building more homeless centers the best solution to the problem of homelessness?

Lesson 20

Sex on the Job[1]

The Lewinsky Effect: Business takes a closer look at executive affairs[2]
By William C. Symonds in Boston

    A few months back, Garry G. Mathiason, senior partner with Littler, Mendelson, Fastiff, Tichy & Mathiason, the nation's largest employment law firm[3], got a call from a very sheepish general counsel for a major company[4]. The president of the company, the counsel said, "is planning to have a consensual affair[5] with one of his employees," but before he does, "he wants to draft a written agreement" stating that the affair is voluntary — to reduce the chance that the woman might file a sexual-harassment suit if they broke up. [6] "You won't believe it," Mathiason assured the nervous counsel. "But we've already drafted a standard form" for just such cases.

    STUNNING. Welcome to the minefield that is office romance in the Nervous Nineties. [7] Sure, President Clinton might survive the scandalous charges that he had an affair with former White House intern Monica S. Lewinsky, even if proved true. But few senior executives think they could do the same. Indeed, while just 43% of the executives responding to a new BUSINESS WEEK/Harris Poll[8] believe an affair with Lewinsky would affect Clinton's "ability to serve as President," 59% say an extramarital affair by a CEO[9] is detrimental.

    While the President of the U. S. is just learning how an alleged office indiscretion might backfire, presidents, CEOs, and other top corporate execs[10] have already discovered that an old-fashioned fling between boss and subordinate can be a fatal distraction. [11] In fact, says Mathiason, "in the last three years, I've been involved in more terminations of CEOs due to claims of sex harassment" than for anything else.

    That's a stunning change. In the old days, a top exec who requested some intimate overtime risked, at most, a slap in the face and the loss of a good secretary. [12] These days the object of the boss's unwanted affection is likely to respond with a sexual-harassment suit. And as Mathiason's client feared, even when a relationship begins with mutual consent, after the breakup, the plaintiff lawyers[13] appear. Elizabeth J. du Fresne, a senior partner at Miami law firm Steel, Hector & Davis, says she settles 10 or 15 such cases a year for over $500,000, and a few that top $1 million — double or triple the number of cases five years ago. Says Susan Meisinger, senior vice-president at the Society for Human Resource Management[14]: "Romance in the office aren't cheap."

    As a result, more companies have adopted policies to minimize the liability. [15] "Businesses that always closed their eyes to office romance ... are having to think about it," says du Fresne. So far, however, less than 30% of companies have a clear policy on relationships between senior execs and their subordinates, according to a January survey by Human Resource Management.

After the Lewinsky scandal, however, it's a safe bet that[16] more companies will make new rules. So what's the best policy? The options range from voluntary disclosure to rigid rules with strict penalties. Intel Corp., for example, is among the companies that explicitly and severely limit office dating between superiors and subordinates. Intel's "non-fraternization guideline," for instance, forbids managers from dating any employee they supervise and warns violators that they may face termination.

But such iron-clad prohibitions "merely drive the relationships underground[17]," says Freada Klein, founder of a Cambridge (Mass.) employee-relations consulting firm. She favors the more flexible policy adopted by companies such as General Motors Corp.[18] There, managers are encouraged to report romantic involvements with subordinates. Usually, GM reacts by "creating a different reporting relationship to protect everyone," says a GM spokesman.

Given today's intense business climate, in which men and women are thrown together for days on end in meetings or on trips, "no company is going to stop Cupid at the front door,"[19] says Eric Greenberg, director of management studies at the American Management Assn.[20] "People meet at work. They date," says Gordon E. Eubanks Jr., chief executive of software maker Symantec Corp.

The good news is that most relationships don't lead to trouble. Eubanks' office romance, for instance, led to marriage. "It's common in Silicon Valley[21]," he says. And elsewhere: 55% of the 617 respondents to the Human Resource Management survey said romances in their companies resulted in marriage. There are many famous examples: Microsoft CEO William H. Gates III[22] met wife Melinda French while she was a product manager at the company. General Motors Chairman John F. Smith Jr. met his wife Lydia when she was briefly assigned to be his secretary in the late 1980s. French quit when she had a baby, and to avoid problems, Lydia Smith left her GM job shortly after meeting her future husband.

Still, when relationships don't end at the altar, "it can get very complicated afterwards," warns Ellen Bravo, co-director of 9to5, National Association of Working Women[23]. Her group receives 15,000 calls a year from non-executive women, many complaining about a relationship with a superior.

The problems only get bigger when the superior is the CEO. Says Patricia Arredondo, president of Boston-based Empowerment Workshops, which offers training on office relationships between the sexes[24]: "It becomes a free-for-all if the CEO can behave this way.[25]" At Astra USA Inc., Chief Executive Lars Bildman became a role model for untoward behavior and a dozen female employees told BUSINESS WEEK in 1996 they had been fondled or propositioned by Bildman or other executives. Bildman was fired after the charges became public in BUSINESS WEEK.

MORALE PROBLEMS. Indeed, even less serious CEO imbroglios spice up the business news.[26] Silicon Valley buzzed for years about charges brought against Oracle Chairman Lawrence J. Ellison by an employee who alleged that he fired her when their affair fizzled.[27] Ellison eventually prevailed in court, but it didn't help the corporate image.

Even if an affair doesn't cause legal problems, it can hurt morale. In 1996, Edward R.

McCracken, then chairman and CEO of Silicon Graphics Inc.[28], began dating a much younger woman who worked in human resources. That's where McCracken had met his wife of 11 years, from whom he was separated. McCracken has said the relationship was proper and above board. But the affair upset other employees, says one former SGI employee: "It's hard to be credible about sexual harassment when the chairman of the company dates somebody who works for him, even indirectly."

Whatever the policy, almost no one feels that Corporate America can relax about affairs of the CEO's heart.[29] If anything, the charges swirling around Clinton "have heightened concerns about the potential for abuse of power" in office romances, says Arredondo. That goes for the Oval Office or the corner office.[30]

From *BusinessWeek*, February 16, 1998
With Steve Ham in San Mateo, Gail DeGeorge in Miami, and bureau reports

I. New Words

altar	['ɔːltə]	n.	（教堂内的）圣坛
counsel	['kaunsəl]	n.	a lawyer advising on legal matters
detrimental	[,detri'mentəl]	adj.	*formal* causing harm or damage
fling	[fliŋ]	n.	a short and not very serious sexual relationship
fondle	['fɔndl]	v.	to gently touch or tenderly stroke
fraternization	[,frætənai'zeiʃən]	n.	亲密关系
indiscretion	[,indis'kreʃən]	n.	不谨慎；言行失检
ironclad	['aiənklæd]	adj.	unable to be contradicted
plaintiff	['pleintif]	n.	a person who begins a lawsuit
prohibition	[,prəuhi'biʃən]	n.	an order stopping something
proposition	[,prɔpə'ziʃən]	v.	to invite (someone) to engage in sexual intercourse
sheepish	['ʃiːpiʃ]	adj.	uncomfortable or embarrassed
termination	[,təːmi'neiʃən]	n.	the act of ending something
untoward	[,ʌntə'wɔːd]	adj.	contrary to what is desired

II. Background Information

性骚扰

美国前总统克林顿与白宫实习生莫妮卡·莱温斯基的性丑闻轰动了全球，激怒了民众，也使他险些遭到弹劾（impeachment）。其实，这并非是他第一件性丑闻。早在他任阿肯色州州长时期就曾对一家宾馆女招待葆拉·琼斯（Paula Jones）进行过性骚扰。

性骚扰（sexual harassment）已成为美国一种社会疾病，肆虐各个领域，涉及各界各个层次。

国会议员中有不少人贪恋女色,要求秘书提供性服务(sexual service)、性优惠(sexual favours)。美国专栏作家贝克曾经指出:"在美国参众两院一直有着'老花心'(old dandies)。他们硬是利用手中权力,或是诱骗,或是强迫性地乱搞女助理和女职员。"这类老色鬼较为典型的是原资深联邦参议员、参议院财政委员会主席鲍博·帕克伍德(Bob Packwood)。他在日记中毫不掩饰地写道:曾与22名女下属有过性关系,与75名女子有过感情关系。还有众议员梅尔·雷诺兹,他的这方面罪行多达20页,他甚至诱骗17岁女孩。

军界的性丑闻更多。海军部自1992年以来性猥亵行为报告有3,500多起,性骚扰控告1,000多份。行为从摸弄女性身体到实施强奸,五花八门什么都有。海军部承认实际情况更糟。1991年海军"尾钩狂欢会"(Tailhook Party)是轰动全国的大丑闻。1995年7月4日美国海军驻守冲绳岛的3名士兵对一名12岁日本少女进行轮奸(gang rape)。

美国校园的性骚扰搅得许多学生无法安心读书。美国妇女法律保护与教育基金会1992年所做的调查报告中介绍了这方面的情况。该会研究人员调查了4,200名9—19岁女生。被调查者申诉说过去的一年里受到性骚扰的人占39%,报告每周遭到一次性骚扰的人占29%。

当今美国的宗教殿堂也受到了性骚扰的玷污。不少神职人员,教会工作人员不是清心寡欲,念经修行,反倒迷恋美色,贪图肉欲。据调查,在过去的10年里美国天主教神父和其他神职人员中有400多人对少女进行过性骚扰和性攻击。华盛顿一名律师承认,美国5.3万名天主教神职人员中,至少有3,000人与少女发生过性关系。

商界这种情况就更多了。不少老板视自己的公司为他们可以为所欲为的王国,对其属下进行性骚扰。

美国性骚扰之所以较为普遍,是因为美国文化中渗透着歧视妇女的观念,社会上色情文化严重泛滥。

III. Notes to the Text

1. Sex on the Job — sexual affairs in the office/workplace;工作场所的风流韵事
2. The Lewinsky Effect: Business takes a closer look at executive affairs — 莱温斯基效应:企业更为重视经理的风流韵事。(① Lewinsky, here, refers to the exposure of Clinton's scandalous sexual affair with Monica Lewinsky. ② affair — extramarital sexual relationship)
3. employment law firm — a company that provides legal services on employment cases 劳工事务律师所
4. general counsel for a major company — 一家大公司的法律总顾问
5. consensual affair — an affair with mutual consent
6. ... the woman might file a sexual-harassment suit if they broke up. — 如果他们关系破裂,女方会提出性骚扰起诉。(sexual-harassment — the unwelcome directing of sexual remarks, looks, or advances, usually at a woman in the workplace)
7. Welcome to the minefield that is office romance in the Nervous Nineties. — 欢迎步入"神经质90年代"公司风流韵事的雷区。(① The imperative opening sentence is used to catch readers' attention. It carries an ironic undertone, suggesting that what is being "welcomed" to is not such a desirable thing after all. ② The phrase "Nervous Nineties"

indicates the character of the changes in social intercourse: what would previously have been seen as casual flirtation or joking can be and has been a cause for people to be fired from jobs or sued for sexual harassment. There is also a phrase in common use, "Nervous Nellie," which refers to a woman who is easily upset by disturbances or changes in her life.)

8. BUSINESS WEEK/Harris Poll — a poll jointly conducted by Business Week and Harris (Harris — a company doing opinion polls, founded by Louis Harris)

9. CEO — shortened form of Chief Executive Officer（首席执行官；执行总裁）

10. exec — *informal* an executive；主管业务的人，经理

11. ... an old-fashioned fling between boss and subordinate can be a fatal distraction. — 过去那种老板对属下调情现在会是断送前程的游戏。(fling — a short and not very serious sexual relationship)

12. In the old days, a top exec who requested some intimate overtime risked, at most, a slap in the face and the loss of a good secretary. — 过去，高层经理要求秘书下班后留下来亲热亲热，最多是遭到一记耳光，失去一个好秘书的后果。(intimate — euphemism for maintaining illicit sexual relationship)

13. the plaintiff lawyers — 原告律师

14. the Society for Human Resource Management — 人力资源管理协会（human resource management — the work of employing, training and helping people in companies)

15. As a result, more companies have adopted policies to minimize the liability. — 因而，更多公司采取措施，最大限度减少这种情况发生的可能。(liability — the state of being susceptible or vulnerable)

16. ... it's a safe bet that... — ... it seems almost certain that...

17. But such iron-clad prohibitions "merely drive the relationships underground... — But such unchangeable rules forbidding executive-subordinate romance only make them carry on such relationships in secret.

18. General Motors Corp. — 通用汽车公司（Founded in 1908, it operates manufacturing and assembly plants and distribution centers throughout the United States, Canada and many other countries.)

19. Given today's intense business climate, ... "no company is going to stop Cupid at the front door..." — 当今公司业务活动频繁，男男女女常常连续几天相聚开会，一起出差，没有任何公司会阻止爱神的进入。(① intense — full of vigorous activity; ② Cupid — the Roman god of love, here referring to romance)

20. director of management studies at the American Management Assn. — 美国企业管理协会管理研究部主任（Assn. — Association）

21. Silicon Valley — 硅谷（美国旧金山东南圣克拉拉谷的别称，美国主要微电子公司集中于此，因微电子工业材料主要为硅片，故名。）

22. Microsoft CEO William H. Gates III — 微软公司执行总裁威廉·H. 盖茨（William H. Gates III — Bill Gates 的正式姓名）

23. co-director of 9to5, National Association of Working Women — 全国日班女工协会副会

长(9-5 has come to refer to the traditional office working hours, from 9 AM to 5 PM. Hence, the association of women who work in offices has adopted it to symbolize their daily time on the job.)

24. ... Boston-based Empowerment Workshops, which offers training on office relationships between the sexes ... — 总部设在波士顿市的"能力培训班",这些研习班提供有关工作场所男女之间应该如何相处的教育。(empowerment — the act of enabling)

25. It becomes a free-for-all if the CEO can behave this way. — 如果公司执行总裁有这种行为,那么全公司人人都会自由自在这么干。(free-for-all — a fight, race, or contest, open to all or in which everybody participates)

26. Indeed, even less serious CEO imbroglios spice up the business news. — 的确,执行总裁所引起的纠纷即使比这要轻,也会增添商业新闻趣味。(① imbroglio — a difficult, embarrassing or confusing situation; ② spice up — to add excitement to sth)

27. Silicon Valley buzzed for years about ... when their affair fizzled. — 硅谷有好几年流传甲骨文公司一名雇员对董事长劳伦斯·J.埃利森的指控,她声称埃利森在他们两人关系告吹时将她解雇。[① Note the author's use of the two onomatopoeic words for vividness and vitality; ② buzz — to make a continuous low sound like the sound of a bee; ③ fizzle — (of a fire) to make a hissing sound that dies out weakly; ④ Oracle — a company which assists customers in setting up e-businesses on the Internet. It is characterized as a "data warehouse".]

28. Silicon Graphics Inc. — 硅图图形公司(It is a company which helps customers design websites for the Internet, employ more detailed computer graphics and assists customers in computer enhancement of power and speed. It is headquartered in Mountain View, California.)

29. Whatever the policy, almost no one feels that Corporate America can relax about affairs of the CEO's heart. — 不管采取什么措施,几乎所有人都认为美国大公司不能对执行总裁的风流韵事放任不管。(① Corporate America — America's large corporations; ② affairs of the heart — love affairs)

30. That goes for the Oval Office or the corner office. — That is true for the president of the United States or the president of a company.

{ Ⅳ. Language Features }

委婉语

本文中有几处使用 office romance,affairs of the heart 替代 sexual relationship between senior execs and subordinates,如:Businesses that always closed their eyes to office romance... are having to think about it. 相比之下,office romance 是一种较为委婉的表达法。

委婉语是用以替代被认为过于露骨,过于伤人或不太悦耳的词或短语。主要有两种:缩小性委婉语和夸张性委婉语。

缩小性委婉语是用较含蓄、性质较轻的词语来表达不便直言的事情。主要表现在以下几个方面：

1. 生、老、病、死。常用 pass away, depart 替代 die；用 elderly people, senior citizens 替代 old people；用 social disease 替代 venereal disease(性病)。

2. 贫穷。英语中"poor"常被"needy"，"underprivileged"，"disadvantaged"替代。

3. 犯罪。burglary(夜盗)被说成是"surreptitious entry"（秘密进入），prison(监狱)被称为"correctional center"(教养中心)。

4. 性或性器官。英语中"have sex"（发生性行为）常被婉称为"make love"（做爱）；"illegitimate child"（私生子）被称作"love child"（爱情生下的孩子）；"pornographic movie"（黄色电影）称为"adult film"（成人电影）；"sexual organs"（生殖器官）说成是"private parts"（阴部）。

夸张性委婉语就是将原词语替换成意思更雅致、更体面、更重要的词语。主要有下列几种：

1. 机构。把 madhouse(疯人院)称作 mental hospital(精神病院)，mental health center(精神健康中心)；把一些实力不雄厚的公司称作 industry(企业)，如 hotel industry(旅馆业)，garbage industry(垃圾清理业)；规模不大的学院称作 university(大学)

2. 职业。把 hairdresser（理发员）说成是 beautician（美容师）；floorsweeper 称作 custodian engineer(房屋管理师)；gardener(园丁)称为 landscaper(园林师)；janitor(看门的)说成 superintendent(监管人)

3. 政治、军事。用一些温和词语掩饰社会问题，美化政府形象。如：economic crisis(经济危机)说成 recession(衰退)，depression(萧条)；strike(罢工)说成 industrial action(工业行动)，industrial dispute(工业纠纷)；slum(贫民窟)说成 substandard housing(不够标准的住房)；relief(救济)说成 welfare(福利)；ghetto(贫民区)说成 inner city(内城区)；air strike(空中打击)说成 air option(制空选择)；ground war(地面战争)说为 ground operation(地面行动)；neutron bomb(中子弹)说成 clean bomb(清洁弹)；aggression(侵略)说成 invasion(进入)或 involvement(介入)；attack(进攻)说成 pacify the area(绥靖)。

上述美化性词语(cosmetic words)在西方报刊中较为常见，在阅读中应予注意。

Ⅴ. Analysis of the Content

1. The president's intention in drafting a written agreement about his office affair is to _____.
   A. secure the commitment to the relationship
   B. make it a life-long bond
   C. express his true love for the woman
   D. reduce the chance of a sexual-harassment case

2. According to the article, most of office romances _____.
   A. lead to lawsuits
   B. cause family breakups
   C. don't lead to trouble
   D. result in the terminations of CEOs

3. So far in America, _____ of companies have a clear policy on workplace affairs.
   A. most
   B. less than 30%
   C. half
   D. none
4. The author believes that the exposure of Clinton's sex scandal produced the effect of _____.
   A. infuriating the American public
   B. arousing Americans' sympathy for Lewinsky
   C. heightening companies' concern about executive affairs
   D. making women office workers more worried
5. More sexual harassment cases occurred at Astra U. S. A. Inc. because _____.
   A. there were more women in the company
   B. the company encouraged office romances
   C. the CEO set a bad example
   D. the company had no rule against such behavior

VI. Questions on the Article

1. Why does the author call office romance a minefield?
2. What change has taken place concerning the consequences of office romance?
3. What measures have American companies taken to cope with the problem?
4. Explain the term of "non-fraternization guidelines."
5. Why did Eric Greenberg say "no company is going to stop Cupid at the front door"?
6. What kind of office romance does not lead to trouble?
7. What effect does CEO's extramarital affair produce on the company if it gets publicized?

VII. Topics for Discussion

1. Should executives be strictly forbidden from office dating?
2. Is office dating a personal problem or a company's problem?

Lesson 21

Crooks Find Net Fertile Ground for Cyber Crime

Web allows gangs to devise new ways to commit old crimes
By Jon Swartz

SAN FRANCISCO — Organized crime rings and petty thieves are flocking to the Internet like start-ups in the go-go '90s, federal authorities say — establishing a multibillion-dollar underground economy in just a few years.[1]

"Willie Sutton used to say he robbed banks because that's where the money is," says FBI Agent Keith Lourdeau, an expert on cyber crime. "The same applies today to crooks and the Internet."

The Internet's growth as an economic engine, particularly for financial transactions, is feeding the felonious frenzy.

Lured by shoddy computer security and the ability to commit crimes from far-flung countries, the Russian mafia and other Eastern European gangs are plunging into spam, phishing schemes, cyber-extortion and the trafficking of stolen goods online,[2] authorities say. Many hire hackers in economically depressed countries, but a growing number are becoming computer savvy to do the dirty work themselves.

Crime syndicates and the Internet are a natural fit, security experts say. Both are global, thrive on flexible networks and require specialization.[3] The Net has allowed offshore gangs to branch into other ventures while devising new ways to commit old crimes, such as money laundering and counterfeiting.

Criminals shop on illicit computer bulletin boards for stolen credit card numbers as they would for books on Amazon.com.[4] They threaten devastating electronic attacks on Web sites unless they are paid. Online bank accounts are under siege. And millions of hijacked computers, or zombies — infected with malicious code under the control of a hacker without the owner's knowledge — perpetrate the schemes without a trail.[5]

Consumers and businesses, as a consequence, lost at least $14 billion to digital thieves last year, although most of the crimes went undetected or unreported, experts say. Spam alone accounted for $10 billion, Ferris Research says. Fraud cost online merchants $2 billion more, Gartner Research says. And phishing — fraudulent e-mail messages and Web sites designed to trick consumers into divulging personal information — gouged consumers by $2 billion in the 12-month period ended in April, Gartner says.[6]

The surge in cyber crime has triggered changes not only in criminal behavior but also in law enforcement.

The FBI, in the midst of beefing up its cyber-division, is investigating 2,700 cyber crime-related cases nationwide, two-thirds of them opened in the past year.[7] Of those cases,

346 individuals have been convicted.

"This is more sophisticated stuff than purse snatching,"[8] FBI Agent Tom Grasso says.

Crime. com

Computer crime has never been so lucrative. With the Internet as ubiquitous as cable TV, there are millions of potential victims banking and shopping online. Contributing to the chaos: security flaws in business, home and university computers, and few effective cyber crime laws in the USA and abroad.[9]

What is more, homeland-security measures designed to tighten U.S. borders and fortify physical infrastructures may have drawn crime syndicates to technology, which is relatively invisible, security experts say.[10] "Crooks like the Internet because it is less violent and carries lighter penalties than loan sharking and drugs," Grasso says.

What makes online endeavors particularly attractive is that crooks and their accomplices don't have to meet. They can collaborate across continents and exploit the computers of innocent bystanders to carry out their crimes. U.S. Rep. Mac Thornberry, R-Texas, chairman of the Homeland Security Committee's cyber-security subcommittee, compares the problem to the rise of street gangs in the 1920s and 1930s.

Cyber-crooks are focusing on:

• **Extortion.** What started out as a digital shakedown of gambling Web sites has expanded[11], federal authorities say.

Nearly one-fifth of 100 small and midsize companies polled this summer say they have been targets of cyber-extortion threats, according to a survey by Carnegie Mellon University's H. John Heinz III School of Public Policy and Management and InformationWeek magazine.[12]

Banks and companies planning initial public stock offerings are the latest targets of shadowy hackers, who demand $20,000 to $50,000 for protection from distributed denial-of-service attacks, which bombard and paralyze a Web site with data.[13] Often, the e-mail threats are issued shortly before an attack, demanding that cash be sent to a Western Union[14] office overseas.

In July, young Russian hackers were arrested for operating an extortion ring that for nearly a year cost British banks as much as $73 million in lost business and damages, government officials in Russia told Itar-Tass news agency[15].

In an attack in the USA last month, the Web site of Authorize.Net, a processor of credit card transactions for thousands of small and midsize businesses, was hit for several days, disrupting service.[16] Authorize.Net rejected several e-mails demanding a "significant amount" of money, says David Schwartz, a spokesman. An unknown number of zombie computers were used in the attack, he said. The FBI is investigating.

Authorize.Net downplayed the attacks, but some of its customers said the withering assaults were costly. "I lost $15,000," says David Hoekje, president of PartsGuy.com, an online retailer of heating and air-conditioning parts.

As cyber-extortion grows, attacks are becoming more sophisticated. Some extortionists monitor how their targets defend themselves, so they can alter attacks. They enlist new zombie computers unfamiliar to the company under siege or change the type of data used in an electronic assault.[17]

• **Fraud.** The most fertile online territory for crooks runs the gamut from credit card theft and phishing to electronic burglary schemes.[18]

In one of the largest Internet fraud investigations, the FBI and international law-enforcement authorities in August obtained a federal grand-jury indictment of a suspected Romanian computer hacker and five Americans on charges they conspired to steal more than $10 million in computer equipment from distributor Ingram Micro in Santa Ana, Calif.

The indictment charges that Calin Mateias, 24, using the alias Dr. Mengele, hacked into Ingram's online ordering system and placed fraudulent orders for computer equipment. The order directed the equipment be sent to dozens of addresses throughout the USA.

Mateias may be extradited to the USA from Romania. The American suspects are awaiting trial.

Big banks and credit card companies are bearing the brunt of Internet-related fraud. More than 60% of computer hacks targeted financial institutions last year, says market researcher IDC[19].

About 30 million credit card numbers have been stolen through computer-security breaches since 1999, resulting in $15 billion in losses, according to the FBI.

"It's like picking someone's pocket before they enter the bank," says Bill Burnham, managing partner at venture firm Softbank Capital Partners.

Banks are loath to discuss break-ins out of fear of spooking customers and are willing to quietly eat losses from fraud[20], says security consultant John Frazzini, a former U.S. Secret Service agent.

Federal authorities in the USA and Great Britain also note a sharp rise in phishing by organized crime as it recognizes how much money can be made with little or no overhead.

A three-year investigation by the FBI and England's National Hi-Tech Crime Unit has led to the arrest of 30 members of an Eastern European crime ring accused of dabbling in phishing and ID theft. The most recent bust was of a high-level member on June 4 who is allegedly in charge of the ring's money laundering, the Department of Justice says.

Another popular scam entails an elaborate shipping network for expensive goods purchased online with stolen credit cards.[21]

Fraudulent online buyers in West Africa have goods shipped to Europe, where an accomplice or legitimate delivery service re-ships the items to West Africa, FBI agents say. Re-shippers are recruited in chat rooms, online job postings and over the phone.[22] They are either paid with counterfeit cashier's checks or allowed to keep some merchandise. Though the scheme requires a cash outlay, it is an inexpensive way to move stolen products without revealing the identity of the original buyer, agents say.

Working with the FBI, Nigerian officials recently seized more than $340,000 in illegally obtained online merchandise and recovered $115,000 in fraudulent cashier's checks issued against U.S. financial institutions. Nearly 20 people were arrested.

A legislative fix?[23]

The computer-crime epidemic has set off a reorganization by agencies such as the FBI and Secret Service[24], as well as a flurry of activity in Congress. Nearly a year after the first federal anti-spam law, bills wending through the House and Senate would give cyber crime fighters more heft and would outlaw phishing and ban spyware, the irritating software that quietly monitors the activities of Internet users.

An anti-phishing bill recently introduced by Sen. Patrick Leahy, D-Vt., would make it a crime to phish. It carries a $250,000 fine and up to five years in jail.

On Oct. 7, the House passed the second bill in three days that would outlaw spyware. It carries a penalty of up to five years in prison for people convicted of installing such programs without a computer user's permission.

"We need to act quickly before this spirals even more out of control," says Rep. Thornberry, co-author of a bill to create a high-ranking position in the Department of Homeland Security. The assistant secretary of cybersecurity would coordinate cyber crime busting with private industry and state and local governments. (Amit Yoran, the nation's cybersecurity chief, abruptly resigned Oct. 1, after a year. He quit, industry observers said, over what he considered a lack of attention paid to cybersecurity within the department.)

And it shouldn't stop there, says Thornberry, who advocates tax incentives and liability protection for corporations that "beef up" cybersecurity. "Threats and vulnerabilities change in a matter of seconds," he says. "Defenses are obsolete unless they're constantly improved."

Whether any of the bills make a dent as law is debatable, given the mixed results of the national Can-Spam law.[25] About three-fourths of e-mail monitored in September by e-mail-security company Postini was spam.

The law has had another unintended result: Spam operators have fled the USA for other countries, where they continue to inundate Americans with e-mail for porn and "miracle" drugs[26].

"The reality is we are just the U. S., and there are nearly 200 countries connected to the Internet. Our laws stop at the border," says Jody Westby, a managing director of PricewaterhouseCoopers' security and privacy practice.

From *USA Today*, October 21, 2004

I. New Words

bust	[bʌst]	v.	*informal* to punch, hit; to crack down arrest a criminal
crook	[kruk]	n.	*informal* 骗子
counterfeit	['kauntəfit]	v.;adj.	伪造；伪造的
dabble	['dæbl]	vi.	涉猎
divulge	[dai'vʌldʒ]	v.	泄露（秘密等）
downplay	['daunplei]	v.	to make sth seem less important
extortion	[iks'tɔːʃən]	n.	勒索，敲诈
extradite	['ekstrədait]	v.	引渡，受……引渡
felonious	[fi'ləunjəs]	adj.	极恶的，重罪的
flurry	['flʌri]	n.	an occasion when there's a lot of activity
gamut	['gæmət]	n.	整个范围；全部
gouge	[gaudʒ]	v.	*AmE informal* to force sb to pay an unfairly high price

hacker	['hækə]	n.	电脑黑客
heft	[heft]	n.	*informal* weight; influence, force
indictment	[in'daitmənt]	n.	起诉；诉状
launder	['lɔ:ndə]	v.	洗（钱）
loan sharking	['ləun,ʃɑ:kiŋ]		放高利贷
lucrative	['lu:krətiv]	adj.	making a large profit
phishing	['fiʃiŋ]	n.	网络钓鱼（一种旨在盗取网络用户银行账户信息等的网上诈骗行为）
savvy	['sævi]	adj.	having practical knowledge of sth
spam	[spæm]	n.	[计]垃圾邮件
spook	[spu:k]	v.	*informal* to frighten sb
spyware	['spaiwɛə]	n.	间谍软件
syndicate	['sindikit]	n.	辛迪加，集团
ubiquitous	[ju:'bikwitəs]	adj.	seeming to be everywhere
zombie	['zɔmbi]	n.	僵尸电脑

Ⅱ. Background Information

网络犯罪

网络技术的发展推动了美国乃至全球信息化的进程，促进了科技文化、经济生产的发展。然而，随着网络触角的不断延伸，网络犯罪也得以在温床中日益滋生。网络犯罪给社会造成了多方面的损失。

目前互联网上最常见的犯罪形式有以下几种：

1. 网上诈骗。所谓网上诈骗（Internet fraud），主要指利用虚假信息或邮件引诱受害人并对其实施金钱或实物诈骗的犯罪行为。普通网民、企业和公共部门都是犯罪人下手的目标群体。

2. 僵尸病毒。该病毒通过连接 IRC 服务器进行通信从而控制被攻陷的计算机。僵尸网络（BotNet），是互联网上受到黑客集中控制的一群计算机，往往被黑客用来发起大规模的网络攻击，如分布式拒绝服务攻击（DDoS）、海量垃圾邮件等，同时黑客控制的这些计算机所保存的信息也都可被黑客随意"取用"。由于发现一个僵尸网络非常困难，因此，它是目前互联网上黑客最青睐的作案工具。

3. 网络钓鱼。网络钓鱼（Phishing，与钓鱼的英语 fishing 发音相近，又名钓鱼法或钓鱼式攻击）是通过大量发送声称来自于银行或其他知名机构的欺骗性垃圾邮件，引诱收信人给出敏感信息（如用户名、口令、账号 ID、ATM PIN 码或信用卡详细信息）的一种攻击方式。

4. 垃圾邮件。垃圾邮件（Spam）是指未经用户许可就强行发送到用户的邮箱中的任何电子邮件。

垃圾邮件一般具有批量发送的特征。其内容包括赚钱信息、成人广告、商业或个人网站广告、电子杂志、连环信等。垃圾邮件可以分为良性和恶性的。良性垃圾邮件是各种宣传广告等对收件人影响不大的信息邮件。恶性垃圾邮件是指具有破坏性的电子邮件。一些有心人会从网上多个 BBS 论坛、新闻组等收集网民的电脑地址,再售予广告商,从而发送垃圾邮件到这些地址。垃圾邮件带来的主要危害是:

1. 占用网络带宽,造成邮件服务器拥塞,进而降低整个网络的运行效率。
2. 侵犯收件人的隐私权,侵占收件人信箱空间,耗费收件人的时间、精力和金钱。
3. 被黑客利用成助纣为虐的工具。2000 年 2 月,黑客攻击雅虎等五大热门网站,用数以亿万计的垃圾邮件猛烈袭击目标,造成被攻击网站网路堵塞,最终瘫痪。
4. 严重影响因特网服务供应商(ISP)的服务形象。调查表明:ISP 每年因垃圾邮件要失去 7.2% 的用户。
5. 妖言惑众,骗人钱财,传播色情等内容的垃圾邮件,对现实社会造成巨大危害。

Ⅲ. Notes to the Text

1. Organized crime rings and petty thieves are flocking ... establishing a multibillion-dollar underground economy in just a few years. — 联邦当局指出,就像经济蓬勃发展的 20 世纪 90 年代新创公司一般,有组织的犯罪团伙和小偷正大批涌入互联网,并在短短几年间就已经形成了一个产值几百亿的地下经济。(① go-go—of a period of time when businesses are growing and people are making money fast;② start-up — a company that is just beginning to operate)

2. Lured by shoddy computer security ... cyber-extortion and the trafficking of stolen goods online. — 由于现在电脑安全性低,技术上可以从遥远的外国进行网络犯罪活动,俄罗斯和其他东欧国家的黑帮便纷纷投入发送垃圾邮件,进行网络钓鱼、网络敲诈和网上交易盗窃物品活动。

3. Both are global, thrive on flexible networks and require specialization. — 两者都有全球化的特点,都依赖灵活的网络,并且专业性强。

4. Criminals shop on illicit computer bulletin boards for stolen credit card numbers as they would for books on Amazon.com. — 罪犯们就像在亚马逊网站上购书一样在非法的电脑公告板上购买被盗的信用卡号码。

5. And millions of hijacked computers ... perpetrate the schemes without a trail. — 此外,数百万被"劫持"的电脑(即所有者并不知道已被恶意代码感染而成为由黑客控制的"僵尸电脑")能不留痕迹地进行网络犯罪。

6. And phishing ... gouged consumers by $2 billion in the 12-month period ended in April, Gartner says. — 截至 4 月份,网络钓鱼(通过欺骗性的电子邮件和网站诱使消费者泄露个人信息)在 12 个月间已经骗走了消费者 20 亿美元的资金。

7. The FBI ... two-thirds of them opened in the past year. — 联邦调查局正在加强网络部门实力,目前在调查全国范围内 2,700 件网络犯罪相关的案子,其中三分之二是去年开始审理的。(beef-up — *informal* to make sth bigger and better)

8. "This is more sophisticated stuff than purse snatching," — "这可比抢钱包这类案子复杂多了。"

9. Contributing to the chaos: security flaws in business, home and university computers, and few effective cyber crime laws in the USA and abroad. — 造成这种混乱的因素是:

商用、家用和学校的电脑存在安全漏洞以及在美国国内和国外几乎没有针对网络犯罪的有效法律。

10. What is more, homeland-security measures ... which is relatively invisible, security experts say. — 此外,安全专家说,加强美国边界安全和基础设施保护的国土安全措施有可能促使犯罪团伙活动转向技术领域,因为该领域具有相对的隐蔽性。

11. What started out as a digital shakedown of gambling Web sites has expanded — 开始只是对赌博网站的敲诈活动现在范畴已经扩大了(shakedown — *informal* the act of getting money from sb by using threats)

12. a survey by Carnegie Mellon University's H. John Heinz III School of Public Policy and Management and InformationWeek magazine. — 由卡内基·梅隆大学的 H. 约翰·海因茨三世公共政策与管理学院和《信息周刊》杂志共同进行的调查。

13. Banks and companies planning initial public stock offerings ... which bombard and paralyze a Web site with data. — 计划出售首次公开发行股票的银行和公司成了潜伏在网络中的黑客们的最新攻击目标。黑客们向他们索要 2 万到 5 万美元不等的免受分布式拒绝服务攻击保护费,这种攻击是用大量数据轰炸受害者的网站并致使瘫痪。

14. Western Union — 西联国际汇款公司(该公司通过全球 200 多个国家和地区的代理网点办理汇款业务)

15. Itar-Tass news agency — 俄通社-塔斯社(俄罗斯官方通讯社,原名塔斯社,1992 年更名)

16. In an attack in the USA last month, the Web site ... was hit for several days, disrupting service. — 上个月在美国发生了一起对 Authorize. Net 网站的袭击,该网站是为数千家中、小型企业提供信用卡交易处理的服务机构。袭击持续了好几天,使其服务中断。

17. They enlist new zombie computers unfamiliar to the company under siege or change the type of data used in an electronic assault. — 他们使用被攻击的公司所不熟悉的新的"僵尸"电脑,或是更换用于网络攻击的数据的类型。

18. The most fertile online territory for crooks runs the gamut from credit card theft and phishing to electronic burglary schemes. — 对于骗子们十分有利可图的活动领域很广,从盗取信用卡,网络钓鱼到网上盗窃。

19. IDC:Internet data center — 互联网数据中心

20. Banks are loath to discuss break-ins out of fear of spooking customers and are willing to quietly eat losses from fraud — 银行由于担心客户产生恐惧往往不愿谈论黑客的侵入,而是愿意默默承受诈骗所造成的损失。

21. Another popular scam entails an elaborate shipping network for expensive goods purchased online with stolen credit cards. — 另一种普遍的诈骗是通过一个很周密的托运网络来转移用所盗的信用卡网上购买的贵重物品。(entail — to make it necessary to do sth)

22. Re-shippers are recruited in chat rooms, online job postings and over the phone. — 这些重新发货人都是通过聊天室、网上招聘公告板和电话通讯等方式被招募来的。

23. A legislative fix? — Is legislation a solution(to the problem of cybercrime)?

24. Secret Service — 美国特工处(该部门原先属于美国财政部,2003 年后隶属于美国国土安全部,主要负责保卫总统,查缉伪钞制造犯及战时进行谍报活动等。)
25. Whether any of the bills make a dent as law is debatable, given the mixed results of the national Can-Spam law. — 考虑到全国反垃圾邮件法带来的后果有好有坏,这些法案究竟能否取得初步成效还是个问题。[①make a dent — to produce an effect;②Can-Spam law — referring to "Controlling the Assault of Non-solicited Pornography and Marketing Law"(2003)]
26. "miracle" drugs — "灵丹妙药"

Ⅳ. Language Features

网络新词常用词缀

本文多处使用由前缀 cyber-(电脑,网络)所构成的派生词,如 cyber-crime,cyber-security,cyber-extortion。

因特网语言中有几个极具派生力的前缀,如:cyber-、E-、hyper-等,由它们构成的新词汇层出不穷,以下是一些常用派生词:

1. 由前缀 E-构成的词
E-page system 电子页系统　　　　　E-paper 电子报
E-business 电子商务　　　　　　　　E-currency 电子货币
2. 由前缀 hyper-构成的词
Hyperlink 超链接　　　　　　　　　hyperaccess 超级访问软件
Hypertext 超文本　　　　　　　　　hypermedia 超媒体
3. 由 cyber-构成的词
cyberculture 电脑文化　　　　　　　cybercommunity 电脑界,网络界
cyber-crime 电脑犯罪　　　　　　　cyber-friend 网友
cyber-star 电脑之星,网络之星　　　　cyber-café 网吧
cyberspeak 网络用语　　　　　　　cybernaut 网络用户

在因特网语言中,有三个非常活跃的词:web,net 和 virtual,它们同其他词结合后生成了大量的复合词:

1. 由 web 生成的复合词
web surf 网上漫游　　　　　　　　web page 网页
webmaster 站点管理员 web TV 网络电视
webcasting 网络播放 website 站点
webwriter 发送电子函件的人 webzine 网络杂志
2. 由 net 生成的复合词
netizen 网民　　　　　　　　　　　netfiles 网络文件
netgroup 网络用户组　　　　　　　net speak 网络用语
nethead 网虫　　　　　　　　　　　net group 网络用户
3. 由 virtual 生成的复合词
virtual Library 虚拟图书馆　　　　　virtual Memory 虚拟内存

virtual community 虚拟社区   virtual university 虚拟大学

V. Analysis of the Content

1. The word "bust" in the sentence "The most recent bust was of a high-level member on June 4 who…" (Para. 31) means _____.
   A. bankruptcy
   B. arrest
   C. demotion
   D. a thing that is not good
2. It can be seen from the article that banks usually respond to cyber break-ins by _____.
   A. reporting them to the police
   B. discussing them openly
   C. quietly eating losses
   D. beefing up cyber-security
3. The latest targets of cyber-extortion are _____.
   A. companies planning initial public stock offerings
   B. start-up companies
   C. small-size companies
   D. shipping companies
4. It can be inferred from the first paragraph that the 1990s in the U.S. was a period of _____.
   A. economic depression
   B. economic boom
   C. social unrest
   D. over-consumption
5. The author's attitude towards the bills passed by the US Congress on cyber-security is _____.
   A. believing
   B. unknown
   C. doubtful
   D. objective

VI. Questions on the Article

1. What is feeding the frenzy of cybercrime?
2. What have lured the Russian mafia and other East European gangs into committing cybercrimes?
3. In what sense are crime syndicates and the Internet a natural fit?
4. What were the losses suffered by consumers and businesses from cybercrimes last year?
5. Why do crooks like the Internet?
6. How sophisticated have cyber-extortion attacks grown?
7. What is the most fertile online territory for crooks?
8. According to the anti-phishing bill recently introduced by Sen. Patrick Leahy, what penalty would phishing carry?
9. What is Rep. Thornberry's view on America's cyber-security?
10. What is the author's view on the effects of the bills passed by the Congress?

VII. Topics for Discussion

1. Is it sensible for the banks to quietly eat losses from cyber-frauds?
2. Can legislation solve the problem of cybercrime?

Lesson 22

Secrets of Success

America's system of higher education is the best in the world. That is because there is no system

It is all too easy to mock American academia. Every week produces a mind-boggling example of intolerance or wackiness. Consider the twin stories of Lawrence Summers[1], one of the world's most distinguished economists, and Ward Churchill, an obscure professor of ethnic studies, which unfolded in parallel earlier this year[2]. Mr Summers was almost forced to resign as president of Harvard University because he had dared to engage in intellectual speculation by arguing, in an informal seminar, that discrimination might not be the only reason why women are under-represented in the higher reaches of science and mathematics. Mr Churchill managed to keep his job at the University of Boulder, Colorado[3], despite a charge sheet[4] including plagiarism, physical intimidation and lying about his ethnicity.

With such colourful headlines, it is easy to lose sight of the real story: that America has the best system of higher education in the world. The Institute of Higher Education at Shanghai's Jiao Tong University ranks the world's universities on a series of objective criteria such as the number of Nobel prizes and articles in prestigious journals. Seventeen of the top 20 universities in that list are American; indeed, so are 35 of the top 50. American universities currently employ 70% of the world's Nobel prize-winners. They produce about 30% of the world's output of articles on science and engineering, according to a survey conducted in 2001, and 44% of the most frequently cited articles.

At the same time, a larger proportion of the population goes on to higher education in America than almost anywhere else, with about a third of college-aged people getting first degrees[5] and about a third of those continuing to get advanced degrees. Non-traditional students also do better than in most other countries. The majority of undergraduates are female; a third come from racial minorities; and more than 40% are aged 25 or over. About 20% come from families with incomes at or below the poverty line. Half attend part-time, and 80% of students work to help support themselves.

Why is America so successful? Wealth clearly has something to do with it. America spends more than twice as much per student as the OECD average (about $22,000 versus $10,000 in 2001), and alumni and philanthropists routinely shower universities with gold.[6] History also plays a part. Americans have always had a passion for higher education. The Puritans established Harvard College in 1636, just two decades after they first arrived in New England.

The main reason for America's success, however, lies in organisation. This is something other countries can copy. But they will not find it easy — particularly if they are developing countries that are bent on state-driven modernisation.[7]

The first principle is that the federal government plays a limited part. America does not have a central plan for its universities. It does not treat its academics as civil servants[8], as do France and Germany. Instead, universities have a wide range of patrons, from state governments to religious bodies, from fee-paying students to generous philanthropists. The academic landscape has been shaped by rich benefactors such as Ezra Cornell, Cornelius Vanderbilt, Johns Hopkins and John D. Rockefeller.[9] And the tradition of philanthropy survives to this day: in fiscal 2004, private donors gave $24.4 billion to universities.

Limited government does not mean indifferent government. The federal government has repeatedly stepped in to turbocharge higher education. The Morrill Land Grant Act[10] of 1862 created land-grant universities across the country. The states poured money into community colleges. The GI Bill[11] of 1946 brought universities within the reach of everyone. The federal government continues to pour billions of dollars into science and research.

The second principle is competition. Universities compete for everything, from students to professors to basketball stars. Professors compete for federal research grants. Students compete for college bursaries or research fellowships. This means that successful institutions cannot rest on their laurels[12].

The third principle is that it is all right to be useful.[13] Bertrand Russell once expressed astonishment at the worldly concerns he encountered at the University of Wisconsin[14]: "When any farmer's turnips go wrong, they send a professor to investigate the failure scientifically." America has always regarded universities as more than ivory towers[15]. Henry Steele Commager, a 20th-century American historian, noted of the average 19th-century American that "education was his religion" — provided that it "be practical and pay dividends".[16]

This emphasis on "paying dividends" remains a prominent feature of academic culture. America has pioneered the art of forging links between academia and industry. American universities earn more than $1 billion a year in royalties and licence fees. More than 170 universities have "business incubators" of some sort, and dozens operate their own venture funds[17].

Nothing quite like it

There is no shortage of things to marvel at in America's higher-education system, from its robustness in the face of external shocks to its overall excellence. No country but America explores such a wide range of subjects (including some dubious ones such as GBLT — gay, bisexual, lesbian and transgender studies). However, what particularly stands out is the system's flexibility and its sheer diversity.

For a demonstration of its flexibility, consider New York University. NYU used to be a commuter school with little money and even less prestige. In the mid-1970s, it was so close to bankruptcy that it had to sell off its largest campus, in the Bronx. But today it is flush with money from fund-raising, "hot" with would-be undergraduates across the country, and famous for recruiting academic superstars.[18] The Shanghai world ranking puts it at number 32.

The academic superstars certainly helped, but two other things proved even more useful. The first was NYU's ability to turn its location in downtown Manhattan into an asset. Lots of universities have fine economics departments, but having the stock exchange nearby adds something extra.[19] The second was the university's ability to spot market niches.

What made all this possible was the fact that power is concentrated in the hands of the central administration. Most universities in other countries distribute power among the professors; American universities have established a counterbalance to the power of the faculty in the person of a president, which allows some of them to act more like entrepreneurial firms than lethargic academic bodies.[20]

The American system's diversity has allowed it to combine excellence with access by providing a wide range of different types of institutions. Only about 100 of America's 3,200 higher-education institutions are research universities. Many of the rest are community colleges that produce little research and offer only two-year courses. But able students can progress from a humble two-year college to a prestigious research university.

To be fair, one reason why America's best universities are so good is that they have borrowed liberally from abroad — particularly from the British residential universities[21] that grew up in Oxford and Cambridge in the Middle Ages, and from Wilhelm von Humboldt's German research university[22] in the early 19th century.

Serpents in paradise[23]

But America's academic paradise harbours plenty of serpents. The political correctness[24] that has plagued Mr Summers is just one example of a deeper problem: America's growing inclination to abandon the very principles that have made it a world leader.

Ross Douthat has recently created a stir with his exposé of Ivy League[25] education, "Privilege: Harvard and the Education of the Ruling Class." High-school students compete furiously to get into Ivy League universities such as Harvard, but Mr Douthat, who graduated from there only three years ago, argues that they are seldom stretched when they arrive.[26] A few professors try to provide overviews of big subjects, but many stick with their pet subjects regardless of what undergraduates need to learn.[27] Mr Douthat wanted to pick a comprehensive list of classes in his chosen subjects, history and literature, but ended up with a weird mish-mash taught by "unengaged professors and overburdened teaching assistants."[28] Looking back on his experience, he feels cheated.

He is not alone. In many ways, undergraduates are the stepchildren of American higher education. Most academics pay more attention to research than to teaching, and most universities continue to neglect their core curriculums in the name of academic choice.

From time to time, universities try to improve the lot of the undergraduate, as Mr Summers is currently doing at Harvard: reforming the core curriculum, taming grade inflation[29] and asking professors to concentrate on teaching rather than self-promotion. But reformers are fighting in hostile territory. The biggest rewards in academic life are reserved for research rather than teaching, not least because research is easier to evaluate; and most students are willing to put up with indifferent teaching so long as they get those vital diplomas.

Complaints about the neglect of undergraduate education are as old as the research university, but the past few years have produced a host of[30] new criticisms of American universities. The first is that universities are no longer as devoted to free inquiry as they ought to be. The persecution of Mr Summers for the sin of intellectual rumination is symptomatic of a wider problem. At a time when America's big political parties are deeply divided over profound questions, from the meaning of "life" to the ethics of pre-emptive war, university professors are overwhelmingly on the side of one political party. Only about 10% of tenured professors[31] say they vote Republican. The liberal majority has repeatedly shown that it is willing to crush dissent on anything from speech codes to the choice of subjects worth studying.

There are signs that scientists, too, are turning against free and open inquiry, though for commercial rather than ideological reasons. Corporate sponsors are attaching strings to their donations in order to prevent competitors from free-riding on their research, such as forcing scientists to delay publication or even blank out crucial passages from published papers.[32] When Novartis[33], a Swiss pharmaceutical giant, agreed to invest $25m in Berkeley's College of Natural Resources, for example, it stipulated that it should get a first look at much of the research carried out by the plant and microbial biology department.

The second criticism is that America's universities are pricing themselves out of the range of ordinary Americans. Between 1971—1972 and 2002—2003, annual tuition costs, in constant 2002 dollars, rose from $840 to $1,735 at public two-year colleges and from $7,966 to $18,273 at private four-year colleges. True, the federal government spends over $100 billion a year on student aid, and elite universities make every effort to subsidise poorer students. One study of admissions to selective colleges shows that, in 2001—2002, students with a median family income paid only 34% of the "sticker" price[34].

Still, the sheer relentlessness of academic inflation is worrisome. Elite colleges have little incentive to compete on price; indeed, they tend to compete by adding expensive accoutrements, such as star professors or state-of-the-art gyms[35], thus pushing up the cost of education still further. And the public universities that played such a valiant role in providing opportunities to underprivileged students are being forced to raise their prices, thanks to the continual squeeze on public funding. The average cost of tuition at public universities rose by 10.5% last year, four times the rate of inflation.

The dramatic rise in the price of American higher education puts a heavy burden on middle-class families who are too rich to qualify for special treatment.[36] It also sends negative signals to poorer parents who may be unaware of all the subsidies available. Deborah Wadsworth, an opinion pollster, points out that universities may be courting a popular backlash. Americans increasingly regard universities as the gatekeepers to good jobs, but they also see them as prohibitively expensive. The result is a steady erosion of public admiration for these formerly much-esteemed institutions.

This points to a third criticism: that universities are becoming bastions of privilege rather than instruments of social mobility.[37] From the 1930s onwards, America's great universities did much to realise the American creed of equality of opportunity. James Bryant Conant[38], Harvard's president from 1933 to 1953, opened up scholarships to academic merit, and the vast post-war expansion of higher education extended Conant's meritocratic principle to millions of students. "Flagship" public universities such as Michigan, Texas and Berkeley, California, provided world-class education for next to nothing.[39]

Meritocracy in retreat

But the march of academic meritocracy has now slowed to a crawl, and, on some fronts, has even turned into a retreat. William Bowen of Princeton University and two colleagues, in a study of admissions to elite universities, found that in the 11 universities for which they had the best data, students from the top income quartile increased their share of places from 39% in 1976 to 50% in 1995. Students from the bottom income quartile also increased their share very slightly: the squeeze came in the middle.

Mr Summers points out that Harvard now offers free tuition to students whose families earn less than $40,000 a year, and greatly reduced fees to students from families earning $40,000—60,000. Other elite universities have followed suit. Yet at the same time those universities give priority to athletes, people applying early (who often come from privileged backgrounds) and the children of alumni ("legacies"). Duke University encourages the offspring of wealthy parents to apply early and considers their applications sympathetically.

The real threat to meritocracy, however, comes not from within the universities but from society at large. One consequence of the squeeze on funding for public universities, created by Americans' reluctance to pay taxes, has been an academic brain drain to the more socially exclusive private universities. In 1987, seven of the 26 top-rated universities in the US News & World Report rankings were public institutions; by 2002, the number had fallen to just four.

The biggest risk to American higher education is the erosion of the competitive principle. The man often cited as the architect of American academia's current success is Vannevar Bush[40], who was director of the office of scientific research and development during the second world war. After the war he insisted that research grants be allocated to universities on the basis of open competition and peer review. But in the 1980s universities began undermining this principle by lobbying their local congressmen for direct appropriations. In 2003, the amount of money from the federal research budget awarded on a non-competitive basis topped $2 billion, up from $1 billion in 2000.

American academia's merits still outweigh its faults. Many American undergraduates are savvy enough to get a first-class education. Many academics resist the temptation to censor ideological minorities. The vast bulk of research grants are allocated on the basis of merit. Yet American universities are acquiring a growing catalogue of bad habits that could one day leave them vulnerable to competitors from other parts of the world — though probably not from Europe, which has overwhelming academic problems of its own.

From *The Economist*, Sep. 10, 2005

I. New Words

academia	[ˌækəˈdiːmjə]	n.	学术界
accoutrements	[əˈkuːtəmənts]	n.	*plural* pieces of equipment
appropriation	[əˌprəupriˈeiʃən]	n.	*formal* a sum of money for a particular purpose
bastion	[ˈbæstiən]	n.	堡垒
bursary	[ˈbəːsəri]	n.	（尤指大学的）奖学金
counterbalance	[ˌkauntəˈbæləns]	n.	抵消；平衡
exposé	[ˌekspəuˈzei]	n.	（丑事、罪恶等的）暴露，揭露
incubator	[ˈinkjubeitə]	n.	孵化器；培养人才的基地

laurels	[ˈlɔːrəlz]	n.	(*plural*) 荣誉；名声
lethargic	[leˈθɑːdʒik]	adj.	having no energy or interest
meritocracy	[ˌmeriˈtɔkrəsi]	n.	英才教育
microbial	[maiˈkrəubiəl]	adj.	微生物的
mind-boggling	[ˈmaindˌbɔɡliŋ]	adj.	difficult to imagine, extremely surprising
mishmash	[ˈmiʃmæʃ]	n.	a mixture with no particular order
niche	[nitʃ]	n.	适当的位置
patron	[ˈpeitrən]	n.	资助人
pharmaceutical	[ˌfɑːməˈsjuːtikəl]	adj.	制药的
pollster	[ˈpəulstə]	n.	民意调查者
quartile	[ˈkwɔːtail]	n.	(统计学)四分位数
robustness	[rəˈbʌstnis]	n.	the state of being strong and healthy
rumination	[ˌruːmiˈneiʃən]	n.	沉思，反复思考
stipulate	[ˈstipjuleit]	v.	规定
stir	[stəː]	n.	轰动；骚动
turbocharge	[ˈtəːbəutʃɑːdʒ]	v.	用涡轮(给发动机)增压；促进
wackiness	[ˈwækinis]	n.	古怪

Ⅱ. Background Information

美国高等教育

美国是世界上高等教育事业最发达的国家之一。自1636年哈佛学院(哈佛大学前身)创立开始已有370多年历史。

美国高校形式多样,常见类型有以下四种：(1) 名牌大学：设有研究生院,能授予博士学位。(2) 四年制学院：以本科教育为主。(3) 社区学院、初级学院和专科学院：提供二、三年制教育。(4) 开放式院校：主要指暑期学校、函授学校、夜校、网上学校,从事普及高等教育任务。

不同类型学校所设学位也不一样。两年制院校给修满60—64学分(credits)的学生授予准学士学位(associate degree)；四年制院校给修满120—128学分的学生授予学士学位(bachelor degree)。更高层次的学位为硕士(master degree)和博士(doctor degree)。

美国之所以在建国后短短的200多年时间内由一个农业国发展成为世界一流的工业大国,从一个地区大国一跃成为当今的世界超级大国,其先进发达的高等教育是一个突出因素。

美国高等教育具有四大特点：

1. 实行自治：美国大学享有不受政府控制的自由,可以自行设置课程,筹集分配经费,聘用任命教授,招收挑选学生。这种自治给高校提供更大的发展空间。

2. 竞争机制：美国高校比欧洲高校具有更强的竞争机制,每年都有对不同层次大学的评审,并就教师阵容、招生质量、图书资料和科研成果等主要项目进行评比打分,挑出各项前20强。

3. 突出科研：大学是美国科研基地,承担了全国3/5的基础研究任务。美国诺贝尔奖获得者有90%集中在大学里。

4. 强调服务：社会服务是美国高等教育的优良传统。高校注重科研成果的转让和推广，与企业保持密切合作关系。通过研发新产品，高校为社会提供服务，既促进企业生产发展，又提高科研人员实践能力，还获得丰厚的经济回报。

Ⅲ. Notes to the Text

1. Lawrence Summers — 劳伦斯·萨默斯（哈佛大学第27任校长，也是该校历史上第一位经济学家校长，曾任世界银行首席经济学家、美国财长等职）
2. which unfolded in parallel earlier this year — 这两条新闻在今年早期同时披露[① in parallel —（happening）at the same time；② unfold — to be gradually made known]
3. University of Boulder, Colorado — 科罗拉多大学波尔得分校（该校是一所公立学校，位于落基山麓风光秀美的波尔得市，拥有学生20,000多人，其中研究生4,000人左右。）
4. charge sheet — 案情记录（a record kept in a police station of charges made）
5. first degree — 学士学位
6. America spends more than twice ... routinely shower universities with gold. — 美国花在每个学生身上的钱是经合组织国家平均数额的两倍以上（2001年约为2.2万美元，而经合组织国家平均数额为1万美元），而且校友和慈善家也经常向大学捐赠巨资。[OECD — 经济合作与发展组织（Organization for Economic Cooperation and Development：a group of industrially advanced countries who work together to develop trade and economic growth. Its members include West Europe, some countries from East Europe and the US, Canada, Mexico, Australia, New Zealand and Japan）]
7. But they will not find it easy — particularly if they are developing countries that are bent on state-driven modernisation. — 不过这样做并不容易——对于正致力于政府操控现代化建设的发展中国家尤其如此。(bent on — completely determined to do sth)
8. It does not treat its academics as civil servants — 美国不把大学教研人员作为公务员对待。(academic — a person who teaches and/or does research at a university or college)
9. The academic landscape has been shaped by rich benefactors such as Ezra Cornell, Cornelius Vanderbilt, Johns Hopkins and John D. Rockefeller. — 埃兹拉·康奈尔、科尼利厄斯·范德比尔特、约翰斯·霍普金斯和约翰·洛克菲勒等富有的捐助者对高校的现状产生了决定性影响。（① Ezra Cornell — 埃兹拉·康奈尔，美参议员、慈善家、联合电报公司创始人，于1865年创立康乃尔大学；② Cornelius Vanderbilt — 科尼利厄斯·范德比尔特，近代美国的航运和铁路大王、金融家、田纳西范德比尔特大学创始人；③ Johns Hopkins — 约翰斯·霍普金斯，美国马里兰州巴尔的摩市银行家，于1876年创立霍普金斯大学；④ John D. Rockfeller — 约翰·洛克菲勒，美国企业家和慈善家、美孚石油公司创办人，洛克菲勒家族创始人。）
10. the Morrill Land Grant Act — 《莫里尔土地赠与法案》（该法案因倡议者莫里尔议员而得名，于1862年在国会通过，它从根本上扩大了所有美国人接受高等教育的机会，其中包括妇女和少数民族。根据此法，各州获准出售联邦土地，并用售地收入资助至少一所公立学院。）
11. the GI Bill — 《退伍军人权利法案》(a law passed in the U.S. in 1944, which makes it

possible for people who have served in the army to continue their education and receive other benefits)

12. rest on their laurels — be satisfied with what they have achieved and stop trying to achieve anything new

13. ... it is all right to be useful. — ……有实用价值就行。

14. Bertrand Russell once expressed astonishment at the worldly concerns he encountered at the University of Wisconsin — 伯特兰·罗素曾对他在威斯康星大学所见对平凡小事的关注表示震惊。[① Bertrand Russell — 伯特兰·罗素(1872 — 1970),英国哲学家、数学家和逻辑学家,20 世纪英国最杰出的思想家之一;② worldly concerns— things affecting ordinary activities of life]

15. ivory tower — 象牙塔(意指超脱现实社会,远离生活之外,凭主观幻想从事学术活动。)

16. Henry Steele Commager, a 20th-century American historian, noted of the average 19th-century American that "education was his religion" — provided that it "be practical and pay dividends". — 美国 20 世纪历史学家亨利·斯蒂尔·康马杰曾认为,对 19 世纪的一般美国人来说,"教育是神圣事业"——条件是它必须"实用并能带来收益"。(Henry Steele Commager — 亨利·斯蒂尔·康马杰,历史学家,美国历史界权威,任教于马塞诸塞州阿默斯特大学,曾获美国历史学会金奖。)

17. venture fund — funds that are invested in a new business which may involve a lot of risk

18. But today it is flush with money from fund-raising, "hot" with would-be undergraduates across the country, and famous for recruiting academic superstars. — 但是今天它已经成为一所拥有大量筹集来资金的、全美高中生毕业生选择热门的高校;同时,它还以聘用学术巨匠而闻名。

19. Lots of universities have fine economics departments, but having the stock exchange nearby adds something extra. — 许多大学都有不错的经济学系,但是地处证券交易所旁边增加了竞争砝码。(纽约大学位于纽约市中心格林尼治村,基本以华盛顿广场为中心地带,向外呈辐射状分散,大部分校舍位于曼哈顿下城、华尔街、联邦储备银行、纽约证券交易所等均坐落于附近。)

20. American universities have established a counterbalance ... act more like entrepreneurial firms than lethargic academic bodies. — 美国大学已经建立了校长个人权力对全体教师权力的平衡体制,这种体制使一些大学运作更像公司企业,而不是毫无生气的学术机构。

21. residential universities — 寄宿制大学

22. Wilhelm von Humboldt's German research university — 德国洪堡研究型大学(德国洪堡大学成立于1810年,前身为柏林大学。它倡导"学术自由"和"教学与研究相结合"的精神,致力于培养学生多方面的人文综合素养,树立了现代大学的完美典范,被誉为"现代大学之母"。)

23. serpents in paradise — 伊甸园里的蛇(基督教《圣经·创世记》中魔鬼化作蛇引诱夏娃偷吃了伊甸园的禁果,在基督教传统中经常成为邪恶的代名词,让人联想到撒旦或魔鬼。这里指美国成功的高等教育体系中也存在着严重的问题。)

24. politically correctness — 政治上正确 (also PC, used to describe language that deliberately tries to avoid offending particular groups such as women and minorities)

25. Ivy League —— 常青藤联合会(指美国东北部的哈佛、耶鲁、哥伦比亚、普林斯顿、布朗、康奈尔、宾夕法尼亚和达特茅斯等8所以学术成就及社会地位著称的名牌大学)

26. ... they are seldom stretched when they arrive. —— 到这里来之后智力很少得到充分开发。(stretch —— to make use of sb's skill or intelligence)

27. A few professors try to provide overviews of big subjects, but many stick with their pet subjects regardless of what undergraduates need to learn. —— 一些教授力图提供重要的学科概观,但很多教授还是只讲他们最爱讲的学科,全然不顾本科生需要学什么。(① big —— important; ② pet subject —— a subject that you particularly like or are interested in)

28. a weird mish-mash taught by "unengaged professors and overburdened teaching assistants" —— 由"空闲的教授和不堪重负的助教"讲授的怪异的大杂烩内容

29. grade inflation —— 分数贬值

30. a host of —— a large number of

31. tenured professors —— 享有终身职位的教授

32. Corporate sponsors are attaching strings ... blank out crucial passages from published papers. —— 为了防止竞争对手从他们的研究中无本获利,公司资助者对他们的捐款设有附加条件,比如强行规定科学家推迟发表研究成果,甚至删除发表论文的关键章节。(① strings —— special conditions or restrictions; ② free-ride —— to obtain sth without cost or effort)

33. Novartis —— 诺华公司(瑞士第一大公司,全球最具创新能力的医药保健公司之一,在全球制药和消费者保健行业的跨国公司中居于领先地位)

34. "sticker" price —— 〈美〉(通常可协商的)标价,标签价

35. state-of-the-art gyms —— 最先进的体育馆(state-of-the-art —— using the most modern and recently developed methods, materials or knowledge)

36. The dramatic rise in the price of American higher education puts a heavy burden on middle-class families who are too rich to qualify for special treatment. —— 美国高等教育费用的急剧上涨给中产阶级家庭带来了沉重的负担,因为他们的收入水平超过了享受特殊照顾的标准。

37. ... that universities are becoming bastions of privilege rather than instruments of social mobility. —— 大学正成为特权的壁垒,而不是社会地位攀升的阶梯。(social mobility —— the ability to move into a different social class, especially up into the higher class)

38. James Bryant Conant —— 科南特(1893—1978)(美国著名教育家、有机化学家,其要素主义教育思想对20世纪五六十年代美国学校的教育改革产生了重大影响,曾任哈佛大学校长)

39. "Flagship" public universities such as Michigan, Texas and Berkeley, California, provided world-class education for next to nothing. —— 像密歇根、得克萨斯、加州(伯克利)一类王牌公立大学几乎不收钱就提供世界一流的教育。(① flagship —— the best and most important one of a group of things; ② world-class —— among the best in the world)

40. Vannevar Bush —— 万尼瓦尔·布什[(1890—1974),美国著名工程师,科学家管理者,以美国"大科学的先驱"而闻名]

Ⅳ. Language Features

新闻英语常用典故

英语典故来自传说、神话、有关的风土民情以及反映这些内容的小说、剧本和诗歌。恰当使用典故可以使语言简明具体或是生动有趣。

本文中"Serpents in paradise"是出自《圣经·创世记》的一则典故,意指美国成功的高等教育体系中存在的严重问题。

《圣经》是基督教的经典,莎士比亚著作是文学的经典,这些经典之作中的主要角色的言行家喻户晓,常被引以为例,成了日常通用语。例如:

Gomorrah 罪恶渊薮;put the new wine in old bottles 旧瓶装新酒(旧形式不能适应新内容);separate the sheep from the goats 辨别善恶;Armageddon 世界末日善恶的决战;much ado about nothing 无事自扰;the widow's mite 少而可贵的贡献;cast pearls before swine 对牛弹琴,明珠暗投;heap coals of fire 以德报怨;Shylock 吝啬的人;Hamlet 优柔寡断的人;Judas 叛徒;Goliath 庞然大物;the writing on the wall 凶兆。

美英报刊中常常使用这类典故。例如:

Motion picture exhibitors have a strong preference for the R (restricted) rating probably on the theory of forbidden fruit. 电影放映商非常喜爱 R 级(17 岁以下观众要由父母或监护人陪同才准许看的)电影,很可能是根据禁果的理论。

这一句中 forbidden fruit 出自《圣经》,现常用来比喻因被禁止反而使人更想得到的东西。

希腊、罗马神话故事在西方人的脑海中留下了很多神和英雄的形象,新闻英语也经常运用这些典故。例如:

Jimmy Carter is a president of the Spartan habit. (*Newsweek*) 吉米·卡特是具有斯巴达式习惯的总统。(Spartan — 斯巴达式的,律己很严的,生活俭朴的)

英文典故另一重要出处就是《伊索寓言》和文学著作。例如:

What Diana clearly didn't understand when she took the fateful step, with all the boldness of an upper-class Alice, through the royal looking class, was that she could never get back into that nice cozy private nursery again. (*Time*)

这一句是从描述戴安娜由幼儿园教师变为"公主"而不得安宁的一段中择出的,作者引用路易斯·卡洛尔(Lewis Carroll)脍炙人口的儿童文学名著 *Alice's Adventures in Wonderland*(《爱丽丝漫游奇境记》)和 *Through the Looking Glass*(《镜子背后》),与戴安娜先前的身份"托儿所阿姨"相呼应,幽默生动,趣味盎然。

Ⅴ. Analysis of the Content

1. The author believes that the main factor in the success of America's higher education is _____.

   A. the organization of America's higher education

   B. long history of Americans' passion for higher education

   C. much more spending on higher education

D. advanced equipments and teaching methods
2. The example of Laurence Summers is cited to illustrate the problem of _____.
   A. decline in academic ethics   B. lack of flexibility
   C. shortage of funds   D. political correctness
3. The major factor in the success of New York University is its _____.
   A. wealth   B. ideal location   C. diversity   D. flexibility
4. The sharp rise in the price of American higher education put a heavy burden especially on students from _____.
   A. lower income families   B. middle class families
   C. upper income families   D. single-parent families
5. To the author's mind, the biggest threat to American higher education is _____.
   A. the erosion of the competitive principle
   B. financial squeeze on public universities
   C. priority to athletes and children of alumni
   D. lack of diversity

VI. Questions on the Article

1. Why was Mr Summers almost forced to resign as president of Harvard University?
2. On what criteria does the Institute of Higher Education at Shanghai Jiao Tong University rank the world's universities? What does the study show about America's higher education?
3. How popularized is American higher education?
4. What kind of role does the federal government play in America's higher education?
5. How is the principle of competition carried out in America's higher education?
6. What are the most outstanding features of America's higher education system?
7. What are the problems in America's higher education?
8. What are the threats to academic meritocracy?
9. What is the author's evaluation of American academia?

VII. Topics for Discussion

1. Should academics pay more attention to research than to teaching?
2. Are universities the gatekeepers to good jobs?

Lesson 23

Tuning Out TV

Advertisers are using a variety of methods to grab consumers' attention

By Betsy Streisand

The nation's top advertisers and network television executives will invade New York City once again this week for what has become the TV industry's most celebrated exercise in failing up: the annual "upfront" market.[1] That's when the Big Six — ABC, CBS, NBC, Fox, UPN, and WB[2] — unveil their new fall schedules to advertisers, who then pony up billions of dollars to prebuy commercial time that costs more and delivers less. Even though network audiences continue to dwindle, the upfront is expected to surpass last year's record haul of $9.5 billion. While the take probably won't represent a double-digit increase like last year's 15 percent jump, it will give the networks all the excuse they need to boast that nothing succeeds like a 30-second TV spot.

Yet behind all the spin about the new shows — most of which will be canceled before you can say *My Big Fat Obnoxious Fiance*[3] — the networks are painfully aware that it is they who are buying time. Under assault from cable, DVDs, and the Internet, CBS, NBC, and the others can't come close to delivering the crowds they once did. And even when hit shows like *The Apprentice* and *CSI* do attract millions of viewers, commercial-zapping digital video recorders like TiVo are waiting in the wings to crash the advertising party.[4] "Advertisers aren't willing anymore to simply put all their money into 30-second spots[5] and cross their fingers," says Kathy Delaney, executive creative director of the ad agency Deutsch, which handles Revlon and Mitsubishi[6]. "Those days are gone."

The new reality of TV is that many of the country's biggest advertisers, including Coca-Cola, General Motors, and Procter & Gamble[7], are finding alternative ways to put their goods and their messages in front of consumers, and they're doing it with some of the money that used to pay for prime-time television commercials[8]. Revlon is running minimovies in theaters, American Express airs short films on its Web site, and General Motors' Hummer H2 gets almost as much face time as the crime specialists on *CSI: Miami*.[9] In a March survey of the Association of National Advertisers[10], more than 40 percent of those asked said they planned to move part of their next-year ad budgets to other outlets, such as the Internet, outdoor advertising, product placement[11], cable, and special events.

Coca-Cola, the onetime king of the commercial, for instance, cut back its spending on TV ads from $269 million in 2001 to $189 million last year, according to TNS Media Intelligence/CMR[12], which tracks ad spending. In addition to online advertising, outdoor ads, and sponsorship of events such as the NCAA[13] basketball tournament, some of that money is being used for the company's new Red Lounges. Located in two shopping malls so far, the lounges are essentially Coke-immersion zones[14] where teenagers can play video games, surf the Web, sprawl on the red sofas, and — what else? — drink Coke. Aside from vending machine[15] sales, which are easily quantifiable, it's hard to measure what these hangouts will do for Coke's bottom line[16]. Not that Coca-Cola is concerned. "We want to be part of our customers' lives every day," says Katie Bayne, Coca-Cola's head of integrated marketing[17]. "We want to connect with them where their passions are."

Ditto for Revlon, which recently began airing two-minute minimovies in theaters featuring Halle Berry[18] and other beauties. "We used to have to really convince clients to think beyond the TV spot," says Delaney. "But it's not so difficult now that they realize that the stronger your brand essence, the less it matters if someone zaps through your commercial on TiVo." Advertisers also are trading in their turf between TV shows for roles in them — and movies, too.[19] The William Morris Agency[20] and Creative Artists Agency[21] now represent dozens of consumer goods companies, including Ford, Anheuser-Busch[22], and Motorola, which they bring to the table when movies, music videos, and TV shows are on the drawing board. When Ice Cube's new movie, *Are We There Yet?*, opens, it will be tough to determine who has the leading role: Ice or his jazzed-up Lincoln Navigator.[23]

Then there is cable. Forget the old argument that all the *Queer Eye for the Straight Guy*[24] showings can't equal one episode of *The Apprentice*. While that may be true, it no longer matters that much. For the first time, cable's aggregate audience will actually top the combined viewership of the Big Six networks, and the Discovery Channels[25] and CNNs of the world are expected to commandeer as much as $1 billion of upfront ad money. "For advertisers interested in target marketing[26], the networks can seem inefficient," says Brad Adgate, senior vice president at Horizon Media, a media buying firm in New York. GM, for example, which reduced its prime-time spending by $40 million last year, is shifting more dollars to cable, the Internet, and other outlets to get its wide range of products in front of as many demographics as possible.

The Internet, which attracted $6.5 billion in ads last year — a 16 percent increase over the year before — is expected to jump an additional 6 percent this year. Online advertising offers not just interactivity but an easy way to mingle content and direct targeting in a subtle fashion — at a fraction of the network price[27]. When visitors to American Express's Web site watch the minifilm starring Jerry Seinfeld[28] and a comically neurotic Superman, for instance, the card[29] is barely mentioned. "There are a lot of people asking what are we accomplishing," says Peter Tortorici, head of TV programming at MindShare, a media services firm. "Who knows, exactly? But we're capturing critical mass and bringing them to our site."

In a world where the average consumer receives 3,000 ad messages a day, simply reaching audiences is no longer enough. Advertisers want to have a one-on-one dialogue with consumers. And while many are content to let celebrities do their pitching, Procter & Gamble, for example, is turning directly to teens. Dubbed the Tremor Nation, its online focus group of more than 200,000 teens weighs in with opinions on everything from product names to packaging of P&G products. Then the word of mouth begins.[30] So far, Tremor has been behind the buzz on CoverGirl's latest lipstick color and Pringles's newest potato chip flavor.[31]

Which is not to say that advertisers won't continue to fork over millions to reach millions in one pop.³² "Network television is still the best medium for building brand awareness and selling products," says Adgate. Some advertisers, including Toyota and Anheuser-Busch, are even slightly increasing their prime-time spending to capitalize on big events like the Summer Olympics. On top of high drama and a wide audience, few things please advertisers more than associating with the feel-good atmosphere created by athletes pursuing their dreams.³³

Even so, broadcasters are worried enough about their future that for the first time ever, they have banded together to promote network television as a whole. There is a lot at stake, and not just the $55 billion that TV collected in advertising revenue last year. The entire business model that has made broadcast television a money-minting machine — sell lots of 30-second commercials for gobs of money and then use the cash to foot the bills for everything else — is in peril.³⁴ "For the price of one spot in a hit show, you can buy a lot of everything else," says Robin Kent, chairman and CEO of Universal McCann³⁵, the global advertising conglomerate. "And even a 1 or 2 percent drop at the networks would have a huge impact."

Join 'em. With that in mind, the networks, too, are adapting. Although DVRs are in fewer than 4 percent of homes, their popularity is growing. And studies show that the average TiVo viewer zaps 77 percent of the commercials out of recorded shows. Since the more popular shows are the ones most likely to be recorded, it is the most expensive commercials that are biting the dust³⁶. So networks are focusing on integrating ads into shows and striking deals to keep ratings makers happy and advertisers in the mix. NBC will soon debut *The Contender*, a boxing contest produced by Reality TV's reigning prince³⁷, Mark Burnett, and DreamWorks Television³⁸. In an unprecedented concession by a network, the show's producers will retain six commercial spots each episode, which they can sell to advertisers who will also get to showcase their product.³⁹ In another unusual deal, consumer products giant Unilever⁴⁰ will produce six episodes of a new ABC drama and license it to the network in return for the ad time.

Not all these newfangled approaches work. Major League Baseball quickly discovered how far afield it had gone earlier this month when it agreed to allow Sony Pictures to promote its upcoming *Spider-Man 2* movie by decorating bases with the *Spider-Man* web⁴¹. Fans threw a fit, and the project was scrapped.⁴² "All sides recognize that things are going to change, but to what and in what way, nobody really knows," says Tortorici. "All we know is that whatever we think the future of TV is, we'll think differently about it a year from now."

From *US News & World Report*, May 24, 2004

Ⅰ. New Words

aggregate	['ægrigeit]	*adj.*	being the total amount of something
commandeer	[,kɔmən'diə]	*v.*	to take someone else's property for your own use
debut	['debju:]	*v.*	to introduce a product to the public for the first time

ditto	['ditəu]	n.	the same
dwindle	['dwindl]	v.	to become gradually less
gob	[gɔb]	n.	a large amount of something
hangout	['hæŋaut]	n.	*informal* a place where sb likes to go often
haul	[hɔ:l]	n.	the amount won or taken at one time
neurotic	[njuə'rɔtik]	adj.	tending to be emotionally unstable
newfangled	['nju:,fæŋgld]	adj.	new and often needlessly novel
pitch	[pitʃ]	v.	*informal* to sell something by saying how good it is
pony	['pəuni]	v.	~ **up** *AmE informal* to pay money for sth
quantifiable	[,kwɔnti'faiəbl]	adj.	可用数量表示的
showcase	['ʃəukeis]	v.	to display prominently, especially to advantage
spin	[spin]	n.	*informal* a way of providing information that makes it seem to be favorable
unveil	[ʌn'veil]	v.	to show or introduce a new plan, product, etc. to the public

Ⅱ. Background Information

美国广告

美国广告业已有200多年历史,广告文化渗透社会各个角落,成为人们生活中不可缺少的组成部分。据美国广告公司协会(American Association of Advertising Agencies)调查,美国人一天通过各种媒体所接触的商业广告多达1,600多条。

美国是广告业最为发达的国家,其广告费在世界独占鳌头。1997年全球广告费为3,795亿美元,而美国的广告费高达1,875亿美元,占全球总额的49.1%!

广告离不开媒体,媒体依赖广告收入,广告与媒体是相互依赖关系(interdependence)。其关系正如电影《杰里•麦奎尔》(Jerry Mcguire)中媒体广告节目制作人与广告业主的一段对话:"Show me the money." — "Show me the audience."

广告主要传统媒体是报纸、杂志、广播和电视,这四种媒体各有特点。

报纸的优点是宣传面广、读者量大、传播及时、制作简单、费用低廉,但缺点是内容庞杂、美感较差、读后便弃。杂志优点是针对性强、较为生动、便于保存,但缺点是传播不及时、读者面较窄。广播优点是快速灵活、宣传面广、制作简单,缺点在于信息易失、缺乏实体感。电视优点是形象生动、快速及时、受众面大、易于留下深刻印象,缺点是信息易失、费用昂贵。

其他广告媒体有直接邮件(direct mail)、户外媒体(outdoor media)、黄页电话簿(yellow pages)、互联网(Internet)。网络广告(online advertising)由于具有迅捷便利、互动性强、价格低廉的优点,增长十分迅猛。2005年网络广告的增长率为11%,高于其他媒体广告。

美国每年的广告费总额中有60%用于支付各种媒体,如2003年媒体广告总收入为

1283.6亿美元。

　　1999年美国广告费用分布情况是:电视占23.4%,报纸占21.7%,直接邮件占19.2%,广播占8%,黄页电话簿占5.9%,杂志占5.3%,商业报占2%,广告牌占0.8%,互联网占0.9%,其他媒体占12.8%。

Ⅲ. Notes to the Text

1. The nation's top advertisers and network television executives … the annual "upfront" market. — 美国主要广告商和电视网络业务主管将在本周再次涌入纽约市参加每年的广告费预付业务洽谈会,这已成为电视业最为出名的失败活动。(upfront — paid in advance)

2. the Big Six — ABC, CBS, NBC, Fox, UPN, and WB: 六大广播公司——美国广播公司、哥伦比亚广播公司、全国广播公司、福克斯广播公司、联合派拉蒙电视网、华纳兄弟广播公司(ABC — American Broadcasting Company; CBS — Columbia Broadcasting System; NBC — National Broadcasting Company; Fox — Fox Broadcasting Company; UPN — United Paramount Network; WB — Warner Bros)

3. *My Big Fat Obnoxious Fiance* — a one-shot television reality show on the Fox Network during the 2003 – 2004 seasons

4. And even when hit shows … are waiting in the wings to crash the advertising party. — 即使《飞黄腾达》和《犯罪现场调查》这类十分风行的电视剧确实吸引数百万电视观众,像 TiVo 一样能跳过广告的数字视频录像机已摆出架势狠狠打击广告业。(①hit shows — extremely popular shows; ②commercial-zapping — advertisement-avoiding; ③crash — to hit sth hard; ④wait in the wings — to be ready to take action; ⑤*The Apprentice* — the hottest American news TV program in 2004, which features 16 candidates who compete for a salary of US＄250,000; ⑥ *CSI — Crime Scene Investigation*,该剧讲述法医运用高科技侦查手段,通过蛛丝马迹破解一个个谜案,将穷凶极恶的罪犯送上法庭。)

5. 30-second spots — 30秒钟广告插播

6. executive creative director of the ad agency Deutsch, which handles Revlon and Mitsubishi — 承办露华浓美容产品和三菱公司产品广告业务的多伊奇广告公司创意部执行主任(①Deutsch — a full-service marketing communications agency;②Revlon — 露华浓公司,生产美容等产品)

7. Procter & Gamble — 美国宝洁公司(该公司以两位创始人姓名命名,生产洗涤剂、清洁剂、一次性尿布和处方药品等)

8. prime-time television commercials — 黄金时段电视商业广告

9. American Express airs short films on its Web site, and General Motors' Hummer H2 gets almost as much face time as the crime specialists on *CSI*: *Miami*. — 美国运通公司在自己的网站上播放短片,通用汽车公司所生产的悍马H2汽车在《犯罪现场调查:迈阿密》电视片中所出现的时间几乎与犯罪分析家一样多。(①American Express — a US company that has a credit card service, exchanges foreign money and sells Traveller's Cheques; ②face time — viewing time; ③Hummer H2 — 悍马H2汽车,车体形象剽悍

10. Association of National Advertisers — 全国广告商协会
11. product placement — the use of particular products in films or television programs in order to advertise them
12. TNS Media Intelligence/CMR — 美国市场调查机构,全球第二大市场研究集团
13. NCAA — National Collegiate Athletic Association(美国)全国大学生体育协会
14. Located in two shopping malls so far, the lounges are essentially Coke-immersion zones — 到目前为止,已在两个大型购物中心设有这种娱乐室,他们实质上是熏陶可口可乐文化的地方。
15. vending machine — 投币式自动售货机
16. bottom line — the amount of money that is a profit or loss after everything has been calculated
17. Coca-Cola's head of integrated marketing — 可口可乐饮料公司综合营销部主任
18. Halle Berry — 美国许多年轻人心目中的偶像,经常担任色情片的角色
19. Advertisers also are trading in their turf between TV shows for roles in them — and movies, too. — 广告商现在把电视节目间的广告时段折价换作电视节目和电影中的角色。(① trade in — to give sth used as part of the payment for sth new; ② turf — referring to commercial time)
20. William Morris Agency —创新艺人经纪公司 (the oldest and largest talent and literary agency in the world)
21. Creative Artists Agency — a talent and literary agency which represents a vast array of actors, musicians, writers, directors, and athletes, as well as a variety of companies and their products
22. Anheuser-Busch — 安海斯-布希公司[创立于1852年,旗下有世界最大的啤酒酿造公司,百威啤酒(Budweiser)是该公司产品之一]
23. When Ice Cube's new movie, *Are We There Yet?*, opens, it will be tough to determine who has the leading role: Ice or his jazzed-up Lincoln Navigator. — 当艺人"冰块酷儿"的新片《小鬼上路》公演的时候,观众很难确定到底是"冰块酷儿"还是他所驾驶的帅气十足的林肯领航员牌车是主角[① Ice Cube — 冰块酷儿(艺人);② *Are We There Yet* — 《小鬼上路》(2005年北美票房冠军家庭喜剧片);③ jazz up — to make sth interesting, lively, enjoyable;④ Lincoln Navigator — 林肯领航员,体型庞大、形象突出、空间宽敞,是美国豪华车代表品牌之一]
24. *Queer Eye for the Straight Guy* —《粉雄救兵》[该片以五个同性恋的男时尚设计师为主角,每一集他们会闯进一个普通的异性恋(也叫直男)男人的家中,全方位地包装这个男人,使他由一个邋遢的男人成为一个时尚、性感、充满自信的都市男人。]
25. Discovery Channels — 探索频道(由美国探索通讯公司 Discovery Communications Inc 或 DCI 经营)
26. target marketing — 目标营销
27. Online advertising offers ... of the network price. — 网上广告不仅提供互动,而且容易把广告内容和直接推销微妙地结合在一起,其费用仅是电视广告的一小部分。
28. Jerry Seinfeld — 杰里·宋飞(一位生活表演在纽约的喜剧演员)

29. the card — referring to American Express credit card

30. Dubbed the Tremor Nation, its online focus group ... Then the word of mouth begins. — 由20多万青少年组成被称作"兴奋民众"的宝洁公司网上焦点群体对宝洁公司产品从品名到包装各个方面发表观点,于是口传广告便开始了。(①focus group — a group of people, specially chosen to represent different classes, who are asked to give opinions about a particular subject; ②weigh in on sth — *informal* to add a remark to a discussion or an argument; ③Tremor — In 2001, P&G started "Tremor," a word-of-mouth marketing program that recruited teens to "pitch" products.)

31. So far, Tremor has been behind the buzz on CoverGirl's latest lipstick color and Pringles's newest potato chip flavor. — 到目前为止,"兴奋民众"一直在推动对封面女郎最新的口红颜色及"品客"新薯片口味的讨论。(①buzz — the sound of people talking especially in an excited way; ②Pringles — "品客"薯片,一种年轻人爱吃的波浪造型,松脆可口的薯片)

32. Which is not to say that advertisers won't continue to fork over millions to reach millions in one pop. — 但这并非说广告商不会继续用数百万美元购买一次能获得数百万受众的广告。(①fork over sth — *AmE informal* to pay especially unwillingly; ②pop — *AmE informal* each particular occasion)

33. On top of high drama and a wide audience, few things please advertisers more than associating with the feel-good atmosphere created by athletes pursuing their dreams. — 除了效果强烈、观众量大之外,使广告商最为满意的是产生关联效应的运动员实现梦想而制造出的那种美好气氛。(①feel-good — making you feel very happy and pleased about life; ②on top of — in addition to)

34. The entire business model ... is in peril. — 广播电视被打造成印钞机,靠出售30秒广告大把赚钱,然后用这些钱来为其他东西买单,现在这个经营模式正面临危险。

35. Universal McCann — 优势麦肯公司 (one of the leading media agencies in Australia with key skills in media planning and buying, and communications architecture)

36. bite the dust — *informal* to fail

37. Reality TV's reigning prince — 真人秀本届王子

38. DreamWorks Television — 梦工厂电视

39. In an unprecedented concession by a network ... showcase their product. — 电视网做出前所未有的让步:电视片制作商每一集保留6个插播广告的时段,他们把这些时段卖给广告商为其产品做广告。

40. Unilever — 联合利华公司 (a widely listed multi-national corporation, formed of Anglo-Dutch parentage, which owns many of the world's consumer product brands in foods, beverages, cleaning agents and personal care products)

41. Major League Baseball quickly discovered ... decorating bases with the *Spider-Man* web. — 全美棒球联合总会这个月允许索尼影视公司用蜘蛛侠网装饰棒球攻垒方式宣传即将公演的《蜘蛛侠2》影片,此后很快便发现这种做法非常错误。(afield — out of the right way)

42. Fans threw a fit, and the project was scrapped. — Fans became very angry, so the

project was canceled.

Ⅳ. Language Features

缩略词(Shortenings)

本文多处使用缩略词(shortenings)，如 ABC，CBS，NBC，WB，DVD，NCAA，DVR 等。
英语的整个发展趋势是逐渐简化,反映在词汇层次上的重叠现象便是大量缩略词的涌现。语言学家埃里克·帕特里奇(Eric Patridge)与西蒙·波特(Simeon Potter)在《变化中的英语》一书中写到:"现实世界上,缩略词大量产生,很难跟踪收集。"出于节约篇幅、精炼语言的需要,新闻报道使用缩略词的频率更高,到处皆可见到。
缩略词形式除拼缀词以外,主要还有三种形式。

1. 截短词(clippings)
这是截除原词的某一(或某些)音节所得的缩略词。例如,

doc(doctor)医　　　　　　　　dozer(bulldozer)推土机
info(information)信息　　　　　net(Internet)因特网
tech(technology)技术　　　　　pop(popular)流行的
vet(veteran)有经验者,老手　　semis(semifinals)半决赛
teens(teenagers)青少年　　　　con(convict)罪犯
ex(ex-husband/wife)前夫/夫人　temp(temporary)临时雇员
hood(neighborhood)街坊　　　 prenups(prenuptial agreement)婚前协议

2. 首字母缩写词(alphabetism)
用词组的每个词第一字母组成并按字母发音的缩略词。例如,

CD(compact disk)光盘　　　　GM(genetically modified)转基因的
HOV(high occupancy vehicle)多乘员车辆
WTO(World Trade Organization)世贸组织
NII(National Information Infrastructure)国家信息机构
BPOC(business process outsourcing)业务流程外包
UAV(unmanned aerial vehicle)无人驾驶机

3. 首字母缩拼词(acronym)
把词组每个词第一个字母组成并拼读为一个词的缩略词。例如,

DIMP(double income money problem)双职工困难家庭
ROM(Read Only Memory)只读存储器
UFO(Unidentified Flying Object)不明飞行物
NOW(National Organization for Women)(美)全国妇女组织
BRIC(Brazil, Russia, India, China)金砖四国
NEET(not in education, employment or training)尼特族(啃老族)

Ⅴ. Analysis of the Content

1. The word "cable" in the second paragraph means _____.

A. a metal rope
   B. a plastic tube containing wires
   C. a message sent by electrical signals
   D. cable television
2. It can be seen from the article that the best medium for building brand awareness and selling products is _____.
   A. network television   B. the Internet
   C. cable television   D. the newspaper
3. The Red Lounges are intended to _____.
   A. provide entertainment for kids
   B. promote Coca-Cola sale
   C. teach teenagers computer skills
   D. enliven the atmosphere of the shopping malls
4. Revlon's new way of advertising is the use of _____.
   A. minimovies in theaters featuring beauties
   B. billboards featuring beauties
   C. celebrities' promotion
   D. cable television.
5. The author's attitude towards network television advertising is _____.
   A. appreciative   B. critical
   C. objective   D. supportive

VI. Questions on the Article

1. How much upfront ad money will network television gain this year?
2. What will the top advertisers and the Big Six television networks do in New York this week?
3. According to the survey of the Association of National Advertisers, what did many advertisers plan to do?
4. What were the changes in Coca-Cola's ways of advertising?
5. How important will cable advertising become?
6. How fast has the Internet advertising been growing?
7. What are the advantages of online advertising?
8. How does Procter & Gamble do advertising?
9. Why are some advertisers, including Toyota and Anheuser-Busch, even slightly increasing the prime-time spending to capitalize on big sports events?
10. What measures are the networks taking to ensure financial revenues from advertising?

VII. Topics for Discussion

1. Is advertising more harmful than beneficial?
2. Can network television keep its present position in advertising?

Lesson 24

Our Titanic Love Affair

A chick-flick[1] period piece with a tragic ending is rewriting the Hollywood rules. It's about to become the first billion-dollar movie. Why are we all sobbing with pleasure?
By David Ansen

EVEN JAMES CAMERON is, he says, "a little bit mystified" by the passionate reaction to his movie. The director of "Titanic" has been tirelessly circling the world to promote his film's opening. Audiences don't always laugh at the same jokes, he's discovered. But whether it's Moscow or Tokyo or Rome, they all cry at the same places. If the tears being shed over "Titanic" could be collected in rain clouds, El Niño[2] would have stiff competition.

The dimensions of the mania, as we well know, are extraordinary. They love it in Slovenia. It's the most successful movie ever in Mexico and Hong Kong. In some towns in France, cinema owners report that their admissions exceed the local population, which means that the French are going to it three or four times — something the French are not supposed to do. Last Saturday in the United States, "Titanic" hit the $350 million mark after 58 days; it took "Jurassic Park"[3] 67 days to break the $300 million mark. What makes this number even more remarkable is that, because of its three-and-a-quarter-hour length, it can show only three times a day. On the Internet, the movie's Web site is averaging 4 million hits daily. By all estimates, before the end of next month "Titanic" will be the first billion-dollar movie ever released.

Movies this popular are usually shunned by the Academy[4], but Cameron's epic is breaking all the rules. The 14 Oscar nominations it received last week — including bids for 22-year-old Kate Winslet and 87-year-old Gloria Stuart[5] — ties the record set 47 years ago by "All About Eve,"[6] a movie it couldn't resemble less. It's the odds-on favorite to win best picture.

In the executive suites of Twentieth Century Fox[7], panic has been replaced by jubilation. Having hedged their bet on the most expensive movie ever made by giving Paramount North American[8] rights for a $65 million investment, Fox had little hope of breaking even[9]. Now both studios are looking at profits that could well surpass $100 million apiece. (Once both studios recoup their investments, all the revenues — including video, television and soundtrack — go into a pot that is split 60—40 in Fox's favor.)

Like all megahits, the movie has become a kind of religion. And as with all religions, you don't worship at the altar just once. Normally, films draw a 2 percent repeat audience; "Titanic" is drawing 20 percent. Consider these highly unusual statistics: 45 percent of all the women under 25 who have seen the movie have seen it again. What's particularly surprised the studios is that 37 percent of the audience is older than 25 — a larger percentage of adults than was expected. In Chicago, 28-year-old Maria Federici is on her way to see it a fifth time with her boyfriend and his mother. "I don't normally see movies twice. This is kind of weird for me,"[10] she confesses. "It's totally a chick flick. You got everything you want — love and a little gore." Its appeal to women is well known, but 40 percent of the audience is male. Federici's boyfriend, Ken Lill, is on his third go-round. "I like action movies[11], but this one touches you," Lill says. "Guys can try to blow it off and say they're coming back just to learn about the Titanic — but that's bogus, it's a movie that touches you."[12] Sixteen-year-old William Rodriguez has a friend who's seen the movie seven times. "He took seven different girls to see it. And he still liked the movie after all those times," Todriguez says. "I don't really like history movies or love stories, but I saw 'Romeo and Juliet'[13] and that was the best. That's why I want to see this one."

Could the dizzying success of "Titanic" mark a sea change[14] in popular culture? It's not, on the face of it, anything a blockbuster Hollywood movie is supposed to be. Look at a list of the 15 top-grossing domestic films[15] in history, from "Star Wars" and "E.T." down through "Independence Day," "Batman" and "Twister."[16] Every one before it has been primarily aimed at guys. Not one of them is a love story. Most are set in the present or the future (only "Raiders of the Lost Ark"[17] is set in the past, but no one thought of it as a period picture[18]). There's nothing you could remotely think of as a tragic romance. None with the exception of "E.T." and "Forrest Gump," even tries to put a lump in your throat.[19] Nor was "Titanic" designed, as so many movies are today, to generate merchandising tie-ins.

Here we are in the midst of a deeply cynical, pre-millennium age, where the smirk of every hip TV host is dripping with irony and Madison Avenue sells its products with edge and attitude,[20] and the country is losing its heart to a movie that's 100 percent cynicism-free. "Titanic's" archetypes of good and evil, its star-crossed lovers, its handcuffed-to-the-post cliffhangers are as foursquare and primal as anything from a D. W. Griffith silent movie.[21] Wasn't this supposed to be the age of Tarantino?[22] It turns out that what young people were starved for was a movie that could make them feel, a movie that could make them weep, a huge, bigger-than-life romantic wallow.[23] With its passionate love story framed by the epic sweep of a true historical event, "Titanic" is the "Gone With the Wind" of its generation. Its God's-eye vistas of human folly and human heroism seem to answer a need to see the world in life-changing perspective.[24]

Gina Latta, an 18-year-old freshman at Lewis & Clark College in Portland, Ore., is more than a little embarrassed at how much she likes "Titanic." "I think the dialogue was incredibly cheesy," she says, before admitting she's seen it four times. Latta, who wears blue nail polish has her ears triple pierced and counts David Lynch's surreal "Lost Highway" among her favorite movies, would not seem to be the sort who would let an Edwardian Age love story get to her, yet she is powerless in its grip.[25] "The first time I saw it, I got out of the theater and I was having a cigarette with a friend and we couldn't stop crying. I was so overwhelmed at how sad it was." Like many other Titanic addicts, she has found herself haunting her local bookstore, surreptitiously reading the many Titanic books on the market. She would have bought them if she had had the money (the $20 paperback of "James Cameron's Titanic" is No. 1 on The New York Times's best-seller list; even its $50 hardback version is a best seller). This grunge-music[26] aficionado has also bought the soundtrack — helping to make it the fastest-selling soundtrack album in history (10 million units have been shipped worldwide). "I'm not obsessed," she assures us. "OK, maybe a little obsessed."

The pundits have been scratching their heads trying to figure out Latta's predicament, the New York Times weighed in with[27] an editorial attributing the film's success to the return of "the dead hero," says Camille Paglia. "People are sick and tired of shallow postmodernist irony and cynicism, people are ready for big passions, grand opera, big sweeping statements[28]. No more of these little independent movies, depressing, depressing, depressing." Pauline Kael puts it another way: "It's square in ways people seem to have been longing for. I'm not one of those people."

Mary Pipher, whose book "Reviving Ophelia[29]: Saving the Selves of Adolescent Girls" has become a bible for mothers of young girls, addresses the movie's appeal to teenagers. "It's not a common American script in the '90s because it's really about those two people having sex. It's really about his helping her become an authentic whole person. There's this tremendously personable[30], handsome man, whose main motivation is to save her life — both literally and figuratively-in the sense of saying, you have a right to have your own life. So the love story taps into the old myth of the damsel in distress being rescued, but it has a very modern spin that's really cool." (Cameron is not surprised that Pipher responded to his film: "She should like the movie. I read her book before I wrote the script.")

For a movie painted in such big bold, unambiguous brushstrokes, it's surprising how differently it's perceived by its fans. "Titanic" seems to hold an endlessly refracting mirror up to its audience. It doesn't just speak to teenage girls grappling with issues of independence. For men like Naoshi Kayashima, a 29-year-old magazine editor in Tokyo, it's a film about male honor. "I was impressed by the way a great number of men on the ship decided to stay on and go down with the ship. Remember those gentlemen who were fully dressed and waiting for their death gracefully? I could not help but cry. To me, it was a movie about how men choose their endings." For some teenage boys, the thrill is cheaper: many slip in after an hour to catch Kate Winslet's nude scene again. One of the movie's more unexpected fans is the theater director Andre Gregory, 63, the star of a movie as tiny as "Titanic" is huge, "My Dinner With Andre."[31] He's seen it three times, accompanied by a roll of toilet paper to staunch his sobs. "Most of my friends I have to say, hate it. I thought the movie was really about that old woman. I was moved that she could fight her way out of a life that was imposed on her by her family, and by society."

In explaining "Titanic's" success, you cannot, of course, discount the heartthrob factor. Coming off "Romeo and Juliet," Leonardo DiCaprio[32] is every adolescent girl's dream come true, his almost feminine beauty establishing him in the great tradition of non-threatening teen pinups. "Even at an early age, girls are looking for sensitive soul mates, a boy who's in some ways like a girl," explains historian Joan Brumberg, author of "The Body Project: An Intimate History of American Girls." "This has been going on for a long time, even before modern media. In the 19th century the equivalent was the adolescent female's infatuation with Lord Byron.[33]"

The thing about Jack Dawson — and what made him difficult to play for a child of the '90s like DiCaprio — is that he doesn't have a dark side.[34] DiCaprio had never played a character without demons. "How do you do that?" DiCaprio says. "I was asking Jim[35]: 'can't we add some dark things to this character?' And he was like, 'No, Leo, you can't. You just have to accept that he is like a ray of light. The character lights up the screen and lights up this girl's life'." "A lot of people who don't know Leo thought he was just playing himself," says Cameron. "Which is so far from the truth. Actors always gravitate to the guy with the biggest problem.[36] He had to mesmerize an audience without any tricks."

Cameron isn't surprised Leonardo didn't get an Oscar nomination, because of his teen-idol image, and because he believes there's a "resentment of too much stardom too fast." But he doesn't think DiCaprio is interested in being a star. "He wants to be an actor's actor. His personal taste in roles is more idiosyncratic." From his brilliant (and Oscar-nominated) turn in "What's Eating Gilbert Grape" to his risky portrayal of the poet Rimbaud[37] in the 1995 flop "Total Eclipse," the resume bears Cameron out. He's a heartthrob in spite of himself. But don't think it's only teenagers who are responding to DiCaprio's sensitivity. For Linda Hodges, a 36-year-old housewife from Alameda, Calif., DiCaprio's ardent, free-spirited hero "embodies the American ideal of man. It's important to know that all men are not total jerks. Love and sacrifice aren't values we see on the screen nowadays."

If this year's Oscar nominations are any reflection, the movie industry seems to share the public's newfound taste for the heartfelt, the straight and the true. In "Good Will Hunting," the brilliant, emotionally wounded hero must break through his protective shell to gain the capacity to love. Audiences weep. In "As Good as It Gets," the brilliant, wounded Scrooge of a hero must break through his neurotic shell to gain the capacity to love. Audiences laugh and weep. The lovable working-class blokes in "The Full Monty" discover their value as husbands, fathers and lovers through the traditionally feminine ritual of the striptease. Audiences weep for joy. If the fifth nominated movie, "L. A. Confidential," strikes darker and more complex chords, it is nonetheless, like "Titanic," a return to classical Hollywood filmmaking, a genre movie whose concerns are moral rather than sensational. You can read all this according to your taste: as a welcome rejection of the cynical and tawdry, a salutary return to romanticism and hope or, as some believe, as an esthetic regression, a retreat to the simplicities and lies of old Hollywood.[38]

Funny how things turn out. It wasn't that long ago that the vultures were circling what many thought would be the biggest fiasco in movie history.[39] When it became clear that "Titanic" couldn't make its summer-release date and was postponed until Christmas — a delay that added $3.5 million in interest to its $200 million budget — the Hollywood oracles prophesied doom. But Cameron's ship is as luck as the real one wasn't. Christmas turned out to be a godsend. "It's a time people are more interested in an emotional experience," Cameron says. And by January and February, the movie had a clear field.[40]

"I'm enjoying the ride," says a vindicated Cameron. "Realistically, I'll probably never experience this again." He's not rushing into another movie after this draining experience. He plans next to write and produce — but not direct — a new version of "Planet of the Apes." DiCaprio is ready for a break, too. He's done four movies in a row: "Romeo and Juliet," "Titanic," "The Man in the Iron Mask" (opening March 20) and a cameo in the next Woody Allen[41] movie, "Celebrity." Winslet just finished a low-budget English film, "Hideous Kinky," in which she plays a hippie mom in the '60s, who takes her kids to live in

Marrakesh. She's getting used to the strange but not unpleasant realization that "I'm suddenly very famous." Gloria Stuart is reveling in the belated glory of an Oscar nomination. "Just imagine — all these years, since 1932, when I came into film, and now it's 1998 and here I am!" Shirley MacLaine just called her to see if she'd be interested in playing a part in the first movie MacLaine will direct.

Still, there is one little thorn in Cameron's side.[42] You might recall that in his single-minded mania to get "Titanic" made exactly the way he wanted it, he gave up not only his fees but his percentage of the profits to keep the studio at bay[43] when his movie went over budget and over schedule. This sacrifice, it's recently been estimated, amounts to some $50 million. "I feel like a chump every time I discuss waiving my deal," he confesses. But now it seems even this misfortune will have a happy ending. Rolling in profits, Fox and Paramount are preparing to "do the right thing." According to one studio insider, "We will do something to make Jim happy. We all believe it is the just thing to do." Talks have begun to reinstate his deal. And though they are not contractually entitled to a bonus, DiCaprio and Winslet each may be the recipients of a million-dollar show of gratitude. When they all stroll down the red carpet on Oscar night, they should have more than enough to smile about.

From *Newsweek*, February 23, 1998

Ⅰ. New Words

aficionado	[ə,fi:sjə'nɑ:dəu]	n.	fan, enthusiastic follower
blockbuster	['blɔk,bʌstə]	n.	a highly successful film or novel
cameo	['kæmiəu]	n.	（电影、电视中）名演员演的小角色
cheesy	['tʃi:zi]	adj.	shabby; in poor taste
chump	[tʃʌmp]	n	a stupid person
damsel	['dæmzəl]	n.	maiden
fiasco	[fi'æskəu]	n.	total failure
gore	[gɔ:]	n.	some unpleasantly violent and bloody scene
heartthrob	['hɑ:tθrɔb]	n.	a man highly attractive to women
idiosyncratic	[,idiəsiŋ'krætik]	adj.	original, distinctive
jerk	[dʒə:k]	n.	*slang* idiot or annoying person
jubilation	[,dʒu:bi'leiʃən]	n.	celebration
megahit	['megəhit]	n.	sth (as a motion picture) that is extremely successful
mesmerize	['mesməraiz]	v.	to fascinate
millennium	[mi'leniəm]	n.	a span of one thousand years
odds-on	['ɔdz'ɔn]	adj.	having or viewed as having a better than even chance to win
primal	['praiməl]	adj.	ancient; fundamental
pundit	['pʌndit]	n.	a man of wisdom and knowledge
smirk	[smə:k]	n.	affected smile

surreptitiously	[ˌsʌrəp'tiʃəsli]	adv.	stealthily, secretly
tawdry	['tɔːdri]	adj.	俗丽的，非常华丽的
tie-in	['taiin]	n.	搭卖的广告，商品
waive	[weiv]	v.	to refrain from something, to give up

Ⅱ. Background Information

美国电影史

电影是美国最流行的娱乐方式之一。

电影在美国第一次出现的时间是1889年。1894年美国开办了第一家电影院。当时的电影与现代电影有天壤之别，只是一种"会动的画片"(motion picture)。

美国早期电影史最重要的人物是大卫·格里菲斯。他被后人称为"导演之父"。从1908年到1921年他拍摄了400多部影片。他常在影片中设置许多悬念(suspense)，使故事引人入胜。其影片结尾模式被称为"最后一分钟营救"(last-minute rescue)，成为以后好莱坞电影常用手法。

早期电影全部都是无声电影(silent movies)，因而这一时期也常称作"默片时代"。当时电影院门票为五分钱，这类电影院因此也称作"五分钱影院"(Nickel Theater)。由于票价低廉，百姓皆能承受，因而电影很快在下层民众中(in the bottom strata of the society)流行开来。当时上流社会认为电影表现粗俗，不屑一顾。因此，电影院便成了下层人聚集地。这种情况直到20世纪20年代才有所改观。随着越来越多的豪华电影院的兴起，上流人士逐步抛弃昔日的鄙视态度。

1923年以后，有声影片(the talkies)问世。1927年华纳兄弟电影制片公司拍摄的《爵士歌王》获得成功。有声电影从此真正立稳脚跟。30年代彩色影片的出现又为电影业增添了光彩。1939年《乱世佳人》的成功充分展示出彩色影片的魅力。

电视的出现虽对电影业构成一大威胁。但电影这一娱乐行业仍然有很大市场。美国现在共有11,000多家电影院和4,000多个汽车电影院(drive-in theaters)。

好莱坞(Hollywood)号称为"世界影都"，这里拍摄出多达75种电影。最能说明好莱坞特色的是西部故事片(Westerns)。这种影片充分反映了美国人的民族性格和精神倾向。

美国电影业迄今已有一百余年历史。推出了许多构思新颖、富有创见、反映时代特色和社会现状的经典作品，如《宾虚传》(Ben-Hurt)、《乱世佳人》(Gone With the Wind)、《公民凯恩》(Citizen Kane)、《音乐之声》(The Sound of Music)。

美国电影市场也充斥了大量渲染暴力与性(sex-and-violence)等质量低劣、黄色下流的影片(pornographic film)。相当多影片不适宜青少年。为了便于控制，电影通常标明类别：G级(general audience)适合所有观众；PG级(parental guidance)，孩子只有在父母指导下才能观看；R级(restricted to persons over 17 unless accompanied by parents)，有控制性的电影；X级(admission denied to persons under 17)，17岁以下者禁止观看的电影。

本文是对1997年奥斯卡获奖影片《泰坦尼克号》成功因素的评论。

III. Notes to the text

1. chick-flick — a movie which mostly women would like
2. El Niño — "厄尔尼诺"现象
3. "Jurassic Park" —《侏罗纪公园》(a motion picture about a plan to build a dinosaur theme park that goes awry, based on a novel by Michael Crichton. Released in 1993, this box-office hit won Academy Awards for visual effects and sound effects.)
4. The Academy — Academy of Motion Picture Arts and Sciences(美国电影艺术科学院), an organization founded in 1927 at Hollywood, California, for the purpose of raising the cultural and technical standards of professional filmmaking. The academy is best known for its annual presentation of special awards of merit, called the Academy Awards. The headquarters of the academy is in Beverly Hills, California.
5. Kate Winslet and Gloria Stuart —《泰坦尼克号》中扮演女主角(Rose)青年和老年时代的两个演员 (It was the first time two actresses were nominated from the same movie for the same character.)
6. "All About Eve" —《彗星美人》[a motion picture about an aging Hollywood star. Released in 1950, it won Academy Awards for Best Picture, Director, Writing, Supporting Actor, Costume Design, and Sound Recording. Eve Harrington (played by Anne Baxter), an aspiring actor, befriends an older, successful star (Bette Davis), and gradually connives her way to stardom by betraying the star she set out to emulate.]
7. Twentieth Century Fox — major American motion-picture studio, formed in 1935 by the merger of Twentieth Century Pictures and the Fox Film Corporation. In 1985 the corporation was sold to Rupert Murdoch.
8. Paramount North American — one of the first and most successful of the Hollywood motion-picture studios
9. to break even — to finish with no losses
10. This is kind of weird for me. — It's rather unusual for me (because I am going to see the film for the fifth time).
11. action movies — 动作片
12. Guys can try to blow it off and say they're coming back just to learn about the Titanic — but that's bogus, it's a movie that touches you. — This sentence says that young men who have seen the film Titanic say they are coming to see it again just to look at the extraordinary set which duplicates the appearance of the original ship. The author says the film has a strong emotional effect on audiences, and the young men are denying that they are emotionally affected by the film.
13. "Romeo and Juliet" —《罗密欧与朱丽叶》(an adaptation of the play by William Shakespeare about two teenage children from warring families who fall in love. Released in 1968, this Academy Award-winning British and Italian joint production was directed by Franco Zeffirelli. Convinced that their families will never allow their marriage, the two lovers attempt to conceal their affair. When the families learn of their affair and a murder results, Romeo is banished from the city. The lovers develop a wild scheme to feign death and elope.)
14. a sea change — a dramatic change

15. 15 top-grossing films — 票房收入前 15 名的电影

16. "Star Wars" —《星球大战》;E. T. —《外星人》(a box-office hit motion picture about a boy who befriends an alien. Released in 1982, the film won Academy Awards for music, sound effects, and visual effects.); Independence Day —《独立日》(a film about aliens attacking Earth and humans giving them the big boot. Academy Award Nominations: Best Sound, Best Visual Effects. Academy Awards in 1996: Best Visual Effects.); Batman —《蝙蝠侠》(该电影由漫画改编而成,蝙蝠侠韦恩平时是个慈善的富翁,当他穿上蝙蝠衣时就成了罪恶的克星、正义的化身。他可以飞檐走壁,穿行黑夜都市,行侠仗义); Twister —《龙卷风暴》(An ex-husband-and-wife team of stormchasers rush to be the first to study the dynamics of tornados in America's heartland. The uncredited lead roles are the tornados, created with eye-dazzling computer generated effects. Michael Crichton contributed the fast-moving story. Academy Award Nominations in 1996: Best Sound, Best Visual Effects.)

17. Raiders of the Lost Ark —《迷失方舟的袭击者》(a box-office hit motion picture about archaeologist Indiana Jones's search for the Ark of the Covenant. Released in 1981, the film won Academy Awards for art direction and its innovative special effects.)

18. a period picture — a film which is set in another time period — like the 1800s or the 1950s

19. None, with the exception of "E. T." and "Forrest Gump," even tries to put a lump in your throat. — Except "E. T." and "Forrest Gump," no film is designed to move the audience. [①a lump in one's throat — a feeling of inability to swallow, caused by pity, sorrow or other strong emotions; ②"Forrest Gump" —《阿甘正传》(The title character leads viewers through an accidental travelogue of American social history from the early 1960s through the present in this revisionist fable. Vietnam, desegregation, Watergate and more are presented from the perspective of Hanks' lovably slow-witted character as he finds himself embroiled in situations he can't quite comprehend. Academy Awards in 1994: Best Picture, Director, Actor and Adapted Screenplay.)]

20. Here we are in the midst of a deeply cynical, pre-millennium age ... sells its products with edge and attitude. — 我们现在正处于世纪之交,这是一个充满虚情假意的年代;注重时尚的电视节目主持人矫揉造作的笑容饱含着讥讽,广告商极力欺骗以推销商品。(① hip TV host — someone whose dress or manners are sophisticated and up to date with the latest trends; ②Madison Avenue — a street in New York City, which stands for the American advertising industry)

21. "Titanic's" archetypes of good and evil, its star-crossed lovers, its handcuffed-to-the-post cliffhangers are as foursquare and primal as anything from a D. W. Griffith silent movie. —《泰坦尼克号》中善良与邪恶的原型,一对命运不济的情人和扣人心弦的惊险场面,完全与格里菲斯所导演的无声片一样真实可信。(① star-crossed — unfortunate; ② handcuffed-to-the-post — suspenseful, thrilling; ③ cliffhanger — a film which is exciting and full of suspense; ④ foursquare and primal — referring to the technique which is a solid basis for film plotting)

22. Tarantino — Quentin Tarantino, a modish film director, whose film is characterized by fastness, stylishness, gaudiness, violence.

23. ...a movie that could make them weep, a huge bigger-than-life romantic wallow. — 一部能使他们动情流泪、沉湎于大大高于现实生活的爱情的影片。("A huge bigger-than-

life-romantic-wallow" is a cynical way of commenting on the intense and somewhat exaggerated emotional component of the film which focused on a love affair between an unhappy rich girl and an exciting poor young man. Their love broke through economic and social barriers but then ended in his death as he sacrificed himself for her after the ship sank.）

24. Its God's-eye vistas of human folly and human heroism seem to answer a need to see the world in life-changing perspective. — The stories of people who are foolish and people who are heroic show us the range of human nature so that we can see the same actions or potential actions in ourselves, thereby teaching us to change our lives for the better and not continue to live in narrow and selfish ways.

25. Latta, who wears blue nail polish, has her ears triple pierced and counts David Lynch's surreal "Lost Highway" among her favorite movies, would not seem to be the sort who would let an Edwardian Age love story get to her, yet she is powerless in its grip. — Latta涂着蓝色的指甲油,扎了三重耳眼,David Lynch的超现实主义电影《妖夜荒踪》是她喜欢的电影之一。她似乎不是能被一部描写爱德华时代的爱情片打动的人,然而,她却被这部电影深深打动了。（①an Edwardian Age love story — referring to the film "Titanic" which depicted a love story that happened in the Edwardian Age; ②powerless in its grip — completely overcome by the movie emotionally; ③"Lost Highway" — 1997年十佳电影之一）

26. grunge-music — 格郎基音乐(a style of rock music that is associated with old-looking, untidy clothes and is characterized by lots of electronic guitars and drums.）

27. to weigh in (with) — to join in an argument

28. big sweeping statement — general, but having deeper, more complex yet widely applicable ideas, related to what in literature studies is called a "universal statement," suggesting it applies to all times and places.

29. Ophelia — 奥菲莉亚(heroine in Shakespeare's tragedy "Hamlet")

30. personable — attractive

31. "My Dinner With Andre" — 《与安德雷吃晚餐》[a motion picture about a long conversation between a playwright and a theater director. Released in 1981, this film was written by Wallace Shawn and Andre Gregory, who play the principal roles in the movie. Over dinner at a restaurant, Wally (played by Shawn) and Andre (Gregory) discuss their philosophies and their experiences.]

32. Leonardo DiCaprio — an actor who plays the part of Jack Dawson (the hero) in "Titanic"

33. Lord Byron — 英国浪漫派诗人拜伦,据说他也具有"女性美"。

34. The thing about Jack Dawson ... is that he doesn't have a dark side. — The character Jack in "Titanic" doesn't have any flaw, so DiCaprio (a contemporary child) found it difficult to play such a character.

35. Jim — James的昵称,此处指《泰坦尼克号》的导演James Cameron

36. Actors always gravitate to the guy with the biggest problem. — Actors like to play a character with dark sides.

37. Rimbaud — French poet, who was born in 1854 and died in 1891

38. ...as a welcome rejection of the cynical and tawdry, a salutary return to romanticism and hope or, as some believe, as an esthetic regression, a retreat to the simplicities and

lies of old Hollywood. —— 是对愤世嫉俗和华而不实风气的可喜摒弃,是浪漫和希望的有益回归;或者如某些人所信的那样是艺术的倒退,是"旧"好莱坞无知和谎言的复活。

39. It wasn't that long ago that the vultures were circling what many thought would be the biggest fiasco in movie history. —— 不久前秃鹫还在上空盘旋,等着这个电影史上最大的失败者寿终正寝时好大饱口福。(Here the film is compared to prey.)

40. ... the movie had a clear field. —— ... the film's way to a big success was free of any obstacle.

41. Woody Allen —— 伍迪·艾伦(American motion-picture director, screenwriter, actor, and author, best known for his bittersweet comic films)

42. Still, there is one little thorn in Cameron's side. —— There is something that keeps upsetting Cameron. (a thorn in one's side/flesh —— a continual cause of annoyance)

43. to keep something at bay —— to keep something under control

IV. Language Features

报刊用喻特色

为了使语言浅显易懂,生动活泼,新闻报道常用比喻性词语(metaphorical words)。本文也是如此,标题就是很好的一例。

西方报刊在选择消息时往往侧重于"能引起情感联系"的趣味新闻。特别是那些能产生威尔伯·施拉姆博士(Dr. Wiber Schramm)所定名为"瞬即心理报酬"(immediate reward)的新闻。在文字应用上也明显反映了这种倾向。暴力、性爱等相关的比喻表达法常被使用。如:用 courting(求爱)比喻 seek friendly relations(寻求友好关系);用 marriage 或 wedding(结婚、联姻)表示 close association 或 union(密切的关系或联盟);用 divorce(离婚)比喻 breakup of relationship(关系破裂);用 flirt(调情)表示 make an insincere proposition of friendly relationship(提出并无诚意的建立友好关系的建议);以 sexy(有性感的)表示 attractive(吸引人的)或 interesting(有趣的)。

新闻报道中"暴力""战争"等比喻词语使用也很普遍。"冲突""辩论""争吵""比赛""竞争"都可能被说成是战争。例如 war on poverty(向贫穷开战); war on cancer(向癌症开战); war on inflation(向通货膨胀开战); war on corruption(向腐败开战); a war of words(舌战); turf war(争夺势力范围战); trade war(贸易战); propaganda war(宣传战); spy war(间谍战); price war(价格战)。其他与暴力相关的比喻词语还有: blitz(闪电战); barrage(齐射式的攻击); offensive(攻势); counterattack(反攻); crossfire(交叉火力); breakthrough(突围); salvo(火枪齐射); attack(进攻); explosion(爆炸); battle(战役); fight(战斗)。例如,

... the "Oppo War" is on. Last week Ross Perot and George Bush engaged in an Oppo skirmish so nasty that they declared a truce with Perot bloodied and the Bush campaign on the offensive, the on-the-record, overt lines of Oppo attack ceased. But the covert hostilities — the private nudges to the press, the hunt for documents — continue. [Oppo war 这里指攻击丑化对手的负面竞选(negative campaigning)](*Newsweek*)

应该指出的是,这类比喻属于夸张词语,如果夸张失度,便会"使读者在他们的连珠炮的震鸣声里很快感到疲倦"。(王佐良,1982:96)

V. Analysis of the Content

1. Among the following statements, _____ is false.
   A. The Academy usually preferred highly popular movies.
   B. The French are not supposed to see the same film more than twice.
   C. The film company, Twentieth Century Fox, didn't anticipate "Titanic" would be a hit.
   D. "Titanic" is a love story.
2. Young people are starved for _____.
   A. action movies   B. epics
   C. tragic romances   D. love stories
3. People loved "Titanic" because _____.
   A. it was a film about independence of women
   B. it was a film about male honor
   C. it was a film which could make them feel and make them weep
   D. all of the above
4. DiCaprio didn't get an Oscar nomination because _____.
   A. he didn't want to be a star   B. he was an actor's actor
   C. he was a heartthrob   D. of his teen-idol image
5. From the article, we know that _____.
   A. "Titanic" was welcomed by people only in the western world
   B. the film studio, the director and all the actors and actresses made a large fortune
   C. the miss of the summer-release deadline was a hidden blessing for the film
   D. none of the above

VI. Questions on the Article

1. Who is James Cameron?
2. Does the Academy favor popular movies?
3. Was "Titanic" designed to put a lump in the audience's throat?
4. Is a love story featured by "Titanic" the theme for most Hollywood movies?
5. What was Gina Latta's predicament?
6. Did Cameron sacrifice anything in directing "Titanic"? What were they?
7. Why was "Titanic" so popular according to an editorial in the *New York Times*?
8. What's your opinion on the dizzying success of "Titanic"?

VII. Topics for Discussion

1. Is the box-office value the best scale to measure the quality of films?
2. Should our country keep the door wide open for Hollywood films?

Lesson 25

What Price Reputation?

Many savvy companies are starting to realize that a good name can be their most important asset — and actually boost the stock price

By Pete Engardio and Michael Arndt

A recent print ad by United Technologies Corp. looks deceptively like an assembly diagram for a model helicopter.[1] Study it more closely, however, and you'll notice that the color schematic of UTC's Sikorsky S-92 copter is embedded with messages aimed at Wall Street.[2]

Text near the engine trumpets 40% lower maintenance costs than comparable helicopters and a "health and usage system" that ensures the S-92 "always operates at peak performance."[3] Next to a view of the cockpit, you learn that the thermal imaging system[4] lets rescuers find people they can't see. Other text notes fuel efficiency that allows "more rescues per gallon" and paint with few compounds that harm the environment. "You don't have to understand everything we do to profit from it," crows the tagline. The underlying theme: UTC is a great investment because it is a leader in innovation and eco-friendly technologies that help the bottom line.[5]

More research went into crafting those messages than you might imagine. The $49 billion Hartford conglomerate has long been frustrated that the strengths of its individual brands may be well known, but as for the publicly traded parent, investor surveys showed "most view us as some sleepy Northeast company," says UTC Communications Vice-President Nancy T. Lintner.[6]

ECO BOOST

So in late 2005, UTC turned to a tiny consulting firm named Communications Consulting Worldwide, led by sociologist Pamela Cohen and former Ernst & Young strategist Jonathan Low,[7] pioneers in the nascent study of how public perceptions affect a company's stock price. A CCW team spent months processing a bewildering amount of assorted data UTC had amassed over the years. It included studies tracking consumer perceptions of its brands[8], employee satisfaction, views of stock analysts and investors, corporate press releases, thousands of newspaper and magazine articles, and two years' worth of UTC financial information and daily stock movements. After feeding the data into an elaborate computer model, Cohen and Low concluded that 27% of UTC's stock market value was attributable to intangibles like its reputation.[9]

The duo determined the way to drive up the stock was to make investors more aware of UTC's environmental responsibility, innovation, and employee training — points the company had not stressed publicly. To make sure investors got the message, UTC plastered the Sikorsky S-92 ads and others like it featuring an Otis elevator, a Pratt & Whitney jet engine, and a hybrid bus with UTC Power fuel cells, on four commuter train stations in Connecticut towns with high concentrations of financiers. [10] "The work we did with CCW guided the development of our ad strategy," says Lintner. "We're very happy with the results."

Call it the new science of reputation management. Corporations have long used sophisticated statistical models to predict everything from how much a new production process would hike efficiency to how much more soap can be sold with an additional $100 million in advertising. But a company's reputation among investors, customers, and the general public traditionally has been regarded as too squishy to measure with hard numbers or manage with any precision, let alone to prove cause and effect. [11]

Many investment pros scoff at suggestions they can be influenced by image manipulation. [12] And to most CEOs, corporate image is not something to fret about — at least, not until a crisis erupts, like an options scandal, employee class action, or ecological disaster[13]. Even when execs try to be proactive, it's often by gut. [14] Want to be viewed as a good corporate citizen? Order up a PR blitz on your charity work or efforts to go green. [15] Eager to land on a magazine's most-admired list? Gin up a strategy to game the selection process. [16]

But a more sophisticated understanding of the power of perception is starting to take hold among savvy corporations. More and more are finding that the way in which the outside world expects a company to behave and perform can be its most important asset. Indeed, a company's reputation for being able to deliver growth, attract top talent, and avoid ethical mishaps can account for much of the 30%-to-70% gap between the book value of most companies and their market capitalizations. [17] Reputation is a big reason Johnson & Johnson trades at a much higher price-earnings ratio than Pfizer, Procter & Gamble than Unilever, and Exxon Mobil than Royal Dutch Shell. [18] And while the value of a reputation is vastly less tangible than property, revenue, or cash, more experts are arguing it is possible not only to quantify it but even to predict how image changes in specific areas will harm or hurt the share price.

Of course, spin alone can't create a lasting public image. A company's message must be grounded in reality, and its reputation is built over years. And if there is a negative image based on a poor record of reliability, safety, or labor relations, "please don't hire a PR company to fix it," says strategy professor Phil Rosenzweig of Switzerland's International Institute for Management Development[19]. "Correct the underlying problem first." The biggest driver of a company's reputation and stock performance is, after all, its financial results, notes Rosenzweig, author of *The Halo Effect*[20], a book that details how quickly reputations can turn.

Smarter communications can, however, help companies with good stories to tell. By most metrics, such as return on equity, profit growth, and product quality, companies like UTC, Southwest Airlines, and United Parcel Service may compare well with top rivals. [21] But unless the message gets through to Wall Street, their stocks may trade lower than they could.

The trick is to decide where to focus amid dozens of factors defining a corporate image. As reputation expert Sandra Macleod of London's Echo Research Ltd. [22] puts it, there are "threshold expectations[23]" that every company must deliver and reinforce, such as good service and financial performance. Beyond that, priorities get fuzzy. Sure, it looks great to tell the world about your innovative culture or that you are the greenest company in your industry. But do these issues really move the needle with your target customers or investors?[24]

That's why companies are trying to get more scientific about reputation management. Many big companies now shell out $2 million a year on image research. This will be a tiny slice of the $4.2 billion spent on PR this year, but such research is growing fast. To get a fix on how companies are seen publicly, they are hiring firms like Factiva and Delahaye that use powerful search engines to track databases of all print, broadcast, and Internet coverage and to search for trends.[25] For around $100,000, for example, Factiva can plow through a database that includes 10,000 mainstream media sources from 150 countries and 14 million blogs and tell clients whether their press is positive or negative on key issues.

MINE OF DATA

A host of small consulting firms including CCW, a subsidiary of Omnicom Group's Fleishman-Hillard PR agency, and KDPaine & Partners, a Durham boutique, mine this data with remarkable precision to steer client corporations to the most effective messages and away from those that should be ignored.[26] "Not long ago, there wasn't much science behind media tracking," says Warren Weeks, CEO of Australian reputation analysis firm Cubit Media Research, whose clients include Microsoft, SAP, and Ford.[27] "With today's technology, we can find every scrap of information on what is said about a company, second by second, and correlate that to movements in the share price."

Work done by Echo Research for SABMiller PLC provides an illustration of the process.[28] The South African beer giant had enjoyed a great reputation among investors for its ability to acquire and manage brewers in fast-growing emerging markets. But SAB's stock suffered a year after its $5.6 billion takeover of Miller Brewing Co. in 2002. First, Echo turned to providers like Factiva and CyberAlert[29], which tracks Internet news and blogs, to collect all articles on SAB appearing in financial media in Britain, the U.S., and South Africa over a one-year period. From the company, Echo secured all stock analyst reports. Echo staff read and analyzed each piece and determined whether the articles or analyst comments were positive, negative, or neutral on key points, such as SAB's financial performance, leadership quality, and ethics. It compared this data against moves in the stock of SAB and its top competitors.

Echo pinpointed which journalists had the most influence on daily stock movements — and which analysts they talked to. It also found a strong correlation between a 57% increase in unfavorable articles in the spring of 2003 and SAB's weak stock price. Digging further, it learned the biggest factor was continuing weakness at Miller. The market expected a faster turnaround, raising doubts about SAB'S U.S. expansion.

Echo recommended that SAB change its communications strategy to talk more consistently about gradual but steady progress at Miller, and thus restore confidence in SAB's leadership. Since mid-2003, SABMiller's stock has soared from around 6 to 24.[30] But the brewer says the stock gains reflect its stronger financial performance: Revenues have doubled since 2003, while operating profits have more than tripled. "Echo's research was considered an expensive expression of what was abundantly obvious to anyone with eyes in their head," says Nigel Fairbrass, SABMiller's media-relations chief. "While I would acknowledge that an ability to specifically evaluate PR activity in stock value sounds seductive, it betrays a misapprehension of the complexities and inefficiencies of equity markets.[31]" Macleod agrees such analysis alone doesn't explain stock moves but says many clients find outside analysis helpful.

Now reputation wonks are trying to take this to the next level — to enable companies to hone their message to attain specific financial outcomes. Procter & Gamble Co., one of the first companies to do consumer research and test marketing, applies statistical tools developed to guide its marketing of soaps and shampoos to promote the P&G corporate brand. Other companies such as UTC, Southwest Airlines, UPS, and AT&T[32] are turning to consultancies like CCW.

CCW's Low and Cohen have spent more than a decade developing ways to measure intangible corporate assets, especially reputation factors that can affect the bottom line. "There are plenty of data measuring the visibility and credibility of a company," says Low. "But there have been no data showing how communications adds value to a company." Says corporate communications professor Paul A. Argenti of Dartmouth's Tuck School of Business, also a CCW partner: "If we can get this right, we have found the holy grail of communications."[33]

The method works like this. Cohen first takes data on a company's daily stock movements for a certain period, say two years. She then collects data on its financial disclosures and economic conditions at both the national and industry level. She runs a statistical model to determine how much of the stock movement is due to financial performance and how much to outside factors such as the economy.

After adjusting for these influences, she loads in less obvious factors.[34] Drawing on reams of data on media coverage, opinion surveys, investor interviews, the company's public statements, reputation rankings in magazines, and other sources, she runs through several dozen reputation-related issues to see if they move the stock. Do messages about the company's employee relations, governance, or environmental efforts have impact, for example? If so, how many cents per share can be explained that way?

SKEPTICISM

Opinions are mixed about how much credence to put in such predictions. UTC is thrilled with CCW's work. Since launching its ad campaign in September, the number of financiers viewing UTC as an innovation leader has leaped by 10 percentage points, says an annual survey by researcher Lippincott Mercer. UTC thinks this may have contributed to the 16% rise in UTC's stock, far outpacing the Standard & Poor's 500-stock index and rival General Electric Corp.[35]

Other companies say it's too early to tell whether their new communications strategies have had any impact on sales or their stock. But investment pros, not surprisingly, are dubious. "Very little, very little," said stock analyst Raymond F. Neidl of Calyon Securities when asked how much he thinks PR influences his investment decisions on Southwest Airlines, which he covers. "The markets are smarter than that."

Perhaps. Yet the fact that corporations are commissioning such intricate work shows image management has come a long way.[36] Just a decade ago, it largely meant crisis management or tracking media references through news clippings. But by the late 1990s, investors began to recognize reputation was in part responsible for the sky-high market values of the likes of Cisco Systems Inc. and Amazon. com Inc. , companies with relatively few brick-and-mortar assets such as factories, machines, and real estate.[37]

Interest really took off after the tech bust and accounting scandals of 2001, which made investors more aware of risks if a company's reputation is trashed by governance and leadership lapses.[38] Companies also realized their shares were increasingly vulnerable to negative publicity over employee and social practices.

This may explain why many once-cagey companies are returning more reporters' phone calls. By shunning the media, P&G realized in the late '90s that it had little influence in the way journalists framed its corporate identity.[39] Now the consumer-products giant says it uses the same approach in crafting its messages to the media that it has used to market its consumer brands. To learn how it's being perceived, P&G commissions surveys of journalists and tests key messages with focus groups. It also makes sure its messages are parlayed to suppliers and employees, and carried in ads and PR. Then it tracks media pickup to adjust its talking points.[40]

Southwest also leaves little to chance. The Dallas carrier[41] already enjoys one of the industry's best reputations, and Wall Street rewards it accordingly. Its $11.4 billion market cap is bigger than the combined value of the two biggest airlines, American and United, a gap that differences in assets like planes and routes don't begin to explain.[42] Still, when Linda Rutherford, Southwest's vice-president for public relations and community affairs, heard Low's pitch at a PR meeting two years ago, she decided to hire CCW to assess whether it was stressing the right points.

After crunching years' worth of data, Cohen and Low flew to Dallas last August with results that were eye-opening. CCW estimated public relations alone could move Southwest's stock up or down by 3.5%, equal to $400 million in market value today. The data also indicated Southwest was getting little return by stressing its budget fares — a familiar story.[43] Instead, there was more upside potential for shares if Southwest stressed its extensive routes and schedules. "We had a bit of an Aha!" Rutherford recalls.[44]

So Southwest has begun emphasizing long-haul flights and frequent service between many cities, points that seldom had gotten press. It also plans a third-quarter ad campaign based on CCW's advice. The effect so far: While airline stocks have fallen more than 15% overall in 2007, Southwest's shares are down only 5%, to about 14.80.

While these experiments are intriguing, the real test of faith in the new science of spin[45] will come when somebody risks serious money on it. Suppose a hedge fund really does unravel the secret that can boost a company's value simply by turning around its reputation — and uses that information to buy and reshape that company's image?[46]

The idea isn't completely far-fetched. Fashion and fragrance companies have long built successful businesses largely on brand image. That's why Fleishman-Hillard Eastern U. S. President Peter J. Verrengia thinks it's inevitable companies will one day manipulate their images with some of the same precision they use to optimize operating performance.[47] "Just as people reengineer corporations, they will reengineer reputations," he predicts. "The tools are becoming available." The question is whether companies are ready to bet their reputations on them.

From *Business Week*, July 9, 2007

Ⅰ. New Words

amass	[əˈmæs]	v.	to collect sth especially in large quantities
assorted	[əˈsɔːtid]	adj.	*AmE* of various different sorts
bewildering	[biˈwildəriŋ]	adj.	令人困惑的
brewer	[ˈbruːə]	n.	(啤酒等的)酿造者
cagey	[ˈkeidʒi]	adj.	not wanting to give sb information
craft	[krɑːft]	v.	to make sth using special skills
credence	[ˈkriːdəns]	n.	*formal* the acceptance of sth as true
crow	[krəu]	v.	to talk about what you have done in a very proud way
crunch	[krʌntʃ]	v.	(computing) to deal with large amounts of data very quickly
duo	[ˈdjuːəu]	n.	two people who perform together
embed	[imˈbed]	v.	to fix sth firmly and deeply in a surface or solid
fuzzy	[ˈfʌzi]	adj.	unclear
hone	[həun]	v.	to develop and improve sth especially a skill over a period of time
lapse	[læps]	n.	a small mistake
long-haul	[ˈlɔŋhɔːl]	adj.	(空运航线)长距离的
mishap	[ˈmishæp]	n.	a small accident or mistake
nascent	[ˈnæsənt]	adj.	coming into existence or just starting to develop
parlay	[ˈpɑːli]	v.	to use or develop money, skills, etc. in a way that makes money or leads to success
pinpoint	[ˈpinpɔint]	v.	to say exactly what the facts about sth really are
pitch	[pitʃ]	n.	*informal* 竭力推销的广告语,商品广告
plow	[plau]	v.	~ **through** to read all of sth even though it is boring and takes a lot of time
proactive	[prəuˈæktiv]	adj.	积极主动的
quantify	[ˈkwɔntifai]	v.	to describe or express sth as an amount or a number
ream	[riːm]	n.	~**s of** a large amount of
seductive	[siˈdʌktiv]	adj.	attractive in a way that makes you want to have or do sth
schematic	[skiˈmætik]	n.	图表
shell	[ʃel]	v.	~ **out for** *informal* to pay a lot of money for sth
tagline	[ˈtæglain]	n.	(产品广告中的)主题句
tangible	[ˈtændʒəbl]	adj.	that can be clearly seen to exist
trash	[træʃ]	v.	*informal* to damage or destroy
wonk	[wɔŋk]	n.	政策专家

Ⅱ. Background Information

企业形象

企业形象是企业在公众心目中的印象,它直接影响企业的股价,关系到企业的发展前景。

企业的良好形象是由多方面因素所决定的。美国公司一般注重以下四个方面的企业形象:产品形象、员工形象、环境形象和服务形象。

1. 产品形象。产品形象是企业形象的重要组成部分,常被称作企业的生命线。产品形象不仅是产品的质量,还包括实际效用、产品品牌、款式、价格、色彩、包装、装潢等诸多方面。最近一些年很多企业十分注重产品的使用操作简便(user-friendliness)。好的产品形象要靠长期精心打造而成。

2. 员工形象。员工形象不仅指员工的服饰外表,还包括员工内在素质、技术水平、服务态度、精神面貌和敬业精神。员工形象好就可以增强企业竞争能力。

3. 环境形象。环境形象不只是指企业的外部工作环境,而且指企业内部的工作关系。整洁优雅、先进现代的工作环境可以促进员工增强信念、重视信誉和提高效率,还可以产生良好视觉效应,使顾客产生好感、增加购欲。管理科学、上下和谐、互相尊重、彼此合作的内部工作环境会使员工奋发向上、开拓进取、增强企业的凝聚力。最近一些年,许多公司重视塑造绿色企业形象、迎合社会环保风尚,以便赢得公众对企业的信任。

4. 服务形象。如果企业只重视售前、售中服务,而忽视售后服务(after-sale service),便会失去顾客的信任和好感。美国许多公司意识到顾客是一种无形资产,可以随时转化为有形资产,带来巨大经济效益。一项调查表明:一个满意的顾客会引发8笔潜在生意,而一个不满意的顾客会动摇25个人的购买意愿。为了使顾客买得舒心、用得放心,做到真正满意,许多公司都保证及时提供商品配件,有的服务口号是"24小时内把零件送到世界各地"。美国很多商店遵照"货物出门、确保满意"原则,顾客如果觉得不合心意,只要商品没有损坏,均可退货。

这些年来,越来越多的美国公司意识到良好的企业形象的重要价值,注重公司商誉的调查研究。为了迎合这种需求,一些专业性商誉研究咨询公司应运而生。这些公司采用高科技手段对媒体大量资料进行分析,找出客户公司商誉所存在的主要问题,提出改进企业形象的措施。客户公司根据商誉咨询公司的建议,采用媒体有针对性地做广告,取得与公众的真正沟通,重塑企业良好商誉,从而提高企业的股值和市场上的竞争力。

Ⅲ. Notes to the Text

1. A recent print ad by United Technologies Corp. looks deceptively like an assembly diagram for a model helicopter. —— 联合技术公司最近所做的一则印刷广告看上去让人误以为是直升机的装配图。(United Technologies Corp. —— a diversified company whose products include carrier heating, air conditioning, aerospace systems, etc.)

2. ... the color schematic of UTC's Sikorsky S-92 copter is embedded with messages aimed at Wall Street. —— 这张联合技术公司 Sikorsky S-92 型直升机的彩色图表中印入针

对投资者的广告信息。(①Sikorsky —— 一家美国飞机和直升机制造商,由俄罗斯裔美国飞行工程师埃格·西科斯基于1923年创办;②Wall Street —— the U.S. stock market, here referring to investors who buy stocks)

3. Text near the engine trumpets 40% lower maintenance costs than comparable helicopters and a "health and usage system" that ensures the S-92 "always operates at peak performance." —— 发动机旁的广告文字宣扬说:这种飞机维修费比同类直升机低40%,其"部件质量和操作系统"确保S-92型直升机"永远在最佳状态下飞行"。(comparable —— similar in category and size)

4. the thermal imaging system —— 热成像系统

5. The underlying theme: UTC is a great investment because it is a leader in innovation and eco-friendly technologies that help the bottom line. —— 这则广告的主题是:联合技术公司在促进利润提高的创新和环保技术方面引领时代,因此是一家投资价值很高的企业。(eco-friendly —— not harmful to the environment)

6. The $49 billion Hartford conglomerate has long been frustrated ... investor surveys showed "most view us as some sleepy Northeast company," says UTC Communications Vice-President Nancy T. Lintner. —— 联合技术公司信息宣传部副主任说,总部设在哈特福特市价值490亿美元的联合大企业长期以来感到失望的是:虽然企业旗下单个品牌十分出名,但对投资者的调查却显示公开上市的母公司"被大部分认为只是东北部一家死气沉沉的公司"。(sleepy —— without much business activity)

7. Communications Consulting Worldwide, led by sociologist Pamela Cohen and former Ernst & Young strategist Jonathan Low —— 由社会学家帕米拉·科恩和曾担任过安永公司策略家乔纳森·洛负责的全球通讯咨询公司(Ernst & Young —— 一家金融服务公司,为客户提供审计、税务和业务外包等服务,1989年由英国Ernst & Whinny公司和美国Arthur & Young公司合并组建而成)

8. consumer perceptions of its brands —— 消费者对其品牌的看法

9. After feeding the data into an elaborate computer model, Cohen and Low concluded that 27% of UTC's stock market value was attributable to intangibles like its reputation. —— 科恩和洛将数据输入一个复杂的计算机模型后得出的结论是:联合技术公司的股票市值中27%是由其商誉这样的无形因素所决定的。(① attributable to —— probably caused by the thing mentioned;② model —— referring to statistical model)

10. To make sure investors got the message, UTC plastered the Sikorsky S-92 ads ... with high concentrations of financiers. —— 为了确保投资者得到这些信息,联合技术公司在康涅狄格州许许多多金融界人士出入的4个通勤火车站贴满了Sikorsky S-92型直升机广告和类似奥的斯电梯、普惠公司喷气机引擎和配有联合技术能源公司燃料电池的混合动力汽车的广告。(plaster —— to spread or stick sth all over a place)

11. But a company's reputation ... has been regarded as too squishy to measure with hard numbers or manage with any precision, let alone to prove cause and effect. —— 但是,一家公司在投资者、顾客和普通大众中的声誉一向被认为难以捉摸,没法用具体数字来计算或进行精确处理,更不用说证明声誉与股价之间的因果关系了。(squishy —— soft and easy to squash, therefore very hard to measure)

12. Many investment pros scoff at suggestions they can be influenced by image manipulation. — 许多投资专家对他们会受到形象操控影响的说法嗤之以鼻。(pro — *informal* a person who works as a professional)

13. ... a crisis erupts, like an options scandal, employee class action, or ecological disaster — 危机的爆发,比如期权丑闻、员工共同起诉或生态灾难(class action — *AmE* a type of lawsuit that is started by a group of people who have the same problem)

14. Even when execs try to be proactive, it's often by gut. — 即使当主管们设法采取积极行动时,常常也是要鼓足勇气的。(gut — courage, determination)

15. Want to be viewed as a good corporate citizen? Order up a PR blitz on your charity work or efforts to go green. — 想要取得优秀企业公民形象么?那就花钱安排公关闪电战,开展慈善和环保活动。(go green — show concern for the environment)

16. Eager to land on a magazine's most-admired list? Gin up a strategy to game the selection process. — 渴望列入杂志最受仰慕的公司排行榜吗?那就想出法子去影响其遴选过程。(①gin up — *AmE informal* to stir up; ②to game — to control or influence by tricks)

17. Indeed, a company's reputation ... can account for much of the 30%-to-70% gap between the book value of most companies and their market capitalizations. — 实际上,一家公司账面价值和市场价值之间所存在的30%到70%的差距有许多成分是由其实现企业增长,吸引优秀人才和避免道德过失的能力方面声誉所造成的。(①capitalization — the total value of a company's shares; ②book value — the value shown by account books)

18. Reputation is a big reason Johnson & Johnson trades at a much higher price-earnings ratio than Pfizer, Procter & Gamble than Unilever, and Exxon Mobil than Royal Dutch Shell. — 强生股票市盈率之所以大大高于辉瑞,宝洁之所以大大高于联合利华,埃克森美孚之所以大大高于荷兰皇家壳牌,商誉是其重要原因。〔①price-earnings ratio — 〔股〕价格收益比率(一种将公司股票的现行市场价格除以每年每股的收益得出的比率),略作p/e ratio;②Johnson & Johnson — 美国强生公司(创立于1887年,是一家规模大、产品多元化的医疗卫生保健品及消费者护理产品公司);③Pfizer — 美国辉瑞公司(创立于1849年,是一家以研究为基础的大型日用消费品公司);④Unilever — 联合利华公司(创立于19世纪90年代,是全球最大的消费品生产企业之一);⑤Exxon Mobil — 美国埃克森美孚公司(创立于1882年,是世界最大的石油公司);⑥Royal Dutch Shell — 荷兰皇家壳牌石油公司(创立于1907年,是著名的大型跨国石油公司)〕

19. Switzerland's International Institute for Management Development — 瑞士国际管理发展研究院

20. *The Halo Effect* — 《光环效应》(作者 Phi Rosenweig,该书全名为:*The Halo Effect and the Eight Other Business Delusions that Deceive Managers*《光环效应以及欺骗管理人员的其他八大商业谬见》)

21. By most metrics, such as return on equity, profit growth, and product quality, companies like UTC, Southwest Airlines, and United Parcel Service may compare well with top rivals. — 联合技术公司,西南航空公司和美国联合包裹公司用大部分标准来衡量都可与业内顶尖公司相媲美,比如其股份回报率、利润增长率和产品质量等等。

[①metric — measure system；②equity — value of a company's shares；③Southwest Airlines — 美国西南航空公司(美国第二大航空公司,该公司在全美航空业不景气的时候,依然一枝独秀,其营业额 2005 年升幅为 26%)。④United Parcel Service — 美国联合包裹运输公司(成立于 1907 年,是世界最大的包裹交付公司)]

22. London's Echo Research Ltd. — 伦敦回声研究股份有限公司

23. threshold expectations — 最低期值

24. But do these issues really move the needle with your target customers or investors? — But do these issues really produce any effect on the customers you aim at?

25. To get a fix on how companies are seen publicly, they are hiring firms like Factiva and ... and Internet coverage and to search for trends. — 为了确切了解公众对公司的看法,它们雇佣 Factiva 和 Delahaye 等公司用强大搜索引擎跟踪所有印刷媒体、广播和网络报导数据库,找出舆论趋势。[①Factiva — 道琼斯路透集团合资公司(该公司成立于 1999 年,提供重要商业新闻和信息。其信息选自 152 个国家,22 种语言资料。);②Delahaye — 美国一家著名的媒体咨询机构]

26. A host of small consulting firms including CCW ... mine this data with remarkable precision to steer client corporations to the most effective messages and away from those that should be ignored. — 有许多家小型咨询公司以出色的精确性进行数据挖掘引导客户公司采用最有效的广告用语,避用那些本应摒弃的用语,这些公司中有美国宏盟集团福莱希乐咨询公司附属公司全球通咨询公司和北卡罗来纳州达勒姆市的小型专业性派恩合股公司。[①Omnicom Group — 美国宏盟集团(一家规模宏大的广告和市场营销企业);②Fleishman-Hillard — 美国福莱希乐咨询公司(美国宏盟集团成员,是一家全球性公关咨询机构);③KDPaine — Katie Delahave Paine;④boutique — a small highly specialized company]

27. Australian reputation analysis firm Cubit Media Research, whose clients include Microsoft, SAP, and Ford. — 澳大利亚商誉分析公司丘比特媒体研究公司,这家公司客户包括微软公司、思爱普公司和福特公司。(SAP — 成立于 1972 年,总部设在德国沃尔多市,是全球最大的企业管理和协同商务解决方案供应商之一)

28. Work done by Echo Research for SABMiller PLC provides an illustration of the process. — 回声研究公司为 SABMiller PLC 公司所做的工作提供了显示这一过程的实例。(SABMiller PLC — 由 South African Breweries 与 Miller Brewing Company 于 2002 年合并而成立的公司,总部设在伦敦,为全球第二大啤酒集团)

29. CyberAlert — 赛门铁克公司(一家著名的数据供应商)

30. Since mid 2003, SABMiller's stock has soared from around 6 to 24. — 自 2003 年年中以来,SABMiller 公司的股价已从每股大约 6 美元飙升至 24 美元。

31. While I would acknowledge that an ability to specifically evaluate PR activity in stock value sounds seductive, it betrays a misapprehension of the complexities and inefficiencies of equity markets. — 虽然我承认具备准确评估公关活动对股票价值影响的能力听上去是有诱惑性,但这也暴露了对股市的复杂性和无效性的误解。(①misapprehension — failure to understand sth；②inefficiency — inability to work satisfactorily)

32. AT&T — American Telephone & Telegraph 美国电话电报公司

33. Says corporate communications professor Paul A. Argenti of Dartmouth's Tuck School of Business, also a CCW partner: "If we can get this right, we have found the holy grail of communications." — 全球通讯咨询公司合作伙伴达特茅斯大学塔克商学院企业通讯学教授保罗·A·阿根提说:"如果我们把这一点搞准,我们就找到了通向通讯圣殿的大门。"(holy grail — the cup or bowl believed to have been used by Jesus Christ before he died, that became a holy thing that people wanted to find. It is often used metaphorically to refer to sth that is extremely difficult to find or obtain.)

34. After adjusting for these influences, she loads in less obvious factors. — 把这些因素计入之后,她又把不太明显的因素数据输入进去。[load in — (computing) to put data or a program into the memory of a computer]

35. UTC thinks this may have contributed to the 16% rise in UTC's stock, far outpacing the Standard & Poor's 500-stock index and rival General Electric Corp. — 联合技术公司认为,公司的股票增长中有16%归功于这个因素,其股价增长幅度大大高于标准普尔500股指和竞争对手通用电气集团。[①Standard & Poor — 标准普尔公司(一家国际著名的信用评级公司,成立于1860年,为金融界提供有关股票的独立分析、见解和信息);②500-stock index — 500家公司股票指数]

36. Yet the fact that corporations are commissioning such intricate work shows image management has come a long way. — 然而公司委托专业机构进行这类错综复杂的研究这一事实显示,形象操控已经取得了巨大进展。(①commission — to formally ask sb to do a task for you; ②have come a long way — have developed or changed a lot)

37. But by the late 1990s, investors began to recognize reputation was in part responsible ... and real estate. — 但是20世纪90年代末,投资者开始意识到思科系统公司和亚马逊之类公司虽然拥有工厂、机器和房地产等实体资产较少,但却有极高的市场价值,其部分原因就是其商誉。[①brick-and-mortar — a building when you are thinking of it in connection with how much it is worth;②Cisco System Inc. — 思科系统公司(一家全球领先的互联网设备供应商);③Amazon.com Inc. — 美国亚马逊公司(一家经营网上零售的网络公司)]

38. Interest really took off ... and leadership lapses. — 随着2001年技术泡沫的破灭和会计丑闻的出现,使得投资者对公司治理和领导的过失所造成的商誉损害带来的风险更加警惕,此后对公司商誉的关注才真正开始。(①the tech bust — referring to the period when IT business was at a low ebb; ② accounting scandals — referring to the accounting scandals of companies such as Enron which overreported the amount of money the company was worth and finally ended in bankruptcy)

39. ... it had little influence in the way journalists framed its corporate identity. — 它在新闻报道对公司的形象塑造方面影响很小。

40. Then it tracks media pickup to adjust its talking points. — 然后跟踪媒体报道改进的情况,再对宣传内容进行调整。(①talking points — items that sb will speak about; ②pickup — improvement)

41. the Dallas carrier — referring to Southwest Airlines whose headquarters is located in

Dallas

42. Its $11.4 billion market cap is bigger ... don't begin to explain. — 它的 114 亿美元市场价值比美航和联航两家大公司的市值总和还要高,这种差距是飞机和路线等资产差别根本解释不了的。(①cap — capitalization;②not begin to do — it's quite impossible to do;③American Airlines — 美利坚航空公司,简称"美航";④United Airlines — 美国联合航空公司)

43. The data also indicated Southwest was getting little return by stressing its budget fares — a familiar story. — 数据还表明,强调机票价格便宜给西南航空公司带来收益很小,因为这种广告十分常见。(budget — low in price)

44. Instead, there was more upside potential for shares if Southwest stressed its extensive routes and schedules. "We had a bit of an Aha!" Rutherford recalls. — 相反,如果西南航空公司宣传强调它的航线更广、航班更多,其股价上升潜能更大。拉瑟福德回忆说,"分析的结果使我们感到兴奋。"(Aha — exclamation used to express pleasure that you have found sth out. Here it is converted into noun in the sense of excitement.)

45. the new science of spin — 新式宣传科学方法(spin — *informal* a way of presenting information in a particular way, especially one that makes your ideas seem very good)

46. Suppose a hedge fund really does unravel the secret ... and uses that information to buy and reshape that company's image? — 假使一家对冲基金确实掌握了仅仅改善公司的商誉就可提高公司价值的秘密并且采用这些信息去获取和重塑公司形象的话,那后果会是怎样?(hedge fund — *AmE* an investment fund set up as a limited partnership for investment private capital speculatively)

47. That's why Fleishman-Hillard Eastern U. S. President Peter J. Verrengia thinks it's inevitable companies will one day manipulate their images with some of the same precision they use to optimize operating performance. — 这就是为什么福莱希勒公司美国东部地区总裁彼得·S.瓦伦吉亚会认为必然会有一天公司要对其形象进行操控,其精确性有些类似公司优化经营运作。(optimize — to make sth as good as it can be)

IV. Language Features

标题句式

本文标题"What Price Reputation"是省略句,其完整形式是:"What Price Is Reputation?"。英语报刊标题语言高度凝练,经常采用省略手段。初读外刊的人由于不了解标题省略方式,往往感到理解困难。新闻标题常常省略下列成分:

1. 冠词

例 1 Actor in Crash (An Actor in a Crash)

例 2 U.S. set for missile attack on Iraq (The U.S. is set for a missile attack on Iraq)

2. 人称代词

例 1 Man quizzed after wife is knifed in sports store(A man is quizzed after his wife is knifed in a sport store)

例2 Anne and Baby Are Well. (Anne and her Baby Are well.)

3. 连系动词

例1 Cops under Fire (Cops Are under Fire)

例2 Bankers Silent (Bankers Keep Silent)

4. 被动语态或进行时的助动词

例1 Pensioner raped, Criminal jailed (A pensioner was raped, the criminal is jailed)

例2 Bulls closing in on sixth title, lead 3—1 (Bulls is closing in on the sixth title, lead 3—1)

标题除采用省略手段精炼句式,还运用下列手段:

1. 使用名词定语,省去前置词

例 Bread Price Rise (A Rise in the Price of Bread)

2. 使用标点符号替代词

1) 运用逗号替代连接词"and"

例 Rubin, Greenspan at odds (Rubin and Greenspan are at odds)

2) 使用冒号替代说意动词

例 Owen: Watch Me Get Better

3) 使用冒号代替连系动词,甚至其他动词

例 Tests: Akiwande has hepatitis B (Tests show Akiwande has hepatitis B)

Ⅴ. Analysis of the Content

1. The word "pitch" in the sentence "Still, when Linda Rutherford, ... heard Low's pitch at a PR meeting two years ago, she decided to hire CCW to assess whether it was stressing the right points." (Para. 26) means _____.
   A. level of a voice   B. throw of a baseball
   C. strength of a feeling   D. promotional talk

2. It can be inferred from Para. 27 that airline advertisements often stress _____.
   A. quality service   B. extensive routes
   C. low prices   D. schedules

3. The attitude of many investment pros towards the influence of image manipulation is _____.
   A. highly supportive   B. dubious
   C. objective   D. oppositional

4. According to the article, interest in image management really began to grow in _____.
   A. the early 1990s   B. the late 1990s
   C. 2001   D. the 1980s

5. Which of the following statements is False according to the article?
   A. A deeper understanding of the power of perception is beginning to take hold among savvy corporations in the U.S.
   B. Most of the companies in the U.S. believe that new communication technologies have great impact on their sales and stock.
   C. Many companies in the U.S. are beginning to see the importance of a good reputation.

D. Corporations in the U. S. have long used sophisticated models to predict the impact of a new production process.

VI. Questions on the Article

1. What is the problem which has been frustrating UTC?
2. What move did UTC take in late 2005?
3. What was the method used by the CCW team in the research?
4. What was the finding and suggestion made by the team's research?
5. What are the benefits brought by UTC's ad campaign?
6. Do most CEOs in the U. S. pay much attention to corporate image?
7. According to Phil Rosenzweig, what should a company do if it has a negative image based on a poor record of reliability, safety or labor relations?
8. How can a company make its image management effective?
9. By what means did Echo help SABMiller's stock to increase from around 6 to 24?
10. What change has taken place in P&G's attitude towards the media?
11. How did CCW's research help southwest to improve its PR? What was the effect of the improvement?

VII. Topics for Discussion

1. Is a company's reputation its most important asset?
2. Were the tech bust and accounting scandals caused by executives' lapses?

Lesson 26

Tech's Kickback Culture[1]

Inside the sweet deals that grease the industry
By Linda Himelstein and Ben Elgin

It was showdown[2] time in the Rockies. On the morning of Mar. 24, 2000, about two dozen engineers at Qwest Communications International Inc.[3] crammed into a conference room high above the Denver skyline for a meeting with the company's president at the time, Afshin Mohebbi. In a three-hour presentation, neatly outlined in a 20-slide PowerPoint presentation, the engineers complained that morale was sagging. They attributed much of the unrest to one festering problem: a growing culture of palm-greasing at Qwest. If top management didn't remedy the problem, the engineers would walk.[4]

The engineers said Qwest executives were receiving lucrative stock offers from companies angling for business. And this could entice them to steer big contracts to companies in which they held investments. According to the slides obtained by *BusinessWeek* and interviews with six of the engineers, Qwest all too often was buying inferior gear — while execs' personal stock holdings shot through the roof.[5] "Decisions were not based on what equipment performed the best or what would fit in best," says Kelly Marshall, a former manager of the lab that tested Internet gear for Qwest. "They were based on who gave stock options[6] to people making the decisions."

Mohebbi heard the engineers out, and they left the meeting with hopes that change was on the way. Little did they know they had stumbled onto a practice that has raged throughout high tech.[7] The booming stock market had minted a new currency: a plethora of preferred and friends-and-family shares from hundreds of high-tech initial public offerings.[8] Much of the industry was lavishing this new payola on the top brass of customers, partners, and suppliers alike — dividing the loyalties of execs between their companies and their personal portfolios.[9] "It's an ethical nightmare," says retired executive Richard Liebhaber, who resigned from Qwest's board in January, 2000.

High-profile cases of IPO payola already have rocked the investment-banking world. During the boom, Wall Street firms allocated coveted IPO shares to the private accounts of CEOs such as Ford Motor Co.'s[10] William Clay Ford and WorldCom Inc.'s[11] Bernard J. Ebbers, allegedly to win future banking business. On Dec. 20, regulators negotiated a $1.4 billion settlement with 10 investment banks that, among other requirements, barred such practices.

But a more pervasive form of palm-greasing has plagued the high-tech industry. A four-month BusinessWeek investigation has revealed hundreds of managers who were granted exclusive stock[12] in companies with which their employers did business. Interviews with 135 current and former executives from 87 companies, including Cisco Systems[13] and EMC[14], reveal an industrywide fever. The influence-peddling spread beyond customers and suppliers — even reaching so-called independent research houses that write industry reports and market forecasts.

Did the market crash put the kibosh on these excesses?[15] Not entirely. Even with fresh IPO currency in short supply, the culture of backroom back-scratching hasn't disappeared.[16] "Companies are continuing to be approached for stock by analysts and others who wield influence," says David Helfrich, a partner at ComVentures, a venture-capital firm[17] in Silicon Valley. Helfrich says two of his portfolio companies[18], which he won't identify, relented to pressure and granted shares to market researchers in the latter half of 2002. Such deals could pick up as the tech economy recovers and IPOs return.[19]

Giving gifts to curry favor in business has long been standard operating procedure — from a round of golf to theater tickets. Neither gifts nor stock grants are against the law. But legal experts say stock allocations[20] create conflicts that put individuals in positions where they could place their own interests ahead of their company's. That's why, long ago, much of the old guard in Corporate America[21] adopted rules to keep such perks from swaying its executives. But at many young tech companies, traditional conflict-of-interest rules are often a work-in-progress — and ignored.[22]

It's the New Economy turned Kickback Economy.[23] Consider a typical deal: After eight top sales executives at storage giant[24] EMC Corp. bought ultracheap, pre-IPO shares in a customer and business partner, StorageNetworks Inc., they started steering contracts to the upstart — including rich deals that some former EMC execs think should have gone to their own company. These contracts brightened the new company's prospects and boosted its stock. While this may have hurt EMC and its stockholders, it produced a windfall of $2 million for at least one of the EMC executives who got those cheap shares.

Just as intoxicating as early-stage shares are offers for so-called "friends-and-family" IPO stock. Such friends-and-family plans allow companies going public to distribute about 5% of their offering to whomever they choose. Those invited get to buy shares at the IPO price — a perk not available to the average investor. At the height of the bubble, IPOs were jumping an average of 65% in their first day of trading, virtually ensuring a large payday.[25] "The money to be made is so significant that it starts to look like outright bribery," says Craig W. Johnson, chairman of Venture Law Group[26], a law firm that specializes in advising high-tech startups.

These divided loyalties may have cost shareholders billions. Companies, along with their bankers, wanted friends-and-family participants to make a tidy profit[27]. For that reason, among others, they may not have sought top dollar for their offerings, according to research collected by Jay R. Ritter, a University of Florida professor of finance. This contributed to a $62 billion disparity between IPO prices and prices one day later for all public offerings[28] in 1999 and 2000. That money could have gone into company coffers, increasing the value for shareholders. "If it weren't for friends and family," says Ritter, "company executives would have pushed for a higher offering price."

Not all companies tolerate backroom dealing. A number of them, including IBM[29], Dell Computer[30], and Nokia[31], long ago established tough rules governing employee investments. Plenty of others, such as Microsoft[32], Sun Microsystems[33], and Computer Associates, put policies in place in the heat of the dot-com boom. Still, many corporate policies remain murky — leaving employees unclear about what's acceptable. "When you're very vague about what the rules are, that's when people get into trouble," says Michael D. Lambert, a former senior vice-president at Dell.

These conflict-of-interest investments rarely lead to an explicit quid pro quo[34]. In some cases, the amounts of stock are minuscule. Then the question becomes: At what point does a nice little thank-you become more like a bribe?

Tech-services upstart[35] NetSolve Inc., for instance, says it doled out chunks of its 1999 IPO to 42 executives at companies that were customers.[36] But no one received more than 100 shares. NetSolve's stock closed up 46% in its first day of trading, meaning 100 shares would have generated an immediate profit of just $600. "It seemed unseemly to say: 'Let us enrich you right before you make a decision about buying NetSolve's services,'" says Kenneth C. Kieley, NetSolve's CFO[37]. "But if someone asked, and everybody was doing this, we didn't want to be impolite."

For startup StorageNetworks, there was nothing small about its pre-IPO stock allocations. In December, 1998, eight EMC sales executives accepted an invitation to buy preferred stock in StorageNetworks for 50 cents a share, according to Securities & Exchange Commission[38] filings. StorageNetworks, a business that operates storage systems for its corporate customers, had the potential to become a customer, a partner, even a competitor to EMC.

After the investments, the EMC sales staff began recommending StorageNetworks to their customers. This business quickly grew to 40% of the startup's $6.3 million revenue in 1999. Thanks in part to this relationship, StorageNetworks was able to command a high share price when it launched its IPO on June 30, 2000. The young company raised $226 million that day. And its shareholders at EMC saw their investments rocket from 50 cents a share to $90.25. EMC sales exec Robin A. Monleon, for instance, turned $50,000 into more than $2 million in just two years, according to SEC filings and insider-trading records.

But as StorageNetworks grew and EMC developed its services arm, the two companies found themselves competing. It got so bad that in June, 2000, just days before the IPO, EMC sent a letter to StorageNetworks complaining that it was poaching its employees and interfering with EMC's customer relationships. "These guys were getting paid millions of dollars to push EMC equipment, not to recommend StorageNetworks," gripes John F. Cunningham, a former EMC board member who says he resigned in 1999 partly because his private complaint to top management about the StorageNetworks investments yielded no action. "No question, it had an impact on their day-to-day decisions. It was a tremendous financial incentive."

An EMC spokesperson says Cunningham never voiced any complaints about the EMC-StorageNetworks investments, nor was he aware of anyone else protesting. He adds that any business lost to StorageNetworks was a drop in the bucket of EMC's $6.7 billion in 1999 revenues. Through a spokesperson, Monleon declines to comment. StorageNetworks didn't return calls.

Tech executives and backers of startup companies admit they used their stock to gain an edge over competitors — or at least to get their foot in the door. Indeed, handing out shares often meant the difference between buyers taking a phone call and banishing it to voice-mail purgatory.[39] "It was a way to say 'thank you' and a way to reach people who we wanted to help us in the future," says Dick Barcus, former president of optical-networking company[40] Tellium Inc., which gave stock to executives at potential customers.

And executives were eager to invest. Take Cisco Systems Inc.'s Deborah Traficante, a former regional sales director who oversaw a sales staff of 150. In 1998, she was invited to buy 85,174 preferred shares in telecom startup MegsINet at 56 cents a share, according to a list of shareholders prepared for the Internal Revenue Service[41] that was obtained by BusinessWeek. The stock purchase came a few months before Cisco loaned MegsINet $12 million to purchase Cisco equipment. When MegsINet was bought 10 months later by CoreComm Ltd., Traficante's stake was worth more than $200,000.

Cisco says Traficante's investment had no impact on its relationship with MegsINet or on its decision to extend financing to the company. And Traficante's attorney says her behavior was appropriate and that she put all her gains back into CoreComm stock. They are now worth less than $300. Cisco did adjust its policy in 2000, however. Now, employees are required to get written permission from their superiors before accepting equity in companies with which they might be involved.

Few industry executives benefited as richly from suppliers' largesse as the brass at Qwest. According to public documents and BusinessWeek interviews, Qwest execs held prime stock positions[42] in at least a half-dozen suppliers, ranging from Foundry Networks to Tellium — much to the chagrin of the company's engineers. Indeed, one slide of their presentation to Mohebbi asks the company to bar vendors from "granting personal options[43] to key decision-making individuals." Mohebbi left Qwest at the end of last year. His home phone has been disconnected, and he could not be reached. Qwest says it has no contact information for Mohebbi.

Qwest's biggest conflict may have involved CoSine Communications Inc. and Shasta Networks, which is owned by Nortel Networks[44]. The two companies were vying to sell hardware to Qwest. Engineers say Shasta's gear cost less and could handle more than 100 times the amount of traffic than could CoSine's offering.[45] Shasta's product also provided access to users connecting through everything from cable modems to digital subscriber lines[46]; CoSine's gear could not. "Shasta was so far beyond where CoSine was that there was no comparison at all at the time," recalls former lab manager Marshall.

While Qwest bought gear from Shasta, it also bought from CoSine. In its initial purchase, Qwest ordered 35 CoSine boxes, recalls one engineer. Many of those boxes, say Qwest engineers, ended up sitting unopened in warehouses.

So why do the deal? Qwest engineers charge it was personal greed. At the time, at least four top Qwest executives, as well as an investment firm controlled by then-Chairman Philip F. Anschutz, held more than 1.6 million preferred shares of CoSine stock, according to public documents. A Qwest spokesperson will say only that the company has new management. Qwest changed its conflict-of-interest policy in late 2002 to prohibit employees from investing in companies that have a connection to Qwest. A spokesman for Anschutz says he is not involved in decisions related to small investments and did not influence the CoSine/Qwest relationship. CoSine declines to comment.

For some Qwest execs, investments in CoSine never paid off. Although the stock popped 63% on its first day of trading, a lockup on preferred shares kept Qwest managers from selling for 180 days.[47] Public records show that only Anschutz Investment Co., made a profit. Anschutz' company bought in at an earlier date (and a lower price), making a tidy $700,000.

Most friends-and-family stock, however, had no such lockup. That's why executives rarely passed on the opportunity.[48] It took Colin Dalzell, an executive at systems integrator MCI Systemhouse, just a few hours to decide to buy the shares offered by e-business software maker Commerce One Inc. in 1999. It turned out to be a wise investment: Dalzell turned $21,000 into $61,000 in a day. His $40,000 profit paid for a 1965 Cobra racing-car kit[49].

Dalzell says the payment wasn't enough to influence his dealings with Commerce One. He had worked with the software maker for years and says his relationship with the company was established long before the IPO. Still, he concedes that a conflict could have arisen. "If it had been for more money, I would have thought more about how much bearing it had," he says.

Friends-and-family stock also cements relationships with market researchers. Juniper Networks, for example, gave IPO shares to analysts at a smattering of research houses, including Yankee Group and RHK, according to Juniper's former director of communications, David Abramson. The idea was to garner favorable attention among influential analysts, he says. Abramson was fired by Juniper in January, 2000, and recently had a lawsuit against the company dismissed. While Juniper declines to comment on the stock allocations, the company says it did not need to buy influence. RHK says its will no longer take stock in companies it covers. Calls to Yankee Group were not returned.

Others dispute that there's anything to clean up. Frank Dzubeck, a networking analyst with his own firm, Communications Network Architects in Washington, D.C., admits he held stock in several startups, including Foundry Networks, Alteon, and Convergent Networks. He says it was payment for consulting services. Dzubeck says that hasn't influenced his opinions and he always discloses his ownership stakes to clients. "I'm always going to give my honest opinion," he says.

Taking Dzubeck at his word may be fine for some. But execs say the best way to guard against conflicts and questionable behavior is for the high-tech industry to adopt sharply chiseled rules[50] that bar stock ownership in companies where business ties exist. As recent events show, one person's conflict can be costly for many.

With Ira Sager in New York

From *BusinessWeek*, February 10, 2003

I. New Words

angle	['æŋgl]	v.	~ **for** to try to get sth by making suggestions
banish	['bænɪʃ]	v.	to force to go away
bearing	['bɛərɪŋ]	n.	关系,关联
chagrin	['ʃægrɪn]	n.	annoyance and disappointment

coffer	[ˈkɔfə]	n.	金库
covet	[ˈkʌvit]	v.	to long to possess
equity	[ˈekwiti]	n.	（某公司的）股权，股本
garner	[ˈɡɑːnə]	v.	*formal* to obtain or collect sth
kickback	[ˈkikbæk]	n.	酬金，回扣
kit	[kit]	n.	成套配件
largesse	[ˌlɑːˈdʒes]	n.	the act or quality of being generous with money
lockup	[ˈlɔkʌp]	n.	股票封闭期
mint	[mint]	v.	铸造（硬币）
minuscule	[ˈminəskjuːl]	adj.	extremely small
palm-greasing	[ˈpɑːmˌɡriːsiŋ]	n.	*slang* bribe offering
perk	[pəːk]	n.	special benefits
plethora	[ˈpleθərə]	n.	an excessive amount
poach	[pəutʃ]	v.	to persuade sb to leave a company and join yours
sag	[sæɡ]	v.	to sink or fall
skyline	[ˈskailain]	n.	空中轮廓线
smattering	[ˈsmætəriŋ]	n.	a small number
sway	[swei]	v.	to influence
unseemly	[ʌnˈsiːmli]	adj.	*formal* not polite or suitable
upstart	[ˈʌpstɑːt]	n.	暴发户
wield	[wiːld]	v.	to have and use (power, influence)
windfall	[ˈwindfɔːl]	n.	an amount of money that sb receives unexpectedly

Ⅱ. Background Information

商业贿赂

经过200多年的发展，美国经济称雄世界，出现了许多规模宏大、实力雄厚的跨国公司。美国之所以经济竞争力如此之强，主要原因在于它具有一整套科学的经营理念，具体表现在注重开拓创新、严格质量管理、紧扣市场需求、积极宣传推销和强调售后服务。但是，美国商界也存在一些问题，贿赂便是其中之一。

商业贿赂是指经营者为争取交易机会，暗中给予交易对方的有关人员和能够影响交易的其他相关人员财物或其他好处的行为，其表现形式有：

（1）馈赠现金和其他物质利益的实物回扣；

（2）提供高消费招待、酒吧包厢享乐、境内外各种名义的旅游机会；

（3）为对方解决住房、工作、提拔职务、出国留学等问题；

（4）为对方安装电话、包租手机、装修住房；

（5）为对方提供明显可营利的业务项目、物资批件及合同；

（6）提供其他非物质性的利益，如"性贿赂"。

除了上述方式之外,还包括假借促销费、宣传费、劳务费等名义,给付对方公司或个人财物;以报销各种费用或冲账的办法给以贿赂等等。

为了解决商业贿赂问题,美国采取了一系列相应措施。从美国的市场运作和社会监管方面来看,主要是靠反垄断机制、公平竞争机制、舆论监督机制、完善法律机制四大机制来杜绝商业贿赂。

美国惩治腐败主要是依靠两支队伍,联邦检察官和州检察官。地方检察长虽然官职不高,但权力很大,因为他们是由选民直接选举产生的,不受制于其他高官。司法部长可以任命特别检察官,调查包括总统在内的任何政府官员。特别检察官一旦上任,就只对法律负责,不听命于任何人。

Ⅲ. Notes to the Text

1. tech's kickback culture —— 高科技行业的回扣风气
2. showdown —— 摊牌
3. Qwest Communications International Inc. —— 奎斯特全球通讯公司(该公司 2007 年被《财富》杂志列为 500 强公司中第 178 名,雇员 37,000,总部设在丹佛市)
4. If top management didn't remedy the problem, the engineers would walk. —— 如果公司高层管理部门再不解决这个问题,那工程师们就要走人。(walk —— to leave a workplace)
5. According to the slides obtained by *BusinessWeek* and interviews with six of the engineers, Qwest all too often was buying inferior gear — while execs' personal stock holdings shot through the roof. —— 根据《商业周刊》获得的幻灯片以及对六名工程师的采访,Qwest 公司经常购买劣质设备,而公司管理人员们的个人股票资产却大幅增加。(shoot through the roof —— to increase very quickly)
6. stock option —— 股票期权(指在规定期前按规定的优惠价格认购一定股数的股票权利)
7. Little did they know they had stumbled onto a practice that has raged throughout high tech. —— 他们根本不知道他们所触及的这种做法在高科技界已经十分盛行了。(① stumble onto sth —— to discover or encounter by chance; ② rage —— to spread very quickly)
8. a plethora of preferred and friends-and-family shares from hundreds of high-tech initial public offerings. —— 数百家高科技公司新股发行时大量派发优先股和亲友股。(① preferred shares —— 优先股,指在公司的利润分配方面较普通股有优先权的股份; ② friends-and-family shares —— 亲友股,指公司配额很小优惠亲友的初次发行利润较高的股份; ③ initial public offerings —— 〈主美〉初次公开发行,首次公开募股)
9. Much of the industry was lavishing this new payola on the top brass of customers, partners, and suppliers alike — dividing the loyalties of execs between their companies and their personal portfolios. —— 高科技行业许多公司给客户、合作伙伴以及供应商高层管理人员慷慨提供这种新式的贿金,这使得公司的管理人员在忠于公司利益和忠于个人投资利益两者之间构成冲突。[① lavish sth on sb —— to give someone a lot of something; ② payola —— a bribe to secure special treatment; ③ personal portfolio —— a collection of shares owned by a particular person]

10. Ford Motor Co. — 福特汽车公司(世界第三大汽车制造公司)
11. WorldCom Inc. — 世界通讯公司(美国第二大长途电话公司,2002 年该公司财务欺诈丑闻震惊美国,其首席执行官被判入狱 25 年)
12. exclusive stock — 独享股票
13. Cisco Systems — 思科公司(该公司为全球领先的电讯网络设备和解决方案供应商)
14. EMC — EMC 公司(该公司为信息储存系统、软件、网络服务供应商,公司名称 E 和 M 字母是两位公司创始人 Egan 与 Mario 的首字母)
15. Did the market crash put the kibosh on these excesses? — 股市行情暴跌是否阻止了这种过分行为的发生?(put the kibosh on — to stop sth from happening)
16. Even with fresh IPO currency in short supply, the culture of backroom back-scratching hasn't disappeared. — 即使起始股发行很少,这种私下优惠交易也未消失。(①back-scratching — giving sb help in return for his help;②IPO — Initial Public Offering)
17. venture-capital firm — 风险投资公司
18. portfolio company — 投资组合公司(a company or entity in which a venture capital firm invests)
19. Such deals could pick up as the tech economy recovers and IPOs return. — 随着高科技经济的复苏以及起始股发行的恢复,这种交易会再次兴起。(pick up — to start again)
20. stock allocation — 股票配发
21. old guard in Corporate America — 美国企业界老牌公司(old guard — those who have worked for a long time and are unwilling to accept new ideas)
22. But at many young tech companies, traditional conflict-of-interest rules are often a work-in-progress — and ignored. — 但是许多新创建的科技公司传统的公共利益冲突处理规则常常尚未完善,并且被无视。
23. It's the New Economy turned Kickback Economy. — "新经济"已转变成了"回扣经济"。
24. storage giant — 信息储存大公司(giant — referring to a very large company)
25. At the height of the bubble, IPOs were jumping an average of 65% in their first day of trading, virtually ensuring a large payday. — 泡沫经济最热的时候,起始股上市第一天平均净值就暴涨 65%,使持股者实际上大赚了一笔钱。(① have a big payday — to earn a lot of money from a game; ② bubble — referring to bubble economy)
26. Venture Law Group — 风险投资法律集团(硅谷著名的法律服务公司)
27. a tidy profit — *informal* a large amount of profit
28. public offerings — 公开募股
29. IBM — International Business Machine(美国)国际商用机器公司
30. Dell Computer — 戴尔计算机公司(生产计算机、服务器、存储器和附件的公司)
31. Nokia — 诺基亚公司(该公司从事移动电话研发、生产和批发业务)
32. Microsoft — 微软公司(世界上最大的软件制造商)
33. Sun Microsystems — 太阳软件系统有限公司(提供为工程工作站、数据存储产品以及相关软件而设计的服务程序的网络服务器公司)
34. quid pro quo — *AmE* something given in return for something else
35. Tech-services upstart — 科技服务新贵

36. it doled out chunks of its 1999 IPO to 42 executives at companies that were customers. —— 该公司将其1999年发行起始股的相当大部分分发给了客户公司的42名管理人员。(dole out —— to give out an amount of money to a number of people)

37. CFO —— Chief Financial Officer 首席财务官

38. Securities & Exchange Commission ——〈美〉美国证券交易委员会

39. Indeed, handing out shares often meant the difference between buyers taking a phone call and banishing it to voice-mail purgatory. —— 的确，分发股票常常造成的区别就像买股票用电话和不用电话而苦等语音邮件。(①purgatory —— *humorous* a situation when you suffer a lot; ②voice mail —— an electronic system which can store telephone messages so that sb can listen to them later)

40. optical-networking company —— 光纤网络公司

41. Internal Revenue Service ——〈美国〉国内收入署

42. prime stock positions —— 最优惠股票行权条件

43. personal option —— 个人期权(option —— 指按规定价格在规定期限内买卖股票的特权)

44. Nortel Networks —— 北电网络公司(该公司为全球提供沉浸式呈现解决方案和高清视频会议解决方案服务)

45. Engineers say Shasta's gear cost less and could handle more than 100 times the amount of traffic than could CoSine's offering. —— 工程师们称Shasta公司生产的设备价格更便宜，通信量是CoSine公司生产的同类产品的一百多倍。

46. Shasta's product also provided access to users connecting through everything from cable modems to digital subscriber lines. —— Shasta公司产品还提供通过线缆调制解调器和数字用户线等各种途径连接进入用户。

47. Although the stock popped 63% on its first day of trading, a lockup on preferred shares kept Qwest managers from selling for 180 days. —— 虽然这只股票交易第一天暴涨63%，但是优先股的冻结使得Qwest公司的经理们在180天内无法抛售。(pop —— to go somewhere quickly, suddenly or for a short time)

48. rarely pass on the opportunity —— 很少推让这种机会

49. 1965 Cobra racing-car kit —— 1965年Cobra牌跑车全套元件

50. sharply chiseled rules —— clearly defined rules (chiseled —— having clear and sharp outlines)

Ⅳ. Language Features

词义变化

在现代英语中"culture"一词使用十分频繁，范围非常宽泛。因此，它的内涵和外延变得十分丰富，界定它的意义也就变得比较困难。Kroeber 和 Kluckhohn 在他们合著的《文化概念和定义评述》一书中曾列举了近300个文化定义。本文标题"Tech's Kickback Culture"可以视作"culture"一词词义泛化的一个例子。这里它具体表示"风气"之意。

词义扩大指词义从特定的意义扩大为普通的意义，主要有以下四种形式：

(1) 词义由特指转到泛指,如:economy(家庭料理 → 经济),orientation(向东 → 方向)。
(2) 词义由具体到抽象,如:arrive(靠岸 → 到达),place(广场 → 地方)。
(3) 术语用作一般词语,如:introvert(性格内向的人 → 不爱交际的人),bottom-line(账本底线 → 基本意思)。
(4) 专有名词成为普通名词,如:watt(瓦特),volt(伏特),xerox(静电复印)。

词义变化除词义扩大现象外,常见的还有词义缩小(specialization)、词义降格(degeneration)和词义升格(elevation)。

词义缩小有以下四种形式。
(1) 词义由一般到特指,如 exploitation(利用→商业色情利用),pill(药片→避孕药片)。
(2) 普通名词用作专有名词,如:the Hill(国会山),the City(伦敦商业区)。
(3) 一般词语用作术语,如:web(电脑网络),virus(电脑病毒),page(网页),server(服务器),memory(存储器)。
(4) 抽象名词用做具体名词,如:youth(青年人),counsel(律师),failure(不及格的学生),terror(令人厌烦的人)。

词义降格指词从原先表示中性意义或褒义转为表示贬义,如:peasant(农民 → 粗野无知的人),vulgar(普通人的 → 庸俗的),propaganda(宣传 → 宣传伎俩),gay(高兴的 → 男同性恋的),hussy(家庭妇女 → 轻佻的女人),villain(村民 → 坏人)。

词义升格指词从原先表示中性意义或贬义转为表示褒义,如:nimble(偷东西手脚敏捷的 → 巧的、敏捷的),shrewd(邪恶的 → 机灵的),craftsman(骗术高明的人 → 名匠),paradise(花园 → 天堂)。最近一些年随着人们健康意识、环保意识的增强,natural(天然的)和 green(绿色的)的词义也就升格,分别产生了"有益健康的"和"环保的"意思。

Ⅴ. Analysis of the Content

1. The term "old guard" in the sentence "That's why, long ago, much of the old guard in corporate America adopted rules to keep such perks from swaying is executive"(Para. 7) means _____.
   A. old soldiers
   B. old-fashioned people
   C. political conservatives
   D. traditional companies
2. Which of the following companies has no regulation against conflict-of-interest investments?
   A. IBM.
   B. Microsoft.
   C. Communication Network Architects.
   D. Computer Associates.
3. Qwest bought 35 boxes of gear from CoSine because _____.
   A. CoSine's products had better quality
   B. CoSine's products provided access to users connecting through everything
   C. CoSine offered better after-sale service
   D. some Quest executives had personal investments in CoSine
4. Which company's executives benefited most from supplier's stocks?
   A. Qwest.
   B. Nokia.
   C. EMC.
   D. Cisco Systems.

5. Which of the following statements is False?
   A. Executives were eager to buy preferred shares.
   B. The problems of palm-greasing raged throughout high tech industry.
   C. Stock offers do not have any effect on market researchers or analysts.
   D. Offering stock is an effective way to win contracts.

VI. Questions on the Article

1. What problem did the engineers at Qwest complain about? What was the cause of the problem?
2. What effects did the lucrative stock offers have on the interests of Qwest according to the engineers?
3. What problems has the four-month *BusinessWeek* investigation revealed?
4. According to legal experts, what problems do stock allocations create?
5. What did much of the old guard in Corporate America do about those stock grants?
6. What effects would friends-and-family IPO stocks have on all public share-holders? Why?
7. What is the intention of start-up companies in offering stocks to executives?
8. What's Cisco's new requirement concerning employees' buying of stocks?
9. How much profit did Zalzell gain from his shares in Commerce One Inc? How much influence did the investments have on his dealings with the company according to his own remarks?
10. What effect does friends-and-family stock have on market researchers and analysts?
11. What's Dzubeck's view on stock ownership?
12. What is the best way to guard against conflicts and questionable behavior for the high-tech industry?

VII. Topics for Discussion

1. Is stock offering a form of bribery?
2. Can America end businesses' kickback culture?

Lesson 27

The Last Kodak Moment?

Kodak is at death's door; Fujifilm, its old rival, is thriving. Why?

Lenin is said to have sneered that a capitalist will sell you the rope to hang him.[1] The quote contains a grain of truth. Capitalists quite often invent the technology that destroys their own business.

Eastman Kodak is a picture-perfect example. It built one of the first digital cameras[2] in 1975. That technology, followed by the development of smartphones that double as cameras, has battered Kodak's old film—and camera-making business almost to death.

Strange to recall, Kodak was the Google of its day.[3] Founded in 1880, it was known for its pioneering technology and innovative marketing. "You press the button, we do the rest," was its slogan in 1888.

By 1976 Kodak accounted for 90% of film and 85% of camera sales in America. Until the 1990s it was regularly rated one of the world's five most valuable brands.

Then came digital photography[4] to replace film, and smartphones to replace cameras. Kodak's revenues peaked at nearly $16 billion in 1996 and its profits at $2.5 billion in 1999. The consensus forecast by analysts is that its revenues in 2011 were $6.2 billion. It recently reported a third-quarter loss of $222m, the ninth quarterly loss in three years. In 1988, Kodak employed over 145,000 workers worldwide; at the last count, barely one-tenth as many. Its share price has fallen by nearly 90% in the past year.

For weeks, rumors have swirled around Rochester, the company town that Kodak still dominates, that unless the firm quickly sells its portfolio of intellectual property, it will go bust.[5] Two announcements on January 10th—that it is restructuring into two business units and suing Apple and HTC over various alleged patent infringements[6]—gave hope to optimists. But the restructuring could be in preparation for Chapter 11 bankruptcy[7].

While Kodak suffers, its long-time rival Fujifilm is doing rather well. The two firms have much in common. Both enjoyed lucrative near-monopolies of their home markets: Kodak selling film in America, Fujifilm in Japan. A good deal of the trade friction during the 1990s between America and Japan sprang from Kodak's desire to keep cheap Japanese film off its patch[8].

Both firms saw their traditional business rendered obsolete. But whereas Kodak has so far failed to adapt adequately, Fujifilm has transformed itself into a solidly profitable business, with a market capitalization[9], even after a rough year, of some $12.6 billion to Kodak's $220m. Why did these two firms fare so differently?

Both saw change coming. Larry Matteson, a former Kodak executive who now teaches at the University of Rochester's Simon School of Business[10], recalls writing a report in 1979 detailing, fairly accurately, how different parts of the market would switch from film to digital, starting with government reconnaissance, then professional photography and finally the mass market, all by 2010. He was only a few years out.[11]

Fujifilm, too, saw omens of digital doom as early as the 1980s. It developed a three-pronged strategy[12]: to squeeze as much money out of the film business as possible, to prepare for the switch to digital and to develop new business lines.

Both firms realized that digital photography itself would not be very profitable. "Wise business people concluded that it was best not to hurry to switch from making 70 cents on the dollar on film to maybe five cents at most in digital," says Mr Matteson. But both firms had to adapt; Kodak was slower.

A culture of complacency

Its culture did not help. Despite its strengths—hefty investment in research, a rigorous approach to manufacturing and good relations with its local community—Kodak had become a complacent monopolist. Fujifilm exposed this weakness by bagging the sponsorship of the 1984 Olympics in Los Angeles while Kodak dithered. The publicity helped Fujifilm's far cheaper film invade Kodak's home market.

Another reason why Kodak was slow to change was that its executives "suffered from a mentality of perfect products, rather than the high-tech mindset of make it, launch it, fix it," says Rosabeth Moss Kanter of Harvard Business School, who has advised the firm. Working in a one-company town did not help, either. Kodak's bosses in Rochester seldom heard much criticism of the firm, she says. Even when Kodak decided to diversify, it took years to make its first acquisition. It created a widely admired venture-capital arm, but never made big enough bets to create breakthroughs, says Ms Kanter.

Bad luck played a role, too. Kodak thought that the thousands of chemicals its researchers had created for use in film might instead be turned into drugs. But its pharmaceutical operations fizzled, and were sold in the 1990s.

Fujifilm diversified more successfully. Film is a bit like skin: both contain collagen. Just as photos fade because of oxidation, cosmetics firms would like you to think that skin is preserved with anti-oxidants. In Fujifilm's library of 200,000 chemical compounds, some 4,000 are related to anti-oxidants. So the company launched a line of cosmetics, called Astalift[13], which is sold in Asia and is being launched in Europe this year.

Fujifilm also sought new outlets for its expertise in film: for example, making optical films for LCD flat-panel screens.[14] It has invested $4 billion in the business since 2000. And this has paid off. In one sort of film, to expand the LCD viewing angle, Fujifilm enjoys a 100% market share.

George Fisher, who served as Kodak's boss from 1993 until 1999, decided that its expertise lay not in chemicals but in imaging. He cranked out digital cameras and offered customers the ability to post and share pictures online.

A brilliant boss might have turned this idea into something like Facebook, but Mr Fisher was not that boss. He failed to outsource much production, which might have made Kodak more nimble and creative. He struggled, too, to adopt Kodak's "razor blade" business model[15]. Kodak sold cheap cameras and relied on customers buying lots of expensive film. (Just as Gillette makes money on the blades, not the razors.) That model obviously does not work with digital cameras. Still, Kodak did eventually build a hefty business out of digital cameras—but it lasted only a few years before camera phones scuppered it.

Kodak also failed to read emerging markets correctly. It hoped that the new Chinese middle class would buy lots of film. They did for a short while, but then decided that digital cameras were cooler. Many leap-frogged from no camera straight to a digital one.

Kodak's leadership has been inconsistent. Its strategy with each of several new chief executives. The latest, Antonio Perez, who took charge in 2005, has focused on turning the firm into a powerhouse of digital printing[16] (something he learnt about at his old firm, Hewlett-Packard, and which Kodak still insists will save it). He also tried to make money from the firm's huge portfolio of intellectual property—hence the lawsuit against Apple.

At Fujifilm, too, technological change sparked an internal power struggle. At first the men in the consumer-film business, who refused to see the looming crisis, prevailed. But the eventual winner was Shigetaka Komori[17], who chided them as "lazy" and "irresponsible" for not preparing better for the digital onslaught. Named boss incrementally between 2000 and 2003, he quickly set about overhauling the firm.

He has spent around $9 billion on 40 companies since 2000. He slashed costs and jobs. In one 18-month stretch, he booked more than ¥250 billion ($3.3 billion) in restructuring costs for depreciation and to shed superfluous distributors, development labs, managers and researchers. [18]"It was a painful experience," says Mr Komori. "But to see the situation as it was, nobody could survive. So we had to reconstruct the business model."

This sort of preemptive action, even softened with generous payouts, is hardly typical of corporate Japan. Few Japanese managers are prepared to act fast, make big cuts and go on a big acquisition spree, observes Kenichi Ohmae, the father of Japanese management consulting[19].

For Mr Komori, it meant unwinding the work of his predecessor, who had handpicked him for the job[20]—a big taboo in Japan. Still, Mr Ohmae reckons that Japan Inc's long-term culture, which involves little shareholder pressure for short-term performance and tolerates huge cash holdings, made it easier for Fujifilm to pursue Mr Komori's vision. American shareholders might not have been so patient. Surprisingly, Kodak acted like a stereotypical change-resistant Japanese firm, while Fujifilm acted like a flexible American one.

Mr Komori says he feels "regret and emotion" about the plight of his "respected competitor." Yet he hints that Kodak was complacent, even when its troubles were obvious. The firm was so confident about its marketing and brand that it tried to take the easy way out, says Mr Komori.

In the 2000s it tried to buy ready-made business, instead of taking the time and expense to develop technologies in-house. And it failed to diversify enough, says Mr Komori: "Kodak aimed to be a digital company, but that is a small business and not enough to support a big company."

Perhaps the challenge was simply too great. "It is a very hard problem. I've not seen any other firm that had such a massive gulf to get across," says Clay Christensen, author of The Innovator's Dilemma[21], an influential business book. "It was such a fundamentally different technology that came in, so there was no way to use the old technology to meet the challenge."

Kodak's blunder was not like the time when Digital Equipment Corporation, an American computer-maker, failed to spot the significance of personal computers because its managers were dozing in their comfy chairs. It was more like "seeing a tsunami coming and there's nothing you can do about it," says Mr Christensen.

Dominant firms in other industries have been killed by smaller shocks, he points out. Of the 316 department-store chains of a few decades ago, only Dayton Hudson has adapted well to the modern world, and only because it started an entirely new business, Target.[22] And that is what creative destruction can do to a business that has changed only gradually—the shops of today would not look alien to time-travelers from 50 years ago, even if their supply chains have changed beyond recognition.

Could Kodak have avoided its current misfortunes? Some say it could have become the equivalent of "Intel Inside" for the smartphone camera—a brand that consumers trust.[23] But Canon and Sony were better placed to achieve that, given their superior intellectual property, and neither has succeeded in doing so.[24]

Unlike people, companies can in theory live for ever. But most die young, because the corporate world, unlike society at large, is a fight to the death. Fujifilm has mastered new tactics and survived. Film went from 60% of its profits in 2000 to basically nothing, yet it found new sources of revenue. Kodak, along with many a great company before it, appears simply to have run its course. After 132 years it is poised, like an old photo, to fade away.

From *The Economist*, Jan. 14th, 2012

Ⅰ. New Words

acquisition	[ˌækwiˈziʃ(ə)n]	n.	the act of getting sth
alien	[ˈeiliən]	adj.	strange, different from what you are used to
anti-oxidant	[ˌæntiˈɔksidənt]	n.	[化] 抗氧(化)剂
batter	[ˈbætə]	v.	to hit sth hard many times
collagen	[ˈkɔlədʒən]	n.	[生化] 胶原(蛋白)
chide	[tʃaid]	v.	*formal* to criticize
comfy	[ˈkʌmfi]	adj.	*informal* comfortable
complacency	[kəmˈpleis(ə)nsi]	n.	a feeling of satisfaction, especially without a good reason
consensus	[kənˈsensəs]	n.	an opinion that all members of a group agree with
crank	[kræŋk]	v.	*informal* ~ **sth out** to produce a lot of sth quickly
dither	[ˈdiðə]	v.	to hesitate about what to do
double	[ˈdʌb(ə)l]	v.	~ **as sth** to have another use or function as well as the main one
fizzle	[ˈfiz(ə)l]	v.	to fail or end disappointingly
hefty	[ˈhefti]	adj.	(an amount of money) large
incrementally	[ˌiŋkrəˈment(ə)li]	adv.	递增地,渐进地
in-house	[ˌinˈhaus]	adj.	within a company or an organization

lawsuit	[ˈlɔːˌsuːt]	n.	诉讼
leap-frog	[ˈliːpˌfrɔg]	v.	to jump over
lucrative	[ˈluːkrətiv]	adj.	producing a large amount of money
mindset	[ˈmaindset]	n.	a fixed state of mind
nimble	[ˈnimb(ə)l]	adj.	able to move quickly and easily
omen	[ˈoumən]	n.	a sign of what is going to happen in the future
onslaught	[ˈɔnˌslɔːt]	n.	a strong and violent attack
outsource	[ˈautsɔːs]	v.	(business) to arrange for sb outside a company to do work or provide goods
overhaul	[ˌouvərˈhɔːl]	v.	全面检修；全面改革
oxidation	[ˌɔksiˈdeiʃ(ə)n]	n.	氧化作用
pharmaceutical	[ˌfɑːməˈsjuːtik(ə)l]	adj.	connected with the making of medicine
picture-perfect	[ˌpiktʃərˈpəːfikt]	adj.	exactly right in appearance or in the way things are done
plight	[plait]	n.	a dangerous or difficult situation
poised	[pɔizd]	adj.	~ to do sth completely ready to do sth
pre-emptive	[priˈemptiv]	adj.	抢先的，先发制人的
render	[ˈrendər]	v.	to cause sb/sth to be in a particular state
reconnaissance	[riˈkɔnisəns]	n.	activity of getting information for military purposes
rigorous	[ˈrigərəs]	adj.	careful, thorough and exact
scupper	[ˈskʌpə]	v.	BrE informal to defeat or ruin
slash	[slæʃ]	v.	to reduce sth by a large amount
spark	[spɑːk]	v.	to cause sth to start or develop, especially suddenly
smartphone	[ˈsmɑːtˌfoun]	n.	智能手机
spree	[spriː]	n.	无节制的狂热行为
spurious	[ˈspjuəriəs]	adj.	based on false ideas or ways of thinking
stereotypical	[ˌsteriouˈtipik(ə)l]	adj.	已成陈规的，老一套的
swirl	[swəːl]	v.	to move around in a circle
sneer	[snir]	v.	to speak as if sth is not worthy of serious attention

Ⅱ. Background Information

"柯达"的破产与"富士"的幸存

柯达公司全称伊士曼柯达公司(Eastman Kodak Company),创建于1880年,总部位于美国罗切斯特市,经营影像产品和相关服务。该公司成立之后长期居于全球影像行业领先地位。

富士胶片公司全称富士胶片株式会社,创建于1934年,总部位于日本东京,是一家综合性影像、信息、文件处理产品和服务的制造和供应商。富士创业初期,曾出于对柯达的仰慕请求与其合作,遭到对方断然拒绝。

两家公司所经营的业务较为相似,然而到了2012年境况却迥然不同。柯达从1997年到2011年公司市值由310亿美元降至21亿美元,十余年蒸发99%,不得不于2012年提出破产保护申请。而富士2012年上半年累计实现销售收入134.38亿美元,营业利润为5.35亿美元。

为何昔日大佬步入穷途末路,而遭遇冷漠蔑视的富士却前途一片光明?

两家公司一盛一衰并非偶然,主要因素如下:

1. 公司文化因素。富士公司危机意识较强,坚信成功只是暂时的,挑战才是永远的,而柯达公司长期以龙头老大自居,危机意识淡薄,只满足胶片领域的改进和领先。

2. 经营模式因素。富士公司幸存和发展的关键在于其多元化经营模式,这一模式不仅减少了企业风险而且有利于顺利转型。富士一直比柯达相对多元,富士胶片业务收入最高时实际上也只占总收入的50%左右。柯达虽早在1976年就开发了数字相机技术,1991年就有了30万像素的数码相机,但到2000年,柯达的数字产品收入也仅占总收入的22%,2002年也只是25%,而这一年富士数字产品收入已达到60%。

3. 企业转型因素。富士根据自身的技术优势,将已有的核心技术和新市场的需求密切结合构建新业务,快速灵活开发有价值的新产品。例如富士将公司的抗氧化技术用以开发化妆品,赢得了可观的市场份额。柯达转型步伐一直很慢,未能及时大力发展数字业务。转型医疗业务时选择的药物研究周期较长,不能很快改变公司亏损局面。

4. 企业环境因素。企业环境不同也是一个重要因素。富士转型成功在一定程度上是由于富士在日本。日本企业管理者传统上实行终身雇佣制,一般是从公司一步一步提拔上来的。他们十分了解公司基本情况,也赢得企业员工的信任和支持。这种环境有利于公司稳定和转型。柯达公司高层管理频繁更迭,导致公司决策和转型难于延续。日本的股东关注企业发展,而不是短期利益,较少对管理层施压。而美国股东常常关注短期利益,容易对企业指手画脚,百般掣肘,从而构成企业转型的障碍。

Ⅲ. Notes to the Text

1. Lenin is said to have sneered that a capitalist will sell you the rope to hang him. —It's based on the following quotation from Vladimir Ilyich Lenin: "The capitalists will sell us the rope with which we will hang them."
2. digital cameras—数码相机

3. Strange to recall, Kodak was the Google of its day.—如今回忆起来觉得很怪,柯达公司在鼎盛时期曾(在技术创新方面)相当于"谷歌"。(Here, Google is used to emphasize Kodak's lead in pioneering technology during the period of its prosperity.)

4. digital photography—数码照相

5. ... unless the firm quickly sells its portfolio of intellectual property, it will go bust.—如果公司不很快出售其拥有的知识资产,就会破产。[①portfolio—holdings in the form of shares, bonds or property; ② intellectual property—anything which a person has invented or has the only right to make or sell; ③bust—bankrupt]

6. suing Apple and HTC over various alleged patent infringements—控告苹果公司和赫斯特电视广播公司侵犯各种专利权(①HTV—Hearst Television, a television broadcasting company of the US; ②infringement—an action that violates a law; ③patent—an official right to be the only person to produce or sell a product)

7. Chapter 11 bankruptcy—(美国)破产法第11章(Chapter 11 bankruptcy—a chapter of the US Bankruptcy Code, which permits reorganization under the bankruptcy laws of the US. It is available to every business.)

8. Kodak's desire to keep cheap Japanese film off its patch—柯达公司阻止日本生产的廉价胶卷进入自己销售区域的欲望(patch—referring to the area of sale)

9. market capitalization—the total value of the issued shares of a publicly traded company 市值

10. University of Rochester's Simon School of Business—罗切斯特大学西蒙商学院

11. He was only a few years out.—他离职才几年。(out—no longer in a position of power)

12. a three-pronged strategy—三管齐下的做法(-pronged—having the number of different directions or ways)

13. Astalift—艾诗缇(富士公司旗下护肤品牌,由富士公司将其生产胶原蛋白的技术、纳米技术和抗氧化技术综合应用所开发出的美容产品)

14. Fujifilm also sought new outlets for its expertise in film: for example, making optical films for LCD flat-panel screens.—富士胶片公司还为其胶片的专长技术寻求新的应用渠道,例如制造液晶平板屏幕的光学薄膜。(①expertise—expert knowledge or skill in a particular field; ②outlet—a way of making good use of sth)

15. "razor blade" business model—"剃须刀片"商业模式[又称"freebie market"(免费赠品销售),意指以低价出售,甚至免费赠送某项商品,目的是为了从该项低价或免费商品的配套商品销售获取利润]

16. turning the firm into a powerhouse of digital printing—把公司转变成强大的数码印刷公司(powerhouse—an organization that has a lot of power)

17. Shigetaka Komori—重隆小森(富士胶片公司首席执行官)

18. In one 18-month stretch, he booked more than ¥250 billion ($3.3 billion) in restructuring costs for depreciation and to shed superfluous distributors, development labs, managers and researchers.—在18个月的时间里他采取降价、削减过剩销售人员、开发实验室、经理和研究员等措施,用于调整的开支超过2,500亿日元(33亿美元)。(① book—to register; ② superfluous—more than you need; ③ depreciation—reduction of

value)

19. Kenichi Ohmae, the father of Japanese management consulting——日本管理咨询学之父大前研——(management consulting——the practice of helping organizations to improve their performance, primarily through the analysis of existing organizational problems)

20. For Mr Komori, it meant unwinding the work of his predecessor, who had handpicked him for the job...——对于重隆小森先生而言,这意味着废除精心挑选他担任总裁职位的前任的工作成效……(①handpick——carefully chosen for a special purpose; ②unwind——to cancel the effect of)

21. Clay Christensen, author of *The Innovator's Dilemma*——《创新者的困境》一书作者克莱顿·M.克里斯坦森(① Clay Christensen——哈佛商学院企业管理学教授 ② *The Innovator's Dilemma*——该书主要意思是即使经营最好的十分注意顾客需求并不断投资开发新技术的公司都有可能被市场或技术上的新变化所影响而遭失败。该书旨在告诉经营者为何有些公司无法回避这样的困境而另一些公司却可以走出困境,一个成功的公司如何在两难境地保证其产品不被新技术挤出市场。)

22. Of the 316 department-store chains of a few decades ago, only Dayton Hudson has adapted well to the modern world, and only because it started an entirely new business, Target.——几十年前的316家百货连销业只有代顿哈德森公司很好地适应现代世界,而且只是因为它开创了全新的企业Target。(Dayton Hudson——founded in 1969 with the merger of the Dayton Company with the J. L. Hudson Company. In 2000, Dayton Hudson changed its name to Target.)

23. Some say it could have become the equivalent of "Intel Inside" for the smartphone camera——a brand that consumers trust.——有些人说柯达可能会成为相当于智能手机上消费者所信赖的"内装英特尔处理器"的标识。(英特尔公司以其处理器而闻名,"Intel Inside"是电脑或智能手机上"内装英特尔处理器"的标识)

24. But Canon and Sony were better placed to achieve that, given their superior intellectual property, and neither has succeeded in doing so.——考虑到"佳能"和"索尼"公司知识资产更加优越,它们更有可能实现这个目的,但两家公司都未能成功办到。(be better placed——to have a better opportunity to do sth)

Ⅳ. Language Features

词性转化(Conversion)

本文有这么一句:"Wise business people concluded that it was best not to hurry to switch from making 70 cents on the dollar on film to maybe five cents at most in digital."该句中"digital"是由原先形容词转化成的名词,意思是"digital photography"(数码照相)。

在英语的发展过程中,词尾基本消失,各种词逐渐失去词类标志。现代英语中各类词之间形态上没有多大区别,因此许多词可以不改变形态,从一种词类转化为另一种词类,从而具有新的意义和作用,成为新词。这种构词法的特点是无需借助词缀就实现词类的转换,故称之为零位派生法(zero derivation)。

词性转化可以节约篇幅,并可使语言生动有力,因而在新闻写作中经常使用。常见的词性转化类型有:

一、名词转化为动词

1. He mouthed fine words about friendship. 他满口是友谊。

2. The White House press secretary is once more backgrounding newsmen for the president. 白宫新闻秘书再次代表总统给新闻记者提供背景。

二、动词或动词词组转化为名词

1. Like today's haves and havenots, we will have a society of the knows and knowsnots.

就像今天社会上有富人和穷人一样,将来社会上会出现有知识的人和无知识的人。

2. (Computer Gap...) These aging choose-nots become a more serious issue when they are teachers in schools.

这些日益变老,又不愿学电脑的人如果在学校当教师的话,那么问题就更为严重了。

三、形容词转化为名词

这种现象十分普遍,在新闻刊物中常常见到舍去名词而将其形容词修饰语用作名词的做法。例如:

undesirables	不受欢迎的人或物	perishables	易腐败的东西
unreachables	不可接近的人	pin-ups	钉在墙上的美女照
variables	易变的东西	unreadables	无法读懂的东西
gays	同性恋者	undecides	未下决心的人
never-marrieds	从未结婚的人	retireds	退了休的人
unwanteds	不想要的人或物	the young marrieds	新婚的年轻人

Ⅴ. Analysis of Content

1. The meaning of the word "out" in the sentence "He was only a few years out." (Para. 9) is _____.
   A. not in the position of power
   B. unemployed
   C. away from the country
   D. unconscious

2. The peak year of Kodak's revenues is _____.
   A. 1999
   B. 1976
   C. 1996
   D. 2011

3. Which of the following statements is NOT true about Kodak?
   A. Kodak failed to see the coming of new technology.
   B. Kodak was slow in responding to the change of technology.
   C. Kodak failed to read emerging markets correctly.
   D. Kodak's leadership changes have weakened its performance.

4. It can be seen from the article that the traditional impression of a typical Japanese company is _____.
   A. change-resistant
   B. flexible
   C. innovative
   D. nimble

5. The article is _____.
   A. an expository writing   B. a news comment
   C. an interpretative news report   D. a straight news report

Ⅵ. Questions on the Article

1. When was Kodak founded? What was it known for?
2. How successful was Kodak's business in the past?
3. What losses did Kodak's business suffer in recent years?
4. How is its long-time rival Fujifilm doing?
5. What do the two firms have in common?
6. Have the two firms reacted to the change in the same way?
7. Why was Kodak slow in reaction?
8. What was the bad luck that Kodak suffered?
9. How did Fujifilm react when it saw omens of digital doom?
10. How did Fujifilm diversify?
11. How has Shigetaka Komori restructured the firm?
12. To the author's mind, what accounts for Fujifilm's survival?

Ⅶ. Topics for Discussion

1. Is diversification of business the most ideal way for a firm's survival?
2. Was Kodak's failure in pharmaceutical operations a matter of bad luck?

Lesson 28

How One Red Hot Retailer Wins Customer Loyalty[1]

Staples[2] low prices made it a $2 billion office-supply retailer almost overnight. Now CEO Stemberg must reinvent the company. His new focus: the customer.

By Rahul Jacob

 Robert Sallada walked into a Staples store in Charlottesville, Virginia, last year, looking for some map pins but not much in the way of service. He expected, he says dismissively, the kind of shopping experience that "Kmart is the epitome of."[3] Staples, after all, is an office-supplies discount store. Turned out the store didn't have the unusual variety of map pins Sallada was after, but the sales associate helping him was quickly on the phone to the manufacturer of a similar pin.[4] After Sallada returned to his 15-employee furniture business, the Staples worker faxed him information on the pins. All this, Sallada marvels, for an order of no more than $20. Says he, still sounding incredulous: " I walked in a few months later, and the clerk remembered my name. It really impressed me." Sallada is now a regular Staples shopper and plans to spend a couple of thousand dollars annually at the store.

 What Sallada and many others now realize is that Staples cares deeply, very deeply, about pleasing customers. Such pampering, combined with great prices, has helped transform Staples from a nobody — the company didn't even exist ten years ago — into America's hottest retailer.[5] In this year's FORTUNE 500, Staples posted the best total return to investors for 1994 among specialist retailers. Analyst James Stoeffel of Smith Barney projects that sales this year will increase 45%, to $2.9 billion, with profits jumping 58%, to $63.1 million. Staples' stock recently traded at about $30, a rich 34 times 1995 estimated earnings.[6]

 But that kind of success doesn't mean Staples can rest easy. Competition is heating up in the rapidly growing, $8 billion office superstore business. Tough competitors like Office Depot and OfficeMax are also cutting costs and boosting service. To keep profits flowing, Staples must reinvent itself, raising customer service to a new level. Says CEO and founder Tom Stemberg, 46: "We clearly need to become more intimate with our customers. We're way better at service than we were two years ago[7], but I don't think we're nearly as good as we need to be."

 But just what is this customer intimacy Stemberg's talking about? In a sense it is very much like one of those value disciplines popularized by consultants Micael Treacy and Fred Wiersema in their best-selling book, *The Discipline of Market Leaders*[8]. Their elegant and occasionally simplistic premise is that companies become market leaders by delivering superior customer value in one of three disciplines — operational excellence, customer intimacy, or product leadership — while meeting industry standards on the other two.[9]

307

While Staples still intends to offer great prices on its paper, pens, fax machines, and other office supplies, its main strategy is to grow by providing customers with the best solutions to their problems. The idea is to emulate customer-intimate companies like Home Depot[10] and Airborne Express. These companies do not pursue one-time transactions; they cultivate relationships.[11] As Treacy and Wiersema put it in their book, "They specialize in satisfying unique needs, which often only they, by virtue of their close relationship with — and intimate knowledge of — the customer, recognize.[12]"

Stemberg didn't always have a passion for the customer. Before he founded Staples, he worked in the grocery business, where he was one of the first to introduce the concept of generic products[13] to food retailing. In the early Eighties he was an executive at Edwards-Finast, a Connecticut supermarket company. But in 1985, in a dispute with the owners, he got fired. Searching for a new career, he contacted one of his old professors at the Harvard business school. The professor suggested he take the modern, efficient distribution methods of the grocery business and apply them to an industry untouched by them. After a bad experience shopping for office supplies, Stemberg decided he'd found his industry.

After raising money from venture capitalists and a former grocery competitor, Stemberg opened the first Staples store in Brighton, Massachusetts, in 1986. His warehouse stores were ugly, but buying power and efficient distribution let him offer customers huge bargains.[14] Sales took off. Today he runs some 375 stores throughout Canada and in 21 states, with heavy clusters in California and the Northeast.

A couple of years ago this charismatic entrepreneur and his top management team realized that competing on price can take you only so far. To outstrip the competition, Staples would have to evolve into a more customer-intimate company. Says Jack Bingleman, in charge of Staples' North American superstores: "When the industry started out, it was not unlike the grocery store industry — a low-cost, no-service, self-serve environment. We are now at a point where low prices and a good selection are not enough. You have to do a better job training your employees and making your stores easier to shop." Adds Martin Hanaka, Staples' president: "We need to develop a service culture that will set us apart.[15]"

So Staples is in the midst of pursuing customer intimacy. The job amounts to a total revamp of the $2 billion company. To achieve it, Stemberg is shaking up his management team, mining a killer database full of customer information, changing his employee reward system, and redesigning all the stores to make them more people-friendly.[16] Here's how he's doing it.

Know your customers better than they know themselves. To get to know its customers, Staples has been compiling lots of information about buying habits and storing it in a massive database. "Retailers usually don't know their customers from Adam[17]," says Frederick Reichheld, who heads the customer-loyalty practice[18] at Bain & Co. "Staples knows better than anybody who their customers are."

To get the information Staples used a membership card, which gave customers a discount on certain items every time they produced it at the register. Each time a customer used the card, Staples collected information about his buying habits. The company, for instance, did well with lawyers and dentists but not with school principals. Staples uses this knowledge to locate new stores where they will be convenient for their customers — such as in neighborhoods with lots of law offices.

Another advantage of knowing who your customers are: You can work on building long-term relationships. Staples wants to do everything it can to get its best customers coming back to its stores. Since the database knows who those folks are, Staples can try to win their loyalty by offering them special discounts. In its Cincinnati stores, for instance, Staples is experimenting with a new rebate card[19] that offers discounts to small-business customers who spend at least $100 a month. The database also alerts Staples to once loyal customers who have left the flock. When a salesperson sees that someone who, say, bought six cases of copier paper for six months has stopped cold, he can call to find out why and to ask if Staples can do anything to win the customer back.

Make your stores more customer friendly. Staples is working hard to see that customers have a pleasant experience shopping in its stores. That isn't a sure thing. Many of the company's older stores are laid out badly, confusing to people trying to find an item quickly, check out, and leave. To fix that, Staples is redesigning all its stores. The remodeled stores boast better lighting, wider aisles, and better signs. They are a hit with consumers; Staples is posting incremental sales gains of 7% in these stores.[20] Says Smith Barney's Stoeffel: "That's a very good number. They need about 2% to break even on the remodeling cost. If you're doing 3½ times that, that's a nice return on business."

Making the stores an easier place to shop is something of an obsession with Jack Bingleman[21], the head of Staples' superstores division. Follow him down the aisle of a Staples store, and he'll pull a box of file folders from the shelf and quickly tick off the information a customer must see immediately: the number of folders, the size and color, and any special features that ought to be highlighted on the box.[22] As it often does, Staples worked with the folder manufacturer to develop packaging that included a window so that the customer can see the color without opening the box. A trivial detail, you sniff. "Retail is detail," counters Bingleman. "When you make the store simple, you can afford to have service where you need it." Freeing up sales associates from the routine — and tedious — queries about pens or copier paper means being able to deploy them in force where good service is needed most: in the electronics section of the store. This is where Staples sells big-ticket items like computers, printers, and fax machines. Those items today account for more than 40% of sales in the stores. The last thing the company wants is a customer walking out of the store because no salesperson was around to explain how a fax or computer worked.

Encourage management to spend its time thinking about the customer. Creating a customer-intimate organization often means changing how management allocates time. Until a couple of years ago, Staples' meetings were dominated by the challenge of getting new stores open on time. The nitty-gritty of customer service often took a back seat to the demands of rapid growth.[23] That's changed, as a recent three-hour sales meeting attended by CEO Stemberg suggests. As the managers sat around the table, the agenda was detail, detail, detail — all aimed at providing customers with better service. Why are the Nautica bags in the stores priced so high ($89.99)? How can the delivery of monthly bonus checks for sales associates be speeded up? Might that not boost morale and improve their attitude when dealing with customers? What's the secret to making Generation X[24] employees better salespeople? (If you think the answer is to be more sympathetic to their whining, you're wrong; company executives believe they like to be trained more than most employees.) A significant portion of the meeting, which is notable for its absence of grandstanding, is taken up by a Staples buyer providing an update on when a popular variety of white-washed office furniture will be available in the stores.[25] Over a video hookup that the company uses regularly and effectively, Dick Neff, the head of California operations, snaps: "We're looking pretty sparse. We need to get that furniture." Stemberg understands that having his managers spend lots of time solving customer problems sends clear signals to everyone about the organization's priorities.

Meetings like this offer a view not only into the style of the company but also into the personality of its founder, Stemberg, who likes to pepper his speech liberally with the phrase "busting my/our/his balls," displays a general impatience with conventional corporate decorum.[26] For instance, Staples' last quarterly management meeting, where informal dress— including sweat shirts — is de rigueur, took place in a church that one manager reported gleefully had been loaned by a parish that uses Staples' parking lot on weekends. Executives projected the company's first-quarter sales results onto the front wall. Numbers were framed incongruously by a cross on one side and a guitar and drum set on the other. (So much for plush off-site meetings.)[27]

Stemberg believes strongly that all resources should be spent on what will please the customer, not on corporate perks. He and all employees buy only coach airline tickets. The company's four-year-old headquarters in Framingham, Massachusetts — "they're already bursting at the seams," a cabdriver volunteered — looks as if it was furnished in a hurry at a garage sale.

Improve customer service by improving incentives. Such frugality is endearing when manifested at your corporate headquarters, but when reflected in the wages of your store sales associates it can trip up the best-laid plans to become a customer-intimate company.[28] Staples' position is that the economics of the discount-store business allow it to pay only the prevailing average wage in the industry. Trouble is, an average wage often translates into average service, one reason retailers like Home Depot pay above the norm. Instead of hiking wages across the board[29], Staples is putting in place bonus packages only for key store employees. Stemberg hopes this will encourage them to improve service in the stores. But he has a way to go. Some customers are not bowled over by the treatment they get.[30] Says Gilda Yolles Mintz, a public relations consultant in New Jersey who describes herself as a big fan of Staples' liberal return policy[31]: "Staples' service is just matter of fact. Maybe it's difficult in this part of the country to get retail staff who seem to be enjoying themselves." Adds Ben Shapiro, a Harvard business school marketing professor who taught Stemberg and has done consulting for Staples and "invested in it — thank God![32]": "Their store service is mixed; it varies a lot by the store and by the individual. If Staples can do better, it can be a differentiator.[33] It's a big opportunity."

To improve employee morale and thus service, Stemberg looked to the outside for talent. Less than a year ago he hired Martin Hanaka, a 20-year Sears[34] veteran, to be his president. Hanaka is a man with a mission.[35] Shedding his white shirt and tie for a sweatshirt, Hanaka has free rein to give Staples the store-level customer focus it lacks.[36]

Hanaka sees his brief as bringing a new discipline to merchandising efforts in particular.[37] This includes increasing the selection in the stores and motivating store managers with bonuses in a mystery-shopper program. He sends consultants incognito into the stores to shop. They evaluate service, indicating how courteous and knowledgeable the clerks were, and even rate their appearance. The managers whose stores score highest see the results in their paychecks.

Uppermost on Hanaka's list of priorities is "celebrating failures," a tip he picked up from Home Depot CEO Bernie Marcus at a FORTUNE conference this spring.[38] The point Hanaka good-humoredly made was that in trying to serve the customer more imaginatively, every so often someone trips up. The danger is the tendency to cover up; not sharing those mistakes prevents other people from learning from your example.

Treat your people as you would like them to treat your customers. It is perhaps not too romantic to say that a sense of filial loyalty is one of Staples' strengths. Over the years Stemberg has formed strong relationships with his senior management team. Ron Sargent remembers Stemberg calling him every night when his newborn son spent a week in intensive care. As his company grows bigger, this CEO's challenge is to maintain that small-company spirit. Though the company has had an employee stock-ownership program[39] since it was founded, motivating employees is about much more than that. Staples has quarterly town hall-style meetings called Stake in Staples, where senior managers report on the company's performance and solicit ideas at different locations. At Staples Direct, a $200 million catalogue business that sells to small-business customers and doubled in size last year, the division is implementing a Direct Effect award program[40]. In it the employees themselves decide who gets bonuses for good service. The unusual thing about this program is that it was designed by the corps of telephone reps who take as many as 85,000 to 100,000 calls from customers every week. The retailer is also spending more heavily across the board on training. Staples Direct has had consultants call up and pretend to be customers; the insights gained have been rolled into the eight hours of training that associates receive every month. Says Jane Biering, vice president of operations, in her energetic, mile-a-minute fashion: "We learned about the importance of tone of voice and not putting people on hold. We learned we're abysmal at what's called up-sells — selling products that are bigger or better, after probing customers about their requirements."[41]

As Staples continues to grow rapidly, will it become a victim of its own success? The company is now vaulting past the 18,000-employee mark. Communicating its passion about customers to all employees is becoming increasingly difficult. Two of the great retail stories of our time, Wal-Mart and Home Depot, owe much of their success to the almost messianic values[42] of their founders. The question for Stemberg, it seems, is whether he can continue to build the same kind of intense relationships with employees and customers. One thing he can bet on: If he doesn't, his customers will be the first to let him know.

From *Fortune*, July 10, 1995

I. New Words

abysmal	[ə'bizməl]	adj.	very bad; terrible
big-ticket	['big,tikit]	adj.	*AmE informal* expensive
charismatic	[,kæriz'mætik]	adj.	able to attract and influence others
coach	[kəutʃ]	n.	*AmE* the cheapest type of seats on a plane or train

cold	[kəuld]	adv.	*AmE* suddenly and completely
de rigueur	[dəri'gə:]	adj.	*French* necessary if you want to be fashionable
economics	[ˌi:kə'nɔmiks]	n.	*plural* 经济情况,经济因素
electronics	[ilek'trɔniks]	n.	电子设备
epitome	[i'pitəmi]	n.	the best possible example
filial	['filjəl]	adj.	of or suitable to a son or daughter
frugality	[fru'gæliti]	n.	tendency to save money
gleeful	['gli:ful]	adj.	really enjoying the fact that something good has happened to you
grandstanding	['grændstændiŋ]	n.	*AmE* an action intended to make people notice and admire you
hookup	['hukʌp]	n.	a temporary connection between two pieces of equipment
incognito	[in'kɔgnitəu]	adv.	without letting people know who you are
incongruous	[in'kɔŋgruəs]	adj.	looking strange and unsuitable
incremental	[ˌinkri'mentl]	adj.	increasing
messianic	[ˌmesi'ænik]	adj.	*formal* marked by idealism and an aggressive crusading spirit
nitty-gritty	['niti'griti]	n.	*informal* **the nitty-gritty** the basic and practical facts of an activity
plush	[plʌʃ]	adj.	*informal* expensive, comfortable and of good quality
rep	[rep]	n.	*informal* a sales representative 推销员
revamp	['ri:'væmp]	n.	*informal* arranging something in a new way so that it appears to be better
sniff	[snif]	v.	to say sth in a complaining way
snap	[snæp]	v.	to say sth quickly in an angry way
solicit	[sə'lisit]	v.	to try to obtain by urgent requests
vault	[vɔ:lt]	v.	**vault past** to leap over
whine	[wain]	v.	to complain in a sad, annoying voice

Ⅱ. Background Information

经营观念

顾客利益至上是美国公司的重要经营观念。美国商界视顾客为衣食父母,把顾客满意(customer satisfaction)作为鉴定公司一切行为的唯一标准,所有经营活动都是以顾客满意为中心。为了更好服务顾客利益,赢得顾客满意,许多企业采取以下措施:

1. 调查市场需求。市场经济规律要求商家必须注重市场需求,否则生产经营的商品无人问津,造成大批积压。美国企业在设计和生产新产品之前总是要做详细的市场调查。研究表明,成功的技术革新和民用新产品中有60%—80%来自顾客的建议。因此,美国商家十分重视顾客意见,开设顾客免费电话服务。

  2. 严格质量管理。质量是企业成功的保证,因而许多企业严格质量管理。麦当劳(MacDonald's)占据了美国快餐市场的 42%,在世界 89 个国家里有 18,000 多家分店。这家快餐业之所以博得大众喜爱成为美国饮食文化的象征,除了快捷服务(fast service)、卫生环境(clean surroundings)和合宜价格(reasonable price)因素以外,很重要的一点便是其质量标准。据说麦当劳所生产的牛肉饼要经过 40 多项检查。

  3. 积极宣传推销。为了促进商品推销,美国商界十分重视商品信息的传播,采用一切媒体大做广告。为了吸引顾客,美国商界十分注重商品的包装(packing)。精明的制造商和经销商意识到,光靠产品好是不够的,要想打开销路,还得有刺激购买欲的包装。因此,他们在商品的包装上狠下工夫,使其色泽和形状都具有诱人的魅力。

  4. 创造购买方便。创造购货方便可以增加商品的销售额。美国商家深知这个道理,千方百计为顾客提供购物方便,开设各种形式方便销售。人们无需出门,通过订单、电话、电脑通知商家所需商品,很快东西就被送上门来。为了使顾客购物放心满意,许多商家提供试用(trial use)。用得满意付款,不满意可以退货。

  5. 提供售后服务(providing after-sales service)。美国商家认为顾客是一种无形资产,这种无形资产能够随时随地转变为有形资产,创造巨大经济效益。美国一项调查表明,一个满意的顾客会引发 8 笔潜在生意,而一个不满意的顾客会动摇 25 个人的购买意愿。许多公司为了让顾客不仅买得舒心而且用得放心,做到真正满意,不但搞好售前服务,并且重视售后服务。

  正是这种顾客利益至上的精神促使美国许多公司不断提高产品质量、服务水准和竞争能力,从而占领一个又一个市场,取得一个又一个成功。

Ⅲ. Notes to the Text

1. How One Red Hot Retailer Wins Customer Loyalty —— 生意火暴零售店,如何赢得顾客心?(① red hot —— *informal* extremely popular; ② loyalty —— a feeling of support)

2. Staples —— 史泰博办公用品公司(1986 年成立,目前已在全球拥有 1,600 余家办公用品超市和仓储分销中心,2004 年破《商业周刊》列为 S & P500 股指表现最优的第 50 位)

3. He expected, he says dismissively, the kind of shopping experience that "Kmart is the epitome of." —— Without hesitation, he says what he expected was the kind of service typical of Kmart. [Kmart —— Kmart Corporation, major American retail chain, marketing general merchandise primarily through discount and variety stores (廉价商店和杂货店)]

4. <u>Turned out the store didn't have the unusual variety of map pins Sallada was after</u>, but the sales associate helping him was quickly on the phone to the manufacturer of a similar pin. —— 萨拉达想要的图钉品种很少见,结果,这家商店没有。但是,为他服务的营业员很快打电话给一种类似图钉的制造商。(画线处为省略句,完整句应为:It turned out that ...)

5. Such pampering, combined with great prices, has helped transform Staples from a nobody ... into America's hottest retailer. —— Such deep care, plus low prices, has helped change Staples from an unimportant retailer into the most popular retailer in America. (① nobody —— someone who is not important and has no influence; ② hot ——

informal popular at a particular point in time)

6. Staples' stock recently traded at about ＄30, a rich 34 times 1995 estimated earnings. — 史泰博文具店的股票最近大约以每股高达 30 美元成交,是 95 年预计收益的 34 倍。

7. We're way better at service than we were two years ago... — 比起两年前,我们的服务要好得多……(way — *adv AmE informal* far or by far)

8. The Discipline of Market Leaders —《市场领先者的修炼》

9. Their elegant and occasionally simplistic premise is that ... while meeting industry standards on the other two. — 他们的前提非常精练,有时显得十分简单,那就是:公司要想成为市场领先者,就要在经营出色、亲密顾客、产品领先这三个项目中能有一个为顾客提供优质服务,而其他两个项目达到行业标准。(① elegant — very clever and simple; ② simplistic — treating difficult subjects in a way that is too simple)

10. Home Depot — 家得宝公司(成立于 1978 年,是全球最大的家居建材零售商)

11. These companies do not pursue one-time transactions; they cultivate relationships. — 这些公司追求的不是一次性交易,他们建立与顾客的关系。

12. They specialize in satisfying unique needs, which often only they ... recognize. — They concentrate on satisfying special needs. Quite often only they know the needs of customers because they keep close contact with customers and have friendly relationship with them.

13. generic products — *AmE* products without a trademark 低价非专利性商品

14. His warehouse stores were ugly, but buying power and efficient distribution let him offer customers huge bargains. — 他的零售商店外观丑陋,但是,由于购买力强,供货迅速,他能为顾客提供非常便宜的东西。

15. We need to develop a service culture that will set us apart. — 我们需要营造一种与众不同的服务氛围。

16. To achieve it, Stemberg ... to make them more people-friendly. — 为了做到这一点,斯坦伯格正在改组他的管理队伍,利用充满顾客信息的优质数据库,改革雇员奖励制度,重新设计所有商店,更加便于人们购物。[① shake up — to make changes in an organization to make it more effective; ② mine — to seek valuable material in; ③ killer — *AmE slang* something that is very good(句中作前置定语); ④ -friendly — not difficult for people to use]

17. Retailers usually don't know their customers from Adam ... — 零售商往往一点儿也不了解他们的顾客……(not know someone from Adam — not know someone at all)

18. ... who heads the customer-loyalty practice — (他)负责联络顾客感情的业务。

19. rebate card — 打折卡(rebate — an amount of money that is returned to you)

20. They are a hit with consumers; Staples is posting incremental sales gains of 7％ in these stores. — Consumers like them very much; Staples announces sales growth of 7％ in these stores.

21. Making the stores an easier place to shop is something of an obsession with Jack Bingleman... — Jack Bingleman has a rather strong and continuous interest in making it easier for customers to buy things in his stores...

22. special features that ought to be highlighted on the box. — 应该在盒子上突出显示的特色。(highlight — to make something easy to notice)
23. The nitty-gritty of customer service often took a back seat to the demands of rapid growth. — The basic needs of customer service were often treated as less important than the demands of rapid growth.
24. Generation X — 无名代 (Please refer to L2)
25. A significant portion of the meeting, which is notable for its absence of grandstanding, is taken up by a Staples buyer providing an update on when a popular variety of white-washed office furniture will be available in the stores. — 值得注意的是,会上不搞哗众取宠,大部分时间由一位史泰博公司采购员提供最新商品信息:一种受人欢迎的白色办公设备什么时候到货。(update — the most recent news)
26. Stemberg, who likes to pepper his speech liberally with the phrase "busting my/our/his balls," displays a general impatience with conventional corporate decorum. — Stemberg, a person who likes to use "busting my/our/his balls" repeatedly in his speech, generally does not care about office manners normally required by corporations. 〔① pepper — to scatter things all through something; ② bust one's balls — *slang* to work very hard or too hard to the extent of personal stress. Literally it means "to break one's testicles (睾丸)." It's inappropriate to use this phrase in a corporate setting. This shows Stemberg's dislike of formal behaviour, and his close relationship with his colleagues. ③ decorum — *formal* correct behavior that shows respect〕
27. Numbers were framed incongruously by a cross on one side and a guitar and drum set on the other. (So much for plush off-site meetings.) — 数字的一边是个十字架,另一边是个吉他和一组鼓,显得很不协调。(在公司外租借豪华会场费用太贵。)(① frame — to surround something with a border; ② off-site meeting — a meeting which does not take place in the buildings of the corporation)
28. Such frugality is endearing when manifested at your corporate headquarters, but when reflected in the wages of your store sales associates it can trip up the best-laid plans to become a customer-intimate company. — 公司总部的这种精打细算会赢得人们的喜爱,但是给公司售货员开工资方面也是这样的话,创建亲密顾客的公司计划再好,也会泡汤。(① endearing — causing to be liked or loved; ② trip up — to make something fail)
29. Instead of hiking wages across the board … — Instead of increasing wages for everybody …
30. But he has a way to go. Some customers are not bowled over by the treatment they get. — But he still needs to make some improvement. Some customers are dissatisfied with the service they get. (bowl over — to please or satisfy someone very much)
31. … who describes herself as a big fan of Staples' liberal return policy … — who says she is greatly interested in Staples' generous return policy … (A liberal return policy refers to offering customers an opportunity to return items they find unacceptable.)
32. … invested in it — thank God! — He made investments in Staples and felt glad to have done so.

33. If Staples can do better, it can be a differentiator. — If Staples can offer better service, it can serve as an example illustrating the differences between Staples' excellent service and the other companies' service.

34. Sears — Sears, Roebuck and Company, one of the world's largest retailers of general merchandise, with retail stores and mail-order operations.

35. Hanaka is a man with a mission. — Hanaka is a man with a strong sense of duty.

36. Shedding his white shirt and tie for a sweatshirt, Hanaka has free rein to give Staples the store-level customer focus it lacks. — Stepping out of office in a sweatshirt, he is completely free to do study of customer needs in the stores, and to focus on customer satisfaction, which has been neglected. (free rein — complete freedom to do a job)

37. Hanaka sees his brief as bringing a new discipline to merchandising efforts in particular. — 哈纳卡认为,他的责任是专门为销售工作提供一种新的规范。(① brief — official instruction about the job; ② discipline — a rule governing activity)

38. Uppermost on Hanaka's list of priorities is "celebrating failures", a tip he picked up from Home Depot CEO Bernie Marcus at a FORTUNE conference this spring. — 哈纳卡要办的事中重中之重是"庆贺失败",这是他在今年春天《财富》杂志组织的会议上从家得宝公司执行总裁伯尼·马库斯那儿学到的好办法。(① uppermost — more important than other things; ② tip — a helpful piece of advice)

39. employee stock-ownership program — 雇员持股计划

40. Direct Effect award program — 当即兑现奖励计划

41. We learned we're abysmal at what's called up-sells — selling products that are bigger or better, after probing customers about their requirements. — 我们知道我们根本不会搞超度销售,即了解顾客需求之后,试图销售数量更多、档次更高的商品。(① abysmal — very bad, terrible; ② up-sell — one of the business jargons to describe "encouraging customers to buy more expensive, higher-quality, more feature-laden items than they originally telephoned to buy.")

42. messianic values — here referring to the business concept of rendering all customers ideal service and ensuring their satisfaction

Ⅳ. Language Features

嵌入结构(embedding)

本文多处使用了嵌入结构。例如:
Such pampering, combined with great prices, has helped transform Staples from a nobody — the company didn't even exist ten years ago — into America's hottest retailer.

新闻报道为了在有限的篇幅内传达更多的消息,采用了多种手段浓缩精炼句式,大量使用嵌入结构是其中的一种主要方式。插入语是嵌入结构中最为常见的形式,插入语的两头既可用逗号亦可用破折号标明。例如:

1. Ken Bush, 54, a state fire marshal, pulled his vehicle onto the shoulder of Route 50

and was struck by two other vehicles. (*The Washington Post*)

2. Edward Krutulis, 34, a Plainfield, Illinois, pharmaceutical sales representative, after lamenting the country's moral condition, said, obviously, President Clinton is not much of a role model for us. (*The International Herald Tribune*)

3. Watergate Hotel, part of Washington's exclusive and notorious Watergate Complex, has been sold to the investment bank Blackstone Group. (*The Washington Times*)

4. In 1996, the most recent year available, there were about 11.8 million registered boats owners. (*USA Today*)

从文体效果来看,使用破折号标出插入成分"更具独立性","给人一种随意感"(David Crystal & Derek Davy,1969)。例如:

1. The mum-and-pop operation — they have two employees besides themselves — is growing at a rate of about 15% a year and last year had sales of $350,000. (*USA Today*)

2. Nevertheless, it's physical evidence — the sticks and stones of murder trials — that delivers crushing blows to a defendant's case, he and other legal experts say. (*The Los Angeles Times*)

3. People are confounded: which Bible will give a particular person — maybe a scholar or a seeker, a harried parent, a struggling student — spiritual nourishment, moral enlightenment and literary pleasure? (*USA Today*)

V. Analysis of the Content

1. Tom Stemberg emphasizes _____ greatly.
   A. customer intimacy   B. operational excellence
   C. market leadership   D. industry standards
2. The advantage of knowing customers is _____.
   A. knowing the buying habits of managers
   B. better location of new stores
   C. building short-term relationships
   D. compiling lots of information about buying habits
3. Stemberg believes that all resources should be focused on _____.
   A. corporate perks   B. holding meetings
   C. pleasing customers   D. headquarters
4. By "celebrating failures", Hanaka means that Staples can _____.
   A. find the mystery shoppers
   B. provide sales associates with entertainment
   C. cover up mistakes
   D. help other people learn from mistakes
5. The big challenge for Staples is _____.
   A. the rapid growth
   B. the competition from Kmart
   C. continuation of the same kind of intense relationship with employees and customers

D. messianic values of Home Depot founder

VI. Questions on the Article

1. Why is Staples a big success in retailing business?
2. Why can't Staples rest easy?
3. What is the main strategy of Staples?
4. How does Staples pursue customer intimacy?
5. How does Staples know its customers?
6. How does Staples make its stores more customer-friendly?
7. What is the style of the Staples company?
8. How does Staples improve incentives?

VII. Topics for Discussion

1. Is it sensible to celebrate failures?
2. Which is the better way to keep employees' loyalty, offering them a higher pay or maintaining good relationship with them?

Lesson 29

The Internet Has Created a New Industrial Revolution
Anyone with a good digital idea can create a successful online business. So are the "Makers," who are harnessing these new technologies, helping to reboot the manufacturing industry?

By Chris Anderson

Back in the early 1940s my grandfather had a great idea. Noting the obsession Californians have with perfectly green front lawns, he decided that what they needed was an automatic sprinkler system. He lavished time and love on it, inventing this and fine-tuning that, and eventually came up with what was essentially an electric clock that could be timed to turn water valves on or off at given times of the day and night.[1] Patent number 2311108 was duly filed in 1943, at which point my grandfather started knocking on manufacturers' doors. It was a long, arduous process. Finally, in 1950, after endless discussions, the Moody Rainmaster hit the stores[2]. It earned my grandfather a modest income.

Recently, I decided to follow in his footsteps, but apply a little 21st-century know-how to the mix.[3] Online I found a few like-minded souls interested in producing an improved water sprinkler.[4] We used open-source software[5] to help us create a sprinkler system not only capable of being operated remotely via an app by worried gardeners on holiday, but also sophisticated enough to factor in the latest local weather forecasts before deciding whether to switch the system on or off. We then sent our designs to an assembly house who duly came up with a smart-looking finished product. It has proved quite popular. It took my grandfather a decade and a small fortune to perfect his device and market it. It took us a few months and $5,000.

And that in a nutshell is the Maker movement[6]—harnessing the Internet and the latest manufacturing technologies to make things. The past 10 years have been about discovering new ways to work together and offer services on the web. The next 10 years will, I believe, be about applying those lessons to the real world. It means that the future doesn't just belong to Internet businesses founded on virtual principles. But to ones that are firmly rooted in the physical world.[7]

This has massive implications not just for would-be entrepreneurs but for national economies. The fact is that any country, if it wants to remain strong, must have a manufacturing base. Even today, about a quarter of the US economy rests on the creation of physical goods. A service economy is all well and good, but eliminate manufacturing and you're a nation of bankers, burger flippers and tour guides.[8] As for software and information industries, they may get all the press, but they employ just a small percentage of the population.

The nascent Maker movement offers a path to reboot manufacturing—not by returning to the giant factories of old, with their armies of employees, but by creating a new kind of manufacturing economy, one shaped more like the web itself: bottom-up, broadly distributed, and highly entrepreneurial. The image of a few smart people changing the world with little more than an Internet connection and an idea increasingly describes manufacturing of the future, too.

It's almost a cliche that anyone with a sufficiently good software idea can create a fabulously successful company on the web.[9] That's because there are practically no barriers preventing entry to entrepreneurship online: if you've got a laptop and a credit card, you're in business. Manufacturing has traditionally been regarded as something else entirely. But over the past few years, something remarkable has begun to happen. The process of making physical stuff has started to look more like the process of making digital stuff.

Various innovations are helping to make this possible. The first, of course, is the crowdsourcing power of the Internet[10]—if you don't know all the answers, there is someone out there who will. Put out a call for help on a blog or online forum, and somewhere there will be an expert prepared to help you. The second innovation is the increasing sophistication of design programs that can take raw ideas and transform them into executable files. Just as word-processing software has become ever simpler and more intuitive for the user, so Cad (computer-aided design)[11] programs are becoming simultaneously more sophisticated and easier to handle. You design something; the Cad program works out how it can be produced.

And then there is the first generation of 3D printers. These take "geometries" on screen (3D objects that are created with the same sorts of tools that Hollywood uses to make computer generated movies) and turn them into objects that you can pick up and use. Some 3D printers extrude molten plastic in layers to make these objects, while others use a laser to harden layers of liquid or powder resin so the product emerges from a bath of the raw material. Yet others can make objects out of any material from glass, steel and bronze to gold, titanium or even cake frosting. You can print a flute or you can print a meal. You can even print human organs of living cells, by squirting a fluid with suspended stem cells on to a support matrix.[12]

What's important here is not so much current reality as potential. 3D printers, laser cutters and "CNC" (computer numerical control)[13] machines, which use a drill bit[14] to shape a block of material, are already sophisticated devices—a few years ago they would have seemed distinctly sci-fi—but I suspect that they resemble the technology of 10 years hence in much the same way that the primitive single-color dot matrix printers[15] of the 1980s resemble the color laser printers we having sitting in our homes today. Even now scientists are talking about creating manufacturing tools that use "structural DNA" to create physical objects. In other words, the technology still has a long journey to make. However, its liberating implications are already there, and I believe that when they are combined with other online innovations, a very powerful manufacturing force is created.

First of all, such technology helps remove the shackles from innovation. Until now, the creative process has been beset with obstacles, from the problems inherent in creating a prototype, to the difficulties of persuading a third party to become involved, to the expense of the final launch.[16] And, of course, there's no guarantee of ultimate success.

Now, however, things are looking rather different, both at the Innovation and the selling stages.

Take Alex Andon, for example. After graduating in 2006, he moved to the San Francisco Bay Area[17] for a biotech job. But his real passion was jellyfish, which he had first encountered while sailing in the British Virgin Islands[18] as a teenager. He quit his job and set up a company in a friend's garage to make custom jellyfish tanks with special pumps (a conventional pump will suck in a jellyfish and rip it to pieces), custom water-flow systems to keep the jellyfish off the sides and colorful LED lighting. That in itself was no small feat.

Where Alex also scored, though, was in his ability to test the market before he launched his product. He opted to go via the crowdfunding website.[19] Kickstarter to see whether people were interested in what he could offer them. If they were, he invited them to help fund his start-up in return for one of his Desktop Jellyfish Tanks at a discount. His aim was to raise $3,000. After a month he had raised more than $130,000. He had managed both to market-test his idea and find his first customers without having to go to the risky expense of first filling a warehouse (or his bedroom) with jellyfish tanks.[20]

It's not difficult to see how Maker technology suits this sort of niche enterprise. The chances are that a savvy and committed market already exists for the right product, and, thanks to the Internet, it's relatively easy to find it. What's more the current manufacturing technology that supports Makers is ideally suited to small batches of bespoke products—from customized plastic toys to tailored clothes. With a conventional factory, you fix on a design and mass produce it; start up is expensive, but mass-production involves compensating economies of scale. With a 3D printer, startup is cheap, but there are no economies of scale to be gained: product number 150 will cost you precisely the same to create as product number 1. That precludes success in the mass market, but does set you up to succeed in a niche market[21] that by its very nature is less price sensitive.

Moreover, you can, if you choose, make every item bespoke: number 150 does not have to be precisely the same in appearance as number 100. And you can manufacture at home, perhaps using your own 3D printer (in the US prices are already dropping to $1,000) or sending your files to a third party fitted out with the necessary kit.

Having said that, I don't believe that Makers enterprises have to remain small-scale. Many, of course, will opt to do so, creating customized goods for a specialist market. Others, though, can utilize all that the Maker technology has to offer to get an enterprise off the ground, road test its products[22], respond to customer feedback, and then build a larger-scale company. What they'll have going for them in addition—and it's something that many larger companies lack-is agility and flexibility built into their DNA.

Imagine a new company, WindCo, making its first product: a small backyardwind turbine generator[23]. They make the first prototype themselves, as well as a handful of others. Then, it's time to go into serious production. WindCo is small, and they don't have sufficient manufacturing capacity themselves, so they outsource to a factory in China that can handle small batches cheaply.

If the product is successful and demand builds, they may well opt to move production back home to cut out delays. If it's astonishingly successful, then they may decide to move production to a different factory in China that specializes in bulk manufacturing.[24] They have to be flexible because their business is constantly evolving. They are able to be flexible because their design files are digital, the tooling costs of setting up a new manufacturing operation are minimal, and they all use the same robotic machinery.

This adaptive business of the future will need to be accommodating in other ways, too. It needs to be in constant contact with its customers and be prepared to respond quickly to their feedback and criticism. It needs to be able to draw on skills wherever they are, not merely on people who happen to be close to home. The co-founder of a small robot aeroplane enterprise I run, for example, is not someone who answered an ad, but an enthusiast who came to my attention when he started posting inspired ideas for improvements on an online forum I was hosting.

That this can work is demonstrated by the success of a Colorado-based company, Sparkfun , which operates in one of the most ruthlessly cut-throat of all areas of business—electronics[25]. Back in 2003 its founder, Nathan Seidle, was an undergraduate engineering student, who was finding it frustratingly difficult to locate electronic components that he needed for his projects. Today, Sparkfun designs and manufactures specialist printed circuit boards, using sophisticated pick-and-place robot machines to assemble them.[26] Its website makes a major feature of its blog, with chatty tutorials and videos from employees, and forums that are full of customers helping one another.

Its employees are young, passionate and appear to totally love their jobs. Dogs and hobbies are indulged at work (though not on the production floor); tattoos and indie punk rock reflect its culture.[27] It's a far cry from the "dark satanic mill" vision of manufacturing—much closer in fact to the maverick image of software companies in their startup days.[28]

And it works. Today Sparkfun has more than 120 employees and annual revenues of around $30 million. It's growing by 50% a year. A basketball-court-sized ground floor is dominated by robotic electronic production lines, running day and night. Daily blog posts and tutorials have turned its retail website into a high-traffic community, with more than 50,000 visitors a day.[29]

The Maker movement has a long way to go before it can really be said to have come of age. But that doesn't mean it should be ignored or regarded solely as a hobbyist's or niche manufacturer's paradise. It represents the first steps in a different way of doing business. Rather than top-down innovation by some of the biggest companies in the world, we're starting to see bottom-up innovation by countless individuals, including amateurs, entrepreneurs and professionals. We've already seen it work before, in bits, from the original PC hobbyists to the web's citizen army. Now the conditions have arrived for it to work again, at even greater, broader scale, in atoms. If the Second Industrial Revolution was the Information Age, then I would argue that a Third Industrial Age is on its way: the age of the Makers.[30]

From *The Guardian*, September 28, 2012

I. New Words

agility	[ə'dʒiləti]	n.	ability to move quickly and easily
arduous	['ɑːdjuəs]	adj.	involving a lot of effort and energy
batch	[bætʃ]	n.	a group of people or things

bespoke	[bi'spəuk]	adj.	(of a product) made especially according to an individual customer's needs
biotech＝biotechnology			生物工艺(学)
bottom-up	['bɔtəmʌp]	adj.	自下而上的
chatty	['tʃæti]	adj.	talking a lot in a friendly way
circuit	['sə:kit]	n.	线路
cliché	['kli:ʃei]	n.	陈词滥调
custom	['kʌstəm]	adj.	specially designed and made for a particular purpose
executable	['eksikju:təbl]	adj.	(computing) (of a file or program) that can be run by a computer
extrude	[ek'stru:d]	v.	挤压出,挤压成,压制
fabulously	['fæbjuləsli]	adv.	*formal* extremely
feat	[fi:t]	n.	an action needing strength, skill or courage
feedback	['fi:dbæk]	n.	反馈
flute	[flu:t]	n.	长笛
frosting	['frɔstiŋ]	n.	(糕饼上的)糖霜混合物
geometry	[dʒi'ɔmətri]	n.	几何(学)
harness	['ha:nis]	v.	to use the force of sth to produce
indie	['indi]	adj.	独立制作的
jellyfish	['dʒelifiʃ]	n.	水母
kit	[kit]	n.	a set of tools or equipment
laptop	['læptɔp]	n.	便携式电脑
LED		abbr.	light emitting diode 发光二极管
molten	['məultən]	adj.	熔化的
nascent	['næsənt]	adj.	*formal* starting to develop
opt	[ɔpt]	v.	to choose to take a particular course of action
patent	['peitənt]	n.	专利,专利权;专利证书
preclude	[pri'klu:d]	v.	to prevent sth from happening
prototype	['prəutəutaip]	n.	原型
reboot	[ˌri:'bu:t]	v.	(of computer) to switch it off and then start it again immediately
resin	['rezin]	n.	树脂
savvy	['sævi]	adj.	having practical knowledge of sth
scifi	['sai'fai]	n.	*informal* science fiction 科幻小说
sophisticated	[sə'fistikeitid]	adj.	深奥微妙的,精致的
sprinkler	['spriŋklə]	n.	洒水器,喷洒器
tank	[tæŋk]	n.	(贮放液体的)箱,槽,罐
titanium	[tai'teiniəm]	n.	(化)钛
top-down	['tɔpdaun]	adj.	自上而下的
tutorial	[tju:'tɔ:riəl]	n.	a computer program giving information on a particular subject

valve	[vælv]	n.	阀门
warehouse	['weəhaus]	n.	仓库
would-be	['wudbi]	adj.	（将要）成为的，未来的

Ⅱ. Background Information

创客运动

本文的作者克里斯·安德森曾如此说道："过去的十年，我们在互联网上寻找新的协作方式和各类服务。下一个十年，该把这些学到的东西用于现实世界。因为未来并不仅仅属于建立在虚拟规则上的网络经济，而是要深深扎根于现实世界。如果第二次工业革命意味着信息时代，那么第三次工业革命则代表创客时代。"

那么何谓创客呢？

所谓"创客"，根据创词者克里斯·安德森的解释，就是那些能够利用互联网将自己的各种创意转变为实际产品的人。他们将会成为未来互联网经济的主力军，推动整个经济社会和相关产业的发展。虽然"创客"这一理念提出的比较晚，我们甚至还无法十分准确定义这场运动，但可以肯定的是，它具有三个变革性的共同点：

第一，在得到准许的情况下，任何人都可以通过广泛认可的设计文件标准将设计传给商业制造服务商，以任何数量规模制造所设计的产品，也可以使用桌面工具自行制造。

第二，人们使用数字桌面工具设计新产品并制作模型样品，即通常所说的"数字DIY"(Do It Yourself)。

第三，"创客"是新兴科技下的产物，具有一定的时代性特征，他们是互联网经济的一代，其所倡导的在开源社区中分享设计成果、开展合作的理念已经成为一种文化规范。

如今，制造业与服务业的界线正变得日益模糊，个性化生产和自动化生产相结合的未来工业生产方式已经登上了历史的舞台。在这种新型生产方式下，劳动成本将变得越来越无足轻重。虽然从历史的角度来说，每一次工业革命，都不是以彻底摧毁一个旧的生产模式而仅仅添加一个新的模式开始的，但预先觉察到先进生产方式的人，毕竟是可以从中获得巨大的效益。所以，从这个角度来说，认识、了解"创客运动"的实质并适当地将它运用到工作当中，对于社会的整体发展大有裨益。

"创客运动"是一种具有划时代意义的新浪潮，将实现全民创造，推动新工业革命。其中，每一个进行或参与创造的人都可以被称作"创客"。以往，凭借准入门槛低、快速创新、创新精神强烈的优势，商业互联网模式所向披靡；现在，"创客运动"的出现更是将这种模式转移到制造业，在改变虚拟世界的同时，彻彻底底地在变革着我们的真实生活。因此，我们应该高度重视并且立刻采取相应的对策。因为以"创客运动"为标志的新工业革命正在拉开序幕，一个新的时代即将到来。

Ⅲ. Notes to the Text

1. He lavished time and love on it, inventing this and fine-tuning that, and eventually came up with what was essentially an electric clock that could be timed to turn water valves on

or off at given times of the day and night. —他花了大量时间和心血制造各种装置,进行种种改进,最终制造出一种电钟,能够在日夜任何时间开启或关闭水阀。(①lavish—to give a lot of sth; ②fine-tune—to make very small changes to sth so that it is as good as it can possibly be; ③come up with—to produce)

2. the Moody Rainmaster hit the stores—穆迪(自动)雨阀上市(hit the stores—to become widely available for sale)

3. Recently, I decided to follow in his footsteps, but apply a little 21st-century know-how to the mix. —最近,我决定仿效他,但在技术组合中应用一些21世纪的知识。(①follow in his footsteps—to follow his example; ②know-how—knowledge about how to do sth; ③mix—a combination of things)

4. Online I found a few like-minded souls interested in producing an improved water sprinkler. —在网上,我找到了一些对改进洒水器感兴趣、有相同想法的人。(like-minded souls—people with the same interests)

5. open-source software—开放源代码软件(简称OSS开源软件,是一种源代码公开的软件)

6. And that in a nutshell is the Maker movement... —简而言之,这就是"创客运动"……[in a nutshell—(to say)in a very clear way, using few words]

7. But to ones that are firmly rooted in the physical world. —而是属于那些牢牢植根于实体世界的企业。

8. A service economy is all well and good, but eliminate manufacturing and you're a nation of bankers, burger flippers and tour guides. —服务型经济虽好,但如果要消除了制造业,一个国家就只剩下了银行业、餐饮业、旅游业之类的行业。(①all well and good—quite good but not exactly what is wanted; ②service economy—economy built on service industry; ③burger flippers—people who sell hamburgers)

9. It's almost a cliche that anyone with a sufficiently good software idea can create a fabulously successful company on the web. —任何人只要有足够好的软件创意就可以在网上创造极为成功的公司,这几乎是人人皆知的事。

10. The first, of course, is the crowdsourcing power of the Internet... —当然,首要的就是互联网的众包能力……(crowdsourcing power—the power of getting help from a large number of people)

11. computer-aided design—电脑辅助设计

12. You can even print human organs of living cells, by squirting a fluid with suspended stem cells on to a support matrix. —你甚至通过在支持阵式上喷射含有悬浮培育的干细胞的流体,打印出活细胞组成的人体器官。(①squirt—to force liquid in a thin fast stream through a narrow opening; ②suspended stem cells—悬浮培育干细胞,是常用的组织干细胞及肿瘤干细胞的体外研究方法)

13. 3D printers, laser cutters and "CNC"(computer numerical control)—3D打印机、激光切割机和电脑数字控制机器

14. drill bit—(机)钻头,扁钻

15. single-color dot matrix printers—单色点阵式打印机(dot matrix—指用来组成图形,字符或数字的点矩阵)

16. Until now, the creative process has been beset with obstacles, from the problems inherent in creating a prototype, to the difficulties of persuading a third party to become involved, to the expense of the final launch. ——至今,这一创造过程遭遇重重障碍,从制造原型固有的问题,说服第三方加入项目的困难到最终筹集生产需要资金。(①beset ——to affect sth in a harmful way; ②inherent ——present naturally as a part of it)

17. the San Francisco Bay Area——圣弗朗西斯科湾区(简称 the Bay Area 湾区,是美国加州西北部的一个大都会区)

18. British Virgin Islands——英属维京群岛

19. He opted to go via the crowdfunding website. ——他选择众筹资金网站方式。

20. He had managed both to market-test his idea and find his first customers without having to go to the risky expense of first filling a warehouse (or his bedroom) with jellyfish tanks. ——他成功地将自己的设想进行市场测试,并且无需冒把仓库或卧室堆满水母水箱的风险就找到了自己的第一批客户。(market-test his idea ——to use the market to test his idea)

21. niche market——利基市场(指由企业的优势细分出来有特定需求的小市场)

22. road test its products——test its products through actual use

23. wind turbine generator——风力涡轮发电机

24. If it's astonishingly successful, then they may decide to move production to a different factory in China that specializes in bulk manufacturing. ——如果取得了惊人成功的话,他们也许会决定将生产任务转交给中国另一家专门大批量生产的工厂。(①specializes in ——does well in; ②bulk ——a large quantity of sth)

25. one of the most ruthlessly cut-throat of all areas of business——electronics——竞争最为残酷激烈的行业之一——电子业(cut-throat ——very fierce and cruel)

26. Today, Sparkfun designs and manufactures specialist printed circuit boards, using sophisticated pick-and-place robot machines to assemble them. ——现今,Sparkfun 公司设计并生产特别印制的电路板,用精密的拾取和放置自动机械装置将它们组装起来。(① sophisticated ——produced or developed with a high level of skill and knowledge; ② Sparkfun——美国最具盛名的零配件供应商)

27. Dogs and hobbies are indulged at work (though not on the production floor); tattoos and indie punk rock reflect its culture. ——上班可以随意带狗,充分发展自己的爱好(但不得在生产车间之内);文身、独立制作朋克摇滚显示他们的气质。(文身、朋克摇滚常体现个性张扬或标新立异,反叛社会的意识形态)

28. It's a far cry from the "dark satanic mill" vision of manufacturing——much closer in fact to the maverick image of software companies in their startup days. ——这与制造业的"阴森邪恶的磨坊"形象全然不同,实际上十分接近软件公司创业阶段富有创新的形象。(① maverick ——a person who does not behave or think like others, but has an independent and unusual opinion; ② dark satanic mill ——The phrase quoted from William Blake's poem is often interpreted as referring to the early Industrial Revolution and its destruction of nature and human relationship.)

29. Daily blog posts and tutorials have turned its retail website into a high-traffic community, with more than 50,000 visitors a day. ——每日的博客发布和使用说明已经将销售网站转变为一个日访问量愈 5 万人次的高频次社交区域。(high-traffic community

—with many people visiting the website)

30. If the Second Industrial Revolution was the Information Age, then I would argue that a Third Industrial Age is on its way: the age of the Makers—如果说第二次工业革命是指信息时代的话,那么我认为第三次工业革命,即"创客时代",正在到来。(on its way — coming)

Ⅳ. Language Features

《卫报》简介

《卫报》(The Guardian)原为《曼彻斯特卫报》(The Manchester Guardian),是一家地方性报纸,创办于 1821 年 5 月。后来该报发展成为全国性报纸,1859 年 7 月改为现名。

《卫报》在欧洲知识界影响很大,是一份严肃、独立的定位于高端市场的主流大报。

为了解决现代人在紧凑空间里读报的麻烦,同时也为了应对电视和网络等媒体的激烈竞争,英国《泰晤士报》和《独立报》都在 2004 年放弃了传统的大版(Broadsheet),改用四开小版(Tabloid)。《卫报》也于 2005 年 9 月改版,不过采用的是比传统大版小又比小版大的"柏林式"(Berliner)。这样做的效果是既保留了大版的严肃风格又不失小报的灵活和便捷。此外,《卫报》还改用全部彩色印刷,其意图是使这张报纸成为英国"最鲜艳"的报纸。

《卫报》政治观点中间偏左,自称政治上"是自由主义的","支持社会变革"。据 2005 年调查,该报读者有 48% 是工党支持者,34% 是民主党支持者。2010 年大选中,该报明确支持自由民主党。

《卫报》在第二次世界大战前明确反对英国政府的绥靖政策,由此获得了较好的声誉和读者信任。对伊拉克战争和阿富汗战争,《卫报》持批评态度,为此赢得大量反战读者。

该报是卫报媒体集团(the Guardian Media Group)的组成部分,2011 年 1 月发行量为 27.9 万,位于《泰晤士报》和《每日邮报》之后。然而,据该报编辑称,《卫报》电子读者数量在全球英语电子报中排行第二,仅次于《纽约时报》,该报网站是 guardian.co.uk。

《卫报》是英国五家大报之一,对于这几家大报英国社会流行的看法如下:

掌权者读《泰晤士报》(The Times is read by the people who run the country.)

权欲者读《卫报》(The Guardian is read by the people who think they ought to run the country.)

达官夫人读《每日邮报》(The Daily Mail is read by the wives of the people who run the country.)

富豪们读《金融时报》(The Financial Times is read by the people who own the country.)

怀旧派读《每日电讯报》(The Daily Express is read by the people who think the country ought to be run as it used to be run.)

《卫报》没有星期日版,但出版小型封面的《卫报周刊》(The Guardian Weekly)。每期《卫报》头版一般是 5—6 篇文章,3—4 张图片,文章几乎是长篇报道,每篇都要转版,转版走向明确标示,有的头版文章仅有图片、标题和版面走向。该报曾获一系列英国新闻奖(British Press Awards)。由于该报根据"监控门"事件揭露者斯诺登提供的大量机密文件所做的监控事件报道,2014 年获得美国普利策新闻奖(Pulitzer Prize)。

《卫报》的网址是 www.guardian.co.uk。

V. Analysis of the Content

1. The phrase "a small fortune" in the sentence "It took my grandfather a decade and a small fortune to perfect his device and market it." (Para. 2) means _____.
   A. a good luck
   B. a bad luck
   C. a small sum of money
   D. a large amount of money
2. How long did it take the author's grandfather to produce the automatic sprinkler system?
   A. About 10 years.
   B. A few months.
   C. 7 Years.
   D. 3 Years.
3. Traditional manufacturing drives down cost of production by _____.
   A. sound management
   B. use of cheap labor
   C. use of low-price raw materials
   D. economy of scale
4. Which of the following is NOT on the author's list of factors helping to start the Maker Movement?
   A. Crowdsourcing power of the Internet.
   B. 3D printers.
   C. Increasing sophistication of design programs.
   D. The government's favorable tax policies.
5. Which of the following statements is NOT true about Makers enterprises?
   A. They have to remain small-scale.
   B. They involve the use of new technology.
   C. Their start-up is cheap.
   D. They have agility and flexibility.

VI. Questions on the Article

1. By what means did the author manage to produce the improved water sprinkler in just a few months?
2. What is the Maker Movement?
3. What is the significance of the Maker Movement?
4. What kinds of physical stuff can 3D printers make now?
5. What does the example of Alex Andon show?
6. What kinds of products is the current manufacturing technology that supports Makers ideally suited to?
7. What does the example of WindCo show?
8. Tell something about the image of Makers enterprises demonstrated by Sparkfun.
9. What are the prospects of the Maker Movement?

VII. Topics for Discussion

1. Does a service economy mean elimination of manufacturing?
2. Was the Second Industrial Revolution the Information Age?

Lesson 30

Think Again: American Nuclear Disarmament
A smaller atomic arsenal isn't just wishful thinking—it's bad strategy.
By Matthew Kroenig

(Abridged)

"Nuclear Weapons Are Cold War Relics."
Not so.

When the Soviet Union collapsed in 1991, the era of nuclear competition seemed to be at an end, and the United States and Russia began to get rid of many weapons they had used to threaten each other for more than 40 years. In 1967, the size of the U.S. nuclear arsenal peaked at 31,255 warheads, but by 2010, under the New Strategic Arms Reduction Treaty (New START)[1] signed with Russia, the United States had promised to deploy no more than 1,550.

In June of this year, U.S. President Barack Obama announced his intention to go even lower, to around 1,000 warheads—a move that would leave the United States with fewer nuclear weapons than at any time since 1953. What's more, influential figures around the world, including erstwhile American hawks, have increasingly supported steps toward total disarmament. In his major 2009 address in Prague, Obama committed "to seek the peace and security of a world without nuclear weapons."

Nuclear reductions and the heady dreams of abolition are driven in part by a belief that nukes are Cold War[2] anachronisms. But it would be incorrect—dangerous, in fact—to assume that the conditions that have allowed the United States to de-emphasize its atomic arsenal will persist. Nuclear weapons are still the most potent military tools on Earth, and they will remain central to geopolitical competition. They have been relatively unimportant in the recent past not because humanity has somehow become more enlightened, but because we have been blessed with a temporary respite from great-power rivalry.

The Soviet Union's collapse left the United States as the world's sole superpower, and America's unmatched conventional military overawed other countries.[3] Nuclear weapons have not been central to America's national security for the past two decades because its primary foes—Serbia, Iraq, Afghanistan, and al Qaeda—did not have them.[4] Whatever America's problems in prosecuting its recent wars, a lack of firepower was not one of them.[5]

But times are changing. Economists predict that China could overtake the United States as the world's largest economy in the coming years, and international relations theory tells us that transitions between reigning hegemons and rising challengers often produce conflict. Already, China has become more assertive in pursuing revisionist claims in East Asia, confronting America's allies, and building military capabilities—including anti-ship ballistic missiles and submarines—tailored for a fight with the United States[6]. In September 2012, a dispute between China and Japan over the Senkaku Islands nearly caused a war that could have easily drawn in the United States.[7] Beijing's contested claims to natural resources in the South China Sea and ever-present tensions with Taiwan could also lead to Sino-U.S. conflict. Even relations with Russia, America's partner in arms control, are becoming more competitive: The civil war in Syria bears every hallmark of a Cold War-style proxy battle.[8] In short, great-power political competition is heating up once again, and as it does, nuclear weapons will once again take center stage.

The writing is already on the wall.[9] Russia, China, India, Pakistan, and North Korea are modernizing or expanding their nuclear arsenals, and Iran is vigorously pursuing its own nuclear capability. As Yale University political scientist Paul Bracken notes, we are entering a "second nuclear age" in which "the whole complexion of global power politics is changing because of the reemergence of nuclear weapons as a vital element of statecraft and power politics." Nostalgia for simpler times can be seductive, but the United States needs a nuclear force that can protect it from the challenges that lie ahead.

"It Takes Only a Handful of Nukes to Deter an Enemy."
Wrong.

Advocates of further cuts argue that a secure second-strike capability—the ability to absorb an attack and retain enough nuclear warheads to launch a devastating response—is sufficient for nuclear deterrence. Although "secure" and "devastating" are imprecise terms, many analysts would say that a few dozen submarine-launched ballistic missiles, each with multiple warheads, is plenty because at-sea subs are difficult to target in a first strike and the firepower provided by, say, 200 nuclear weapons is impressive. By their logic, anything more is "overkill" that can be cut with little loss to U.S. security.

Although it is possible that no sane leader would intentionally start a nuclear war with a state that possesses even a small deterrent force, nuclear-armed states still have conflicting interests that can lead to crises.[10] And it turns out that, contrary to widely held assumptions, the nuclear balance of power is critically important to how such disputes are resolved.

Recently, I methodically reviewed the relationship between the size of a country's nuclear arsenal and its security. In a statistical analysis of all nuclear-armed countries from 1945 to 2001, I found that the state with more warheads was only one-third as likely to be challenged militarily by other countries and more than 10 times more likely to prevail in a crisis—that is, to achieve its basic political goals—when it was challenged. Moreover, I found that the size of this advantage increased along with the margin of superiority. States with vastly more nukes (95 percent of the two countries' total warheads) were more than 17 times more likely to win. These findings held even after accounting for disparities in conventional military power, political stakes, geographical proximity, type of political system, population, territorial size, history of past disputes, and other factors that could have influenced the outcomes.

When the United States operated from a position of nuclear strength during the Cold War, it stopped the Soviet Union from building a nuclear submarine base in Cuba in 1970 and deterred Moscow from increasing support to its Arab allies in the 1967 and 1973 Arab-Israeli wars[11]. By contrast, when the nuclear balance was less favorable to Washington, it was unable to achieve clear victories in crises against the Soviet Union—for example, failing to roll back Moscow's 1979 invasion of Afghanistan[12].

In addition, qualitative evidence from the past 70 years shows that leaders pay close attention to the nuclear balance of power, that they believe superiority enhances their position, and that a nuclear advantage often translates into a geopolitical advantage. During the Cuban missile crisis[13], American nuclear superiority helped compel Moscow to withdraw its missiles from the island. As Gen. Maxwell Taylor, then chairman of the Joint Chiefs of Staff[14], wrote in a memo to Defense Secretary Robert McNamara, "We have the strategic advantage in our general war capabilities... This is no time to run scared." Similarly, Secretary of State Dean Rusk argued, "One thing Mr. Khrushchev may have in mind is that he knows that we have a substantial nuclear superiority, but he also knows that we don't really live under fear of his nuclear weapons to the extent that he has to live under fear of ours."

We see similar patterns in South Asia. When asked years later why Pakistan ultimately withdrew its forces from Indian Kashmir during the 1999 Kargil crisis[15], former Indian Defense Minister George Fernandes cited his country's nuclear superiority. In the event of a nuclear exchange, he said, "We may have lost a part of our population ... [but] Pakistan may have been completely wiped out."

This may sound crazy. To most people, "But you should see the other guy"[16] would be scant consolation for losing perhaps millions of one's fellow citizens. But the truth is that nuclear war might well be more devastating for one country than for the other, even if both sides can inflict "unacceptable" damage. As Cold War nuclear strategist Herman Kahn wrote, "Few people differentiate between having 10 million dead, 50 million dead, or 100 million dead. It all seems too horrible. However, it does not take much imagination to see that there is a difference."

This is not to argue that leaders of countries with bigger arsenals believe they can fight and win nuclear wars. The logic is more subtle.[17] Nuclear states coerce each other through brinkmanship. They heighten crises, raising the risk of nuclear war until one side backs down and the other gets its way. At each stage of the crisis, leaders make gut-wrenching calculations about whether to escalate, thereby risking a catastrophic nuclear war, or to submit, throwing an important geopolitical victory to their opponent. If the costs of nuclear war are higher for one state than another, then giving in will always look more attractive to leaders in the inferior position—whatever payoff they might get from escalating would always be offset by a higher potential cost.

So, on average, we should expect that leaders with fewer nukes at their disposal will be more likely to cave during a crisis. And this is exactly what the data show.

Competition between nuclear powers is like a game of chicken, and in a game of chicken, we should expect the smaller car to swerve first, even if a crash would be disastrous for both.[18] The United States has always driven a Hummer[19], but it is trading it in for a Prius[20], even though games of chicken are likely for decades to come. Rather than cutting its forces, the United States should, as President John F. Kennedy promised, maintain a nuclear arsenal "second to none."

"But Doesn't Superiority Increase the Risk of War in the First Place?"
Don't be so sure.

It is true that many strategists have long argued that having a nuclear arsenal "second to none" could increase the risk of nuclear war. Their logic is simple: If a state has a "first-strike advantage"—that is, the ability to launch a nuclear attack that disarms its opponent and leaves it(itself) relatively invulnerable to retaliation—then, in a crisis, it might be tempted to start a nuclear war. Alternatively, the weaker state might be tempted to use its weapons first, lest it lose them altogether. By this reasoning, nuclear superiority is dangerous for everyone, and the most stable situation is one in which both sides have survivable arsenals of roughly the same size, leaving both vulnerable.

Today, it is still widely believed that it is a bad idea for the United States to possess a nuclear advantage over Russia, and the Obama administration's 2010 Nuclear Posture Review[21] identified "strategic stability" as a primary goal. That is why New START and Obama's proposed follow-on agreement aim for equal limits on the United States and Russia. Some analysts also apply this logic to China, over which the United States has tremendous nuclear superiority. (China is thought to have a mere 50 or so warheads capable of reaching the United States.)

But an American first-strike advantage is just that, an advantage, and arguments that try to make a vice out of a virtue rest on tortured logic[22]. After all, the United States possesses a first-strike advantage against the world's 184 non-nuclear states, and it doesn't wring its hands about that. Would Americans be better off if these countries could hold them hostage with nuclear threats? No. Would they feel better if North Korea's missile tests did not routinely fail, giving the Hermit Kingdom[23] a more reliable ability to nuke Los Angeles? Of course not. Then why is the United States so fearful of pursuing superiority over Russia and China?

The answer often given is that, while the United States can trust itself not to start a nuclear war, it doesn't want to make a Russian or Chinese leader feel the need to "use 'em or lose' em." But this fear is unfounded. A leader in a position of inferiority—inferiority so extreme that his country could be vulnerable to a disarming first strike—has a choice of launching a nuclear war he will surely lose or simply conceding the contested issue. Faced with that choice, there is every reason to believe he will back down. Indeed, this is exactly the dynamic that my research demonstrates. To make any other decision, a leader would have to be either crazy or at the end of his rope. But if either were the case, nuclear parity would, if anything, make him more likely to gamble on nuclear war.

In sum, a U.S. nuclear advantage is a major problem—if you are one of Washington's adversaries.

"But a Smaller Arsenal Will Help the United States Discourage Nuclear Proliferation."
Keep dreaming.

Proponents of deep cuts claim that a smaller arsenal will help the United States stop the spread of nuclear weapons to rogue states[24] and terrorists because having so many nuclear weapons makes it difficult (if not hypocritical) to tell, say, Iran that it cannot have any or to convince non-nuclear countries (such as Brazil and Turkey) to help pressure Iran.

This argument makes sense at a superficial level, but on closer inspection it falls apart. As Iran's leaders decide whether to push forward with, or put limits on, their nuclear program, they likely consider whether nuclear weapons would improve their security, whether they have the technical capability to produce nuclear weapons, whether they could withstand economic sanctions or military strikes from the United States and its allies, and a host of other factors. The size of the U.S. nuclear arsenal would not affect any of these calculations.

Similarly, in considering whether to pressure Tehran, Turkey likely considers the threat posed by a nuclear Iran, whether it can actually affect Iranian policy, how curtailing trade with Iran would hurt its economy, and how its Iran policy will affect relations with other countries. But, again, it is implausible to think that if Washington possessed 1,000 warheads instead of 1,550, Turkey would suddenly get tougher with Iran.

In my research, I systematically searched for a correlation between the size of the U.S. nuclear arsenal and a variety of measurable nonproliferation outcomes: state decisions to explore, pursue, and acquire nuclear weapons; voting on nonproliferation issues in the United Nations Security Council; and the transfer of sensitive nuclear technology to non-nuclear-weapon states. I couldn't find any evidence of a relationship. The United States has been cutting the size of its nuclear arsenal since the late 1960s, but there is no reason to believe that its cuts have slowed or reversed proliferation. In fact, the most important diplomatic breakthrough in stopping the spread of nukes—the opening for signature of the Nuclear Non-Proliferation Treaty (NPT)[25]—occurred in 1968, at nearly the peak of the U.S. arsenal's size. And, remember, 177 countries have never pursued nuclear weapons at any point, including when the United States possessed more than 30,000 warheads.

Some advocates argue that many states signed the NPT only because it mandates cuts to existing nuclear arsenals, but in fact the NPT does not require cuts or disarmament. It simply requires all states to "pursue negotiations in good faith" on measures relating to disarmament. So though the United States can by all means pursue negotiations, it should not come to a deal that further reduces its nuclear stockpile until the world has been made safe for disarmament—and that, unfortunately, will not happen anytime soon.

"The U.S. Can Save Money by Shrinking Its Nuclear Arsenal."
Don't count on it.

In the climate of budget austerity now afflicting Washington, some supporters of nuclear cuts turn to another, nonstrategic argument to advance their case, saying that reducing the size of the nuclear arsenal would save money. But it would not save much, and it might even cost more.

It is important to understand that warhead reductions alone will not result in savings. As any employee of the U.S. national nuclear laboratories can tell you, the cost of nuclear weapons is in the infrastructure; the warheads, in comparison, are virtually free. If the United States is going to retain even a handful of nuclear weapons, it will need national laboratories with scientists and technicians, delivery vehicles, military units trained to handle nuclear weapons, and many other capabilities. These are large, fixed costs regardless of the number of warheads in the arsenal.

Moreover, reducing the number of nuclear weapons the United States deploys can actually result in short-term budget increases. Reducing arsenal size means pulling missiles out of silos, dismantling retired warheads, and decommissioning and decontaminating nuclear facilities. All of this costs money.

It would only be by failing to fully modernize the systems that deliver the warheads—intercontinental ballistic missiles, bombers, and submarines—that the United States could hope to save money. But unless it completely disarms or kills a leg of this triad, the country's aging missiles, bombers, and subs will need to be upgraded. Delaying the modernization of delivery vehicles, as some have suggested, would save only an estimated $3.9 billion annually over 10 years, an amount that is nothing short of trivial compared with the overall U.S. defense budget[26], which is roughly $600 billion per year.

Over the long term, the budget-savings argument becomes even less compelling. Nuclear weapons provide a lot of bang for the buck[27], literally and figuratively. President Dwight Eisenhower's "New Look" policy[28] in the 1950s emphasized nuclear weapons—as does current Russian military doctrine—because they are less costly than comparable conventional capabilities. If the United States continues to cut its nuclear arsenal, it will need to develop new conventional capabilities to fill the roles and missions previously performed by nuclear weapons. At present, nuclear weapons provide a strategic deterrent at a cost of only about 4 percent of the defense budget. Do we really think equivalent conventional forces would be more cost-efficient?

Furthermore, only if we think the United States can maintain a diminished nuclear force indefinitely is it plausible to think that nuclear cuts will save money, but this would be an unwise bet given that other countries are moving in the opposite direction. In 1989, the Energy Department shut down its only plutonium-pit manufacturing plant at Rocky Flats, Colorado. Decommissioning and decontaminating the facility cost taxpayers $7 billion. In 2007, however, the department restored pit-manufacturing capability at a cost of billions of dollars, and it is seeking billions more for a new facility. This poor decision teaches a broader lesson: It would be much more costly to cut now and build back up later, rather than simply recapitalize current capabilities.

To justify kneecapping the U.S. arsenal as we enter a second nuclear age, the savings would have to be overwhelming. But they are not. As Deputy Defense Secretary Ashton Carter recently said, "Nuclear weapons don't actually cost that much ... You don't save a lot of money by having arms control."

Instead of striving for the smallest possible arsenal in the erroneous belief that less is better, the United States should strive to maintain clear nuclear superiority over its adversaries. Ideally, this means the ability to wipe out an enemy's nuclear forces before they can be used and to annihilate its homeland—because the more devastating that adversaries find the prospect of nuclear war, the less likely they will be to start trouble. Where this is not possible, the United States must aim for a posture that limits damage to the U.S. homeland to the greatest extent possible and that at least ensures destruction of an adversary.

That means the United States should refrain from additional nuclear reductions and should maintain the "hedge" force of weapons it keeps in reserve. The Obama administration must also follow through on its promise to fully modernize U.S. nuclear infrastructure. Finally, the country must prepare for the possibility that if China or other strategic competitors continue to expand their nuclear arsenals, the United States might once again have to build up its strategic forces. You don't bring a knife to a gunfight, and America shouldn't bring a crippled nuclear arsenal to the second nuclear age.

From *Foreign Policy*, September 3rd, 2013

Ⅰ. New Words

anachronism	[ə'nækrə,nizəm]	n.	an idea that seems old fashioned and does not belong to the present
arsenal	['ɑːsənəl]	n.	武器库
assertive	[ə'səːtiv]	adj.	武断的；过于自信的
austerity	[ɔ'steriti]	n.	（国家开支）紧缩；严格的节制消费
bipartizan	[,baipɑːti'zæn]	adj.	两党（或派）的；为两党所拥护的
brinksmanship	['briŋksmənʃip]	n.	边缘政策（冒险把危急形势推到极限）
cave	[keiv]	v.	~ in to collapse
coerce	[kəu'əːs]	v.	to force sb to do sth by using threats
complexion	[kəm'plekʃn]	n.	the general character of sth
decommission	[,diːkə'miʃn]	v.	使核武器退役
deploy	[di'plɔi]	v.	to spread or arrange for military use
devastating	['devəsteitiŋ]	adj.	causing a lot of destruction
dismantle	[dis'mæntl]	v.	to take apart a machine
disparity	[di'spærəti]	n.	*formal* a difference
erstwhile	['əːstwail]	adj.	*formal* former
follow-on	['fɔləu,ɔn]	adj.	后继的
geopolitical	[,dʒiːəpə'litikəl]	adj.	地缘政治的
heady	['hedi]	adj.	excited in a way that makes you do things without worrying about the possible results
hallmark	['hɔːl,mɑːk]	n.	a feature or quality that is typical of sth
hegemony	[hi'dʒeməni]	n.	支配权，霸权
host	[həust]	n.	a large number
implausible	[im'plɔːzibl]	adj.	not seeming reasonable or likely to be true
infrastructure	['infrə,strʌktʃə]	n.	基础结构，基础设施
kneecap	['niːkæp]	v.	to cripple
mandate	['mæn,deit]	v.	to require by a law
methodical	[mi'θɔdikəl]	adj.	done in a careful and logical way
nostalgia	[nɔ'stældʒiə]	n.	恋旧，怀旧
overawe	[,əuvə'ɔː]	v.	to impress someone so much as to make him nervous or frightened
nuke	[njuːk]	n.	a nuclear weapon
parity	['pærəti]	n.	the state of being equal
payoff	['pei,ɔːf]	n.	报偿
pit	[pit]	n.	（地面的）坑，洞，矿井
proliferate	[prəu'lifəreit]	v.	to increase rapidly in number or amount

proximity	[prɔk'simiti]	n.	the state of being near
reign	[rein]	v.	to rule as king, queen, emperor
respite	['respit]	n.	a pause or rest from sth difficult or unpleasant
revisionist	[ri'viʒənist]	adj.	修正主义的,持修正论的
plutonium	[pluːˈtəuniəm]	n.	[化]钚(放射性元素)
roll	[rəul]	v.	~ **back** to force sth back
sanction	['sæŋkʃən]	n.	an official order that limits trade, contract with authority
scant	[skænt]	adj.	hardly enough
silo	['sailəu]	n.	(导弹)发射井
triad	['traiəd]	n.	三位一体,三合一战略力量
wring	[riŋ]	v.	~ **one's hands** 苦恼(或悲痛、绝望)地绞扭双手

Ⅱ. Background Information

美国核裁军

自 1945 年美国研制原子弹并在日本使用后,国际社会就开始了核军备控制活动。1946 年 1 月,联合国大会通过的第一个决议就要求消灭原子武器并确保和平利用原子能。20 世纪 60 年代中期,中国出于防御目的,开始拥有核武器。从此,世界核国家增加到美国、苏联、法国、英国和中国五个。但是美苏所拥有的核弹头数量占世界核弹头库存总数的 97%。

冷战期间,美苏两国奉行核威慑、核讹诈政策,进行核军备竞赛。在此期间,两国举行了限制核武器谈判并签订了一些核军备控制的条约和协议。如:1963 年美苏签订了《部分禁止核试验条约》(Partial Test Ban Treaty);1968 年双方签订了《防止核武器扩散条约》(Treaty on the Non-proliferation of Nuclear Weapons);1969 年双方在芬兰赫尔辛基举行第一轮限制战略武器会谈(First Round of Strategic Arms Limitation Talks,简称 SALT Ⅰ),这一轮会谈导致《反导条约》(Anti-Ballistic Missile Treaty)和《进攻性战略武器的临时协议》(Interim Accord on Offensive Strategic Weapons)的签订。此后,双方又进行第二轮限制战略武器会谈。1979 年美苏签署了《第二轮限制战略武器会谈协定》(SALT Ⅱ Agreement)。该协定由于苏联此后入侵阿富汗,美国参议院拒绝签署。

尽管双方举行了一系列会谈,也签订了相关协议,但核军备并未得到有效控制,反呈增加趋势。核力量曾增大到十分荒唐的地步。美苏两方所拥有的核弹头数量都超过 3 万枚,达到"超饱和"状态,各方所拥有的核力量足够摧毁对方 10 余次!

80 年代中期起,美苏开始加快控制核军备步伐。1991 年双方签订了《削减和限制进攻性战略武器条约》,又称《第一阶段削减战略武器条约》(START Ⅰ Agreement)。条约规定:双方把各自拥有的核弹头削减至不超过 6,000 枚,运载工具减至不超过 1,600 件。1993 年美俄签署了第二阶段削减战略武器条约,即《进一步削减战略武器条约》(Further Strategic Reduction Talks Agreement)。该条约规定美俄拥有进攻性战略武器上的核弹头分别削减至 3,500 枚和 3,000 枚。之后美俄关系急剧恶化,两国迟迟未交条约批准文件。2010 年 4 月美俄签署了《新削减战略武器条约》(New START Treaty)。该条约规定：双方部署的核弹头数量不超过1550枚；用于发射弹头的发射工具数量不超过800架；已部署的洲际导弹不超过700枚；已部署的潜基弹道导弹不超过700枚；已部署的可挂载核武器的重型轰炸机不超过700架；削减目标在生效后7年之内完成；条约有效期为10年；期满后可延期5年。

美国以基辛格为首的有识之士提出世界无核武器目标，这一呼吁得到不少政界、军界官员和学者的支持。然而，美国要求政府增强核军备的右翼势力也十分活跃。他们叫嚣："美国必须确保核力量的绝对优势。"这股势力不断给政府施加压力。因此，核裁军的道路依然存在重要障碍。

Ⅲ. Notes to the Text

1. New START—《新削减战略武器条约》(该条约替代2009年12月5日到期的《削减战略武器条约》，条约有效期为10年，并可延长5年)
2. Cold War—(第二次世界大战后为争夺世界霸权的)美苏冷战(时期)
3. The Soviet Union's collapse left the United States as the world's sole superpower, and America's unmatched conventional military overawed other countries. —苏联的解体使美国成了世界上唯一的超级大国，而美国的无与伦比的常规军事力量使其他国家感到胆战心惊。(①sole—only；②overawe—to impress sb so much that they feel very nervous or frightened)
4. Nuclear weapons have not been central to America's national security for the past two decades because its primary foes—Serbia, Iraq, Afghanistan, and al Qaeda—did not have them. —过去的20年里核武器并不是美国国家安全的最主要手段，因为美国的几个主要敌人——塞尔维亚、伊拉克、阿富汗和基地组织没有核武器。
5. Whatever America's problems in prosecuting its recent wars, a lack of firepower was not one of them. —美国所进行的最近几场战争，不管存在着什么样的问题，火力不足不在其中。(prosecute—to carry out)
6. building military capabilities—including anti-ship ballistic missiles and submarines—tailored for a fight with the United States—打造专门用于对美作战的军事力量，包括反舰弹道导弹和潜艇(tailored for—made or adapted for a particular purpose)
7. In September 2012, a dispute between China and Japan over the Senkaku Islands nearly caused a war that could have easily drawn in the United States. —2012年9月，中日之间一场关于钓鱼岛(尖阁列岛)的争议差点引发了一场很容易把美国牵入的战争。
8. The civil war in Syria bears every hallmark of a Cold War-style proxy battle. —叙利亚内战具有冷战式由第三方代理大国战争的特征(①hallmark—a feature that is typical of sth；②proxy battle—a conflict where third parties fight on behalf of more powerful parties)
9. The writing is already on the wall. —凶兆已经出现。(used to describe a situation in which there are signs that sth is going to have problems or that it is going to fail)
10. Although it is possible that no sane leader would intentionally start a nuclear war with a state that possesses even a small deterrent force, nuclear-armed states still have

conflicting interests that can lead to crises. —尽管没有一个明智的国家领导人会故意对只拥有很小核威慑力量的国家发起核战争,但是拥有核武器国家之间还是存在能够导致危机的利益冲突。

11. the 1967 and 1973 Arab-Israeli wars—1967 年和 1973 年阿以战争(①the 1967 Arab-Israeli War —也称第三次中东战争。埃及、约旦和叙利亚遭到失败,以色列占领埃及控制的加沙地带和西奈半岛,约旦控制的约旦河西岸和耶路撒冷旧城,叙利亚控制的戈兰高地。按照联合国安理会 242 号决议,以色列必须归还所占领土,但以色列只归还了部分领土;②1973 Arab-Israeli War—也称第四次中东战争。埃及与叙利亚决议收复六年前以色列所占领地。开始埃及、叙利亚占上风,但局势很快逆转,最终以色列获胜。)

12. failing to roll back Moscow's 1979 invasion of Afghanistan—未能迫使苏联放弃 1979 年对阿富汗的入侵(Moscow's 1979 invasion of Afghanistan—At the end of Dec. 1979, the Soviet Union sent thousands of troops into Afghanistan and assumed control of Kabul and large portions of the country. The conflict in Afghanistan lasted 9 years.)

13. the Cuban missile crisis—古巴导弹危机(1962 年美国、古巴和苏联之间的一场危机,直接原因是苏联在古巴部署导弹。最终达成的协议是苏联撤回部署在古巴的导弹。美国宣布不再对古巴进行任何入侵行动并撤回部署在土耳其和意大利的导弹。)

14. the chairman of the Joint Chiefs of Staff—参谋长联席会议主席

15. the 1999 Kargil crisis—卡吉尔危机(also known as the Kargil Conflict/War. It was an armed conflict between India and Pakistan that took place between May and July in 1999 in the Kargil district of Kashmir and elsewhere along the line of control.)

16. "But you should see the other guy"... —但是对手的情况更糟……(The sentence is a way of saying "Though I have suffered from injury, the opponent's injury is much greater." It is intended to seek consolation.)

17. This is not to argue that leaders of countries with bigger arsenals believe they can fight and win nuclear wars. The logic is more subtle. —这并不是说拥有更多核武器国家的领导人相信他们可以发起并且打赢核战争。其中的道理更为复杂。(①logic—sensible reason;②subtle—not easy to explain)

18. Competition between nuclear powers is like a game of chicken, and in a game of chicken, we should expect the smaller car to swerve first, even if a crash would be disastrous for both. —核武器强国之间的竞争就像是一场驾车胆量比试,在这场比试中,尽管撞车对于双方来说都会造成灾祸,结果应该是比较小的车先退让。(①chicken—a dare or challenge to do sth dangerous as a test of courage;②swerve—to change direction suddenly in order to avoid hitting)

19. Hummer—悍马车(美国 AGM 公司生产的越野车。其特点是马力大,结构硬,体积较大,乘员较多。)

20. Prius—普锐斯车(日本丰田公司生产的一款混合动力车,其特点是重量较轻,油耗低,环保性能较好)

21. Nuclear Posture Review—核态势评估报告(a legislatively-mandated review that establishes U.S. nuclear policy, strategy, capabilities and force posture for the next ten years)

22. arguments that try to make a vice out of a virtue rest on tortured logic—试图把美好的东西变成邪恶的东西的论说是以歪曲的逻辑作为基础的

23. Hermit Kingdom—隐士王国（a term applied to any country, organization or society which walls itself off, from the rest of the world）

24. rogue states—流氓国家（a term used by the U.S. government for over 10 years in reference to countries such as Iran and the People's Republic of Korea）

25. the Nuclear Non-Proliferation Treaty（NPT）—《不扩散核武器条约》（该条约于1968年7月1日由英、美、苏和其他59个国家缔结签署,其宗旨是防止核扩散,推动核裁军和促进和平利用核能的国际合作）

26. an amount that is nothing short of trivial compared with the overall U.S. defense budget—这个数额比起美国国防总预算而言全然不足挂齿（①trivial—unimportant；②nothing short of—nothing less than）

27. Nuclear weapons provide a lot of bang for the buck…—钱花在核武器上更加有价值……（bang for the buck—better value for the money you spend）

28. "New Look" policy—"新面貌"政策（referring to Dwight Eisenhower's policy on balancing the Cold War military commitments of the U.S. with the nation's financial resources. The policy emphasized reliance on strategic nuclear weapons to deter potential threats, both conventional and nuclear, from the Soviet Union.）

Ⅳ. Language Features

外报外刊中意识形态的表现

新闻话语也是意识形态的话语。西方主要报刊基本是资本主义垄断集团手中的媒体。它们向读者灌输的是这些特权集团的意识形态和观念。

外报外刊的意识形态和观念反映在文章篇章、句式、用词和配置的图片及其说明文字上,其中词汇层面表现得更为明显。常用的手法是委婉语和负面词语的使用。西方报刊通常使用温和词语来掩盖己方存在的问题和矛盾。在国际新闻报道中,对顺乎美国心意的国家常用褒义词语,如"democratic system"（民主体制）,"a country ruled by law"（法治国家）。对于意识形态不同的国家常用贬义词语,如"dictatorial regime"（独裁政权）,"totalitarian government"（极权政府）。"意识形态通过伪装自己的性质,装扮成另一种东西发挥作用,其作用方式最隐蔽时才最有效。"西方报刊意识形态的语言表现方式常常十分隐晦,如使用信息来源不明的引语："It is said that……""It is reported that…""According to reliable sources…""Authorities say that…""Witnesses say that…"在转述中,援引报道所涉及人物的话时,作者通过情感色彩的"说"意动词使用,既使报道显得客观又影响读者的情感和态度。我们还常常发现西方报刊常采用"被动句式""静态动词"等方式来弱化自己所反感的新闻事件效果。

本文是篇评论。社论、评论在西方报刊中占有重要地位,常被称作"报刊的心脏"。评论与报道的最大区别在于主观发挥,作者观点鲜明、直言不讳。本文所代表的是美国极右分子对核军备的观点。作者提出:虽然冷战已经结束,但是核战争威胁依然存在;美国核武力越强,安全越有保障;美国核优势不会增加核战争风险;削减核武器不会阻止核扩散,无益减少美国财政开支;主张美国不要再削减核武器,同时要进一步更新核武器设施,确保拥有一支全球绝对第一的核力量。

作者把我国经济实力的增强说成构成对美国安全的威胁,肆意夸大其他国家的核武力的威胁,全然否定和贬低削减核武器对缓和世界紧张局势和美国国防开支所起的重大作用,其用意是要美国保住其核军备的绝对优势,使美国成为可以在世界为所欲为的核霸主。如果美国步入这些极右分子所设计的轨道,其结果必然引起世界新一轮更大规模的核军备竞赛。

本文在用词方面也显示了作者对我国和其他一些持有与美国不同政见国家的敌意,如把我国维护领海主权和国家统一歪曲为"contested claims to natural resources in the South China Sea and ever present tensions with Taiwan",把某些不同体制国家污蔑为"rogue nations"等。

V. Analysis of the Content

1. The author's list of countries modernizing and expanding nuclear arsenals does not include _____.
   A. India   B. Russia
   C. Britain   D. North Korea
2. It can be seen from the article that many analysts in the U.S. would like to reduce the number of nuclear weapons down to _____.
   A. around 200   B. 1000
   C. 1550   D. 500
3. To the author's mind, what led to the Soviet Union's withdrawal of missiles from Cuba was _____.
   A. Cuban people's demands   B. pressure from the whole world
   C. U.S. nuclear superiority   D. the Soviet Union's financial difficulty
4. Which of the following is NOT a part of the triad?
   A. Land-based missiles.   B. Missile-carrying submarines.
   C. Strategic bombers.   D. Satellites.
5. Which of the following is NOT the author's view?
   A. Nuclear weapons have always been central to America's national security.
   B. Nuclear weapons are still the most potent military tools in the world.
   C. Nuclear superiority is important to present geopolitical competition.
   D. Nuclear weapons are more cost-efficient than conventional forces.

VI. Questions on the Article

1. How many nuclear warheads did the U.S. have in 1967? How many nuclear warheads had the U.S. promised to deploy under NEW START by 2010?
2. What did the Obama administration intend to do about the nuclear arsenal?
3. What is the partial reason for the ideas of nuclear reduction and abolition?
4. According to the author, what problem does transition between reigning hegemons and rising challengers often produce?

5. To the author's mind, what does his qualitative evidence from the past 70 years show?
6. What does the "first-strike advantage" refer to?
7. What does the secure second-strike capability mean?
8. What does the author think of the relationship between the size of the U. S. nuclear arsenal and nuclear proliferation?
9. What did President Eisenhower's "New Look" policy emphasize?
10. What does the author suggest the U. S. should do about its nuclear force?

Ⅶ. Topics for Discussion

1. Which increases the risk of war, nuclear superiority or nuclear parity?
2. Is a smaller atomic arsenal bad strategy for the U. S. ?

Lesson 31

On the Horizon: Are the next generation of UAVs ready to take off?

With the likes of Reaper and Shadow[1] now established on the modern battlefield, manufacturers and operators alike are looking at what comes next. Huw Williams canvasses the opinion of some of the leaders in the field and looks at what the future may hold.

(Abridged)

By Huw Williams

During the last few years a number of events and milestones have passed that have affected the development of the next generation of unmanned aerial vehicles (UAVs) both positively and negatively.

Late 2012 saw the first flight of the pan-European Neuron combat UAV demonstrator and the US Navy's (USN's) X-47B programme continuing apace, with successful catapult take-off trials and the embarkation of the platform onboard an aircraft carrier.[2] Conversely, events in Iran in December 2011 provided a setback, with the clandestine, cutting edge RQ-170 Sentinel[3] downed in the desert near the Afghan border. If Iran's claims that they were able to "hijack" the aircraft are true then clearly much work is needed in securing UAVs from electronic attack.

While UAVs continue to have their doubters, their role during the Iraq and Afghanistan conflicts[4] has cemented their place in the inventories of many countries. However, the development of new systems is now at tipping point and a sneak peak (**peek**) of what the next generation may offer has been provided by the latest demonstrations.[5] Ultimately, the discriminator may not be what technologies can be developed, but rather if militaries have the inclination and the means to invest the capital required.[6]

Industry is unable, or unwilling, to take the bold step without the support of the military and an outline of what capabilities will be required of future platforms. Fortunately, the USN—arguably the most proactive service in examining future systems— is to announce the requirements for its Unmanned Carrier Launched Airborne Surveillance and Strike System (UCLASS)[7] in early 2013, and this will likely provide an indication of what most users will be looking for.

"The question will no longer be if the UAV is good or not, the question will be what kind of added value does it give to the end user. In that sense we see a trend in which customers all over the world are talking about mission systems and not only about aircraft performance ... about what kind of missions it can perform," Elad Aharonson, General Manager of Elbit Systems[8]' Unmanned Aerial Systems (UAS) Division, told *IHS Jane's*[9], adding, "in that sense we see more and more technology going onboard UAVs ... now we're talking about a lot of other sensors and missions systems, such as communications intelligence payloads for finding radios and cell phones and listening to them, electronics intelligence also, which can detect and locate radar and other transmitting systems." In addition to these Aharonson says there is interest in equipping UAVs with radars, both synthetic aperture systems[10] and naval radars.

"On the military side the mission sets that we've seen are in benign airspace environments, so certainly one thing would be the ability to operate in high-threat environments," Bob Ruszkowski, Director of UCLASS programme development at Lockheed Martin[11] said. "Another aspect that we feel needs to be addressed is the ability to self-deploy across international airspace; we also believe they need to have open architectures so that upgrades can be done in a portable way.[12] I think some of the missions that we might see unmanned aircraft growing into on the military side might be more specialised. For example we've seen a lot of ISR[13] missions that unmanned systems are addressing. I think you'll start to see more in the electronic warfare realm, or other types of intelligence gathering. I think it will be many years before we see a growth into air-to-air missions, but certainly we'll see more air-to-ground operations and the ability to interoperate with manned aircraft in combined operations. Right now they are very segregated—we see them as being more closely integrated and synergised."

The ability for the next generation of UAVs to operate in contested and hostile airspace is a key capability, Ruszkowski explained. "When you look at the national strategy of the United States and its pivoting to the Pacific, you can see that the environment in that part of the world and the potential adversaries are much more demanding than say in Afghanistan and Iraq. Given that, I would posit that in a crisis or wartime scenario in the South China Sea you would probably see very few of the current generation of UAVs deployed, because quite frankly they would have very limited utility. For those future scenarios the systems that are deployed—be they manned or unmanned—are going to have to have some measure of survivability, stealth if you will. Our conviction is that the next generation of UAVs absolutely has to have some form of stealth capability or survivability capability in order to be useful across a wider range of operational scenarios."

While stealth is one option, future UAVs are likely to receive some of the defensive capabilities that are already possessed by manned aircraft, in the form of their own aid suites.[14] While there are benefits to both aspects of survivability, Aharonson is cautious of putting too much emphasis on the former in particular: "[stealth] is one direction that some customers are going to. But I'm not sure it will be the most common way because it makes UAVs very expensive, and one of the advantages of a UAV over a manned aircraft is the price... Because you don't have people on board you can take more risks, to make it stealthy or to put all of the protection you see on manned aircraft I'm not sure will be clever, but maybe some other means of reducing the ability of anti-aircraft systems to detect it."

Future capabilities

High performance, in terms of speed, is not inherent in the vast majority of UAVs, and only recently is attention being paid to this, with the emphasis largely being on endurance. However, future systems may need to be able to transit quickly to and through an area of operations and will need engines that can provide this capability. "The reality is that the [UAV] systems business is not quite big enough yet to be the driver for new propulsion concepts, at least for the bigger aircraft. We are dependent on what manned aviation does. For example, if we're developing a platform like our UCAS [unmanned combat air system] vehicle, we take a jet engine that exists already out of a manned aircraft and employ it in the unmanned aircraft design ... It's not a bad thing, it's really expensive to develop a new engine," explained Chris Hernandez, Chief Technology officer & Vice President of Technology Development for Northrop Grumman[15].

The newest member of General Atomics' Predator family, the Predator C Avenger, features a Pratt and Whitney turbofan engine.[16] This promises a top speed in excess of 400 kt for the aircraft and has reportedly already been acquired by the US Air Force (USAF).

Alternative fuel and power research for UAVs has been ongoing for some time and is covering the full range of systems from small manportable to large high-altitude, long endurance (HALE) systems[17].

At the smaller end of the spectrum the focus is on providing an alternative method for powering small electric engines. Earlier this year Lockheed Martin demonstrated the ability to power its Stalker UAV[18] with a laser beam. Working with LaserMotive[19] — a specialist in the field — the Stalker UAS was modified for an indoor flight test to incorporate a system that makes it possible to wirelessly transfer energy over long distances using laser light to provide a continual source of power to the UAS. At this level much attention is also being given to fuel cells[20] in the place of traditional batteries.

At the other end of the scale, alternative fuel systems are being examined that will provide endurance for a number of days. Hydrogen-fuelled systems[21] and solar power are under consideration.

Boeing[22] is looking to its hydrogen-fuelled Phantom Eye[23] platform to provide an endurance of up to four days at an altitude of 65,000 ft[24] and a payload capacity of 450 lb[25] (204kg). The propulsion system is a custom four-cylinder, 2.3 litre unit capable of developing 150 hp.[26] However, the Phantom Eye programme has not been without its issues. In June of this year it flew at an altitude of 4,080 ft and reached a cruising speed of 62 kt, but the landing proved hazardous with the landing gear breaking. A planned operational Phantom Eye will be 40% larger, and will be able to carry a 1,000 lb payload for about 10 days, or 2,000 lb over seven days.

Other efforts have not faired (**fared**) so well. AeroVironment's Global Observer[27] aircraft has not been flight trialled[28] since crashing in April 2011. Also hydrogen fuelled, the aircraft in the trial had a 175 ft (53m) wingspan and a payload capacity of up to 400 lb. However, it is expected that the largest variant will have a wingspan of about 259 ft and a payload of more than 1,000 lb.

Global Observer was developed under a USD 120 million Joint Capability Technology Demonstration programme to meet an urgent national security need for a persistent stratospheric platform, the funding for which came from six unnamed US government agencies.[29] US Special Operations Command[30] made the award in 2007 and the programme was due to complete on 31 March 2011. Communications, intelligence, surveillance and reconnaissance payloads are targeted for integration into the UAV, including the USAF's Joint Aerial Layer Network (JALN) Tactical Communications Suite (TCS)[31].

There is much competition to develop UAVs with an extended endurance, mainly due to their potential to fill a number of the roles undertaken by more expensive satellites, as well as the fact that they can easily be reroled and equipped with different payloads.

Operations for the UAV would see aircraft cycled on and off station, with each having an endurance of 5 to 7 days, typically flying at altitudes of between 55,000 ft and 65,000 ft, where they will be above weather systems.[32] Two aircraft could alternate over any location on the globe, providing seamless coverage for an indefinite period and quasi-satellite capabilities.

Other platforms competing in this area include QinetiQ's solar-powered Zephyr[33], which has demonstrated its ability to fly for more than 14 days at an altitude of more than 70,000 ft. However, work on Zephyr has concluded and little is known of plans to develop the system further. While Zephyr has proven the utility of solar-powered aircraft, limitations remain on these aircraft, due to power requirements they are restricted to the latitudes in which they can fly: too far North or South and the sun's strength is not sufficiently strong.

A flexible approach

Stealth capabilities, high performance engines, and advanced payloads may be the elements of next generation UAVs that catch the eye, but changes will be required in the computing and communications capabilities and architecture that underpin these advanced aspects if the aircraft are to have any utility.

"We want an open systems architecture with a plug-and-play capability, and probably the best example of that is our FireBird aircraft.[34] That aircraft was designed around the processing and sensors. We looked at [the design principle of] that airplane as being 'what I really need to do is get these sensors up into the airspace and be able to process the data—now build me an airplane around it.' The architecture of the processing is really an Ethernet-based system[35], it literally is a plug-and-play system … Our customers want us to have tremendous flexibility in the payloads that we put on these UAVs so the processing architecture must be amenable to accepting things on the fly, understand what they are, what they need, and make them work," explained Hernandez.

Computing power and the ability to do as much on-board processing as possible is a sought-after aspect of contemporary UAVs and will certainly be a factor in the design of the next generation.[36] The benefit of adding a plethora of advanced payloads to UAVs will be greatly diminished if there is information overload at the operator's end. Aharonson believes that we will see more and more applications in which on-board processing is important, mainly because the data-link will become a bottleneck: "you cannot transmit all of the data that these sensors can gather with the current datalinks because of the technology or the spectrum limitations. We want a lot of the processing to be done onboard, and sometimes we may want sensors to talk to each other onboard without any input from the GCS [ground control station]."

Ruszokowski supports this notion, believing that solving issues with bandwidth will be key: "I think we're waiting for the step change in communications-bandwidth management. A lot of the unmanned operations today saturate many of the communications infrastructures, so the idea of being able to streamline information and perhaps do more on-board processing and letting the operators not have to monitor the video streams in real time, 24/7, and (原文 having to) destroy or delete data once it's stored as we run out of space.[37] I think the step change[38] there is managing the information better and making it less manpower intensive on the ground so that we're taking the 'manned' out of the 'unmanned.'"

Hernandez posited that one aspect needing to be addressed is the protection of UAVs from cyber attacks, a threat that has been made real with viruses targeting US systems (this purportedly being the method used by Iran to take control over the ill fated RQ-17). Avionics designs, he asserted, must be impervious to this fledgling offensive capability.[39]

Dreaming of autonomy

The issue of increased autonomy is the stuff of dreams and nightmares in equal measure.[40] Improvements in this area are likely to feature in the future, but there seems to be little appetite for handing over significantly more responsibility for mission control to the systems themselves. Warren Henderson, Director of Advanced Boeing Military Aircraft Business Development for Phantom works[41], points to his company's Common Open Mission management Command-and-Control (COMC2) system[42] as a component of its autonomy strategy: "[it] is designed to be the core command-and-control system for a full range of unmanned platforms. COMC2, which was successfully used during the first Phantom Eye flight in June, provides for rapid fielding and improved efficiency by eliminating redundant ground systems and allowing for the operation of multiple unmanned airborne platforms by a single manager. It also reduces overall costs."

According to Hernandez, autonomy will be crucial to enabling different mission profiles for manned and unmanned aircraft, "Autonomy becomes important for a lot of reasons, one of them being communications, there are times when you lose communications and it's good to know that your system can continue to do what it was supposed to do until you can regain communication ... More importantly autonomy is going to open up the mission space; it's going to allow us to do things that we couldn't previously do."

Aharonson believes that the emphasis will be on using autonomy to reduce the workload of operators, "customers always want to have a man in the loop.[43] The system should be very easy to operate and reliable. They don't want the operator to be a pilot in the sense that they fly the UAV—they want the operator in the loop for safety reasons and emergency procedures and to oversee the mission. I don't see a lot of requirements for totally autonomous UAVs—I would say the opposite. People always want the operator in the loop, but want reduced workload, to make it easier to operate and provide the means to focus on the mission and not fly the UAV—the system should fly the aircraft."

It is not only the larger, high-end UAV sector that is receiving consideration. The small systems that have been deployed in large numbers in support of infantry and mounted reconnaissance units may not be destined to possess the stealth and other advanced capabilities of their larger siblings, but requirements for a widened mission set are appearing. "The market is not developing as we perceived five to eight years ago. First of all, you don't see a lot of tenders for mini UAVs, I see many customers putting a lot of requirements on a bird of 5 or 6 kg, and mini UAVs becoming like tactical UAVs. For example, requirements for encryption of the datalink or having emergency procedures and advanced payloads—all on a small bird of 5 or 6 kg. We are going in that direction, we will have more advanced datalinks and payloads, more reliable take-off and landing, connectivity between the UAV and the C4I systems[44] of infantry or manoeuvring forces. This kind of UAV is organic to the unit, so that connectivity is very important," explained Aharonson.

AeroVironment, manufacturer of two of the most prevalent small UAVs—Raven and Puma—are focusing on power and payloads.[45] "We've conducted numerous tests using fuel cell systems and other technologies to successfully extend flight duration. Increasing energy density in advanced batteries has the potential to extend flight duration or allow for greater payload capacity ... new payloads such as chemical, biological and radiological agent detectors[46] will expand the utility of small UASs," said Steve Gitlin, company vice-president.

However, Aharonson cautioned against the push to miniaturise, believing that customers' requirements for manportability can have negative affect (**effect**) on the capabilities provided: "Is it so important that mini UAVs be manportable? Or is it good enough to have them carried aboard a ground vehicle? It gives you a lot of flexibility if you have a vehicle—then you can have a little bigger UAV with much better operational performance."

The performance improvements promised by the next generation of UAVs will by no means lead to sweeping changes to the UAV landscape. While existing systems may not be effective in all future battlespaces, they will still have utility. Therefore it is likely that, as is the case now, there will be a tiering of assets. While a Reaper or Predator may not be suited to operating in contested airspace for example, that does not mean the inventory should be completely replaced with systems that can.

From *Jane's International Defence Review*[47], January, 2013

Ⅰ. New Words

amenable	[əˈmiːnəb(ə)l]	adj.	open to influence, suggestion or advice
augment	[ɔːgˈmənt]	v.	to increase the amount, size or value of sth
avionics	[eiviˈɔniks]	n.	plural 航空电子学
canvass	[ˈkænvəs]	v.	to find out the opinions of people by conducting a survey
catapult	[ˈkætəpʌlt]	v.	弹射
clandestine	[klænˈdestin]	adj.	secret, private, concealed
conversely	[kənˈvəːsli]	adv.	相反
cylinder	[ˈsilində(r)]	n.	汽缸
data-link	[ˈdeitəliŋk]	n.	[计]数据自动传输装置
encryption	[inˈkripʃn]	n.	加密
fielding	[ˈfiːldiŋ]	n.	the act of sending troops to the field
hijack	[ˈhaidʒæk]	v.	劫持
incorporate	[inˈkɔːpəreit]	v.	to include or be included as part of a large unit
integrated	[ˈintigreitid]	adj.	整体的,互相协调的
interoperate	[ˌintəˈɔpəreit]	v.	to operate interactively
inventory	[ˈinvəntəri]	n.	a detailed list of all the items in a place

manportable	[mæn'pɔːtəbl]	adj.	便于人携带的
miniaturise	['miniətjuəraiz]	v.	to make a much smaller version of sth
mounted	['mauntid]	adj.	set up or adjusted for use
overload	['əuvələud]	n.	an excessive load or burden; too great a load
payload	['peiləud]	n.	the instruments, equipment, etc., carried by an aircraft
pivot	['pivət]	v.	to turn as on a pivot; to hinge
plethora	['pleθərə]	n.	an amount that is greater than is needed
posit	['pɔzit]	v.	to lay down as a basis for argument
proactive	[prəu'æktiv]	adj.	积极主动的
propulsion	[prəu'pʌlʃən]	n.	the action of driving or pushing forward or onward
purportedly	[pə'pɔːtidli]	adv.	据称
scenario	[si'nɑːriəu]	n.	设想,方案;事态,局面
sensor	['sensə]	n.	传感器
sought-after	['sɔːtɑːftə(r)]	adj.	wanted by many people because it is of good quality
stratospheric	[strætə'sferik]	adj.	平流层的,同温层的
sweeping	['swiːpiŋ]	adj.	having an important effect on a large part of sth
synergise	['sinədʒaiz]	v.	协同
tiering	['tiəriŋ]	n.	arrangement in rows
transit	['trænsit]	v.	to be moved or carried from one place to another
underpin	[ˌʌndə'pin]	v.	to support

Ⅱ. Background Information

无人机的发展趋势

无人机指的是利用无线电遥控设备和机上自备的程序控制装置操纵的不载人飞机。

无人机功能主要分为五类,包括靶机、侦察、战斗、后勤和研发,参与的任务也从起初单纯的情报、监视、侦察三种任务扩展到电子干扰、通信截听、中继通信、军事打击、武力压制、突破敌军空防、战场搜救、战区空中导弹防御、网络中心战等任务。

由于无人机具有用途广泛、成本较低、效费比高、使用方便、无人员伤亡、机动性能较强等特点,它们备受各军事强国青睐。

近些年来,高新技术的发展促进了无人机进一步的研发和改进。无人机的发展呈现出以下主要趋势:隐身化、智能化、远程化和武装化。

一、隐身化。

未来无人机飞行区域防空火力威胁日益增强,无人机要想提高生存能力就必须增强自身隐身性能。因此,无人机在研制中应用了许多先进的隐身技术。一是采用复合材料、雷达吸波材料和低噪音发动机。二是采用限制红外光反射技术,在机身表面涂上能够吸收红外光的特别油漆并在发动机燃料中注入防红外辐射的化学制剂。三是减少机身雷达反射面。四是采用充电表面涂层,使其具有变色特性。

二、智能化。

无人机智能化就是"无人机自我作出决定的能力"。这种能力不仅使无人机能够按照指令或预先编制的程序来完成预定的作战任务,对已知的威胁目标做出及时自主的反应,还能对随时出现的突发情况做出及时的反应。

与有人机相比,无人机具有更高的机动性和更灵活的作战方式,但最大难题在于无人机对作战态势的自动分析处理信息和对飞行姿态的准确自动控制以及对敌我目标的准确判断。要提高无人机的适用范围,就必须提高自主性,这就需要采用先进设备提升无人机的"战场感知性能",使其适应未来的复杂战场。

三、远程化。

高空长航可以提高无人机的生存力和侦查能力,可使无人机不断扩大应用范畴。一些专家认为,高空长航时无人机将会成为大气层侦查网络的一个重要组成部分。同时,提高无人机的飞行速度也是降低敌方拦截武器的拦截概率的主要途径。目前,各军事强国正加强提高无人机的高空长航能力和飞行速度的研究。据报道,美国"全球鹰"(Global Hawk)无人机的航程为 2.6 万公里,续航时间达 42 小时,能在 1.8 万米高空飞行,最大飞行速度 740 公里/小时,可从美国本土基地飞往全球的目标连续侦察 24 小时,是当今世界上无人机中最大续航纪录保持者。

四、武装化。

武装无人机是无人机的一个重要发展方向。由于无人机能预先靠前部署,可以在所防卫目标较远的距离上摧毁来袭导弹,从而能够克服一般导弹反应时间长,拦截距离近,拦截成功后的残骸对防卫目标仍有损害的缺点。武装无人机可担任轰炸目标、对地攻击和空中格斗等军事任务。

无人机虽然有诸多优势,但目前还存在一定的劣势,包括独立作战能力不足,存在单点失效性,战损率较高,飞行航线一般比较固定,容易受到干扰,与地面指挥通信存在信号延迟和信号安全难以保证等弱点。然而,由于无人机避免了载有飞行员带来的限制,同时又可以遂行多种任务,它在未来战场中将会发挥更大作用。

Ⅲ. Notes to the Text

1. Reaper and Shadow—"死神"和"影子"无人机(① Reaper—MQ-9 Reaper, formerly named Predator B, the first hunter-killer UAV designed for long-endurance, high-altitude surveillance; ② Shadow—RQ-7B, used for reconnaissance, surveillance, target acquisition and battle damage assessment. Launched from a trailer-mounted pneumatic catapult, it is recovered with the aid of arresting gear similar to jets on an aircraft carrier.)

2. Late 2012 saw the first flight of the pan-European Neuron combat UAV demonstrator

and the US Navy's (USN's) X-47B programme continuing apace, with successful catapult take-off trials and the embarkation of the platform onboard an aircraft carrier.—2012年末泛欧"神经元"作战无人机首次飞行演示,美国海军 X-47B 项目持续快速进行,航母甲板上(无人机)弹射起飞试验和着落成功。[① the pan-European Neuron combat UAV—an experimental Unmanned Combat Air Vehicle (UCAV) being developed with international cooperation, led by the French company Dassault Aviation; ② X-47B programme—referring to the development of a demonstration unmanned combat air vehicle (UCAV) designed for carrier-based operations; ③ embarkation—the act of getting onto a ship; ④ demonstrator—a device used to demonstrate the product to customers]

3. RQ-170 Sentinel—RQ-170"哨兵"[an unmanned aerial vehicle (UAV) that Lockheed Martin developed and that the United States Air Force (USAF) operates for the Central Intelligence Agency]

4. the Iraq and Afghanistan conflicts—伊拉克和阿富汗冲突(referring to the two wars started by the U. S. in 2003 and in 2001 respectively)

5. However, the development of new systems is now at tipping point and a sneak peak (**peek**) of what the next generation may offer has been provided by the latest demonstrations.—然而,新系统的发展正处于一个转折点,最近的演示让我们窥见下一代无人机可能具备的革新。(① tipping point—the crisis stage in a process, when a significant change takes place; ② sneak peek—an opportunity to see sth before it is officially available)

6. Ultimately, the discriminator may not be what technologies can be developed, but rather if militaries have the inclination and the means to invest the capital required.—最终决定因素也许不是什么样的技术能被研发出来,而是军方是否愿意并有钱投入所需要的资金。

7. Unmanned Carrier Launched Airborne Surveillance and Strike System (UCLASS)—航母发射无人驾驶空中侦察攻击系统

8. Elbit Systems—艾尔比特系统公司(Elbit Systems Ltd. is a defense electronics manufacturer and integrator. Established in 1967, it is based in Haifa, Israel.)

9. *IHS Jane's*—《IHS 简氏防务周刊》(IHS is a company based in Douglas County, Colorado, U. S. Its brands include Jane's Information Group.)

10. synthetic aperture systems—合成孔径(雷达)系统(一种高分辨率成像雷达,可在能见度极低的气候条件下得到类似光学照相的高分辨率雷达图像)

11. Lockheed Martin—洛克希德·马丁(美国航空航天公司)(a major American aerospace company producing military aircraft, missiles, space satellites, space-launch systems, information and technology services, and electronic products)

12. … we also believe they need to have open architectures so that upgrades can be done in a portable way. —……我们还认为它们必须有开放式体系结构,以便可以(通用)组合式升级。(① open architecture—a type of computer architecture or software architecture that is designed to make adding, upgrading or changing components easy; ② portable—that can be run on two or more kinds of computers or with two or more kinds of operating systems)

13. ISR—intelligence, surveillance and reconnaissance
14. While stealth is one option, future UAVs are likely to receive some of the defensive capabilities that are already possessed by manned aircraft, in the form of their own aid suites. —虽然隐身是一种选择,未来的无人机可能会配备有人驾驶飞机已经具备的一些防卫能力,体现在无人机自身辅助系统。
15. Northrop Grumman—诺斯罗普·格鲁门公司(an American global aerospace and defense technology company formed by the 1994 purchase of Grumman by Northrop)
16. The newest member of General Atomics' Predator family, the Predator C Avenger, features a Pratt and Whitney turbofan engine. —通用原子技术公司生产的捕食者系列的新成员"捕食者"C型"复仇者"的特色是采用"普惠"公司生产的涡轮风扇发动机。[① General Atomics—a nuclear physics and defense contractor headquartered in San Diego, California. General Atomics develops systems ranging from the nuclear fuel cycle to remotely operated surveillance aircraft, airborne sensors, and advanced electric, electronic, wireless and laser technologies; ② the Predator C Avenger—a developmental unmanned combat air vehicle built by General Atomics Aeronautical Systems for the United States military; ③ Pratt & Whitney—a U.S.-based aerospace manufacturer with global service operations, a subsidiary of United Technologies Corporation (UTC), whose aircraft engines are widely used in both civil aviation (especially airlines) and military aviation]
17. high-altitude, long endurance (HALE) systems—高空长航系统
18. Stalker UAV—"潜行者"无人机(a hand-launched, electrically-powered unmanned aerial vehicle developed by Lockheed Martin Skunk Works)
19. LaserMotive "激光动力"公司(a U.S. engineering firm developing technologies for efficiently transmitting power via lasers, a form of wireless energy transfer commonly called "laser power beaming")
20. fuel cells—cells that produce electricity 燃料电池
21. hydrogen-fuelled systems—氢燃料系统
22. Boeing—波音公司(an American multinational corporation that designs, manufactures and sells fixed-wing aircraft, helicopters, rockets and satellites and provides leasing and product support services)
23. Phantom Eye—幻影之眼[The Boeing Phantom Eye is a high-altitude, long-endurance (HALE) unmanned aerial vehicle liquid hydrogen-powered spy plane developed by Boeing Phantom Works.]
24. ft—a written abbreviation for foot
25. lb—a written abbreviation for pound, a unit of weight
26. The propulsion system is a custom four-cylinder, 2.3 litre unit capable of developing 150 hp. —动力系统是定制的4缸,2.3升排量能产生150马力的单位。(hp—an abbreviation for horsepower, a unit of power equal to 746 watts)
27. AeroVironment's Global Observer—航空环境公司研发的"全球观察者"无人机(① AeroVironment—AeroVironment, Inc. is a technology company in California, that is

primarily involved in energy systems, electric vehicle systems, and unmanned aerial vehicles; ② Global Observer—a high-altitude, long-endurance unmanned aerial vehicle, designed to operate as a stratospheric geosynchronous satellite system with regional coverage)

28. flight trial—飞行测试
29. Global Observer was developed under a USD 120 million Joint Capability Technology Demonstration programme to meet an urgent national security need for a persistent stratospheric platform, the funding for which came from six unnamed US government agencies.—"全球观察者"是一项按照为满足国家对永久性同温层平台的紧迫安全需要,资金为1亿2千万美元"联合能力技术演示项目"而研制的,其资金来自6个匿名的美国国家机构。(① USD—U. S. Dollars; ② Global Observer—the first UAV with the ability to provide persistent communication and surveillance over any location on the globe; ③ Joint Capability Technology Demonstration programme—a program of examining the military utility and providing an assessment of a new technology)
30. US Special Operations Command—美国特种作战司令部
31. the USAF's Joint Aerial Layer Network (JALN) Tactical Communications Suite (TCS)—美国空军联合空中层网络战术通讯系统
32. Operations for the UAV would see aircraft cycled on and off station, with each having an endurance of 5 to 7 days, typically flying at altitudes of between 55,000 ft and 65,000 ft, where they will be above weather systems.—将来的无人机在执行行动时,会在机场上周而复始地降落和起飞,每架都能续航5—7天,通常飞行高度是55,000—65,000英尺。在这个高度上,无人机不受天气系统的影响。(① cycle—to occur over and over again in the same order; ② typically—usually; ③ above sth—not affected by sth)
33. QinetiQ's solar-powered Zephyr—奈奎蒂克公司生产的太阳能动力的"微风"无人机(① QinetiQ—a British multinational defence technology company; ② Zephyr—a lightweight solar-powered UAV. The military uses the vehicle for reconnaissance and communications platforms. Civilian and scientific programmes use it for Earth observation.)
34. We want an open systems architecture with a plug-and-play capability, and probably the best example of that is our FireBird aircraft.—我们想要具有随插即用能力的开放体系结构。这方面可能最好的样板便是"火鸟"飞机。[① plug-and-play—(of computer equipment) ready to use immediately when connected to a computer; ② FireBird—an intelligence gathering aircraft which can be flown remotely or by a pilot. The aircraft has the ability to simultaneously view infrared imagery, gather real time high definition video, use radar and eavesdrop on communications.]
35. an Ethernet-based system——种基于"以太网"的系统(Ethernet——种电脑局域网,是当今现有局域采用最广的通信协议标准)
36. Computing power and the ability to do as much on-board processing as possible is a sought-after aspect of contemporary UAVs and will certainly be a factor in the design of the next generation.—计算能力和在机上处理尽可能多信息的能力是当代无人机很受欢

迎的特色,因而必将是下一代无人机设计的要素。(① on-board—on an aircraft;② sought-after—wanted by many because of the good quality)

37. A lot of the unmanned operations today saturate many of the communications infrastructures, so the idea of being able to streamline information and perhaps do more on-board processing and letting the operators not have to monitor the video streams in real time, 24/7, and (原文 having to) destroy or delete data once it's stored as we run out of space. —当今许多无人机充满很多通讯设施,故而产生这样的想法:使(无人机)具备提炼信息,也许做更多的机上信息处理的能力,能让(地面)操作人员不必每天24小时不停实时监看视频信息流,当信息储存到缺乏空间时又得销毁或删除数据。(① saturate—to fill sth completely with sth;② infrastructure—the essential elements forming the basis of a system;③ 24/7—for 24 hours a day, 7 days a week)

38. step change—阶跃变化(a significant change, especially an improvement)

39. Avionics designs, he asserted, must be impervious to this fledgling offensive capability. —他断言,航电系统设计必须具备这种新的攻击的抗受能力。(① avionics—electronic devices in an aircraft;② impervious—not affected by sth harmful;③ fledgling—new)

40. The issue of increased autonomy is the stuff of dreams and nightmares in equal measure. —提高无人机自主性既是美梦也同样是噩梦。

41. Director of Advanced Boeing Military Aircraft Business Development for Phantom works—波音公司先进军用飞机业务"幻影"无人机研发工程主管(Phantom—a high-altitude, long-endurance UAV designed to provide advanced intelligence and reconnaissance work)

42. Common Open Mission management Command-and-Control (COMC2) system—常见开放任务管理指挥控制系统

43. Aharonson believes that the emphasis will be on using autonomy to reduce the workload of operators, "customers always want to have a man in the loop…" —阿哈龙森认为重点将放在用(无人机)自主性减轻操作员的工作负担,"客户总是想要在执行任务圈子中有人……"(in the loop—part of a group dealing with sth important)

44. C4I systems—指挥、控制、通信、计算机和军事情报系统[The acronym C4I stands for command, control, communications, computers, and (military) intelligence.]

45. AeroVironment, manufacturer of two of the most prevalent small UAVs—Raven and Puma—are focusing on power and payloads. —航空环境公司是一家制造两种最为常见小型无人机("乌鸦"和"美洲豹")的公司。这家制造商特别重视无人机的动力和有效载荷。(① Raven—a small hand-launched remote-controlled unmanned aerial vehicle developed for the U.S. military, but now adopted by the military forces of many other countries;② Puma—a small, battery powered, American hand-launched unmanned aircraft system. Its primary mission is surveillance and intelligence gathering using an electro-optical and infrared video camera.)

46. chemical, biological and radiological agent detectors—化学试剂、生物试剂、放射性试剂探测器

47. *Jane's International Defence Review*—《简式国际防务评论》(a monthly magazine reporting on military news and technology, a unit of Jane's Information Group)

Ⅳ. Language Features

前置定语(premodification)

本文多处使用前置定语,例如:air-to-ground operations, high-altitude, long-endurance system, air-to-air mission, plug-and-play capability, high-threat environment, on-board processing, solar-powered aircraft, hydrogen-fueled systems。前置定语不仅可以替代短语,还可以替代定语从句,是精炼句式的十分有效手段。

例如:an all-male club (a club whose members are all male) 男子俱乐部
　　　once-poor farmers (farmers who were once poor) 曾经贫穷的农民

在现代英语中,前置定语使用频率日趋增加。由于它可以浓缩结构,节约篇幅,因而深得新闻写作人员青睐。《美国新闻与世界报道》专栏作家约翰·利奥(John Leo)曾在一篇新闻语言评论文章中称前置定语为"新闻语言的基本成分"。

从结构上看,新闻英语的前置定语大致可分六类:

1. 名词短语作前置定语
mom-and-pop store 夫妻店　　　　　　　a dead-end job 没有奔头的工作
long-fiber food 长纤维食物　　　　　　　waste-to-energy power plant 垃圾发电厂

2. 动词短语作前置定语
a stand-up meeting 站着开的会议　　　　start-up costs 启动费用
drive-by shooting 开车射击　　　　　　　a go-with-the-stream person 随波逐流的人

3. 形容词短语作前置定语
a decade-long shortage 持续十年的短缺　　war-weary citizen 厌倦战争的公民
fire-proof material 耐火材料　　　　　　　sugar-free drink 不含糖饮料

4. 前置短语作前置定语
on-the-job problem 工作时出的问题　　　on-site service 现场服务
on-the-spot investigation 现场调查　　　under-the-counter dealing 台下交易

5. 分词短语作前置定语
turned-on audience 激动的观众　　　　　land-based missile 陆基导弹
sexually-transmitted disease 性渠道传染的疾病
full-blown case 爆发性疾病

6. 句子作前置定语
a seeing-is-believing attitude 眼见为实的态度
the three-strikes-you're-out law "事不过三"法(犯罪三次,终身监禁)

V. Analysis of the Content

1. Which of the following branches of the U. S. Army is the most proactive in examining future military systems?
   A. The Army.
   B. The Navy.
   C. The Air Force.
   D. The Marine Corps.
2. The author's list of elements of next generation UAVs does NOT include _____.
   A. ability to strike
   B. stealth capability
   C. high performance engines
   D. advanced payloads
3. It can be seen from the article that the best example of UAVs having an open system architecture with a plug-and-play capability is _____.
   A. Phantom
   B. FireBird
   C. Predator
   D. Shadow
4. Which of the following kinds of energies is Not mentioned in the article's discussion of alternative energy for UAVs?
   A. laser light
   B. hydrogen fuel
   C. biofuel
   D. solar power
5. Aharonson's view on UAVs' stealth capability is _____.
   A. highly critical
   B. strongly supportive
   C. cautious
   D. unknown

VI. Questions on the Article

1. According to the author, what may be the discriminator of the development of UAVs' new systems?
2. Why is stealth capability stressed now?
3. What advantage does open structure offer to UAVs?
4. What kind of UAV is the Predator C Avenger? What accounts for its top speed?
5. Why is there much competition to develop UAVs with an extended endurance?
6. What are the limitations to solar-powered UAVs?
7. Why will the ability to do as much on-board data processing certainly be a factor in the design of next generation UAVs?
8. What suggestion does Ruszokowski make concerning the bottleneck of communication?
9. What does Aharonson think of UAV's autonomy?

VII. Topics for Discussion

1. Does the use of UAVs increase the likelihood of wars?
2. Will UAVs replace all manned aircraft in the future?

Lesson 32

Big Power Goes Local[1]

A grass-roots movement to generate power in towns and basements is challenging the energy industry's status quo.

By Stefan Theil

In the late 1990s, the town of Freiamt in Germany's Black Forest decided to take the fight against global warming into its own hands.[2] Three hundred of the town's 4,300 residents chipped in to buy the four 80-meter-tall Enercon wind turbines[3] that now top the surrounding hills, generating 1.8 megawatts each. An additional 270 families put solar collectors[4] on their roofs to heat water and power their homes. Three businesses — two sawmills and a bakery — whose land abuts a gurgling stream have installed old-fashioned water wheels, each providing an additional 15 kilowatts.

To make up for shortfalls when the sun doesn't shine or the wind doesn't blow, one of the local farmers invested in a "biogas" fermenter, which uses enzymes to turn grain and agricultural waste such as manure and chaff into methane. The gas, in turn, fires up an electricity generator. And rather than simply release heat given off in the process into the air, as conventional power plants do, the generator pumps the waste heat into nearby homes, where it's used for water and space heating, through pipes laid by volunteers. But the prize for Freiamt's most creative source of energy surely goes to Walter Schneider, a local dairy farmer. To harness the energy set free when the milk from his 50 cows is chilled before transport, Schneider installed a heat exchanger[5] that uses the heat from the cow's milk to warm the water he needs for cleaning and showering. Today, the Freiamters are proudly self-sufficient. What's more, in 2007 they generated an extra 2.3 million kilowatt-hours beyond the 12 million they consumed. They sold the surplus, enough for an additional 200 homes, back to the national grid.

Freiamt is no hippie commune trying to shut itself off from the world.[6] It's at the forefront of a growing and thoroughly modern trend. Whether to save the climate or save money — or a combination of both — homeowners, businesses and entire communities around the world are increasingly generating their own energy. From Tokyo, where homeowners have begun installing the first commercial fuel cells[7], to California's Million Solar Roofs program[8], to towns like Freiamt, the new word in energy is think small and go local.

The global electricity industry is still dominated by big, fossil-fuel-fired utilities, no question.[9] They account for 67 percent of all electricity generation worldwide. And the International Energy Agency's World Energy Outlook[10], published in December, predicts in its "alternative scenario" that even if governments push energy and efficiency savings hard, big coal and gas power plants will provide half of all new generating capacity coming on line by 2030 — and locally generated power will make up less than 20 percent. But other experts say the IEA projection could shift as massive new investment in energy research bears fruit and governments liberalize the energy markets that have so far favored centralized utilities. In 2006, locally generated "micropower" passed nuclear power in terms of total electricity generated, supplying 16 percent of the globe's power.[11] Amory Lovins, founder of the Rocky Mountain Institute[12], estimates that one third of the generating capacity installed each year is local.

Some energy economists now foresee an "alternative alternative" scenario, in which governments break the hold that fossil-fueled utilities have on the market.[13] Nikolaus Richter, networks specialist at Germany's Wuppertal Institute for Climate Research[14], says liberalized energy markets, combined with new technologies, could break the "carbon lock-in" — the preference for existing energy technology based on experience, legislation and vested interests.[15] There's evidence that this state-sponsored revolution is underway.

Rising fuel costs and climate worries are making businesses and households think a lot harder about how they get their power. Governments are pushing the trend with subsidies and by opening up protected electricity markets that have so far favored the big utilities. In January, the European Commission made opening up power grids to locally produced energy one of several measures to boost the bloc's energy efficiency 20 percent by 2020.[16] The vision of local communities generating their own power is also a crucial part of Sweden's ambitious program to wean the country off all oil and gas imports by 2020. In the past few years, more than three dozen countries, including Germany, Spain, Brazil and Indonesia, have created "feed-in tariffs"[17] — guaranteed rates at which public utilities must buy power from wind, sun, waste or biomass from private citizens or local cooperatives.

Ironically, these state subsidies seem to be the fastest and most effective way to create mass markets for new, efficient sources of energy. They break the monopoly of utilities over the electrical grid by allowing virtually anyone to sell their power. That creates an opening for local-generation technologies such as wind turbines, solar panels and household-size boilers cogenerating power and heat in the basement,[18] which are now hitting the market in significant numbers at declining prices. Critics argue that many of these technologies are still far from competitive and depend on the continued flow of subsidies.

The idea of generating power locally, where it's needed, is as old as power itself. In the late 1800s, light-bulb inventor Thomas Edison envisioned efficient cogeneration of heat and power for every home and business, and even drew up plans for a self-sufficient home powered by a wind generator. However, it was George Westinghouse's vision of a giant hub-and-spoke system of centralized electricity plants and a vast network of power lines and transformer stations to distribute power that won the day.[19] The central plants' efficiency was abominable, and much of the power was lost in transit from electrical resistance in the wires. That didn't matter in an age when fossil fuels were cheap, the environment didn't count and central planning was in vogue.

That equation is changing. The most powerful argument for generating local power is efficiency. The average power plant converts only about 30 percent of the energy content of fossil fuel into power — the rest is lost directly from the plant as heat to the atmosphere or cooling water. Of the power generated, 7 percent is then lost from transmission lines.

The newest, state-of-the-art power plants can reduce direct losses of heat to about 45 percent. Create power locally, even with fossil fuels, and not only do you cut transmission losses but you can also recapture waste heat to boil water or to heat homes. "Trigeneration" machines in schools and hospitals use generated heat to extract power, heating and, in a process that absorbs heat by boiling a liquid coolant, air conditioning out of a single fuel course, raising efficiency to about 90 percent.[20] Do the math: tripling efficiency from 30 to 90 percent cuts fuel needs (and carbon emissions) by two thirds. Add better insulation or more-efficient appliances and local generation could cut the fuel required to heat and power homes and businesses to a small fraction of today's.

The poster child of local power is Denmark, the world's most energy-efficient nation.[21] This resource-poor country began mandating local cogeneration of heat and power in the 1980s. In the 1990s, the Danish Parliament was the first in the world to create "a feed-in tariff" promoting local sources of alternative energy. Today, with less than one third of the nation's power generated by big utilities, Denmark uses less energy to generate each dollar of GDP than any other country in the world.

Increasingly, other governments are following suit. Thanks to a feed-in tariff established in 2004, Germany has become the world leader in solar power. In three years, 400,000 households and small businesses have installed 3,000 megawatts of solar generating capacity, enough to replace six conventional power plants. Germany is today the world's biggest market for photovoltaics and solar thermal collectors; the runners-up are Japan and Spain, which also have feed-in tariffs.

Although these programs are based on tax credits and subsidies, they have jump-started the market for photovoltaics, spurring entrepreneurs to bring prices down to where solar power is expected to be competitive with conventional power generation by 2010.[22] As a result, solar is no longer confined to off-grid niche markets like remote cabins or pocket calculators.[23] The majority of new solar installations are now directly connected to the grid.

Opening up those grids hasn't been easy. Not only do utility companies jealously guard their turf, but there are technical complications as well.[24] Power plants can be turned on and off, but countless local generators working independently of one another can't match demand at any given time (at least not until there are better ways to store power).

New technology is being developed to solve this problem. The Scandinavian countries have connected their power grids across their borders. Now, when a gale blows through Denmark's wind farms, hydroelectric turbines in Norway shut down.[25] Ireland and Scotland are working on a similar network. The Germans last year tested a "virtual utility" that uses the Internet to monitor power generation at hundreds of dispersed local facilities producing solar, wind and biogas power, turning reserve generating capacity on and off to match demand[26].

In Denmark, grid operator Energinet is developing the next step: using "smart meters"[27] and variable prices depending on the time of day, sunshine and wind speed, to create a self-regulating grid no longer dependent on a central utility — a kind of "energy Internet." "Moving to a decentralized smart grid is like shifting from analog to digital[28]," says John Balbach, managing partner at Cleantech, a Silicon Valley venture-capital firm[29]. "We'll be there in 10 years."

In the lucrative global power market, utilities in many other countries aren't always happy about the newcomers. Most French and German utility oligopolies have little interest in opening their grids. Since they own both the transmission network and the power plants, they naturally want to sell as much of their own power as possible. Local-power advocates accuse them of using technical norms and licensing procedures to keep new sources off the grid. That's why the European Commission is pressing member states to create separate companies to run the grid, as the Scandinavians have done.

The market would take care of the rest, says Richter. In late February Germany's biggest utility, Eon, announced it would pre-empt the EU mandate by selling its high-voltage grid.[30] The surprise announcement is a step in the right direction — but by keeping ownership of the "last mile" of power lines to customers, Eon maintains substantial control over the market. Germany and France, in particular, oppose any further liberalization.

The battle is creating some unlikely allies. Equipment manufacturers such as Germany's Bosch and New Zealand's WhisperGen hope to push superefficient household "microcogeneration" units onto the market.[31] These units work like regular boilers for hot water and heat — except that they generate additional electricity that can be sold back to the grid, cutting household electricity consumption by at least 20 percent. Since the boilers run on gas, some gas utilities are helping to distribute them. Their hope, says Richter, is that future energy savings come at the cost of the power companies, not the gas utilities.

Though local production is growing mainly in electricity, some communities are starting to feed their own locally produced "biogas" into the existing network of gas pipes. After more than a decade of wrangling with the local natural-gas utility, the German town of Aachen became the first to pump biogas made from corn and rye — which yields twice the energy per unit of land as corn-based ethanol — into the city network. Replacing natural gas imported from Siberia, the biogas is enough to supply gas for 5,000 households. Other European towns are following suit, and German lawmakers are developing a law that would open up the gas-pipeline network to locally produced biogas. In America, too, several trends are pushing local power. New green policies[32], from Texas's generous tax credits for wind generators, to California's Million Solar Roofs program, have helped kick-start a long-dormant market.

Yet the developing world has the most promising markets for do-it-yourself power. With the long-distance power network underdeveloped (in rural India or China) or nonexistent (as in much of Africa), local generation allows communities and businesses to leapfrog multibillion-dollar investments in power plants and transmission lines. In February, the Indian government announced a new project to fund biomass and wind generators for rural communities. China is expected to pass Germany as the world's biggest manufacturer of photovoltaics in 2009. For now, China's production is for export to Western countries, but China's entry into the solar market has raised hopes that prices will see another fall, to where solar starts making economic sense in China, too.

Critics of local power point to the high costs of current generating technology. With the exception of wind turbines, few of the new local power sources are yet competitive with traditional power plants. Their growth is still largely due to tax credits, renewables mandates and above-market feed-in tariffs.[33] Consumers and taxpayers in Germany, to take just one example, are paying more than $6.2 billion a year to subsidize local and renewable power.

Defenders say the laws and subsidies are needed to jump-start the market; they can be slowly phased out as production revs up and equipment prices come down.[34] The benefits of cutting imports and emissions should also be factored into the equation[35], they say, not to mention the estimated $300 billion in annual subsidies to the global utility industry. What's more, local power production could save much of the $22 trillion the IEA estimates is necessary to upgrade the distribution infrastructure by 2030. "You don't need to invest in a big grid if you have a lot of micropower," says an executive at Denmark's Energinet.

Will all this amount to a "paradigm switch" from central utilities to local power?[36] "Technology might be disruptive, but changing behavior in the way we use energy is only going to be incremental," says Vinod Khosla, a leading California venture capitalist. All those increments — the thousands of communities like Freiamt producing and selling power — add up to a whole lot of change.

With Patrick Falby and Jesse Ellison

From *Newsweek*, April 21, 2008

I. New Words

abominable	[ə'bɔminəbl]	adj.	糟透的，低劣的
above-market	[ə,bʌv'mɑːkit]	adj.	高于市场价的
abut	[ə'bʌt]	v.	to be next to sth
biogas	['baiəugæs]	n.	生物气
chaff	[tʃɑːf]	n.	谷壳，糠；切细的干草
chip	[tʃip]	v.	~ **in** to join in
coolant	['kuːlənt]	n.	冷却剂
dormant	['dɔːmənt]	adj.	not active or growing now
enzyme	['enzaim]	n.	〔生物〕酶
fermenter	[fə'mentə]	n.	发酵桶，发酵罐
gale	[geil]	n.	大风(7级—8级的风，尤指8级风)
grid	[grid]	n.	（输电）系统网络
gurgle	['gəːgl]	v.	to make a sound like water flowing quickly through a narrow space
insulation	[,insju'leiʃən]	n.	〔物〕绝缘
kick-start	['kik,stɑːt]	v.	to do sth to help an activity start or develop more quickly
leapfrog	['liːpfrɔg]	v.	跳跃，跳过
oligopoly	[,ɔli'gɔpəli]	n.	〔经〕寡头卖主垄断
photovoltaic	[,fəutəuvɔl'teiik]	n.	光生伏打电池；太阳电池
rev	[rev]	v.	~ **up** to make an engine work faster
rye	[rai]	n.	黑麦
shortfall	['ʃɔːtfɔːl]	n.	缺少；差额
wrangle	['ræŋgl]	v.	to argue angrily, and usually for a long time about sth

| wean | [wiːn] | v. | to make sb gradually stop using sth |
| runner-up | [ˌrʌnəˈʌp] | n. | a person or team that finishes second in a race or competition |

Ⅱ. Background Information

能源与环境

在人类活动的不断扩张、对于物质享受的不断追求的同时，所使用的能源量急剧增长，也使人类所居住的环境遭到严重的破坏。大量能源的消耗导致了温室效应、大气污染、酸雨的增加、废弃的放射性物质的扩散和地表水的毒性增长。

温室效应已经对人类构成严重威胁。根据科学研究，二氧化碳是人类产生的最重要的温室气体，约占总量的2/3，因而是造成温室效应的罪魁祸首。

目前世界上有75%的能源供给靠燃烧原油、煤和天然气来获取，这些能源所制造出的二氧化碳量很大，燃烧1吨油或煤就排放出3吨二氧化碳。据调查，全球每年向大气中排放的二氧化碳大约为230亿吨，比20世纪增加了20%，至今仍以每年0.5%的速度递增。

温室气体的增加导致一系列灾难。首先，温室效应(greenhouse effect)造成全球温度上升。气候变化专门委员会(IPCC)一份研究报告指出，当前全球的平均温度已经达到1000年来的历史最高值。近25年升温出现加速。如这一趋势持续下去，到2100年气温将升高1~3.5℃。全球变暖导致海冰与雪盖面积减少以及冰川缩小、海平面上升，使得大片陆地被淹没。除此之外，温室效应还会导致水循环的破坏、森林的转移与萎缩以及人类健康状况的恶化。

20世纪80年代开始，许多国家政府、科学家和公众对这一问题给予了高度关注。1997年12月，在日本京都召开了联合国气候大会，与会的100多个国家通过了《京都议定书》(Kyoto Protocol)。该议定书规定：在2008至2012年期间，39个工业发达国家的温室气体的排放量要在1990年的基础上平均削减5.2%，其中美国削减7%，欧盟8%，日本6%。2007年12月在印度尼西亚巴厘岛(Bali)又召开了最新一次联合国气候大会。会议对于2012年《京都议定书》到期后国际社会实施的温室气体减排的谈判进程做出了框架安排。美国是世界上最大的温室气体排放国，其排放量占全球总量的1/4以上。但是，美国政府却以"人类活动导致气候变化具有不确定性"为由，拒绝签署《京都议定书》。

减少温室气体的排放主要办法是减少能源浪费和采用绿色能源。

目前各个国家能源使用过程中浪费十分严重。美国经济所浪费的能源大约有56%，电力业高达66%。煤和天然气燃烧发电过程散失大量热能，电力传输过程中又损耗10%。一些专家主张地方发电，这样既可以大大降低传输电力的消耗，又可以更为灵活地使用环境友好型(environment-friendly)能源，并且能更好地综合利用能源。

不少国家已经开始使用生物燃料(biofuel)。然而实践证明，生物燃料的大量使用也会带来相应问题。玉米用于制造的燃料只能替代汽油的12%和柴油的6%。环境保护者发现用玉米生产乙醇过程中也要消耗同样量的能源。此外，大量使用玉米、大豆生产燃料必然使人类的粮食、动物的饲料供应紧张，导致粮食、牛肉、猪肉、禽蛋价格大幅上涨。

很多专家呼吁人类要充分利用太阳能。实际上，不少国家正在设法大规模开发和利用太阳能。美国计划到2050年，光伏技术将提供30亿千瓦的电力，供应全国69%的电力和35%

的总能量。

与太阳能相比,风能发电成本较低,但其弱点是发电量波动不定。科学家们深信:只要政府大力支持,采用先进技术,风力发电的弱点可以克服,太阳能发电的成本会大幅降下来,人类绿色能源的梦想是可以实现的。

Ⅲ. Notes to the Text

1. Big Power Goes Local — 大型发电地方化
2. In the late 1990s, the town of Freiamt in Germany's Black Forest decided to take the fight against global warming into its own hands. — 20世纪90年代末期,德国黑林山镇决定用自己力量抗击全球变暖。(Black Forest — an area of southwest Germany where there is a very large forest, which is a popular place for tourists)
3. the four 80-meter-tall Enercon wind turbines — 四台80米高Enercon牌风力发电机组
4. solar collectors — 太阳能集热器
5. heat exchanger — 热交换器
6. Freiamt is no hippie commune trying to shut itself off from the world. — 弗瑞艾默特镇并非是一个试图与世隔绝的嬉皮士群居区。(hippie commune — a group of people rejecting the way most people live in western society, and living together, sharing responsibilities and possessions)
7. fuel cells — (由气体燃料与氧化剂反应直接产生电能的)燃料电池
8. California's Million Solar Roofs program — 加州的"百万装有太阳能电池板屋顶"项目(On August 21, 2006, Arnold Schwarzenegger, California's state governor signed the Million Solar Roofs bill which mandates that solar panels become a standard option for all new home buyers.)
9. The global electricity industry is still dominated by big, fossil-fuel-fired utilities, no question. — 毋庸置疑,全球电力行业依然由大型火力发电厂主宰。
10. the International Energy Agency's World Energy Outlook — 国际能源署出版的《世界能源展望》[the International Energy Agency — 国际能源署是一家旨在实施国际能源计划的机构,与1974年11月在经济合作与发展组织(Organization for Economic Cooperation and Development)的框架下成立,总部设在法国巴黎。]
11. In 2006, locally generated "micropower" passed nuclear power in terms of total electricity generated, supplying 16 percent of the globe's power. — 2006年,地方"小型发电"总发电量超过了核能源的总发电量,占全球发电量的16%。
12. the Rocky Mountain Institute — 落基山研究院
13. Some energy economists now foresee an "alternative alternative" scenario, ... on the market. — 一些能源经济学家已经预见一种更加另类的情况,即政府打破火力发电厂的垄断。(alternative alternative — The first "alternative" is used here for emphasis.)
14. Germany's Wuppertal Institute for Climate Research — 德国乌帕塔尔气候研究院(该机构全称为 Wuppertal Institute for Climate, Environment and Energy Research)
15. ... liberalized energy markets ... legislation and vested interests. — 放开能源市场,结

合新技术可以打破"碳垄断",即基于经验、法律和既得利益对现有能源技术的偏爱。(lock-in — dominance of a product or technology not because its cost is low or performance is good but because it enjoys the benefits of scale)

16. In January, the European Commission made opening up power grids to locally produced energy one of several measures to boost the bloc's energy efficiency 20 percent by 2020. — 一月份,欧盟委员会将电力网对地方产电开放作为 2020 年前能效提高 20% 的几项措施之一。

17. feed-in tariffs — compensation paid to owners of renewable energy systems when energy from their systems is sold to the public grid(再生性能源发电)入网价格(tariff — fixed price)

18. That creates an opening for local-generation technologies such as wind turbines, solar panels and household-size boilers cogenerating power and heat in the basement, ... — 这项措施为地方发电技术发展提供了好机会,这些技术有风力涡轮机、太阳电池板和地下室安装的同时发热发电的家用锅炉。(opening — a good opportunity for sb or sth)

19. However, it was George Westinghouse's vision ... to distribute power that won the day. — 然而,最终获胜的却是乔治·威斯汀豪斯所提出的设想,即采用大型中枢辐射系统结构,由中心发电厂通过巨大网络输电线和变电站向各地送电。[①Westinghouse — 威斯汀豪斯(1849 — 1914),美国发明家、企业家,发明空气制动器(1869)等,创办威斯汀豪斯电气公司,又译"西屋电气公司"(1886),一生获专利 400 项;②win the day — to finally be successful]

20. "Trigeneration" machines in schools and hospitals use generated heat to extract power, heating and, in a process that absorbs heat by boiling a liquid coolant, air conditioning out of a single fuel course, raising efficiency to about 90 percent. — 学校和医院的热电冷三联产机器在燃料一次性使用过程中利用燃料产生的热发电、制热和通过煮沸液态冷却剂吸热来进行空气调节,使能效提高到 90% 左右。

21. The poster child of local power is Denmark, the world's most energy-efficient nation. — 地方发电的典型是节能最好的国家丹麦。(poster child — a person who is seen as representing a particular quality)

22. Although these programs are based on tax credits and subsidies, ... bring prices down to where solar power is expected to be competitive with conventional power generation by 2010. — 虽然这些项目基于课税扣除和政府补贴,但是它们推动了太阳电池市场的发展,促使企业家把太阳能电价格在 2010 年前降到可与常规电相竞争的水平。(①tax credit — a sum of money that is taken off the amount of tax you must pay;②jump-start — to help a process or activity start)

23. As a result, solar is no longer confined to off-grid niche markets like remote cabins or pocket calculators. — 因此,太阳能电不再限于用在像遥远的小木屋和袖珍计算器那样的不能入网的小专业市场。(niche market — a small area of trade within the economy often involving specialized products)

24. Not only do utility companies jealously guard their turf, but there are technical complications as well. — 不但电力公司小心守护自己的领域,而且在技术方面还存

在困难。(① turf — an area that you think of as being your own; ② jealously — carefully)

25. Now, when a gale blows through Denmark's wind farms, hydroelectric turbines in Norway shut down. — 现在,当大风吹过丹麦风力发电厂时,挪威的水力发电涡轮机就关闭。

26. turning reserve generating capacity on and off to match demand — 根据需求启用和关闭备用发电能力。

27. smart meters — 智能计量器

28. Moving to a decentralized smart grid is like shifting from analog to digital — 采用分散的智能电网就像由模拟化转为数字化

29. a Silicon Valley venture-capital firm — 硅谷一家风险投资公司

30. In late February Germany's biggest utility, Eon, announced it would pre-empt the EU mandate by selling its high-voltage grid. — 二月末,德国最大的电力公司 Eon 公司宣布将在欧盟规定做出之前采取行动,将其高压电网出售。(pre-empt — to do sth before sb else does)

31. Equipment manufacturers such as Germany's Bosch and New Zealand's WhisperGen hope to push superefficient household "micro-cogeneration" units onto the market. — 德国博世公司和新西兰 WhisperGen 公司之类的设备制造商希望把超高效节能的家用微型电热二联发电机组推向市场。(micro-cogeneration unit — a unit that integrates a heat pump and generator into a simple package delivering air conditioning, space heating, electrical power generation and hot water)

32. green policies — 有利环境保护的政策

33. Their growth is still largely due to tax credits, renewables mandates and above-market feed-in tariffs. — 它们的发展依然主要依靠课税扣除、使用再生能源的政府规定和高于市场价的(地方电力)入网价格。[① tax credit — a sum of money that is taken of the amount of tax you must pay; ② renewables — renewable energies]

34. ... they can be slowly phased out as production revs up and equipment prices come down. — 随着设备生产加快、设备价格下降,这些法令和补贴将慢慢被取消。(phase out — to gradually stop using or providing something)

35. The benefits of cutting imports and emissions should also be factored into the equation — 减少电力进口和废气排放也应该作为综合考虑的因素(factor — to include a particular fact when you are thinking about sth)

36. Will all this amount to a "paradigm switch" from central utilities to local power? — 这一切是否构成由中央电力业到地方电力业的范式变化?(paradigm — a pattern of sth)

{ Ⅳ. Language Features }

习语活用

本教材 27 课标题活用了习语"marriage of convenience"(权宜婚姻)。

英语习语浩如烟海。这些习语中有相当一部分由于过度使用而苍白无力,或因时间过长而腐气浓厚。在现代英美报刊中,作者为了摈弃因袭,刻意求新,或者为了简洁明快、节约篇幅,或是为了形象幽默、增强效果,常常将习语活用。

英语习语活用后的形式从字典中很难寻到释义,但它们并非变幻莫测,毫无规则。了解其活用形式对提高外刊阅读能力十分有益。一般说来,报刊英语中习语活用形式可以归纳为四种:节缩、扩展、套用、拆用。下面分别举例作以说明。

1. 节缩

这是把原习语缩短使用,报刊常常借助前置定语来节缩。例如,

Employees foster nose-to-the-grindstone strategies.

这里,"nose-to-the-grindstone"是习语"keep one's nose to the grindstone"(使某人埋头从事辛苦劳动)的节缩形式。

2. 扩展

在习语中夹字,使其增加新意。

例 1. Inside Rosalyn's velvet glove is a stainless hand.

这一句中,作者不仅在原习语"the iron hand in the velvet glove"加上"stainless",而且把"iron"改为"steel",使整个句子语气强烈,趣味盎然,(美国前总统)卡特夫人罗莎琳外柔内刚的本性便活脱脱地刻画出来。

例 2. Many government-sponsored agencies are now jumping on the exercise bandwagon and coaxing reluctant spectators to join the fun.

句中"jump on the exercise bandwagon"是由习语"jump on the bandwagon"扩展而成,加上"exercise"这个词就增加一层新意,表示"在运动方面赶浪头"。

3. 套用

套用是通过改变习语中的个别词来表达新意和加强语意。例如,

Salaries did increase. But so did the race to keep up with the Wangs.

这一句摘自《新闻周刊》一篇关于中国改革开放之后人民生活状况的报道,作者用 Wangs 替代原习语中的 Joneses,染上鲜明的民族色彩,产生了活泼风趣的效果。

4. 拆用

拆用就是将原习语的成分拆开加以活用。这样既可避免照搬陈旧形式,又可生出新意。例如,

They have a mountain of high-resounding resolve and a molehill of results.

本句是原习语"make a mountain out of a molehill"的拆用形式,整句意思是:他们的决心很大,调子很高,但收效甚微。

V. Analysis of the Content

1. Freiamt's main purpose in producing power was to _____.
    A. fight against global warming   B. save money
    C. break the control of power utilities   D. solve the power shortage problem
2. According to the article, the most energy-efficient nation in the world is _____.
    A. Japan   B. the U.S.   C. Denmark   D. Germany

3. Which of the following countries will be the world's biggest manufacture of photovoltaics in 2009?

   A. China.　　　B. Germany.　　　C. India.　　　D. The U. S.

4. From the article we know that the local power source competitive with traditional power plants is _____.

   A. solar collectors　　　　　　B. wind turbines
   C. biogas　　　　　　　　　　D. water wheels

5. It can be seen from the article, the main obstacle to local power generation is _____.

   A. high costs　　　　　　　　B. utility companies' opposition
   C. technical complications　　 D. lack of public support

Ⅵ. Questions on the Article

1. By what means does the town of Freiamt produce power?
2. Who dominates the global electricity industry?
3. What is the IEA projection of global power generation by 2030?
4. What was European Commission's purpose in adopting the measure of opening up power grids?
5. What does the "alternative alternative" scenario refer to?
6. What effect do the state subsidies produce on power generation?
7. What was Thomas Edison's idea of power generation? What was Westinghouse's vision of power generation?
8. What are the advantages of local power over central utilities?
9. How has Germany been using solar power?
10. Why is it difficult to open up grids?
11. What measures have been taken to solve the technical problems?
12. Why does the author say that the developing world has the most promising markets for local power?
13. What are the factors listed by defenders in their argument for local power generation?

Ⅶ. Topics for Discussion

1. Should power generation be localized?
2. Should governments provide subsidies for local power generation?

Lesson 33

A Hopeful Continent

After a decade's great improvement, African lives will be even better in the next ten years.

(Abridged)

Three students are hunched over an iPad at a beach café on Senegal's Cap-Vert peninsula, the westernmost tip of the world's poorest continent.[1] They are reading online news stories about Moldova, one of Europe's most miserable countries. One headline reads: "Four drunken soldiers rape woman." Another says Moldovan men have a 19% chance of dying from excessive drinking and 58% will die from smoking-related diseases. Others deal with sex-trafficking[2]. Such stories have become a staple of Africa's thriving media, along with austerity tales from Greece. They inspire pity and disbelief, just as tales of disease and disorder in Africa have long done in the rich world.

Sitting on the outskirts of Dakar, Senegal's capital, the three students sip cappuccinos and look out over a paved road shaded by palm trees where restaurants with white tablecloths serve green-spotted crabs. A local artist is hawking framed pictures of semi-clad peasant girls under a string of coloured lights. This is where slave ships used to depart for the New World[3]. "Way over there, do they know how much has changed?" asks one of the students, pointing beyond the oil tankers on the distant horizon.

This special report will paint a picture at odds with Western images of Africa.[4] War, famine and dictators have become rarer. People still struggle to make ends meet, just as they do in China and India. They don't always have enough to eat, they may lack education, they despair at daily injustices and some want to emigrate. But most Africans no longer fear a violent or premature end and can hope to see their children do well. That applies across much of the continent, including the sub-Saharan part[5].

African statistics are often unreliable, but broadly the numbers suggest that human development in sub-Saharan Africa has made huge leaps. Secondary-school enrolment grew by 48% between 2000 and 2008 after many states expanded their education programmes and scrapped school fees. Over the past decade malaria deaths in some of the worst-affected countries have declined by 30% and HIV infections by up to 74%. Life expectancy across Africa has increased by about 10% and child mortality rates in most countries have been falling steeply.

A booming economy has made a big difference. Over the past ten years real income per person has increased by more than 30%, whereas in the previous 20 years it shrank by nearly 10%. Africa is the world's fastest-growing continent just now. Over the next decade its GDP is expected to rise by an average of 6% a year, not least thanks to foreign direct investment. FDI[6] has gone from ＄15 billion in 2002 to ＄37 billion in 2006 and ＄46 billion in 2012.

Many goods and services that used to be scarce, including telephones, are now widely available. Africa has three mobile phones for every four people, the same as India. By 2017 nearly 30％ of households are expected to have a television set, an almost fivefold increase over ten years. Nigeria produces more movies than America does. Film-makers, novelists, designers, musicians and artists thrive in a new climate of hope. Opinion polls show that almost two-thirds of Africans think this year will be better than last, double the European rate.

Africa is too big to follow one script, so its countries are taking different routes to becoming better places. In Senegal the key is a vibrant democracy. From the humid beaches of Cap-Vert to the flyblown desert interior, politicians conduct election campaigns that Western voters would recognise. They make extravagant promises, some of which they will even keep. Crucially, they respect democratic institutions. When President Abdoulaye Wade last year tried to stand for a third term, in breach of term limits, he was ridiculed.[7] A popular cartoon showed him in a bar ordering a third cup of coffee and removing a sign saying, "Everyone just two cups." More than two dozen opposition candidates formed a united front and inflicted a stinging defeat on him, which he swiftly accepted. Dakar celebrated wildly, then went back to work the next day.

At the end of the cold war only three African countries (out of 53 at the time) had democracies; since then the number has risen to 25, of varying shades[8], and many more countries hold imperfect but worthwhile elections (22 in 2012 alone). Only four out of now 55 countries—Eritrea, Swaziland, Libya and Somalia—lack a multi-party constitution, and the last two will get one soon. Armies mostly stay in their barracks. Big-man leaders are becoming rarer, though some authoritarian states survive.[9] And on the whole more democracy has led to better governance: politicians who want to be re-elected need to show results.

Ways to salvation

Where democracy has struggled to establish itself, African countries have taken three other paths to improving their citizens' lives. First, many have stopped fighting. War and civil strife have declined dramatically. Local conflicts occasionally flare up, but in the past decade Africa's wars have become a lot less deadly. Perennial hotspots such as Angola, Chad, Eritrea, Liberia and Sierra Leone are quiet, leaving millions better off, and even Congo, Somalia and Sudan are much less violent than they used to be. Parts of Mali were seized by Islamists last year, then liberated by French troops in January, though unrest continues. The number of coups, which averaged 20 per decade in 1960—90, has fallen to an average of ten.

Second, more private citizens are engaging with politics, some in civil-society groups, others in aid efforts or as protesters. The beginnings of the Arab spring in north Africa two years ago inspired the rest of the continent. In Angola youth activists invoke the events farther north. In Senegal a group of rap artists formed the nucleus of the coalition that ousted Mr Wade.[10]

Third, Africa's retreat from socialist economic models has generally made everyone better off. Some countries, such as Ethiopia and Rwanda, still put the state in the lead.

Meles Zenawi, Ethiopia's prime minister from 1995 until his death last year, achieved impressive gains by taking development into his own (occasionally bloodstained) hands. Others, such as Kenya and Nigeria, have empowered private business by removing red tape[11]. Yet others are benefiting from a commodities boom, driven by increased demand from China, which has become Africa's biggest trading partner. Over the past decade African trade with China has risen from $11 billion to $166 billion. Copper-rich Zambia and oil-soaked Ghana are using full coffers to pay for new schools and hospitals, even if some of the money is stolen along the way.

Inevitably, Africa's rise is being hyped. Boosters proclaim an "African century" and talk of "the China of tomorrow" or "a new India." Sceptics retort that Africa has seen false dawns before.[12] They fear that foreign investors will exploit locals and that the continent will be "not lifted but looted." They also worry that many officials are corrupt, and that those who are straight often lack expertise, putting them at a disadvantage in negotiations with investors.

So who is right? To find out, your correspondent travelled overland across the continent from Dakar to Cape Town, taking in regional centres such as Lagos, Nairobi and Johannesburg as well as plenty of bush and desert. Each part of the trip focused on one of the big themes with which the continent is grappling—political violence, governance, economic development—as outlined in the articles that follow.

The journey covered some 15,800 miles (25,400km) on rivers, railways and roads, almost all of them paved and open for business. Not once was your correspondent asked for a bribe along the way, though a few drivers may have given small gratuities to policemen. The trip took 112 days, and on all but nine of them e-mail by smartphone was available. It was rarely dangerous or difficult. Borders were easily crossed and visas could be had for a few dollars on the spot or within a day in the nearest capital. By contrast, in 2001, when Paul Theroux researched his epic travel book, *Dark Star Safari: Overland from Cairo to Cape Town*[13], he was shot at, forced into detours and subjected to endless discomforts.

Another decade from now a traveller may well see an end to hunger in some African countries, steeply rising agricultural production in others, the start of industrial manufacturing for export, the emergence of a broad retail sector, more integrated transport networks[14], fairer elections, more effective governments, widespread access to technology even among many of the poor and ever-rising commodity incomes. Not everywhere. This report covers plenty of places where progress falls short.[15] But their number is shrinking.

Wait for it

The biggest reason to be hopeful is that it takes time for results from past investment to come through, and many such benefits have yet to materialise. Billions have already been put into roads and schools over the past decade; the tech revolution has only just reached the more remote corners of the continent; plenty of new oilfields and gold mines have been tapped but are not yet producing revenues. The aid pipeline too is fairly full. The Bill and Melinda Gates Foundation[16] alone has invested $1.7 billion in Africa since 2006 but acknowledges that "it takes years and years to shift the system." Some aid will be wasted, some new roads will remain empty and more than a few barrels of oil will be stolen. Yet whereas currently not even half of Africa's countries are what the World Bank calls "middle income" (defined as at least $1,000 per person a year), by 2025 the bank expects most

African countries to have reached that stage.

As the hand-painted number 3 bus pulls out of Cap-Vert and travels through the streets of Dakar, the views, bathed in buttery late-afternoon sunlight, reflect aspects of Africa's current triumphs and tribulations. On the left are new tenement buildings[17] with running water for the urban poor. On a hill to the right stands a 160-foot (49-metre) bronze statue of a man with a muscular torso resembling Mr Wade in his younger years on which he spent $27m of public money. The bus leaves the capital behind and chugs on, passing craggy cliffs and flooded pastures, single-room huts and mangrove forests. Several hours later it crosses a muddy creek near the city of Ziguinchor, heading south towards Guinea-Bissau.

Leaving the ivorian commercial capital, Abidjan[18], at 7am, you run straight into what is known as the civil-servant rush hour. The president has decreed that administrators must be at their desks by 7:30am, and most are. A Western ambassador says disbelievingly, "If you are five minutes late for a meeting, you have missed the first five minutes. " Having travelled to the office on elevated dual carriageways[19], civil servants leap into lifts and ride up to their desks on the upper floors of modern glass towers. Some sneakily keep an iPad or some other electronic gadget with which to while away the time.

Governance in Côte d'Ivoire is rarely as good as it looks. Bribes still solve problems faster than meetings. The opposition spitefully boycotted the most recent elections. Deep cleavages run across the political landscape. And yet the national accounts are in order, debts are coming down and new roads are being built. This is the picture in much of Africa. The allocation of power is becoming fairer and its use more competent, as in Ghana, though there is much more to do, especially in resource-rich nations like Nigeria.

African governments are beginning to accept the importance of good governance, not least for improving the lot of the poor. Rulers travelling on presidential planes strut their stuff at the World Economic Forum in Davos and declare their undying interest in "capacity-building."[20] Behind the jargon a remarkable change is taking place. The default means of allocating power in Africa now is to hold elections[21], and elections are generally becoming fairer. Sceptics rightly bemoan voter fraud and intimidation, and plenty of polls are still stolen. But the margins of victory that autocrats dare to award themselves are shrinking. Indeed, quite a few have discovered, in forced retirement, that by allowing notional democracy they have started something they cannot stop.

Until 1991 it was almost unknown for a ruling party to be peacefully ousted at the polls. Since Benin ticked up a first in that year it has happened almost three dozen times. In many countries such an event cements tentative gains, as it did in Ghana in 1992 and again in 2000. Crossing the border from Côte d'Ivoire into Ghana, the visitor immediately becomes aware that democratic expression here is unrestrained. An election is under way and supporters of the ruling party and the opposition cheerfully line one side of the road each, holding megaphones and waving banners. Opinion polls put the two main parties neck-and-neck even though the present government has achieved impressive economic growth: GDP increased by 14% in 2011.

After a few hours on the road, just past the city of Takoradi, the country's economic turbo-charger comes into view. Pipelines run along the road and diggers make huge holes for storage tanks. A vast oilfield has been found nearby, but celebrations were muted. Ghanaians know that a resource bonanza can be dangerous and politicians may get greedy, so administrators are now being trained in handling a large influx of oil revenues.[22] At a leafy campus with neatly trimmed grass on the outskirts of Accra, the capital, they learn about transparency, accountability and the intricacies of transfer pricing[23].

This stuff matters. Some of the biggest obstacles to better governance are not murderous tyrants but a lack of bureaucratic competence and a divided opposition. Ageing autocrats die eventually, but bad habits will not go away of their own accord.[24] Robert Mugabe, Zimbabwe's dictator, now aged 89, could be deposed if rivals, with whom he has been forced to share power since the most recent election, were better at their jobs. Still, in neighbouring Zambia opposition politicians outmanoeuvred a tired government in 2011 and took office.

Luckily, competence is on the rise in Africa. White elephants are still being created, but are now generally designed to serve larger and more inclusive groups of people.[25] South Africa's football stadiums built for the 2010 World Cup[26] are in that category, as are many new dams and airports.

Politicians and officials are learning new skills to run such projects. It is hard to quantify the change, but traipsing in and out of ministries across the continent builds up a measure of confidence.[27] There are plenty of shortcomings and allegations of corruption, but in a fair number of African countries the bureaucracies are not far behind standards in, say, India.

Transport management in particular has become much better. A bus ride from Accra across three African borders in one day is instructive. Departing at sunrise, the 15-seater[28] easily crosses into Togo where it passes well-run port installations and warehouses. An hour later it arrives in Benin. The driver ignores the outstretched hands of traffic policemen. After a few more hours the bus reaches Nigeria amid throngs of packed lorries on their way to Onitsha, Africa's largest market. Most of the bus passengers are professionals, including several telecoms engineers who commute weekly. All four countries have sensible transit policies and trade actively with each other.

What has brought about this change? Across Africa both voters and leaders are better educated than they were even half a generation ago. Many of those in power are the first in their families with a university degree. Standards of political debate have risen thanks to better schools, modern media and the return of diaspora members who bring new ideas with them.

One lesson in particular seems to have sunk in: the need for solid and durable institutions.[29] In the past, good practice all too often lapsed quickly after a change of incumbent. Foreign advisers ram home the need for institution-building.[30] "Everyone is nagging us about it, from TB to Mo," says an Oxford-educated official, referring to Tony Blair, a former British prime minister who now runs an African governance initiative, and Mo Ibrahim, an Anglo-Sudanese telecoms billionaire who awards prizes for political leadership.

Size matters here. Benin is nicely democratic—it has more political parties than cities—but with a mere 9m people it carries little weight. Nigeria, on the other hand, has 160m, so along with Kenya and South Africa it sets the tone in regional meetings and institutions—and it still struggles to get things right. When the parliament's speaker needed a bit of extra cash before leaving office in 2011 (on top of more than $1m a year he got in pay and expenses) he gave himself a $65m government loan. He was charged but later acquitted.

Nigeria is famous for corruption, yet at issue is more than thievery.[31] Members of the elite systematically loot state coffers, then subvert the electoral system to protect themselves.[32] Everybody knows it, and a few straight arrows in the government talk about it openly.[33] Perhaps half the substantial (but misreported) oil revenues of Africa's biggest oil producer go missing. Moderate estimates suggest that at least $4 billion—8 billion is stolen every year, money that could pay for schools and hospitals. One official reckons the country has lost more than $380 billion since independence in 1960. Yet not a single politician has been imprisoned for graft. The day that Nigeria works properly, the battle for Africa's future will have been won.

From *The Economist*, March 2nd, 2013

Ⅰ. New Words

acquit	[ə'kwit]	v.	to decide and state officially in court that someone is not guilty of a crime
booster	['buːstə]	n.	积极的支持者
breach	[briːtʃ]	n.	a failure to do sth that must be done by law
chug	[tʃʌg]	v.	(of a vehicle) to move while making a low repeated knocking sound
cappuccino	[ˌkæpu'tʃiːnəu]	n.	卡布奇诺咖啡
craggy	['krægi]	adj.	very steep and covered in rough rocks
detour	['diːtuə]	n.	a longer route that you take in order to avoid a problem
diaspora	[dai'æspərə]	n.	the spreading of people from a national group or culture to other areas
flyblown	['flaibləun]	adj.	*Br. E* dirty and in bad condition
grapple	['græpəl]	v.	to fight or struggle with someone, holding them tightly
gratuity	[grə'tjuːiti]	n.	money given to sb for service
intricacy	['intrikəsi]	n.	the state of containing a large number of parts or details
materialize	[mə'tiəriəlaiz]	v.	to start to exist as expected or planned
mute	[mjuːt]	v.	to make the sound of sth quieter
oust	[aust]	v.	to force someone out of a position of power
outmanoeuvre	[ˌautmə'nuːvə]	v.	to gain an advantage over someone by using cleverer or more skilful plans or methods
scrap	[skræp]	v.	to throw away (sth useless or worn-out)
semi-clad	['semiklæd]	adj.	半身穿着衣服的
sneakily	['sniːkili]	adv.	secretly

spitefully	[ˈspaitfuli]	adv.	胸怀恶意地
staple	[ˈsteipəl]	n.	~ of sth a large and important part of sth
tap	[tæp]	v.	to make use of sth
throng	[θrɔŋ]	n.	a mass of things
torso	[ˈtɔːsəu]	n.	（人体的）躯干雕塑像
tribulation	[ˌtribjuˈleiʃn]	n.	great trouble or suffering
vibrant	[ˈvaibrənt]	adj.	full of life or energy
Abidjan	[æbiˈrɑːŋ]		阿比让（科特迪瓦最大都市和经济首都）
Accra	[əˈkrɑː]		阿克拉（加纳首都）
Angola	[ænˈgəulə]		安哥拉（非洲西南部国家）
Benin	[bəˈnin]		贝宁（西非国家）
Cape Town	[ˈkeiptaun]		开普敦（南非西南部港市）
Cap-Vert	[ˈkæpvəːt]		佛得角（区）（塞内加尔）
Chad	[tʃæd]		乍得（非洲中北部国家）
Dakar	[dəˈkɑː(r)]		达喀尔（塞内加尔首都）
Eritrea	[ˌeriˈtriə]		厄立特里亚（东非国家）
Ghana	[ˈgɑːnə]		加纳（西非国家）
Guinea Bissau	[ˌginibisau]		几内亚比绍（西非国家）
Johannesburg	[dʒəuˈhænisbəːg]		约翰内斯堡（南非东北部城市）
Lagos	[ˈleigəs]		拉各斯（尼日利亚西南部港市）
Liberia	[laiˈbiəriə]		利比里亚（西非国家）
Libya	[ˈlibiə]		利比亚（北非国家）
Moldova	[mɔlˈdɔːvə]		摩尔多瓦（欧洲东南部国家）
Nairobi	[naiˈrəubi]		内罗毕（肯尼亚首都）
Onitsha	[ˈɔnitsa]		奥尼查（尼日利亚城市）
Senegal	[ˌseniˈgɔːl]		塞内加尔（西非国家）
Sierre Leone	[siéərəliáuni]		塞拉利昂（西非国家）
Somalia	[səuˈmɑːliə]		索马里（东非国家）
Sudan	[suːˈdæn]		苏丹（非洲东北部国家）
Swaziland	[ˈswɑːzilænd]		斯威士兰（非洲东南部国家）
Takoradi	[ˌtɑːkəˈrɑːdi]		塔科拉迪（加纳西南部港市）
Togo	[ˈtəugəu]		多哥（西非国家）
Zambia	[ˈzæmbiə]		赞比亚（非洲中南部国家）
ziguinchor	[zigwinˈtʃɔː]		济金绍尔（塞内加尔的一个行政区）

Ⅱ. Background Information

非洲的崛起

非洲约占世界陆地总面积的 20%，是仅次于亚洲的第二大洲，世界上最年轻的大陆。非洲历史悠久，其中埃及是四大文明古国之一。15 世纪西方殖民主义者入侵非洲，统治长达四百多年，非洲人民生活在没有自由和民主的极度贫困之中。从 16 世纪到 19 世纪，西方殖民者将两千多万非洲黑人贩运到美洲当奴隶,致使大量劳动力缺失,导致了非洲经济的长期落后。西方列强运用武力抢占非洲的土地和资源,进而完全瓜分非洲,建立起野蛮、残酷的殖民统治。二战后,非洲的独立浪潮从北非兴起。非洲国家的独立瓦解了世界殖民体系,成为世界上最大的发展中国家集团,也为非洲经济的发展提供了最基本的条件。非洲被称为"富饶的大陆",其矿藏资源十分丰富,黄金、铀、钻石、铜、铝、石油和天然气等资源都很充足。非洲还有占大约60%的世界未使用耕地,这些土地的开垦和种植有望成为世界的粮仓。

进入21世纪,非洲经济发展加速,特别是最近几年,速度快于其他大洲。当前非洲的人均国民收入已经超过印度,有十多个非洲国家的人均国民收入已经超过中国,在54个非洲国家中,大约1/3国家的年度GDP增速超过6%。

非洲发展快速以及后力强劲的原因不只归功于其丰富的自然资源,还有其良好的外部条件与巨大发展潜力。首先,新兴消费阶层扩大,内需不断增长,市场机会巨大。非洲大陆有52个人口达到或超过100万的城市——与西欧的同类城市数相当。在非洲前十大经济体中,服务业产值占GDP的40%。其次,政局日趋稳定。在过去的10年里,非洲的债务和通货膨胀问题得到显著缓解,这得益于非洲各国政府广泛采用市场经济体制。政变次数自1990年以来已急剧下降。再次,非洲的人口红利,海外专业人员回归等因素使非洲企业家素质有所提高。非洲劳动力将在10年内激增到1.63亿;到2035年,非洲劳动力人数将超过中国。此外,与世界上其他地方的同龄人相比,非洲劳动力的赡养责任要更轻一些。第四,非洲内部贸易处于起步期。当前,只有11%的非洲贸易发生在当地,这一比例是所有贸易区域中最低的。非洲的政治和资源限制因素使其与外界隔离,但新一批有竞争力的泛非公司和领导者正在改变这一格局。第五,非洲20%的政府开支用于教育。教育水准是判定激增的劳动力是福是祸的关键因素。2008年,非洲小学入学率已达76%,10年间上升了14个百分点。中学入学率仍然较低,仅为35%,但这已经增长了10个百分点。

另外,一些世界环境下的因素也加速了非洲的崛起,例如:外贸因素,特别是来自中国的需求不断增长;技术革新因素,如非洲与发达国家间的光缆通讯,提高了非洲人的劳动生产率,使非洲人增加了收入,促进了非洲的崛起。

Ⅲ. Notes to the Text

1. Three students are hunched over an iPad at a beach café on Senegal's Cap-Vert peninsula, the westernmost tip of the world's poorest continent.——在世界最穷洲的最西端的塞内加尔佛得角半岛的一家沙滩咖啡馆里,三个学生弓着身一起在玩iPad。
2. sex-trafficking——a form of commercial sex act induced by force, fraud or coercion 性交易
3. the New World——referring to the North, Central and South America
4. This special report will paint a picture at odds with Western images of Africa.——这份特别报道将描绘出与西方人心目中非洲形象不同的画面。(at odds with——different from)
5. the sub-Saharan part——撒哈拉沙漠以南的非洲地区
6. FDI——Foreign Direct Investment 外国直接投资
7. When President Abdoulaye Wade last year tried to stand for a third term, in breach of term limits, he was ridiculed.——去年阿卜杜拉耶·瓦德总统违反任期限制试图第三次连任时遭到嘲弄。(① Abdoulaye Wade——1926— , a Senegalese politician who was

President of Senegal from 2000 to 2012 ②breach—a failure to do sth that must be done by law）

8. varying shades—different kinds
9. Big-man leaders are becoming rarer, though some authoritarian states survive. —独裁领袖越来越少,但还是有些专制国家存在。(① big-man leaders—dictatorial leaders; ② authoritarian—demanding total obedience)
10. In Senegal a group of rap artists formed the nucleus of the coalition that ousted Mr Wade. —在塞内加尔一个以一组说唱艺术家为核心组成的联合群体把瓦德先生赶下了台。(① nucleus—a small, important group at the centre of a larger group or organization; ②oust—to force sb out of a position of power)
11. red tape—繁文缛节
12. Sceptics retort that Africa has seen false dawns before. —持怀疑态度的人反驳道,非洲在此之前也出现过虚幻的希望。(false dawn—a situation in which sth good seems likely to happen, but it does not)
13. *Dark Star Safari*: *Overland from Cairo to Cape Town*—《灾星之旅——从开罗到开普敦的陆地艰难之行》(The book is based on the author's travel in Africa from Cairo to Cape Town, down the Neil, through Sudan and Ethiopia, to Kenya, Uganda, and ultimately to the tip of South Africa. The author described Africa as "hungrier, poorer, less educated, more pessimistic, more corrupt.")
14. more integrated transport networks—更加完整的运输网络
15. This report covers plenty of places where progress falls short— 这篇报道提到许多进步不足的地方。(fall short—to fail to reach the standard you expected or need)
16. The Bill and Melinda Gates Foundation—比尔和梅琳达盖茨基金会
17. tenement buildings—出租住宅,经济公寓
18. Abidjan—阿比让(the former capital city and currently the economic city of Ivory Coast)
19. elevated dual carriageways—有中央分隔带的高架复式车行道(dual carriageways—a main road on which the traffic travelling in opposite directions is kept apart by a central band or separation)
20. Rulers travelling on presidential planes strut their stuff at the World Economic Forum in Davos and declare their undying interest in "capacity-building." —乘坐总统专机出行的统治者在达沃斯世界经济论坛上炫耀他们的物品,宣称他们永远关注"能力建设"。〔① strut—to proudly show; ② capacity-building— strengthening of the skills, competence and abilities of people and communities; ③ the World Economic Forum—简称 WEF,是一个以基金会形式成立的非营利组织,成立于 1971 年,以每年冬季在瑞士滑雪胜地达沃斯举办的年会(俗称达沃斯论坛)闻名于世〕
21. The default means of allocating power in Africa now is to hold elections... —现在非洲既定分配权力的方式是举行选举……(default— what exists if you do not change it intentionally by performing an action)

22. Ghanaians know that a resource bonanza can be dangerous and politicians may get greedy, so administrators are now being trained in handling a large influx of oil revenues. —加纳人知道丰富的资源财富会产生促使政客变得贪婪的危险,所以管理人员正在接受如何管控大笔石油收入的培训

23. transfer pricing—转让定价(指关联企业之间在销售货物、提供劳务、转让无形资产等制定的价格)

24. Ageing autocrats die eventually, but bad habits will not go away of their own accord. —上年纪的独裁者最终要离开人世的,但坏的习惯却不会自动消失。(of one's own accord—without being asked, forced)

25. White elephants are still being created, but are now generally designed to serve larger and more inclusive groups of people. —无价值的工程依然在建,但现在这些工程一般用以服务更大、更广的群体。(① white elephant—sth that is useless and unwanted, especially sth that is big and costly; ② inclusive— including a wide range of people)

26. the 2010 World Cup—referring to the 2010 World Cup Tournament

27. It is hard to quantify the change, but traipsing in and out of ministries across the continent builds up a measure of confidence. —这种变化很难用数字表示,但到整个非洲的政府部门慢慢走一走,看一看,就会建立一定信心。(① traipse—to walk somewhere slowly; ② a measure of—a particular amount of sth especially a fairly large amount)

28. the 15-seater—a car with 15 seats

29. One lesson in particular seems to have sunk in: the need for solid and durable institutions. —特别有一个教训看来已被人们所意识到:那就是建立牢固持久体制的必要性。(sink in—to be fully understood or realized)

30. In the past, good practice all too often lapsed quickly after a change of incumbent. Foreign advisers ram home the need for institution-building. —过去,执政者更换后,好的做法通常便会转瞬即逝。外国顾问反复强调建立制度的必要性。(① lapse—to end officially or legally by not being continued; ② ram home—to emphasize an idea very strongly to make sure people listen to it)

31. Nigeria is famous for corruption, yet at issue is more than thievery. —尼日利亚的腐败臭名昭著,这个问题比偷窃更为亟待解决。(at issue—to be considered)

32. Members of the elite systematically loot state coffers, then subvert the electoral system to protect themselves. —精英们有计划、有步骤地洗劫着国库,接着推翻选举制度来保护自己。(① state coffer—the money that a government has available to spend; ② subvert—to try to destroy the power and influence of the established system)

33. Everybody knows it, and a few straight arrows in the government talk about it openly. —这件事人人皆知,政府里只有几个诚实的人公开谈论。(straight arrow—a morally good, honest person)

Ⅳ. Language Features

拼缀词

本文中"geopolitics"是由"geography"和"politics"两个词剪裁复合而成的拼缀词。在现代英语中,这类拼缀词日趋增多。由于拼缀法(blending)既可使文字活泼,又可节约用词,它在新闻英语中十分常用。

例1. Robodocs and Mousecalls [robodoc—robot + doctor(机器医生,这里指远程运用电脑行医);mousecall 是由 mouse + call 复合而成的词,意思是运用鼠标(电脑)出诊]

例2. Holidazed? It's not the happiest time of the year for every one. (holidazed—holiday + dazed 节日忙得头脑发昏)

拼缀词大致可分为以下四类:

1. 前词首部 + 后词尾部,例如:
botel(boat + hotel) 水上旅馆
taikonaut(taikong+astronaut)(中国)太空人,宇航员
medicide(medical + suicide) 医助安乐死
guestimate(guess + estimate) 约略估计
fremy(friend + enemy)友敌
webonomics(web + economics)网络经济

2. 前词全部 + 后词尾部,例如:
screenager(screen + teenager) 屏幕青少年(从小就看电视、玩电脑的青少年)
eyelyzer (eye + analyzer)眼部测醉器
workfare(work + welfare) 工作福利制
filmdom(film + kingdom) 电影王国
newsgram(news + program) 新闻节目
staycation(stay + vacation)在家休假

3. 前词首部 + 后词全部,例如:
exerhead(exercise + head) 运动狂
medicare(medical + care) 医疗照顾
telescript(television + script) 电视广播稿
t-can(trash + can) 垃圾箱
ecotourism(ecological + tourism)生态旅游
cenbank(central + bank)央行

4. 前词首部 + 后词首部,例如:
interpol(international + police) 国际警察
elint(electronic + intelligence) 以电子侦察手段获取情报
comsat(communication + satellite) 通讯卫星
sitcom(situation comedy) 情景喜剧
neocon(neo + conservative)新保守主义者
robodoc(robot + doctor)机器人医生

Ⅴ. Analysis of the Content

1. The meaning of the word "straight" in the sentence "They also worry that many officials

are corrupt, and that those who are straight often lack expertise, putting them at a disadvantage in negotiations with investors."(Para. 12) is _____.

   A. simple
   B. correct
   C. honest
   D. serious

2. According to the article, which of the following countries is noted for unrestrained democratic expression?

   A. Ghana.
   B. Côte d'Ivoire.
   C. Angola.
   D. Senegal.

3. Which of the following is NOT on the author's list of paths to the improvement of citizens' lives?

   A. End of fighting.
   B. Citizens' participation in politics.
   C. Retreat from socialist economic models.
   D. Elevation of citizens' education level.

4. Which of the following statements is NOT true about the correspondent's journey in Africa?

   A. The journey was rarely dangerous or difficult.
   B. The journey took over 100 days.
   C. The correspondent traveled by train and plane.
   D. It was easy to get visas.

5. Which lesson in particular seems to have been learnt by African countries?

   A. The need for solid and durable institutions.
   B. The need for capacity-building.
   C. The need for independence.
   D. The need for fast economic development.

Ⅵ. Questions on the Article

1. What kind of picture will *The Economist*'s special report paint?
2. What do statistics show about human development in Sub-Saharan Africa?
3. How fast is Africa's economy growing now and expected to grow over the next decade?
4. What changes have taken place in Africans' life?
5. What is the biggest reason to be hopeful about Africa's future?
6. How is governance in Côte d'Ivoire?
7. What effort is Ghana making to improve officials' governance?
8. Which country sets the tone in regional meetings and institutions? Why?
9. Which country is famous for corruption? How serious is the problem according to the article?

Ⅶ. Topics for Discussion

1. Should African countries model their system after western political systems?
2. Is corruption unavoidable in the process of economic development?

Lesson 34

Return of the Samurai

Japan's popular, assertive Prime Minister wants to change the country's security stance, and Tokyo is baring its muscles[1].
By Beech, Hannah/Naha Air base

(Abridged)

Riceman was on high alert. So was Vader (as in Darth), a Japanese fighter pilot whose sinister call sign belies his smiling countenance.[2] At Naha Air Base[3], perched on the subtropical tail of the Japanese archipelago, F-15 pilots from the 204th tactical fighter squadron know what the sudden, hushed message broadcast over the loudspeakers one rainy afternoon in September means: another emergency fighter-jet mission for a nation that technically doesn't even possess a conventional military.[4] Territorial tensions between Japan and China have intensified over a scattering of islands in the East China Sea, which Japan administers but to which China lays historic claim. As a result, the squall-prone skies over Naha have darkened with the shadow of scrambled jets overhead.[5] "The stress level has increased," says Atsushi "Riceman" Takahashi, a veteran fighter pilot who now instructs younger charges.[6] "The scramblings show our pride in securing our domain."

From April to June, 69 Japanese jets were deployed because of perceived threats from China, compared with just 15 during the same period last year. September was just as busy, with Japan's Self-Defense Force (SDF)[7] responding to the first confirmed flight of a Chinese drone over Japan, the first reported flight of Chinese bombers on a course not far from Naha and a flotilla of Chinese coast-guard vessels sailing through waters near the disputed islands—called Senkaku by the Japanese and Diaoyu by the Chinese. "Going up [in an F-15] makes me feel like I'm really playing a part in national defense," says Kohta "Vader" Araki. "The responsibility is very heavy."

Naha Air Base borders Okinawa prefecture's main civilian airport, thronged with sunburned holiday seekers in flowered shirts. Commercial planes with colorful logos touch down just as gray camouflage F-15s roar into the sky. It is an incongruous scene in a nation that is divided over its martial past and future. After World War II, Japan's DNA was shaped into a pacifist helix, reinforced by a constitution that renounces war altogether.[8] The charter was imposed by the victorious Americans, who wanted to ensure that Japan would not repeat its imperialist rampage across Asia. In exchange, the U.S. charged itself with maintaining Japan's national security. Japan was free to achieve its postwar economic miracle.

Now, under hawkish Prime Minister Shinzo Abe[9], Japan is expanding its military footprint and speaking out more forcefully against nations it sees as threatening its sovereignty, most notably China. For Abe and other conservatives in the ruling Liberal Democratic Party (LDP), Japan's samurai spirit is just as integral to the national makeup as any paeans to peace.[10] A rewrite of the constitution, which has been interpreted as forbidding anything but defensive military maneuvers, is difficult—any change requires a two-thirds majority in both houses of the legislature, then a public referendum.[11]

But this past summer, Abe said pursuing such an amendment was his "historic mission." Pacifism is still the reflexive stance in Japan—just look at all those kids automatically flashing peace signs in photos. At the same time, a real debate is emerging about whether Japan can finally evolve into a normal country with normal armed forces. "The constitution says Japan doesn't possess an army, navy or air force," Shigeru Ishiba[12], secretary general of the LDP, tells TIME. "Is that true? Japan does have an army, a navy, an air force. We have lots of warplanes and tanks. Let's stop telling a lie. The constitution and the reality of Japan are different. I think it is now necessary to make our constitution reflect the reality of Japan."

New Cop on the Beat[13]

Japan's sterner posture—no more deferential bows—comes at a time of shifting geopolitics in Asia. China has already claimed economic superiority over Japan, replacing it as the world's second largest economy three years ago. Now, with confident leadership in place, Beijing is flexing its muscle over everything from trade to territory. Meanwhile, the U. S.—the historically pre-eminent—if geographically remote—regional policeman has promised to refocus its attentions on Asia by deploying 60% of its naval vessels there by 2020, up from 50%. But this "rebalancing"—as the Obama Administration is now calling what was originally sold as a "pivot" to Asia—depends on Washington's attentions not being dominated by the Middle East, as well as an American unwillingness to endure further overseas adventures. "When we think 10 years, 20 years or 30 years from now, the power of the U. S. will decline," says Ishiba, noting the cuts in American military spending.

Enter Japan. Buoyed by a rare electoral mandate in two consecutive elections, Abe and his LDP envision a world in which Japan cannot only stand firm against rivals like China but also share with an ascendant continent its national values: Democracy! Peace! Love for cute stuff!

Yet while the U. S. has enjoyed relative goodwill in the region, Japan's relations with some of its neighbors are still poisoned by the decidedly unpeaceful, undemocratic way in which it tried to fashion a Greater East Asia Co-Prosperity Sphere[14] more than seven decades ago. Animosity lingers because, unlike Germans, Japanese politicians can be equivocal about their nation's wartime guilt. Also, leaders in China and South Korea, countries especially brutalized by Japan, profit politically from stoking anti-Japanese public sentiment. "The phantom of militarism is rising once more in Japan," warned an August editorial in the People's Daily, a Chinese Communist Party mouthpiece. Even the U. S.—which is treaty-bound to defend Japan in case of attack, maintains military bases in the country and presumably isn't averse to someone else needling China for a change—seems wary. "U. S. policymakers have sent clear signals to Abe that a further drift to the nationalist side is not welcome," says Koichi Nakano, a politics professor at Sophia University in Tokyo.

Still, Abe's combative stance has won him some surprising allies. He has strengthened economic ties with nations like India and Burma that are keen to hedge against China Inc[15]. Southeast Asian nations are looking to Japan to counter China's growing military might, even if they once suffered under the boot of the imperial Japanese army.

In July, Abe received a warm welcome in the Philippines, where Japanese soldiers had presided over the murderous 1942 Bataan death march[16]. Manila is embroiled in its own territorial conflict with Beijing over disputed isles and shoals in the South China Sea, a vast waterway that China claims as nearly all its own. Abe came to town with promises of 10 cutters to upgrade the Philippine coast guard. In September, Japanese warships docked in Philippine ports, followed by U.S. armed forces who conducted joint war games with their Philippine counterparts. (In the early 1990s, U.S. military bases in the Philippines were closed because of local opposition, but the current government has indicated interest in a renewed American military presence.) "Japan has every right to enhance its military capability due to China's provocation," says Clarita Carlos, a former president of the National Defense College of the Philippines[17]. "The Chinese are always playing the we-were-colonized-by-the-Japanese card. All of us have been there. We do remember, but we also know how to forgive."

Security Fixation[18]

Besides forgiveness, Japan needs revival. The country has been wounded by more than two decades of economic stagnation and was hit hard by the 2011 earthquake, tsunami and nuclear crisis that claimed nearly 20,000 lives. Abe, who during his first stint as Prime Minister in 2006 became the nation's youngest postwar leader, has projected himself as a bold changemaker. Since taking office again in December, he has launched a reform program, dubbed Abenomics[19], that aims to use monetary expansion and fiscal stimulus to goose Japan's long-deflated economy. In September, the national mood was buoyed when Tokyo was awarded the 2020 Olympics, despite international concerns over radioactive water leaking from a tsunami-damaged nuclear power plant. "I want to make the Olympics a trigger," Abe said, "for sweeping away 15 years of deflation and economic decline." In a February speech in Washington, he proclaimed, "Japan is back."

Indeed, the LDP's slogan is "Restore Japan," and Abe has explicitly linked any economic recovery to Japan's ability to protect its sovereignty. "Japan's beautiful seas and its territory are under threat, and young people are having trouble finding hope in the future amid an economic slump," he said in September 2012, as the Senkaku-Diaoyu row with China heated up. [20]"I promise to protect Japan's land and sea, and the lives of the Japanese people, no matter what." This year, Japan's defense budget increased for the first time in 11 years—by a paltry 0.8%, yes, but a clear signal from the Abe administration of the importance it places on national security. In August, the Defense Ministry requested a 3% rise in next year's spending, which would be the biggest jump in more than two decades.

Despite the SDF's constitutional limitations on any offensive use of force, Japan already boasts the world's fifth highest defense coffers. This summer, the Defense Ministry unveiled the Izumo[21], Japan's biggest warship of the postwar era, which resembles an aircraft carrier; plans are afoot to form a new amphibious corps of soldiers and a fleet of surveillance drones. Abe is also pushing for the formation of a Japanese National-Security Council. On Sept. 17, he made a plea for the rhetorically tortured concept of "active pacifism," or collective self-defense, in which Japan can come to the aid of its military allies should they come under attack.[22] The liberal newspaper *Asahi Shimbun*[23] editorialized, "[Collective self-defense] would represent a radical departure from the basic security policy principle of postwar Japan and a gross deviation from its pacifist creed."

Japan's official position on the disputed isles——which are located in waters rich in oil and natural gas—is that, well, it hasn't budged one bit. "Japan has never changed our attitude toward issues of our territorial waters and land," Defense Minister Itsunori Onodera[24] tells TIME. "It is China today that is trying to change this." But the latest tension ratcheted up after the Japanese government nationalized three of the contested islands a year ago. The purchase was aimed, says the Japanese government, at preventing the islands from falling into the hands of Tokyo's nationalist governor, who was threatening to buy the outcroppings from their private Japanese owners. Beijing took exception to the nationalization[25], and forays by Chinese planes and vessels have increased markedly since then. Abe's administration is now considering stationing personnel on the isles, which have been uninhabited since before World War II—a move that will surely further anger Chinese. "We can't avert our eyes from the reality: a flurry of provocations against our country's sovereignty," Abe said in mid-September, referring to Japan's territorial spat with China. "I'm pushing for the regeneration of our country's security by looking squarely at reality."

Man with a Past

With his soft face and panda-set eyes[26], Abe, 59, is known as an obotchan[27], which roughly translates to "little boy," referring to his privileged lineage as the son of a Foreign Minister and the grandson of a Prime Minister. In truth, there aren't many leading politicians in Japan who aren't obotchan—nepotism flourishes in Tokyo's halls of power.[28] But Abe seems especially weighted with a sense of his conservative family's mission, particularly his grandfather Nobusuke Kishi's desire to amend Article 9 of the constitution, which is read as banning Japan from possessing an offensive military force.[29] "From a young age, Abe had it in his mind that he would be the one who would bring the postwar regime to an end," says Hitoshi Tanaka, a former Deputy Foreign Minister.

Abe's sense of history and destiny for Japan backfired for him during his first stint as PM. "Abe misread the public mood about nationalism," says Koichi Nakano, a politics professor at Sophia University in Tokyo[30]. "People were more concerned about the economy, and he focused on the wrong thing." Abe's popularity plunged, even as he pursued a patriotic agenda and supported a textbook that played down Japanese wartime atrocities. A year after taking office, amid financial scandals involving his Cabinet members, Abe resigned in tears. He later blamed a rare intestinal ailment for his retreat.

Abe's surprise exit was hardly the kind of fortitude expected from a young political shogun.[31] In his 2.0 version, he continues to sound the nationalist bell.[32] In 2012, he visited the controversial Yasukuni Shrine[33], where Japan's war dead, including top war criminals, are memorialized—although he has so far declined to worship there while serving as Prime Minister. (Abe's grandfather Kishi was arrested as a suspected war criminal by Allied occupation forces but never charged.) During last year's political campaign, Abe suggested the need to revise two official Japanese apologies for the nation's cruel wartime record, including one for the imperial Japanese army's systematic sexual enslavement of Asian "comfort women[34]."

This time, however, Abe's popularity is high. About 7 in 10 Japanese have a favorable opinion of him, according to a July Pew poll—unusually robust in a nation that serially dumps its leaders after brief periods in office. In May, a self-assured Abe was even moved to clamber into the cockpit of a Japanese military jet and flash a thumbs-up sign. The resulting image wasn't quite Michael Dukakis in a tank. But the notion of Abe as proud commander in chief felt forced—and it didn't help neighborly relations that the jet trainer chosen for the photo op was numbered 731, the same digits as a notorious Japanese military unit that unleashed germ warfare on Manchuria. [35]

Anti-Chinese sentiment is soaring in Japan. Nevertheless, a significant percentage of Japanese remain allergic to any military buildup, particularly those who personally experienced the ravages of war. Only a minority of Japanese support constitutional revision. There is also a grudging understanding that Japan—especially an aging, depopulating Japan—needs China economically far more than the other way around. "Our biggest national interest is reviving our economy, and Japan is not in a position to be isolated by this question of [wartime] history," says former Deputy Foreign Minister Tanaka[36]. "I am very concerned about these careless right-wing statements by people inside government."

It's true that Abe's party triumphed in recent polls. But the LDP[37] won the past two ballots with fewer votes than when it was trounced in 2009 by the former ruling Democratic Party of Japan[38] (DPJ). The LDP's most recent electoral victories owed more to voters' disgust with the DPJ than an endorsement of Abe's worldview. "The last two elections were about the economy, the economy, the economy," says Taro Kono, an LDP legislator. Still, the Abe administration has articulated a consistent theme: Japan's economic and military futures are inextricably tied. "Abe is very up-front about his personal philosophy, which is that he's interested in a strong state that can defend its people and compete internationally," says Tobias Harris, a Washington-based Japan analyst with Teneo Intelligence[39]. Harris notes the historical precedent of 19th century Japanese modernizers who reformed a once closed nation under the motto "Rich nation, strong military." "[Those reformers] believed that if they didn't modernize, they would be gobbled up by the imperial powers; Abe brings that thinking to the 21st century. That's very dangerous."

Right Is Might[40]

One of the unlikely showcases of Japan's military prowess is a radar facility that looms like a giant golf ball, atop a hill overlooking sugarcane fields and picture-postcard beaches. [41] The SDF base, on Okinawa's Miyako Island[42], is a frontline one, and its 160 personnel have been particularly busy since the Senkaku-Diaoyu tiff escalated last year. Living full time on the typhoon-battered base isn't easy.

But the soldiers' hardship posting is at least more appreciated now by the Japanese public. Approval for the SDF has skyrocketed in recent years, particularly after soldiers aided the 2011 natural-disaster-relief effort. A popular TV drama this year followed the fictional love lives of a female TV director and an SDF officer. In a nation obsessed with all things cute, the SDF promotes itself through cartoon mascots named Pickles and Parsley. (Pickles and parsley are strong but ultimately pleasing tastes, just like the SDF, apparently.) "People used to call us 'tax robbers' before," says Air Self-Defense Force Major Yasuhisa Furuta. "Now the situation is totally different." SDF enlistment is up, and its veterans even serve in parliament—the likes of Masahisa Sato, a mustachioed retired colonel who commanded Japanese peacekeepers in Iraq. Unsurprisingly, Sato supports a constitutional revision. "When I entered the SDF 30 years ago, I never imagined that we could be discussing constitutional reform so openly," he says. "Japan is becoming an ordinary country, and the SDF an ordinary military."

That spooks many Okinawans, who inhabit what was once a kingdom called Ryukyu[43] that paid tribute to imperial China. By the late 19th century, though, Okinawa had been absorbed into Japan. (Chinese academics and military officers have postulated that China has territorial rights not just to the Senkaku-Diaoyu Islands but to all of Okinawa.) At the end of World War II, in the horrific Battle of Okinawa, the Japanese military forced tens of thousands of Okinawans into combat, some even compelled to commit suicide in the face of the Allied assault. Local animosity toward Japanese troops, even under the guise of the SDF, lingers—not to mention discomfort with the 25,000 Americans on U.S. military bases on Okinawan soil.[44] "Japan is a very scary country, a warrior culture," says former Okinawa governor Masahide Ota. "The most important lesson from the Battle of Okinawa[45] is that the Japanese military will never protect the local people."

On the island of Ishigaki[46], which has administrative jurisdiction over what Japan calls the Senkaku, Mayor Yoshitaka Nakayama appears open to building an SDF base to better protect the disputed islets. "I am concerned that China is trying to expand its territorial interests," he says. "Since such a country exists in our neighborhood, we have to enhance our defense." Kameichi Uehara, head of the local fishermen's union, doesn't see the threat. "I've never heard of any Chinese boats giving any trouble to us." Local historian Shizuo Ota concurs. "I don't think China has provoked the Senkaku issue," he says. "It's rightist groups from Japan that are causing most of the problems."

From *Time*, October 7th, 2013

Ⅰ. New Words

allergic	[ə'lə:dʒik]	adj	**be ~ to sth** *informal, humorous* to have a strong dislike for sth
amphibious	[æm'fibiəs]	adj.	两栖的
archipelago	[ɑ:ki'peləgəu]	n.	群岛,列岛
ascendant	[ə'sendənt]	adj.	becoming more powerful
assertive	[ə'sə:tiv]	adj.	expressing or tending to express strong opinions
averse	[ə'və:s]	adj.	**not ~ to sth or to do sth** liking sth or wanting to do sth
avert	[ə'və:t]	v.	**~ one's eyes from sth** to turn one's eyes away from sth
budge	[bʌdʒ]	v.	to change your opinion about sth
cutter	['kʌtə]	n.	(海岸警卫队)小型武装快艇
coffer	['kɔfə]	n.	资金,金库
concur	[kən'kə:]	v.	to agree

deferential	[ˌdefəˈrenʃəl]	adj.	恭敬的
depopulate	[diːˈpɔpjuleit]	v.	to decrease the number of people living in a place
embroil	[imˈbrɔil]	v.	使(自己或他人)卷入纠纷
equivocal	[iˈkwivəkəl]	adj.	模棱两可的,含糊其辞的
flotilla	[fləuˈtilə]	n.	小舰队
foray	[ˈfɔrei]	n.	突袭
gobble	[ˈgɔbl]	v.	to eat very quickly
goose	[guːs]	v.	to make sth move or work faster
hush	[hʌʃ]	v.	to make sb/sth become quieter
hawkish	[ˈhɔːkiʃ]	adj.	鹰派的,强硬派的
incongruous	[inˈkɔŋgruəs]	adj.	strange or surprising in relation to the surroundings
intestinal	[inˈtestinəl]	adj.	肠的;肠内的
lineage	[ˈliniidʒ]	n.	直系后裔;家系,家族
logo	[ˈlɔgəu]	n.	(路标、广告等用的)标识
mascot	[ˈmæsˌkət]	n.	吉祥物;福神
mustachioed	[məˈstæʃiəud]	adj.	有八字胡的
needle	[ˈniːdl]	v.	刺激,激怒
outcropping	[ˈautˌkrɔpiŋ]	n.	[地]露出地表
paltry	[ˈpɔːltri]	adj.	worthless or worthlessly small
perch	[pəːtʃ]	v.	**～ed on sth** 坐落在……之上
pivot	[ˈpivət]	n.	枢轴;中枢
prefecture	[ˈpriːfektʃə]	n.	专区,县
postulate	[ˈpɔstjuleit]	v.	to suggest or accept sth as a basis for further reasoning
rampage	[ˈræmpeidʒ]	n.	狂暴行径
ravage	[ˈrævidʒ]	n.	*formal* the destruction caused by sth
reflexive	[riˈfleksiv]	adj.	(本能)反应的
ratchet	[ˈrætʃit]	v.	**～ sth up** to increase or make sth increase by small amounts
shoal	[ʃəul]	n.	[常作-s] 暗礁
spat	[spæt]	n.	口角,小争吵
spook	[spuːk]	v.	吓唬,恐吓
squadron	[ˈskwɔdrən]	n.	飞行中队
stance	[stæns]	n.	姿态,态度
stint	[stint]	n.	工作期限,规定的任期
stoke	[stəuk]	v.	煽动,激起
throng	[θrɔŋ]	v.	to go or be present somewhere in large numbers
tiff	[tif]	n.	a slight argument
trounce	[trauns]	v.	to defeat sb completely
tsunami	[tsuːˈnaːmi]	n.	海啸,地震海啸

upfront　　　[ʌpˈfrʌnt]　　　*adj.*　　　~ **about sth** not trying to hide what you think or do

Ⅱ. Background Information

日本军国主义的复活

日本军国主义源远流长,根深蒂固,它的形成和发展是有多种因素的。

日本武士道是日本军国主义的思想根源。武士道既是日本武士的人生观和世界观,又是武士应尽的义务和职责,包括效忠君王、崇尚武艺和绝对服从等封建道德。武士是日本封建政权存在的基础,曾主导日本政权数百年。武士道文化在日本长期盛行,对日本政治和社会生活各个方面的影响极其深远。

日本军国主义有厚重的历史根源。日本是一个军事封建色彩十分浓厚的国家,有着一脉相承的军国战略思维传统。日本是一个自然资源极其贫乏的岛国,对外拥有很强的扩张欲望。长期的内战和对外扩张的实践为日本孕育了军国主义肥沃的历史土壤。

日本军国主义还有很深的社会根源。天皇制的确立为军国主义提供了制度基础,而神道教将日本军国主义加以推广,使其深入到日本人内心之中,成为宣扬军国主义的精神工具。

日本民族特性也是军国主义产生和存在的一个重要因素。唯我独尊的特征使日本人产生民族优越感和"日本中心论"观念。这种民族特性一旦走向极端便会导致军国主义的形成和发展。

二战后日本虽经和平改革、制定和平宪法,取消了组建军队和对外宣战的权利并建立了由文官主导的政府,削弱了军方对国家和政府的决策影响,但是天皇制得到保留。这种不彻底的变革为军国主义的复活提供了体制可能性。

日本军国主义近年来抬头与美国不无关联。冷战期间,美国出于全球争霸和遏制苏联和中国的目的,转而扶植日本成为美国的战略桥头堡。日本军事力量得到强化,军国主义思想得以保留。只要右翼势力掌权,军国主义便有可能复活。

安倍晋三重任首相之后发誓要领导日本重现往日辉煌,恢复强大兴盛。上台后不久安倍便发起了一场经济改革,并公开把经济复苏与增强日本国防关联在一起。他还公然提出要修改日本和平宪法,声称修宪是其"历史任务"。不久前,日本自民党安全保障相关人员会议通过了新版《防卫计划大纲》和《国家安全保障战略》。日本政府将集体自卫写入新版《防卫计划大纲》。两年来,安倍政府连续增加国防预算。2014 年国防预算高达 4.88 兆日元(约合 2,814 亿人民币),创日本历史新高。2013 年 8 月 15 日是日本战败投降纪念日。安倍政府多名内阁成员不顾国际舆论强烈反对,祭拜了供奉着 14 名日本战犯牌位的靖国神社,为二战罪魁祸首招魂。近年来,日本与邻国军事争斗不断:与俄罗斯争夺南千群岛主权,与我国争夺钓鱼岛和东海主权,与韩国争夺独岛主权。种种迹象表明,日本军国主义正在复活。

Ⅲ. Notes to the Text

1. Tokyo is baring its muscles—Japan is showing its military power
2. So was Vader (as in Darth), a Japanese fighter pilot whose sinister call sign belies his

smiling countenance. ——瓦德同样如此(呼号取自《星球大战》角色达斯·瓦德)。他是日本歼击机驾驶员,他的可怕呼号和他微笑的面容完全不相配。[①call sign——referring to Vader; ②Darth——Darth Vader(旧译黑武士或达斯·瓦德)原名天行者阿纳金(Anakin Skywalker),是电影《星球大战》里最重要的角色之一,他的两次改变决定了光明与黑暗两股势力的消长; ③belie——to give a false impression of sth; ④countenance——a person's face]

3. Naha Air Base——那霸空军基地(an airbase of Japan's Air Self-Defense Force)

4. ...technically doesn't even possess a conventional military.——……从严格意义上讲甚至没有一支常规军。(technically——according to a strict interpretation of laws)

5. As a result, the squall-prone skies over Naha have darkened with the shadow of scrambled jets overhead. ——那易刮飓风的天空又投上了紧急起飞的喷气式飞机的阴影,变得非常暗淡。(① squall-prone——likely to suffer a sudden strong wind often bringing rain or snow; ② scramble——to get a plane into the air in an emergency)

6. ...a veteran fighter pilot who now instructs younger charges. ——……一名经验丰富的歼击机飞行员,现在指导年轻新手。(charge——a person under the care and management of sb)

7. Self-Defense Force (SDF)——日本自卫队

8. After World War II, Japan's DNA was shaped into a pacifist helix, reinforced by a constitution that renounces war altogether. ——二战后,日本在国家性质上已变为类似蜗牛的和平主义,这种性质被全然放弃发动战争的宪法所强化。(① DNA——used as a metaphor for the fundamental aspect of one's nature which is unlikely ever to change; ② altogether——completely; ③ Constitution——指《日本国宪法》,又称《战后宪法》《和平宪法》,1946年11月3日公布。宪法第9条规定放弃向别国发动战争。)

9. Prime Minister Shinzo Abe——日本首相安倍晋三

10. For Abe and other conservatives in the ruling Liberal Democratic Party (LDP), Japan's samurai spirit is just as integral to the national makeup as any paeans to peace. ——对于安倍和执政的自民党其他保守派人而言,日本的武士精神是日本民族不可或缺的一部分,就像赞歌对于和平一样。(① integral to sth——being an essential part of sth; ② paeans——a song of praise)

11. A rewrite of the constitution, which has been interpreted as forbidding anything but defensive military maneuvers, is difficult——any change requires a two-thirds majority in both houses of the legislature, then a public referendum. ——宪法被解释为禁止除防御性军事演练以外的任何军事行动。修改宪法十分困难,任何修改都需要参、众两院三分之二多数人的赞成,还要进行公投。

12. Shigeru Ishiba——石破茂(自民党秘书长,前日本防卫大臣)

13. New Cop on the Beat——新的警察在巡逻(① New Cop——referring to the US; ② the beat——the area of a city that a policeman regularly walks around)

14. Greater East Asia Co-Prosperity Sphere——大东亚共荣圈(日本帝国主义在第二次世界大战期间炮制的侵略和奴役亚洲人民的殖民主义计划)

15. China Inc——referring to China as an economic power

16. Bataan death march——forced march of 90,000 to 108,000 American and Filipino prisoners

of war by the Japanese in the Philippines from Bataan Camp which began on April 19, 1942 during WW Ⅱ. All told, approximately 2,500—10,000 Filipino and 100—650 American prisoners of war died before they could reach their destination.

17. National Defense College of the Philippines—菲律宾国防学院
18. security fixation—excessive concern for Japan's security
19. Abenomics—安倍经济学(指日本第96任首相安倍晋三2012年底上台后加速实施的一系列刺激经济政策,最引人注目的就是宽松货币,日元汇率加速贬值)
20. ...as the Senkaku-Diaoyu row with China heated up. —……与中国有关尖阁列岛/钓鱼岛之争升温(① row—a serious disagreement; ② heat up—to be more intense; ③ Senkaku—Japanese translation of the English term "Pinnacle Islands")
21. Izumo—Izumo-class helicopter destroyer 出云级直升机驱逐舰
22. On Sept. 17, he made a plea for the rhetorically tortured concept of "active pacifism," or collective self-defense, in which Japan can come to the aid of its military allies should they come under attack. —9月17日,他恳求(国会)接受意思被歪曲了的"积极和平主义"概念,或者是集体自卫。这个概念是:日本能够在军事盟友遭受攻击时对其提供军事援助。(①plea (for sth)—an urgent emotional request; ②collective self-defense—referring to Japan's legitimate use of its armed forces to help defend its close allies when they are under military attack. What Abe really intends to do is to give Japan a more muscular military posture and allow greater scope of action for its defensive forces. It's part of the ambition to break away from the restriction on Japanese military role.)
23. *Asahi Shimbun*—《朝日新闻报》(日本三大综合性对开报纸之一,1879年1月创刊)
24. Itsunori Onodera—日本防卫大臣小野寺五典
25. Beijing took exception to the nationalization—China was very angry about the nationalization
26. panda-set eyes—熊猫眼(referring to dark under-eye circles)
27. obotchan—son (used for other people's sons in Japanese); a young member of a family, especially a famous or important one
28. ...nepotism flourishes in Tokyo's halls of power. —……裙带关系在日本官场上十分盛行。(①nepotism—the practice of giving one's relatives unfair advantages; ② flourish—to be active and common; ③ halls of power—referring to the field of politics)
29. But Abe seems especially weighted with a sense of his conservative family's mission, particularly his grandfather Nobusuke Kishi's desire to amend Article 9 of the constitution, which is read as banning Japan from possessing an offensive military force. —但是,安倍看来特别感到肩负其保守家族所赋予的使命,尤其是其外祖父岸信介要修改日本宪法第9条款的愿望,这一条款被解释为禁止日本拥有进攻性军事力量。[① be weighted with—to be given a heavy load; ②Nobusuke Kishi—岸信介(甲级战犯,曾在盟军战争监狱关押3年,获释之后两度组阁,担任首相)]
30. Sophia University in Tokyo—东京索菲娅大学(日本称其为"上智大学")
31. Abe's surprise exit was hardly the kind of fortitude expected from a young political shogun. —安倍出人意料的退出并不是人们所期待一名年轻好斗的政客所要表现出的那

种刚毅。(①shogun—a metaphor for a militant; ② fortitude—firm courage)

32. In his 2.0 version, he continues to sound the nationalist bell. —安倍变本加厉继续重弹民族主义老调。(2.0 version—an improved version, here used as a metaphor for a more intense display of nationalism)

33. Yasukuni Shrine—靖国神社

34. comfort women—慰安妇(women and girls forced into sexual slavery by the Japanese Imperial Army during WWⅡ)

35. The resulting image wasn't quite Michael Dukakis in a tank. But the notion of Abe as proud commander in chief felt forced—and it didn't help neighborly relations that the jet trainer chosen for the photo op was numbered 731, the same digits as a notorious Japanese military unit that unleashed germ warfare on Manchuria. —结果照片形象和站在坦克里的迈克尔·杜卡基斯形象不太一样。但是,安倍作为显赫的最高统帅的形象给人感觉很勉强,并且这不利于改善邻国关系,因为选择拍照的教练喷气机编号为731,这个数字与曾经对满洲发动细菌战而臭名昭著的日本部队番号数字相同。(① Michael Dukakis—the longest serving Governor in Massachusetts history. In 1988, he was the Democratic nominee for President, but lost to the Republican candidate, the then vice-President George H. W. Bush. One of the factors in his defeat was the disastrous photo taken when he stood at the helm of a tank. The photo was used in TV ads by the Bush campaign as evidence that Dukakis would not make a good commander-in-chief. He was widely mocked for his martial posturing and silly image; ② photo op—photo opportunity, an occasion when a famous person arranges to be photographed doing sth that will impress the public; ③ unleash—to cause; ④ Manchuria—a term used in the past to refer to Northeast China; ⑤ forced—unnatural)

36. Tanaka—前副外相田中仁

37. LDP— the Liberal Democratic Party 自民党(a major conservative political party in Japan)

38. Democratic Party of Japan—日本民主党(a centrist political party founded in 1998 by the merger of several opposition parties)

39. Teneo Intelligence——家政治风险咨询公司(a US-based corporate advisory firm that offers strategic communications, investment banking, business intelligence and restructuring services)

40. Right Is Might—creative use of the idiom "Might is right" in the sense that only the right faction focuses on military build-up

41. One of the unlikely showcases of Japan's military prowess is a radar facility that looms like a giant golf ball, atop a hill overlooking sugarcane fields and picture-postcard beaches. —一个令人难以置信,展示日本军事威力的装备是个雷达设施,它隐隐约约看上去像一个巨大的高尔夫球,坐落在一座俯瞰着甘蔗田和海滩的小山顶上,海滩宛如美术明信片上的画。(① showcase—sth that presents one's abilities in an attractive way ;② prowess—outstanding ability)

42. the SDF base, Okinawa's Miyako Island—冲绳宫右岛的自卫队军事基地

43. Ryukyu—琉球群岛(位于中国台湾与日本之间)
44. Local animosity toward Japanese troops, even under the guise of the SDF, lingers—not to mention discomfort with the 25,000 Americans on U.S. military bases on Okinawan soil.—当地居民对于即使在自卫队伪装下的日本军队的敌对情绪仍然存在,更不用说对那些驻扎在冲绳土地上的美军基地里的 25,000 个美国人的不爽之感了。(① animosity—strong dislike or hostility; ② linger—to continue to exit; ③ discomfort—a feeling of being uncomfortable mentally)
45. Battle of Okinawa—冲绳战役(the largest amphibious assault in the Pacific War of WW Ⅱ. It lasted 82 days.)
46. Ishigaki—石垣岛

Ⅳ. Language Features

借代

本课多处使用"借代",如用 Tokyo 替代 Japan, Beijing 替代 China。这种语言现象被称作借代。

借代是新闻写作中所常用的修辞手段,它可以节省篇幅,避免重复,增加语言的形象性和表达效果。

在报刊上常见的借代形式有以下几种:

1. 借地名代机构。例如:
Capitol(Hill)/ Hill — 国会山(美国国会)　　White House— 白宫(美国政府)
Whitehall— 白厅(英国政府)　　Elysee— 爱丽舍宫(法国政府)

2. 借地名代行业、社会阶层。例如:
Wall Street— 华尔街(美国金融市场)　　Hollywood— 好莱坞(美国电影业)
Beverly Hill— 贝佛利山(美国明星阶层)　　Broadway— 百老汇大街〔(纽约市或美国)戏剧业〕
Madison Avenue— 麦迪逊大街(美国广告业)

3. 借商标、品牌、店名代相关物。例如:
Cadillac— 卡迪拉克(汽车)　　McDonald's — 麦当劳(快餐)

4. 借所具特色代某国、某机构。例如:
the bear— 前苏联　　Big Apple— 大苹果城(纽约市)
Dice City— 赌城(拉斯维加斯市)　　Motor City— 汽车城(底特律市)

5. 借典型姓氏代某人或某国。例如:
Ivan— 伊凡(俄罗斯人)　　Wang— 王(中国人)
John Bull— 约翰牛(英国人)　　John Doe— 约翰·多伊(美国人)

6. 借人名、地名、国名代相关事件。例如:
Hello, Kuwait. Goodbye, Vietnam.　　欢迎你呀,海湾战争胜利的捷报!见鬼去吧,越战失败的耻辱!

The court drills a crack in the foundation of Roe.　　最高法院在罗诉威德案决定的基础上钻出了裂缝。

V. Analysis of the Content

1. The meaning of the word "charge" in the sentence "... Takahashi, a veteran fighter pilot who now instructs young charges." (Para. 1) is _____.
   A. a task
   B. a debt to be paid
   C. a person under one's management
   D. a project
2. The cop in the subhead "New Cop on the Beat" refers to _____.
   A. Abe
   B. LDP
   C. the Self Defense Force
   D. the U.S.
3. The author changes the idiom "might is right" into "right is might" to express the idea that _____.
   A. having the power to do something gives you the right to do it
   B. having the right to do something gives you the power to do it
   C. military build-up is right
   D. only the right faction focuses on military build-up
4. Which of the following is NOT the author's view on Abe?
   A. Sensible.
   B. Hawkish.
   C. Conservative.
   D. Nationalist.
5. It can be seen from the article that Okinawans' feeling about the revival of nationalism in Japan is _____.
   A. fear
   B. pride
   C. non-committal
   D. unknown

VI. Questions on the Article

1. Where is Naha Air Base located?
2. How is the situation at Naha Air Base now?
3. According to the author, what is the reason for the stress level increase?
4. What is the chief aim of the Constitution?
5. Under what circumstances can any change of the Constitution be made?
6. What is the family's influence on Abe's present political stand?
7. What has Abe done about Japan's economy since taking office?
8. What has Abe done to boost Japan's military strength?
9. What effect did the photo of Abe in the cockpit of a Japanese military jet produce on neighborly relations?
10. How do local people in Okinawa feel about Japanese troops?

VII. Topics for Discussion

1. Can Abe realize his ambition of having the Constitution amended in his way?
2. What will be the real effect of the US government's way of handling international affairs in Asia, helping to maintain regional peace or intensifying international conflicts?

Lesson 35

The Lost Youth of Europe[1]

The continent's boomers are retiring, leaving a bitter legacy for the generation that comes next, which increasingly feels locked out of the European dream.[2]

By William Underhill and Tracy McNicoll

It's election time in France, and the promises are flowing fast. If you believe the candidates, young voters are in line for a fat slice of state largesse, no matter who wins the vote.[3] On offer from Nicolas Sarkozy[4], the right's presidential candidate: interest-free loans for young entrepreneurs and a 300-a-month allowance for training. Not to be outbid, his rival, meanwhile, the Socialists' Ségolène Royal[5], has pledged more housing, 10,000 loans and guaranteed jobs or training after six months of unemployment. As Royal told a party rally last week: "As a mother, I want for all children born and raised in France what I wanted for my own children."

They now seem unlikely to get it. Young adults in France, like their contemporaries across Europe, face a slew of problems never experienced by their middle-aged leaders. Consider: a 30-year-old Frenchman earned 15 percent less than a 50-year-old in 1975; now he earns 40 percent less. Over the same period, the number of graduates unemployed two years after college has risen from 6 percent to 25 percent, even if they typically have better degrees. Thirty-year-olds in 2001 were saving 9 percent of their incomes, down from 18 percent just six years before. Young people who snag stable jobs, gain access to credit and buy homes later in life are particularly angry that the older generations continue to rack up public debts for which they will get the bill.[6] And they are very skeptical of the pledges of boomer-generation[7] politicians. "If all this were financially possible, it would have been done long ago," says Clément Pitton, the 23-year-old leader of Impulsion Concorde[8], which recently circulated a petition declaring "We will not pay your debt."

Pitton's sentiments are increasingly shared by the children of Europe's baby boomers, a generation sometimes called the baby losers. Not only will they be forced to pick up the tab for a welfare system that offers far more to the elderly than to the young, but they will be forced to do so with less: Europe's economy remains skewed in favor of the old and its politicians have been shy about pushing painful reforms that might correct the balance.[9] No wonder one recent poll in France showed that only 5 percent believed young people had a better chance of succeeding than their parents. Europe, it seems, is increasingly split — not along class or racial lines, but between its young and its old.

As the rift grows so does awareness. Just browse the media or visit the bookstores. In France, the shelves groan with works bemoaning the "Génération Précaire" — the Precarious Generation[10]. Two boomer authors warned in a book released this December, "Our Children

Will Hate Us." In Britain, think tanks turn out reports on "Maggie's Children" — the unfortunates born in the affluent Thatcher[11] years — or the IPOD Generation[12]: the newcomers to the job market who find themselves "Insecure, Pressured, Overtaxed and Debt-Ridden."

Small wonder Europe's young are losing faith in their leaders. In a recent report for the Policy Exchange[13] think tank, David Willetts, the Conservative Party's education spokesman, concluded, "A young person could be forgiven for thinking [there's] a conspiracy by the middle-aged against the young." There may not be any concerted plot, but it's clear who's to blame for today's sorry situation: the boomers. The sunlit decades of postwar prosperity saw the creation of generous welfare states across Europe. Dynamic economies assured the boomers secure employment (Germans still like to speak of "job owners") and hefty pensions on retirement. But this good fortune came at a price[14]. The same labor rules that protect the jobs of the middle-aged shut out the young. And dwindling birthrates mean there will soon be fewer workers to support the retirees.

So will the boomers renounce — or at least share — their benefits? Unlikely, says leading French sociologist Louis Chauvel. "The baby boomers didn't [intend] to do this to young people, but I don't see a willingness to get them out of the situation either." Such intransigence looks even more unfair given the disparities in wealth and lifestyle. The boomers are living it up; many have used their generous pensions to opt out of the labor market altogether.[15] Only 30 percent of Belgians older than 55 still work, for example. A report by the London-based think tank Reform put the issue plainly. "People over 50 are developing the lifestyles of teenagers."

As they slack off, their children's woes are multiplying. Germans now talk of "Generation Intern" as well-educated graduates increasingly accept unpaid jobs in the quest for elusive permanent posts. Such challenges breed despair. Ask Daniel Knapp. Born in Germany, he speaks four languages fluently and holds a master's degree from the London School of Economics[16]. But he's spent the last six months chasing jobs in London, Berlin and Brussels — unsuccessfully. "I feel as if I'm simply draining my family's resources. It seems my degrees only qualify me for further education but not really a job."

Some countries have so far avoided the malaise. In Ireland, the birthrate peaked late and the strong economy still provides jobs for all. In fact, "this is the first generation to have grown up in Ireland with no question that they would be able to find a job in the country," says Tony Fahey of the Economic and Social Research Institute[17] in Dublin. Ditto for Spain, where everyone is enjoying the new prosperity and a welfare system vastly expanded since the end of the Franco regime[18]. "[The young here] don't live worse than their parents; in fact they live much better," says Federico Steinberg, an economist at the Autonomous University of Madrid[19].

But even the happy Irish and Spanish share a housing problem. Across the continent, spiraling property prices and poor job prospects are conspiring to keep youngsters living at home. According to the Italian Institute of Social Medicine, 45 percent of the country's 30- to 34-year-olds still sleep in their old beds and enjoy Mama's home cooking. In France, the proportion of 24-year-olds now living with their parents has almost doubled since 1975, to 65 percent. Even in the U.K., with its enviable record of job creation, the average age of the first-time home buyer has climbed from 26 in 1976 to 34 today. Property prices are now eight times higher than the median earnings of the ordinary twentysomething.

This great homecoming — by what the press in Britain has dubbed the "Boomerang Generation[20]" — points to one more troubling shift. Lacking well-paid jobs, the young have been thrown back on the generosity of their parents.[21] That's fine for the middle class, but much worse for the poor. "Progress was once produced by the state; now it comes from family solidarity," says 28-year-old Aurore Wanlin of London's Centre for European Reform. But don't look to the politicians for action. Sure, pension reform is close to the top of most national agendas. Last week the Italian Prime Minister Romano Prodi declared, "Italy should feel a moral duty to … prevent an entire generation from facing life without certainties."

But money for the young will have to come from somewhere, and tinkering with boomers' privileges presents a tricky political challenge. After all, their numbers are increasing and so is their clout. They're overrepresented in government: the average age of the British M. P.[22] is now over 50, up two years since Labour[23] came to power in 1997, and in 2002, only 15 percent of the members in France's lower house of Parliament was under 45. Boomers are also better organized. And, says John Curtice of the University of Strathclyde[24] in Scotland, "Older people are a popular cause and are generally regarded as a deserving group."

Ironically, Europe's young don't seem to favor cutting their parents' benefits; they want the same treatment. Last year French youths mobbed the streets to protest a new bill that aimed to create more employment but offered less security; the proposal was defeated. Says Wanlin: "Their aspiration is to get the same protection for themselves." If the economics don't work out, that's a problem for the politicians — not the young. Indeed, even some boomers recognize the flaws in the status quo[25]. "The worst thing," says French author and former political advisor Bernard Spitz, "would be if we lived contentedly with our debts and our early retirements, telling ourselves the young will pay, just like we told ourselves 'Germany will pay' after the Treaty of Versailles[26]." As Europe has learned before, a bad peace only leads to more war — even between generations.

From *Newsweek*, March 12, 2007

I. New Words

bemoan	[bi'məun]	v.	to complain that you are not happy about sth
browse	[brauz]	v.	浏览
concerted	[kən'sə:tid]	adj.	done in a planned way by a group
conspire	[kən'spaiə]	v.	to plan sth harmful secretly
disparity	[dis'pæriti]	n.	a difference, especially an unfair one
dub	[dʌb]	v.	把……称为,给……绰号
hefty	['hefti]	adj.	large
interest-free	['intristfri:]	adj.	无息的
intern	['intə:n]	n.	实习生
intransigence	[in'trænsidʒəns]	n.	unwillingness to change opinions or behavior

largesse	[ˈlɑːdʒes]	n.	the quality of being generous
malaise	[mæˈleiz]	n.	the problems affecting a particular group
mob	[mɔb]	v.	to crowd around especially in anger
outbid	[ˌautˈbid]	v.	to offer more (money) than sb else in order to get sth
renounce	[riˈnauns]	v.	放弃
rift	[rift]	n.	a serious disagreement which separates two groups
slew	[sluː]	n.	**a ~ of** *informal* a large number of
spiraling	[ˈspaiərəliŋ]	adj.	螺旋上升的
tab	[tæb]	n.	a bill for goods you receive but pay for later
tinker	[ˈtiŋkə]	v.	~ **with** to make small changes to sth to repair it
tricky	[ˈtriki]	adj.	difficult to do or deal with
woe	[wəu]	n.	trouble; great unhappiness

Ⅱ. Background Information

困扰欧洲的两大问题

福利重负和青年失业是困扰欧洲的两大问题。

从20世纪50至60年代开始,在经历了第二次世界大战的巨大创伤之后,许多西欧和北欧的发达国家逐步建立了以高福利为特色的社会保障制度。福利项目覆盖儿童抚养、医疗保障、住房补助、失业救济和养老保险等社会生活的方方面面,常被称为"从摇篮到坟墓"的福利体系。这些福利政策在稳定政治局势,恢复发展生产,减少生活贫困和缓和社会矛盾等方面发挥了积极作用,同时也具有深刻的人道主义内涵。

然而进入到21世纪后,欧洲引以为自豪的福利制度出现了严重的问题,也成为社会发展的制约。许多西欧国家建立福利制度是以照顾失业人口、健康保险和其他社会福利措施作为首要任务,没有有效地创造广泛的就业机会。欧洲许多国家的福利政策允许失业者可以长期领取政府补助,再加上政府提供的廉租房,解决失业人员的温饱已经没有问题。另外,许多西欧国家每年拨出大量资金鼓励生育。按照目前的生育补助标准,一个家庭如果生了4个孩子,仅靠生育补助加上失业补助就可以过上比较不错的生活。这种优厚的社会福利构成了沉重的财政负担。更为严重的是,欧洲社会已经开始步入老龄化阶段。婴儿潮一代的欧洲人已经逐渐离开工作岗位,享受国家提供的各种福利项目。2005年欧洲的老年人口占总人口的25%,预计2050年将达到50%,庞大的老年人口将使欧洲各福利国家承担巨大的经济压力。

欧洲社会所面临的另一严重问题是失业问题,年青人失业的情况尤其严重。欧盟各国青年人的失业率平均为17.4%。年轻人失业率超过20%的欧洲国家有法国、比利时、西班牙、希腊、意大利和芬兰,远远高于美国11%的失业率。然而年青一代的欧洲人在欧洲经济不景气的大环境下不仅不容易找到工作,而且工作所赚到的钱也并不比失业在家的人多多少。他们还要承担高额的税款,为老一辈人支付高额的税金,替他们买单,这使得他们对老一辈人依靠福利的生活方式非常不满,严重地影响了他们工作的积极性。不少年轻人大学毕业后并不急于找工作,而是待在家里。

这种失业率的增加以及就业后待遇的下降使得欧洲年轻人陷入了一种两难的境地。近年来,欧洲一些国家,例如英国、法国,为了提高整体竞争力已经开始进行一些社会改革,但是改革并不是一帆风顺。降低福利的改革不仅遭到了老一代人的反对,而且引起了一些年轻人的谴责。法国青年就曾上街游行反对旨在增加就业机会但会降低福利的法律。可以看出,解决欧洲福利国家的就业与福利的矛盾的改革还有很长的路要走。

Ⅲ. Notes to the Text

1. The Lost Youth of Europe — 欧洲迷惘的青年(The author here likens the young generation of Europe to the Lost Generation of America who became adults during or just after WWI and suffered social and emotional disadvantages as a result.)
2. The continent's boomers are retiring ... out of the European dream. — 欧洲婴儿潮代人正在陆续退休,他们为后一代人所留下的是苦难,让后一代人越来越感到他们被排斥在欧洲梦之外。(lock sb out — to prevent sb from entering)
3. If you believe the candidates, young voters are in line for a fat slice of state largesse, no matter who wins the vote. — 如果你相信这些候选人的话,那么无论谁赢得大选,年轻的投票者们都会得到国家丰厚的馈赠。(be in line for sth — to be likely to get something good)
4. Nicolas Sarkozy — 尼古拉·萨科齐[(1955—),法国右派人民运动联盟党(UMP Party)主席,现任法国总统]
5. Ségolène Royal — 塞格琳·罗雅尔(法国社会党政治家)
6. Young people who ... will get the bill. — 那些年纪较大时才找到稳定的工作,拿到贷款购买住房的年轻人感到特别恼火,因为老一辈的人继续使国家债台高筑,而这些都需要他们买单。(①snag — AmE to succeed in getting sth quickly; ②rack up — to gradually increase in amount)
7. boomer-generation — 婴儿潮代(Please refer to Background Information of Lesson 2)
8. Impulsion Concorde — a French think tank on national politics created in June 2005
9. Not only will they be forced to pick up the tab ... that might correct the balance. — 欧洲的福利体制给老年人提供的福利比年轻人多得多,可是年轻人不仅被迫要为这种福利体系买单,而且他们所得的报酬更少,因为欧洲的经济仍然对老年人倾斜,那些政客们很怕推行艰难的改革,而这些改革可能会纠正不公正的局面。(①pick up the tab for — to pay money for something; ②skew — to change or influence sth with the result that is not fair; ③shy about sth — afraid of doing or being involved in sth)
10. the Precarious Generation — 简称 Generation P (a generation that is forced to complete a number of poorly paid internships instead of getting fixed employment after studying. They have minimal legal protection, and work long hours but they can be fired with very little notice and for no given reason.)
11. Thatcher — Margaret Thatcher, UK's first woman Prime Minister
12. IPOD Generation — Insecure, Pressured, Over-taxed, and Debt-ridden (This term was

first used in the Reform report "*The Class of 2005 — the IPOD Generation*", written by Professor Nick Bosanquet and Blair Gibbs)

13. Policy Exchange — "政策交流"思想库 (a conservative-leaning think tank)
14. at a price — 以很高的代价
15. The boomers are living it up; many have used their generous pensions to opt out of the labor market altogether. — 婴儿潮代人在尽情享乐，许多人依靠丰厚的养老金全然不干活。(① live it up — to engage in festive pleasures or extravagances; ② opt out of — to choose not to participate in something)
16. London School of Economics — 伦敦政治经济学院(全称为 London School of Economics and Political Science，1900 年成为伦敦大学的一部分)
17. the Economic and Social Research Institute — 社会经济研究所(It was founded in 1959 and opened in 1960 by the Irish Government with the funding support from the US-based Ford Foundation. It focuses on Ireland's economic and social development.)
18. the Franco regime — 佛朗哥政权[Franco (1892—1975)，a Spanish military leader and Right Wing politician]
19. the Autonomous University of Madrid — 西班牙马德里自治大学
20. Boomerang Generation — 还巢儿代
21. Lacking well-paid jobs, the young have been thrown back on the generosity of their parents. — 由于没有报酬好的工作，许多年轻人得重新依靠父母的慷慨帮助。(throw back — to cause to depend, make reliant)
22. M. P. — member of Parliament
23. Labour — 工党 (Labour refers to Labour Party.)
24. the University of Strathclyde — 斯特拉思克莱德大学(规模名列苏格兰第三)
25. the status quo — 现状
26. the Treaty of Versailles — 凡尔赛条约(a peace agreement made in 1919 at Versailles in France, following the defeat of Germany in WWI, between the Allies and Germany. According to the treaty, Germany had to pay a great number of reparations.)

Ⅳ. Language Features

名词定语

本文多处使用名词定语，如：election time, welfare system, boomer authors, job prospects, home buyer, pension reform, property prices。

新闻写作中常常使用名词定语，这是因为它是精炼句式的有效方式，从下面两例便可看出这一功效：

diet pill (the kind of pill which helps people to reduce weight)

boom generation (the generation born between 1946 and 1964, when many more babies were born than in other periods)

翻开报纸便可发现名词定语到处可见。熟悉这一语言现象并掌握对它的判断能力可以提高对英语报刊的理解水平。例如：

power game 权力游戏	turf war 势力范围之争
property tax 财产税	tube strike 地铁工人罢工
perk city 特权城（指国会）	poverty line 贫困线
interest group 利益集团	minimum wage 法定最低工资
pressure group 压力集团	convenience food 方便食品
health insurance 医疗保险	stone killer 铁石心肠的杀手
TV violence 电视暴力	scare talk 吓人之谈
remarriage rate 再婚率	drug dealer 毒品犯
sex worker 妓女	emergency shelter（应急）收容所
supervision agency 审批机构	refugee law 难民法
breast cancer surgery 乳腺癌手术	race riot 种族骚乱
workplace crime 工作场所犯罪	job training 职业培训
child abuse 虐待孩子	cardboard condos 纸板箱居住区
welfare mother 靠救济生活的母亲	gun control law 限制枪支法
street gang 黑帮	abortion advocate 主张堕胎者
teen sex 青少年性行为	clothing drive 募集衣物活动
discount store 减价商店	panic buying 抢购

语言学家对名词定语褒贬不一，有的指责名词定语造成理解困难，读者往往难从表层确定语意，必须联系深层结构理解。有人赞扬名词定语可以浓缩句式、节省篇幅、避免句式拖沓繁冗。

语言学家西蒙·波特（Simeon Potter）在他所著的《变化中的英语》（*Changing English*）一书中指出名词定语是现代英语的发展趋势，同时他也告诫：在名词定语使用方面"为了语意明晰和句式美观不要累积使用超过三个"。

V. Analysis of the Content

1. The sentence "People over 50 are developing the lifestyle of teenagers" (in Paragraph 6) emphasizes the fact that European baby boomers _____.
   A. slack off
   B. have childlike innocence
   C. are vigorous
   D. are nostalgic for teenagers' life

2. Which of the following terms does not relate to youth of any European country?
   A. The Precarious Generation.
   B. Generation Intern.
   C. The Boomerang Generation.
   D. Generation X.

3. It's very hard to change the welfare system of European countries mainly because _____.
   A. the system is sound
   B. the system is supported by all generations
   C. Baby Boomers have great political influence
   D. the need for the change is not strongly felt

4. According to the author, Europe is increasingly split between _____.

A. different classes   B. different races
   C. the younger and the older people   D. different ranks
5. The author's attitude towards the younger generation in Europe is _____.
   A. sympathetic   B. critical
   C. derisive   D. unknown

Ⅵ. Questions on the Article

1. What promises did the two French presidential candidates make during the election campaign?
2. What problems are the French young adults faced with?
3. According to the article, what is the problem with Europe's economy?
4. What was the background to the present welfare system?
5. Why does the welfare system pose a heavy burden on the younger generation?
6. How is the job situation for Germany's well-educated graduates?
7. Which countries fare better? Why?
8. Why does the press dub the younger generation in Europe as the "Boomerang Generation"?
9. Why does tinkering with boomers' privileges present a tricky political challenge?
10. What do Europe's young people want to do about the boomers' benefits according to the author?

Ⅶ. Topics for Discussion

1. Is it fair for 30-year-olds to earn 40 percent less than 50-year-olds?
2. Should European countries change their present welfare system?

Lesson 36

At Daggers Drawn[1]

First bananas, now beef, soon genetically modified foods. America and Europe are at war over trade.

Trade relations between America and Europe have rarely been so bad. Even as they fight side-by-side against Serbia[2], they are taking aim at each other across the Atlantic. They are embroiled in a battle over hormone-treated beef. They are at loggerheads over genetically modified crops.[3] They have fallen out over noisy aircraft, mobile telephones and data privacy.[4] They are coming to blows over aerospace subsidies and champagne. And they have yet to patch up their split over bananas.

True, transatlantic trade tiffs are nothing new. Indeed, some friction is perhaps inevitable between the world's top two trading entities, which do trade of around $400 billion a year with each other. But this is different. The mood in both Washington and Brussels[5] is resentful and uncompromising. Events could easily get out of hand. The current conflict is about more than just hormones in beef or aircraft noise. It is a battle about how far countries are willing to accept constraints on domestic policy in sensitive areas such as food safety or environmental protection for the sake of free trade.

The battle is putting huge strains on the World Trade Organisation.[6] The body that polices world trade cannot function properly unless America and Europe accept its writ. But the WTO itself is in crisis over its member countries' inability to agree on a new director general. It is now leaderless and fractured; supporters of the two rival candidates are engaged in a slanging match rather than a search for compromise. The longer this drags on, the more its credibility will be undermined.

The timing of the recent clashes is partly chance. Long-standing wrangles over bananas and beef have finally worked their way through the WTO's dispute-settlement mechanism. On April 6th the WTO ruled for the third time that the European Union must amend its banana-import rules, which discriminate unfairly against American fruit distributors.[7] On April 19th the WTO gave America the go-ahead to slap retaliatory sanctions[8] against $191m of European imports — the first time it has sanctioned such a move.

The WTO has also ruled that the EU must lift its ban on hormone-treated beef by May 13th, because there is no convincing scientific evidence that the hormones are dangerous. America is planning to impose sanctions on around $300m of European imports, mainly foodstuffs and motorcycles, if the EU shows no signs of complying with the WTO's ruling by then. Last week the EU hit back with a new report claiming that the hormones could cause cancer. It also raised the stakes after hormones were found in imports of supposedly hormone-free American beef. It is threatening to ban all American beef on June 15th unless

America can provide watertight guarantees that it is hormone-free.

Last week the Europeans also issued new restrictions on noisy aeroplanes that will hit American companies particularly hard, although the new rules will not take effect until next year. America in turn launched two new WTO cases against the EU. One is over subsidies to Airbus, Boeing's rival in aerospace. The other is over EU rules on geographical labels, which prevent, for instance, Californian fizzy wines being called champagne.[9]

But there is more to this than unfortunate coincidence. These bust-ups are a consequence of mercantilist policies exacerbated by political weakness and the increasingly legalistic nature of the WTO.[10] America and Europe (like most countries) tend to see trade as a zero-sum game. They aim to pry open markets for their exporters while protecting their domestic industries from import competition as far as possible. Access to their markets is granted only in exchange for access to others'. Such policies are wrong-headed, since a country as a whole gains by opening its markets unilaterally. But they are pervasive, since industries that fear foreign competitors tend to lobby governments harder than the disparate millions of consumers who benefit from cheaper imports.

America's mercantilist urges were once tempered by Cold War considerations and the liberal convictions of presidents and other senior politicians. But Cold War reflexes are now all but dead and, hemmed in by an increasingly protectionist Congress, Bill Clinton's administration (with the exception of Robert Rubin, the Treasury secretary) does not have the stomach or the inclination to make a stand for liberal policies.[11] As Sylvia Ostry of the University of Toronto puts it: "America doesn't have a trade policy. It has clients."

As for the EU, it has never been particularly keen on free trade. Over half its budget goes on the explicitly protectionist Common Agricultural Policy (CAP). Trade barriers between EU member states have been removed less out of a liberal belief in free trade than with the aim of creating a large, protected market for European firms. Under American prodding, the EU has grudgingly agreed to liberalise over the years. But now that American policy is essentially mercantilist, the EU is comfortable playing the same game.

When trade is viewed as a zero-sum game, one side is perforce a loser. Yet, when both sides are of roughly equal strength, neither feels compelled to back down. Europe's economic clout now matches America's, so the United States can no longer rely on having its own way. And now that the EU has its own currency, the euro, to match the dollar, it has become even more reluctant to yield to American pressure.

Political weakness is part of the problem too. America is gearing up for the presidential election next year. Its ballooning trade deficit, a record $262 billion in the year to February, has made trade a sensitive political issue. Charlene Barshefsky, America's trade supremo, says it has reached "red-alert" level; even Mr. Rubin says it is "economically and politically unsustainable." The concern is largely misplaced, since the soaring deficit is caused not by foreign wickedness but by rapid economic growth in America combined with sluggish growth elsewhere. Yet Congress is up in arms; and since the administration cannot do anything to curb the deficit's rise, it must act tough in other ways. Europe is an obvious target: it has a hefty (and rising) surplus and it has done little to stimulate its economy at a time when recession-hit emerging economies urgently need to export more to rich countries.

European politicians are hamstrung as well. Economic growth is sluggish, unemployment remains high. The European Commission, which handles trade policy for the

15 EU states, is mired in scandal[12]; big decisions are on hold until a new set of commissioners is appointed some time later this year. Sir Leon Brittan, the EU's liberal-minded trade commissioner, does not have as much clout as he once did; he was already due to leave at the end of the year. EU trade policy is in any case highly inflexible. In principle, it is decided by a qualified majority vote of member states, but in practice decisions are usually reached by consensus. If a country fears it will be outvoted on a trade issue, it usually threatens to block a decision that requires unanimity, according to Patrick Messerlin of the Institut d'Etudes Politiques[13] in Paris. EU governments are often "conscious that reform is needed but are unable to deliver," he says. In the banana case, for example, France and Spain have successfully blocked German attempts to compromise with America.

The increasing legalisation of the WTO is making matters worse. True, the WTO's dispute-settlement mechanism often helps to resolve trade quarrels, since countries commit themselves to comply with the rulings of its impartial panels. America, for instance, lifted its restrictions on imports of Costa Rican underwear after the WTO ruled the restrictions were illegal. But, when governments lack the political will to comply and are too big to be bullied into doing so, the mechanism can be counterproductive. Assigning blame to one side reinforces mercantilist thinking and can make it harder to reach a face-saving political compromise.

One reason why the banana case has proved so difficult to resolve is that the EU has been reluctant to accept publicly that it has lost. It has so far put off complying by using legal delaying tactics that the WTO's ambiguous rules make possible. And it has tried to muddy the waters by launching two WTO cases of its own against America, over its premature and excessive retaliation against European imports on March 3rd, and over its Section 301 law, which sets a unilateral timetable for American retaliation that may pre-empt the WTO's. America too has dug its heels in.[14] It will not settle for anything less than the full victory the WTO has awarded it, even though the dispute is damaging relations with the EU and undermining the WTO. Its sanctions against European imports are also hurting American consumers, who are now paying twice as much as they once did for Louis Vuitton[15] handbags and German coffee-making machines.

A big beef[16]

There is a bigger reason, however, why America and Europe cannot agree on trade. They are fighting a new kind of trade dispute about sensitive policy issues, such as food safety and environmental protection, that were once exclusively domestic. Such quarrels have come to the fore because countries' economies are now so closely intertwined through trade and investment that almost any government policy can have a discriminatory impact on foreign companies. They are particularly tricky, not least because governments are reluctant to compromise their ability to pursue other aims as well as free trade.[17]

Consider the difference between a traditional trade quarrel, such as a dispute over restrictions on steel imports, and the battle over hormone-treated beef. Traditional disputes are rather simple. They are usually about explicitly protectionist measures, such as import tariffs or quotas, that keep out foreign goods at the border. The costs of such measures (higher prices and less choice for consumers) are reasonably easy to quantify; they typically outweigh the benefits (fatter company profits and tariff revenues for governments).[18] Even mercantilist governments should be able to resolve such narrowly economic disputes. One way is to buy off steel companies and unions with economic goodies. Another is to exchange access to domestic markets for access to foreign ones.

The new trade disputes are rather more complicated. They are about more than economics: typically they are about social issues too. They are usually about domestic regulations that have international effects rather than about border controls: Europe has banned all hormone-treated beef, not just America's. Such regulations are not wholly protectionist. Although Europe's ban does keep out American imports and is partly motivated by a desire to protect inefficient European farmers, it is also a response to public fears about food safety.

The costs of the ban (higher beef prices, less choice) are quite easy to establish. But the benefits are not: the value of safer food is hard to quantify and reasonable people may put widely different prices on it. Indeed some of the new actors in such disputes, such as consumer-rights activists and environmental groups, may not be susceptible to economic reasoning.[19] So even liberal governments may have trouble resolving such quarrels. They may be particularly wary of setting precedents that they may later regret: the beef war is widely seen as a forerunner for a larger battle about genetically modified crops. Indeed, many may feel that such disputes intrude too far on national sovereignty, and thus refuse to accept that international trade rules should trump domestic political considerations.

The multilateral trading system recognises that governments have legitimate aims other than free trade.[20] It was founded in 1948, when memories of the 1930s were still fresh. Governments were keen to liberalise international trade, but were wary of giving up policy tools that might help them prevent another slump. So a delicate compromise was struck. Governments agreed to be bound by multilateral rules in order to free trade internationally, but retained the right to set their own policies domestically.

In the 1950s and 1960s, the compromise worked well. Countries agreed to lower their most blatant barriers to trade, such as import tariffs or quotas imposed at the border, while intervening at will, with taxes, subsidies and regulations, in their domestic economies. But by the 1970s, problems began to emerge. As border barriers fell, it became clear that domestic regulations were also a big impediment to trade: a subsidy or a discriminatory rule could shut out imports just as effectively as a tariff. Moreover, governments began to abuse these loopholes for protectionist ends: anti-dumping cases and import-restricting regulations proliferated.[21] So the focus of trade policy turned to limiting such abuses.

Twenty years on, the compromise is in tatters. The problem is how to craft a new compromise that secures the huge benefits of free trade while respecting countries' rights to pursue other aims. It is a delicate balancing act. Trample too much on domestic sovereignty and popular support for free trade will evaporate. Tread too lightly and it will be open season for protectionism.[22] Broadly, the solution is for governments to pursue their political aims in ways that harm the rest of the world as little as possible. But that is often tough to achieve in practice.

Struggling to cope

The rows between American and Europe are taking their toll on the WTO.[23] The banana case has exposed flaws in its dispute-settlement rules, which do not specify what countries must do to comply with its rulings. This ambiguity allows recalcitrant losers to drag out cases almost at will. The EU is exploiting this legal wiggle-room in the beef case too. It is refusing simply to lift its ban. Instead it proposes to do one of three things: to allow in hormone-treated beef as long as it is labelled as such; to offer America temporary compensation while further research on the potential risks of hormones is conducted; or to impose a temporary ban on the grounds that there is not yet sufficient scientific evidence to show that hormones are safe.

America would probably settle for a labelling scheme, as long as it does not imply that its beef is unsafe. But the labelling option looks like a non-starter now that the EU alleges the hormones cause cancer. America may also accept compensation, though the EU has yet to make any firm offer. But a temporary ban would invite American retaliation, since the beef case has been dragging on for more than ten years, and there is still no convincing evidence that hormones in beef are unsafe.

At a practical level too, the WTO is struggling to cope. It has a small staff and a budget of only $80m, the equivalent of the IMF[24]'s travel budget. The twists and turns of the banana and beef cases have over-stretched it and hampered preparations for the big WTO summit in Seattle in late November.[25] The summit will set the political blueprint for a new round of trade-liberalisation negotiations that kicks off in Geneva next January. Among the items on the agenda are agriculture, services and industrial tariffs, although the EU would like to broaden the talks to cover issues such as investment and competition policy.

Prospects for the new round look bleak in any case. Many developing countries feel short-changed by previous negotiations. Bruised by financial turmoil, they are far from keen on further liberalisation. The main problem on the European side is agriculture. The timid Berlin summit deal on CAP reform last month highlighted the EU's reluctance to open up its heavily protected farming sector, a key demand by America and many developing countries. But the biggest problem is that America, which has driven all previous efforts at multilateral liberalisation, is now a laggard not a leader. Congress has repeatedly denied President Clinton "fast-track" negotiating authority: the power to strike trade deals that Congress cannot subsequently amend. Without it, the administration cannot negotiate credibly, because any deals it strikes with other countries may subsequently be unpicked on Capitol Hill.[26] Worse, America is insisting that any WTO deal must include provisions on enforceable labour and environmental standards, which are anathema to most countries.

But the WTO now has a more pressing problem. It is leaderless. Its members cannot agree on a successor to Renato Ruggiero, the mercurial Italian whose term as head of the WTO ended on April 30th. In front is Mike Moore, who was briefly New Zealand's prime minister in 1990 and, as trade minister in 1980s, transformed his country from a protectionist backwater to a paragon of free trade.[27] He has strong support from both America and France, an unlikely combination. Many other European countries and Latin America are also behind him. The other candidate is Supachai Panitchpakdi. He is a Thai deputy prime minister and a former banker. His support comes from Japan, Asia and Mexico. Africa and the Caribbean are almost evenly split.

Talks have broken down in acrimony. Some developing countries, which feel that the new WTO's director general should come from a poor country for once, are stubbornly blocking the appointment of Mr. Moore, who now leads Mr. Supachai by a margin of over two to one. Thailand insists that Mr. Supachai will not pull out and angrily protests that America has conspired to block his candidacy. Tempers are running high: the Zimbabwean ambassador said the Americans were lobbing "Scud missiles[28]" at the Third World; and the WTO's press corps has been gagged at Mexico's insistence. Unless this dispute is resolved quickly, the WTO's reputation will be dealt a hammer-blow.

The four-year old WTO is at a crossroads. It has become a quasi-judicial body, an embryo world government whose rulings on world trade are supposed to be binding even on America and the EU. Yet it is now being asked to arbitrate on matters which are intensely political. It lacks the legitimacy to do so. The world needs the WTO, without which a catastrophic retreat into protectionism is all too likely. But the WTO cannot be expected to set the world to rights[28] without the political support of America and Europe.

From *The Economist*, May 8th, 1999

Ⅰ. New Words

acrimony	['ækriməni]	n.	*formal* anger and unpleasantness
anathema	[ə'næθimə]	n.	something that is detested
balloon	[bə'lu:n]	v.	to become larger in amount
Costa Rican	['kɔstə'ri:kən]	adj.	哥斯达黎加的
disparate	['dispərit]	adj.	*formal* very different in kind
distributor	[dis'tribjutə]	n.	批发商,批发公司
embroil	[im'brɔil]	v.	*usually passive* to involve someone in a difficult situation
embryo	['embriəu]	n.	胚;萌芽期
exacerbate	[ig'zæsəbeit]	v.	to make a bad situation worse
fizzy	['fizi]	adj.	containing bubbles
forerunner	['fɔ:,rʌnə]	n.	预兆,先兆
gag	[gæg]	v.	to stop people expressing their opinions
gear	[giə]	v.	**gear up** to prepare well for something you have to do
goody	['gudi]	n.	sth attractive, good, or desirable
hamstring	['hæmstriŋ]	v.	to restrict someone's activities
hem	[hem]	v.	**hem in** to prevent from moving or changing
impediment	[im'pedimənt]	n.	a situation that makes it difficult for sth to make progress
laggard	['lægəd]	n.	*old-fashioned* someone that is very slow
lob	[lɔb]	v.	*informal* to throw something
loggerhead	['lɔgəhed]	n.	**at loggerheads with** (与……)不和,相争
mercurial	[mə:'kjuəriəl]	adj.	*literary* changing suddenly and unexpectedly
muddy	['mʌdi]	v.	**muddy the waters/the issue** to make something more complicated
non-starter	['nɔn'sta:tə]	n.	*informal* an idea, plan etc that has no chance of success
paragon	['pærəgən]	n.	a model of excellence or perfection

405

patch	[pætʃ]	v.	**patch up** to end an argument
perforce	[pə'fɔːs]	adv.	*literary* of necessity
pervasive	[pə'veisiv]	adj.	existing or spreading everywhere
press corps	['preskɔː]	n.	记者团
prod	[prɔd]	v.	to strongly encourage sb to do sth
provision	[prə'viʒən]	n.	a condition in an agreement or law
pry	[prai]	v.	**pry open** to force sth open
recalcitrant	[ri'kælsitrənt]	adj.	refusing to do what you are told to do
slanging match	['slæŋiŋˌmætʃ]	n.	an angry argument in which people insult each other
sluggish	['slʌgiʃ]	adj.	moving more slowly than normal
supremo	[sjuː'priːməu]	n.	*BrE informal* 最高统治者
tatters	['tætəz]	n.	**in tatters** ruined or badly damaged
temper	['tempə]	v.	to moderate; to lessen the intensity or extremeness of
tiff	[tif]	n.	a slight argument
wrangle	['ræŋgl]	n.	a noisy and angry argument
writ	[rit]	n.	an order in writing
wiggle-room	['wigəlrum]	n.	回旋余地
zero-sum game	[ˌziərəu-'sʌmˌgeim]	n.	零和赛局，零合游戏

Ⅱ. Background Information

世贸组织

世贸组织，即世界贸易组织(the World Trade Organization，简称 WTO)，其前身是关税和贸易总协定，简称为关贸总协定(General Agreement on Tariffs and Trade，缩略词为 GATT)。

关贸总协定最初是53个国家签订的关于全球贸易规则的一项协议，在1948年成为全球贸易组织的名称，并一直沿用到世界贸易组织的成立。该组织总部设在瑞士日内瓦。其宗旨是加强成员国之间的经贸合作，实施最惠国待遇(according most-favored nation treatment)、降低关税(lowering tariff)、减少进出口配额限制(reducing restrictions on import and export quotas)、消除贸易壁垒和贸易上的差别对待(removing trade obstacles and eliminating discrimination in trade)，促进自由贸易(promoting free trade)。

在关贸总协定存在的近50年时间里，共进行了八轮(eight rounds)多边贸易谈判(multilateral trade talks)。前四轮谈判进行较为顺利，均在半年左右时间内达成协议。随着世界经济实力对比发生变化，多边贸易谈判日趋复杂，时间也越拉越长：第五轮耗时1年半，第六轮3年，第七轮6年多，最后一轮长达近8年！

关贸总协定所主持的多边贸易谈判虽然困难重重、争论不休，但也产生了积极作用：降低了关税和促进了世界贸易额的增长。根据统计，到1975年，缔约国之间工业制成品(manufactured products)的关税总水平已从该组织成立之初时的40%降至10%。从1945年到20世纪末,世界贸易额增长了16倍。

进入20世纪80年代之后,世界贸易范围扩大,种类增多。与此同时,贸易保护主义重新抬头,使得全球及多边贸易体制受到威胁。为了加强和扩展世界贸易,关贸总协定缔约国与1986年9月达成协议,发起了第八轮全球多边贸易谈判。经过各方共同努力,这轮谈判的最后文件终于在1994年4月15日签署,同时还签署了关于建立世界贸易组织取代关贸总协定的协议。该协议于1995年1月1日生效,世界贸易组织也由此诞生。

世界贸易组织的职能:管理和执行多边贸易协定(multilateral trade agreements);作为多边贸易谈判的讲坛,解决贸易争端;同其他有关的国际机构进行合作。

到2014年6月底,该组织成员国数量已增至160个。总部仍然设在日内瓦。最高决策权力机构至少每两年召开一次部长大会,下设负责日常工作的总理事会和秘书处。我国于2001年12月1日成为该组织正式成员国。

Ⅲ. Notes to the Text

1. At daggers drawn — 剑拔弩张(at daggers drawn — in a state of open hostility)
2. Even as they fight side-by-side against Serbia... — 甚至当他们共同与塞尔维亚战斗的时候……(It refers to the joint military action by the U.S. and NATO against the Milosevic government in Serbia.)
3. They are embroiled in a battle over hormone-treated beef. They are at loggerheads over genetically modified crops. — 关于激素牛肉,他们陷入纷争。关于转基因农作物,他们存在很大分歧。
4. They have fallen out over noisy aircraft, mobile telephones and data privacy. — 关于噪音飞机、移动电话和信息保密,他们陷入争吵。(fall out — to have a quarrel)
5. Brussels — Brussels is the capital of Belgium, host to the European Union and the headquarters of NATO. It refers to EU in the context.
6. The battle is putting huge strains on the World Trade Organisation. — 这场争端给世界贸易组织带来了巨大的困难。(strain — a problem or difficulty caused when something is used too much)
7. On April 6th the WTO ruled ... against American fruit distributors. — 4月6日,世界贸易组织第三次做出裁决,要求欧洲联盟必须修改香蕉进口规定,因为这些规定不够公正,歧视美国的水果商。
8. On April 19th the WTO gave America the go-ahead to slap retaliatory sanctions ... — On April 19th the WTO gave America the permission to quickly impose revengeful sanctions ...
9. America in turn launched two new WTO cases against the EU. ... called champagne. — 美国反过来向世贸组织提出了两项针对欧盟的新的诉讼:一项是关于对"空中客车"的补贴,"空中客车"是波音在航空领域的竞争对手;另一项是有关欧洲联盟的地域商标规定,例如,不准加利福尼亚生产的汽酒使用"香槟"这个名称。[① Airbus — 空中客车公司,由欧洲宇航防务集团所拥有,成立于1970年,以便和美国公司竞争。其成员包括来自法国、德国、英国和西班牙的公司。总部设在法国南部城市图卢兹(Toulouse)。

② Boeing — 波音公司,20 世纪下半叶全世界最大的商用飞机制造商,总部设在美国西雅图。]

10. These bust-ups are a consequence of mercantilist policies exacerbated by political weakness and the increasingly legalistic nature of the WTO. — These quarrels result from commercial policies worsened by the WTO's political weakness and increasing focus on small legal details. [① bust-up — *informal* a very bad quarrel; ② mercantilist — of mercantilism (商业主义的) (mercantilism — 16 至 18 世纪欧洲国家普遍奉行的经济理论。这种理论认为,贸易必须是顺差,即出口额大于进口额。因此,商业主义的贸易政策是保护主义政策,鼓励出口,抵制进口。商业主义理论和措施为资本主义的早期发展提供了有利条件。后来,商业主义遭到自由主义政策提倡者的批评,他们认为,内贸和外贸对于商人和大众都有利。)]

11. But Cold War reflexes are now all but dead and ... the inclination to make a stand for liberal policies. — 但是,冷战期间的思维方式现在几乎完全消失了,国会越来越实行贸易保护主义。受到它的制约,克林顿政府没有坚决捍卫自由主义政策的愿望或意向。[① have no stomach for — to not have the desire to do sth; ② protectionist — of protectionism (protectionism — 保护主义政策,主要通过关税、补贴、进口配额等手段来限制国外进口。保护主义政策旨在保护国内某些行业免受国外竞争的威胁。) ③ liberal — of, favoring, or based upon the principles of liberalism (liberalism — 自由主义,经济学理论的一种,强调个人自由经营不受限制,其基础是自由竞争、市场自我调节。)]

12. The European Commission, which handles trade policy for the 15 EU states, is mired in scandal ... — 欧洲委员会处理 15 个欧盟国家的贸易政策,现已陷入丑闻之中。(be mired in — to be in a very difficult situation)

13. Institut d'Etudes Politiques — 巴黎政治学院

14. America too has dug its heels in. — 美国也拒绝让步。(dig one's heels in — to refuse to do something)

15. Louis Vuitton — 路易威登皮件公司 (a French luxury leather-goods company)

16. a big beef — a big complaint (beef — *informal* a complaint)

17. They are particularly tricky ... as well as free trade. — They are particularly difficult to deal with, especially because governments are unwilling to weaken their ability to achieve not only free trade but also other aims.

18. The costs of such measures ... fatter company profits and tariff revenues for governments). — 这些措施的代价(对于消费者来说商品价格较高,选择性较小)比较容易衡量;代价一般大于收益(更高的公司利润和政府关税收入)。(outweigh — to be more important or valuable than something else)

19. Indeed some of the new actors in such disputes ... economic reasoning. — 事实上这些争端的一些新的参与者,比如说保护消费者权利活动者和环保团体,不大会受经济因素的影响。

20. The multilateral trading system recognises that governments have legitimate aims other than free trade. — 这个多边贸易机构承认成员国政府除自由贸易之外还具有制定国内

政策的权利。(legitimate — having the right to set domestic policies)

21. Moreover, governments began to abuse these loopholes for protectionist ends: anti-dumping cases and import-restricting regulations proliferated. — 此外,政府开始为了保护主义的目的利用这些漏洞,所以反倾销案例和限制进口措施迅速增加。(anti-dumping — designed to discourage the import and sale of foreign goods at prices well below domestic prices)

22. Trample too much on domestic sovereignty... for protectionism. — If the WTO pays too little attention to domestic sovereignty, people's support for free trade will gradually disappear. If the WTO pays too much attention to domestic sovereignty, then all the governments will be free to practice protectionism.

23. The rows between America and Europe are taking their toll on the WTO. — The strong disagreements between America and Europe are producing a very bad effect on the WTO.

24. IMF — International Monetary Fund (联合国)国际货币基金组织(略作 IMF)

25. The twists and turns of the banana and beef cases... in Seattle in late November. — 有关香蕉和牛肉的诉讼有了意外的曲折变化,这种变化搞得世贸组织疲惫不堪,阻碍了11月底将在西雅图举行的世贸组织大型最高级会议的筹备工作。

26. Without it, the administration cannot negotiate credibly, because any deals it strikes with other countries may subsequently be unpicked on Capitol Hill. — Without the "fast-track" negotiating authority, the government cannot be fully trusted in negotiations, because any agreement it reaches with other countries may be voted down afterwards by the Congress. (unpicked — not selected, not agreed)

27. ...transformed his country from a protectionist backwater to a paragon of free trade. — ……将他的国家从一种施行贸易保护主义的,与外界隔绝的状态转变为完美的自由贸易典范。(backwater — an isolated or backward place)

28. Scud missiles — 飞毛腿导弹

29. But the WTO cannot be expected to set the world to rights... — But the WTO cannot be expected to make the world return to normal again...

Ⅳ. Language Features

经贸常用术语

本课涉及经贸术语较多,如:free trade(自由贸易),protectionism(贸易保护主义),WTO(世界贸易组织)。伴随改革开放规模扩大,对外贸易越来越重要,这里介绍报刊上常见的经贸术语。例如:

incorporated company 股份有限公司　　joint stock company 合股公司
board of directors 董事会　　　　　　　International Monetary Fund 国际货币基金组织
half-finished goods 半制成品　　　　　　most-favored nation clause 最惠国条款
barter trade 易货交易　　　　　　　　　intermediary trade 中介贸易

export items 出口项目
foreign trade contract 外贸合同
letter of credit 信用证
delivery order 交货单
due date 到期日
cash payment against document 凭单据付
C. O. D(cash on delivery)货到付款
forward exchange 远期外汇
mail transfer 信汇
rebate 回扣
letter of authority 授权书
limited company 有限公司
chamber of commerce 商会
business standing 商业信用状况
manufactured goods 制造品
entrepot trade 转口贸易
protective trade 保护贸易
sales contract 销售合同
quality certificate 品质证明书
bill of lading 提单
documents against acceptance 承兑交单
account receivable(应收款)
bill of exchange 汇票
postal money order 邮政汇票
bill payable 应付票据
letter of guarantee 保证书

order form 订单
inspection certificate 检验证明书
consignee 收货人
document against payment 付款交单
account payable 应付款
d/s(days after sight)见票后若干日付款
foreign exchange 外汇
IOU(I owe you)借据
traveler check 旅行支票
C. C.(carbon copy)复打副本
R. S. V. P.(*répondez s'il vous plaît*)请签复
affiliated company 附属公司、联号
commission agent 佣金代理人
exportable goods 可出口货物
bilateral trade 双边贸易
direct trade 直接贸易
export mode 出口方式
commodity inspection 商品检验
consignor 发货人
date expiry 有效日期、限期
through bill of lading 联运提单
rate of exchange 汇率
telegraphic transfer 电汇
D/N(debit note)欠款通知单
in duplicate 一式两份

{ Ⅴ. Analysis of the Content }

1. The author believes that if WTO's crisis over the selection of its leader drags on, _____.
   A. WTO's member countries will withdraw from the organization
   B. WTO will stop functioning
   C. WTO will be dismembered
   D. WTO's credibility will be undermined
2. The key reason for the EU's reluctance to yield to American pressure is that _____.
   A. the EU's economic power now matches America's
   B. trade is viewed as a zero-sum game
   C. the EU has its own currency to match the dollar
   D. the United States can no longer rely on having its own way

3. According to the article, in the multinational trading system, governments _____.
   A. do not have legitimate aims other than free trade
   B. are totally bound by multilateral rules
   C. retain their right to set their own policies domestically
   D. have to give up policy tools
4. From the article, we know the main trade problem on the European side is _____.
   A. Airbus   B. beef
   C. agriculture   D. CAP reform
5. Which of the following statements is wrong according to the report?
   A. WTO has become a quasi-judicial body.
   B. WTO lacks the legitimacy to arbitrate on matters which are intensely political.
   C. Without the WTO a retreat into protectionism is all too likely.
   D. The WTO has the legitimacy to arbitrate on intensely political matters.

VI. Questions on the Article

1. List some of the products which Euro-U.S. trade conflicts concern.
2. Why is the current conflict over hormone-treated beef and genetically modified crops something new?
3. List the three recent rulings made by the WTO.
4. Why does America practice mercantilist policies?
5. Why does the EU practice mercantilist policies according to the article?
6. List the problems faced by European politicians.
7. Why does the author say "the increasing legalization of the WTO is making matters worse"?
8. Why is the banana case so difficult to resolve?
9. What is the bigger reason why America and Europe cannot agree on trade?
10. What are the features of traditional trade disputes? And what are the solutions?
11. Why are new trade disputes hard to resolve?
12. How did the compromise work in the multilateral trading system in the 1950s and 1960s? Why?
13. What does the EU propose in the beef case?
14. What is the influence of the banana and beef cases on WTO?

VII. Topics for Discussion

1. Should WTO increase its power of regulating world trade?
2. Should a country apply protectionism in times of domestic economic crisis?